Artificial Intelligence

Rob Callan

First published 2003 by
PALGRAVE MACMILLAN
Houndmills, Basingstoke, Hampshire RG21 6XS and
175 Fifth Avenue, New York, N. Y. 10010
Companies and representatives throughout the world

PALGRAVE MACMILLAN is the global academic imprint of the Palgrave Macmillan division of St. Martin's Press, LLC and of Palgrave Macmillan Ltd. Macmillan® is a registered trademark in the United States, United Kingdom and other countries. Palgrave is a registered trademark in the European Union and other countries.

ISBN 0–333–80136–9

This book is printed on paper suitable for recycling and made from fully managed and sustained forest sources.

A catalogue record for this book is available from the British Library.

10 9 8 7 6 5 4 3 2
12 11 10 09 08 07 06 05 04

Printed and bound in Great Britain by

Ashford Colour Press Ltd, Gosport

Contents

Preface

Featured on the cover of this book is a picture of ASIMO, a humanoid robot made by Honda in Japan. Standing at a height of just over 1 metre, ASIMO can walk like a human, negotiate stairs competently and understand a limited set of commands. Another humanoid robot, SDR-4X, produced by Sony, can also move in a human-like manner and pick itself up when it falls, has stereo digital cameras for learning to recognize faces and for obstacle avoidance, and possesses speech recognition so that it can respond to voice input. These robots represent significant technology advances and, although the initial application is for entertainment, their longer term application is as personal aids. These robots are impressive, and reminiscent perhaps of the robots in science fiction films that can think and behave like humans. But ASIMO and SDR-4X are far from thinking machines. In fact, their level of intelligence is quite basic.

In the foreseeable future the subsequent generations of robots spawned by ASIMO and SDR-4X will not present any threat of superior intelligence. These future robots will, however, be equipped with a growing level of intelligence so that they can fit more naturally within our own environment. They will be able to do more and more complex tasks so that they become valuable aids in our everyday life. Before they can emerge from their current confinement as entertainers they will need a complex array of artificial intelligent modules. They will need knowledge of the environment in which they operate so that they can understand what their sensors are monitoring and so that they can behave rationally. They will need some level of human communication so that they understand requests, they will need the ability to formulate plans of action sequences and recognize objects so that they can navigate round a building, and they will need to be able to adapt their behaviour by learning rather than being pre-programmed.

In a nutshell, this book introduces the range of artificial intelligence elements that future robots must possess as embedded implementations if they are to behave intelligently. Embedding intelligence into robots is just one application out of many that motivates artificial intelligence technologists. Other applications include automated navigation for autonomous vehicles, object recognition and tracking, job shop scheduling, assistance with air traffic control, medical diagnosis and machine health diagnosis, automated travel plan agents, language communication, and many others. Any application that requires human-like intelligence is an application for artificial intelligence.

This book is a modern introduction to artificial intelligence for both undergraduate students and anyone who wishes to gain an appreciation of what artificial intelligence is about. There are a number of books on this subject. So why use this book? There are a number of reasons:

- If you are like me, then your understanding of a subject is enhanced when you consult a number of texts that present topics in slightly different ways. There is always a place for new books!
- This book provides an up-to-date treatment of those topics that have evolved significantly in the last few years. For example, Bayesian reasoning is used in many modern applications, and so this topic is treated in some depth. Neural networks are also key tools for artificial intelligence and they should occupy their fair share of space.

- This book aims to strike a balance between providing enough depth so that readers can start to implement artificial intelligence techniques but not so much depth so that readers become overwhelmed.
- The book is self-contained as far as is practically possible and assumes a minimal background in mathematics.
- This book has a well-supported dedicated website.

Organization of this text

Chapter 1 provides an overview of what artificial intelligence is about and the approaches to modelling intelligence. A brief overview of knowledge representation is also given. In older texts, knowledge representation would be treated in one or more dedicated chapters, but for a modern text this no longer seems to provide the best introduction; instead, representation is presented within the context of each topic. The next three chapters in the second part of the book cover some fundamental topics that are required for later chapters. Chapter 2 introduces propositional and predicate calculus. We see how to represent simple forms of knowledge and how to reason using this knowledge. Chapter 3 covers the basics of search. All forms of inferencing can be viewed as a type of search. When we solve a task with little knowledge the search can be quite intensive, but our aim is to learn and gain new knowledge that can be utilized so that search becomes more efficient (learning is covered in later chapters). Chapter 4 introduces techniques to mechanize reasoning with logical expressions. The Prolog programming language is a prime example of what can be achieved through this type of implementation.

The third part of the book looks at reasoning under uncertainty. The ability to reason in uncertain situations is fundamentally important. Original approaches to modelling uncertainty were somewhat ad hoc, but today's methods are more theoretically sound. In Chapters 5 and 6 we introduce Bayesian networks. These networks are beginning to find many applications and are proving to be important practical tools, and therefore we spend two chapters covering the basics and introducing techniques that form the basis for commercial applications. Chapter 7 covers other models of uncertainty including fuzzy logic, Dempster–Shafer theory and non-numerical approaches.

The fourth part of the book looks at methods for making decisions. Chapter 8 introduces decision networks (also called influence diagrams). These networks combine utility theory with probabilistic inference to derive optimum decisions. Chapters 9 and 10 cover planning. In Chapter 9 we concentrate on what planning is and then introduce what is called propositional planning. Chapter 10 discusses practical aspects of planning, such as handling constraints and uncertainty, and the need for more knowledge-rich representations. Chapters 8, 9 and 10 are really about making decisions on what actions should be taken in order to achieve desired goals.

Part 5 is all about learning. For autonomous systems learning is important. We need machines that can adapt their behaviour from experience. You would not consider very intelligent a colleague who kept making the same mistakes or could not improve his or her performance at different tasks. But learning is also required when we cannot access task-solving knowledge. For example, nobody could tell you how to ride a bike. You had to learn this skill for yourself. And there are many situations in which a machine must learn for itself how to perform a task. Learning is also of interest for discovering hidden patterns in large sets of data. For example, supermarkets collect a huge amount of data about customers and their buying habits. These data can be used to identify trends and to determine how best to target marketing and to plan the layout of stores. Chapter 11 provides an overview of what learning is and the different types of learning, and takes a general look at learning as searching. Chapter 12 introduces decision trees. Decision trees are found in applications that use data mining. Chapter 13 presents inductive logic programming (ILP). In simple terms, ILP is the idea of automatically generating Prolog programs (or similar type of logic programs). The potential applications are enormous, but it is probably fair to say that the techniques are not as mature as some of the other learning techniques that are introduced. Reinforcement learning, introduced in Chapter 14, is about getting machines to learn optimum decision sequences, such as letting a robot discover the best way to navigate its way round a building. Chapters 15 and 16 introduce some of the popular connectionist methods for learning with neural networks and, finally, Chapter 17 looks at genetic algorithms, which are inspired by biological evolution.

The sixth part of the book introduces those aspects of intelligence that need to build on many of the techniques introduced in earlier chapters. These higher levels of intelligent functioning include natural language understanding, speech recognition and vision. Chapter 18 provides an introduction to natural language understanding. The elements covered in this chapter include different types of knowledge required, a brief reminder of the different parts of speech, bottom-up and top-down parsing, the basics of semantic processing using the logical form and the need for context analysis. Chapter 19 extends the material introduced in Chapter 18. Chart parsing is introduced, the requirement for semantic features is explained, the material on context analysis is extended and finally a brief overview of statistical techniques is given. Chapter 20 looks at the functional elements of speech processing, and the hidden Markov model is explained in some detail. Chapter 21 introduces the functional elements of vision for object recognition. The chapter takes a brief look at the extraction of salient object features, segmentation and the classification of objects.

The seventh part of the book looks at some topics that play a supporting role in artificial intelligence. Chapter 22 introduces intelligent agents. 'Intelligent agent' was very much a buzz term a few years ago, and near enough all elements of artificial intelligence started to be introduced in the context of agents. A theory of intelligence can be constructed using the concept of agents but the concept can be usefully employed in the implementation of intelligent systems. A skilled software engineer will understand that agents provide a significant conceptual leap beyond today's notion of a software component. Chapter 23 is more like a short essay on some philosophical questions of artificial intelligence. The book concludes with Chapter 24. This chapter introduces a number of applications with the aim of showing that artificial intelligence has matured to a point where it is proving its utility in a ever-expanding array of real-world tasks.

Some of the chapters provide more depth than might be required for a first course in artificial intelligence. It is suggested that a first course might make use the following chapters: 1, 2, 3, 5, 9, 11, 12, 15, 18 and 21. The book can be used in a number of ways depending on the course emphasis. The introduction to each part will explain any subject prerequisites. The dependencies between chapters are given in the table overleaf.

Chapter	Chapters required to be read first	Chapters that would be useful to read first
1		
2		
3	2	
4	2, 3 up to section 3.4	
5		2
6	5	
7	2	
8	5	
9	2, 3	
10	2, 3, 9	5, 7
11	2, 3	
12	11, 2	
13	2, 3, 4, 11	
14	11	5
15	11	
16	15	5
17		2, 3
18	2	
19	2, 18	5
20		5
21	2, 11	Useful to study Chapters 5, 12, 15

PART 1

Introduction

Chapter 1 provides an overview of what artificial intelligence (AI) is. The applications of AI techniques are implemented through software. The difference between an AI application and other software applications is explained. The two broad paradigms of connectionist AI and symbolic or traditional AI are explained.

Introduction

This book is an introduction to techniques that are being used to build machines that manipulate information. These machines are being used today in a wide variety of applications, such as monitoring credit card fraud, making autonomous decisions on space missions, watching for attacks from computer network hackers, diagnosing faults in aircraft, enabling human–machine speech interfaces, and making the characters in a video game behave in a more human-like way. All of these machines are the result of technologists working in the field of artificial intelligence (AI). AI has become an important engineering discipline for building machines that can assist us and entertain us. But AI is not just about engineering; it is also a science that aims to further our understanding of our own and other animal intelligence. You may ask 'Is not the ultimate aim of AI to build machines that think like us, are mobile, perceive what is going on around them, can communicate with us, and have limbs similar to ours so that they can do the sort of physical things that we do – a humanoid?' In some sense, AI is about striving to build this type of machine. The technologies required to build such machines are being developed. There are robots that look like humans in spacesuits that walk and climb stairs, and robots that express emotion. Aspects of perception such as seeing and listening are being heavily researched, along with all of the other elements that make up intelligence, e.g. reasoning, learning, language communication, planning, decision making, and common-sense. We are still a long way from building a humanoid, and we do not really know whether it will be possible to build artificial machines that think like us and have an understanding about the world in the same way that we understand our world. But we are building machines that today assist us in many aspects of our daily life and we can be sure that AI will infiltrate our lives more and more in the coming years without us even knowing. We can also be sure that these machines will be better than us at many tasks in much the same way that the calculator is better than any human is at arithmetic computations.

The aim of this chapter is to provide a little more of the background of what AI is about.

1.1 AI emerges from the laboratory

In 1965, a team headed by Edward Feigenbaum and Robert Lindsay started work on a computer system to assist chemists to determine the molecular structure of complex organic compounds. Their system was not programmed in a conventional manner. Instead, it used a body of knowledge, the kind of knowledge possessed by chemists, to help solve the problems it was presented with. The system was an expert at analysing molecular structure and it was the start of **expert systems**, computer programs that have expert knowledge in specialized domains.

The system developed by Feigenbaum and his team was called DENDRAL. Determining the molecular structure of a compound involves finding out which atoms are present and how these atoms are connected together. Chemists can obtain data about a compound by breaking it up into fragments using a device called a mass spectrometer. The results of mass spectrometry provide clues as to the chemical composition of the fragments and how many types of each fragment there are. The problem for the chemist is that each fragment can correspond to several different types of substructure and yet all of these substructures must fit together into a single global structure. In theory, the chemist could test to see which combinations of substructures fit together to form the global structure. The problem is that there are too many possible combinations to make this approach practical. The problem is a little like being presented with a photograph of someone's face that has been cut into many squares and jumbled up. There are many ways in which the squares can fit together but only one fit reproduces the face. If the photograph has been separated into four equal segments then there are 24 possible combinations of fit (ignoring rotations). The number of combinations increases rapidly with the number of segments. An exhaustive search would entail a systematic rearrangement of the pieces until the fit forms the image of the face. The search time can be significantly reduced if knowledge can be used. For example, in the face reconstruction task there are many constraints suggested by knowledge of real faces. For instance, the ears are to the left and right of the eyes, the eyes are approximately in line and above the nose, which is above the mouth, etc. DENDRAL used its knowledge base to constrain the search and help chemists discover the molecular structure of a compound.

A few years later, work started on another expert system for suggesting which micro-organism was causing a blood infection and how the infection should be treated. The system was named MYCIN. Tests are performed to gather data about the infection a patient has. One such test involves growing bacterial cultures from a sample taken from the location of the infection. These cultures can provide morphological features and staining characteristics of the organism. MYCIN's knowledge can then be applied to these clues about the infection to diagnose the likely organism and to suggest treatment. Like DENDRAL, MYCIN's knowledge was encoded as a set of IF...THEN rules. These rules consist of a set of conditions and a conclusion. If all of the conditions hold (are true) then the conclusion holds. A typical rule in MYCIN is:

> IF
>> The stain of the organism is Gram negative
> AND   The morphology of the organism is rod
> AND   The aerobicity of the organism is aerobic
>
> THEN   There is strong evidence to suggest that the class of organism is Enterobacteriaceae

When reasoning, an expert system will usually apply many rules. The conclusion from one rule can form part of the IF condition of another rule. For example, the following two rules might form part of an expert system for diagnosing a fault with a car engine:

> 1   IF
>> The engine will not turn over
> AND   The lights do not come on
>
> THEN   The battery is dead

> 2   IF
>> The battery is dead
>
> THEN   The car will not start

If rule 1 concludes that the battery is dead, then rule 2 will conclude that the car will not start.

DENDRAL and MYCIN were the first of many expert systems. These systems represented the first truly large-scale commercialization of AI technology. Large corporations started to develop expert systems to mimic the reasoning performed by human domain experts. The boom years for the traditional expert system were the 1980s. The boom was short-lived however. Too many people jumped on the bandwagon and started to suggest expert systems for applications for which they were not suited. Expert systems were good at tackling specific types of problem, but they represented only part of the AI technology under development. Many overestimated what expert systems were capable of, probably because expert systems were offshoots of the field whose aim is to equip machines with human-like intelligence.

Expert systems are in commercial use today, but it is now rare for an application to be called an expert system. To many in industry, the title 'expert system' still conjures up a perception of what the technology offered in the 1980s and yet there have been some significant advances since. For example, the MYCIN rule presented earlier had its conclusion couched in uncertainty – *there is strong evidence to suggest...* The car rules, although written here as black and white conclusions, are lacking in diagnostic reasoning. Again, the knowledge base has to have knowledge of how likely a conclusion is when the conditions in the IF part hold. There were techniques for handling uncertain knowledge in early expert systems, but the approaches were somewhat ad hoc. Today, good probabilistic-based techniques exist. The tools of today also offer many advances over early systems because software engineering techniques have made significant advances in the last 10–15 years. The term '**knowledge-based system**' is more likely to be used today rather than 'expert system'.

1.2 What is an AI application?

Those early expert systems represent the essence of an AI application. An AI application is designed to mimic some aspect of human intelligence, whether that be reasoning, learning, perceiving, communicating, or planning. All of these facets of human intelligence rely on knowledge. They must also be flexible so that they can respond to events that were not foreseen by the developers of the system. An AI program is not like a database program that queries for information from a table, it is not like a spreadsheet program that computes total sales by category of item, and it is not like a program for constructing and sending emails. All of these programs follow clearly defined sequences of instructions determined by what the user requests. In these conventionally programmed systems, it is possible to predict what the user will want to do and program the instructions accordingly. AI programs are somewhat different. Programs are still constructed by programmers, but the program they implement must be able to execute in a way that is highly flexible. Consider the task faced by a medical domain expert, a doctor. Often a patient presents a minor complaint that may easily be treated by prescription. There is usually no single treatment for any one complaint. A patient may not respond well to one form of medication or may suffer side-effects. Sometimes a doctor may not be sure what is causing the symptoms but believes that the cause belongs to a certain class of complaint that normally responds to a particular form of treatment. A doctor may decide that there is value in carrying out tests to assist the diagnosis. He or she may decide that a patient needs to be referred for more specialist consultation.

So what makes the programming of an artificial doctor different from, say, a program for filing and calculating your tax return? In many ways, the two domain tasks are similar. They both require elicitation of data concerning an individual. The doctor needs to know about symptoms and may perform tests to gather further data. The tax return program needs data concerning earnings, personal circumstances, expenses, etc. Both the medical and tax domains require expert knowledge. The doctor has gained a large amount of knowledge over many years of training. There are many rules regarding tax and a tax expert has good knowledge of these rules. Both types of domain expert seek to derive information from data and knowledge. The doctor hopes to identify the cause of the complaint and prescribe a treatment; the tax expert seeks to compute money owed to the tax office or money to be refunded to the individual. The real differences between the two domains lies in the amount of knowledge the expert requires, the type of data and number of exceptional circumstances, the consequences of a mistake, and the complexity of decision making. Earnings when filing a tax return are easily computed. The symptoms a patient suffers cannot always be so precisely described: symptoms may vary in severity, symptoms may come and go, and aspects of the data may be unknown (e.g. a negative test result might reduce the likelihood of some condition being present but the test may not be conclusive). A mistake on a tax return can always be recovered, possibly in the next tax year. A mistake in diagnosing a patient may not be so easily rectified. A doctor may need to consider many decisions, like the need for additional tests, and the type of treatment, etc. The other major difference between the tax domain problem and the medical one is that a doctor will use a wide range of other information such as a patient's history and information derived through their own perceptions from vision, and listening. In summary, programming an artificial doctor cannot be tackled using conventional techniques.

Back in the 1980s, there were suggestions for more sinister applications of expert systems. Some people, for example, contemplated putting expert systems onboard missiles. The missile would be given a specific target and, should the target not be found, the expert system could decide if an alternative target existed or if the missile should return home to be recovered. At that time this form of application was ambitious. For a start, the system would need to reliably recognize legitimate targets, and this is no easy task. There is though a growing need for complex reasoning on autonomous vehicles. There is currently much funding and development of unmanned aircraft. These air vehicles have been used in recent conflicts for surveillance. Development is also under way on unmanned air combat vehicles. Many believe that the new Joint Strike Fighter currently in development will be the last manned combat aircraft to be produced on a large scale. There will be a drive for autonomous reasoning so that an aircraft can respond quickly and appropriately to events. Eventually, this reasoning will also extend to the aircraft's health so that it can take appropriate action should it develop a fault or suffer battle damage.

An application needs AI technology when there is no clear recipe of how to perform a task given all the circumstances that might arise. If you can sit down and put together a list of instructions that can state for a task, when X occurs do Y, then you may not need AI. Most technology applications today get along without AI, but they desire it just like man desired speed and progressed from horseback to mechanized transport. For example, today you do your banking by phone. You can dial in, enter a pass code, find out your balance, and pay a bill. The more involved the transaction is, the more awkward the interface becomes. You have to wait for a question to be asked, respond by entering data through the keypad, and, if all is okay, you go to the next stage. No need for AI here. But would you not prefer to do all this by speaking? It would certainly be quicker. The greater challenge though is when you want to do a transaction or make an enquiry that is not on the menu. You are then referred to a human operator. If you want a bank loan and the computer sees that all the right boxes are ticked then the loan can be approved. The computer always has a default instruction, 'any exceptional circumstances refer to bank'. The computer might have a rule that says, 'you need to have been in employment for at least 1 year'. If you are a talented young graduate 3 months into a new job then surely the bank wants you as a customer? Of course it does, but you are still an exception requiring human attention!

An AI application is in simple terms a system that possesses knowledge about an application domain, takes in data from its environment, and reasons about these data to derive information. This information is then used to make decisions and act. Often a human will make the decision and perform the action but technology is developing so that more of this responsibility resides in the machine. Expert systems are good examples of what the essence of AI is, but an expert system is just one example of AI being applied to real-world problems. Other applications require vision, speech recognition, learning, mobility, etc. A specific expert system may also use these technologies.

1.3 What is AI?

Hopefully the preceding paragraphs have given some idea as to what AI is all about, but we have not directly tackled the question of what AI is. There is no crisp definition of AI, and a number of people have attempted to express what the aim of AI is. Marvin Minsky, the co-founder of the AI lab at the Massachusetts Institute of Technology (MIT), gives one such view of AI:

AI is the science of making machines do things that would require intelligence if done by men.

The machine is usually a digital computer.

It is generally recognized that AI became established as a scientific discipline at a conference in 1956 when a small group of like-minded scientists gathered to discuss their work and ideas. The fundamental underpinnings of the subject were to develop over the following years. It was John McCarthy, one of the organizers of the conference, who labelled the new discipline 'artificial intelligence'. The central hypothesis of traditional AI, known as the **physical symbol system hypothesis**, is that any facet of human intelligence can be understood and described precisely enough for a machine to simulate it. The world is to be represented internally by the machine using symbolic structures. Intelligence then emerges as a process of transforming these structures. Consider, for example, language communication. We use symbols (words) to refer to objects in the world and other aspects such as actions (e.g. running), time, emotion, and so on. A computer simulation of this form of communication can be implemented in a way that is similar to having a computer read the following mathematical expression and understand how to produce an answer:

$$[(x-2/y)+3]$$

A program would parse this expression to make sure that it can recognize it, and out of this parse it might form a tree structure like the one shown in Figure 1.1. To give an answer, the program needs to recognize a number and needs to know what to do with the mathematical operators $/, +$ and $-$. These operators have meanings, and their meanings are the mathematical operations divide, add, and subtract. The program can recognize these symbols and call functions that implement these mathematical operators. The tree is scanned in a certain order to produce what is called Polish notation. Once this notation is derived, the calculation is simple: the expression is scanned from right to left and when an operator is encountered it is applied to the two operands to its right. Many language programs operate in a similar way by parsing sentences into tree structures. They then transform the trees into other structures that can represent the meaning. For example, suppose we have a database table with the following entry:

Relation	Argument 1	Argument 2
own	caroline	mia

We could write a simple program that could answer:

What does Caroline own?

The program could parse the sentence into the following form:

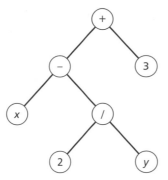

Figure 1.1 A tree representation of the expression $((x - 2/y) + 3)$.

own(caroline, X)

The program could then look up the table to see where it finds a match for the relation *own* and the first argument *caroline*. In this example, the variable *X* would be assigned the value *Mia* (because a variable can refer to any object) and the system would respond with 'mia'. The above expression is asking what can match with *own(caroline, X)*. The database contains the relation *own(caroline, mia)*. The variable *X* can match with any other symbol, which in this case is 'mia'.

The physical symbol system hypothesis is still waiting to be proved. Today, machines can perform useful language communication, but they still fall far short of what a young child is capable of. Many would argue that the physical symbol system hypothesis is not sufficient to replicate human intelligence. There is a big question over whether internal representations are adequate to prime a machine with enough understanding so that it can reason intelligently. For example, can we really describe a garden tree to a computer using structures that convey features such as texture, size, and rooted in the ground? Or does the machine need to have its own perception of the world so that it can learn for itself what a tree is? Consider the challenge of how to represent a chair inside a machine. Four legs to which is attached a small surface upon which a backrest may be present? I would not describe my sofa as having four legs, and what about a more unusual design of chair that has two sloping legs and stabilizing feet. How then do we find it relatively easy to recognize an object as a chair even when we have not seen some unusual design before? Perhaps we see these objects as comfortable spots to park our weary limbs and perhaps on some occasions we use the context of our surroundings, like a restaurant, where we can expect to be seated, or the selection of dining suites in a furniture store.

AI is both an engineering and scientific discipline. Most people in AI want to build machines that require human-like intelligence. Others within AI want to understand more about human intelligence. The two interests are, of course, complementary. The act of building applications can tell us much about intelligent processes, and discovering more about ourselves through more direct methods such as psychological studies or the biology of the brain gives us insight in how to build intelligent machines.

If your interest in AI is to build a human-like agent to do the household chores then you should be encouraged. This is a noble challenge, and success would surely capture the interest of the world at large. In reality, such machines are still a long way off. Whether these machines await a huge scale of effort similar to the first manned missions to the moon, who knows? It might be that we have the fundamental collection of techniques already. It might be that we need to radically rethink some aspects of AI. Notwithstanding the considerable challenges facing AI researchers, there is great interest in what AI can do for real-world applications. This interest is also growing. The problem-solving techniques developed within the discipline of AI tackle hard problems and in some areas the performance is better than that of humans. Some examples of the types of application are listed below.

- Systems have been demonstrated that can perform as well as humans in restricted domains of medical diagnostics.
- Machines can now recognize speech to a level competent enough for continuous dictation.
- Unmanned space vehicles have flown that use AI-based planning to allow onboard autonomous reasoning.
- Machine learning is used to detect credit card fraud.
- Large corporations use data mining to hunt out information in huge databases. Such applications assist companies such as supermarkets to devise their sales strategies.
- Machines have been trained to recognize individuals from images of their faces.
- Machines can also track the eye and mouth movement of an individual who is speaking and moving their head.
- Topics of interest in news stories can be filtered and summarized by machines.
- Gaming companies actively employ AI technologists to program human-like traits into the agents of a game.

This is just a small sample of the sort of problems AI is tackling. Some of the technology areas are more advanced than others. Often the domain of application is very restricted and the environment controlled. For example, you might be able to communicate with a machine to enquire of tourist information within a city but you would not be able to widen the conversation and talk about the weather, employment opportunities, or sport.

AI is largely about building machine programs that can simulate some aspect of human intelligence. There are algorithms for reasoning, learning, planning, speech recognition, vision, and language understanding. AI takes from and gives back to many disciplines that include mathematics, psychology, neurobiology, philosophy, computer science, and linguistics. There are many professions that have an interest in AI, such as medicine, engineering, and law.

1.4 Different models of intelligence

AI has sometimes been partitioned by different researchers into various camps that hold a particular view of how human intelligence is best modelled. Models of intelligence have been influenced by different subjects, such as mathematical logic, psychology, biology, statistics and economics. These influences can be seen in the subjects presented in this book. The logical and psychological models have influenced much of what is referred to as **traditional AI** or **classical AI**. An example of biologically inspired AI is **connectionist AI**, in which the computing elements resemble an abstraction of our own neural circuitry. Neural networks are the computing tools of connectionists. Most work on connectionist architectures has been done in the last 20–30 years. Early work on neural networks predates the 1956 conference at which AI was born, but traditional AI is so called because neural networks played a minor role in the formative years of AI. Connectionism has really boomed since the late 1980s.

Neural networks are structures that consist of many simple processing nodes connected via weighted links. The nodes and links form a network. The type of processing performed by a node varies depending on the node type, but the processing is usually very restricted, often doing nothing more than summing signals sent from other nodes and transforming this sum into an output. This output can then be sent on to other nodes or to some interface that communicates with a user. The weighted links can inhibit or strengthen a signal transmitted between nodes. The fascination with these networks is that they can perform complex tasks and yet they are constructed out of very simple elements. Of course, a computer at a fundamental level is also composed of simple elements such as sequences of bits which are subjected to simple operations.

To get anything useful out of a computer, it has to be programmed, and the more complex the task the more complex the instruction set that has to be entered. A neural network is simulated on a computer using a conventional program, but the network is not explicitly instructed in how to perform a task. Think for a moment about the rules in an expert system. These systems are constructed using a tool known as a shell. The shell is a high-level programming environment that permits the programmer to write a set of rules and test these rules. The shell has an inference engine, which is a program that knows how to use the rules to reason and derive conclusions. The rules represent the programmer's knowledge but the inference engine is the same whatever the domain of application. The shell is similar to a spreadsheet program: you can enter data into a spreadsheet and state what you want to be done, but there is a lower level program that interprets your instructions. The rules in an expert system are explicit instructions: if condition a holds and condition b holds then you can conclude c. A neural network, on the other hand, is not usually explicitly programmed. Instead, you feed the network with examples of the sort of data it is to process and you tell it what you expect it to output for each example. The network then attempts to adjust its weighted connections to comply with your wishes. For example, you could program an expert system with rules to credit score a bank loan applicant. The rule base would be fed data about the applicant, such as salary and current debt, and rules would be used to derive a conclusion that indicates whether or not the applicant is successful. In contrast, a neural network would be trained using known case histories. For each example, the network is fed with input data (the same data fed to the rule base) and the network is told for each example whether or not that individual was a successful applicant. Over time the network adjusts its weighted connections so that for each case it can output a successful or unsuccessful applicant. The network is basically told: given this type of data I want you to produce this result. Neural networks are largely self-programming devices – they learn. We should note here that there are also many learning techniques that fall within the traditional or symbolic AI paradigm.

We may suppose that neural networks ought to be the mainstay of AI in view of their abstract similarity to our own computing hardware. The situation at present is that our engineering skills in traditional AI techniques are more widely applicable. A pragmatist will use neural networks for some tasks and traditional approaches for others. We could get tangled in endless debate over which paradigm will yield the most fruitful results in the future. Some traditionalists argue that neural networks offer nothing new other than a platform for program implementation. They believe that at a functional level our reasoning operates along the same lines as traditional symbol manipulation. We think in a language and this language is similar in form and operation to logic or rules. Some connectionists argue that the traditional approach of symbolizing representations is ultimately restricted. For instance, symbols that are text based fail to capture the contextual information that is necessary for much intelligent reasoning. For example, a watch could be described differently depending on the context of how it is to be utilized. It may be desirable for an everyday watch to have a range of functions and be robust, but for a dress watch look and style may be more important than the range of functions it offers.

Connectionism does computation in a different way to computing with symbols, which is the mainstay of computing as we know it today. While some still look for an all-encompassing theory for building intelligence and will argue for a paradigm like symbolism or connectionism, there is an emerging consensus that intelligent machines will need multiple approaches to modelling aspects of human intelligence. Furthermore, there is no longer a clear divide of techniques between symbolism and connectionism. This can be seen in areas where the role of statistics is gaining more emphasis.

1.5 Representation

We reason, plan, learn, and perceive about objects and events in the external world. Somehow we hold representations of the events and objects in our mind. If you are planning a dinner party you must hold in your thought process some representation concerning objects that will form the menu and other objects that represent your guests. A machine simulation of intelligence will also need representations of the external world. A great facet of human intelligence is that we can reason by simulating actions in the real world. This simulation is important because we can predict things that might happen and do not put ourselves at disadvantage through trial and error. Suppose you want to rescue a cat from a tree. You can reason about the use of a ladder, whether the ladder is long enough, whether the cat has the temperament to let you pick her up, whether you can balance with the cat, etc. Trial and error means that you do not give much thought about what you are about to do and you go ahead in the hope that somehow everything fits together. To do this reasoning, we need to represent knowledge about the world. We need internal representations, substitutes for things, such as the cat, the ladder, and the tree. We also hold some representation for abstract things such as fear, distress, or love. The thought of losing our beloved cat might cause us to overcome a fear of heights.

The whole science of AI has largely revolved around issues of knowledge representation. That said, there is a school of people within AI building machines without concern for specifics of knowledge representation. These machines are not built with the purpose of reasoning in the same way as humans. These machines use pattern recognition, and the association of meaning to a pattern is achieved through interacting with the environment. The idea is for these machines to exhibit intelligent behaviour, but their processes may be very different to our own. For example, a neural network can be fed sentences with no knowledge of word category such as noun or verb, and yet it develops its own internal representations that exhibit patterns for verbs and inanimate and animate objects. We may suppose that teachers use much expert knowledge when marking students' essays and that they follow a complex chain of reasoning that uses this knowledge. It is not uncommon for a teacher to explain how a mark was derived. Such explanation suggests access to expert knowledge. It is surprising then to know that a purely pattern-based text system that has no explicitly programmed domain expertise can automatically grade students' essays and that the grades correlate highly with those given by expert markers. Pattern-based reasoners still possess a representation, but their representations are not necessarily accessible by us. We may not be able to open and inspect their knowledge base in the same way you could with a rule-based expert system. In a rule-based system the rules are syntactic structures that we can read and interpret. The elements that represent the knowledge in a pattern-based reasoner may look totally meaningless to us. It is a bit like looking at the internal representation a computer has of a photograph. In the computer the photograph is a huge array of numbers. Looking at these numbers means nothing to us, but when the computer displays the photograph these numbers are transformed into colour and intensity levels that reveal the image and its meaning.

Applications that exhibit intelligent behaviour are being built without concern for explicitly structuring the representation of domain knowledge. However, the representation of knowledge has played a key role in the development of intelligent machines, and it continues, and will continue, to do so. For any application, you need to understand what the objectives are and then you need to decide which problem-solving strategy offers the best approach – the application may require explicitly programmed knowledge or the system may be able to learn such that its behaviour, once trained, offers the intelligent simulation that the application demands. A whole chapter could have been written about knowledge representation, but instead I have taken the approach of dealing with representation implicitly in the context of different problem-solving strategies. Although representation will be specifically discussed only rarely, it is always there in the background, be it in the form of logical structures or some semantically enriched graph structure. It is, however, important to have an understanding of what is meant by knowledge representation as the term crops up time and again.

A representation, by definition, is a substitute for the real thing. A street map of a town is a representation. The map holds just enough detail for the purpose it is intended – finding a street and navigating between locations. You do not get an image of what the town looks like and you are not supplied with irrelevant information such as the routing of telecommunication cables. Pilots use maps to plan flight paths, but their maps look quite different from ground-based maps. An air map shows key ground features such as major roads and railways, but it also contains information concerning restricted airspace and hazards to flight. The information represented by an air map can be used to work out a heading to be flown. Pilots are trained to navigate. They operate in many ways like a programmed machine. They have access to a functional tool, the flight computer, and have a representation of key data to which they apply their navigational inference. The answer they derive also depends on data received at the time of planning, e.g. wind direction and speed.

Knowledge-based inference machines work in a similar way. They represent knowledge and they have a program that knows how to apply this knowledge to case-specific data to derive answers.

There are many forms of representation; three types will be briefly discussed and then some general points will be considered. Later chapters will include more detail of specific forms of representations such as logic, connectionist networks, natural language grammars, and causal networks.

1.5.1 Production systems

A **production system** is made up of IF … THEN rules. The IF part of the rule will contain one or more conditions and is called the **antecedent**. The THEN part is the **consequent**. A number of these rules exist in long-term memory (are stored when the system is not running), and the **working memory** holds information that is currently being processed. The basic mechanism of inferencing (reasoning) is to match the information in the working memory with rule antecedents in long-term memory. If a rule matches, then it is triggered, and if a triggered rule is fired its consequent is added to working memory and this new information may cause other rules to fire. Sometimes **conflict resolution strategies** are defined should more than one rule be triggered. The strategies determine which one of the triggered rules to fire.

An example of a production rule is:

```
IF      X has skin
AND     X eats food
AND     X breathes

THEN X is an animal
```

In this rule the antecedent has three conditions. The rule also contains a variable, X, that can refer to any object.

Figure 1.2 shows a simple example of how matching and rule firing is used to achieve inferencing.

1.5.2 Semantic networks

A **semantic network** consists of nodes that denote concepts or objects, links between the nodes that denote object relations (also called associations), and link labels that denote specific relations. For

```
┌─────────────────────────────────────┐  ┌─────────────────────────────────────┐
│ Long-term memory                     │  │ Working memory                      │
│                                      │  │                                     │
│  1. IF        clothes are wet        │  │ clothes are dirty                   │
│     AND       day is sunny           │  │ 20 dirty items                      │
│                                      │  │ day is sunny                        │
│     THEN      dry clothes outside    │  │                                     │
│                                      │  │ step 1: match with rule 3           │
│  2. IF        clothes are wet        │  │                                     │
│     AND       day is wet             │  │ clothes are dirty                   │
│                                      │  │ 20 dirty items                      │
│     THEN      dry clothes in dryer   │  │ day is sunny                        │
│                                      │  │ wash clothes                        │
│  3. IF        clothes are dirty      │  │                                     │
│     AND       more than 15 dirty items│ │ step 2: match with rule 4           │
│                                      │  │                                     │
│     THEN      wash clothes           │  │ clothes are dirty                   │
│                                      │  │ 20 dirty items                      │
│  4. IF        wash clothes           │  │ day is sunny                        │
│                                      │  │ wash clothes                        │
│     THEN      clothes wet            │  │ wet clothes                         │
│                                      │  │                                     │
│                                      │  │ step 3: match with rule 1           │
│                                      │  │                                     │
│                                      │  │ clothes are dirty                   │
│                                      │  │ 20 dirty items                      │
│                                      │  │ day is sunny                        │
│                                      │  │ wash clothes                        │
│                                      │  │ wet clothes                         │
│                                      │  │ dry clothes outside                 │
└─────────────────────────────────────┘  └─────────────────────────────────────┘
```

Figure 1.2 Example working of a small production system. Data come into the working memory and are matched against rules in the long-term memory. When a rule is fired, its conclusion is added to the working memory and this newly derived information can lead to the firing of other rules.

example, Figure 1.3 shows a semantic network for representing the concept arch. An arch consists of three parts: a top and two sides. The sides, which must not be touching, support the top. If the objects for the tops and sides are allowed to be of any type, the semantic network in Figure 1.3 provides a general description that can be used to recognize any arch. For example, the sides could be cylindrical and the top could be a pitched roof.

The labelled links can be used to express various forms of relations. These could be structural, such as *is-part-of* or *x-contains-y*, subtyping, as in *ako* (a kind of), similarity based, in which a numeric weight indicates the strength of association between one object and another, or more complex, e.g. *hit*, *loves*, and *go*. Another example of a semantic network is shown in Figure 1.4.

1.5.3   Frames and object-oriented concepts

Marvin Minsky proposed the concept of **frames** to represent stereotypical situations. You have, for example, an expectation of what will be found in a kitchen, e.g. a cooker, storage cupboards, a sink, and various forms of utensils. Events can also be described in terms of stereotypical situations.

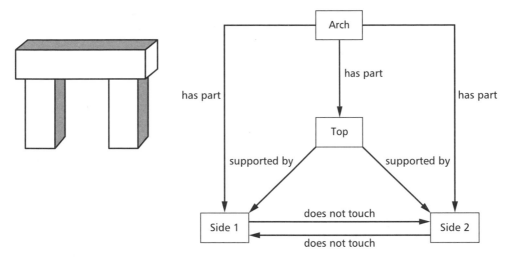

Figure 1.3 A semantic network for the concept arch (Winston, 1970).

Eating at a restaurant generally entails being seated, selecting from the menu, order taking, eating, and paying the bill. Minsky proposed frames as structures that could be called up from memory and adapted when a new situation is encountered. The frame would be adapted by changing certain features, such as the colour of the walls in a kitchen or whether the floor is tiled or carpeted. A frame could also have properties that must be present for the frame to be applicable to the situation. A kitchen frame may insist on the presence of a sink and a cooking appliance. Frames could also be linked together to organize knowledge and express relations.

The concept of frames can be found in the more general object-oriented programming paradigm that is popular today. The terminology of frames is different from that of the object-oriented school, and the motivation for frames is to perform inferencing, which is a specific type of computational task that is not generally required in the wider field of object-oriented programming. Nonetheless, we shall introduce a number of key object-oriented concepts as they support the structures and mechanisms that are suggested by frames. Indeed, many AI systems are implemented using an object-oriented language. The wider concepts of object-oriented techniques are also being utilized in some advanced frameworks for inferencing, one example being an extension to structuring probabilistic causal inferencing, which is introduced in Chapters 5 and 6.

An **object** can be used to denote anything we wish. It could be a concrete concept such as a book or car, or something more abstract, e.g. shape. A **class** provides a framework for describing a type of object. The class is the blueprint, much as a drawing is a blueprint for a house. An object is an **instantiation** of a class. For instance, a book has features such as title, author, publication date, and publisher. The class 'book' provides a generic description using features, but an instance is an object that has values assigned to these features. Instead of the term 'feature', the word '**property**' is used to denote an attribute of an object. Properties are pieces of information about an object, such as colour, author, publisher, and number of pages. **Methods** describe behaviour in that they declare what an object can do. For example, a book object might have a list of keywords that describe the book's content. The list of keywords is a property, but a method could be used to see if a particular word exists in the list of keywords. A graphical object that is part of a user interface will have methods such as *draw*, *move*, *hide*, and *resize*.

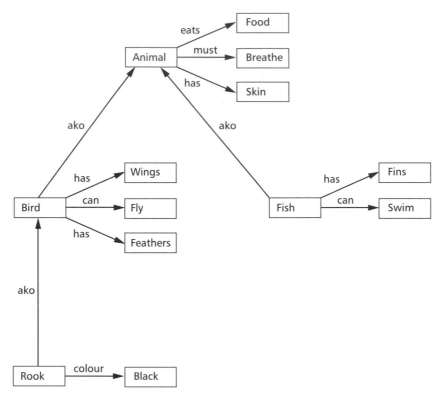

Figure 1.4 Semantic network showing some animal concepts and properties. This network is an efficient way of memorizing data. For example, we do not need to store explicitly the knowledge that a bird must breath. We can infer this fact because a bird is a kind of animal and animals must breath.

There may be some confusion as to the granularity of an object. For example, this text is an instance of the class 'book', but there are many instances that are all copies of this text. The important thing is that an object should be identifiable and so every object should have some property that is unique. A library may contain many copies of the same book, but everyone can be uniquely identified in terms of a number.

Objects can be linked (associated). One special type of association is **inheritance**. Class is synonymous with **type** and inheritance is used to define type specialization. This text is of type book, but a book is a subtype of a more general class called publication. All publications have a title, publisher, and date. Journals, newspapers, and books are all **subtypes** of publication, and they differ from each other in the way that they specialize publication. A book has a property that is a list of chapters, whereas a journal will contain a list of papers. The publication class is said to be a **parent** of book, journal, and newspaper. Also, book and journal can be referred to as **child** classes, or **derived** classes, or **specializations**, or **subtypes**, or **subclasses**. Inheritance is a special form of association because it usually has built-in support that allocates by default all properties and methods found in a parent class to a derived class. For example, in Figure 1.4, bird is derived from animal and so all birds have properties *must-breath*, *eats-food*, and *has-skin*. There are restrictions that can be enforced to determine which properties and methods are inherited, but this is detail that need not concern us here. Any other form of association can be modelled. The links that form associations are usually implemented by having a property in one object hold a reference to the associated object.

Another useful feature of objects is that they can be programmed to respond to events. Probably the most commonly encountered event with computers is the press of a key when typing or the click of a mouse button. An event will invoke a method that describes how the object should respond. Clicking the mouse on part of a window might cause the window to close. When the water in a kettle boils (an event), the kettle should switch itself off after a short delay.

A method can have different behaviour depending on the type of object being processed. The method for drawing an object to the screen is dependent on the shape of the object. For instance, the draw method for a circle-shaped object is different to that for a cube.

The object-oriented paradigm is excellent for modelling and implementing programs. There is growing demand for software components that can be used in different applications. The component may be a learning algorithm, a component for displaying graph structures and executing graphical operations, or a component that filters emails and routes them to particular storage folders. The object-oriented programming paradigm and component software techniques are of practical interest to AI in that they are tools that assist in building large complex systems out of smaller parts.

There are many real-world examples that can be modelled using object-oriented techniques. Consider simulating a lift system with two lift shafts. The objects are the two lifts, the people using the lifts, the request service panels on each floor, and the control panels inside each lift. The behaviour of each lift can be described using methods (e.g. move up, move down, and wait). The behaviour can also be constrained in terms of control logic rules. For example, 'if moving down and a request for service to a lower floor is received after a request to move to a higher floor, continue to move down'. Passenger requests issued in the lift or on the various service levels are events. A request to go to a particular floor is an event that the lift must handle along with all other events. Responding to events in strict order of receipt is not likely to be efficient, and so some careful control logic is applied. A sophisticated simulation might get both lift objects communicating in an attempt to optimize the service to customers. The simulation allows engineers to see how the lifts respond to different scenarios of user demand.

1.5.4   Key features of a representation

Davis *et al.* (1993) state that a knowledge representation is best understood in terms of five distinct roles that it plays:

1   A representation is a substitute. The substitute allows us to think rather than act. For instance, we often play out scenarios in our own minds to reason about the consequences of our actions. Planning an evening out requires substitutes for venues, transport, friends, likes and dislikes, etc.

2   A representation suggests in what way you should think about the world. For example, a procedural representation for instructions to change a car's wheel would be written as a sequence of instructions: apply handbrake, loosen nuts, jack car, and so on. Representing this type of knowledge using objects does not appear so natural. On the other hand, modelling knowledge concerning the components that make up a car engine might fit naturally with an object description. Some objects are composed of other objects and there exist objects of the same type, such as hoses, pistons, etc.

3   A representation is a fragmentary theory of intelligent reasoning. Representations are based on theories about what reasoning is. Often these theories are incomplete or are generated by some

small insight, for example observations of behaviour from psychological studies. Prolog is an AI programming language that has a representation rooted in mathematical logic. Knowledge is represented in Prolog using logical expressions and these expressions support reasoning, as we shall see in later chapters. The rules in expert systems are inspired by psychological studies of how domain experts reason. Connectionist networks are biologically inspired. Causal networks use statistical reasoning. All of these representations present a view on what reasoning is and how it is to be done. A connectionist view is that knowledge can be represented in the weighted connections of nodes and that inference is basically achieved by pattern association.

4   A knowledge representation is a medium for efficient computation. A representation is useful only if we can compute with it. Much research concerns the efficiency of the computation. Often efficiency is judged in terms of space (memory requirements) and speed of inference. The question of efficiency is very important for real-world applications.

5   A knowledge representation is a medium of human expression. A representation is a way for us to impart knowledge to our machines. It is also a way for humans to exchange and share knowledge with one another. Software engineers are familiar with this role for representation. They will often use a modelling language to document the design of a program and to communicate ideas with other members of the team. They will judge a representation on how easy it is to express things, how concise the representation is, and how readable it is to others.

Further reading

For a good overview of work in AI during the first 40 years see Grevier (1993). Grevier also provides a good general and readable introduction to AI, as does Copeland (1993), albeit from a more philosophical perspective. An interesting read on intelligence and a general discussion about its computational modelling is provided in Davis (1998).

A general book on representation is Ringland and Duce (1988). Davis *et al.* (1993) explore in depth the nature of representation. For specific discussions of various representation formalisms see Collins and Quillian (1969) for semantic networks, Minsky (1975) for frames and Schank and Abelson (1977) for scripts. An early example of learning semantic structures is Winston (1970).

A general read on some of the capabilities of connectionist architectures is Clark (1993). An example of intelligent-type behaviour without explicit programming of knowledge is Brooks (1991). Two examples of text processing without explicit knowledge of language are Elman (1990) and Deerwester *et al.* (1990).

PART 2

Logic and Search

This part introduces some material that is fundamental to many AI topics. Chapter 2 introduces logic. No prior knowledge of the subject is assumed. Deductive inferencing in propositional logic is introduced. The representation language of first-order logic follows. Chapter 3 introduces search. All forms of reasoning involve search. Blind and heuristic search over tree structures is introduced first, which is then followed by function optimization before finally introducing constraint-based search using propositional satisfiability. No prior knowledge is assumed. Chapter 4 explores the practical implementation of logical inferencing. Resolution in propositional logic is introduced and then extended to first-order logic. Unification is then explained, following which Prolog is introduced before taking a more detailed look at how a language like Prolog implements reasoning. Chapter 2 is a prerequisite for Chapter 4.

Logic

Logic is one of the basic disciplines of computer science. Logic is primarily concerned with reasoning about the truth of statements. Consider the following three sentences:

1   All horses have four legs.
2   Misty is a horse.
3   Therefore Misty has four legs.

The third sentence is a **conclusion** and the first two sentences are called the **premises**. In logic, the third sentence is said to be a **valid deduction** if the conclusion is true in every situation in which the premises are true. In essence, logic is used to reason about the truth values of sentences. A sentence can be assigned a truth value of true (T) of false (F). Consider a second example:

1   John is a pilot.
2   Gary is a pilot.
3   John is a pilot and Gary is a pilot.

The third sentence is composed from the first two sentences. Using the reasoning apparatus of logic we can determine the truth value of the third sentence from knowing the truth values of the first two sentences.

This chapter introduces propositional and predicate logic. Propositional logic is the simplest of logics and therefore the basis for carrying out deduction is introduced using propositional logic. Predicate logic is introduced in the form of the first-order predicate calculus (FOPC). The material on FOPC is concerned with the syntax and meaning of the language. In Chapter 4 we shall extend the methods for reasoning with both forms of logic.

2.1 Propositional logic

'**Proposition**' is the term more commonly used to refer to a statement. An **atomic proposition** (or atom) is the smallest entity to which a value of true or false can be assigned. For example, the following are propositions:

Copper is a metal.
Manchester is a city in England.
Tom is a cat.

Reference to an encyclopaedia will assert that the first two propositions each have a value of 'true'. The truth value of the third proposition depends on the object that Tom is a reference to. If I had a cat

I shall order the steak or fish, or both the steak and fish.

The truth table for not (also called **negation**) is:

A	¬A
T	F
F	T

Negating a proposition has the effect of inverting the truth value: the negation of T is F, and the negation of F is T.

Expressions of the form **if … then** are denoted by the symbol →, which is called **implication**. Its definition is given below:

A	B	A → B
T	T	T
T	F	F
F	T	T
F	F	T

In an expression of the form:

$$p \rightarrow q$$

p is called the **antecedent** and q the **consequent**. The expression is given a value of F only in situations in which the antecedent is true and the consequent is false. The definition for implication is not as straightforward for us to understand. Consider the following sentences:

1   If $(3<5)$ Then $(5>3)$.
2   If the moon is made of cheese Then $(5>3)$.
3   If the moon is made of cheese Then $(5<3)$.

According to the definition of implication, all three of the above sentences would be given a value T. Propositional expressions do not have to make any sense in terms of their association with the real world. We can therefore evaluate expressions that involve the moon, cheese and mathematical operators. The following sentence will be given a value F only in the situation in which *I am hungry* but *do not eat*.

If I am hungry Then I eat.

If I were to make the above statement, but do not eat when I am hungry then I have lied. The above statement implies that I eat when hungry. I could also eat when I am not hungry – I do not have to be hungry to eat – but I must eat if I am hungry for the above statement to be truthful.

The last connective to be defined is **if and only if**:

A	B	$A \leftrightarrow B$
T	T	T
T	F	F
F	T	F
F	F	T

This connective is sometimes called double implication. Two propositions (arguments) must have the same truth values for the expression to evaluate to true. Consider the following:

> If my head is in China Then I am in China.

This should be written more strictly as:

> My head is in China if and only if I am in China.

or

> I am in China if and only if my head is in China.

Implication would allow the possibility of me being in China without my head.

2.1.2 Truth tables

The logical connectives have been defined using truth tables. Truth tables provide a mechanical means for a complex expression to be evaluated (for its truth value to be determined).

Example 1 ● ● ● ● ●

Find the complete set of truth values for all possible truth assignments to p and q in the following expression:

$$(p \rightarrow q) \wedge (q \rightarrow p)$$

The expression has two propositions and four rows are needed in the truth table so that each combination of truth assignment can be evaluated:

1	2	3	4	5
p	q	$(p \rightarrow q)$	$(q \rightarrow p)$	$(p \rightarrow q) \wedge (q \rightarrow p)$
T	T	T	T	T
T	F	F	T	F
F	T	T	F	F
F	F	T	T	T

Columns 3 and 4 are found directly from the definition for implication. Column 5 is found by taking the *and* of columns 3 and 4.

● ● ● ● ●

Example 2 ● ● ● ● ●

Find the truth table for:

$$((p \rightarrow q) \wedge (q \rightarrow p)) \rightarrow (p \rightarrow q)$$

1	2	3	4	5
p	q	$(p \rightarrow q) \wedge (q \rightarrow p)$	$(p \rightarrow q)$	$3 \rightarrow 4$
T	T	T	T	T
T	F	F	F	T
F	T	F	T	T
F	F	T	T	T

The fifth column is the implication of columns 3 and 4, where column 3 is the antecedent. All the values in column 5 are T and so the expression always evaluates to T no matter what the truth values of p and q. Such an expression is called a **tautology**. Some other tautologies are:

$$p \rightarrow p$$
$$(p \wedge q) \rightarrow p$$
$$(\neg (\neg p)) \rightarrow p$$

The complement of a tautology is a **contradiction,** where every row of the truth table for an expression has a value F no matter what the truth value assignments of the component propositions.
Box 2.1 states a general procedure for forming the truth table.

● ● ● ● ●

Example 3 ● ● ● ● ●

Find the truth table for:

$$(p \vee q) \wedge (p \vee r)$$

There are three propositional symbols and the truth table will need eight rows:

p	q	r	$p \vee q$	$p \vee r$	$(p \vee q) \wedge (p \vee r)$
T	T	T	T	T	T
T	T	F	T	T	T
T	F	T	T	T	T
T	F	F	T	T	T
F	T	T	T	T	T
F	T	F	T	F	F
F	F	T	F	T	F
F	F	F	F	F	F

● ● ● ● ●

Box 2.1 Procedure for finding the truth table of an expression

The procedure for finding the truth table for an expression can be given as a number of basic steps:

- Count the number of atomic propositions, *n*.
- Calculate the number of required rows from 2^n.
- Fill in the columns for each atom with T and F. Notice that the last atom follows the sequence TFTF..., the second from last TTFFTTFF..., the third from last TTTTFFFF..., etc. So the successive Ts and Fs go in powers of 2.
- Form the other columns by breaking the expression into simple component parts. For instance, if given:

$$((A \wedge B) \rightarrow C) \rightarrow (A \rightarrow (B \rightarrow C))$$

we see that the middle implication has the expressions $((A \wedge B) \rightarrow C)$ and $(A \rightarrow (B \rightarrow C))$ either side and so we need columns for both of these expressions. Before computing the truth values for these columns we need to break down the expressions further for $A \wedge B$ and $B \rightarrow C$. The truth values for each column are then computed using the truth table definitions for the basic connectives.

2.1.3 Equivalences

If two expressions have the same truth table they are said to be **equivalent**. The symbol $\equiv$ is used to denote equivalence. For example:

$$(p \vee q) \wedge (p \vee r)$$

is equivalent to:

$$(p \vee (q \wedge r))$$

This can be checked by finding the truth table for $(p \vee (q \wedge r))$ and showing that the resultant table is the same as the previous example $((p \vee q) \wedge (p \vee r))$.

The following equivalences are known as **De Morgan's laws**:

$$\neg \neg A \equiv A$$
$$\neg (A \vee B) \equiv \neg A \wedge \neg B$$
$$\neg (A \wedge B) \equiv \neg A \vee \neg B$$

Another example is:

$$(A \rightarrow B) \equiv \neg A \vee B$$

The following sentences are logically equivalent:

If you don't go then I go.

Go or I shall go.

Identifying equivalences is useful for simplifying complex expressions. Some other equivalences are given in Box 2.2.

There are a number of other logical connectives that we could define but we shall not have to be concerned with these. In fact, any propositional expression can be expressed in a logical equivalent form using only *and* ($\wedge$) and *negation* ($\neg$).[1] We shall make great use of equivalences in Chapter 4 when we look at automated reasoning.

Brackets are used to indicate the order in which logical connectives should be applied. For example, the brackets in $(A \wedge B) \rightarrow C$ indicate that A should be *and* first with B before applying implication. Brackets are useful for making the order of connectives explicit, but they can be dropped if the order of precedence is made clear (see Box 2.3).

2.1.4   Formally representing English sentences

English sentences can be formalized by using propositional logic. The process is to identify the smallest parts of a sentence that can be assigned truth values and to denote these parts using propositional symbols. The different parts can then be linked using the connectives. The words 'and' and 'or' will often map directly onto the logical connectives *and* and *or*. The word 'but' expresses a conjunction and can be represented using *and*. Implication can be identified in sentences that have the forms:

> If A, then B.
> A implies B.
> A only if B
> B follows from A
> B is a necessary condition for A.

Propositional logic is useful for representing only certain aspects of English. We shall look further at representing English using logic later in this chapter and in Chapters 18 and 19.

2.1.5   Arguments and validity

An argument states that a conclusion follows logically from its premises. The argument is said to be **valid** if the conclusion can be proved to follow logically from the premises.

By definition, an argument with premises $A_1, \dots A_n$ and conclusion B is logically valid when

$$(A_1 \wedge, \dots, \wedge A_n) \rightarrow B$$

is a tautology, otherwise the argument is invalid.

Example 4 ● ● ● ● ●

1   John's keys are in the car or hung up in the office.
2   John's keys are not in the car.
3   Therefore, John's keys are hung up in the office.

---

[1]For example $((p \vee q) \rightarrow r)$ can be written as $\neg(\neg(\neg p \wedge \neg q) \wedge \neg r)$.

Box 2.2 Some logical equivalences

$A \wedge \neg A \equiv F$	Law of contradiction
$A \vee \neg A \equiv T$	Tautology
$\neg \neg A \equiv A$	Double negation
$A \wedge B \equiv B \wedge A$	Commutativity
$A \vee B \equiv B \vee A$	Commutativity
$A \wedge (B \vee C) \equiv (A \wedge B) \vee (A \wedge C)$	Distributivity
$A \vee (B \wedge C) \equiv (A \vee B) \wedge (A \vee C)$	Distributivity
$A \wedge (A \vee B) \equiv A$	Absorption
$A \vee (A \wedge B) \equiv A$	Absorption

Box 2.3 Order of precedence

The order of precedence is $\neg$, $\wedge$, $\vee$, $\rightarrow$, $\leftrightarrow$, which means that if there are no brackets then $\neg$ should be applied before $\wedge$, which should be applied before $\vee$, and so on. For example:

$A \wedge B \rightarrow C$ is the same as $(A \wedge B) \rightarrow C$

$A \wedge B \vee \neg C$ is the same as $(A \wedge B) \vee (\neg C)$

$A \vee B \wedge C$ is the same as $A \vee (B \wedge C)$

The third sentence is a conclusion that follows from the first two sentences (premises). Using the symbols p for 'John's keys are in the car' and q for 'John's keys are hung up in the office', the sentences are:

1   $p \vee q$
2   $\neg p$
3   q

The argument is formally presented as:

$$((p \vee q) \wedge \neg p) \rightarrow q$$

The argument is expressed by taking the conjunction of the premises and stating that this conjunction implies the conclusion.

The truth table for this argument is:

p	q	$p \vee q$	$\neg p$	$((p \vee q) \wedge \neg p)$	$((p \vee q) \wedge \neg p) \rightarrow q$
T	T	T	F	F	T
T	F	T	F	F	T
F	T	T	T	T	T
F	F	F	T	F	T

The expression is a tautology and this shows that the argument is valid.

An alternative way of presenting the proof that the argument is valid is to show that the negated conclusion is inconsistent with the premises. To do this we symbolize the argument by taking the conjunction of the negated conclusion and premises. If the truth table is a contradiction then the argument is valid.

● ● ● ● ●

Example 5   ● ● ● ● ●

Prove the argument in Example 4 by showing that the negation of the conclusion is incompatible with the premises.

The argument is formulated as follows:

$$(p \vee q) \wedge \neg p \wedge \neg q$$

The truth table for this expression is:

p	q	$p \vee q$	$\neg p$	$\neg q$	$((p \vee q) \wedge \neg p)$	$(p \vee q) \wedge \neg p \wedge \neg q$
T	T	T	F	F	F	F
T	F	T	F	T	F	F
F	T	T	T	F	T	F
F	F	F	T	T	F	F

The strategy of checking to see that a negated conclusion is inconsistent with its premises is called a **refutation**.

● ● ● ● ●

Example 6   ● ● ● ● ●

Symbolize the following argument:

> If the interest rate increases then the mortgage rate increases. If the mortgage rate increases then house sales will fall. Either the interest rate will increase or the mortgage rate will increase, therefore house sales will fall.

The first step is to identify the conclusion. The conclusion is the final statement that says *house sales will fall*. The above argument is claiming that this conclusion follows from the previous statements. So the argument is:

1   If the interest rate increases then the mortgage rate increases.
2   If the mortgage rate increases then house sales will fall.
3   Either the interest rate will increases or the mortgage rate will increase.
4   House sales will fall.

> p – interest rate increases
> q – mortgage rate increases
> r – house sales will fall.

Using logic connectives we get:

1   $p \rightarrow q$
2   $q \rightarrow r$
3   $p \lor q$
4   r

The premises and conclusion are now clearly identified. Taking the conjunction of the premises as implying the conclusion gives:

$$((p \rightarrow q) \land (q \rightarrow r) \land (p \lor q)) \rightarrow r$$

● ● ● ● ●

2.1.6   Deduction

We used truth tables to prove that a conclusion follows logically from its premises. In the case of large problems, the manual use of truth tables becomes cumbersome. An alternative approach is to use intuition within a controlled framework for reasoning to reach a proof. By a controlled framework, we mean the definition of a set of rules that specify what is allowable at each step of the proof. A step consists of deriving a new expression from those that already exist. The rules to be used are known as **rules of deduction**. A proof using rules of deduction is a little bit like playing a strategy game. A game has rules that state what you can and cannot do. At each step of a game you change something (e.g. the state of the board in a game of chess), but what you change must conform to the rules. The more complicated the game, the more difficult the decision on what to change, but the decision usually gets better (and often easier) with experience. Proofs using the rules of deduction also get easier with experience.

Some of the rules of deduction are given in Table 2.2; we shall say more about these rules later. The rules are symbolized using A, B, C and the logical connectives. A, B, C can represent any logical expression. The expression below the line can be deduced when the expressions above the line have been either deduced or assumed. For example, the rule *and introduction* states that 'if A has been assumed or deduced, and B has been assumed or deduced, then $A \land B$ can be deduced'. For example, if we have deduced that *Steven is on the train* and *David is on the train* then we can deduce that *Steven and David are on the train*. The *or elimination* rule looks more complicated on first inspection. The rule states that 'if C follows from A and C follows from B then C follows from either A or B'.

When using rules of deduction, it is more common to talk about a conclusion being derived from a set of assumptions.[2] When C can be derived from a set of assumptions it is written as:

$$\{A_1, A_2, ..., A_n\} \vdash C$$

The symbol $\vdash$ is called the **turnstile**.

Example 7   ● ● ● ● ●

It should be reasonably clear that C can be derived from the following three assumptions.

1   $A \rightarrow B$
2   $B \rightarrow C$
3   A

---

[2]The assumptions may also be referred to as the set of hypotheses.

Table 2.2 Rules of deduction

∧ elimination	$\dfrac{A \wedge B}{A}$ and $\dfrac{A \wedge B}{B}$
∧ introduction	$\dfrac{A, B}{A \wedge B}$
∨ elimination	$\dfrac{A \rightarrow C, B \rightarrow C, A \vee B}{C}$
∨ introduction	$\dfrac{A}{A \vee B}$ and $\dfrac{B}{A \vee B}$
Modus ponens	$\dfrac{A, A \rightarrow B}{B}$
Double negation	$\dfrac{\neg\neg A}{A}$

The assumptions state that C follows from B, and B follows from A. As A is an assumption (given in statement 3), then B follows and C follows in turn. The rules of deduction allow this proof to be shown formally (i.e. in strict accordance with the rules). The derivation is as follows:

4   B can be derived from assumptions 1 and 3 and the rule modus ponens:

$$\frac{A, A \rightarrow B}{B}$$

5   From step 4 and assumption 2, C can be derived using modus ponens:

$$\frac{B, B \rightarrow C}{C}$$

● ● ● ● ●

There are two basic types of deduction rule: **introduction rules** and **elimination rules**. The introduction rules allow us to combine different elements (propositions) by introducing conjunction, disjunction, implication, etc. The elimination rules allow us to break complex propositions into simpler forms. The rules must conform exactly with the truth table definitions for the connectives.

Conjunction rules

From the truth table for conjunction, we know that if

$A = \text{T}$ and $B = \text{T}$

then

$$A \wedge B = T$$

The first rule is $\wedge \mathbf{I}$ (and introduction):

$$(\wedge \mathbf{I}) \frac{A, B}{A \wedge B}$$

This rule states that if $A = T$ and $B = T$, we can conclude that $A \wedge B = T$. We can also see that if we know $A \wedge B = T$, then $A = T$ and $B = T$ because, according to the truth table, $A \wedge B = T$ only when both arguments are true. This leads to the $\wedge \mathbf{E}$ (and elimination) rule:

$$(\wedge \mathbf{E}) \frac{A \wedge B}{A} \text{ and } \frac{A \wedge B}{B}$$

So, if it is assumed that $A \wedge B$ is true or $A \wedge B$ has been derived, then A must be true and B must also be true.

Disjunction rules

The truth table definition for disjunction (or) states that if either $A = T$ or $B = T$ then $A \vee B = T$.

$$(\vee \mathbf{I}) \frac{A}{A \vee B} \text{ and } \frac{B}{A \vee B}$$

There are many ways in which an element can be eliminated from $A \vee B$. If we know $A \vee B = T$ and we know $\neg A$ we can conclude B:

$$(\vee \mathbf{E}) \frac{A \vee B, \neg A}{B} \text{ and } \frac{A \vee B, \neg B}{A}$$

The rule that is usually adopted as the standard rule for or elimination is:

$$(\vee \mathbf{E}) \frac{A \rightarrow C, B \rightarrow C, A \vee B}{C}$$

This rule states that if C follows from A and C follows from B and we know A or B then we can conclude (derive) C.

Implication rules

The truth table for implication shows that $A \rightarrow B = T$ when either $A = F$ or $B = T$. This leads to the introduction rules for implication:

$$(\rightarrow \mathbf{I}) \frac{\neg A}{A \rightarrow B} \text{ and } \frac{B}{A \rightarrow B}$$

From the same line of reasoning:

$$(\rightarrow \mathbf{E})\frac{A \rightarrow B}{\neg A \vee B}$$

The rule that is more standard for $(\rightarrow \mathbf{E})$ is the familiar modus ponens:

$$(\rightarrow \mathbf{E})\frac{A, A \rightarrow B}{B}$$

Example 8 ● ● ● ● ●

Show that r can be derived from the following assumptions:

1   $(p \wedge s) \rightarrow q$
2   p
3   s
4   $q \rightarrow r$

The argument proceeds as follows:

5   $(p \wedge s)$ from assumptions 2 and 3 and $\wedge \boldsymbol{I}$.
6   q from assumption 1 and step 5, using modus ponens.
7   r from step 6 and assumption 4, using modus ponens.

It is common practice to show the argument using the following style of notation:

$$\frac{\dfrac{p, s}{p \wedge s} \qquad p \wedge s \rightarrow q}{\dfrac{q \qquad\qquad\qquad q \rightarrow r}{r}}$$

Expressions below a line are derived from the two expressions that appear immediately above the line.

● ● ● ● ●

The rules of deduction are meant to reflect the way that we reason about logical arguments. There will often be many solutions to proving an argument – some more elegant than others.

In the derivation of a proof, additional assumptions are sometimes made. For example, given the assumptions:

1   $p \rightarrow q$
2   $q \rightarrow r$

it may appear intuitive that $p \rightarrow r$, but how is this to be proved? Another form of the implication introduction rule is:

$(\rightarrow \mathbf{I})$ if $\dfrac{\{\text{assumptions}\}, A}{B}$ is valid then $\dfrac{\{\text{assumptions}\}}{A \rightarrow B}$ is also valid

If we substitute p for A, r for B, and can show that r follows from the assumptions and p, then $p \rightarrow r$. Although we are not given p as an assumption, we are interested in showing what follows if p were an assumption. Therefore, we assume p. The argument proceeds as follows:

3   p assumption.
4   q from 1, 3, and modus ponens.
5   r from 4 and 2, using modus ponens.

Hence, we have shown that from the original assumptions (1 and 2), along with p, we can derive r. Therefore, from the original assumptions (statements 1 and 2) and p, r has been derived and (according to the $\rightarrow \boldsymbol{I}$ rule) $p \rightarrow$ r is therefore valid.

2.1.7   Soundness and completeness

Any procedure for deriving proofs in propositional logic should be sound and complete. In simple terms, a **sound** procedure means that you cannot prove things that are false and **completeness** means that you have enough rules so that any true derivation can be proved. Before discussing soundness and completeness further, it is useful to introduce a few other terms.

Any propositional expression that can be built from the set of logical symbols is called a **formula**. The following are all formulas:

p
$(p \wedge q) \rightarrow r$
$\neg s$
$p \vee q$

A **model** for propositional logic will map every formula to a value of T or F. By map, we mean there will exist a function(s) that can be applied to assign a truth value to any formula. A model is defined using a **valuation function**. Models and valuation functions have already been used, though not explained, through the truth tables. Each row in a truth table corresponds to a model and a valuation function assigns a value of T or F to a formula. For a formula with a single proposition there are two models – a valuation function for negation, for example, will map p = T to F and p = F to T. A formula with two propositional symbols (e.g. p and q) will have four models (the same as the number of rows required to define a truth table).

Truth tables provide one procedure for conducting proofs that are sound. Are the rules of deduction sound? A rule is sound provided that it can never be used to prove something unless it is true in all possible models. That is, for any model for which the premises are true, the conclusion must also be true. Consider the rule modus ponens:

$(\rightarrow \mathbf{E}) \dfrac{A, A \rightarrow B}{B}$

The truth table for implication is:

Models	A	B	$A \rightarrow B$
1	T	T	T
2	T	F	F
3	F	T	T
4	F	F	T

The only model in which the premises (A and $A \rightarrow B$) are both true is model 1, and the conclusion B is also true.

A set of formulas is said to be **consistent** if there is a model that assigns every formula a value of T. For example, the set:

$$\{p, p \wedge q, p \rightarrow q\}$$

is consistent. The model, in which $p = $ T and $q = $ T, will assign all formula in the set a value T (as can be confirmed from the truth tables). This model is said to **satisfy** the set of formulas.

Another term that we shall need later in the book is **entailment**. A formula A is said to entail B (written $A \vdash B$) if and only if B is assigned T in all models that satisfy A. In other words, if the conclusion must be true when the premises are true, the premises are said to entail the conclusion. A proof system is said to be **complete** if it can prove a conclusion from its premises whenever its premises entail the conclusion.

2.2 Predicate calculus

The first part of this chapter introduced the simplest form of logic called propositional logic (or propositional calculus). The language of propositional logic is limited in expressiveness and is therefore not a good choice for representing many situations. Consider the following sentence:

If John is in China then John's left and right arms are in China.

Symbolizing the above sentence using propositional logic:

p to denote John is in China
q to denote John's left arm is in China
r to denote John's right arm is in China
$p \rightarrow (q \wedge r)$

The representation fails to represent the association between the individual propositions: p, q and r all refer to something being in China and q and r are referring to an arm belonging to John. We can easily spot another representational deficiency of propositional logic when trying to show that the following argument is valid:

Every dog has a master.
Sadie is a dog.
Therefore Sadie has a master.

Using propositional logic we would have an argument of the form:

$$A$$
$$\underline{B}$$
$$C$$

The symbolized argument is not valid and yet we can see that the original premises must surely imply the conclusion that *Sadie has a master*.

This section presents a more expressive type of logic called **first-order predicate calculus** (FOPC). FOPC builds upon propositional logic, and much of what was presented in the first part of this chapter carries over to FOPC.

2.2.1 Representation using FOPC

FOPC enables us to denote objects, properties of objects, and relationships between objects. It also allows a limited form of quantification – that is, an indication of how many objects we are dealing with.

An object corresponds loosely to a noun in the English language. An object might be a physical thing that exists in the real world or it might be an abstract concept. A pen is an object, you and I are objects, this book is an object, the world is an object, your father is an object, etc. Relations describe associations between objects. For example:

London is *west* of Paris.
Sydney opera house is *in* Australia.
Steven is sat *opposite* David.
Sally is the *owner* of a large yacht.

Predicate is the word used in FOPC to describe the symbols used when we make claims about objects and relations between objects. For example:

west(london, paris)	London is west of Paris
girl(caroline)	Caroline is a girl
country(canada)	Canada is a country
tall(mark)	Mark is tall

All of the above expressions are of the form:

$$predicate\_name(a_1, a_2, \ldots)$$

Each has a predicate name followed by one or more **arguments** enclosed in parenthesis. The number of arguments refers to the **arity** of the predicate. For example, *girl* is a unary predicate and has arity 1, *west* is a binary predicate and has arity 2. The name given to a predicate is really one of personal choice, but good practice would insist that names should ideally convey some meaning when read by another person. In this book, a predicate's name must start with a lowercase letter. A named object must start with a lowercase letter – this is contrary to many texts but we adopt this convention to maintain consistency with other material presented in the book. The set of names used to refer to objects are called **constants**.

An expression of the form:

$$predicate\_name(a_1, a_2, \ldots)$$

is known as an **atomic sentence**. Compound (more complex) sentences can be constructed by linking atomic sentences through the logic connectives presented earlier.

Example 9 ● ● ● ● ●

Express the following in FOPC:

1   Sadie is not a person.
2   David sits opposite Steven.
3   If Sadie is a dog and Duncan owns Sadie then Duncan is Sadie's master.

1   $\neg$ person(sadie)
2   sits_opposite(david, steven)
3   (dog(sadie) $\wedge$ owns(duncan, sadie)) $\rightarrow$ master(duncan, sadie)

● ● ● ● ●

Quantifiers

Consider the following sentence:

All dogs like bones.

There are two aspects to this sentence that we have not yet dealt with. First, the sentence refers to more than one object (dogs) and none of these objects is named; second, the sentence refers to *all* dogs. In the absence of any other information we have to assume that *all dogs* is a reference to every dog that exists in the world. Suppose we are talking about the dogs owned by John, which are named in the following set

{Lara, Jasper, Max}

The above set defines the **domain** of objects within the world with which we are concerned. Given this world, *All dogs like bones* can be represented as

likes(lara, bones) $\wedge$ likes(jasper, bones) $\wedge$ likes(max, bones)

This could be represented more concisely as

$\forall$ X. ((dog(X) $\wedge$ owns(john, X)) $\rightarrow$ likes(X, bones))

The symbol $\forall$ is called the **universal** quantifier and stands for *all* or *everything*. The variable X is needed when reference is made to unnamed objects. A variable can refer to any object in the domain. Our variables will consist either of a single uppercase letter or a string[3] that starts with an uppercase letter.

During a conversation with a friend you become less precise about object reference once it is clear what the objects of discussion are. For example:

---

[3] A string is a sequence of characters from the alphabet.

I listened to that CD that I borrowed from Kelly. That CD I borrowed from Kelly sounds great.

is too formal compared with:

I listened to that CD that I borrowed from Kelly. It sounds great.

Expressions can be simplified provided object reference is clear. For example, if it is known that John's dogs are the domain of interest, then:

$$\forall X.(dog(X) \rightarrow likes(X, bones))$$

can be used in place of:

$$\forall X.((dog(X) \wedge owns(john, X)) \rightarrow likes(X, bones))$$

If it is clear that all the objects in the domain are dogs, then a further simplification is:

$$\forall X.(likes(X, bones))$$

Suppose John states the following (when referring to his dogs):

There is a dog that likes bones.

This sentence means that John has at least one dog that likes bones. There could, in fact, be more than one dog that likes bones, but all that can be assumed is that there is at least a dog with an appetite for bones. This would be represented as follows:

$$\exists X.(dog(X) \wedge likes(X, bones))$$

The symbol $\exists$ is called the **existential** quantifier and stands for *there exists* or *at least one*. Given the domain of John's dogs. we could have used a less concise representation:

$$likes(lara, bones) \vee likes(jasper, bones) \vee likes(max, bones)$$

Here are some more examples:

Every boy likes football.
$$\forall X.(boy(X) \rightarrow likes(X, football))$$

There is a winning competitor.
$$\exists X.(competitor(X) \wedge winner(X))$$

Some person stole the money.
$$\exists X.(person(X) \wedge stole(X, money))$$

There is a number between 10 and 20.
$$\exists X.(number(X) \wedge between(X, 10, 20))$$

All members either sing or dance.
$\forall$ X.(member(X) $\rightarrow$ (sing(X) $\vee$ dance(X)))

Everybody loves someone.
$\forall$ X.$\exists$ Y (loves(X, Y))
or, more explicitly,
$\forall$ X.(person(X) $\rightarrow$ $\exists$ Y. (person(Y) $\wedge$ loves(X, Y)))

Someone is loved by everyone.
$\exists$ X.$\forall$ Y. (loves(Y, X))

Note that the order of quantifiers is important, as illustrated by the two sentences (symbolized above):

Everybody loves someone.
Someone is loved by everyone.

From the above examples it can be seen that $\forall$ is usually used with $\rightarrow$. Let us return to our set of dogs:

{Lara, Jasper, Max}

Suppose that the above set is expanded to include John's cats, Tigs and Mia:

{Lara, Jasper, Max, Tigs, Mia}

Let this new set be the domain of objects that can appear in the model. The expression:

All dogs like bones.

can be written:

(dog(lara) $\rightarrow$ likes(lara, bones)) $\wedge$
(dog(jasper) $\rightarrow$ likes(jasper, bones)) $\wedge$
(dog(max) $\rightarrow$ likes(max, bones)) $\wedge$
(dog(tigs) $\rightarrow$ likes(tigs, bones)) $\wedge$
(dog(mia) $\rightarrow$ likes(mia, bones))

The claim being made is that for any predicate on the left of the implication that has a value of T, the predicate on the right of the implication must have a value of T for the sentence to be valid. Note that Tigs and Mia appear in the above conjunction because they are objects within the domain of concern. The predicate *dog(tigs)* has a truth value F, and therefore no claim is made about whether or not Tigs likes bones – Tigs might like bones but the claim is about the dogs. When the more concise representation is used:

$\forall$ X.(dog(X) $\rightarrow$ likes(X, bones))

the variable *X* is subject to the test of being a dog. If *X* is not a dog, then no claim is made with regards to liking bones – the object that X refers to might like bones even when X is not a dog, but no claim is being made about such an instance.

Consider the sentence:

> There is a dog that likes bones.

With reference to the same domain:

> (dog(lara) $\land$ likes(lara, bones)) $\lor$
> (dog(jasper) $\land$ likes(jasper, bones)) $\lor$
> (dog(max) $\land$ likes(max, bones)) $\lor$
> (dog(tigs) $\land$ likes(tigs, bones)) $\lor$
> (dog(mia) $\land$ likes(mia, bones))

The expression is true provided that at least one of the component sentences is true. This captures the notion of the existential quantification. The concise form is:

> $\exists X.(\text{dog}(X) \land \text{likes}(X, \text{bones}))$

Quantifiers and negation

A universally quantified expression has an equivalent existentially quantified expression and vice versa. For example:

> Everyone likes football $\qquad \forall X. \text{likes}(X, \text{football})$

is the same as saying:

> There is no one who does not like football $\qquad \neg \exists X. \neg \text{likes}(X, \text{football})$

There are a set of rules known as **De Morgan's rules** that express the equivalences between the two quantifiers (Box 2.4).

Functions

There is another useful construct in FOPC, which is called a **function**. Functions, like predicates,

---

Box 2.4 De Morgan's rules

If P denotes a predicate, the rules are:

$$\forall x \neg P \equiv \neg \exists x P$$

$$\neg \forall x P \equiv \exists x \neg P$$

$$\forall x P \equiv \neg \exists x \neg P$$

$$\exists x P \equiv \neg \forall x \neg P$$

take one or more arguments. Functions are useful for referring to objects that are not named. For example, if we wish to refer to Caroline's father we could use:

> father(caroline)

We can think of a function as returning a reference to an object. Functions can be applied recursively. For example, Caroline's grandfather could be referred to as:

> father(father(caroline))

People have names, and the name is usually the convenient reference symbol. Many objects do not have names and functions provide a way to reference these objects. For example:

> broken(rightLeg(sandra))

could be used to represent *Sandra's right leg is broken.*

2.2.2   Well-formed formulas

FOPC expressions are constructed from a set of reserved symbols and other symbols that we are free to create. The reserved symbols are the logical connectives and quantifiers. Symbols are created to denote predicate names, function names and named objects. The other type of symbol is a variable. The construction of a logic expression must follow a set of rules that defines how symbols can be combined. The collection of symbols, the rules for how they can be combined, and the meaning of symbols constitute a language. FOPC is a language. The purpose of a language is to facilitate communication, and this communication is assured only when formulas conform to the language rules and the participants in the communication understand the meaning of the symbols used. Any formula that conforms to the set of language rules is said to be well formed. All expressions in FOPC need to be **well-formed formulas** (wff).

A formula in the FOPC language is constructed from a subset of the following symbol types (the language is denoted by L):

1   A set of predicate symbols L_{PRED} with each symbol having a specified arity.
2   A set of constant symbols L_{CONST}.
3   A set of variable symbols L_{VAR}.
4   A set of function symbols, L_{FUNC}, each with a specified arity.
5   Quantifiers $\forall$ and $\exists$.
6   Set of connectives $\rightarrow, \leftrightarrow, \wedge, \vee, \neg$.

Constants, variables and functions are all called **terms**. Terms denote objects.

7   Any member of L_{CONST} or L_{VAR} is a member of L_{TERM}. A member, f, of L_{FUNC} yields a term $t = f(t_1, \ldots t_n)$. t is a member of L_{TERM}.

Formulas are well formed only when the following rules are satisfied:

1   If p is a member of L_{PRED} with arity n, and $t_1, \ldots t_n$ are members of L_{TERM}, then $p(t_1, \ldots t_n)$ is a well-formed formula.

2   If *A* and *B* are well-formed formulas then so too are:
   $A \rightarrow B$
   $A \leftrightarrow B$
   $A \wedge B$
   $A \vee B$
   $\neg A$
3   If *A* is a well-formed formula and *X* is a member of L_{VAR}, then the following are well formed:
   a $\forall X.A$
   b $\exists X.A$

Example 10 ● ● ● ● ●

Using the language rules given above along with the following sets

L_{CONST} {helen, debbie}
L_{VAR} {X}
L_{PRED} {(pretty, arity = 1), (intelligent, arity = 1)}
L_{FUNC} {(mother, arity = 1)}

state which of the following is a well-formed formula:

1   pretty(helen)
2   pretty(mother(helen))
3   pretty(debbie)
4   pretty(helen) ∧ friend(helen, jenny)
5    $\exists X.$ (girl(X) ∧ pretty(X, Y))
6   pretty(helen, debbie)
7   pretty(suzzana)

All of the above are well formed apart from:

•   Sentence 4 – friend is not defined in the predicate set and Jenny is not listed as a term.
•   Sentence 5 – pretty has the wrong number of arguments and *Y* is not a variable.
•   Sentence 7 – Suzzana is not a term.

● ● ● ● ●

Scoping

Consider the following wffs:

$B(X)$
$\forall X.B(X)$
$\forall X.B(X, Y)$

The *X* in *B(X)* is said to be free while the X in $\forall X.B(X)$ is said to be **bound**. The X in $\forall X.B(X, Y)$ is bound but *Y* is said to be **free**.

In a formula of the form $\forall X.\varphi$, where φ is a wff, φ is said to be the scope of the quantifier. Brackets are used to help identify scope:

$\forall X.(B(X, Y) \to A(X))$ The scope of $\forall X$ is $B(X, Y) \to A(X)$.

$\forall X.B(X, Y) \to A(X)$ The scope of $\forall X$ is $B(X, Y)$

$\forall X.(B(X, Y) \to \exists Y. C(Y))$ The scope of $\forall X$ is $B(X, Y) \to \exists Y. C(Y)$ and the scope of $\exists Y$ is $C(Y)$

When a variable X occurs within the scope of a quantifier, X is said to be bound. A variable that is not bound is said to be free. Note that in

$$\forall X.(B(X, Y) \to \exists Y. C(Y))$$

X is bound, the first occurrence of Y is free but the second occurrence of Y is bound.

The notion of scoping and free variables is important when we come to replacing variables with other variables or terms. If the intended meaning is not to be distorted, only the free occurrences of a variable can be replaced. For example:

$$\forall X.(B(X, Y) \to \exists X. C(X))$$

is true only when $B(X, Y) \to \exists X. C(X)$ is true for every X. The scope of $\forall X$ is the subformula:

$$B(X, Y) \to \exists X. C(X)$$

In this subformula, the X in $B(X, Y)$ but not in $\exists X. C(X)$. is free. Let us return to the set of John's dogs to see an example:

{Lara, Jasper, Max}

and the formula:

$$\forall X.(dog(X) \to \exists X. small(X))$$

This formula is equivalent to:

$(dog(lara) \to \exists X.small(X)) \wedge$
$(dog(jasper) \to \exists X.small(X)) \wedge$
$(dog(max) \to \exists X.small(X))$

The subformula $\exists X.small(X)$ can be expanded:

$(dog(lara) \to (small(lara) \vee small(jasper) \vee small(max))) \wedge$
$(dog(jasper) \to (small(lara) \vee small(jasper) \vee small(max))) \wedge$
$(dog(max) \to (small(lara) \vee small(jasper) \vee small(max)))$

2.2.3   The truth of sentences

Up until now we have been concerned with syntax – how sentences should be symbolized and how the various symbols of FOPC can be strung together. We have not dealt with meaning (or semantics as it is more typically called). A means of **interpretation** is required for a formula to have meaning. You cannot understand any written language without the ability to interpret what is written (or perhaps spoken or signed). The symbols in a FOPC formula have to be interpreted in order for a truth value to be assigned to the formula. So what does interpretation in FOPC involve? An interpretation involves a non-empty set of objects called the domain and a set of relationships over the domain. A set of functions may also operate over the domain. To make all this a little more concrete, consider again the dogs that John owns:

> {Lara, Jasper, Max}

A few more facts about these dogs will help to illustrate the notion of interpretation:

> Jasper and Max are male.
> Lara is the mother of Jasper.
> Jasper is bigger than Max.
> Max is bigger than Lara.

These facts can be symbolized as:

> male(jasper), male(max)
> lara = mother(jasper)
> bigger(jasper, max)
> bigger(max, lara)

The first important point about constant symbols is that they are a substitution (a reference) for an object. For example, the name *lara* is a symbol that is used to reference the real dog called Lara. The symbol *lara* is said to map onto the real dog (labelled Lara). Correct mapping is important for an interpretation. Suppose, for example, that you know two people called John, one a teacher, the other a student. The correct interpretation of a sentence with the symbol *John* relies on the correct mapping or association with the person being referred to (either the teacher or student, or perhaps some other John).

The domain of objects shall be denoted by D:

> D = {lara, jasper, max}

Relationships and functions also have to be mapped. The symbol $\mapsto$ shall be used to denote a mapping.

> dog $\mapsto$ {lara, jasper, max}
> male $\mapsto$ {jasper, max}
> bigger $\mapsto$ {(jasper, max), (max, lara)}
> mother $\mapsto$ {jasper $\mapsto$ lara}

Predicates are **n-ary** (arity *n*) relations on D. The predicate *dog* is 1-ary, *male* is 1-ary and *bigger* 2-ary. The mappings reflect this. For example, the predicate *bigger* is a mapping to a set of ordered pairs: each pair denotes two arguments to the predicate. Note that *mother* is a function that maps one element of D into another element.

An interpretation for the primary types of symbols of FOPC can now be given in Table 2.3.

The truth value of *dog(lara)* depends on whether *lara* is a member of the mapping *dog – lara* is and so *dog(lara)* can be assigned a value T. The truth value of *bigger(jasper, max)* is T because the

Table 2.3 Interpretation for the primary types of FOPC

FOPC symbol type	Interpretation over a non-empty domain D
Constant	Element of D
n-ary function name	Mapping of *n*-tuples of D into an element of D
n-ary predicate name	Sets with *n*-tuples of elements of D
Quantifier	Set D

pair *(jasper, max)* is a member of the mapping *bigger*. The truth value of *male(mother(jasper))* is F: the mapping *mother* maps *jasper* to *lara – male(lara)* is assigned F because *lara* is not a member of the mapping *male*.

The meaning assigned to a predicate is said to be **extensional** as opposed to **intensional**. Extensional refers to a meaning that is given in terms of a set (extension) – the set of *n*-tuple elements that are members of the predicate mapping. Intensional meaning describes the properties (characteristics) that elements of the set share. For example, consider the domain:

$$\{1, 2, 5, 4, 6, 9, 12\}$$

The extensional meaning of *even number* would be the set:

$$\{2, 4, 6, 12\}$$

The intensional meaning would describe the set in terms of an understanding of what an even number is – a member of the set is even if it is divisible by 2.

Valuations and satisfaction

The interpretation involving constant terms and function terms has been dealt with but what about variable terms? A variable is mapped onto the elements D in the same manner as for the other types of term. Consider the domain:

$$D = \{0, 1, 2, 3, 4, 5\}$$

Let the relation less than '<' be denoted *lt*.

$$lt \mapsto \{(0, 1), (0, 2), (0, 3), (0, 4), (0, 5), (1, 2), (1, 3) \ldots\}$$

The formula *lt*(0, 1) appears in the mapping for *lt* and is said to be **satisfied,** and the tuple (0, 1) is said to satisfy the relation *lt*. Clearly, (1, 0) does not satisfy *lt*. Suppose that the function *inc(X)* returns value $X + 1$. The following formula is satisfied:

$$lt(0, inc(0)).$$

When dealing with connectives, the question of satisfaction follows naturally from their definitions:

1    $\neg lt(2, 1)$ is satisfied because *lt(2, 1)* is not satisfied.

2   *lt(1, 2)∧lt(1, 3)* is satisfied because both arguments are satisfied.

3   *lt(2, 1)∨lt(1, 3)* is satisfied because one of the arguments, *lt(1, 3)*, is satisfied.

4   *lt(2, 1)→lt(1, 3)* is satisfied. A formula of the form *A→B* is satisfied if either ¬*A* or *B* is satisfied.

5   ∀*X.(even(X)→lt(X, 5))* is satisfied because for every substitution of *X* (those numbers listed in the set) all even numbers are less than 5.

6   ∃*X.(odd(X)∧lt(X, 3))* is satisfied under the substitution *X*=1 because 1 is odd and less than 3.

Summary

A proposition is a sentence and an atomic proposition is the smallest entity to which a value of true or false can be assigned. Atomic propositions can be joined using logical connectives to form complex expressions. These connectives are *and*, *or*, *if ... then* and *if and only if*. The definitions for these connectives are expressed using truth tables. Truth tables can also be used to evaluate the truth value of a complex expression.

An argument is said to be valid if the conclusion can be shown to follow logically from the premises. A truth table can be used to prove a valid argument. Rules of deduction can also be used to prove valid arguments, but the use of these rules relies on experience.

A sound reasoning procedure means that you cannot prove things that are false, and completeness means that you have enough rules of deduction so that any true derivation can be proved.

First-order predicate calculus (FOPC) uses variables, quantifiers and predicates to provide a more expressive language than propositional logic. With FOPC it is possible to represent the association between propositions, which would not be possible using propositional logic. Predicates describe properties of objects and relationships between objects. There are two types of quantifier. The universal quantifier represents *for all* (or *everything*) and the existential quantifier represents *there exists* (or *at least one*). A FOPC formula is interpreted to assign a truth value. An interpretation involves checking for a mapping from formula symbols into sets defining the domains' objects and relationships. For example, *dog(sadie)* is true provided *dog* is a valid predicate and *sadie* appears in the set of domain objects that are dogs.

Further reading

For books on logic see Quine (1982), Manna and Waldinger (1985), Genesereth and Nilsson (1987), Kelly (1997) and Gabbay (1998).

Exercises

1   Evaluate the truth of the following sentences:

   a   If the UK population is 100 then Micky Mouse is the prime minister.
   b   9=2 or 4>3.
   c   If east is 090 degrees and south is 180 degrees then west is 270 degrees.

---

2   Use a truth table to prove the laws of distributivity.

3   Symbolize the following sentences as propositional formulas:

    a   Margaret likes John and John likes Margaret.
    b   David hating football implies David hates rugby.
    c   Bread will be delivered today only if we have breakfast.

4   Check the validity of the following argument using a truth table.

If woody runs then woody wins the race
either woody ran or bella ran
bella did not run
therefore woody won the race

5   Show that the following expression is sound

$$(\rightarrow \mathbf{E}) \frac{A, A \rightarrow B}{B}$$

6   Symbolize the sentences in exercise 3 as predicate formulas.

7   Symbolize the following sentences as predicate formulas:

    a   Manchester is north of London and London is north of Southampton.
    b   London is not north of Coventry.
    c   If city A is north of city B and city C north of city A then city C is north of city B.
    d   No cat likes to swim.
    e   Some cats swim.
    f   Caroline's father likes wine.
    g   Everyone is liked by someone.

CHAPTER 3

Search

The problem-solving strategies presented throughout this book involve search. A problem is presented, the problem is then represented in a form suited to some problem-solving strategy, and the algorithm that implements the strategy is invoked to search for a solution. Search in AI is conceptually no different to our everyday understanding of the word 'search', in which we refer to a specific type of activity such as searching for lost car keys. If when at home we always put our keys in the same place, then we know where we can expect to find them and proceed directly to their location. If we have been absent-minded, then the keys might be somewhere else, in which case we need to perform a search. Many of our everyday activities are not described by us as searching, but a machine implementation of these activities would be described as such: arranging a business meeting between colleagues is a search for a day and time when everybody is free; finding a route to drive from point A to point B; deciding on the next move in a game of chess; planning your working day so that you complete everything that needs doing. You might question whether some activities really involve any form of search. For example, a robot production line for making sandwiches could simply follow a list of instructions: butter two slices of bread, spread pickle on one slice, top with grated cheese, place the other slice of bread on top, cut in half, and wrap. But we are interested in building machines with some intelligence that can respond in a useful way when the unexpected happens. If you were presented with a large wedge of cheese you would know that it needs to be grated or sliced before being placed in the sandwich. A dumb machine might place the whole wedge between bread. A production line usually has limited flexibility and if something changes the production stops and machines are reprogrammed. To be flexible, machines need the ability to search for a problem-solving strategy.

This chapter introduces techniques for searching. These techniques usually form part of a wider problem-solving strategy and so they will be illustrated in the context of toy problems.

3.1 Introduction

One dictionary definition of search is 'look for something whose presence is suspected'. In AI, that something is typically referred to as a **goal**. The whole process of searching is usually presented as a number of steps that describe a connection between the point at which the search starts and the goal. For example, finding a route to drive from London to Edinburgh can be described as a sequence of steps, with each step being a segment along the route. The goal is Edinburgh and the start is London. Each step could be described as a town or city along the route. If you open a map and work your way from London, connecting different cities until you finally reached Edinburgh, then you will have found a solution (a route) to your problem. As you search for your route, you move between cities and towns to form links. Each move changes the state of the search: at one moment you are positioned on London, next on Birmingham, then Leeds, and so on. Finding a goal does not always imply a successful search. The route you have found may fail to achieve a higher level goal of reaching Edinburgh within 6 hours. The quality of a solution will need to be judged and one solution may be rejected in favour of finding another. How the quality is measured depends on the problem. If your objective is to reach Edinburgh with the least fuel consumed then you want to find the shortest route; if, on the other hand, you want to get there in the shortest time, the shortest route may not be optimum if the route is more congested or restricted in terms of speed limits.

In the route-finding problem, the goal state is explicit. Consider what the goal is when searching for your next move in a game of chess. You imagine different sequences of moves that will take you from the existing board state (configuration of your pieces and your opponent's pieces) to a state that puts you in a stronger position. You can make only one move at a time, but you think a few moves ahead in order to predict what the consequences of your next move might be. If it is possible to win the game from one more move then your search had better locate this move as the overriding goal is to win. If the win is a few moves away then you want your next move to be one that maximizes you chance of winning. In this scenario there is no explicit goal state to look for. Instead, you have to evaluate each move in terms of the advantage you believe it gives you.

A little thought about both of the above search problems should bring to mind a number of issues that will be of concern when implementing search strategies. Consider how many routes exist between London and Edinburgh. In practice, all routes cannot be found and there is therefore no guarantee that the route with the shortest distance will be located. The number of board states in chess is huge. A machine will be limited in the amount of memory it can devote to searching and for most problems it will be constrained in the time it is allowed to search. Search strategies are often analysed in terms of time and space (memory) complexity. They are also analysed in terms of the quality of a solution (called **optimality**). If minimum route distance is our objective, then we should prefer a search strategy over other strategies if on average it returns shorter routes. Another important criterion for judging search strategies is **completeness**. If a search strategy is complete then it is guaranteed to find a solution if one exists.

Knowledge plays a big role in most problem-solving strategies, and this knowledge also extends to common-sense reasoning. For example, common-sense tells us that a search for a road route between London and Newport, Isle of Wight, is futile because no bridges or tunnels connect the island with the mainland. We can find a reasonably optimal road route between two towns from inspecting a map even though there may be thousands of possible routes to select from. We have an understanding of the spatial relationship between the two towns and we have a sense of direction that must be taken to move from one town to the other. This knowledge constrains the search; we rule out many options because they appear to be clearly less optimal than other routes. Knowledge constrains searching and knowledge is the key to making search on real-world tasks tractable.

3.2 Some classical AI problems

There are a number of classical toy problems that have been traditionally used in AI to illustrate search. We shall mention two of them in order to make clear some of the terminology used throughout the rest of the chapter.

3.2.1 The eight-tile puzzle

The eight-tile puzzle is a 3×3 grid that has eight tiles and one blank space into which an adjacent tile may be pushed. The objective of the puzzle is to start with the tiles in some random configuration and then move them about until the goal configuration is reached. The puzzle is shown in Figure 3.1. You may well have played with this puzzle, but if we wish to simulate this play using a computer a number of things will need to be represented:

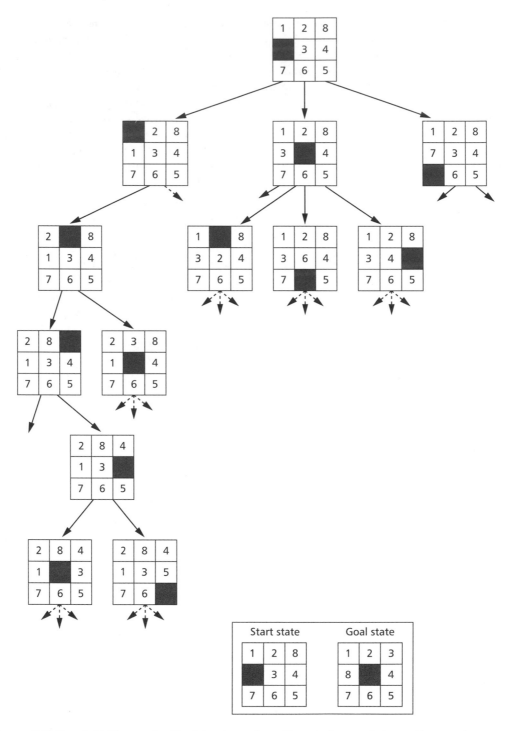

Figure 3.1 The eight-tile puzzle. The tree shows transitions between states as the search attempts to find a path from the start to the goal state.

- **States**. A state represents how the world looks at a point in time. The term 'world' is used to refer to the objects that are contained by the problem, which in this example is the grid and tiles. A state in the eight-tile puzzle is simply a configuration of the tiles.
- **Operator**. The state of the world has to change if anything is to be achieved. A search involves executing actions, and actions change things. The action of moving a tile changes the configuration and hence the state. These changes will be simulated in memory before they are executed for real. A chess-playing computer performs the search in memory and executes its next move once the search is complete. An operator describes an action that might be executed. For example, in the eight-tile puzzle a tile can be moved only if it is adjacent to the blank square. The operators describe possible moves, but some operators might not be executable at a point in time. We could describe four operators for each of the eight tiles: move up, move down, move left and move right. The operator to move tile 2 down can only be executed when the blank square is below tile 2. An operator has to be represented, and we should like the representation to be efficient for the purpose of programming the problem into a machine. The eight-tile puzzle can be represented by four operators if we consider the blank tile to be the one that is moved. Of course, the blank tile is not real, but moving a real tile has the effect of changing where the blank square appears. So the operators are: blank move up, down, left or right.
- **Goal state**. The goal state needs to be recognized, and for this we need a test. In the case of the eight-tile puzzle the test could be a simple match between the current state and the goal state stored in memory.
- **Cost**. A search will always have some measure of quality that is generally referred to as optimality. The measure of optimality depends on the problem, but the measure is usually expressed as a cost. One example cost is the time to search. It would be preferable to have a search strategy that could find the goal in the eight-tile puzzle in the least number of moves. Such a strategy is more optimal than others that take longer. The cost of travelling between two points might be expressed either in time, or distance, or monetary expense.

The **initial state** is the state from where the search commences. The initial state together with the search operators define all other states that can be reached. The set of all reachable states defines the **state space**.

For many problems, the sequence of actions that were taken to reach the goal is of interest. For route planning, the route is the sequence of towns or cities that are used as landmarks along the route from the start to the destination. In the drive from London to Edinburgh, the towns and cities are the states that are generated during the search. For many types of problem it is useful to draw a picture of how a solution is arrived at. In Figure 3.1, such a picture has been drawn in the form of a tree. Only part of the tree is shown. The start state forms the initial root of the tree. Emerging from the root node are three branches that lead to other states. Each branch denotes the application of an operator that moves from the current state to a new state. From the start state, the blank square can move in only one of three directions and hence the three branches. From each new state other states can be generated by applying operators. Continuing this process generates a tree. A path in the tree is any sequence of states that is met by taking a branch from the start state and following the directions of the arrows. Many paths exist, and the objective of searching is to find a path that meets the cost criterion in the shortest time. Sometimes the branches are labelled with weights that denote costs. A road map conveys costs by showing the kilometres between two points. The map may also show costs in terms of estimated time to travel between two points.

Trees are very useful structures for searching because they provide an abstraction that suggest many types of search algorithms. In this chapter we shall look at a few of these algorithms. Abstraction is important for finding algorithms that can be applied to many different problems.

3.2.2 *Missionaries and cannibals*

In this problem, three missionaries and three cannibals have to be ferried across a river, but the boat can only take one or two at a time. The missionaries must never be outnumbered by the cannibals. The opposite banks of the river can be labelled A and B. The goal state is all of the missionaries and cannibals at B. We could denote a missionary by *m* and a cannibal by *c* – for this problem there is no need to represent individuals. It is now possible to list the operators. Each operator is restricted to one or two people in the boat and the combinations are:

m	one missionary in the boat
m, m	two missionaries in the boat
c	one cannibal in the boat
c, c	two cannibals in the boat
m, c	one missionary and one cannibal in the boat

This search is also usefully pictured as a tree. The start state could be denoted as:

$$A = \{m, m, m, c, c, c\}$$

and the goal state as:

$$B = \{m, m, m, c, c, c\}$$

An intermediate state will contain a subset of $\{m, m, m, c, c, c\}$.

In this chapter, search algorithms are split into two broad categories. In the first category, searching is seen as a way to move about a tree structure looking for the goal. This category includes blind searching and informed search, in which information is used to guess which moves to take. In the second category, the algorithms can be pictured as operating in a space of states, the landscape of which is described by some function which is to be optimized – a solution is some optimal point within the landscape.

3.3 Tree-based algorithms

3.3.1 *Blind search*

Blind searching algorithms perform a methodical exhaustive search. No information is used in guiding the search and they proceed using a fixed strategy for generating states and testing for the goal. Two simple algorithms are introduced: **breadth-first search** and **depth-first search**.

Breadth-first search

Breadth-first search starts at the root and explores the whole of one level in the tree before moving on to the next level. Each node within a level is visited in a left to right order. For the tree in Figure 3.2 the order in which nodes are visited is:

A B C D E F G H I J K L M N O P Q

The algorithm for implementing breadth-first search is given in Figure 3.3 and makes use of two structures. The first is a queue, *toVisit*, which holds a record of which nodes to visit next. The

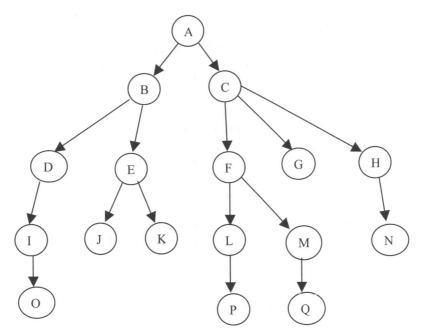

Figure 3.2 A simple search tree for an abstract (imaginary) problem. Each state is labelled and the goal state is taken to be Q.

```
PROCEDURE BreadthFirstSearch(Tree tree, Node root, Goal goal, List alreadyVisited)

        Node current
        Queue toVisit

        add root to toVisit

        while toVisit is not empty
                current ← first node on toVisit
                remove first node from toVisit
                if current = goal
                        add current to alreadyVisited
                        return true
                end if
                for each child node C of current
                        add C to toVisit
                end for
                add current to alreadyVisited
        end while
```

Figure 3.3 Algorithm for implementing breadth-first search.

second is a list called *alreadyVisited*, which records each node that has been visited. The queue is a first-in–first-out (FIFO) data structure, which means that the next element to be removed will be the one that was placed earliest onto the queue. A search using this algorithm is illustrated in Figure 3.4 for the tree in Figure 3.2. The goal node is taken to be the node labelled Q.

Depth-first search

Depth-first search is similar to bread-first search but, as the name implies, it goes deep into the tree following the descendants of a node before returning to explore siblings. The order of search for the tree in Figure 3.2 is:

> A B D I O E J K C F L P M Q G H N

The algorithm for depth-first search is given in Figure 3.5 and the population of the data structures is shown in Figure 3.6. Note that the algorithm is the same as that for breadth-first search except that *toVisit* is now a stack. The stack is a last-in–first-out (LIFO) data structure. The next element to be removed will be the element that was added last.

It is convenient to illustrate the concepts of searching as though the tree is a preconfigured structure. In practice, the tree is actually generated dynamically as the search progresses. Figure 3.7 illustrates the order in which nodes are expanded for breadth-first and depth-first search.

Comparing breadth-first and depth-first search

Breadth-first search is guaranteed to find the goal, if it exists, and in the case that there are several paths to the goal it will find the shortest path as it exhausts one level before progressing to the next. With depth-first search there is no such guarantee because, for an infinite tree, it could wander aimlessly forever, never returning to explore other branches from where it started. However, nodes that have been expanded have to be stored in memory, and breadth-first search consumes more memory than depth-first search. To see this, consider the binary tree in Figure 3.8. Each node has two child

toVisit	alreadyVisited
[A]	[]
[B, C]	[A]
[C, D, E]	[A, B]
[D, E, F, G, H]	[A, B, C]
[E, F, G, H, I]	[A, B, C, D]
[F, G, H, I, J, K]	[A, B, C, D, E]
[G, H, I, J, K, L, M]	[A, B, C, D, E, F]
[H, I, J, K, L, M]	[A, B, C, D, E, F, G]
[I, J, K, L, M, N]	[A, B, C, D, E, F, G, H]
[J, K, L, M, N, O]	[A, B, C, D, E, F, G, H, I]
[K, L, M, N, O]	[A, B, C, D, E, F, G, H, I, J]
[L, M, N, O]	[A, B, C, D, E, F, G, H, I, J, K]
[M, N, O, P]	[A, B, C, D, E, F, G, H, I, J, K, L]
[N, O, P, Q]	[A, B, C, D, E, F, G, H, I, J, K, L, M]
[O, P, Q]	[A, B, C, D, E, F, G, H, I, J, K, L, M, N]
[P, Q]	[A, B, C, D, E, F, G, H, I, J, K, L, M, N, O]
[Q]	[A, B, C, D, E, F, G, H, I, J, K, L, M, N, O, P]

Figure 3.4 How the queue of states *toVisit* and the *alreadyVisited* list develop during execution of the breadth-first algorithm on the tree in Figure 3.2.

```
PROCEDURE DepthFirstSearch(Tree tree, Node root, Goal goal, List alreadyVisited)

        Node current
        Stack toVisit

        add root to toVisit

        while toVisit is not empty
                current ← first node on toVisit
                remove first node from toVisit
                if current = goal
                        add current to alreadyVisited
                        return true
                end if
                for each child node C of current
                        add C to toVisit
                end for
                add current to alreadyVisited
        end while
```

Figure 3.5 Algorithm for implementing depth-first search.

toVisit	alreadyVisited
[A]	[]
[B, C]	[A]
[D, E, C]	[A, B]
[I, E, C,]	[A, B, D]
[O, E, C]	[A, B, D, I]
[E, C,]	[A, B, D, I, O]
[J, K, C]	[A, B, D, I, O, E]
[K, C]	[A, B, D, I, O, E, J]
[C,]	[A, B, D, I, O, E, J, K]
[F, G, H]	[A, B, D, I, O, E, J, K, C]
[L, M, G, H]	[A, B, D, I, O, E, J, K, C, F]
[P, M, G, H]	[A, B, D, I, O, E, J, K, C, F, L]
[M, G, H]	[A, B, D, I, O, E, J, K, C, F, L, P]
[Q, G, H]	[A, B, D, I, O, E, J, K, C, F, L, P, M]

Figure 3.6 How the stack of states *toVisit* and the *alreadyVisited* list develop during execution of the depth-first algorithm on the tree in Figure 3.2.

nodes. When breadth-first search starts to explore the last level, depth 3, it will have expanded all of the nodes at level 2 and so *toVisit* will contain eight nodes waiting to be visited. Depth-first search, on the other hand, will contain:

HIEC

When it then moves across at level 3, depth-first will hold:

JKC

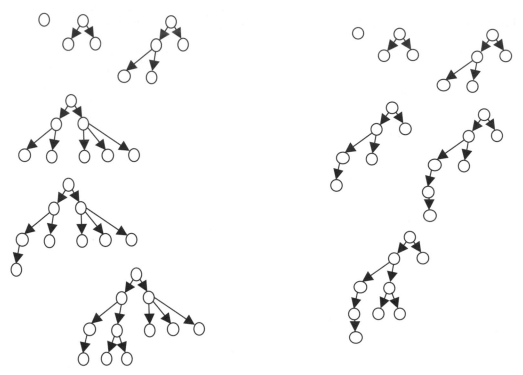

Figure 3.7 Illustration of the search tree shown in Figure 3.2 being generated dynamically as the search progresses for breadth-first search on the left and depth-first search on the right. The whole search is not shown and hence the tree is not yet complete.

once node E has been expanded. Breadth-first search must hold nodes proportional to b^d in memory, where b is the branching factor (in this case 2) and d is the depth. For example, level 3 contains 2^3 nodes and at level 12 breadth-first search will have to hold in memory 2^{12} nodes on *toVisit*. Depth-first search requires in the order of bh nodes to be stored, where h is the maximum depth of the tree.

Iterative-deepening search

Breadth-first search is expensive in terms of both memory and time. Depth-first search, on the other hand, is not guaranteed to find a solution and may never terminate if it follows an infinitely deep path that does not contain the goal. A simple modification of depth-first search is to limit the depth of the search. For example, if the limit were set to 10, the search would not explore any nodes at a depth greater than 10. One difficulty, though, is choosing a sensible limit for the maximum depth. Iterative deepening avoids making this choice in that it keeps performing depth-first search starting with a limit of 0 and then increasing the limit by 1 for every repeat of the search. For example, in Figure 3.8 the search at each step would be as follows:

Limit	Order of visiting nodes
0	A
1	A B C
2	A B D E C F G
3	A B D H I E J K C F L M G N M

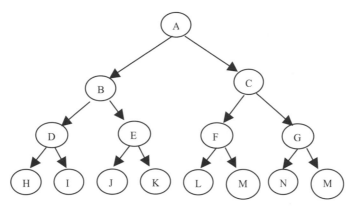

Figure 3.8 A binary search tree.

Starting the search from scratch each time with a new limit might appear to be wasting effort as some nodes are repeatedly expanded. However, if the branching factor is high, the overhead becomes negligible because levels that are deep contain many more nodes relative to shallower levels and the number of times a node is expanded is correlated with its depth – shallower nodes are expanded more often.

The algorithms for breadth-first and depth-first search presented in Figures 3.3 and 3.5 use more memory than is strictly necessary because the *alreadyVisited* list was maintained. If each node has a reference to its parent, then the path taken to reach a goal can always be traced back after the search has completed. However, maintaining the *alreadyVisited* list is useful for many practical search problems, the reason being that many search spaces correspond more to a graph than to a tree, and this means that paths can be repeated. Consider Figure 3.9, which is a modification of the tree in Figure 3.2. The addition of the dotted arrows means that different paths can lead to the same nodes. The structure in Figure 3.9 is a graph as opposed to a tree. It can be transformed into a tree by allowing nodes to be repeated. To do this we would draw a repeated node for I as a child of E and a repeated O as a child of I (that is a grandchild of E). Nodes M and Q would also be repeated as descendants of H. Obviously, this repetition generates a larger tree, and it is wasteful to repeat searches along paths that have already been explored. Figure 3.10 combines the search algorithms for breadth-first and depth-first searches into a more generalized search algorithm. This general algorithm has *toVisit* templated to indicate that it can be any data structure that is of type *DS* (data structure for searching). Note also that a check has been added before a child node is put on *toVisit*. This check ensures that work is not repeated by checking to see if the node appears on either *alreadyVisited* or *toVisit*.

3.3.2   Heuristic search

Blind searching is an exhaustive exploration of the search space. Imagine the eight-tile puzzle in which you are blindfolded. You move a single tile and a friend looks at the puzzle and tells you whether it is a goal state. If it is not, you move another tile and continue in this fashion. Not much fun, but given enough time you might hit upon the solution. Indeed, with good luck you could find the solution quickly. Blindfolding you is not quite analogous to the blind search algorithms we have looked at. These algorithms are more systematic in that they explore the search space in a regulated fashion and they can work with large amounts of memory so that they do not go down paths already explored. Your friend is likely to get tired, and her capacity for memorizing what has been before

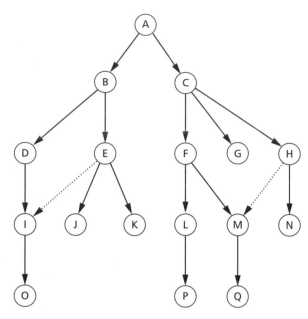

Figure 3.9 A search graph. The tree becomes a graph because the dotted links form cycles – if the links are undirected (no arrows). The path B, E , I, D, B forms a cycle.

```
PROCEDURE Search(Tree tree, Node root, Goal goal, List alreadyVisited)

        Node current
        <DS> toVisit

        add root to toVisit

        while toVisit is not empty
                current ← first node on toVisit
                remove first node from toVisit
                if current = goal
                        add current to alreadyVisited
                        return true
                end if
                for each child node C of current
                        if C is not on alreadyVisited and not on toVisit
                                add C to toVisit
                        end if
                end for
                add current to alreadyVisited
        end while
```

Figure 3.10 A more generalized search algorithm combining the search algorithms for breadth-first and depth-first search.

cannot match a machine. If you take the blindfold off, you will have an advantage over the blind search algorithms. You can make predictions as to which move will take you closer to the goal. Your predictions might not always be good, but on average you will be able to get to the goal in fewer moves than if you were blindfolded. If you play with the puzzle often enough, you will start to detect patterns. You will spot configurations of the tiles that are familiar and your predictions will improve. Without the blindfold you are using information about the search space to control the direction of the search. The more experienced you are, the more information you can employ. For most games, experience counts.

A **heuristic** function is a rule that will return a value for a node that indicates how promising the search will be if it explores paths that emerge from that node. Suppose you are looking for a music CD of some band that was released a number of years ago and you are familiar with the record shops in London. If you think the chance of finding the CD is rare you might start at the stores with the largest stock of CDs. Your heuristic function (which in this case comes from your knowledge of the stores) returns a value that indicates the size of the store. If you are searching for a CD that most stores are likely to keep in stock your criterion might be to search for the cheapest price. You therefore order the search in terms of discount – those shops that usually discount most get visited first.

As a node is expanded, a heuristic function can be called to evaluate how promising the search will be if the paths leading from that node are explored. All the nodes on *toVisit* can be ordered according to the values that the function returns for each node. Depending on the way the problem is expressed, either nodes with lower evaluations or nodes with higher evaluations are preferred. It is more usual to treat the value returned by a function as a cost and look to minimize the cost. Therefore, problems are usually expressed so that nodes with lower values take precedence over those with higher values. **Best-first search** is a search that orders the search on the basis of node preference. The search can be implemented using the algorithm in Figure 3.10, where *toVisit* is now a priority queue. A priority queue will order its elements according to some precedence. Best-first search can be implemented so that every time a child is placed on *toVisit* all of the nodes are ordered so that the lowest cost node is always the next node to be removed. The heuristic function determines the cost and therefore the ordering of nodes. The order of node visits is illustrated for the tree in Figure 3.11. The tree has nodes indicating the cost. You should not try to reason about the numbers – they are for illustration only. The order of node visits is given in Figure 3.12.

A* search

When searching, a child node is generated by applying an operator to the parent node. As nodes represent states, the branch connecting two nodes denotes a state transformation. A path in a search tree therefore represents a succession of state transitions. A cost can be associated with the operator for expanding a node. The cost of a path can then be evaluated by summing the cost for each operation along that path. The simplest form of cost function is to return a cost of 1 for every application of an operator. The cost, then, of a path to a node n is the depth of node n. If cost is based on the depth of a node then breadth-first search is guaranteed to find the cheapest path to the goal. Let us denote this cost function as $g(n)$. So $g(n)$ is the cost of the path from the root node to node n. Let us now denote our heuristic function as $h(n)$. The function $h(n)$ returns the cost of going from node n to the goal node.

A search that is controlled only by $g(n)$ minimizes the cost of the path so far and so it is optimal. If the cost of every move (application of an operator) is always 1, best-first search reduces to breadth-first search and is guaranteed to find the shortest path from the start to a goal node. However, the search can be very time-consuming without good heuristics to suggest which paths to try first. To see

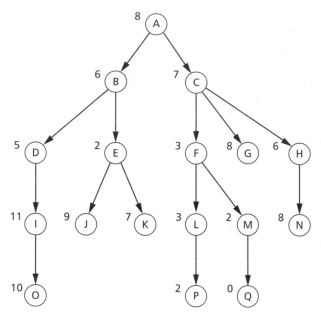

Figure 3.11 This tree has been populated with costs to illustrate heuristic search.

[(A, 8)]	[]
[(B, 6), (C, 7)]	[(A, 8)]
[(E, 2), (D, 5), (C, 7)]	[(A, 8), (B, 6)]
[(D, 5), (C, 7), (K, 7), (J, 9)]	[(A, 8), (B, 6), (E, 2)]
[(C, 7), (K, 7), (J, 9), (I, 11)]	[(A, 8), (B, 6), (E, 2), (D, 5)]
[(F, 3), (H, 6), (K, 7), (G, 8), (J, 9), (I, 11)]	[(A, 8), (B, 6), (E, 2), (D, 5), (C, 7)]
[(M, 2), (L, 3), (H, 6), (K, 7), (G, 8), (J, 9), (I, 11)]	[(A, 8), (B, 6), (E, 2), (D, 5), (C, 7), (F, 3)]
[(Q, 0), (L, 3), (H, 6), (K, 7), (G, 8), (J, 9), (I, 11)]	[(A, 8), (B, 6), (E, 2), (D, 5), (C, 7), (F, 3) (M, 2)]

Figure 3.12 The order of node visits for the tree in Figure 3.11 as determined by a best-first search.

this, imagine that an artificial ant has to find a way from grid location 11 (the start) to grid location 15 (the finish), in Figure 3.13. The ant can change its state by moving to an adjacent square. The filled-in squares are wells and therefore off-limits. The ant can only move vertically or horizontally. The length of the shortest path is 6:

11–16–17–18–19–20–15

Suppose that every move costs the ant 1 unit in effort, unless it moves south, in which case the effort is 2. Figure 3.14 shows two possible paths to the goal state (square 15). The cost of effort in reaching a node is given in parenthesis. We want the search to be optimal in terms of effort spent. Suppose the heuristic is based on $g(n)$, the cost expended so far. The ant opts to move to square 6 because it costs less to move north than to move south. The search starts looking along the leftmost branch in Figure 3.14, swapping between least-cost nodes on either branch, until it expands node 5,

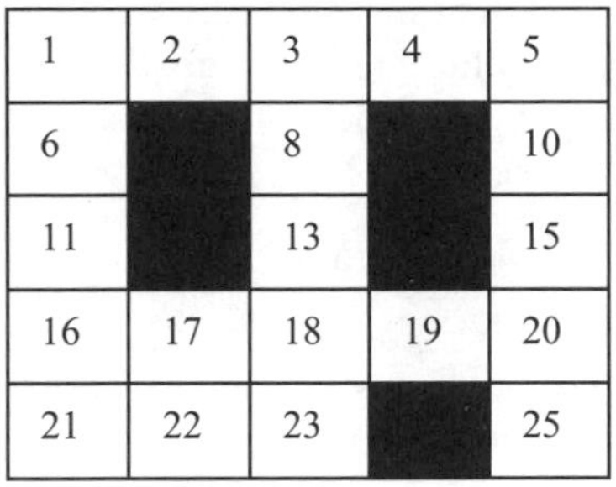

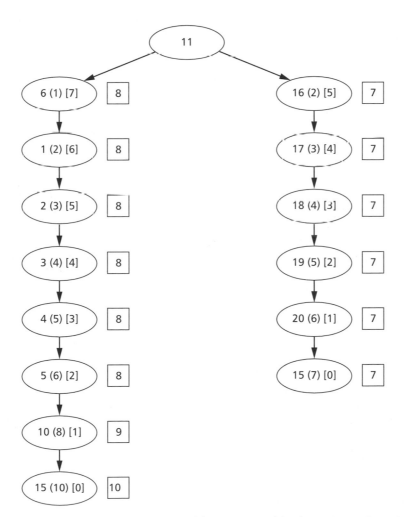

Figure 3.13 An ant has to navigate its way from square 11 to square 15. It cannot enter the dark squares as they represent wells.

Figure 3.14 The costs of two paths for the problem expressed in Figure 3.13. The value in (…) is $g(n)$, that in […] is $h(n)$ and that outside the node the sum of $g(n)$ and $h(n)$.

at which point the search stays on the right-hand branch. An optimal solution has been found but it is not very efficient. It would be more efficient if the heuristic $h(n)$ could be used in addition to $g(n)$ so that the heuristic function includes an estimate of the cost from node n to the goal. A heuristic function that combines $g(n)$ and $h(n)$ is:

$$f(n) = g(n) + h(n)$$

The function $f(n)$ provides an estimated cost of the cheapest solution through node n. It sums the cost of the path from the start node to node n, with the cheapest path estimate from n to the goal. If the function $h(n)$ never overestimates the cost of reaching the goal, then $h(n)$ is said to be **admissible**. If best-first search uses $f(n)$ as the heuristic function and $h(n)$ is admissible, the search is known as **A* search**.

3.4 Search expressed as function optimization

Many problems that occur in AI are a form of function optimization. The output of these functions is a value that indicates the desirability of the state as defined by the function inputs. We shall consider two problems to explain what this means.

In Table 3.1, the distances between various UK cities are given in matrix form. For example, the distance from Bristol to Northampton is 53 miles. A classical optimization problem is the travelling salesman problem (TSP). The task is to find a route that passes through all of the cities a salesman has to visit such that the distance of the route is a minimum (or close to). Table 3.2 lists all possible routes through the cities Southampton, Bristol, London, Northampton and Cambridge. The salesman starts at Southampton and finishes at Southampton.

As the number of cities is small, it is possible to exhaustively compute the distance for each route and find the optimal route. It does not take too many cities before the task becomes impossible to search exhaustively. Since, for large search spaces, an exhaustive search is impractical, it is not possible to guarantee finding the optimum solution, but we would still like a solution that is reasonably optimal. So, for the travelling salesman, it would not be possible to guarantee finding the shortest route, but the search should return a route that is shorter than most others.

Each string in Table 3.2 specifies a tour (route) the salesman could take. Each tour is a state in the search space. An algorithm for searching will need to generate states and evaluate the desirability of a state. For the TSP, the function to be evaluated is the distance corresponding to a state. The tricky part is generating the states during searching. Ideally, we would like each new state that is generated to be more optimal than the last. For example, suppose Table 3.2 were sorted in descending order by distance. The tours with the largest distance are S N L B C S and S C B L N S, and these would appear first in the table. Suppose the first tour is randomly generated and appears at row i in the sorted table. We would like the next tour to be generated to be one below row i, say row j, and the one following row j to be below row j, and so on. Figure 3.15(a) is a plot of the tour distance against tour after sorting in descending order. The points on the curve correspond to a tour. The points have been joined for visual impact, but the function is discrete and not continuous as the line might suggest. There are no tours, for example, that lie between any two points because we have exhaustively evaluated every possible tour. If the states could be generated as suggested in Figure 3.15(a), then the direction of searching would be known; however, as, in practice, this direction is not known heuristics have to be used. The search space in practice appears more like that shown in Figure 3.15(b). Here we can visualize the search space because there are not many states and each state has been described by a single parameter (a string denoting the tour).

The charts in Figure 3.15 are somewhat misleading because the shape of the search surface is

Table 3.1 Matrix of distances between UK cities

	S	B	L	N	C
S		134	80	169	131
B			120	53	97
L				131	60
N					86
C					

S, Southampton; B, Bristol; L, London; N, Northampton; C, Cambridge.

Table 3.2 Possible routes through the cities given in Table 3.1

S B L N C S	134 + 120 + 131 + 86 + 131 = 602
S B L C N S	134 + 120 + 60 + 86 + 169 = 569
S B C L N S	134 + 97 + 60 + 131 + 169 = 591
S B C N L S	134 + 97 + 86 + 131 + 80 = 528
S B N L C S	134 + 53 + 131 + 60 + 131 = 509
S B N C L S	134 + 53 + 86 + 60 + 80 = 413
S L B N C S	80 + 120 + 53 + 86 + 131 = 470
S L B C N S	80 + 120 + 97 + 86 + 169 = 552
S L C B N S	80 + 60 + 97 + 53 + 169 = 459
S L C N B S	80 + 60 + 86 + 53 + 134 = 413
S L N B C S	80 + 131 + 53 + 97 + 131 = 492
S L N C B S	80 + 131 + 86 + 97 + 134 = 528
S N L B C S	169 + 131 + 120 + 97 + 131 = 648
S N L C B S	169 + 131 + 60 + 97 + 134 = 591
S N C L B S	169 + 86 + 60 + 120 + 134 = 569
S N C B L S	169 + 86 + 97 + 120 + 80 = 552
S N B L C S	169 + 53 + 120 + 60 + 131 = 533
S N B C L S	169 + 53 + 97 + 60 + 80 = 459
S C L N B S	131 + 60 + 131 + 53 + 134 = 509
S C L B N S	131 + 60 + 120 + 53 + 169 = 533
S C B L N S	131 + 97 + 120 + 131 + 169 = 648
S C B N L S	131 + 97 + 53 + 131 + 80 = 492
S C N L B S	131 + 86 + 131 + 120 + 134 = 602
S C N B L S	131 + 86 + 53 + 120 + 80 = 470

(a)

(b)

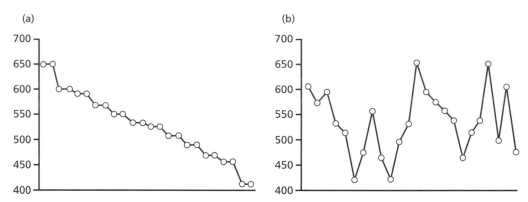

Figure 3.15 (a) Each dot is a tour. The tours have been sorted by length. (b) This chart reflects a random exploration of tours. The chart shows that a pure random exploration can vary widely between good and poor solutions.

determined by the order in which the states are explored. The horizontal axis denotes time and the positions of states along this axis in Figure 3.15(b) are not determined by any ordinal relation between the states – each state has been generated in random order. Contrast this with the problem that is introduced next.

Figure 3.16 shows a number of points that are randomly scattered about the line $y = x$. A least-squares fit to the data is shown, and it will be observed that the slope is still approximately 1 and the intercept is just below $y = 0$. The general equation of a straight line is:

$$y = ax + b$$

where a is the slope and b the intercept. The line can also be written as:

(a)

(b)

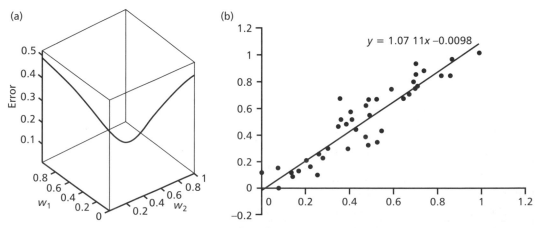

Figure 3.16 The line in (b) shows an optimum fit for the data points. This fit can be found by using fast analytical techniques, but it can also be found using search. Search is the adopted approach for problems for which a good mathematical model does not exist. Graph (a) shows how the error of the fit varies for different line parameters.

$$0 = w_1 x + w_2 y + w_0$$

with $a = -(w_1/w_2)$ and $b = -(w_0/w_2)$.

Each w_i is called a weight. Fitting a line to the data points requires the weights to be found. To make the problem simpler, we shall ignore the weight w_0 and assume that the line passes through the origin – the fit will be approximate. A simple way to find the other two weights is to generate candidate weights and then substitute each point into the equation:

$$e_n = w_1 x_n + w_2 y_n$$

where e is the error and n is a point. Any point that lies on the line will have zero error. Ideally, all points would lie on the line and the error would be zero, but obviously a straight line cannot fit all of the points. There will therefore be an error, but we should like this error to be minimum. For each candidate set of weights the average squared error is calculated:

$$E = \frac{1}{N} \sum_n e_n^2$$

where N is the total number of points. The set of weights that give the minimum value of E is selected as the best fit. We do not want to waste time by generating any random set of weights on each trial, and so we must control the search. An easy way of doing this is to imagine a line that sweeps like the hand of a clock but in an anticlockwise direction. The line starts aligned with the x-axis and stops when vertical. Each line defines a candidate set of weights and the number of candidates is determined by the extent to which the line is allowed to sweep at each step. Of course, this is a naive method of line fitting, but many real applications use an approach that is not dissimilar for fitting functions to data. The task for these applications is to find some controlled procedure that generates candidate weights that improve on the previous set.

In Figure 3.16, a curve has been plotted of E against the weights. The weights that correspond to the lowest point on the curve provide the optimum fit (within the resolution determined by how much the candidate line is allowed to sweep). Only one curve is shown in Figure 3.16 but there will be many curves that could be generated with a minimum point that will provide an optimum fit. These curves will collectively form a surface that looks like a valley. Our search for weights that provide the optimum fit is a search over this surface. The surface forms a landscape which in the current example is smooth but for many (if not most) problems this surface will be complex with many peaks and troughs. The task of optimization is to find the lowest point in this landscape. Any point in the landscape represents a state during the search and if the algorithm for searching is to be useful we would like to move from the current location on the curve towards the minimum point as fast as possible. There are many algorithms designed to do such a job and we shall look at one in the next section. There is another widely adopted approach called gradient descent that we shall meet in Chapter 15. The objective of gradient descent is to move in the direction that provides the maximum rate of change in the evaluation function. For a point on a curve, the direction of maximum change is given by the gradient.

3.4.1 Simulated annealing

Imagine a scaled model of a mountainous terrain with many valleys and peaks. Any location along this terrain can be described by coordinates along the directions north–south and east–west. The model is sat on the floor in a large room. You drop a ping-pong ball onto the terrain and it bounces about until it runs out of energy. The ball initially has a lot of energy and it can hop over high ridges, but as its energy runs out it becomes more limited to where it can bounce until it gets stuck in a valley and eventually settles in a localized bowl of the valley.

The mountainous terrain can be thought of as a cost function of two parameters. The values of the parameters describe the coordinates of where the ball bounces and finally comes to rest. Somewhere in the terrain will be a location for which no other location is lower. Such a point is called a **global minimum**. There will be many other low points. The lowest point within some region like a valley is called a **local minimum**. The ideal solution is where the cost is a global minimum. Spotting the global minimum on our model is possible, but for many real problems the surface of the cost function will be too large to explore exhaustively.

Our bouncing ball will generally find some low point. Where the ball settles will depend on the initial energy it is given and the coordinates of where it starts. The ball is highly unlikely to settle in a global minimum, but it would be great if we could impart some kind of heuristic control on the ball so that the ball finds a reasonably good minimum.

We would like an algorithm that mimics the ping-pong ball, with some control as to what the ball does. Such an algorithm exists and it is called **simulated annealing**. Simulated annealing has become widely used in recent years for tackling a number of optimization problems, but the algorithm originates from work done by Metropolis and colleagues in 1953. The procedure is called simulated annealing because of the analogy with a physical process that occurs when a material is heated to a high temperature and then slowly cooled. The material must be heated to a high enough temperature so that the material's atoms have enough energy to move about in a random manner. The material is then cooled using a cooling schedule designed so that the material's atoms achieve low-energy states and line up in an orderly fashion. If the material is cooled too quickly the atoms can become frozen in random orientations. The annealing of metals is done in manufacturing to toughen the material.

Simulated annealing really refers to a class of algorithms, but they can be seen as variants of the Metropolis algorithm.

Figure 3.17 shows the curve of a hypothetical function of one variable. The function has several minima. We shall describe a simple version of the Metropolis algorithm by imagining a ball that wanders over the landscape of this function searching for a minimum. The ball has some start location. The algorithm iterates over the following steps.

1   Subject the ball to a small random displacement.
2   The change in energy ΔE is computed as $x_{new} - x_{old}$, where x is the height of the ball (value returned by the function).
3   If ΔE is less than or equal to 0, the new position is accepted and the procedure is started again from step 1.
4   If ΔE is greater than 0 (ball has moved higher) its new position is accepted according to some probability distribution:
   a   Generate a random number between 0 and 1.
   b   If the number is less than $\exp[-(\Delta E/T)]$ then the new position of the ball is accepted. If the position is not accepted the ball returns to its old position.
5   Return to step 1.

The distribution $\exp[-(\Delta E/T)]$ denotes the probability of the ball being able to change its energy when the temperature is T. As the algorithm iterates, the temperature is slowly lowered from its initial value. Allowing the ball occasionally to move to a higher position allows the ball the oppor-

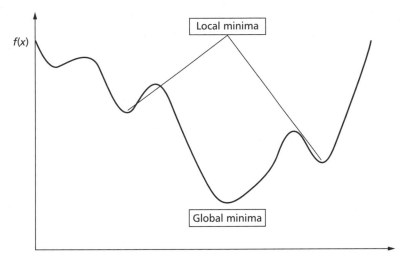

Figure 3.17 Illustration of local and global minima.

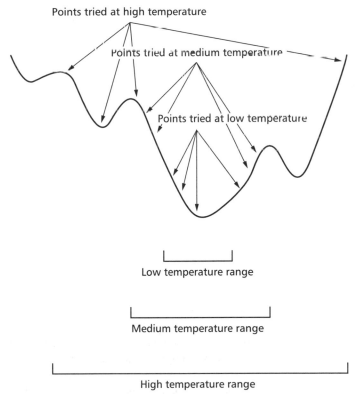

Figure 3.18 Finding global minima using simulated annealing.

tunity to escape from a valley, but as the temperature is lowered there is less opportunity for escape and the ball will seek a lower position within its current valley (see Figure 3.18). The algorithm can terminate when T attains a value of 0. The temperature has to drop according to some specified schedule.

Kirkpatrick *et al.* (1983) provide some simple rules:

1   The initial temperature is set high enough so that nearly all changes in position are accepted.
2   The temperature is decremented according to:
    a $T_k = \alpha T_{k-1}$, $k = 1, 2 \ldots$, where α typically lies between 0.8 and 0.99.
    b   The temperature is decremented so that, on average, there are 10 accepted changes in position at each temperature.
3   If the desired number of accepted changes in position has not been achieved after three successive changes in temperature, then the algorithm stops.

3.4.2   Representing problems

The travelling salesman problem has become a classical test for optimization algorithms. A simple way to represent this problem is to use a sequence that lists the cities in order of visits. The algorithm can start with a randomly selected list such as:

S N B L C S

The Metropolis algorithm can be used to find a solution. We need a method for generating a new state (a new tour) from the existing state and a method for calculating the change in energy. The cost is the length of the tour. A new state can be generated by selecting two cities at random and swapping their positions (the first and last states are never chosen because the tour is to start and finish at S). For example:

S N B L C S swap B and C generates new state S N C L B S

The energy can be computed as the length of the tour. If a new state generates a reduction in tour length (or the length remains the same) it is accepted. If the new state generates a longer tour then it is accepted according to the distribution $\exp[-(\Delta E/T)]$.

An algorithm for the TSP is given in Figure 3.19.

3.4.3   Constraint satisfaction

Many problems can be viewed as a search for a goal that satisfies constraints. You might need to plan a journey from London to Edinburgh with a constraint that you arrive in time for a meeting or that the cost of your journey fits within a budget. Constraints can sometimes be used to effect a reduction in the size of the search space. For example, you might immediately rule out the possibility of flying to Edinburgh because of cost.

Many real-world problems involve satisfying constraints. You may need to arrange a meeting with fellow students within the constraints that the meeting be held this week but it must not clash with scheduled lectures. Scheduling problems usually involve many constraints, such as budgets, time, labour and material resources, etc. Vehicle designs are subjected to many constraints, e.g. fuel efficiency, passenger comfort, luggage capacity, safety and aesthetic qualities.

In this section we shall study a particular form of searching with constraints known as **propo-**

```
PROCEDURE TSP(Tour, Schedule, T₀)

Temperature T ← T₀

while not frozen
            Tour_new ← random new state derived from Tour
            ΔE← Tour_new -Tour
            if ΔE ≤ 0
                        Tour ← Tour_new
            end if
            else
                        choose a random number r between 0 and 1
                        if r < exp(−ΔE/T)
                                    Tour ← Tour_new
                        end if
            end else
            call Schedule
end while
```

Figure 3.19 An algorithm for the TSP. Schedule determines how the temperature drops.

sitional **satisfiability** (SAT). The problem is expressed as a propositional formula and the search looks for an assignment for the variables that makes the formula true. Many types of problem can be solved using SAT. In recent years, SAT methods have been applied to planning problems.

Formulas are often expressed in conjunctive normal form (CNF) (see Chapter 4). A CNF formula consists of a conjunction of clauses and a clause is a disjunction of literals. Consider the following:

> You and two colleagues are interviewing three candidates (A, B, and C) for positions in your company as software engineers. You have a number of vacancies to fill. It could be the case that all candidates are suitable for employment or that none is. At the end of the interview you want to satisfy your own recommendations and those of your colleagues. You believe that you should employ either A or C or both. Your first colleague states that if you employ A then you must employ B (either you employ B or don't employ A). Your second colleague states that you should not employ both B and C.

The desires of you and your work colleagues are constraints on who should be employed. The employment of one person can depend on another. For example, one of your colleagues is insisting that you do not employ A without also employing B. We can represent these constraints as a formula in CNF:

$$(A \lor C) \land (\neg A \lor B) \land (\neg B \lor \neg C)$$

There are two choices that satisfy everyone's desires. You employ candidates A and B but not C or you only employ C. With this assignment the formula evaluates to true, as can be seen in the truth table shown in Table 3.3.

For three propositional symbols an exhaustive search for the assignment is trivial. Once we approach 20 symbols we are starting to consume a good deal of computing time and pragmatic considerations rule out exhaustive searching. SAT algorithms are techniques for finding propositional assignments.

Table 3.3 Truth table evaluation of $(A \lor C) \land (\neg A \lor B) \land (\neg B \lor \neg C)$

A	B	C	$A \lor C$	$\neg A \lor B$	$\neg B \lor \neg C$
1	1	1	1	1	0
1	1	0	1	1	1
1	0	1	1	0	1
1	0	0	1	0	1
0	1	1	1	1	0
0	1	0	0	1	1
0	0	1	1	1	1
0	0	0	0	1	1

There are many SAT algorithms. One example is **GSAT** (see Figure 3.20). GSAT starts with a random truth assignment to the formula Σ and then changes the assignment of the literal that gives the largest increase in the number of satisfied clauses. In essence, this is hill-climbing,[1] but GSAT can move sideways if it finds that it cannot continue to climb. The sideways move is achieved by flipping the truth assignment of a literal that maintains the score (the number of satisfied clauses).

If GSAT fails to escape a local minimum, then the search can restart with a new random assignment. Allowing things to get worse (increasing the number of unsatisfied clauses) is sometimes a better strategy to escape local minima. A strategy similar to that of simulated annealing can be employed. A random walk (Selman *et al.* 1993) is such a strategy. The algorithm follows GSAT but the flipping of a variable is done according to:

> With probability p, pick a variable occurring in some unsatisfied clause and flip its truth assignment.
> With probability $1-p$, flip a variable that minimizes the number of unsatisfied clauses (standard GSAT strategy).

PROCEDURE GSAT(Σ, max_restarts, max_flips)

for i ←1 to max_restarts
    A ← random truth assignment of literals in Σ
    for j ←1 to max_flips
        if A satisfies Σ
            return A
        end if
        A ← A with variable flipped that minimises the number of unsatisfied clauses
    end for
end for
return failure

Figure 3.20 GSAT algorithm.

---

[1]Hill-climbing looks to maximize cost as opposed to minimizing it. Hill-climbing search is a heuristic search that always seeks to improve on the existing state with the next move – it never makes a move to a less desirable state. If the search reaches a local ridge, it will get stuck because all successive moves take the search down (make things worse) before being able to move back up (improving).

Summary

There are many search strategies, and they all aim to transform the existing state to some desirable goal state. For some problems, the sequence of steps in performing the transformation is important, as, for example, when finding a route between two places. For other problems, the sequence of steps is not of interest, but for all problems we should like the search to be efficient in space and time. Many problems are usefully represented as tree structures, in which a node denotes a state and a branch a legal operator that transforms one state into another. Two blind search algorithms, breadth-first and depth-first, will exhaustively search a tree. Most problems require heuristic search in which information is used to guide the search. Heuristics are used to evaluate states and the most promising evaluations are targeted for searching first. Two heuristic search algorithms explored in this chapter were best-first search and A* search.

Many types of task can be represented as function optimization. Like heuristic search, the desirability of a state can be evaluated as a cost. Most optimization tasks are expressed in such a form that the most desirable state is the one with minimum cost. Function optimization can be pictured as a landscape that is covered with different-sized peaks and valleys. Each axis of the landscape corresponds to a function parameter, and a point on the landscape denotes a cost. The aim of the search is to move from the current location in this landscape to a low point (ideally the lowest). One algorithm for function optimization is simulated annealing. For most of the time, simulated annealing moves the current position to a lower cost, but occasionally it will allow things to get worse and for the cost to increase so that local minima can be escaped. As the search continues, the amount by which the current state (point on the landscape) can change is progressively restricted.

Propositional satisfiability is a technique that aims to find a truth assignment to each literal in a propositional formula that satisfies the goal. For a large number of literals, there are many combinations of truth assignment and most (if not all) assignments will fail to satisfy the goal.

Further reading

AI researchers were very active in search techniques from the start. Nilsson (1971) gives a good insight into the early work.

The travelling salesman problem has been tackled by numerous approaches. Two examples using optimization are Johnson and McGeoch (1997) and Fredman *et al.* (1995). The Metropolis algorithm was presented in Metropolis *et al.* (1953). Example papers on SAT include Selman *et al.* (1992, 1993). For an overview of SAT methods see Gent and Walsh (1999).

Exercises

1   Sketch out part of the search space for noughts and crosses (tic tac toe). What is the minimum number of states a breadth-first search would need to explore before a solution might be found? What is the minimum number of states a depth-first search would need to explore before a solution might be found?

2   The figure below is a sketch for a version of the towers of Hanoi problem. There are three pegs and three disks. Each disk is of a different size. The task is to get all of the disks from the first

peg onto the third peg. One disk at a time can be moved, but at no point is a disk allowed to be placed on a smaller disk. Explore the search space. What is the minimum number of moves to complete this problem?

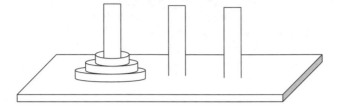

3   Implement a breadth-first search. Use the search to explore the minimum number of moves with the towers of Hanoi using three pegs and two disks, three pegs and three disks, three pegs and four disks, and three pegs and five disks. Can you guess a relationship between the number of moves to the shortest solution and the number of disks and pegs?

4   There are four towns, {A, B, C, D}, which are all connected to each other. The distances between the towns are listed below:

	A	B	C	D
A		10	15	20
B			12	9
C				5
D				

a   What is the shortest route between A and D?
b   What strategy would you use to avoid exploring every state?
c   What would be the maximum number of states in the search for six towns all connected to each other?

5   The search tree in Figure 3.2 has the following costs:

A (15)   B (12)   C (10)   D (11)
E (12)   F (7)   G (8)   H (5)
I (10)   J (9)   K (9)   L (4)
M (5)   N (5)   O (8)   P (3)
Q (0)

Show all steps in a best-first search.

6   Implement A* search for the problem in exercise 4.

7   Get hold of a map of the London Underground. Try and devise a search strategy to automatically find a route between two stations. What sort of knowledge might you build into the strategy?

8 If, for the Metropolis algorithm, the maximum change in energy is 10, what value of T would you start with to ensure that nearly all the initial changes in energy were acceptable?

9 Implement the Metropolis algorithm. Model a ball with an initial height of 20 units. Select a value of T and a temperature schedule, and plot the height of the ball as the program iterates round each cycle of the algorithm.

CHAPTER 4

Automating Logical Reasoning

In Chapter 2 we saw how to perform deductive reasoning using propositional formulas. One approach used truth tables and the other used rules of deduction. The rules of deduction are not best suited for a machine implementation of reasoning. The use of these rules requires experience, and representing this experience in a knowledge base would not be easy. The truth tables provide a mechanistic approach to deduction but become impractical when a large number of terms are involved and a richer language like predicate calculus is used.

In this chapter, we introduce a procedure that is suitable for implementing a machine logical reasoner. The procedure is called resolution and it is first illustrated on propositional formulas. The attraction of resolution is its simplicity. In order for logical expressions to be resolved, they must first be rewritten into a standard form. This rewriting relies on logical equivalences to remove implication and if-only-if connectives. Disjunctive components can then be grouped into sets and resolution executed through simple set operations. Next, we look at applying resolution to first-order predicate calculus formulas. The procedure is the same as for propositional logic but some more work is required to handle quantifiers and variables. Finally, the briefest of introductions to Prolog is given. Prolog is a programming language that uses resolution during program execution and it demonstrates the wide application of the techniques introduced in this chapter.

We should note that this chapter deals only with logical expressions. We deal with other forms of automated reasoning elsewhere in the book. One other form of automated reasoning that we shall explore in some detail is the Bayesian approach, which is now finding many real-world applications.

4.1 Resolution in propositional logic

A few definitions are required before resolution is introduced.

Propositional formulas are made up of propositional symbols that denote simple sentences (or statements). Each one of these symbols is called an **atomic formula** or **atom**. For example, in:

$$p \wedge q$$

p is an atom and so is q. An atom, or the negation of an atom, is a **literal**:

p	a literal, also called a **positive literal**
$\neg p$	a literal, also called a **negative literal**

This chapter is concerned with the fundamental ideas behind automating the process of reasoning with logical expressions. It will assist the implementation if all logical sentences can be put into a similar form. In Chapter 2, it was shown that the logical connectives within a formula can be replaced with an alternative set of connectives, for example $A \rightarrow B$ can be written equivalently as $\neg A \vee B$. It would simplify matters if the number of connectives were to be limited. Formulas can be rewritten into one of two standard forms: **conjunctive normal form** (CNF) or **disjunctive normal form** (DNF).

A well-formed formula in conjunctive normal form is a conjunction of disjunctions of literals. For example,

$$(p \vee q \vee r) \wedge (s \vee \neg p) \wedge (p \vee t)$$

The symbols within the brackets consist only of positive and negative literals, which are connected using disjunction ($\vee$), and the bracketed groups of symbols are connected using conjunction ($\wedge$).

A well-formed formula in disjunctive normal form is a disjunction of conjunctions of literals. For example:

$$(p \wedge q \wedge r) \vee (s \wedge \neg p) \vee (p \wedge t)$$

We need concern ourselves only with one of these forms, and our choice will be the conjunctive normal form. Note that a formula in conjunctive normal form has the structure:

$$C_1 \wedge C_2 \wedge \ldots \wedge C_n$$

where each C_i is called a **clause**. A clause is a disjunction of literals and may consist of a single literal.

The question now is how to transform any wff into CNF. The conversion can involve up to five stages:

1   Eliminate $\leftrightarrow$ by noting the equivalence relation:

$$A \leftrightarrow B \equiv (A \rightarrow B) \wedge (B \rightarrow A)$$

2   Eliminate implication, $\rightarrow$, by noting that:

$$A \rightarrow B \equiv \neg A \vee B$$

3   Move negation, $\neg$, using De Morgan's laws. Negation can only appear immediately before a literal:

$$\neg(A \vee B) \equiv \neg A \wedge \neg B$$
$$\neg(A \wedge B) \equiv \neg A \vee \neg B$$

4   Eliminate double negation:

$$\neg\neg A \equiv A$$

5   Distribute $\wedge$ over $\vee$ by using the distributive law:

$$A \vee (B \wedge C) \equiv (A \vee B) \wedge (A \vee C)$$

Example 1 ● ● ● ● ●

Convert the following formula into CNF:

$$(\neg p \wedge (\neg q \rightarrow r)) \rightarrow s$$

Rewrite implication: the formula is of the form $A \rightarrow s$ to $(\neg A \vee s)$:

$$\neg (\neg p \wedge (\neg q \rightarrow r)) \vee s$$

Rewrite $(\neg q \rightarrow r)$ to $q \vee r$:

$$\neg (\neg p \wedge (q \vee r)) \vee s$$

Move negation in:

$$(\neg \neg p \vee (\neg q \wedge \neg r)) \vee s$$

$$(p \vee (\neg q \wedge \neg r)) \vee s$$

Distribute:

$$(p \vee (\neg q \wedge \neg r)) \text{ is of the form } A \vee (B \wedge C)$$

$$(p \vee \neg q) \wedge (p \vee \neg r)$$

$$((p \vee \neg q) \wedge (p \vee \neg r)) \vee s$$

Similarly:

$$((p \vee \neg q) \vee s) \wedge ((p \vee \neg r) \vee s)$$

Cleaning up the brackets:

$$(p \vee \neg q \vee s) \wedge (p \vee \neg r \vee s)$$

● ● ● ● ●

4.1.1   Resolution

Our main interest in logic is to be able to derive new formulas from existing formulas, perform deductions, carry out proofs and check the validity of arguments. In Chapter 2, truth tables provided a mechanical way to prove that a conclusion follows logically from its premises. The rules of deduction provided an alternative strategy to truth tables but required some skill that develops only with experience. A technique called refutation was also introduced, in which the strategy is to show that a negated conclusion is inconsistent with its premises. For example, the following argument:

$\{(p \vee q), \neg p)\} \vdash q$

is in the form:

$\{A_1, A_2, \dots , A_n\} \vdash C$

which, you will recall from Chapter 2, means that q can be derived from the assumptions and one way to prove this is to show that the negation of the conclusion, q, is inconsistent with the assumptions. This inconsistency can be expressed as:

$((p \vee q) \wedge \neg p) \wedge \neg q \vDash \bot$

where the symbol $\bot$ is called **falsum,** which is a constant that has value 'false'. The above expression states that falsum follows from the premises. The proof is readily seen if the formula is put into normal form:

$(p \vee q) \wedge \neg p \wedge \neg q$

This expression will give falsum: for the first clause, $(p \vee q)$, to be true, either p or q must be true. But if p is true the whole expression is a contradiction because $p \wedge \neg p$ is a contradiction and the same argument applies to q. This insight of spotting when a positive literal exists in one clause and its negation in another gives rise to a technique known as **resolution refutation**. Resolution refutation basically involves the following steps:

1 Represent each clause as a set and the expression as a set of sets:

$\{\{p, q\}\}, \{\neg p\}, \{\neg q\}\}$

2 Look for **complementary pairs** of literals that reside in different sets. For example, p and $\neg p$ are a complementary pair.

3 Resolve the clauses containing the complementary pair to give the **resolvent**. A resolvent of two clauses C_1 and C_2, containing complementary literals L and $\neg L$ respectively, is defined as:

$\text{res}(C_1, C_2) = C_1 - \{L\} \cup C_2 - \{\neg L\}$

where '$-$' means set difference. In other words, the resolvent is a new set formed by the union of the two sets with the complementary pair removed. For example:

$\{p, q\}$ and $\{\neg p\}$ can be resolved to give $\{q\}$

4 Continue resolving clauses until either no more resolutions exist or the empty clause is derived, which indicates falsum (the clauses are incompatible).

Resolution starts with an initial set S of clauses from which new clauses are derived. A new clause is derived by resolving two existing clauses. These existing clauses must either be members of S or a clause that has been derived earlier in the proof.

Resolution steps are often shown using a diagram. The steps for resolving:

$(p \vee q) \wedge \neg p \wedge \neg q$

are shown in Figure 4.1.

A complementary technique is called **resolution deduction**. The procedure is the same as resolution refutation but we are interested in what formula can be derived instead of looking for the empty set after all resolutions have been made. This is easily illustrated through the old example:

$\{(p \vee q), \neg p)\} \vdash q$

We want to show that q can be derived from its set of premises $\{(p \vee q), \neg p)\}$. The refutation procedure states that the conclusion is first negated and then added to the set of premises and resolved. The deduction procedure simply resolves the original set of premises to see if the conclusion can be derived. Clearly, it does as the resolution of the two clauses $\{p, q\}$ and $\{\neg p\}$ gives $\{q\}$.

Example 2 ● ● ● ● ●

Show using resolution that statement 3 follows from statements 1 and 2.

1   If the car starts then the battery is not dead, if the car was not pushed.
2   If the battery is not dead the lights have power.
3   If the car starts and the car was not pushed then the lights have power.

The following symbols will be used.

  p – car starts
  q – battery dead
  r – car pushed
  t – lights have power

Symbolizing the statements gives:

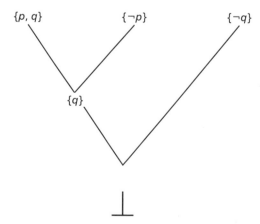

Figure 4.1 Illustrating resolution refutation. A refutation argument is constructed by showing that the negated conclusion is incompatible with the premises. If resolving clauses leads to the empty set, then the clauses are incompatible.

1   $p \rightarrow (\neg r \rightarrow \neg q)$
2   $\neg q \rightarrow t$
3   $(p \wedge \neg r) \rightarrow t$

The statements are now put in CNF and then sets of conjunctive clauses:

1   $\{\neg p, r, \neg q\}$
2   $\{q, t\}$
3   $\{\neg p, r, t\}$

It can be seen that 3 is easily derived from 1 and 2 – it is the union of 1 and 2 without q. Note also that statement 1 could have been written:

If the car starts and the car was not pushed then the battery is not dead.

In propositional form:

$(p \wedge \neg r) \rightarrow \neg q$

Which reduces to the CNF (in set form) $\{\neg p, r, \neg q\}$.

●   ●   ●   ●   ●

4.2 Resolution in FOPC

As we have seen, resolution is a straightforward procedure, and it is suitable for the computer implementation of logic programs. First-order predicate calculus (FOPC) is far more expressive than propositional logic, and so we would like to able to apply resolution to formulas in FOPC. The procedure for applying resolution to FOPC formulas is essentially the same as for the propositional case. There is, however, some additional work to handle variables and quantifiers. The first step is to get a formula into normal form.

The definition of a literal for the predicate case is:

$P(X_1, X_2, ..., X_n)$ is a literal (positive), where P is a predicate with one or more arguments.
$\neg P(X_1, X_2, ..., X_n)$ is a literal (negative).

The definition for the conjunctive normal form (CNF) is that given earlier:

A wff is in CNF if it is a conjunction of disjunction of literals.

A clause is a finite disjunction of literals and may consist of a single literal, in which case it is a **unit clause**. For example, a clause containing $A(X_1, X_2)$ would be a unit clause.

Normalization requires the removal of existential quantifiers, and the procedure for doing this is called **skolemization**. A formula in which all existential quantifiers have been removed is said to be **skolemized**. Skolemization will be explained shortly.

4.2.1 *Procedure for normalization of FOPC formulas*

The procedure for normalizing a FOPC formula is:

1   Eliminate $\leftrightarrow$ by noting the equivalence relation:

$$A \leftrightarrow B \equiv (A \rightarrow B) \wedge (B \rightarrow A)$$

2   Eliminate implication $\rightarrow$ by noting that:

$$A \rightarrow B \equiv \neg A \vee B$$

3   Move negation $\neg$ using De Morgan's laws. Negation can only appear immediately before a literal:

$$\neg (A \vee B) \equiv \neg A \wedge \neg B$$
$$\neg (A \wedge B) \equiv \neg A \vee \neg B$$
$$\neg \exists x P \equiv \forall x \neg P$$
$$\neg \forall x \mathrm{P} \equiv \exists x \neg P$$

4   Eliminate double negation:

$$\neg \neg A \equiv A$$

5   If necessary rename bound variables. If two quantifiers share the same variable naming, then rename one of the variables. The idea here is to make sure that each quantifier binds a unique variable. For example:

$$\forall X. P(X) \vee \exists X.\ Q(X)$$

rename to

$$\forall X. P(X) \vee \exists Y.\ Q(Y)$$

6   Move quantifiers to the left. The set of equivalences listed in Box 4.1 can be used to do this. A wff that has all of its quantifiers to the left is said to be in **prenex** normal form.
7   Eliminate existential quantifiers. This is done using skolemization, which is introduced next.
8   Drop the universal prefix. This can be done because we assume at this stage that all remaining variables are universally quantified.
9   Distribute $\wedge$ over $\vee$ by using the distributive law:

$$A \vee (B \wedge C) \equiv (A \vee B) \wedge (A \vee C)$$

Note that:

$$\forall X. A(X) \vee \forall X. B(X)$$

is not equivalent to

$$\forall X.(A(X) \vee B(X))$$

Box 4.1 Equivalences that can be used to bring quantifiers to the left.

1    $\forall X.A(X) \wedge B \equiv \forall X.(A(X) \wedge B)$
2. $\forall X.A(X) \vee B \equiv \forall X.(A(X) \vee B)$
3    $\exists X.A(X) \wedge B \equiv \exists X.(A(X) \wedge B)$
4    $\exists X.A(X) \vee B \equiv \exists X.(A(X) \vee B)$
5    $\forall X.A(X) \wedge \forall X.B(X) \equiv \forall X.(A(X) \wedge B(X))$
6    $\exists X.A(X) \vee \exists X.B(X) \equiv \exists X.(A(X) \vee B(X))$
7    $Q_1X.A(X) \wedge Q_2Y.B(Y) \equiv Q_1X.Q_2Y(A(X) \wedge B(Y))$

Q_1 and Q_2 can be replaced by either $\forall$ or $\exists$, giving a total of four combination for this equivalence.

8    $Q_1X.A(X) \vee Q_2Y.B(Y) \equiv Q_1X.Q_2Y(A(X) \vee B(Y))$

Q_1 and Q_2 can be replaced by either $\forall$ or $\exists$, giving a total of four combination for this equivalence.

---

and

$$\exists X.A(X) \wedge \exists X.B(X)$$

is not equivalent to

$$\exists X.(A(X) \wedge B(X))$$

In these situations one of the bound variables needs to be renamed. For example:

$$\forall X.A(X) \vee \forall X.B(X)$$

could be rewritten as:

$$\forall X.A(X) \vee \forall Y.B(Y)$$

4.2.2   Skolemization

A wff of the form $\exists X. P(X)$ is stating that there exits some X with property P. The formula is satisfied by a single constant that has property P. Suppose this constant is called c; then $\exists X. P(X)$ can be replaced by P(c). For example, suppose X has the domain:

{john, mary, sally, david, steven}

Obviously, $\exists X. boy(X)$ is true and so are *boy(john)*, *boy(david)*, *boy(steven)*. $\exists X. boy(X)$ is the same as

boy(john) $\vee$ boy(david) $\vee$ boy(steven)

So for $\exists X.\ boy(X)$ to hold it has to be satisfied by some constant and that constant could be John, David or Steven. When the existential quantifier is dropped by replacing X with a constant, c, we have to use a constant that has not already been used. To see this consider the following:

> boy(c)
> $\exists X.\ girl(X)$

If X were to be replaced with c then the formula becomes 'there is a boy who is also a girl'. This is not the meaning of the formula, which states: there is a boy labelled c and there is a girl who could be c or some other person in the domain. The point to remember is that an existentially quantified variable can be replaced with a constant but that constant must be a new one.

Consider now the following predicate, which involves both quantifier types:

> $\forall X.\ \exists Y.\ P(X, Y)$

for all of X there exists a Y that has the relationship P. For example, *everyone has a mother* has this form of relationship. Another example is, *every man loves a woman*:

> $\forall X.\ (man(X) \rightarrow \exists Y.(woman(Y) \wedge loves(X, Y)))$

which can be written as:

> $\forall X.\ \exists Y.\ (man(X) \rightarrow (woman(Y) \wedge loves(X, Y)))$

The existential quantifier cannot now be replaced by a constant. Doing so would imply that every man loves the same woman (whatever woman the constant is a label for). Suppose instead that the existential variable is replaced by a function that maps each X to the woman who is loved. The function could be:

> woman_loved(X)

which is meant to return (refer) to the woman that X loves. Since X is a variable, this function can return a different woman (or the same woman in some instances) for each X. The choice of function name is one of personal choice and it could simply be labelled f instead of *woman_loved*. Eliminating the existential quantifier gives:

> $\forall X.\ (man(X) \rightarrow (woman(f(X)) \wedge loves(X, f(X))))$

using the shorter version f. The function f is called a **skolem** function. Finally, consider the following situation:

> $\forall X.\ \forall Y.\ \exists Z.\ P(X, Y, Z)$

The existential quantifier is now preceded by two universal quantifiers and so it must be replaced by a skolem function that has both of the universally quantified variables as arguments:

> $\forall X.\ \forall Y.\ P(X, Y, f(X, Y))$

Example 3 ● ● ● ● ●

Convert the following formula into normal form:

$$\exists X.p(X) \rightarrow \exists X.q(X)$$

Eliminate implication:

$$\neg \exists X.p(X) \lor \exists X.q(X)$$

Move negation before literal:

$$\forall X. \neg p(X) \lor \exists X.q(X)$$

Rename variable:

$$\forall X. \neg p(X) \lor \exists Y.q(Y)$$

Noting form 8 in Box 4.1:

$$\forall X. \exists Y.(\neg p(X) \lor q(Y))$$

Skolemize:

$$\forall X. (\neg p(X) \lor q(c))$$

Drop the prefix

$$(\neg p(X) \lor q(c))$$

● ● ● ● ●

Example 4 ● ● ● ● ●

Convert the following formula into normal form:

$$\forall X. (p(X) \rightarrow \exists Y.(q(Y) \land r(X, Y)))$$

Step 2 (from normalization procedure) – remove implication:

$$\forall X. (\neg p(X) \lor \exists Y.(q(Y) \land r(X, Y)))$$

Step 6 – move quantifiers left:

$$\forall X. \exists Y. (\neg p(X) \lor (q(Y) \land r(X, Y)))$$

Step 7 – remove existential variable:

$$\forall X. (\neg p(X) \vee (q(f(X)) \wedge r(X, f(X))))$$

Step 8 – drop prefix:

$$(\neg p(X) \vee (q(f(X)) \wedge r(X, f(X))))$$

Step 9 – distribute:

$$((\neg p(X) \vee q(f(X))) \wedge (\neg p(X) \vee r(X, f(X))))$$

●   ●   ●   ●   ●

4.2.3   Unification

Suppose that we have a domain with a large number of constants and a number of variables (universally quantified). Substitutions will usually be required during the course of resolution because we shall often be reasoning about individual objects or a subset of objects. The number of possible substitutions could be huge, and if we proceeded to use random substitutions the amount of computation required would lead to an impractical implementation for real-world applications. Unification is a systematic way of performing substitutions in order to make two literals look similar.

The essence of unification is to try and see if two literals match. For example, the following rule says that someone who is a mother is also a parent:

$$\text{mother}(X, Y) \rightarrow \text{parent}(X, Y).$$

In order to test whether an individual is a parent it is necessary to match the literals in the rule. Suppose that we know that Pam is the mother of Carol:

$$\text{mother}(pam, carol)$$

It is easy to see that Pam is also a parent of Carol and that parenthood can be deduced by applying the above rule once Pam is substituted for X and Carol for Y. In place of substitution we sometimes talk about variables being **bound**. A bound variable is a variable that references something else, which is either a constant or another variable. In the above example, X was bound to Pam and is denoted by writing X/pam.

Resolution needs to recognize if literals can match. If two literals in different clauses match and one is the complement (negation) of the other, then the literals can be resolved. For two literals to match they must satisfy the following conditions:

1   Name and number of arguments. The predicate names must match exactly (character by character). For example, *mother* and *motherOf* are considered different predicates. The number of arguments (arity) must also match.
2   If the predicate names match, the next step is to check the arguments. Any functions must match according to 1. This leaves constants and variables for which there are the following possibilities:
    i   constant b, constant c. Constants b and c match only if they match character by character (e.g. john matches john but john does not match johN).
    ii   constant b, variable X. If the variable is unbound then they will match and the variable is

bound to the constant X/b. If the variable is already bound then b and X match only if the constant that X is bound to matches b (constant/constant match).

iii variable X, variable Y. If X and Y are both unbound then they match, and if one variable later gets bound then the other is also bound. If one of the variables is currently bound and the other unbound then the variables match and the unbound variable will get bound to the same constant. Two bound variables must conform to a 'constant, constant' match.

Some example matches are listed below. More examples will be given throughout the remainder of this chapter.

mother(X, Y) and father(W, Z)	do not match because they have different predicate names
path(X, Y) and path(X, Y, Z)	do not match because they have different numbers of arguments
mother(X, Y) and mother(pam, W)	match with bindings X/pam Y/W
mother(X/pam, Y) and mother(jane, Z)	do not match because X is bound to pam and pam does not match jane

The process of matching and binding variables is called **unification**. Two literals unify if there is a substitution that makes the two literals look the same. So:

mother(pam, Y) and mother(X, W)

unify and the set of substitutions is {X/pam, Y/W}. The set of substitutions is called a **unifier**. We require a unification algorithm to automate the whole procedure. This algorithm should return the **most general unifier**. The most general unifier is the set that makes the least substitutions for the literals to match. For example, the mother literals will match with the unifier {pam/X, Y/carol, W/carol}, but this unifier is less general than {X/pam, Y/W}. The unification algorithm is given in Figure 4.2. The compound expression refers to a predicate or function expression, with *op* denoting the predicate or function name and *args op* the arguments. Variables and the values that they are bound to are stored in a unification table (UT). ADD_UT will add an entry to UT and GET_VAL will return the value for a variable stored in UT or will return the variable if the variable is not bound.

Example 5 ● ● ● ● ●

Find the most general unifier of the two literals:

p(X, f(Y)) and p(a, f(b))

The stack starts with the following pair:

<p(X, f(Y)), p(a, f(b))>

Each element of the pair is a compound expression. Both predicates have the same name *p* and the same number of arguments, i.e. two. The stack is therefore populated with the following pairs:

<X, a> <f(Y), f(b)>

```
PROCEDURE UNIFY(exp₁, exp₂)

while S is not empty
        pop the first pair <s₁, s₂>
        if s₁ is a variable
                s₁ ← GET_VAL(s₁)
        end if
        if s₂ is a variable
                s₂ ← GET_VAL(s₂)
        end if
        if s₁ and s₂ are constants and s₁ != s₂
                return fail
        end if
        else  if s₁ is a variable and s₁ != s₂
                if s₁ occurs in s₂
                        return fail
                end if
                ADD_UT(s₁, s₂)
        end if
        else if s₂ is a variable and s₂ != s₁
                if s₂ occurs in s₁
                        return fail
                end if
                ADD_UT(s₂, s₁)
        end if
        else if s₁ and s₂ are both compound expressions
                if not(op₁ = op₂)
                        return fail
                end if
                if not(args op₁ = args op₂)
                        return fail
                end if
                pair arguments and push onto S
        end if
end while
return success

// S is a stack populated with pairs of expressions to be matched
```

Figure 4.2 Algorithm for unification. The compound expression refers to a predicate or function expression, with op denoting the predicate or function name and args op the arguments. Variables and the values that they are bound to are stored in a unification table (UT). ADD_UT will add an entry to UT and GET_VAL will return the value for a variable stored in UT or will return the variable if the variable is not bound

The UT is still empty at this stage, and so GET_VAL for X simply returns X. X is not bound and therefore can match with the constant a. The UT is updated:

Variable	Value
X	a

The next pair is popped. Both elements of the pair are functions with the same name and one argument. The arguments are removed and placed as a pair on the stack. The final call is for:

<Y, b>

Y is not in UT and will match with *b*.

Variable	Value
X	a
Y	b

The most general unifier is X/a and Y/b.

● ● ● ● ●

Example 6 ● ● ● ● ●

Find the most general unifier for:

p(X, X, f(a)) and p(Y, g(f(b)), Z)

The predicate names match and so do the number of arguments. The pairs on the stack are:

<X, Y> <X, g(f(b))> <f(a), Z>

Pop <X, Y>. *X* is not in UT and *Y* is not. Therefore, they match.

Variable	Value
X	Y

Pop <X, g(f(b))>. Return value for *X* which is *Y*. *Y* can match with g(f(b)).

Variable	Value
X	Y
Y	g(f(b))

Pop <f(a), Z>. *Z* is not in UT and can match with f(a).

Variable	Value
X	Y
Y	g(f(b))
Z	f(a)

● ● ● ● ●

Example 7 ● ● ● ● ●

In this example we shall put all of the various elements introduced into practice. Three statements are given below followed by a question that needs to be answered.

> All friends of Graham like wine.
> Everyone who likes wine drinks alcohol.
> Tony is a friend of Graham.
> Does Tony like alcohol?

First we need to represent all sentences in FOPC.

> $\forall X.$ (friend(X, graham) $\rightarrow$ like(X, wine))
> $\forall X.$ (like(X, wine) $\rightarrow$ drink(X, alcohol))
> friend(tony, graham)

In normal form:

> $\neg$ friend(X, graham) $\vee$ like(X, wine)
> $\neg$ like(Y, wine) $\vee$ drink(Y, alcohol)
> friend(tony, graham)

Putting into sets of clauses:

> {$\neg$ friend(X, graham), like(X, wine)}
> {$\neg$ like(Y, wine), drink(Y, alcohol)}
> {friend(tony, graham)}

The resolution steps are presented as a diagram in Figure 4.3. Resolution deduction has been used to show that Tony does like alcohol.

● ● ● ● ●

Example 8 ● ● ● ● ●

This example is a slight modification to Example 7. This example is a little more precise in that it states that a friend of Graham will like at least one kind of wine.

> All friends of Graham like some wine.
> Everyone who likes wine drinks alcohol.
> Tony is a friend of Graham.

1 $\forall X.$ (friend(X, graham) $\rightarrow \exists Y.($ wine(Y) $\wedge$ like(X, Y)))
2 $\forall X. \exists Y.$ (wine(Y) $\wedge$ like(X, Y) $\rightarrow$ drink(X, alcohol))
3 friend(tony, graham).

Normalize 1
Remove implication:

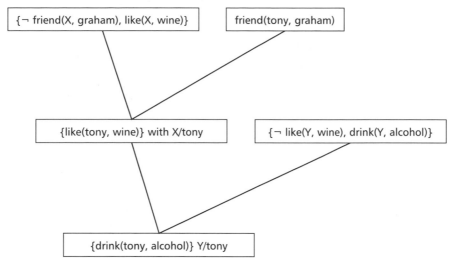

Figure 4.3 The resolution steps for Example 7.

$$\forall X. (\neg \text{friend}(X, \text{graham}) \vee \exists Y. (\text{wine}(Y) \wedge \text{like}(X, Y)))$$

Move quantifiers left:

$$\forall X. \exists Y. (\neg \text{friend}(X, \text{graham}) \vee (\text{wine}(Y) \wedge \text{like}(X, Y)))$$

Skolemize:

$$\forall X. (\neg \text{friend}(X, \text{graham}) \vee (\text{wine}(f(X)) \wedge \text{like}(X, f(X))))$$

Drop prefix:

$$(\neg \text{friend}(X, \text{graham}) \vee (\text{wine}(f(X)) \wedge \text{like}(X, f(X))))$$

Distribute:

$$(\neg \text{friend}(X, \text{graham}) \vee \text{wine}(f(X))) \wedge (\neg \text{friend}(X, \text{graham}) \vee \text{like}(X, f(X)))$$

Normalize 2

$$\forall X. \exists Y. (\text{wine}(Y) \wedge \text{like}(X, Y) \rightarrow \text{drink}(X, \text{alcohol}))$$

Eliminate implication:

$$\forall X. \exists Y. \neg ((\text{wine}(Y) \wedge \text{like}(X, Y)) \vee \text{drink}(X, \text{alcohol}))$$

Move negation:

$$\forall X. \exists Y. (\neg \text{wine}(Y) \vee \neg \text{like}(X, Y) \vee \text{drink}(X, \text{alcohol}))$$

Skolemize:

$$\forall X(\neg wine(f(X)) \vee \neg like(X, f(X)) \vee drink(X, alcohol))$$

Drop prefix:

$$(\neg wine(f(X)) \vee \neg like(X, f(X)) \vee drink(X, alcohol))$$

We now have:

$$(\neg friend(X, graham) \vee wine(f(X))) \wedge (\neg friend(X, graham) \vee like(X, f(X)))$$
$$(\neg wine(f(X)) \vee \neg like(X, f(X)) \vee drink(X, alcohol))$$
$$friend(tony, graham).$$

Forming sets:

1   $\{\neg friend(X, graham), wine(f(X))\}$
2   $\{\neg friend(X, graham), like(X, f(X))\}$
3   $\{\neg wine(f(X)), \neg like(X, f(X)), drink(X, alcohol)\}$
4   $\{friend(tony, graham)\}$

At this stage we are going to introduce one final useful rule for normalizing:

Rename variables so that different names are used in different clauses.

This rule is useful because during resolution we will have to perform substitutions. With the sets as they are, a substitution for X will change all the sets and yet we want to keep clauses in their most general form. Hopefully, the need for this will become more apparent when we look at Prolog, but for now we shall accept the rule as the correct thing to do.

1   $\{\neg friend(X, graham), wine(f(X))\}$
2   $\{\neg friend(Y, graham), like(Y, f(Y))\}$
3   $\{\neg wine(f(Z)), \neg like(Z, f(Z)), drink(Z, alcohol)\}$
4   $\{friend(tony, graham)\}$

We can now perform resolution:

5   $\{wine(f(tony))\}$ from 1 and 4 using the substitution X/tony
6   $\{ like(tony, f(tony))\}$ from 2 and 4 using the substitution Y/tony
7   $\{\neg like(tony, f(tony)), drink(tony, alcohol)\}$ from 3 and 5 Z/tony
8   $\{drink(tony, alcohol)\}$ from 6 and 7

4.3 Prolog

Prolog is a programming language that is based on predicate calculus. Prolog is a **declarative** language, which basically means that a programmer is concerned with describing a problem rather than with specifying a set of instructions to solve the problem. A Prolog program is a collection of clauses in which each clause is either a fact or a rule. The clauses code properties and relationships between objects.

The syntax for Prolog is close to that of predicate calculus. The following are example facts:

metal(copper)	Copper is a metal
likes(john, mary)	John likes Mary
between(manchester, london, edinburgh)	Manchester is between London and Edinburgh
city(washington)	Washington is a city
city(washington, usa)	Washington is a city in the USA

Constants start with a lowercase character and variables start with an uppercase character.

There are some differences between Prolog and predicate calculus in the symbols used for writing rules. The key symbolic differences are shown in Table 4.1.

The predicate '**not**' is not a faithful representation of negation. We can think of 'not' as performing a test on the argument – the truth value returned is 'false' if the argument is evaluated as true and 'true' if the argument is evaluated as false. In Prolog, one would not assert a negated fact. For example, if Fido is a dog we might express the following as facts in predicate calculus:

dog(fido)
$\neg$cat(fido)

In Prolog, the fact that Fido is not a cat would not be entered into the database. If asked the question 'is Fido a cat?'

cat(fido)

Prolog would respond 'no'. Prolog responds automatically with 'no' to anything it has not been explicitly told and cannot prove using its rules. As Prolog has not been told that Fido is a cat and it

Table 4.1 Key symbolic differences between FOPC and Prolog

FOPC	Prolog
Conjunction $\wedge$	Comma ,
Disjunction $\vee$	An *or* condition is expressed by writing two rules. For example, instead of:
	IF the battery is flat or there is no fuel THEN the car won't start
	Use:
	IF the battery is flat THEN the car won't start IF there is no fuel THEN the car won't start
Negation $\neg$	**not** : this is a predicate built into Prolog compilers. For example:
	not(girl(X)) succeeds when girl(X) fails.
If premises then conclusion $\rightarrow$	Conclusion if premises :-

has no rules to prove that Fido is a cat, Prolog assumes that Fido is not a cat. This form of assumption is known as the **closed world assumption**.

Prolog programs are invoked by asking a question. The editing environment for building a Prolog program provides the programmer with a prompt from where questions can be asked. The prompt is a question mark, '?'. Questions are asked with reference to facts and rules that reside in what is called the database. Suppose the database contains the following facts:

```
likes(john, mary).
likes(john, meg).
likes(david, mary).
likes(mary, david).
```

The following questions can be asked:

- Does John like Mary?

    ?- likes(john, mary).

    Prolog would respond with yes because there is a match with an existing fact. To ask questions of the database, the user needs to have knowledge of what terms are used to denote objects, relationships and properties. For example, it is no good asking:

    ?- like(john, mary).

    because *like* does not match *likes*. Prolog uses unification to answer questions relating to facts.

- Who does John like?

    ?- likes(john, Who).

    X (or *Y* or *Z*, …) could be used in place of Who. We are free to name the variables as we wish provided they start with an uppercase character. The answer to this question would be:

    ```
    likes(john, mary).
    likes(john, meg).
    ```

- Who likes Mary?

    ?- likes(Who, mary).

    The answer would be

    ```
    likes(john, mary).
    likes(david, mary).
    ```

- Who likes who?

?- likes(X, Y).

Produces

likes(john, mary).
likes(john, meg).
likes(david, mary).
likes(mary, david).

All of the above answers have been produced by unification. Prolog will only match the question clause with one database clause at a time. If more than one answer is available, then the user has to prompt for the answer. To prompt for alternative answers (if they exist), the user enters the symbol ';'. For example, the following is a trace of the output to a question:

?- likes(john, Who).
Who = mary ;
Who = meg.

Prolog responded with one answer and waited. After the user entered the prompt symbol ';' a second answer (*Who = meg*) was provided.

Matching between clauses can be checked without a database. The symbol used by Prolog to test for matching is '='. For example, the query:

?- like(john, meg) = like(john, X).

produces the response:

X = meg

which indicates that the two clauses match with *X* bound to *meg*. A selection of matches is shown in Figure 4.4.

A rule in FOPC is written using implication. The rule is of the form:

IF premises THEN conclusion

In Prolog rules are written in a backward sense:

conclusion IF premises

For example, *All of Graham's friends like wine* is written in FOPC as:

if someone is a friend of Graham then that someone likes wine
$\forall$X. (friend(X, graham) $\rightarrow$ like(X, wine))

and in Prolog as:

someone likes wine if that someone is a friend of Graham
like(X, wine) :- friend(X, graham).

```
?- like(john, mary) = like(john, mary).
yes

 ?- like(john, meg) = like(john, mary).
no

 ?- like(john, meg) = like(john, X).
X = meg

 ?- like(john, meg) = like(X, Y).
X = john ,
Y = meg

 ?- like(john, X) = like(john, Y).
X = Y = _

 ?- X = meg, like(john, X) = like(john, Y).
X = Y = meg

 ?- like(john, mary) = love(john, mary).
no

 ?- like(john, mary) = like(john, mary, X).
no

 ?- owns(graham, book(neurocomputing, author(nielsen)), neural_nets) = owns(X, Y, Z).
X = graham ,
Y = book(neurocomputing,author(nielsen)) ,
Z = neural_nets

 ?-owns(graham, book(neurocomputing, author(nielsen)), neural_nets) = owns(X, book(Y1, Y2), Z).
X = graham ,
Y1 = neurocomputing ,
Y2 = author(nielsen) ,
Z = neural_nets
```

Figure 4.4 The listing shows Prolog being asked whether two clauses match. Prolog responds with 'no' for no match or 'yes' for a match or if the clauses match and involve variables the bindings are shown. The symbol ' _ ' is an anonymous variable (unnamed).

Figure 4.5 shows a Prolog program that represents the following sentences:

Tony is a friend of Graham.
All friends of Graham like wine.
Everyone who likes wine drinks alcohol.

The following is a list of questions asked of the program:

```
?- drinks(tony, alcohol).
yes

?- drinks(tony, X).
```

```
friend(tony, graham).
likes(X, wine) :- friend(X, graham).
drinks(X, alcohol) :- likes(X, wine).
```

Figure 4.5 Example Prolog program.

X = alcohol

?- drinks(X, alcohol).
X = tony

To see how Prolog executes a program it is instructive to look at the last query. Prolog answers a question by performing backward reasoning, which is goal-directed search. The query *drinks(X, alcohol)* is a goal that Prolog attempts to satisfy. Prolog will first attempt to satisfy the goal by seeking to match against any facts. There are no facts in the program of the form *drinks(X, Y)*. Next, Prolog attempts to match the head of a rule (the head appears to the left of the symbol ':-'). Prolog can match with the head of the rule:

drinks(X, alcohol) :- likes(X, wine).

The head of a rule can be satisfied only when all of the conditions in the body (right-hand side) of the rule have been satisfied. Each condition is a subgoal. The drinks rule only has one condition. The subgoal is:

likes(X, wine)

Prolog now tries to satisfy this subgoal, *likes(X, wine)*. There are no matching facts but there is a rule that will match:

likes(X, wine) :- friend(X, graham).

The new subgoal *friend(X, graham)* must now be satisfied. This subgoal matches the fact:

friend(tony, graham).

and *X* is bound to *tony*. Prolog will now trace back through the subgoals binding relevant variables. The inference steps are shown in Figure 4.6.

Prolog will treat the variables in a rule as being local to that rule (the scope of the variable is the rule). Although, from a programmer's point of view, the same variable name may be used in more than one rule, internally Prolog gives the variables in each rule a unique identity.

Another small Prolog program is given next. This program encodes the graph structure shown in Figure 4.7. The graph is known as a **directed acyclic graph** (DAG) because all of the edges have a direction and there are no cycles, which means that it is not possible to trace a path[1] from a node back to itself. Example paths are:

---

[1]A path is a sequence of nodes where the first node is called the start node and the last node the end (finish) node.

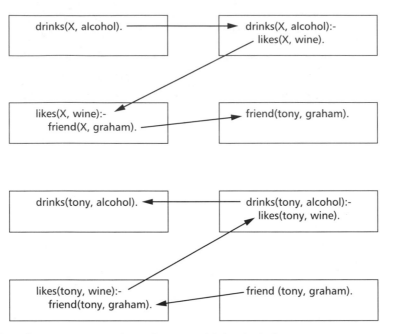

Figure 4.6 The inference steps to show that Tony drinks alcohol.

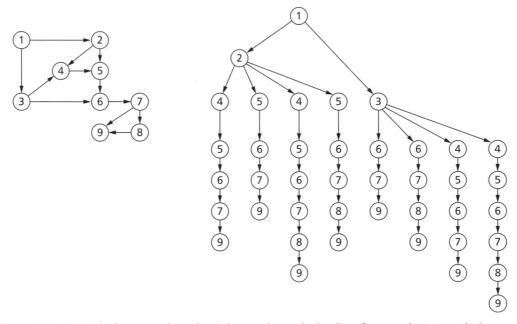

Figure 4.7 A DAG is shown and on the right are the paths leading from node 1 to node 9.

1, 2, 5, 6, 7, 9
5, 6, 7, 8
1, 3, 4, 5, 6

Note that 1, 2, 4, 3 is not a legal path because the direction of the edge between 3 and 4 goes from 3 to 4 and not 4 to 3.

The program is shown in Figure 4.8. The structure of the graph is encoded using a predicate called *edge*. There is an *edge* fact corresponding to each edge in the graph. The order of the arguments is important. The first argument is the *from node* and the second the *to node*. It would be tedious to list all of the possible paths in the graph. Rules are used to infer the existence of a path. There are two rules that deduce the existence of a path between a *Start* node and an *End* node. There is a path between two nodes when either of the following conditions are met:

1   There is a direct edge between the start and end node.
2   There is an edge between the start and some intermediate node, and the intermediate node has a path to the end node.

The second rule is recursive because the body contains a predicate that has the same form (name and number of arguments) as the rule head. The following query and response indicates how many paths there are from node 1 to all of the other nodes. For example, 5 appears three times in the list because there are three paths from node 1 to node 5.

```
?- path(1, X).
X = 2 ;
X = 3 ;
X = 4 ;
X = 5 ;
X = 5 ;
X = 6 ;
X = 7 ;
```

```
edge(1, 2).
edge(1, 3).
edge(2, 4).
edge(2, 5).
edge(3, 4).
edge(3, 6).
edge(4, 5).
edge(5, 6).
edge(6, 7).
edge(7, 8).
edge(7, 9).
edge(8, 9).

path(Start, End) :- edge(Start, End).
path(Start, End) :- edge(Start, IntNode), path(IntNode, End).
```

Figure 4.8 A Prolog program that has a set of 'edge' facts to represent the graph in Figure 4.7 and two rules to infer the existence of a path between two nodes.

X = 8 ;
X = 9 ;
X = 9 ;
X = 6 ;
X = 7 ;
X = 8 ;
X = 9 ;
X = 9 ;
X = 4 ;
X = 6 ;
X = 5 ;
X = 6 ;
X = 7 ;
X = 8 ;
X = 9 ;
X = 9 ;
X = 7 ;
X = 8 ;
X = 9 ;
X = 9 ;

We can get Prolog to print out the path by augmenting the rules with a built-in predicate for writing to the screen:

path(Start, End) :- edge(Start, End), write(Start), write(End).
path(Start, End) :- write(Start), edge(Start, IntNode), path(IntNode, End).

The query

?- path(1, 9).

produces

1 2 4 5 6 7 9 yes

4.3.1 A closer look at prolog inferencing

It may come as no surprise to be told that Prolog's reasoning is based on resolution and unification. Prolog handles a query as though it were a statement that needs to be proved. The details of how Prolog goes about a proof is hidden from the programmer, but the programmer will usually have an option to trace how Prolog has arrived at an answer.

All of Prolog's rules are in the form *conclusion IF set of conditions satisfied*:

$$C :\text{-} C_1, C_2, ..., C_n$$

The comma represents conjunction. Disjunctive conditions are represented by separate rules. For example:

X is the parent of Y if either X is the father of Y or X is the mother of Y
parent(X, Y) :- father(X, Y).
parent(X, Y) :- mother(X, Y).

A pure[2] Prolog program would consist of a set of **Horn clauses**. A Horn clause is a clause that contains at most one positive literal. It is easy to see that a pure Prolog program consists only of Horn clauses. A fact is clearly a positive literal. Rules are of the form (although written backwards) $p \rightarrow q$, which is the equivalent of $\neg p \vee q$ (a clause with a single positive literal q. So, a Prolog rule:

$$C :- C_1, C_2, ..., C_n$$

is equivalent to:

$$C_1 \wedge C_2 \wedge ... \wedge C_n \rightarrow C$$

which is equivalent to:

$$\neg (C_1 \wedge C_2 \wedge ... \wedge C_n) \vee C$$

which is equivalent to:

$$(\neg C_1 \vee \neg C_2 \vee ... \vee \neg C_n) \vee C$$

and written as a set of clauses:

$$\{\neg C_1, \neg C_2, ..., \neg C_n, \vee C\}$$

Figure 4.9 takes the Prolog program listed in Figure 4.8, converts it into CNF and then uses resolution to show that there is a path between nodes 1 and 6. Every time a rule is matched, new variables are used. For example, the first time clauses at line 14 are matched, the variables are called $Z1$, $W1$ and $U1$. The second time they are called $Z2$, $W2$ and $U2$, and so on. If this renaming of variables did not happen then line 18 in the proof would fail. The Z in line 16 is bound to the value 1 and in line 18 a value of 2 is being matched with Z. Without creating new variables the match would obviously fail because Z has been set to 1 and this does not match with 2. The point to remember is that variables are local to the rule and new variable names should be instantiated (created) every time the rule is matched. This also emphasizes the point made earlier that, during unification, variables should remain in their most general form. To keep the solution short we cheated a little and made selective choices of which clauses to match in the database – Prolog will work first through the facts in order, and then the rules in order. Alternative choices for resolving clauses exist. For example, at step 19 we could have chosen to match 3 and 18, which would result in $\neg$edge(4, 6) at step 20. The proof would have failed because there is no edge from node 4 to 6. Prolog does not give up but tries alternatives by examining the last step and seeing if there is an alternative choice which will lead to a proof. Prolog can keep going further and further back (e.g. moving back from step 19 to 16) to try alternatives. This strategy is called backtracking. Step 17 could have matched 16 with 2, giving $\neg$path(3, 6). This choice would lead to a shorter proof because the path from node 1 to 6 via 3 is of length 2 (can be done in two moves).

---

[2]Prolog is not pure because it supports a library of predicates to support procedural aspects of programming (e.g. reading and writing to devices such as the screen).

```
 1.  edge(1, 2).
 2.  edge(1, 3).
 3.  edge(2, 4).
 4.  edge(2, 5).
 5.  edge(3, 4).
 6.  edge(3, 6).
 7.  edge(4, 5).
 8.  edge(5, 6).
 9.  edge(6, 7).
10.  edge(7, 8).
11.  edge(7, 9).
12.  edge(8, 9).

13.  {path(X, Y), ¬ edge(X, Y)}
14.  {path(Z, W), ¬ edge(Z, U), ¬ path(U, W)}

15.  ¬ path(1, 6).
16.  { ¬ edge(1, U1), ¬ path(U1, 6)} Z1/1 W1/6 from 14 and 15
17.  { ¬ path(2, 6)} 1 and 16 with U1/2
18.  { ¬ edge(2, U2), ¬ path(U2, 6)} Z2/2 W2/6 from 14 and 17
19.  { ¬ path(5, 6)} U2/5 from 18 and 4
20.  { ¬ edge(5, 6)} X1/5, Y2/6 from 19 and 13
21.  from 8 and 20
```

Figure 4.9 The Prolog program from Figure 4.8 converted to CNF. Resolution is used to show that a path exists between nodes 1 and 6.

Prolog's resolution strategy is known as linear resolution. This means that Prolog always resolves the clause derived at the last step with either a fact or rule contained in the original program.

Prolog's search for a solution is depth first. The direction of search is best explained in terms of the original program structure (not in normal form). Given a goal to be proved (i.e. a query), Prolog attempts to match the goal with a fact. If this fails, Prolog matches the head of a rule and then tries to satisfy each condition in the rule body in a left to right manner. Suppose a rule has three conditions in the body. Prolog attempts to satisfy the leftmost condition first, and to do this it treats the condition as a subgoal which has to be matched against a fact or the head of a rule. If the subgoal is matched against a rule, then another subgoal is generated. A program is given in Figure 4.10 and the search is illustrated in Figure 4.11 for the query *is Caroline a descendant of Sandra?*

During a search, Prolog may reach a dead-end. For example, step 6 in Figure 4.11 is a failure and so Prolog tries an alternative. At any stage of the search Prolog may have a choice. Each choice represents a branch in a search tree. At step 6 Prolog had two choices for the parent clause. The first choice is to match the arguments with a fact of fatherhood and the second to match with motherhood. If at any stage all of the choices fail, then Prolog can step backwards to a previous choice point and try an alternative. If all of the choices not tried before lead to failure, then Prolog can back up further and can continue doing this until all options have been exhausted. This method of searching is **backtracking**. Suppose an additional fact was added to the Program in Figure 4.10:

mother(barbara, caroline).
father(graham, caroline).
mother(sandra, jane).
mother(sandra, barbara).

```
            mother(barbara, caroline).
            father(graham, caroline).
            mother(sandra, barbara).

            descendant(X, Y) :- parent(Y, X).
            descendant(X, Y) :- parent(Y, Z), parent(Z, X).
            parent(X, Y) :- father(X, Y).
            parent(X, Y) :- mother(X, Y).
```

Figure 4.10 A simple Prolog program that represents some family relationships.

```
?-descendant(caroline, sandra).

No facts can be matched so try rules.

First rule with a head that matches.
1. descendant(X1/caroline, Y1/sandra) :- parent(Y1/sandra, X1/caroline).

Attempt to match the right hand side of step 1.
2. parent(X2/sandra, Y2/caroline) :- father(X2/sandra, Y2/caroline).  fails to match

3. parent(X2/sandra, Y2/caroline) :- mother(X2/sandra, Y2/caroline).  fails to match

Failed so far so now the second descendant rule is tried.
4. descendant(X3/caroline, Y3/sandra) :-
            parent(Y3/sandra, Z3), parent(Z3, X3/caroline).

5. Attempting to match the first condition in step 4.
parent(X4/Y3/sandra, Y4/Z3) :-
            father(X4/Y3/sandra, Y4/Z3).  fails
parent(X4/Y3/sandra, Y4/Z3) :-
            mother(X4/Y3/sandra, Y4/Z3).  succeeds with Y4/Z3/barbara

Succeeded in matching the first condition of the second rule so now trying to match the second condition with
bindings parent(barbara, X3/caroline).

6. parent(X5/barbara, Y5/X3/caroline) :- father(X5/barbara, Y5/X3/caroline). fail.
7. parent(X5/barbara, Y5/X3/caroline) :- mother(X5/barbara, Y5/X3/caroline) success.
```

Figure 4.11 A trace of the search using the program listed in Figure 4.10 to prove that Caroline is a descendant of Sandra.

This fact, *mother(sandra, jane)*, happens to be positioned before the fact that is instrumental in proving that Caroline descends from Sandra. The proof would proceed as before, but when Prolog tries to satisfy the second condition in the rule:

descendant(X, Y) :- parent(Y, Z), parent(Z, X).

it has the following bindings:

> descendant(X/caroline, Y/sandra) :-
>> parent(Y/sandra, Z/jane), parent(Z/jane, X/caroline).

There is no match for parent(Z/jane, X/caroline) and Prolog backs up. The previous choice point looked to match parent(Y/sandra, Z). There are two choices that can be seen (via the use of the parent rules):

> mother(Y/sandra, jane)
> mother(Y/sandra, barbara)

The first choice failed and Prolog remembers this. It now tries the second choice, which leads to success because *parent(Z/barbara, X/caroline)* can be satisfied.

Forward and backward chaining

Search is an attempt to find a sequence of operations that will connect some initial start state to a goal state. Using the logical rules of deduction to prove a statement is a search: the initial state is the set of logical expressions and the goal is the statement that is to be proved. During the search, operations are performed to derive new logical expressions. Search can proceed in one of two ways: forward from the start state or backward from the goal state.

Reasoning using a forward search is sometimes called **forward chaining** or **data-driven** search. A backward-directed search is sometimes called **backward chaining** or **goal-driven** search. The choice of forward or backward reasoning depends to some extent on the nature of the task. A doctor, for example, could use either type of reasoning. Suppose a patient comes into the surgery feeling unwell. The doctor may decide to perform a number of tests to gather data. She may take the patient's temperature, blood pressure, etc. She can use the results of these tests to infer something of the patient's condition and may then decide on further tests if she is still unsure as to what is making the patient unwell. In practice, a pure forward search would not be performed by a diagnostician (e.g. a doctor) because there are a huge number of medical conditions, with a huge number of tests. It is more natural to suspect that the patient is suffering from a small subset of conditions and then to test to see if results confirm the condition. For example, if there has been a recent outbreak of meningitis and a patient exhibits some symptoms of meningitis, the doctor can use meningitis as a goal to be proved. She has knowledge of what symptoms the patient may exhibit with meningitis and these symptoms can be checked for. On rarer occasions, the medical profession might be baffled as to the cause of symptoms. Their initial goals to be proved sometimes fail because test results do not confirm what was suspected. In this situation, the search becomes heavily data driven as more and more tests are conducted to gather more data in the hope of narrowing the search for the cause.

Suppose you are making travel plans and want to travel from Southampton in the UK by train to Rome in Italy. There is no direct train and you have in front of you a European train travel guide that lists stations along with arrivals and departures. You have a search problem and you want to find a sequence of steps (train journeys) that will take you from your initial state (in Southampton) to your goal state in Rome. You could start the search in a forward sense from Southampton or you could start working backwards from Rome. Which is the best choice? Well there is no way to guarantee which direction of search is best. You could perhaps make a reasonable guess by making some assumptions. Southampton is a small city with one centrally located station. It has few direct destinations. Rome on the other hand is a large city, with possibly more than one station and many choices of departure. With no other knowledge, your best option would be to start working forward because there are fewer options[3] for destinations and you have less chance of making a poor choice. In practice, you would probably do a combined search of switching back and forth between a forward and backward search.

Prolog performs a backward search. Prolog could have been designed so that the rules are written in a forward sense. In terms of automating the search there would be no difference in identifying the head of the clause for a goal-directed search even if the rules were written in a forward sense. Backward chaining is a natural search strategy for Prolog because a problem is presented as a query to be answered. The search can focus on those facts and rules that can answer the query. Forward chaining would be appropriate if a new fact were to be added to the database and we wished to see what conclusions could be derived from the addition of the new fact.

Summary

Automating reasoning with logical expressions has been presented as a process of resolution and unification. Resolution is a mechanistic process for cancelling terms in sets of clauses. Resolution refutation is a proof procedure that attempts to prove that the negated conclusion is inconsistent with the assumptions. If, during a refutation proof, all terms can be cancelled and the empty clause derived, then the conclusion is valid.

To perform resolution, logical expressions are put into a standard form. The conjunctive normal form (CNF) rewrites a set of formulas as a conjunction of clauses, with each clause being a disjunction of literals. To rewrite first-order predicate calculus (FOPC) formulas into CNF takes a little more work to remove quantifiers. The existential quantifier is removed using a procedure called skolemization. When resolving propositional formulas, the identification of which literal pairs can be cancelled is straightforward – we identify a literal in one clause that is the negation of a literal in another clause. The matching of FOPC literals is more complicated because variables are involved, and these variables can be bound to other variables or constants. Unification provides a mechanistic procedure for matching FOPC literals.

Further reading

Unification and resolution were introduced by Robinson (1965). For a good introduction to resolution see Kelly (1997). Spivey (1996) goes into some detail about resolution and unification to show how a simple Prolog interpreter is built. Knight (1989) provides a survey of unification. For books on Prolog see Clocksin and Mellish (1994) and Bratko (2000). For a history of the early years in logic programming see Kowalski (1988). For a book on automated reasoning see Wos *et al.* (1992).

---

[3]The **branching factor** refers to the number of states that can be reached from any other state. For trees with all internal nodes having n branches the branching factor is n. The forward search in this example is expected to have cities (and therefore states) with a lower branching factor than the backward search.

Exercises

1   Convert the following formulas into CNF:

    a $((p \wedge q) \vee r) \to s$
    b $(p \to \neg r) \to s$

2   Using both resolution refutation and resolution deduction show that statement (d) follows from statements (a), (b) and (c):

    a   John has beer only if he is happy.
    b   If Kate is with John then John has beer.
    c   Kate is with John.
    d   John is happy.

3   Convert the following formulas to CNF:

$$\forall X. (p(X) \to q(X, Y))$$
$$\forall X. (p(X) \to \exists Y. (q(X, Y) \vee r(Y)))$$

4   Use resolution to show that Sadie is a German Shepherd.

    All of Duncan's dogs are German Shepherds.
    Sadie is one of Duncan's dogs.

PART 3

Uncertainty

This part of the book introduces reasoning under uncertainty. The majority of real-world AI applications have to handle uncertainty. Uncertainty can arise because knowledge is incomplete or data are missing. A medical diagnosis might be uncertain because more than one medical condition is suggested by the observable symptoms. Tests are usually performed to reduce the uncertainty. There is inherent uncertainty in perceiving speech or objects. Words can sound like other words, background noise can interrupt communication, and the speech dialect may be unfamiliar to the listener. The uncertainty with speech is reduced by using other information such as cues from speaker gestures and the context of the subject being talked about. The outcome of an action is also usually uncertain. Your car may not start when the ignition is turned. The lift may not be working in a department store. Uncertainty adds to the complexity of reasoning. For example, a robot might plan to use a lift for getting between floors but if the lift is out of action it will need to revise how it is to transit between levels.

Chapter 5 introduces Bayesian networks. No prior knowledge is assumed: the basics of probability theory are covered. Bayesian networks have proved to be popular tools for implementing real-world applications. For this reason, the following chapter, Chapter 6, takes a more detailed look at the implementation of Bayesian networks. Chapter 7 introduces other approaches to modelling uncertainty. Fuzzy logic, in a strict sense, is not a method for modelling uncertainty, but it fits more neatly within this part of the book given that many talk of fuzzy logic in the context of uncertainty (because of fuzzy sets). Dempster–Shafer theory is introduced next. Dempster–Shafer theory is used in some applications of data fusion in which the signals from different sensors are combined to increase the accuracy of predicted classification (as in recognizing an object, for example). Finally, non-numerical approaches are briefly reviewed.

CHAPTER 5

Bayesian Networks I

Daily life is full of uncertainties. You order a taxi for 12 o'clock and expect it to turn up, but there is a possibility that it won't show at all. A manufacturer of television sets issues a warranty in the expectation that the set will still be working in 1 year from the date of purchase, but it knows that a percentage of sets are likely to develop faults. Insurance companies price the cost of house contents insurance on the basis of crime and accident statistics. These companies price the cost of insurance in the expectation that they will make a profit because the number of claims will be limited. We purchase insurance because we know that theft or accidents can cost much more than a premium. Decisions are being made all the time in an uncertain world. These uncertainties arise because data are incomplete and because the outcomes of many actions are not easy to predict. Data may be missing because it is not possible or practicable to measure everything, or it might be missing because it is related to a future event and is therefore not available. You can never know everything about events that might influence your taxi not showing. Perhaps the taxi firm forgot about you, or the driver had an accident, or flooding blocked a road, etc. We all know about the uncertainty of weather prediction but forecasting has improved with the availability of satellite images and radar. These additional weather-monitoring technologies provide more data to give improved accuracy in the forecast.

Suppose Graham has an ornamental water fountain that he has just purchased for the garden. The fountain is operated by a solar panel. The fountain works only when the sun is out. Graham is having friends round tomorrow for a barbecue and hopes to show off the fountain. There are, however, sources of uncertainty as to whether he will succeed. The main uncertainty would appear to be the dependency on the weather, but there is also a possibility that the fountain will develop a malfunction. If Graham leaves the fountain outside overnight there is a chance that somebody will pinch it. If, at the time of the barbecue, the sun is out and the feature is still in the garden then Graham is certain the water will flow except for a low probability of a malfunction with the device. Just before the barbecue Graham knows the status of the weather and is more certain of the outcome of the fountain working.

Let us consider one other example of a living room with two switches controlling a single light in the centre of the room. The room has a door at either end and a switch is located next to each of the doors so that the light can be operated on entering and leaving the room irrespective of the door used. The combinations of the switches and the light being on or off are given below:

Switch 1	Switch 2	Light
Up	Up	On
Down	Up	Off
Up	Down	Off
Down	Down	On

For the light to be on, both switches need to be up or down. However, the light working depends on the light bulb functioning, the circuit fuse being okay, no malfunction in the wiring and no power cut. So, if you were blindfolded and told the position of the switches, you would guess that the light is almost certainly on but you cannot be completely sure because of the other influencing factors. If you were told that the electricity was flowing to the bulb, and the bulb was working and there was no other malfunction you could say with certainty whether the light was on if told the position of both switches. Given that there is no malfunction, and the position of the light switches, the decision as to whether or not the light is on is deterministic. If however, you only knew the position of one of the light switches you cannot determine if the light is on. If you were in fact ignorant of the existence of switch 2, and kept a record of when the light was on along with the state of switch 1, the lighting would appear stochastic. Sometimes the light is on when the switch is down and sometimes the light is off. Knowing only about the single switch means that your knowledge of the lighting system is incomplete.

In this chapter, we introduce **Bayesian networks,** also called probabilistic networks or belief networks for reasoning under uncertainty. Bayesian networks are proving to be powerful tools with many application domains, including medical diagnosis, troubleshooting computer hardware faults, parent tracing for cattle and many more.

The concept of Bayesian networks is introduced first. Basic probability theory is then briefly reviewed. Bayesian networks are essentially a compact way of representing a joint probability distribution over a set of variables. The network allows us to inspect a line of reasoning and the network structure leads to the compact representation of probabilities. The fundamental properties of Bayesian networks are introduced using two examples. A technique for implementing Bayesian networks that is the basis for many commercial applications follows.

5.1 Introduction

We start by considering a diagnostic scenario.

There are many types of application that involve diagnosis, whether it be a patient suffering some condition such as back pain or a helicopter experiencing excessive vibration. A diagnostic system seeks to identify the cause of the observed effects. In this section, a small model for a car diagnostic system is used to provide an introduction to the concept of a Bayesian network.

The following rule:

1   IF state(battery, dead) Then state(car_start, false)

expresses that a dead battery is a cause for a car not to start. The effect (car will not start) can be deduced from the cause (battery is dead). The rule is deterministic as, without doubt, a dead battery will prevent the car from starting.[1] Diagnostic reasoning is primarily **abductive** – given the effect (car will not start), find the likely cause – but a diagnostic system will often need the ability to reason in the other direction from cause to effect. For example, a user may wish to predict the likely effects given that the car is in a certain condition.

Causal knowledge is usually transitive, which means that if A is a cause of B and B a cause of C then A is a cause of C. This can be seen in the following two rules:

2   IF state(spark_plugs, fouled) Then state(spark_quality, bad)
3   IF state(spark_quality, bad) Then state(car_start, false)

---

[1]Assuming that no other way of starting is available (e.g. pushing).

The fouled spark plugs are a cause for the car not to start. The plugs might be fouled due to the fuel mixture being too rich, in which case the primary (root) cause would be the fuel system.

Notice that in rules 2 and 3 a vague term, *bad*, has been introduced. *Bad* is a qualitative term that cannot be given a precise definition and does not correspond to a single value. Also, rule 3 is underspecified: a bad spark quality will not necessarily mean that the car has no chance of starting. Therefore, the rules as presented above are not a sufficient representation for diagnostic reasoning. The representation should allow for uncertainties to be modelled and should allow reasoning in a forward and backward direction. It has proved difficult to satisfy these requirements using conventional rule-based approaches. An alternative representation that is gaining in popularity is a Bayesian network. A small part of a car diagnostic network is shown in Figure 5.1.

Nodes in the network are more typically referred to as **variables**. Each variable is given a number of discrete states. So the variable *Battery Voltage* has three states: *Strong*, *Weak* or *Dead*. The arrows connecting variables indicate causal influence. So the condition of the *Battery Voltage* has a causal influence on the condition of the *Headlights*. Each state of a variable has an associated

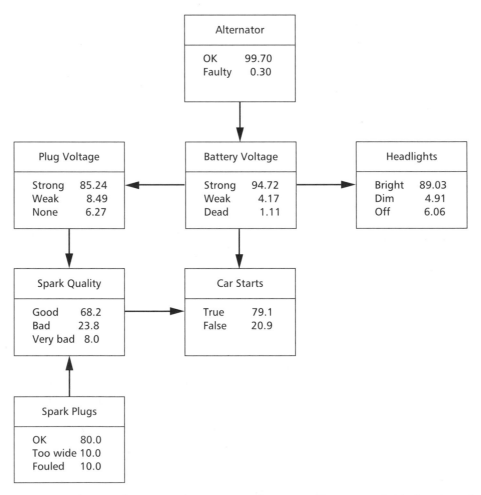

Figure 5.1 A causal network representing reasons why a car will not start. Behind each node is a probability distribution. For example, Battery Voltage is conditional on Alternator for which six values need to be given {(OK, Strong), (OK, Weak), (OK, Dead), (Faulty, Strong), ...}.

real value, which represents the probability of that state occurring. In Figure 5.1, the probabilities have been scaled as percentages. So, if the *Battery Voltage* were to be tested, we would expect that approximately 95% of the time to find that the voltage is strong. It is also expected that 79% of the time the car will start.

If the states of any variables are known, then these data are entered as **evidence** (also referred to as **findings**). For example, if a car does not start this can be entered as evidence by setting *Car Starts = False* (True then becomes 0, and False becomes 100%). After evidence is entered, the network probabilities are updated. After entering evidence that the car will not start, the *Battery_Voltage* being strong is 80% confident and the *Spark_Plugs* being okay is 45% confident. The spark plugs therefore are the most likely cause for the car not starting (see Figure 5.2). However, on entering evidence that the headlights have been tested and found not to be working, the confidences are now shown in Figure 5.3 to be: *Battery_Voltage = Strong* (40%) and *Spark_Plugs = Okay* (63%). Additional evidence has reversed the belief in the direct cause. A good diagnostic reasoning system would issue a recommendation to test the headlights even though it believes the headlights should

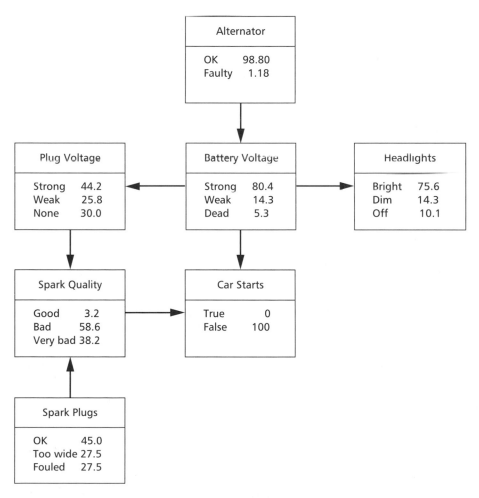

Figure 5.2 Car Starts is false has been entered as evidence.

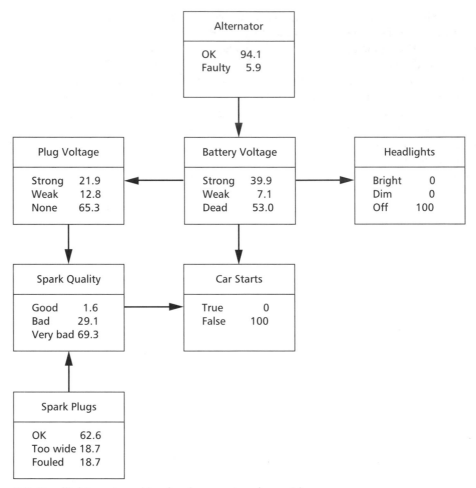

Figure 5.3 Headlights not working has been entered as evidence.

be working. The system would infer that this is a low-cost test and is justifiable if it reduces the possibility of a wrong diagnosis or performing more expensive tests.

Another example: Mary late for work

Mary catches a bus every morning to the train station, where she catches a train to work. Some mornings the bus is late and sometimes the train is late. The bus is late more often than the train, but if either mode of transport should be late it does not necessarily mean that Mary is late for work.

The train or the bus being late is a cause for Mary being late for work and can be represented by the following two rules:

IF bus is late THEN Mary is late for work

IF train is late THEN Mary is late for work

We might want to use the knowledge about Mary in a predictive way to assess the likelihood of her being late should she miss the bus. Alternatively, the knowledge can be used in a diagnostic way to find the most likely cause when we observe that Mary is late for work. The difficulty with modelling this type of knowledge using a conventional rule-based system has already been mentioned, but it is instructive to explore further why using rules is difficult.

In a rule-based system, knowledge is modular or local to rules: rules stand alone and are executed only when their conditions are satisfied; however, once executed, it is not easy to revoke any conclusions that conflict with new evidence. For instance, in the car example, initially the spark plugs are the likely cause of the car not starting, but the battery becomes the most likely cause on entering further evidence that the lights are not working. The new evidence, that the lights are not working, has worked against the previous conclusion that the spark plugs are the likely cause for the car not starting. The point is that knowledge contained in different rules can be associated in subtle ways. Returning to the two rules for Mary, we know that the bus being late and the train being late are independent of one another. That is, the operation of the train service is not affected by the operation of the bus service and vice versa. If, though, we are performing diagnostic reasoning, the conditions of the two rules can be associated. If, for example, we know that Mary is late for work, then our belief in the train being late increases, and so too does our belief in the bus being late. If we should subsequently hear that the bus was late then our belief in the train being late should decrease.

A requirement to reason in both directions can also lead to subtle problems. For instance, consider the following two rules:

IF the bus is late THEN Mary is late
IF Mary is late THEN the train is late

Knowing that the bus is late will conclude Mary is late which invokes the second rule to conclude that the train is late. The rules use the evidence for the bus being late to conclude that the train is late and yet both services are independent. Individual rules cannot be built without considering how all the rules will respond together and this becomes increasingly difficult as the number of variables grow.

● ● ● ● ●

5.2 A short overview of basic probability theory

5.2.1 Basic axioms

A probability is the assignment of a real number to the occurrence of an event. The set of all possible outcomes is called the **sample space**. The probability $P(A)$ of an event A is a real number:

$$P(A) \geq 0 \tag{5.1}$$

Also:

$$P(A) + P(\overline{A}) = 1 \tag{5.2}$$

where $P(\overline{A})$ is **not A.**

So, for example, if event A is that a balanced coin lands heads up and event B it lands tails up, then:

$P(A)=0.5, P(B)=0.5$
$P(A)+P(B)=1$

If two events are mutually exclusive then:

$P(A \text{ or } B)=P(A)+P(B)$ (5.3)

5.2.2 Random variables

A **random variable** is a variable that can exist in one of a finite number of mutually exclusive states. Associated with each state is a real number that gives the probability of the variable being in a particular state. For example, a balanced die can be in one of six states, and each state has a probability of 1/6. A variable of interest to hay fever sufferers is the pollen count. For the purpose of a weather report, the pollen count might be classed as low, medium or high. Probabilities for each one of these states might be given for a particular geographic region as:

$P(\text{Pollen}=\text{low})=0.7$
$P(\text{Pollen}=\text{medium})=0.2$
$P(\text{Pollen}=\text{high})=0.1$

Each probability is a real number between 0 and 1 and the sum of all states is 1. The probabilities can be written in the form of a **probability distribution** as:

$P(\text{Pollen})=(0.7, 0.2, 0.1)$

More formally, we say that if V is a variable with states $v_1, v_2, \ldots, v_n$, then $P(V)$ is a probability distribution over these states. And if $\phi(v_i)$ denotes the probability of V being in state v_i, then:

$P(V)=(\phi(v_1), \phi(v_2), \ldots, \phi(v_n))$

$\phi(v_i) \geq 0$

$$\sum_{i=1}^{n} \phi(v_i) = 1$$

There are many situations in which a distribution involves two or more variables. Suppose there are two variables, X and Y, and variable X can be in one of three states and variable Y can be in one of two states. Thus, there are 3×2 (= 6) combined states for both X and Y. For example, if X denotes pollen count and Y denotes cloud cover, the following table might represent the possible combinations:

	$X=\text{low}$	$X=\text{medium}$	$X=\text{high}$
$Y=\text{cloudy}$	0.5	0.01	0.01
$Y=\text{sunny}$	0.2	0.19	0.09

The table represents the **joint probability distribution,** $P(X, Y)$, for X and Y. All states in the table are mutually exclusive, and all entries in the table must sum to 1. The probability for $P(Y=\text{cloudy})$ can be found by summing all entries in the first row:

$$P(Y=\text{cloudy})=0.5+0.01+0.01=0.52$$

The probability $P(X=\text{low})$ can be found by summing all entries in the first column:

$$P(X=\text{low})=0.5+0.2=0.7$$

5.2.3   Prior and posterior probabilities

This chapter is concerned with reasoning under uncertainty and beliefs about situations change in the light of new evidence. For instance, we can assign a **prior** probability to represent our belief in the likelihood of Mary being late for work. The probability is assigned in the absence of any evidence. If evidence should be received that informs us that the train is late, then the probability of Mary being late will change. The new probability that is computed when given evidence is called the **posterior** probability.

5.2.4   Conditional dependence

Suppose that there are two washing machine manufacturers and a study has been undertaken to find the number of machines that develop a fault within 1 year of purchase. The results of the study are summarized below:

	Manufacturer A	Manufacturer B	Total
Number with fault	200	300	500
Number with no fault	29 800	19 700	49 500
Total	30 000	20 000	50 000

The table represents the frequency of past faults and can be used to calculate the probability of a future event such as a fault developing within 1 year of purchasing a new machine:

$$P(F)=(500/50\,000)=0.01$$
$$P(N)=(49\,500/50\,000)=0.99$$

where $P(F)$ is the probability of a fault and $P(N)$ is the probability of no fault.

Notice that if every element in the table (apart from the totals) is divided by 50 000 then all elements add to 1 and the table gives the joint probability distribution for $P(\text{Manufacturer, Fault})$.

A probability that is usually of interest is the probability of a purchaser's machine developing a fault given that the purchaser bought from manufacturer A. The notation:

$$P(A|B)$$

is used to express the probability of event A given event B. The **fundamental rule** relates conditional probability to the joint probability:

$$P(A|B)P(B)=P(A, B) \text{ or } P(A|B)=[P(A, B)/P(B)] \qquad (5.4)$$

So, the probability of a fault developing given a purchase from manufacturer A is:

$$P(F|A)=(200/50\,000)\times(30\,000/50\,000)^{-1}=0.0067$$

and for manufacturer B:

$$P(F|A)=(300/50\,000)\times(20\,000/50\,000)^{-1}=0.015$$

So, if you purchase from manufacturer B you more than double the probability of your machine developing a fault.

As a final example consider that someone has thrown a balanced coin three times in succession and written the outcomes on a piece of paper. The sample space is:

$$S=\{HHH, HTH, THH, TTH, HHT, HTT, THT, TTT\}$$

If we were asked for the probability of HHH being on the paper we would quote the probability as:

$$P(HHH)=1/8$$

or, more strictly, as:

$$P(HHH|S)=1/8$$

Suppose that we want the probability of three heads given that at least two heads were thrown. The sample space for two heads, calling the event B, is:

$$B=\{HHH, HTH, THH, HHT\}$$

So the probability of HHH, given B, is $1/4$. Using eqn (5.4), this would be calculated thus:

$$P(HHH|B)=P(HHH, B)\times 1/P(B)=1/8 \times (1/2)^{-1}=1/4$$

Bayes' rule

From the fundamental rule it follows that:

$$P(B|A)=P(A, B)/P(A)$$

which leads to:

$$P(B|A)=[P(A|B)P(B)]/P(A) \qquad (5.5)$$

Equation (5.5) is known as Bayes' rule.

Bayes' rule is an important rule since it allows us to reason about probabilities in both directions. Say, for example, you wanted a predictive estimate of somebody having lung cancer given that they were suffering from back pain. People suffer from back pain for all kinds of reasons, and it would be a waste of precious resources to test for lung cancer in everyone who walks into a doctor's surgery complaining of back pain. However, given that a person is suffering from lung cancer you can more easily estimate the probability of them suffering back pain, and Bayes' rule, along with prior probabilities of lung cancer and back pain, can be used to estimate the probability of lung cancer given back pain.

Bayes' rule is the basis for reasoning in Bayesian networks.

Independence

In the example *Mary is late for work,* the lateness of the train and bus are independent in that the state of one mode of transport does not influence the state of the other. Variables A and C are **independent** given B if:

$$P(A|B) = P(A|B, C)$$

So if B is known then knowledge of C will not alter the probability of A.

Chain rule

If $P(V_1, V_2, ..., V_n)$ is a joint probability distribution over the variables $V_1, V_2, ..., V_n$ then:

$$P(V_1, V_2, ..., V_n) = P(V_n | V_{n-1}, ..., V_1)\, P(V_{n-1} | V_{n-2}, ..., V_1)\, ...\, P(V_2 | V_1) P(V_1) \tag{5.6}$$

Equation (5.6) is called the **chain rule** and is a way of factoring a joint distribution into a product of conditional probabilities. There are as many different factorizations as there are orderings of variables. For example:

$$P(A, B, C) = P(A|B, C) \cdot P(B|C) \cdot P(C)$$

or:

$$P(B, A, C) = P(B|A, C) \cdot P(A|C) \cdot P(C)$$

Other orderings for $P(A, B, C)$ include $\{P(A, C, B), P(B, C, A), P(C, A, B), P(C, B, A)\}$. The chain rule is used in Bayesian networks for building a compact representation of a joint probability distribution.

5.3 The Bayesian network

Let us return to our earlier example of Mary being late for work. We could model our beliefs in the states of the variables in terms of probabilities. We might, for example, have a record of how often the bus has been late and use this information to calculate the probability of the bus being late. Alternatively, in the absence of any records, we might assign a number between 0 and 1 that represents our belief in that the bus will be late. If we believe that the bus has a poor record of time-keeping then we might assign a relatively high value to $P(\text{bus} = \text{late})$. We assign prior probabilities to the variables *Bus* and *Train* for their two states of being late and not being late. We also need values for our beliefs in Mary being late when we know the state of the bus or train. Each variable can be in one of two states: late or on time. So, for the variable Mary, we need to assign probabilities for eight states:

Mary is late given that the bus is on time and the train is on time,
Mary is late given that the bus is on time and the train is late,
Mary is late given that the bus is late and the train is on time,
Mary is late given that the bus is late and the train is late,
Mary is on time given that the bus is on time and the train is on time,
Mary is on time given that the bus is on time and the train is late,
Mary is on time given that the bus is late and the train is on time,
Mary is on time given that the bus is late and the train is late,

The probabilities for each of the variables are shown in Figure 5.4.

According to the chain rule the joint probability distribution can be found from:

$$P(Mary, Bus, Train) = P(Mary|Bus, Train)P(Bus|Train)P(Train)$$

The joint probability distribution is shown in Table 5.1 and can be used to perform reasoning. For instance, the probability of Mary being late for work is 0.15 (accurate to two decimal places) and is found by summing all the entries in the product column corresponding to Mary being late.

Given that Mary is late, what is the probability of this being due to a late bus? The probability needed is $P(Bus = late|Mary = late)$. This calculation is found by summing entries in the product column that match both Mary being late and the bus being late and dividing by the sum of all products matching Mary being late:

$$P(Bus = late|Mary = late) = 0.081/0.150 = 0.54$$

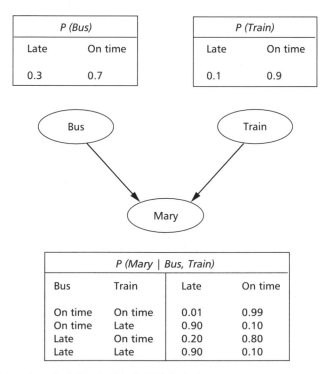

Figure 5.4 Conditional probability tables for *Mary is late*.

Table 5.1 The joint probability distribution for the network shown in Figure 5.4

Bus	Train	Mary	P(Mary| Bus, Train)	P(Bus | Train)	P(Train)	Product
On time	On time	On time	0.99	0.70	0.90	0.6237
On time	Late	On time	0.10	0.70	0.10	0.007
Late	On time	On time	0.80	0.30	0.90	0.216
Late	Late	On time	0.10	0.30	0.10	0.003
On time	On time	Late	0.01	0.70	0.90	0.0063
On time	Late	Late	0.90	0.70	0.10	0.063
Late	On time	Late	0.20	0.30	0.90	0.054
Late	Late	Late	0.90	0.30	0.10	0.027

A similar calculation for the train being responsible for Mary's lateness gives 0.6. Given that Mary is late and the bus was late, then the probability of the train being responsible is 0.33. This is computed by dividing the product value matching:

(Bus = late, Train = late, Mary = late)

by the sum of the products matching:

(Bus – late, Mary = late)

$$P(Train= late \,|\, Mary = late, \; Bus = late) = 0.027/(0.027 + 0.054) = 0.33$$

In the type of scenario under consideration, we are not concerned with exact numerical values of the calculations but we do want to see that the relative size of probabilities match our expectations. For example, we would think it less likely that the train is responsible for Mary being late upon learning that the bus was late, and this reasoning is reflected in the calculations because our belief in the train being late drops from 0.6 to 0.33 upon learning that the bus was late.

5.3.1   D-separation

There are three types of connection in a causal network: converging, diverging and serial. The way in which information can pass through these connections leads to a concept known as **d-separation.** We can use d-separation to read off conditional independencies: if nodes A and B are d-separated, then $P(A|B, e) = P(A|e)$, where e is evidence.

Converging connections

The example with Mary being late for work is a converging connection. In this example, we can reason that the train and bus states are conditionally independent unless we know the state of Mary. If, for example, we know that Mary is late and we know the state of the train, then this will influence our belief in the state of the bus. With a converging connection, like that shown in Figure 5.5, if nothing is known about the state of C then its parents (A and B) are independent: knowledge of A has no influence on B and knowledge of B has no influence on A. If, however, the state of C is known then the parents become conditionally dependent.

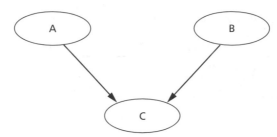

Figure 5.5 A and B are independent unless information about C or a descendant of C has been received.

When the state of a node is known we say that evidence about that node has been received. Evidence can be transmitted through the converging connection (variable *C*) only if either the variable *C* or one of its descendants has received evidence. In other words, *A* and *B* are independent unless evidence about *C* is received. Variables *A* and *B* are said to be d-separated.

Diverging connections

It is known that icy roads can cause Joe or Sara to have an accident. The network of cause and effect is shown in Figure 5.6. Suppose that the state of the road is unknown when we hear that Joe has had an accident. This evidence that Joe has had an accident will influence our belief in Sara having an accident (that is, Sara is more likely to have an accident if Joe has had an accident). If, on the other hand, we know the state of the road is icy, then subsequent knowledge of Joe having an accident will not influence our belief in Sara having an accident. It is the icy roads that increase the risk of an accident then knowledge of the road condition influences our belief in the risk of both Joe and Sara having an accident. If we do not know the state of the roads but learn that either Joe or Sara has had an accident this increases our belief in the roads being icy and hence our belief in the other person being at risk.

In the diverging connection of Figure 5.6, influence can pass between the children of *A* unless the state of *A* is known. So evidence can be transmitted through a diverging connection unless evidence about that connection has been received. In other words, *B* and *C* are dependent and become independent when evidence about *A* is received. *B* and *C* are said to be d-separated given *A*.

Serial connections

A serial connection is shown in Figure 5.7. It is known that smoking increases the risk of lung cancer and lung cancer can cause shortness of breath. Knowing that someone has been a long-term smoker

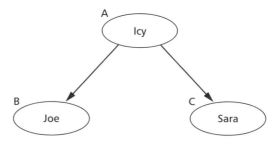

Figure 5.6 B and C are dependent unless evidence is received about A.

increases our belief that they might suffer from lung cancer, which in turn influences our belief that they may suffer from breathing difficulties. Similarly, knowing that someone has breathing difficulty increases our suspicion of lung cancer and that the person is a smoker. However, if we know that someone has lung cancer, knowing that they smoke is not going to further our belief that they might have breathing difficulty.

Evidence may be transmitted through a serial connection unless the state of the variable in the connection is known. In other words, A and C are dependent and become independent upon receiving evidence about B. A and C are d-separated given B.

The Bayesian network representation is more useful than simply working with the complete distribution over all variables because it conveys the structure of knowledge and it also carries semantic information that is lost when dealing with a joint probability distribution table. Also, the structuring of knowledge enables us to see if a more compact representation of the joint distribution can be found through observing d-separation. For example, in *Mary is late for work*, we know that the status of the bus is independent of the status of the train and they become associated only if we have evidence about Mary being late for work. Knowing the independence of bus and train allows the joint distribution to be written as:

$$P(Mary, Bus, Train) = P(Mary \mid Bus, Train)\,P(Bus)P(Train)$$

We can use this form of the distribution to calculate $P(Bus = late, Train \mid Mary = late)$. From Bayes' rule we have:

$$P(Mary, Bus, Train) = \frac{P(Bus = late, Train, Mary = late)}{P(Mary = late)} = \frac{0.054 + 0.027}{0.1503} = 0.54$$

Note that:

$P(Bus = late, Train, Mary = late) = P(Bus = late, Train = ontime, Mary = late) + P(Bus = late, Train = late, Mary = late)$

Example: office is unlocked

Steven and David share an office at the university where they both teach. Steven is usually the first to arrive at work and so he expects to find the office locked. Occasionally, David will arrive at work before Steven and if David is in the office Steven will find the office unlocked. Sometimes the early-morning cleaner forgets to lock the office, and on rare occasions the office will be found unlocked for some other reason. When David is in work it is usual to find his computer switched on.

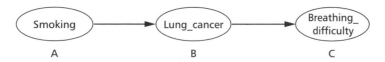

Figure 5.7 Serial connection. A and C are dependent unless evidence about B is received.

Steven is interested in modelling the above scenario and he is going to model it from what he observes. The variables for the model and their possible states are:

David – in or out
Office – locked or unlocked
Cleaner – left office locked or unlocked
Computer – on or off

Steven does not appear as a variable because the model is being built from his view. The variables are the objects of interest. These objects are associated in a causal sense:

David and the cleaner can both be the cause of the office being found unlocked.
David is the cause of the computer being found on or off.

The associations can be modelled with the diagram depicted in Figure 5.8. The diagram represents the structural model which conveys the organization of knowledge about the scenario. The structural model also conveys dependencies in that the state of the office depends on the actions of both David and the cleaner and the state of the computer depends on the action of David.

Before Steven can reason with his uncertainty model he needs to assign probabilities to the various states of the variables. He assigns the probabilities by making subjective assessments based on experience. Steven could keep a detailed account over the period of a year (or more) to estimate the various probabilities, but he opts for a subjective assessment of probabilities. For instance, if Steven finds the office unlocked this will increase his expectation of finding David's computer switched on and increase his suspicion of the cleaner having left the office unlocked. Upon discovering the computer switched on, his belief in the cleaner being responsible will decrease. The subjective probabilities are given in the network diagram.

● ● ● ● ●

A general result for the joint probability distribution of a network, which makes use of independence assumptions, is given next.

For a set of variables $U\{V_1, V_2, ..., V_n\}$ the joint probability distribution $P(U)$ is the product of all conditional probabilities:

$$P(U) = \prod_i P(V_i | parents(V_i)) \tag{5.7}$$

Equation (5.7) is the chain rule written in a concise form by taking account of independence.

So returning to our office example, the probability distribution of the model can be written as:

$$P(U) = P(Office | David, Cleaner)P(Computer | David)P(David)P(Computer)$$

Again the distribution can be represented as a table that captures all the states in which the variables can be combined. Each variable of Steven's model can be in one of two states, and so there are 2^n combinations (n is the number of variables). The distribution is given in Table 5.2. The table can be used to calculate the probabilities of interest. For instance, to find the probability of the office being unlocked, all the values in the product column are summed for rows corresponding to Office = unlocked. To calculate the probability of the computer being on given that the office is

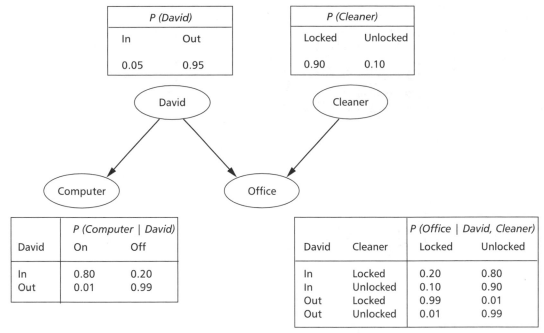

Figure 5.8 The network structure and tables for *Office is unlocked*.

unlocked, the sum of all products corresponding to Office = unlocked and Computer = on is divided by the summed product for Office = unlocked:

$$P(Computer = on \mid Office = unlocked) = \frac{P(Computer = on, Office = unlocked)}{P(Office = unlocked)} = \frac{0.0334}{0.1431} = 0.234$$

It becomes impractical for real applications to generate a distribution table that includes all variables. Like all good approaches to difficult problems, we desire a method to structure a solution. A network solution conveys the causal associations, conveys dependencies and makes the management of real-world applications more feasible.

If the network is a tree, as is the case with the two examples presented so far, then we can implement the calculation of probabilities through a series of message passes. Instead of defining a joint probability distribution table over all variables, we keep a table for a variable local to a node. When evidence is received, as in the case of the office being found unlocked, we pass information to other nodes in the tree. The message passing uses the fundamental rule to compute updated beliefs for each variable in the tree. In the following sections we define the Bayesian network and then illustrate the messaging-passing procedure.

5.3.2   Definition of a Bayesian network

A Bayesian network is a graph in which each node represents a variable. Each variable has an associated conditional probability table. The network along with the tables provides a decomposed representation of the joint probability distribution for the variables.

A Bayesian network over a set of variables $U\{V_1, V_2, \ldots, V_n\}$ consists of:

Table 5.2 The joint probability distribution for *Office is unlocked*

David	Cleaner	Office	Computer	P(David)	P(Cleaner)	P(Office | David, Cleaner)	P(Computer | David)	Product
In	Unlocked	Locked	On	0.05	0.1	0.1	0.8	0.0004
In	Locked	Locked	On	0.05	0.9	0.2	0.8	0.0072
Out	Unlocked	Locked	On	0.95	0.1	0.01	0.01	0.0000095
Out	Locked	Locked	On	0.95	0.9	0.99	0.01	0.0084645
In	Unlocked	Unlocked	On	0.05	0.1	0.9	0.8	0.0036
In	Locked	Unlocked	On	0.05	0.9	0.8	0.8	0.0288
Out	Unlocked	Unlocked	On	0.95	0.1	0.99	0.01	0.0009405
Out	Locked	Unlocked	On	0.95	0.9	0.01	0.01	0.0000855
In	Unlocked	Locked	Off	0.05	0.1	0.1	0.2	0.0001
In	Locked	Locked	Off	0.05	0.9	0.2	0.2	0.0018
Out	Unlocked	Locked	Off	0.95	0.1	0.01	0.99	0.0009405
Out	Locked	Locked	Off	0.95	0.9	0.99	0.99	0.8379855
In	Unlocked	Unlocked	Off	0.05	0.1	0.9	0.2	0.0009
In	Locked	Unlocked	Off	0.05	0.9	0.8	0.2	0.0072
Out	Unlocked	Unlocked	Off	0.95	0.1	0.99	0.99	0.0931095
Out	Locked	Unlocked	Off	0.95	0.9	0.01	0.99	0.0084645

- A **directed acyclic graph** (DAG). Each node of the graph represents a variable. The interaction that can occur between variables is restricted by a set of independent assertions that are encoded by the structure.
- A quantification. Each variable is quantified with a conditional probability table. The probabilities over all states for a variable add up to 1.

5.3.3   An algorithm for implementing Bayesian network updates

This section presents a technique for implementing exact inferencing in Bayesian networks. The technique is first explained, and then illustrated by example. Algorithms for the more general case are given in Chapter 6.

Exact inferencing is performed using a secondary structure. The DAG is transformed into a tree (the secondary structure), which is a more convenient representation of the joint distribution encoded by the DAG.

A Bayesian network is given in Figure 5.9 – this DAG is already a tree but the tree we require has a different structure and is shown on the right in Figure 5.9. The joint distribution can be found using equation 5.7:

$$P(U) = P(B|A)P(C|A)P(D|C)P(E|C)P(A)$$

The figure also shows a **cluster tree,** which is a collection of cluster nodes[2] containing variables from the Bayesian network. The cluster tree also contains separator nodes called **sepsets,** which for the moment can be ignored. A cluster tree corresponding to a Bayesian network is constructed by forming a collection of cluster nodes with the condition that for each variable V there is at least one cluster node that contains V and the parents of V. For example, variable B has an associated cluster node BA: the cluster node contains B and its parent – we shall see later how the clusters and tree are formed. Once the cluster nodes have been formed they are arranged into a tree with separators (sepsets). Each sepset contains the variables that are common to its adjacent nodes. The cluster nodes and sepsets are then assigned tables. The size of the table corresponds to the combinations of

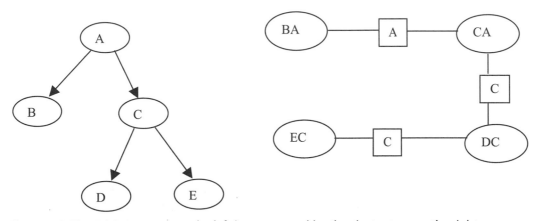

Figure 5.9 The DAG structure on the left is represented by the cluster tree on the right.

---

[2]In graph theory the node in a graph is often called a vertex, but we shall use node for both graphs and trees. We also use the terms 'link' and 'edge' interchangeably.

all variable states. For example, in Figure 5.9, all variables have two states and therefore each cluster node table will have four entries and each sepset two entries. Once the tables are formed, they are initialized by setting each element of the table to a value of 1. Finally, for each variable V, a single cluster node containing V and the parents of V is selected and multiplied by:

$P(V|Parents(V))$

Once the tables have been multiplied out, the tables in the cluster tree of Figure 5.9 will have tables corresponding to:

$BA = P(B|A)P(A)$, $CA = P(C|A)$, $DC = P(D|C)$, $EC = P(E|C)$

The above multiplications come about because A and B are assigned to BA, C to CA, D to DC and E to EC. The product of the cluster node tables in the cluster tree gives the joint distribution of the equivalent Bayesian network.

Any cluster tree that corresponds to a Bayesian network over U (a set of variables) is a representation of $P(U)$, and $P(U)$ is computed by taking the product of each cluster table and dividing by the product of each sepset table:

$$P(U) = \frac{\prod_i C_i}{\prod_j S_j}$$

where C_i is the table for a cluster and S_j is the table for a sepset. We will not show how to multiply and divide tables here, but these will be illustrated by the examples presented later.

Initially the sepsets contain only values of 1 and so division by the sepsets makes no difference to the result. However, division by the sepsets is required when information is transmitted through the tree so that the cluster tree remains a faithful representation of $P(U)$. The product of all cluster tables divided by the product of all separator tables remains invariant when information is transmitted through the tree.

A cluster tree for the *office is unlocked* example is shown in Figure 5.10. The cluster tree shown is not the only one that could be constructed. The probability distribution for a variable can be calculated from any cluster or sepset that contains the variable. For instance, the probability distribution for David is readily seen in the sepset, but it can also be found using either cluster because David is a member of both clusters. The probability distribution of a variable from any cluster or sepset table containing that variable is computed using **marginalization**:

$$P(V) = \sum_{T \setminus V} \phi(T) \tag{5.8}$$

V is the variable whose distribution is to be computed and T is the table for the cluster or sepset that contains V. The notation $T \setminus V$ denotes that the sum is performed on table T where the entries in T match with the subset V. For example, the distribution for David can be found from the cluster (David, Office, Cleaner) as follows:

$P(David = in) = 0.0005 + 0.009 + 0.0045 + 0.036 = 0.05$

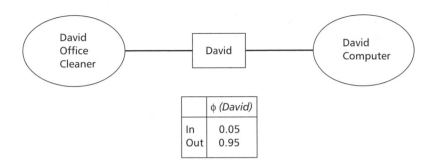

David	Cleaner	Office	φ (David, Cleaner, Office)
In	Unlocked	Locked	0.00050
In	Locked	Locked	0.00900
Out	Unlocked	Locked	0.00095
Out	Locked	Locked	0.84645
In	Unlocked	Unlocked	0.00450
In	Locked	Unlocked	0.03600
Out	Unlocked	Unlocked	0.09405
Out	Locked	Unlocked	0.00855

David	Computer	φ (David, Computer)
In	On	0.0400
In	Off	0.0100
Out	On	0.0095
Out	Off	0.9405

Figure 5.10 Secondary structure (known as a cluster tree) for the *Office is unlocked.*

$$P(David = out) = 0.00095 + 0.84645 + 0.09405 + 0.00855 = 0.95$$

You should also confirm that you get the same result for $P(David)$ using the cluster (David, Computer).

This cluster tree can also be used to perform reasoning when evidence about the state of a variable is received.

The procedure for finding the joint distributions is summarized below:

1   Convert the DAG to a cluster tree.
2   Form a table for each cluster and sepset. The number of entries in the table will correspond to the number of state combinations over each member variable. Set each entry to a value of 1.
3   Assign each variable to exactly one cluster; the cluster must have the variable and the parents of that variable as members.
4   Initialize each cluster table by multiplying for each assigned variable, i:

$$P(V_i | parents(V_i))$$

5   Pass messages around the tree until the tree is consistent. When a message is passed to a sepset, S, from a cluster, C, a new sepset table is calculated according to:

$$\phi(S) = \sum_{C_i \setminus S} \phi(C_i)$$

and when a sepset S passes a message to cluster j, a new cluster is calculated by multiplying the old cluster by the sepset and dividing by the old sepset table:

$$\phi(C_j) = \phi(C_j)\frac{\phi(S)}{\phi(S^{old})}$$

Algorithms for forming the cluster tree and message passing are given in Chapter 6. The procedure for two simple examples is illustrated next.

Example 1 ● ● ● ● ●

Figure 5.11 is a network with three variables, A, B and C. All variables are binary. The conditional tables are:

A	
a_1	0.3
a_2	0.7

A	B	
	b_1	b_2
a_1	a_1b_1 (0.2)	a_1b_2 (0.8)
a_2	a_2b_1 (0.4)	a_2b_2 (0.6)

A	C	
	c_1	c_2
a_1	a_1c_1 (0.1)	a_1c_2 (0.9)
a_2	a_2c_1 (0.5)	a_2c_2 (0.5)

The clusters are (in practice there would be one cluster but two are created for illustration)

for variable B – BA
for variable C – CA

There is a single sepset table with variable A linking BA and CA. Variable A is assigned to BA.
There is a table for each cluster node. Each cluster contains two binary variables, and so the

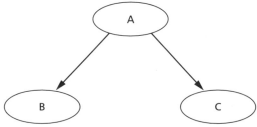

Figure 5.11 A simple Bayesian network used for Example 1.

number of entries in each will be 4, one for each combination of states. The table entries are set to 1 and are initialized by multiplying each entry by each member variable according to:

$P(V|parents(V))$

BA	
a_1b_1	$1.0 \times 0.2 \times 0.3 = 0.06$
a_1b_2	$1.0 \times 0.8 \times 0.3 = 0.24$
a_2b_1	$1.0 \times 0.4 \times 0.7 = 0.28$
a_2b_2	$1.0 \times 0.6 \times 0.7 = 0.42$

We have already assigned A to BA and therefore CA is:

CA	
a_1c_1	$1.0 \times 0.1 = 0.1$
a_1c_2	$1.0 \times 0.9 = 0.9$
a_2c_1	$1.0 \times 0.5 = 0.5$
a_2c_2	$1.0 \times 0.5 = 0.5$

The sepset is initialized to values of 1:

Sepset A	
a_1	1.0
a_2	1.0

Message passing can start from either cluster. Starting from BA, the sepset table is found by marginalizing on BA:

Sepset A	
a_1	0.3
a_2	0.7

CA is then updated by multiplying its table by the new sepset and then dividing by the old sepset. Each entry in CA is multiplied according to which state of A (a_1 or a_2) it matches. The old sepset only has entries of 1.0 and therefore the division will not alter any entry:

New CA	
a_1c_1	$0.1 \times 0.3 = 0.03$
a_1c_2	$0.9 \times 0.3 = 0.27$
a_2c_1	$0.5 \times 0.7 = 0.35$
a_2c_2	$0.5 \times 0.7 = 0.35$

Both CA and BA contain the same information on the sepset. In other words, marginalizing either cluster produces the same result for the entries in the sepset table. Further message passing alters nothing (because the old and new sepset tables are the same).

Any table containing A can now be marginalized to find the states of A. The distribution for B is found by marginalizing on BA and for C by marginalizing on CA.

We can check that the distribution in the cluster tree represents the distribution over all variables in the original graph. To do this, we divide the product of the cluster tables by the product of the sepset tables.

To find the product of BA and CA we create a new table with one entry for each intersection of tables BA and CA. An intersection corresponds to entries that share a variable. For example, a_1b_1 and a_1c_1 share the variable a_1 and so an entry is created for $a_1b_1c_1$.

BACA
$a_1b_1c_1$
$a_1b_1c_2$
$a_1b_2c_1$
$a_1b_2c_2$
$a_2b_1c_1$
$a_2b_1c_2$
$a_2b_2c_1$
$a_2b_2c_2$

The corresponding entries are then multiplied:

BACA	
$a_1b_1c_1$	$0.06 \times 0.03 = 0.0018$
$a_1b_1c_2$	$0.06 \times 0.27 = 0.0162$
$a_1b_2c_1$	$0.24 \times 0.03 = 0.0072$
$a_1b_2c_2$	$0.24 \times 0.27 = 0.0648$
$a_2b_1c_1$	$0.28 \times 0.35 = 0.098$
$a_2b_1c_2$	$0.28 \times 0.35 = 0.098$
$a_2b_2c_1$	$0.42 \times 0.35 = 0.147$
$a_2b_2c_2$	$0.42 \times 0.35 = 0.147$

Finally, this table is divided by the sepset:

BACA/A	
$a_1 b_1 c_1$	$0.0018/0.3 = 0.006$
$a_1 b_1 c_2$	$0.0162/0.3 = 0.054$
$a_1 b_2 c_1$	$0.0072/0.3 = 0.024$
$a_1 b_2 c_2$	$0.0648/0.3 = 0.216$
$a_2 b_1 c_1$	$0.098/0.7 = 0.14$
$a_2 b_1 c_2$	$0.098/0.7 = 0.14$
$a_2 b_2 c_1$	$0.147/0.7 = 0.21$
$a_2 b_2 c_2$	$0.147/0.7 = 0.21$

This table represents the complete joint distribution, and the distribution for any variable can be found by marginalizing on this table.

Example 2 • • • • •

The procedure for the *office is unlocked* example will now be illustrated (refer to Figure 5.10).
Set each cluster and sepset entry to a value of 1:

David	Cleaner	Office	ϕ(*David, Cleaner, Office*)
In	Unlocked	Locked	1
In	Locked	Locked	1
Out	Unlocked	Locked	1
Out	Locked	Locked	1
In	Unlocked	Unlocked	1
In	Locked	Unlocked	1
Out	Unlocked	Unlocked	1
Out	Locked	Unlocked	1

David	Computer	ϕ(*David, Computer*)
In	On	1
In	Off	1
Out	On	1
Out	Off	1

	ϕ(*David*)
In	1
Out	1

The variables will be assigned to clusters as follows. Cleaner can be assigned only to ϕ(*David,*

Cleaner, Office) as it is the only cluster that has Cleaner as a member. Office will also be assigned to the same cluster because it is only this cluster that contains Office and both parents (David and Cleaner).

Computer has to be assigned to ϕ(*David, Computer*). We have a choice of where to assign David, but we make an arbitrary choice and choose the same cluster as Computer.

So:

ϕ(*David, Cleaner, Office*)

has to be multiplied by:

P(Cleaner)P(Office|David, Cleaner)

and:

ϕ(*David, Computer*)

multiplied by *P(David)P(Computer|David)*.

Referring back to Figure 5.8, the products are given below:

David	Cleaner	Office	ϕ(*David, Cleaner, Office*)
In	Unlocked	Locked	$1 \times 0.1 \times 0.1 = 0.01$
In	Locked	Locked	$1 \times 0.9 \times 0.2 = 0.18$
Out	Unlocked	Locked	$1 \times 0.1 \times 0.01 = 0.001$
Out	Locked	Locked	$1 \times 0.9 \times 0.99 = 0.891$
In	Unlocked	Unlocked	$1 \times 0.1 \times 0.9 = 0.09$
In	Locked	Unlocked	$1 \times 0.9 \times 0.8 = 0.72$
Out	Unlocked	Unlocked	$1 \times 0.1 \times 0.99 = 0.099$
Out	Locked	Unlocked	$1 \times 0.9 \times 0.01 = 0.009$

David	Computer	ϕ(*David, Computer*)
In	On	$1 \times 0.05 \times 0.8 = 0.04$
In	Off	$1 \times 0.05 \times 0.2 = 0.01$
Out	On	$1 \times 0.95 \times 0.01 = 0.0095$
Out	Off	$1 \times 0.95 \times 0.99 = 0.9405$

Initialization is now complete.

A message will be passed from ϕ(*David, Cleaner, Office*) to ϕ(*David, Computer*) and then in the opposite direction.

From ϕ(David, Cleaner, Office) to ϕ(David, Computer)

The new sepset table is found from marginalizing on ϕ(*David, Cleaner, Office*). So we sum each value in ϕ(*David, Cleaner, Office*) that is consistent with the sepset.

$$\Sigma\phi(David = in) = 0.01 + 0.18 + 0.09 + 0.72 = 1$$

$$\Sigma\phi(David = out) = 0.001 + 0.891 + 0.099 + 0.009 = 1$$

The sepset table stays the same and so $\phi(David, Computer)$ will not be updated.

From ϕ(David, Computer) to ϕ(David, Cleaner, Office)

The new sepset table is found from marginalizing on $\phi(David, Computer)$.

$$\Sigma\phi(David = in) = 0.04 + 0.01 = 0.05$$

$$\Sigma\phi(David = out) = 0.0095 + 0.9405 = 0.95$$

	ϕ(David)
In	0.05
Out	0.95

$\phi(David, Cleaner, Office)$ is now multiplied by the sepset. Dividing by the old sepset has no effect as all values are 1. Multiplication is achieved by multiplying consistent rows. So, wherever the cluster table has David=in we multiply by 0.05, and for David=out we multiply by 0.95.

David	Cleaner	Office	ϕ(David, Cleaner, Office)
In	Unlocked	Locked	$0.01 \times 0.05 = 0.0005$
In	Locked	Locked	$0.18 \times 0.05 = 0.009$
Out	Unlocked	Locked	$0.001 \times 0.95 = 0.00095$
Out	Locked	Locked	$0.891 \times 0.95 = 0.84645$
In	Unlocked	Unlocked	$0.09 \times 0.05 = 0.0045$
In	Locked	Unlocked	$0.72 \times 0.05 = 0.036$
Out	Unlocked	Unlocked	$0.099 \times 0.95 = 0.09405$
Out	Locked	Unlocked	$0.009 \times 0.95 = 0.00855$

The probability distribution for each variable can be found from marginalizing its associated cluster. For example:

$$P(Office) = (0.0005, 0.0045) + (0.009, 0.036) + (0.00095, 0.09405) + (0.84645, 0.00855) = (0.8569, 0.1431)$$

Note that the first value in parenthesis corresponds to Office=locked and the second to Office=unlocked.

Also, for Cleaner:

$$P(Cleaner) = (0.0005, 0.009) + (0.00095, 0.84645) + (0.0045, 0.036) + (0.09405, 0.00855) = (0.1, 0.9)$$

The order of values in parenthesis is (Cleaner=unlocked, Cleaner=locked).

Summary

- Knowledge is represented in a Bayesian network by constructing a graph in which nodes (vertices) represent objects or events of interest and the links (edges) represent the association of causal influences between objects and events.
- Bayes' rule is the basis for reasoning in Bayesian networks.
- The joint probability distribution for a Bayesian network gives the probability for all combinations of variable states (a node represents a variable). The joint probability distribution is given by:

$$P(U) = \Pi P(V_i | parents(V_i))$$

- The computer implementation of a Bayesian network for exact inferencing relies on representing the joint distribution using a cluster tree. The cluster tree consists of nodes that are clusters of variables. Adjacent nodes are linked via sepsets that contain variables formed from the intersection of the adjacent nodes. Each cluster and sepset is quantified with a table.
- Information is passed round the tree using message passing. Messages are passed to ensure that the information held in the various cluster and sepset tables is consistent.
- Once the cluster tree is consistent, the joint distribution of the original DAG is found by:

$$P(U) = \frac{\prod_i C_i}{\prod_j S_j}$$

Exercises

1

	$X = x_1$	$i = x_2$
$Y = y_1$	0.02	0.30
$Y = y_2$	0.14	0.32
$Y = y_3$	0.10	0.12

Given the above joint distribution for X and Y calculate:
a $P(X = x_1)$
b $P(Y = y_2)$
c $P(Y = y_2 | X = x_1)$

2   Given that $P(a|b) = 0.5$, $P(a) = 0.3$, $P(b) = 0.4$ calculate $P(b|a)$.

3   In Example 1, Figure 5.11, the sepset is redundant and the distribution would in practice be modelled using a single-cluster table. Use a single-cluster table to compute $P(A)$, $P(B)$ and $P(C)$ for the network sketched below.

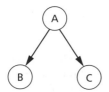

A	B = T	B = F
T	0.3	0.7
F	0.45	0.55

A	C = T	C = F
T	0.8	0.2
F	0.6	0.4

A = T	A = F
0.9	0.1

4   Express the joint probability distribution for the network below using the chain rule.

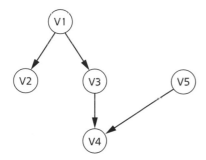

5   Given that evidence about C has been received, what can you say about the dependency between A and B in the following DAGs?

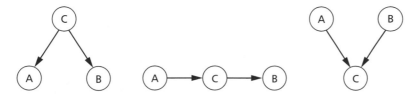

6   Implement a program to check that a graph is a DAG.

7   Implement a program that for small networks will compute the distribution using a single-cluster table (i.e. a table representing all state combinations).

8   Construct a network for modelling the following scenario. Construct your own probability distributions.

Paul parks his car at work in one of two car parks. He has noticed that his car alarm has a tendency to be triggered when parked in the park at the rear of the building. It will also be triggered (very rarely) when parked in front of the building. Paul suspects the alarm is triggered by heavy goods vehicles using the depot adjacent to the rear of the building. The alarm is not always triggered but it is triggered more frequently when the depot is busy. This depot is most active during early hours of the evening (when Paul has left work) but Wednesdays and Fridays are also busier than other days.

CHAPTER 6

Bayesian Networks II

The last chapter introduced Bayesian networks. A technique based on cluster trees was also presented for calculating the joint distribution of a network. This chapter presents the technique for the more general case and gives algorithms for finding the cluster tree and for message passing.

The junction tree, which is a more restricted version of a cluster tree, is introduced first. An algorithm for finding the junction tree is given. The technique for quantifying the junction tree follows. Quantification involves defining the cluster and sepset tables, after which message passing is performed to ensure that the junction tree is consistent. A consistent junction tree is a representation of the joint distribution of all variables described in the original network structure. We conclude exact inferencing with a technique for handling evidence. The techniques presented form the basis of many commercial applications of Bayesian networks.

Finally we take a brief look at inexact inferencing.

6.1 Constructing the cluster tree

If, for each pair of nodes V and W in a cluster tree, the intersection $V \cap W$ is contained in every node that lies on the path between V and W, then the cluster tree is a **junction tree**. This additional requirement that a junction tree has over a cluster tree is necessary to ensure global consistency. If a variable A is placed in more than one location in a cluster tree, there needs to be a way of passing information on A between the two locations. The junction tree constraint ensures that information about A can be passed between the two locations because each node found on the path will contain A.

Using the junction tree approach, inferencing with a Bayesian network is achieved in two stages:

1   The original network is a DAG that is transformed into the junction tree. The nodes of the junction tree are clusters of variables and each edge is associated with a sepset that holds the intersection of the adjacent (or neighbouring) nodes. Also, all nodes on the path between variables V and W contain $V \cap W$.

2   The tables for each cluster and sepset are initialized and then messages are propagated between adjacent clusters until a consistent junction tree emerges. Message passing rearranges the information stored in a table. When a cluster sends information to an adjacent cluster, it does so via the sepset. The sepset holds information that is common to the adjacent clusters and, when the information held in the tables of both clusters and the sepset is the same, then the link connecting the two clusters is said to be **consistent**. When a link is consistent, a message will have no effect on the information held in the table of a cluster or sepset that receives the message.

If, when you drop the directions of the edges in a DAG, you obtain a tree the DAG is said to be

singly connected. The generation of a junction tree from a singly connected DAG is reasonably straightforward:

- For any variable with one or more parents you form a cluster containing the variable and its parents.
- For any two clusters that contain a common variable you create a link and the link has a sepset that contains the common variable.

The procedure is illustrated for the tree in Figure 6.1. A further example is given in Figure 6.2. Notice that in this example we do not yet have a tree because it contains a cycle. All sepsets on the cycle contain the same variable (*D*), and any one link can be removed to obtain the tree. For instance, removing the link from *ABD* to *DF* creates the junction tree. If the cycle contains different sepsets then the cycle cannot be broken. In this situation the graph has to be modified by adding links. A more general procedure for constructing the junction tree is given next.

A variable and its parents are identified when a cluster is formed. This association between a variable and its parents can be represented using a graph by taking the original DAG, dropping the directions of links and then adding a link between any variables that have a common child. The resultant graph is called the **moral** graph. The moral graphs for Figures 6.1 and 6.2 are shown in Figure 6.3. The moral graph identifies the initial clusters, but it will not resolve the cycles for the DAG in Figure 6.4, whose junction graph is shown in Figure 6.5. The problem arises because the DAG has variables that have more than one causal link sharing a common ancestor. For example, both *C* and *D* can cause *E*, and both have *A* as a common ancestor. To resolve cycles resulting from multicausal links, the graph needs to be further transformed by adding links that are called **fill-ins**. The fill-ins are added to the moral graph to create what is called a **triangulated** graph. A graph is

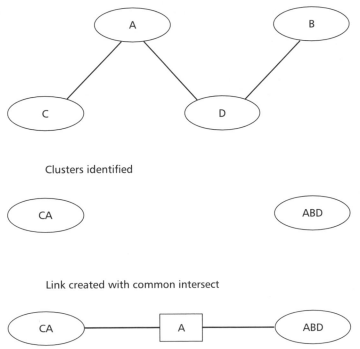

Clusters identified

Link created with common intersect

Figure 6.1 Transformation of a singly connected network into a junction tree. C has parent A and D has parents A and B.

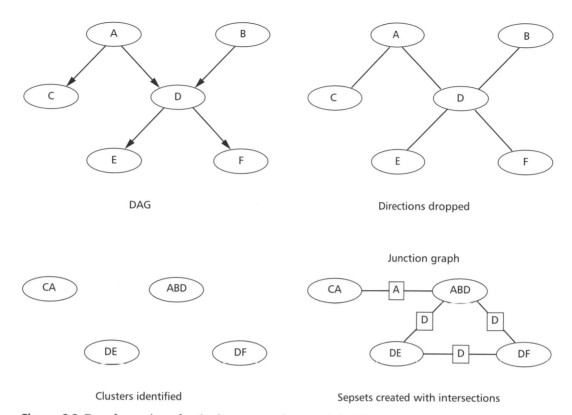

Figure 6.2 Transformation of a singly connected network (DAG) into a junction graph. To generate the tree the cycle in the Junction graph has to be broken. This can be achieved by removing any one of the D links.

triangulated if any cycle of length greater than 3 has a chord.[1] For instance, the path C,F,G,E,C in the moral graph of Figure 6.5 is a cycle of length 4 but it has a chord linking E and F, whereas the cycle A,B,D,C is also a cycle of length 4 but has no chord. A chord can be added between B and C or between A and D. Figure 6.6 shows a fill-in between B and C (chord) and the resultant junction graph (we shall see shortly how to form the junction graph but for now we concentrate on constructing the triangulated graph). The two cycles can be broken by removing the link between ABC and CDE in the first cycle because C is common to each link in the cycle and similarly with the link between CDE and EFG. The removal of these links is permitted because information that is associated with a link can be passed via another path. For example, the link connecting CDE to EFG has a sepset containing E, but information about E can be passed via sepsets CE and EF.

A check can be made as to whether a graph is triangulated by making use of the following definition:

> If all the nodes in a graph can be eliminated one by one without adding any links then the graph is triangulated.

---

[1] A path in a graph is a sequence of distinct vertices (nodes) $V_1, \ldots V_n$ where successive vertices in the sequence are adjacent. If the first and last vertex are the same then the path is a cycle. A chord in a cycle is a link between two vertices which are not successive in the cycle.

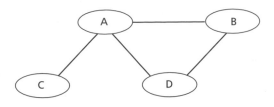

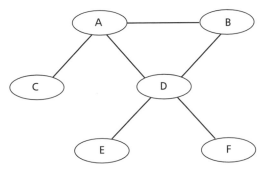

Figure 6.3 The moral graphs for the graph in Figure 6.1 (top) and the graph in Figure 6.2 (bottom).

A node can be eliminated provided all of its adjacent nodes are pairwise linked. Removing that node and its links eliminates a node.

The procedure for constructing the junction tree from a DAG can be summarized as:

1 Drop the direction of each link (edge).
2 For each node identify any parents and connect each pair of parent nodes by adding undirected links to create the moral graph.
3 Form the triangulated graph by adding fill-in links so that each cycle of length greater than 3 has a chord.
4 From the triangulated graph identify the clusters.
5 Connect the clusters to form an undirected tree by linking clusters through appropriate sepsets.

Algorithm

The algorithm for triangulation is:

1 Make a copy of the moral graph and call it Gc.
2 Select a node from Gc. The node selected should be the one that forms a cluster with the least number of links to be added (the cluster will contain the node and its adjacent nodes and all

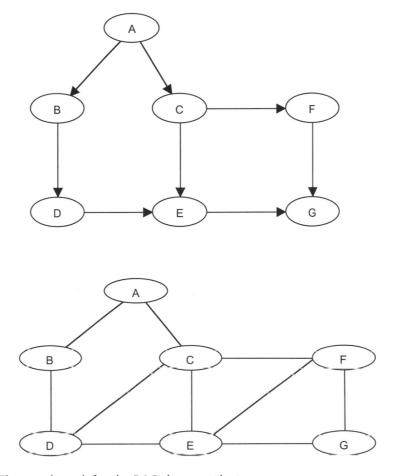

Figure 6.4 The moral graph for the DAG shown at the top.

cluster nodes should be linked). If there is a tie, choose the node that creates the cluster with the smallest weight. The weight of a node is the number of elements in its table and the weight of a cluster is the product of all constituent node weights.

3   Link all nodes for the cluster identified in step 2. For each link added, add the corresponding link to the moral graph.

4   Remove the node selected in step 2 from Gc.

5   If the cluster is not a subset of a previous cluster then save the cluster.

6   Repeat from step 2 until there are no nodes left in Gc.

The algorithm for triangulating a DAG is given in Figure 6.7.

The above algorithm is illustrated in Figure 6.8 for the triangulation of the DAG shown in Figure 6.4. The created clusters are shown below:

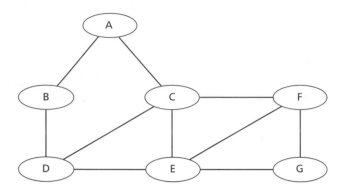

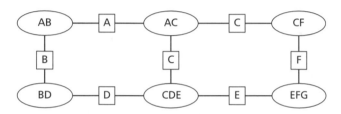

Figure 6.5 The junction graph (at the bottom) is derived from the moral graph (shown at the top).

Eliminated node	Cluster created	Links added	Saved cluster
G	EFG	None	EFG
F	CEF	None	CEF
E	CDE	None	CDE
A	ABC	B-C	ABC
B	BCD	None	BCD
C	CD		Subset
D	D		Subset

6.1.1 Linking clusters and sepsets

The final stage in building the junction tree requires the sepsets to be identified and linked to the adjacent clusters. Before we can illustrate this procedure we define two terms:

- **Mass**. The mass of a sepset is the number of variables it contains.
- **Cost**. The cost of a sepset is the weight of the two clusters it links. The weight of a cluster is the number of elements in its table.

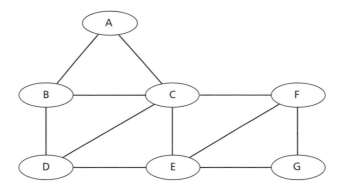

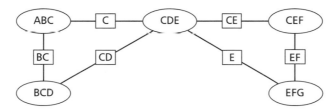

Figure 6.6 The junction graph (at the bottom) is derived from the triangulated graph (shown at the top).

For n-clusters we generate an n by n array and label each column and row with a cluster. Each element of the array holds the intersection of the row and column clusters. Continuing with the previous example, the array is given below:

	EFG	CEF	CDE	ABC	BCD
EFG		EF	E	–	–
CEF			CE	C	C
CDE				C	CD
ABC					BC
BCD					

Note that the diagonal entries link a cluster to itself and so these elements are empty. Only the upper triangle of the array is required because the array is symmetric.

The resultant array holds candidate sepsets. A number of these sepsets need to be chosen to form the junction tree. The sepset with the largest mass is chosen, with any ties being resolved by selecting the sepset with the lowest cost. The selected sepset is then inserted between the clusters that correspond to its row and column index.

The graph Gm is the moral graph which is transformed to the triangulated graph

PROCEDURE Triangulate(Gm)
Graph Gc
Graph cluster
Graph copyCluster
Stack savedClusters

Gc ← Gm

while Gc contains more than one node
        SelectNode(Gc, n)
        add n to cluster
        add each adjacent node of n to cluster
        connect all nodes in cluster
        connect all nodes in Gm that are connected in cluster
        connect all nodes in Gc that are connected in cluster
        if cluster is not a subset of already saved cluster
                copyCluster ← cluster
                push copyCluster onto savedClusters
        end if
        delete n from Gc
        delete all nodes and edges in cluster
end while

Procedure **SelectNode**(Gc, n)
Gc graph, n node
Graph cluster
Node selectNode
numberNodes ← number of nodes in Gc
numberEdges ← number edges in Gc
maxEdgesToAdd ← numberNodes (numberNodes – 1) – numberEdges
maxWeight ← weight of Gc

for each node n in Gc
        cluster ← n and all of the adjacent nodes to n plus the edges
        if maximum edges to add to cluster < maxEdgesToAdd
                selectedNode ← n
                maxEdgesToAdd ← maximum edges to add to cluster
        end if
        else if maximum edges to add to cluster = maxEdgesToAdd
                if weight of cluster < maxWeight
                        selectedNode ← n
                        maxWeight ← weight of cluster
                end if
        end else if
end for

Figure 6.7 Algorithm for triangulating a DAG.

In the above example all the clusters have the same cost. It is easy to see from the array table in this example that the selected sepsets are:

    EF linking EFG and CEF
    CE linking CEF and CDE

CD linking CDE and BCD

BC linking ABC and BCD

6.2 Quantifying the junction tree

For the junction tree to be quantified it has to be made **consistent**. For the tree to be consistent it needs to satisfy two properties.

1   The tree encodes the joint probability distribution as the product of the cluster tables divided by the product of the sepset tables:

$$P(U) = \frac{\prod_i C_i}{\prod_j S_j}$$

2   A sepset and its adjacent clusters are consistent, which means that any sepset table can be generated by marginalizing any adjacent cluster:

$$\phi(S) = \sum_{C \setminus S} \phi(C)$$

The symbol ϕ is used to denote the table of distribution values.

The junction tree is made consistent by first initializing all cluster and sepset tables followed by a series of message passes. Initialization is performed as follows:

1   For each cluster and sepset create a table that will encode all combinations of the n variables. Add a column to record the probability distribution of the table $\phi(T)$ and set each value in this column to 1.

$$\phi(T) \leftarrow 1$$

2   For each variable V identify a cluster that contains both V and the parents of V. Multiply $\phi(T)$ by $P(V|parents\ of\ V)$:

$$\phi(T) \leftarrow \phi(T)P(V|parents\ of\ V)$$

After initialization a series of message passes are performed to make the clusters and sepsets locally consistent. Message passing must be done so that the following ordering constraints are satisfied:

A cluster C can send exactly one message to an adjacent cluster and can only send that message when C has received a message from each of its other adjacent clusters.

A message will be passed in both directions of each link after which the tree will be consistent.

In Hugin propagation (Jensen, 1996), message passing is achieved by calling two procedures:

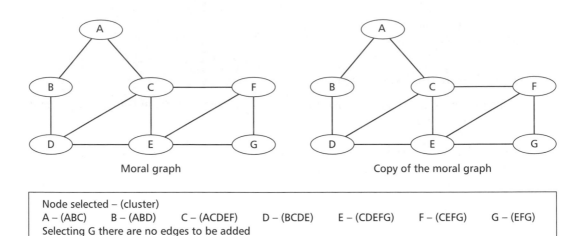

Moral graph   Copy of the moral graph

Node selected – (cluster)
A – (ABC)   B – (ABD)   C – (ACDEF)   D – (BCDE)   E – (CDEFG)   F – (CEFG)   G – (EFG)
Selecting G there are no edges to be added

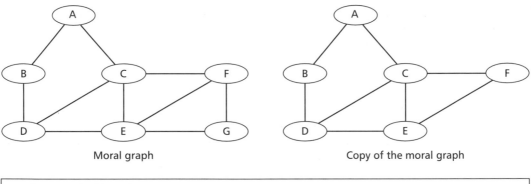

Moral graph   Copy of the moral graph

Node selected – (cluster)
A – (ABC)   B – (ABD)   C – (ACDEF)   D – (BCDE)   E – (CDEF)   F – (CEF)
Selecting F there are no edges to be added

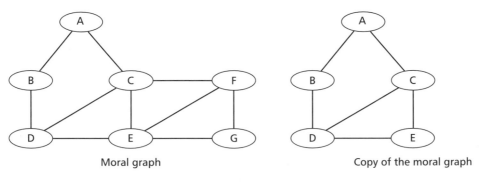

Moral graph   Copy of the moral graph

Node selected – (cluster)
A – (ABC)   B – (ABD)   C – (ACDE)   D – (BCDE)   E – (CDE)
Selecting E there are no edges to be added

Figure 6.8

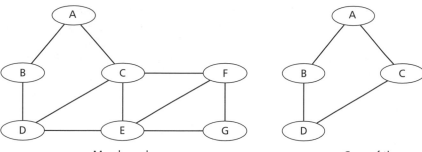

Moral graph   Copy of the moral graph

Node selected – (cluster)
A – (ABC)   B – (ABD)   C – (ACD)   D – (BCD)
All clusters would require a single edge to be added. The first cluster corresponding to selecting node
A is chosen. Link is added between B abd C.

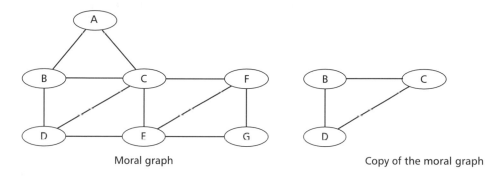

Moral graph   Copy of the moral graph

Node selected – (cluster)
B – (BCD)   C – (BCD)   D – (BCD)
No edges require adding for any cluster and all have the same weight and so the first node B is selected.

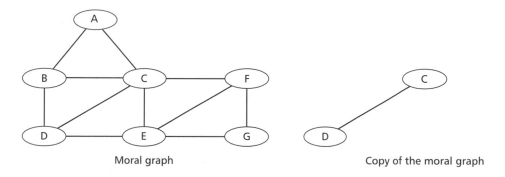

Moral graph   Copy of the moral graph

Node selected – (cluster)
C – (CD)   D – (CD)
C is selected and the final step selects node D.

COLLECT_EVIDENCE(C) and DISTRIBUTE_EVIDENCE(C). An arbitrary cluster C is selected and COLLECT_EVIDENCE is called followed by DISTRIBUTE_EVIDENCE. These algorithms are given in Figure 6.9. The order of message passing for a tree is illustrated in Figure 6.10.

A message is passed from cluster C_i to cluster C_j via sepset S under a process called **absorption**. Absorption is performed using the following procedure:

Make a copy of the sepset table

$$\phi(S^C) \leftarrow \phi(S)$$

Calculate a new sepset table by marginalizing on C_i:

$$\phi(S) = \sum_{C_i \backslash S} \phi(C_i)$$

Calculate a new table for C_j by taking the product of its old table with the sepset table divided by the old sepset table:

$$\phi(C_j) = \phi(C_j) \frac{\phi(S)}{\phi(S^c)}$$

PROCEDURE COLLECT_EVIDENCE(C)
        foreach adjacent cluster Ci COLLECT_EVIDENCE(Ci)
        pass message from Ci

PROCEDURE DISTRIBUTE_EVIDENCE(C)
        pass message from C
        foreach adjacent cluster Ci DISTRIBUTE_EVIDENCE(Ci)

Figure 6.9 Algorithms for message passing in a junction tree.

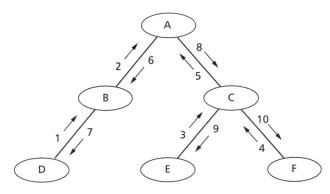

Figure 6.10 The order of message passes is illustrated. Messages 1 to 5 are invoked by COLLECT_EVIDENCE and 6 to 10 by DISTRIBUTE_EVIDENCE. COLLECT_EVIDENCE is called on node A.

An example

The computational steps to create a consistent junction tree for the tree in Figure 6.11 are illustrated in Figure 6.12. Figure 6.12(a) shows how the tables are initialized. Figure 6.12(b) illustrates COLLECT_EVIDENCE(EFG). DISTRIBUTE_EVIDENCE is not shown because in this example it does not change the information in the tables. The probability distributions for A, B and C are computed below by marginalizing on cluster ABC.

A	B	C	$\phi(A, B, C)$
On	On	On	0.06
On	Off	On	0.24
Off	On	On	0.28
Off	Off	On	0.07
On	On	Off	0.04
On	Off	Off	0.16
Off	On	Off	0.12
Off	Off	Off	0.03

$$P(A=on)=0.06+0.24+0.04+0.16=0.5$$
$$P(A=off)=0.28+0.07+0.12+0.03=0.5$$
$$P(B=on)=0.06+0.28+0.04+0.12=0.5$$
$$P(B=off)=0.24+0.07+0.16+0.03=0.5$$
$$P(C=on)=0.06+0.24+0.28+0.07=0.65$$
$$P(C=off)=0.04+0.16+0.12+0.03=0.35$$

6.3 Handling evidence

We have seen how to transform a network into a tree structure and then how to compute the probability distribution for any variable of interest, but we have not yet seen how to update beliefs when given evidence. For instance, in the *office is locked* example in Chapter 5, we might wish to know the probability of the computer being on given that the office is unlocked. For convenience, the junction tree and initialized tables are shown in Figure 6.13.

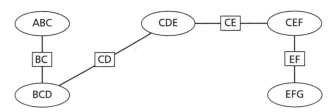

Figure 6.11 The junction tree for the DAG shown in Figure 6.4.

(a)

A	B	C	P(A)	P(B|A)	P(C|A)	φ (A, B, C)
On	On	On	0.5	0.2	0.6	0.06
On	Off	On	0.5	0.8	0.6	0.24
Off	On	On	0.5	0.8	0.7	0.28
Off	Off	On	0.5	0.2	0.7	0.07
On	On	Off	0.5	0.2	0.4	0.04
On	Off	Off	0.5	0.8	0.4	0.16
Off	On	Off	0.5	0.8	0.3	0.12
Off	Off	Off	0.5	0.2	0.3	0.03

B	C	φ (B, C)
On	On	1
On	Off	1
Off	On	1
Off	Off	1

B	C	D	P(D|B)	φ (B, C, D)
On	On	On	0.5	0.5
On	Off	On	0.5	0.5
Off	On	On	0.8	0.8
Off	Off	On	0.8	0.8
On	On	Off	0.5	0.5
On	Off	Off	0.5	0.5
Off	On	Off	0.2	0.2
Off	Off	Off	0.2	0.2

C	D	φ (C, D)
On	On	1
On	Off	1
Off	On	1
Off	Off	1

C	D	E	P(E|CD)	φ (C, D, E)
On	On	On	0.99	0.99
On	Off	On	0.8	0.8
Off	On	On	0.9	0.9
Off	Off	On	0.9	0.9
On	On	Off	0.01	0.01
On	Off	Off	0.2	0.2
Off	On	Off	0.1	0.1
Off	Off	Off	0.1	0.1

C	E	φ (C, E)
On	On	1
On	Off	1
Off	On	1
Off	Off	1

C	E	F	P(F|C)	φ (C, E, F)
On	On	On	0.95	0.95
On	Off	On	0.95	0.95
Off	On	On	0.9	0.9
Off	Off	On	0.9	0.9
On	On	Off	0.05	0.05
On	Off	Off	0.05	0.05
Off	On	Off	0.1	0.1
Off	Off	Off	0.1	0.1

E	F	φ (E, F)
On	On	1
On	Off	1
Off	On	1
Off	Off	1

E	F	G	P(G|EF)	φ (E, F, G)
On	On	On	0.95	0.95
On	Off	On	0.95	0.95
Off	On	On	0.95	0.95
Off	Off	On	0.9	0.9
On	On	Off	0.05	0.05
On	Off	Off	0.05	0.05
Off	On	Off	0.05	0.05
Off	Off	Off	0.1	0.1

Figure 6.12 (a) Initialization of the junction tree. (b) COLLECT_EVIDENCE starting with cluster EFG. Note that EFG is considered the route so each adjacent node is called recursively first. The first message is passed therefore from ABC to BCD via sepset BC.

(b)

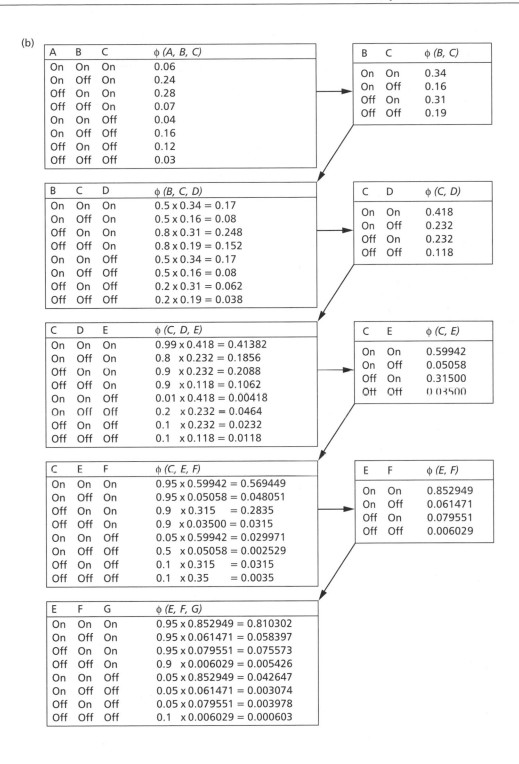

A	B	C	φ (A, B, C)
On	On	On	0.06
On	Off	On	0.24
Off	On	On	0.28
Off	Off	On	0.07
On	On	Off	0.04
On	Off	Off	0.16
Off	On	Off	0.12
Off	Off	Off	0.03

B	C	φ (B, C)
On	On	0.34
On	Off	0.16
Off	On	0.31
Off	Off	0.19

B	C	D	φ (B, C, D)
On	On	On	0.5 x 0.34 = 0.17
On	Off	On	0.5 x 0.16 = 0.08
Off	On	On	0.8 x 0.31 = 0.248
Off	Off	On	0.8 x 0.19 = 0.152
On	On	Off	0.5 x 0.34 = 0.17
On	Off	Off	0.5 x 0.16 = 0.08
Off	On	Off	0.2 x 0.31 = 0.062
Off	Off	Off	0.2 x 0.19 = 0.038

C	D	φ (C, D)
On	On	0.418
On	Off	0.232
Off	On	0.232
Off	Off	0.118

C	D	E	φ (C, D, E)
On	On	On	0.99 x 0.418 = 0.41382
On	Off	On	0.8 x 0.232 = 0.1856
Off	On	On	0.9 x 0.232 = 0.2088
Off	Off	On	0.9 x 0.118 = 0.1062
On	On	Off	0.01 x 0.418 = 0.00418
On	Off	Off	0.2 x 0.232 = 0.0464
Off	On	Off	0.1 x 0.232 = 0.0232
Off	Off	Off	0.1 x 0.118 = 0.0118

C	E	φ (C, E)
On	On	0.59942
On	Off	0.05058
Off	On	0.31500
Off	Off	0.03500

C	E	F	φ (C, E, F)
On	On	On	0.95 x 0.59942 = 0.569449
On	Off	On	0.95 x 0.05058 = 0.048051
Off	On	On	0.9 x 0.315 = 0.2835
Off	Off	On	0.9 x 0.03500 = 0.0315
On	On	Off	0.05 x 0.59942 = 0.029971
On	Off	Off	0.5 x 0.05058 = 0.002529
Off	On	Off	0.1 x 0.315 = 0.0315
Off	Off	Off	0.1 x 0.35 = 0.0035

E	F	φ (E, F)
On	On	0.852949
On	Off	0.061471
Off	On	0.079551
Off	Off	0.006029

E	F	G	φ (E, F, G)
On	On	On	0.95 x 0.852949 = 0.810302
On	Off	On	0.95 x 0.061471 = 0.058397
Off	On	On	0.95 x 0.079551 = 0.075573
Off	Off	On	0.9 x 0.006029 = 0.005426
On	On	Off	0.05 x 0.852949 = 0.042647
On	Off	Off	0.05 x 0.061471 = 0.003074
Off	On	Off	0.05 x 0.079551 = 0.003978
Off	Off	Off	0.1 x 0.006029 = 0.000603

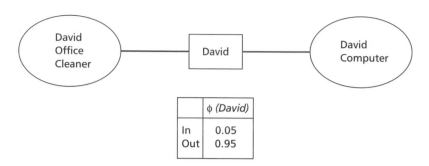

	φ (David)
In	0.05
Out	0.95

David	Cleaner	Office	φ (David, Cleaner, Office)
In	Unlocked	Locked	0.00050
In	Locked	Locked	0.00900
Out	Unlocked	Locked	0.00095
Out	Locked	Locked	0.84645
In	Unlocked	Unlocked	0.00450
In	Locked	Unlocked	0.03600
Out	Unlocked	Unlocked	0.09405
Out	Locked	Unlocked	0.00855

David	Computer	φ (David, Computer)
In	On	0.0400
In	Off	0.0100
Out	On	0.0095
Out	Off	0.9405

Figure 6.13 The initialised junction tree for the *office is locked* example.

Evidence is handled by adding an extra column to a table for each variable contained in the cluster that we have evidence for and then entering a value of 1 in each row corresponding to the state we have evidence for and 0 elsewhere. The probability distribution is then multiplied by the evidence column when initializing:

David	Cleaner	Office	Evidence on office	φ(David, Cleaner, Office)	φ(David, Cleaner, Office) × Evidence
In	Unlocked	Locked	0	0.00050	0
In	Locked	Locked	0	0.00900	0
Out	Unlocked	Locked	0	0.00095	0
Out	Locked	Locked	0	0.84645	0
In	Unlocked	Unlocked	1	0.00450	0.00450
In	Locked	Unlocked	1	0.03600	0.03600
Out	Unlocked	Unlocked	1	0.09405	0.09405
Out	Locked	Unlocked	1	0.00855	0.00855
					0.1431

David	Computer	φ(David, Computer)
In	On	0.0400
In	Off	0.0100
Out	On	0.0095
Out	Off	0.9405

Message passing

From ϕ(David, Cleaner, Office) to ϕ(David, Computer)

	ϕ(*David*)
In	0.0405/0.1431 = 0.28302
Out	0.1026/0.1431 = 0.71698

David	Computer	ϕ(*David, Computer*)
In	On	0.0400×0.28302/0.05 = 0.226416
In	Off	0.0100×0.28302/0.05 = 0.056604
Out	On	0.0095×0.71698/0.95 = 0.0071698
Out	Off	0.9405×0.71698/0.95 = 0.7098102

From ϕ(David, Computer) to ϕ(David, Cleaner, Office)

	ϕ(*David*)
In	0.28302
Out	0.71698

The old and new sepset values are the same and so ϕ(*David*, *Cleaner*, *Office*) remains the same.

After the tree is consistent we are in a position to calculate probabilities as before provided that we normalize any computed value. When we compute the probability distribution for any variable *V* given evidence *e* we are computing $P(V|e)$, where *e* in this example is Office=unlocked. When we marginalize a cluster into a variable V with evidence we are computing:

$$P(V,e) = \sum_{C \backslash V} \phi(C)$$

So to find $P(V|e)$ from $P(V, e)$, we need to normalize as follows:

$$P(V|e) = \frac{P(V,e)}{\sum_{v} P(V,e)}$$

For example, to find $P(\text{Computer}=\text{on}|\text{Office}=\text{unlocked})$ we can use ϕ(*David, Computer*) as follows:

$$P(computer = on \,|\, Office = unlocked) = \frac{0.226416 + 0.0071698}{0.226416 + 0.056604 + 0.0071698 + 0.7098102} = 0.2336$$

6.4 Inexact inferencing

It is possible for very large networks to exceed hardware availability in terms of the memory required to store cluster tables. There are, for example, in excess of one million combinations for a cluster containing 20 binary variables. When such a limitation exists, stochastic techniques can be employed to provide an approximation to the distributions.

The basic stochastic approach is quite straightforward to implement and requires no transformation of the network to produce a secondary structure such as a cluster tree. The stochastic approach uses a random number generator and the conditional distributions in a Bayesian model to determine which state each of the variables are in. The assignment of a state to each variable is called a sample. A large number of samples are generated, and for each variable a count is maintained that records the number of times the variable has been in each of its possible states. After all samples have been generated, the probabilities are easily extracted. Consider again the *Mary is late for work* example introduced in Chapter 5 and shown in Figure 6.14. Each of the variables {Bus, Train, Mary} has a distribution table. A random number, r_1, between 0 and 1 is generated. If r_1 is less than 0.3 (P(Bus=late)) then the state of the *Bus* is *late*. If r_1 is equal to or greater than 0.3 then the state of the *Bus* is *on time*. A second random number, r_2, is generated, and if r_2 is less than 0.1 (P(Train=late)) then the state of the *Train* is *late*; otherwise the state is *on time*. A third random number is then generated to sample the state for *Mary*. Suppose $r_1 = 0.2$ and $r_2 = 0.4$, then the *Bus* is *late* and the *Train* is *on time*. The conditional distribution for *Mary* given that the *Bus* is *late* and the *Train* is *on time* is {late=0.2, on time=0.8}. If r_3 is less than 0.2 then the state for *Mary* is *late*. So if $r_3 = 0.15$ then the state for *Mary* is *late*. The sample then has (Bus=late, Train=on time, Mary=late). Another sample is then generated using a different set of random numbers. The only statistics that need to be stored are the state counts for each variable – the number of times the bus is late and the number of times the bus is on time – with similar counts also being stored for the *train* and *Mary*. After a large number, m, of samples have been generated the probability for each variable is simply the state count divided by m. Table 6.1 shows the counts for 1000 samples. If more samples are generated, the probabilities will converge towards those values obtained using an exact solution.

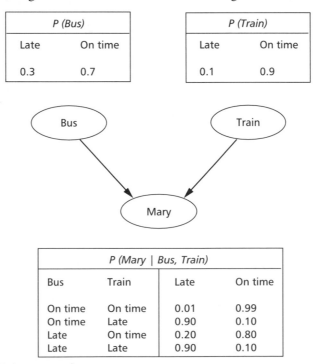

Figure 6.14 *Mary is late* example.

Table 6.1 Counts for 1000 samples for the *Mary is late* example

	Bus	Train	Mary
On time	694 (0.69)	906 (0.91)	858 (0.86)
Late	306 (0.31)	94 (0.09)	142 (0.14)

Evidence can be handled by simply discarding those samples that do not match with the evidence. For example, if it is known that *Mary* is *late*, then any sample that has *Mary* in the state of *on time* will be discarded.

The practical difficulty with simple stochastic simulation is the time it takes to extract a large number of samples for configurations of evidence that have a low probability of occurring. For example, in the *office is locked* example shown in Figure 6.13, the probability of (David=out, Cleaner=unlocked, Computer=on) is 0.001. This means that, on average, only 1 in about 1000 generated samples will match the configuration. So, to generate 100 stored samples will require 100 000 samples to be generated.

One method for dealing with the problem of rare configurations is to use **Gibbs sampling**. Gibbs sampling starts with a configuration that is consistent with the evidence and then randomly changes the states of free variables (i.e. those without evidence) in causal order. Suppose the Bayesian model is that given in Figure 6.15 and all variables are binary with states $\{y, n\}$. If the evidence is $C = n$ and $E = y$, the starting configuration might be $(A=y, B=y, C=n, D=y, E=y, F=n)$. The first free variable is A. We need to compute the probability of A given all the other variables, that is:

$$P(A \mid B=y, C=n, D-y, E-y, F=n)$$

The network structure indicates independence and it is enough to compute:

$$P(A \mid B=y, C=n, D=y)$$

Say the result is $(P(A=y)=0.3, P(A=n)=0.7)$. If the first random number generated is 0.25 then A will stay in the state y. The next free variable is B, and so $P(B \mid A=y, D=y)$ is computed and the state of B is determined according to the next random number to be generated. The process is

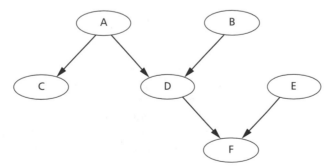

Figure 6.15 A network structure to illustrate Gibbs sampling.

repeated for D and then F. The states of each variable have then been sampled once. The process is repeated m times and the counts maintained as before. Note that the distribution:

$$P(A \mid B = \text{y}, C = \text{n}, D = \text{y}, E = \text{y}, F = \text{n})$$

can be found by multiplying out the tables that contain A and then normalizing.

Even using Gibbs sampling there are problems. One problem is that the simulation can get stuck and some configurations may not be reached. Stochastic simulation remains an active research area. Both exact and inexact inferencing are used in commercial applications.

Summary

- The implementation of exact inferencing is performed by operating on a transformation of the original DAG called a junction tree.
- Clusters and sepsets are identified during a triangulation of the DAG.
- The junction tree is quantified by assigning each variable to one cluster table only and performing the following update for each assigned variable:

$$P(U) = \prod_i P(V_i \mid parents(V_i))$$

- The junction tree is made consistent using message passing. The message passing is performed using the recursive algorithms COLLECT_EVIDENCE and DISTRIBUTE_EVIDENCE.
- Once the cluster tree is consistent, the joint distribution of the original DAG is found by

$$P(U) = \frac{\prod_i C_i}{\prod_j S_j}$$

- Evidence is handled by multiplying the entries in a table by the value 1 when the entry matches the state for which evidence exists and 0 otherwise. Message passing is then executed to obtain a consistent tree.
- An inexact form of inferencing can be performed using stochastic sampling.

Further reading

Bayesian networks were introduced as a form of expert system by Pearl (1986). For a reference on triangulation in graphs see Golumbic (1980). Propagation methods in Bayesian networks have been developed by a number of authors including Lauritzen and Spiegelhalter (1988) and Jensen *et al.* (1990). Forward sampling was proposed by Henrion (1988). Geman and Geman (1984) applied Gibbs sampling to image restoration. A good introduction to inferencing in Bayesian networks can be found in Huang and Darwiche (1994).

Williamson (2001) explores the idea of using Bayesian networks for logical reasoning.

There has been a lot of interest in Bayesian network learning. References include Buntine (1994), Heckerman (1996) and Friedman and Koller (2000). For a comprehensive book on causation and learning see Spirtes *et al.* (2000).

Exercises

1   For the graph below:
    a   Sketch the moral graph.
    b   Give a triangulation of the graph.
    c   Extract the clusters and sepsets.
    d   Construct the junction tree
    e   Indicate the order of message passing.

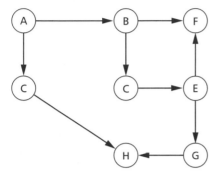

2   Implement a program to perform triangulation.

3   Experiment by running the program developed in exercise 2 on different DAG structures with and without the node elimination criteria (SelectNode procedure). Note any observations regarding the size of the generated cluster tables.

4   Treat all variables in exercise 1 as having binary states.
    a   Generate the distributions for each variable (any values will do).
    b   Express the distribution using the chain rule
    c   If the distribution were to be represented by one large table, what size would it be?
    d   Quantify the junction tree.

CHAPTER 7

Other Approaches to Uncertainty

Much space has been given to the Bayesian approach for reasoning under uncertainty. There are many problems within AI that are cast within the Bayesian framework and it is an important subject. However, there are other approaches to reasoning under uncertainty, and this chapter takes a brief overview of some of these topics. We start with fuzzy logic. To some extent, fuzzy logic is a bit of a misfit in this chapter in that its application is not usually to problems involving uncertainty. Inputs to a fuzzy logic reasoner are normally known with a high degree of certainty. The fuzzy aspect concerns the way in which the input data are described to the reasoner and does not refer to data being incomplete. Many people talk about fuzzy logic in the context of uncertainty and so it is included here. Also, the underlying set theory is relevant to another type of reasoning under uncertainty called possibility theory. We then take a look at Dempster–Shafer theory. This is followed by a brief look at non-monotonic logic and truth maintenance systems.

7.1 Fuzzy logic

First-order predicate calculus is a logic in which an interpretation requires mapping symbols into sets in order to assign a truth value. For example, you are not an astronaut unless you are a member of the set that lists all astronauts. The notion of set membership in first-order logic is a crisp one – an object is either a member of a set or it is not. During the 1960s, Lotfi Zadeh introduced the notion of partial set membership. The idea was to provide a reasoning mechanism that could use fuzzy variables. Knowledge is represented in the form of IF…THEN rules, but symbols need not have crisply defined sets. For example, the rate of calorie burn for someone taking exercise on a bike in a health club might be expressed by rules of the form:

    If speed = high AND load = high Then burn = very fast
    If speed = moderate AND load = high Then burn = fast

These rules are not working with precisely defined values. Each variable (*speed*, *load*, *burn*) is assigned a fuzzy value such as *high*, *moderate*, *fast*, etc. These fuzzy values cover a range of measured values. For example, *speed* on a bike might be expressed in km/h and *high* might span the range 48–72 km/h and the value *slow* might cover the range 0–24 km/h. The variable *load* is meant to refer to resistance (e.g. simulated road incline) and the value *high* would correspond to a range that is appropriate for this variable – determined perhaps by the proportion of people who find that load setting hard work.

Our everyday language is full of fuzzy descriptors or what shall now be called **linguistic values** or simply values, for example *old*, *tall*, *short*, *intelligent*, *warm*, *hot*, etc. For example, *height* is often measured in centimetres and *tall* and *short* describe regions within this continuous scale. The values *tall* and *short* might be separated by the value *average*. Being fuzzy means that there is no clear boundary between the end of one value and the start of another. There is no recognized height at which someone stops being of *average* height and is suddenly classed as *tall*. Similarly, a value of one degree does not really distinguish something being *warm* from something being *hot*. There are no universally defined boundaries for linguistic values and yet we have a good idea of what to expect if we touch a plate that someone has declared to be *very hot*.

Linguistic values are context dependent in that the range of values they are defined over depends on the variable with which they are associated. For example, the range of temperatures covered by a value *hot* in the context of today's weather will be very different to that used when describing the temperature of an oven. Of course, other contextual factors also have an influence on the definition of a linguistic value, e.g. the country whose weather we are describing. Contextual issues for any application are taken into account with a function that is defined for each linguistic variable value. The purpose of a function is to map (convert) a measured value into a linguistic value (for example, 0 °C into freezing). Most applications of fuzzy logic are in the domain of engineering control such as controlling the autocruise of a car or the cycle of a washing machine or the autofocus of a camera or the stability of a tilting train, etc. For these applications, the continuous variables are measured parameters such as *speed*, *angle*, *load*, *light intensity*, etc. The fuzzy rules represent control knowledge and the task of inferencing is to map a series of input variables to a controlling output variable. For example, a car cruise controller might use *speed* and *acceleration* as input variables and *throttle adjustment* as an output variable. The mapping from a measured value to a linguistic value is done using a **fuzzy membership** function. A membership function exists for each linguistic variable value, and the output of that function is a degree of membership. The degree of membership is a measure of strength of association that a measured value has with some linguistic value. You might, for example, consider a height of 178 cm to be associated with both *average* and *tall* but the association with *tall* to be stronger.

7.1.1   *Fuzzy membership*

Set membership in first-order logic is binary, with a value of 0 (false) being assigned if an object is not a member and a value of 1 (true) if an object is a member. Fuzzy set membership can range between 0 and 1. The actual value between 0 and 1 expresses a degree of membership. Each linguistic value corresponds to a fuzzy set. The notation $\mu_A(x)$ is used to denote the degree of membership that value x has with linguistic value A. A membership value of 0.8 would mean that an object has a good association with the set and its association is stronger than for an object with degree of membership 0.6. A membership function is used to map a value from a continuous scale into one or more discrete values along with a degree of membership. A simple function for describing *tall* women is given in Figure 7.1. According to this membership function, a height of 165 cm would have a degree of membership 0.5:

$$\mu_{tall}(165) = 0.5$$

A **fuzzy membership function** maps every object x from the universe of discourse X to a number between 0 and 1. The membership function for a set A is denoted by mA(x), and for an object x it returns a number between 0 and 1; this number gives the degree of membership. We express this more formally as:

$$\mu_A(x) : X \rightarrow [0,1]$$

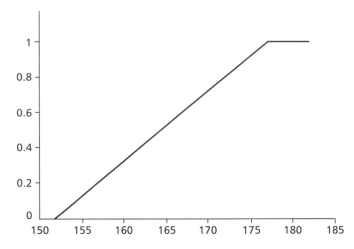

Figure 7.1 Fuzzy membership function describing tall women.

Any woman below 152 cm is not considered tall. Any woman greater than 177 cm is clearly considered tall with degree of membership of 1. Heights in between have a linearly increasing degree of membership. This membership function has a plateau where all people above 177 cm are considered tall. This plateau exists because in this example there is no value other than tall for people beyond a certain height (there is no *very tall* value for example). This is a somewhat arbitrary choice of membership function. The actual function would depend on the context of the application. For example, there are variations in height associated with nationality, and what you or I might consider as tall could be considered as short in the context of a basketball team.

There are a number of different shapes of membership functions. They can be triangular, or normally distributed, or logistic (S-shaped), or some other shape. Membership functions for a parameter will tend to overlap – thus creating a fuzzy boundary between one value finishing and another starting. For example, suppose we wish to discretize the temperature of water over the range 0–100 °C using the values *cold*, *warm* and *hot*. There will be some overlap between *cold* and *warm* and between *warm* and hot, as illustrated in Figure 7.2. According to the definition in Figure 7.2, a value of 80 °C would be classified as *warm* with a degree of membership 0.2 and *hot* with a degree of membership 0.5.

Although degree of membership is expressed as a value between 0 and 1, it should not be confused with probability. The measured value is usually precise (unless there is noise or some other problem such as sensor failure) and a fuzzy function associates a precise (crisp) value with one or more fuzzy (not crisp) values. There is no uncertainty in the input data. On the other hand, probability associates an uncertain quantity with a crisp set. For example, probability can be used to express the uncertainty that the next person to leave a university building is under 25 years of age. The person has not yet been identified and their age is unknown. The set (under 25) is a crisp set in that a particular value of age is either a member or not. This is a different problem to that which exists when we wish to associate a linguistic value that has no crisp definition with the age of an identified person. Once the person is identified their age is known precisely (well, to within the specified precision – years, months, or days, etc.).

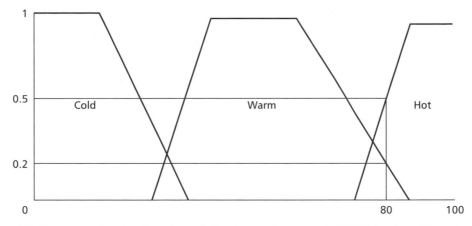

Figure 7.2 Three membership functions defined over the range 0–100°C for describing the temperature of water.

7.1.2   Stages in fuzzy inferencing

A fuzzy controller consists of a set of rules of the form IF…THEN and an inferencing procedure. The **antecedent** relates to the input variables (such as speed and acceleration) and the **conclusion** relates to the output variable (e.g. throttle adjustment). The IF part of rules are matched with the input values. For example, returning to the exercise bike, the rule:

If speed = slow AND load = low Then burn = low

will match with input values (speed = slow) and (load = low). The actual inputs are values measured on a continuous scale and so the first task is to map these measured values into linguistic values. The mapping provides a degree of membership. These membership values have to be combined somehow to indicate the strength in which the antecedent supports the conclusion. The strength in the conclusion is then mapped into a crisp output value. The output for the bike rule given above is a precise indication of the rate at which calories are being burned, but for a control application the output produces an action (for example, adjust the throttle to maintain the car's speed). The stages in inferencing are explained in more detail below followed by an illustrated example.

Fuzzification

The numeric value for each input variable is described in terms of fuzzy sets. Each input value is associated with one or more linguistic values and a degree of association is given.

Match with rules

The IF part of a rule relates to measured inputs and the conclusion to controlling outputs. The IF part contains one or more linguistic variables and each variable has a linguistic value. Variables can be joined using conjunction or disjunction. A rule is turned on when all of the variable linguistic values in its antecedent match with the linguistic values identified during fuzzification. For example, suppose a person's height is 180 cm and age is 25. The height might be associated with linguistic values *average* and *tall* and age with linguistic value *young*. All of the following rules would match:

If height=average AND age=young Then
If height=average Then
If height=tall AND age=young Then
If height=tall Then
If age=young Then

but the following would not match:

If age=old Then
If height=short AND age=young Then
If height=tall AND age=old Then

A rule that matches the inputs is said to be switched on.

Determine the degree to which the conclusion is supported

Each rule that is switched on will have a degree of membership for each linguistic value. If a rule contains a single variable value in its antecedent then the degree to which the conclusion is supported is simply the degree of membership with the antecedent. If the rule contains more than one variable then the degree of membership for all linguistic variable values need to be combined to compute the degree of support for the conclusion. The rule for combination is determined by the logical connectives. These rules are defined in Boxes 7.1 and 7.2.

For example, suppose John has the following degree of membership with tall and young:

$$\mu_{tall}(john)=0.35 \qquad \mu_{young}(john)=0.75$$

The rule with antecedent:

height=tall AND age=young

would evaluate to a value 0.35 and the rule:

height=tall OR age=young

would evaluate to a value 0.75.

Box 7.1 Rule for ANDing two variables

The result of **AND**ing two variable values A and B is the intersection of the two sets A and B. The intersection of two fuzzy sets A and B is another fuzzy set with membership function

$$\mu_{A \cap B}(x) = \min(\mu_A(x), \mu_B(x))$$

This definition says that the degree of membership of A∩B is the minimum of the two values $\mu_A(x)$ and $\mu_B(x)$. In other words, the conjunction of two membership values is the lower of the two.

Box 7.2 Rule for ORing two variables

The result of **OR**ing two variable values *A* and *B* is the union of the two sets *A* and *B*. The union of two fuzzy sets *A* and *B* is another fuzzy set with membership function:

$$\mu_{A \cup B}(x) = \max(\mu_A(x), \mu_B(x))$$

   This definition says that the degree of membership of $A \cup B$ is the maximum of the two values $\mu_A(x)$ and $\mu_B(x)$. In other words, the disjunction of two membership values is the larger of the two.

Combining all rule outputs

Each rule that is switched on implies a degree of support for its conclusion. It is typical practice to fire all rules and combine their implied effects to produce a single crisp output value.

Example 1 • • • • •

We shall use a hypothetical car cruise controller as an example to illustrate the inferencing process. The cruise controller is an automated method for maintaining a car's speed when on a long open stretch of road. The driver selects the desired speed and it is the job of the controller to maintain this speed. The road condition will vary throughout the journey, the road might climb or descend, and the controller should adjust the throttle to maintain the desired speed. There are two input variables: speed and acceleration. The speed variable is calculated as the error between the desired speed and the actual speed:

   Speed Error = Actual − Desired

The error can be *zero*, *positive* (too fast) or *negative* (too slow). Acceleration is considered zero if the car's speed is constant over a specified time interval (say 2 seconds), positive if the car is increasing in speed and negative if the car is slowing.
   The rules and notation are given below:

   se – speed error
   acc – acceleration
   Z – zero
   P – positive
   C – constant
   RS – reduce small amount
   RH – reduce high amount
   IS – increase small amount
   IH – increase high amount

   If se=Z and acc=Z Then throttle=C
   If se=Z and acc=P Then throttle=RS
   If se=Z and acc=N Then throttle=IS

   If se=P and acc=Z Then throttle=RS

If se=P and acc=P Then throttle=RH
If se=P and acc=N Then throttle=C

If se=N and acc=Z Then throttle=IS
If se=N and acc=P Then throttle=C
If se=N and acc=N Then throttle=IH

The rules can be presented in a concise format called a rule matrix. The matrix is shown in Figure 7.3.

The fuzzy sets for the inputs and the output are defined in Figure 7.4. The first step is to take the speed error and acceleration and determine which rules can be fired. Suppose that the speed has error 0 but the acceleration is 8 units. Examination of Figure 7.4 shows that a zero speed error only produces membership of the *zero* state and the degree of membership is 1. The state *negative* ends at the value 0 and the state *positive* begins at value 0 and so membership of these states is not implied. The acceleration of 8 indicates membership of states *zero* and *positive* with degree 0.2 and 0.6 respectively. Rules that have the following terms in their antecedent will fire:

se=Z and acc=Z

or

se=Z and acc=P

Examination of the rule matrix shows that two rules can fire. These two rules correspond to the entries (Z, Z) and (Z, P), where the first entry corresponds to speed error and the second to acceleration. The rules are:

If se=Z and acc=Z Then throttle=C
If se=Z and acc=P Then throttle=RS

The input variables are assumed to have been precisely measured. The speed error is clearly a member of the *zero* state with membership degree 1, but there is fuzziness in terms of the linguistic values for acceleration. The value for acceleration has an association with the state *zero* and an even stronger association with the state *positive*. The terms in the rule are joined using AND. So the support for the conclusion from each rule is quantified by taking the minimum of both terms in the antecedent:

		acc		
		Z	P	N
	Z	C	RS	IS
se	P	RS	RH	C
	N	IS	C	IH

Figure 7.3 A rule matrix. Each rule in this example has two conditions in its antecedent (se and acc). The value of se indexes into a row and the value for acc indexes into a column. The conclusion for a rule is the intersection of values in its row and column indices.

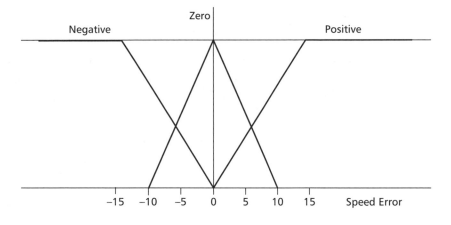

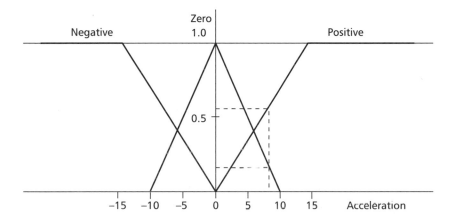

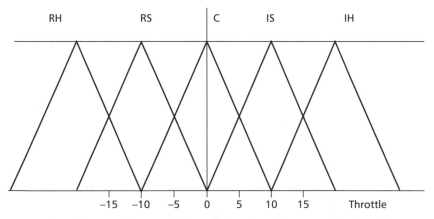

Figure 7.4 Fuzzy functions used in Example 1 to describe the parameters Speed Error, Acceleration and Throttle (adjustment).

membership of C is min(1, 0.2)=0.2
membership of RS is min(1, 0.6)=0.6

There are two recommended actions: to keep the throttle constant or to reduce the throttle by a small amount. There is stronger support for reducing the throttle with a quantified value of 0.6. The task now is to combine the outputs from these two rules.

The output from the controller should be a precise value that indicates the throttle adjustment. Combining the rules to produce this precise value is called **defuzzification**. There are several methods for defuzzification but a popular choice is to find the centre of gravity and this is the method illustrated in this example. Figure 7.5 shows the membership functions for the throttle adjustment corresponding to *Constant (C)* and *Reduce Small Amount (RS)*. These functions have been chopped of at a height of 0.2 and 0.6 respectively. The area under each function represents the strength in each conclusion and the value by which to adjust the throttle is the value on the horizontal axis that is perpendicular to the centre of gravity of these combined areas. This value is found from the following equation:

$$u = \frac{\sum_i b_i \int \mu_i}{\sum_i \int \mu_i}$$

(7.1)

where i indexes over each output function (conclusion), b_i denotes the centre of function i and

$$\int \mu_i$$

is the area under the membership function. The general equation for computing the area under a function involves integration, but in our case the functions are triangular and so the calculation is simply:

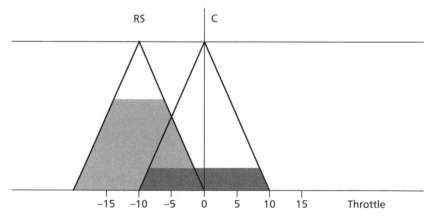

Figure 7.5 The output of the combined functions is read from the horizontal axis at the point corresponding to the centre of gravity of the total shaded area.

$$w\left(h - \frac{h^2}{2}\right)$$

where w is the width of the triangle base and h is the height at which the function is cut off. The value of w for each function in this example is 20. Substituting the values into eqn (7.1) for the two output functions gives:

$$u = \frac{(-10)(8.4) + (0)(3.6)}{8.4 + 3.6}$$

So, the two original inputs (0, 8) for the speed error and acceleration produce a throttle reduction of 7 units.

● ● ● ● ●

7.2 Dempster–Shafer theory

Bayesian reasoning allows us to state our belief in a hypothesis and our belief in that same hypothesis when some new data are received. **Dempster–Shafer theory (D–S)** also provides an assessment of belief in some hypothesis which can be modified in the light of new data. Unlike Bayesian reasoning, D–S takes into account the fact that it may not be possible to assign a belief to every hypothesis set.

We shall explain D–S by imagining the following scenario:

> Mrs Jones has a carton of cream delivered along with the milk very early in the morning on some days of the week. On most mornings following delivery of the cream, the carton is found open and the content is gone. Mrs Jones believes that the culprit is one of three animals that stalk the area. One animal is a dog, the other a cat and the third a fox. Occasionally a neighbour will catch sight of the thief in the act, but the delivery is before daylight and no neighbour has been certain about their sighting.

There are three suspects:

Dog – d, Cat – c, Fox – f

and each suspect represents a hypothesis. Only a single animal is responsible for the theft.

The set of hypotheses is called the **frame of discernment** Θ. In this example:

$\Theta = \{d, c, f\}$

The thief is either the dog or the cat or the fox. D–S is not limited to assigning a belief to only dog, cat or fox but can assign beliefs to any element that is a member of the power set of Θ. The belief in an element, x, is referred to as a **probability mass** denoted, $m(x)$.

The power set of Θ is the set of all subsets of Θ and is denoted by 2^Θ:

$2^\Theta = \{\varnothing, \{d\}, \{c\}, \{f\}, \{d, c\}, \{d, f\}, \{c, f\}, \Theta\}$

where $\varnothing$ denotes the empty set. The power set expresses all possibilities. For example, {d} is the hypothesis that the dog takes the cream and {d, f} is the hypothesis that the culprit is either the dog or the fox.

There are restrictions on the values of $m(x)$:

$$\sum_{x \in 2^{\theta}} m(x) = 1$$

$$m(\varnothing) = 0$$

which state that the total mass must sum to 1 and that the empty set is not possible (the closed world assumption which means that no animal other than the dog, fox or cat is stealing the cream). Any subset x that has a non-zero value for $m(x)$ is called a **focal element**.

Suppose neighbour 1 states that she believes it is either the dog or cat with probability 0.8. So $m(\{d, c\}) = 0.8$. The probability must sum to 1 and so 0.2 has to be assigned somehow to the other hypotheses sets. The best we can do without any other information is to assign it to the whole frame of discernment $m(\{d, c, f\}) = 0.2$.

On the following night, another neighbour spots the thief and states that she believes that it was either the cat or fox with probability 0.7. How should these new data be combined with the original data? D–S theory states that the original mass is combined with the new mass according to the rule

$$m(C) = \sum_{C = A \cap B} m(A)m(B) \tag{7.2}$$

A is the set of focal elements identified by neighbour 1 and B those by neighbour 2. This equation states that there is a set C of focal elements formed by the intersection of the sets in A and B and the mass assigned to an element in C is the product of the intersecting masses. The result of applying eqn (7.2) is given in Table 7.1.

We shall use the notation m^n to indicate that evidence has been encountered at step n. The first step was from neighbour 1 and the second from neighbour 2, which are combined to give a new belief at step 3. So:

$m^3(\{c\}) = 0.56$
$m^3(\{d, c\}) = 0.24$
$m^3(\{c, f\}) = 0.14$
$m^3(\{d, c, f\}) = 0.06$

Two probability measures are provided which assess the **belief (Bel)** and **plausibility (Pl)** of any set of hypotheses:

Table 7.1 The probability masses from neighbours 1 and 2 are combined

		Neighbour 2	
		$m(\{c, f\}) = 0.7$	$m(\{d, c, f\}) = 0.3$
Neighbour 1	$m(\{d, c\}) = 0.8$	$m(\{c\}) = 0.56$	$m(\{d, c\}) = 0.24$
	$m(\{d, c, f\}) = 0.2$	$m(\{c, f\}) = 0.14$	$m(\{d, c, f\}) = 0.06$

$$Bel(A) = \sum_{B \subseteq A} m(B) \tag{7.3}$$

$$Pl(A) = \sum_{B \cap A \neq \emptyset} m(B) \tag{7.4}$$

These two measures represent lower and upper bounds on the belief in a set of hypotheses. So the belief in the cat being the culprit is the sum of the masses where the set of hypotheses is a subset of {c}, which in this case is simply:

Bel({c})=0.56

The plausibility is the sum of all masses that contain cat as a member:

Pl({c})=0.56+0.24+0.14+0.06=1.0

The belief and plausibility in the dog are:

Bel({d})=0
Pl({d})=0.24+0.06=0.3

The belief and plausibility in the fox are:

Bel({f})=0
Pl({f})=0.14+0.06=0.2

The belief and plausibility in it being either the dog or cat are:

Bel({d, c})=0.56+0.24=0.8
Pl({d, c})=0.56+0.24+0.14+0.06=1.0

Suppose now that a third neighbour reports seeing something and states that it was the fox with belief 0.6. The updated masses are given in Table 7.2.

Table 7.2 is problematic because there are two null entries that indicate an empty intersection between the existing focal elements and the new evidence. In other words, the empty set has a mass which violates the earlier condition that it is not possible to have belief in something outside of the

Table 7.2 Combining evidence from neighbour 3 with the evidence derived from combining the sightings of neighbours 1 and 2

		Neighbour 3	
		$m^4(\{f\})=0.6$	$m^4(\{d, c, f\}) = 0.4$
	$m^3(\{c\}) = 0.56$	null	$m^5(\{c\}) = 0.224$
Existing focal elements	$m^3(\{d, c\}) = 0.24$	null	$m^5(\{d, c\}) = 0.096$
	$m^3(\{c, f\}) = 0.14$	$m^5(\{f\}) = 0.084$	$m^5(\{c, f\}) = 0.056$
	$m^3(\{d, c, f\}) = 0.06$	$m^5(\{f\}) = 0.036$	$m^5(\{d, c, f\}) = 0.024$

sets of hypotheses. The suggested way around this problem is to normalize the entries using the following equation

$$m^{n+2}(C) = \frac{\displaystyle\sum_{A \cap B = C} m^n(A)m^{n+1}(B)}{\displaystyle\sum_{A \cap B \neq \varnothing} m^n(A)m^{n+1}(B)} \quad (7.5)$$

For our example, this equation suggests that we should divide each new focal element by the sum of all focal elements that do not have a null entry. All we are doing is ensuring that the null entries have a mass of zero and that all other new focal elements sum to 1. The denominator is:

$$0.084 + 0.036 + 0.224 + 0.096 + 0.056 + 0.024 = 0.52$$

Each newly calculated focal element in Table 7.2 is now updated by dividing by 0.52. The updated values are given in Table 7.3. The final beliefs and plausibilities for each set of hypotheses after all three neighbours have given evidence are listed in Table 7.4.

7.3 Non-numerical approaches

First-order logic is monotonic in that the database of assertions grows monotonically. This means that once something is proved the proof remains valid. New propositions may be derived, but these assertions get added to the database and nothing in the database is ever removed: once something is proved it stays proved. A non-monotonic reasoning system will allow an assertion that was derived

Table 7.3 The entries in Table 7.2 after normalization using eqn (7.5)

		Neighbour 3	
		$m^4(\{f\}) = 0.6$	$m^4(\{d, c, f\}) = 0.4$
	$m^3(\{c\}) = 0.56$	null	$m^5(\{c\}) = 0.431$
Existing focal elements	$m^3(\{d, c\}) = 0.24$	null	$m^5(\{d, c\}) = 0.185$
	$m^3(\{c, f\}) = 0.14$	$m^5(\{f\}) = 0.162$	$m^5(\{c, f\}) = 0.108$
	$m^3(\{d, c, f\}) = 0.06$	$m^5(\{f\}) = 0.069$	$m^5(\{d, c, f\}) = 0.046$

Table 7.4 The beliefs and plausibilities derived from Table 7.3

	Belief	Plausibility
{d}	0	0.231
{c}	0.431	0.770
{f}	0.231	0.385
{d, c}	0.616	0.770
{d, f}	0.231	0.570
{c, f}	0.770	1.0
{d, c, f}	1.0	1.0

earlier to be removed from the database. In practical reasoning systems, assumptions are often made from which new assertions are derived. If an assumption is later found to be incorrect then the assertion may no longer be valid. For example, it might be reasonable to assume that the cost of your mortgage will increase if interest rates rise. So concluding that your disposable income is reduced on the assumption that your mortgage costs have increased is incorrect if you later find that your lender has kept the mortgage interest rate the same. Assumptions allow rules to be used for inferencing even though we may be uncertain as to the truth values of some clauses.

Non-monotonic reasoning permits conclusions to be derived even when information is missing. A purely logic-based approach to non-monotonic reasoning treats statements as though they are either completely true or completely false or completely unknown. Unlike the probabilistic-based approaches we have studied there are no partially held beliefs.

One non-monotonic rule of inferencing is **abduction,** which allows the antecedent to be concluded when the conclusion is true provided that doing so is consistent. For example, the rule:

$$\text{hasFoodPoisoning}(X) \rightarrow \text{sick}(X)$$

allows us to conclude that X has food poisoning if we know that X is sick, provided that nothing else conflicts with concluding food poisoning. Food poisoning could be a reasonable conclusion if several people are sick and they have all recently eaten food from the same source. Abductive reasoning is often used in a diagnostic scenario, as in this example, but drawing black and white conclusions about the antecedent can be troublesome in practice. You might feel reasonably confident in concluding the cause of sickness but you cannot be certain because there are other causes even though in this scenario these other causes are less likely. If you discover that in a party of people all of those who are sick ate mussels apart from John who is sick but ate steak, as did other people in the party, your conclusion in the cause of John's sickness is weakened but John could still have food poisoning.

Another approach to non-monotonic logic is to use a modal operator M that allows a statement to be assumed to be true for the purpose of deriving a conclusion provided that the assumption is consistent with everything else that is known. Consider the rule:

$$(\text{have(food)} \wedge \text{working(oven)}) \rightarrow \text{meal}(Y)$$

This rule states that a meal of some description will be provided if there is food and the oven is working. If you are planning a last-minute dinner party you will normally concentrate on planning what to cook and/or shopping for the food. You are unlikely to test if the oven is working before you invite guests. The oven is usually very reliable and therefore you assume that it is working. So the rule could be written as:

$$(\text{have(food)} \wedge M(\text{working(oven)})) \rightarrow \text{meal}(Y)$$

which means that you will assume that the oven is working provided that this assumption is consistent. If you have a gas oven and you know the gas is switched off because of a leak then the assumption is not consistent with what else is known. Checking for consistency is not straightforward. One way to check is to see if $\neg working(oven)$ can be proved and if this proof fails we take *working(oven)* to be consistent. This approach can be limited because it is based on the premise that the knowledge base is sufficiently complete to test the proof of $\neg working(oven)$. In practice, the knowledge base is never complete.

Supporting non-monotonic inferencing in a practical reasoning system is challenging. Suppose we make an assumption A that is used to derive B. B is later used to derive new conclusions E and H. If we later find that A is invalid, we need to retract A and all of the conclusions that have been derived using A. Other derived facts that did not depend on A remain valid. There is therefore a lot of book-keeping to be done. We could envisage implementing this book-keeping using backtracking to trace back through derivations undoing those that are now invalid. Backtracking is chronological in that the last derivation is inspected first, then the second to last, and so on. This chronological approach can be expensive in terms of computing time, and it would be better if the search for retraction were targeted at those proofs that are logically dependent on the facts that are now known to be invalid. Such a search is called **dependency-directed backtracking**, and one way to implement this to support non-monotonic inferencing is to use a **truth maintenance system** (TMS). To illustrate the idea we shall use rules that capture the following:

> An animal that likes cream is a suspect. A prime suspect is an animal that is a suspect and is out at night. An animal is out at night if it is a cat.

So far we are assuming monotonic inferencing. The structure of the knowledge is shown in Figure 7.6. The root node and internal nodes are conclusions. The arrows leading into a node show the antecedent. These rules could be expressed more concisely but we are to imagine that the rules form part of a much larger knowledge base. Let us now modify the example slightly to make the reasoning non-monotonic.

> An animal that likes cream is a suspect. A prime suspect is an animal that is a suspect and is out at night. An animal is out at night if it is a cat unless the cat is kept in.

The rules are written below using a backward notation (quantification is ignored here):

prime_suspect(X) ← suspect(X) ∧ out(X, night)
suspect(X) ← animal(X) ∧ likes(X, cream)
out(X, night) ← cat(X) UNLESS(kept_in(X))

The third rule is non-monotonic in that a cat is always thought to be out at night unless we are told otherwise (that it is kept in).

A TMS uses a network structure. Any derived assertion has a justification. A justification consists of an IN list and an OUT list, which are connected to the justification via '+' and '−' links

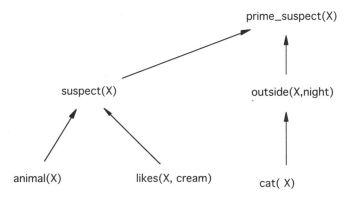

Figure 7.6 A network depicting three simple rules that can be used to derive a prime suspect.

respectively. The tree is given in Figure 7.7. In a TMS network, an assertion is believed when the justification is valid. The justification is valid if every assertion in the IN list is believed and none of those in the OUT list is believed to be true. An assertion is non-monotonic if its OUT list is not empty or if any assertion in its IN list is non-monotonic. In Figure 7.7, *prime_suspect(tiggs)* and *outside(tiggs)* are non-monotonic assertions. The assertion *outside(tiggs)* is non-monotonic because it has an assertion in its OUT list. *prime_suspect(tiggs)* is recursively non-monotonic because it has *outside(tiggs)* (which is non-monotonic) in its IN list. Tiggs is a prime suspect because each assertion can be justified. We know for a fact that Tiggs is an animal, he likes cream and he is a cat, and we assume that he is not kept in.

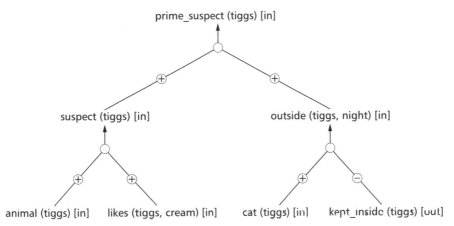

Figure 7.7 A simplified diagram illustrating the principle of a truth maintenance system (TMS). An assertion has a justification. If an assertion is justified it is labelled as [in] otherwise it is labelled as [out]. For example, outside(tiggs, night) is justified and its justification consists of two input nodes, cat(tiggs) and kept_inside(tiggs). Justification nodes that have links labelled '+' are part of an IN list and those labelled with a '–' are part of an OUT list. A node is justified only if all members of the IN list are believed and no member in the OUT list is believed. So Tiggs is believed to be out at night because we believe he is a cat and we do not believe he is kept inside.

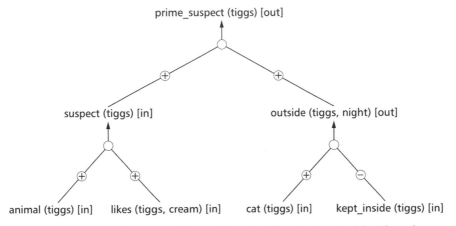

Figure 7.8 We have now received new information that Tiggs is kept inside. The relevant node changes to an [in] label, and this in turn changes the belief in Tiggs being outside at night and being a prime suspect.

Suppose we learn that Tiggs is kept indoors at night. This has now changed our belief in Tiggs being out. We now believe the assertion (kept_inside(tiggs)) in the OUT list that forms part of the justification for asserting that Tiggs is outside. We can no longer assert that Tiggs is outside and can no longer assert therefore that Tiggs is a prime suspect. The network has been updated as shown in Figure 7.8. Note that the assertion that Tiggs is a suspect is still valid.

Summary

Fuzzy logic is typically applied to control problems in which a set of input variable values are used to determine the value of a controlling variable such as the throttle adjustment on a car's autocruise. A set of IF … THEN rules describe the controlling logic. The variable values in these rules can have fuzzy boundaries – the boundaries between one variable value and another can overlap. The advantage of this fuzzy approach is that a small number of rules can handle many different combinations of input values. A variable will usually be continuous (e.g. temperature). Linguistic values for a variable (such as cold, warm, hot, etc. for temperature) are defined in terms of fuzzy sets, on to which a measured value can be mapped. The mapping of the variables on to linguistic values determines which rules get matched and fired to determine the value of the controlling variable.

Dempster–Shafer theory is a probabilistic approach to assessing the belief in a hypothesis by combining evidence. The set of possible hypotheses is called the frame of discernment. Dempster–Shafer theory assigns an upper and lower belief to each subset of hypotheses drawn from the frame of discernment.

There are non-probabilistic approaches to reasoning under uncertainty. Logic-based approaches allow clauses to be assumed true until such time they are found to be false. Conventional logic-based reasoners are monotonic, which means that once something is concluded it cannot be retracted. Non-monotonic logics allow earlier derived conclusions to be retracted. The book-keeping is tricky with these systems as retracting a conclusion can also affect subsequent derivations that used the conclusion. Truth maintenance systems provide one approach to this book-keeping.

Further reading

Zadeh introduced fuzzy sets (Zadeh, 1965, 1973). Books on fuzzy logic include Kosko (1994) and Passino and Yurkovich (1998). Elkan (1993) comments on the potential limitations of fuzzy logic when systems need to scale up.

For information on Dempster–Shafer theory see Dempster (1967, 1968) and Shafer (1976).

For further information on non-monotonic logic see Gabbay (1998), McDermott and Doyle (1980) and Minker (1993) and for truth maintenance systems Doyle (1979), McAllester (1980) and de Kleer (1986).

For possibility theory see Zadeh (1978) and Smets (1999), who provides a general overview of uncertainty.

Exercises

1   Given the following function:

$$f(x) = \frac{1}{1 + e^{-x}}$$

a   Compute $\mu(3)$, $\mu(-2)$, $\mu(-1)$ and $\mu(4)$.

b   Adapt the function for use as a membership function to group middle-aged people. Take middle-age membership as >0.98 for age 50 and a low membership of approximately 0.1 at age 38. The function should cut off so that no-one is a member below age 35 or above age 55.

2   The membership functions for the autocruise controller were sketched. These functions are defined more precisely below:

Speed error (se) and acceleration (acc)

$$\mu_{NEG}(x) = \begin{cases} 1 \text{ if } x \le -10 \\ 0 \text{ if } x \ge 0 \\ -0.075\, x \text{ if } 0 < x < -10 \end{cases}$$

$$\mu_{POS}(x) = \begin{cases} 1 \text{ if } x > 10 \\ 0 \text{ if } x \le 0 \\ 0.075x \text{ if } 0 < x < 1(\end{cases}$$

$$\mu_{ZERO}(x) = \begin{cases} 1 \text{ if } x \le 10 \text{ or } x > 10 \\ 0.1x + 1 \text{ if } -10 < x \le 0 \\ -0.1x + 1 \text{ if } 0 < x \le 10 \end{cases}$$

Each throttle membership function has positive slope $0.1x + 1$ and negative slope $-0.1x + 1$. The functions are centred as follows:

RH	−20
RS	−10
C	0
IS	10
IH	20

Compute the throttle adjustment for a speed error of 2 and acceleration error of −1.

3   Using the example scenario for Dempster–Shafer in section 7.2, compute the beliefs if neighbour 1 reports (d, f) 0.9 and neighbour 2 (c, f) 0.6.

4   Compute the beliefs if a third neighbour adds to the evidence in exercise 3 with (f) 0.7.

PART 4

Deciding on Actions

This part of the book is essentially about deciding which actions to take. A robot, for example, cannot be pre-programmed with deterministic problem-solving knowledge because events within its environment will be unpredictable. It will meet problems that it will have to work round. The robot needs to decide for itself what actions it needs to take in order to achieve a goal. Autonomous vehicles also need to plan sequences of actions. For example, an autonomous space vehicle would need to decide for itself which systems it could power down if it was short on power to achieve a task. The vehicle would need the ability to predict the consequences of its actions and how these consequences are likely to impact on what it needs to achieve.

There are different approaches to modelling decision actions depending on the nature of the task. In Chapter 8, we look at an extension to the Bayesian network model in which two new types of node are introduced: decision nodes and utility nodes. Utility nodes allow the desirability of different outcomes to be modelled. Utility values can be encoded as costs, and costs can be scaled to represent how desirable a state is. The actual costs for states are predicted on the basis of utility values for states and the likelihoods of states being instantiated. You could, for example, model the likelihood of your car developing a fault if it were not serviced. There would be costs associated with servicing and costs associated with a fault developing. Other costs could model the desire to have a reliable vehicle. Such a model could predict whether a service is an optimal decision (your objective being to save money in the long term but to maintain a reliable vehicle). You would, of course, require statistics for the likelihood of your car developing a fault with and without a service. Chapter 5 is a prerequisite for Chapter 8.

Planning systems model an action's preconditions and effects and search for a sequence of actions that will achieve desired goals — a goal might be achieved through the effect of an action. For example, the action of striking a fence post with a heavy hammer has the effect of pushing the post into the ground. A precondition of this action is that the post be positioned where required and the ultimate goal would be to have the post positioned to the required depth. Chapter 9 introduces the basics of propositional planning. A state-of-the-art algorithm is also introduced. Chapter 10 discusses more practical issues with planning for real-world problems like the need to handle uncertain events and the role of knowledge-rich planners.

CHAPTER **8**

Decision Networks

A Bayesian network is a probabilistic model of some part of the world. Bayesian network models reflect the changes in beliefs of the state of the world upon receiving new evidence. Evidence provides data, and Bayesian network models combine knowledge with the data to provide information. This information is really only of value if it is used to change the state of the world through one or more actions. For example, Should money be lent to a loan applicant? Should I service my car? Should a specific test be performed on a patient? In these examples, we are required to decide upon which action to take. Through actions, we aim to change the state of the world in some desirable way. For example, lending money when the risk of default is low will provide a profit on interest earned, servicing a car at optimal intervals should reduce maintenance costs without jeopardizing mechanical reliability, and performing a test on a patient could help to diagnose a disease more accurately so that appropriate medication can be administered. A **utility** measure is adopted to indicate the desirability of some outcome. The utility measure may be expressed in monetary terms, but need not be. In an uncertain world, there is no guarantee that the outcome of an action will be beneficial. You may, for example, put your car into a garage for tuning in the hope that it will fix an intermittent stall problem, but if tuning does not work you have paid out money for no return.

We can think of two fundamental types of decision, a decision to acquire more information to further reduce uncertainty or a decision to do something. The first type is sometimes called a **test** decision and the second an **action** decision. The distinction may not always be clear as a test will obviously call for some type of action, for example taking a patient's blood pressure. There are two types of action decision, **intervening** or **non-intervening**. An intervening action will change the states of some variables whereas a non-intervening action will not. An example of an intervening action is to change the tyres on a car during a race when the weather conditions are varying from sunny to wet. Racing cars have different tyres for wet and dry conditions, and the tyres can have a large influence on performance. In this example, the decision network would be recommending actions to improve performance and the action will obviously influence performance variables. An action to launch the space shuttle cannot influence a launch decision network as the network has no further function once the launch is under way. The launch action in this scenario is a non-intervening action.

We commence this chapter with the modelling of non-intervening actions and follow with intervening actions. We shall concentrate on single-action variables. The extension to multiple actions is straightforward, but to keep the examples manageable we only state the procedure for multiple actions. Applications of decision networks will usually model multiple actions. In this chapter, we assume that there is no delay between executing actions. In other words, we shall not consider sequences of actions in which the state of the world changes between the execution of the first action and the second. Finally, we introduce test decisions.

8.1 Non-intervening actions

A non-intervening action with one determining variable is the simplest situation to consider first.

Example 1 ● ● ● ● ●

A manufacturer of submersible fibreoptic telecommunication cable is confident of finishing a contract on time. On completion, a ship docks alongside the factory and cable is loaded for laying. A bonus of 100 units is available to be split between the staff if the contract is completed on time. The contract has gone very well and the factory manager has been told that, if the cable ships 1 week ahead of time, there will a 200-unit bonus. To bring the ship into port 1 week early and have the ship idle costs 100 units, which would wipe out any staff bonus if the cable is not ready to load. The staff will not be pleased at losing a bonus, but the potential of doubling the bonus is tempting. The probability of having the cable fully completed (including all testing) is estimated by the manager to be Pfinish(yes=0.68, no=0.32).

The decision, then, is whether or not to bring the ship into port early. The decision is made on the basis of the expected reward for an action. The action for which the expected reward is maximum is the optimal action. The utilities for this problem are taken as a direct mapping from the bonus and cost of having the ship in early.

A model for the example is given in Figure 8.1. The determining variable is *finish* (finish manufacturing on time) with two states, *yes* and *no*. There is a single action node, *call-ship*, with two actions (*do nothing, call ship into port early*). The action node is non-intervening because neither action has an influence on the status of manufacturing. We shall use a rectangle to denote an action node and a diamond to denote a utility node.

The utility node has a value specified for each combination of its parent nodes. These values are specified as in Table 8.1.

The expected utility from taking action a is:

$$EU(a) = \sum_{h \in H} U(a,h)p(h) \tag{8.1}$$

and the optimal action is:

$$Opt(A) = \arg \max EU(a) \tag{8.2}$$

where h denotes each state of the determining variable and $U(a, h)$ is the utility for action a when the state is h. The notation 'arg max' means the value of a that maximizes the expected utility.

For this example $U(a,h)$ is given in Table 8.1. There are two actions: *do nothing*, dn, and *call ship*

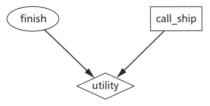

Figure 8.1 A simple decision network with a single determining variable (finish) a single action node (call_ship) and a single utility node.

Table 8.1 Utility values for deciding whether to call the ship in to load early. The values depend on whether manufacturing finished on time

		Do nothing	Call the ship in early
Finish	Yes	100	200
	No	100	0

early, se. The hypothesis is represented by the variable *finish* and it has two states (values) – *yes*, and *no*.

$$EU(dn) = (100 \times 0.68) + (100 \times 0.32)$$
$$= 100$$

$$EU(se) = (200 \times 0.68) + (0 \times 0.32)$$
$$= 136$$

The optimum action is therefore to bring the ship in early as the expected utility is higher than doing nothing.

In practice, the model in Figure 8.1 would have many more nodes that would influence the determining variable, such as the reliability of production machinery, the expected test results (all cable has to be tested), etc. These nodes will complicate the model, but their effect is to influence the determining variable and the calculation of which action is optimum remains simple.

● ● ● ● ●

8.1.1 Multiple non-intervening actions

There may be more than one non-intervening action within a network. There could, for example, be two hypothesis variables, each with their own action nodes. Such a situation could be modelled by combining both action nodes into a single action node. The problem with this approach is the increasing complexity with increasing number of actions. For instance, for two action nodes each having two actions, there would be four combinations in total. For a network with many actions, the number of combinations would become cumbersome to model as a single action node. The simpler approach is to solve each decision locally (as above). For example, suppose there are two hypothesis variables, H_1 and H_2, and associated action nodes (A_1 and A_2) and utility nodes (U_1 and U_2). If:

$$U(A_1, A_2, H_1, H_2) = U_1(A_1, H_1) + U_2(A_2, H_2)$$

Then:

1   $MEU(A_1, A_2) = MEU(A_1) + MEU(A_2)$
2   $Opt(A_1, A_2) = (Opt(A_1), Opt(A_2))$

In other words, the maximum expected utility for actions A_1 and A_2 together is simply the sum of the maximum expected utilities of the actions executed on their own.

8.2 Intervening actions

Intervening actions will influence variables within a network and thus can have an influence on the hypothesis variable. An example is shown in Figure 8.2. Action A has an influence on variables V_1 and V_3, which in turn influence the hypothesis variable.

The expected utility for an action given evidence e is given in eqn (8.3), and the optimum action is given in eqn (8.4).

$$EU(a|e) = \sum_{h \in H} U(h)p(h|a,e) \tag{8.3}$$

$$Opt(A|e) = \arg\max_{a \in A} EU(a|e) \tag{8.4}$$

Equations (8.3) and (8.4) reflect that evidence e has been received and some action a belonging to the set A has been executed.

Example 2 ● ● ● ● ●

We shall use a simple example in which an action node impacts directly on the hypothesis node H.

We have a potted plant that lives outside. It is a reasonably hardy type of plant but can suffer damage through repeated exposure to a hard frost. We have three possible actions that can be performed (do nothing, provide simple insulation for the pot or place the plant in a greenhouse).

The model is given in Figure 8.3. The hypothesis variable is whether or not the plant survives. The *survive* variable has a probability specified for each given action, and these are listed in Table 8.2.

We shall take the utility simply to be what the plant is worth to us. The plant has matured over 5 years, and to replace it with a similar-sized plant would be £80. So, if the plant survives, we could say that this is worth £80, and that the scenario that the plant dies has value zero. It might appear more natural to put a value of zero for survival and –£80 (a loss) if the plant dies. Either way is acceptable provided consistency throughout the model is maintained.

A simple way to compute the optimal action is to calculate $p(H|a)$ for each possible action. In our example, these values are already given because the actions impact directly on H. The expected utilities are therefore:

$$EU(\text{do nothing}) = (0.6 \times 80) + (0.4 \times 0) = 48$$

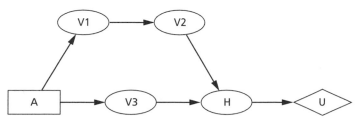

Figure 8.2 A is an intervening action that can impact on variables V1 and V3, which in turn can influence the hypothesis variable H.

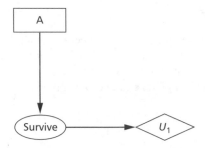

Figure 8.3 The action to protect the plant directly influences the plant's chance of surviving the winter. The action that gives the maximum expected chance of survival will in this example be the optimal action. U_1 represents the utility value for surviving the winter.

Table 8.2 Probabilities of the potted plant surviving given different actions for providing insulation against frost

Action	Survive	
	Yes	No
Do nothing	0.6	0.4
Simple insulation	0.85	0.15
Greenhouse	0.95	0.05

$$\text{EU(simple insulation)} = (0.85 \times 80) + (0.15 \times 0) = 68$$
$$\text{EU(greenhouse)} = (0.95 \times 80) + (0.05 \times 0) = 76$$

The calculation of the utility values in this example is redundant because the highest utility will be produced by the action that provides the maximum chance of survival.

Suppose we do not possess any insulation material or greenhouse and have to purchase these items. We now have a model as shown in Figure 8.4. Suppose the cost of the greenhouse is £100 and the cost of the insulation is £10. These are costs and therefore can be modelled as negative utility values. The calculations are as before but now the material costs have to be subtracted:

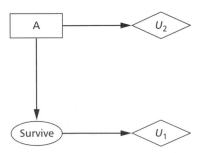

Figure 8.4 A utility node U_2 has been added to the network in Figure 8.3 to model the direct costs of the different actions.

EU(do nothing)$=(0.6 \times 80)+(0.4 \times 0)=48 - 0=48$
EU(simple insulation)$=(0.85 \times 80)+(0.15 \times 0)=68 - 10=58$
EU(greenhouse)$=(0.95 \times 80)+(0.05 \times 0)=76 - 100=-24$

The optimum action now is to provide simple insulation instead of the more costly action to greenhouse the plant even though this latter action gives greater chance of survival.

● ● ● ● ●

Example 3   ● ● ● ● ●

Suppose we have an expensive plant that can suffer from insect infestation. The risk is such that 30% of all plants will get infested. Once infested there are a number of actions that can be taken: wash the leaves with a soap solution, apply an insecticide spray or do nothing. The model is given in Figure 8.5.

Two infestation nodes are shown: *infestation* and *infestation_p*. The node *infestation_p* models the infestation after treatment. The probabilities for *infestation_p* are given in Table 8.3. If the plant is infested and no action is taken then the plant will remain infested.

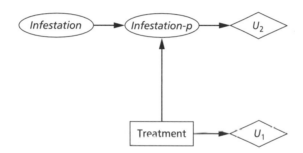

Figure 8.5 A network to model a plant with infestation from insects. A single action node specifies different forms of treatment and each treatment has a cost that is modelled in the node U_1. Treatment has an impact on the expectation of infestation remaining and this is modelled by using the node *infestation_p*. The node U_2 represents the value of the plant surviving.

Table 8.3 Probabilities of the plant remaining infested given its state of infestation and remedy action

Infestation	Action	Infestation_p Yes	No
Yes	Do nothing	1	0
No	Do nothing	0	1
Yes	Wash	0.4	0.6
No	Wash	0	1
Yes	Insecticide	0.15	0.85
No	Insecticide	0	1

The effect of each action is simulated. This simulation provides the probability of the hypothesis variable, *infestation_p*, under each action. The probabilities are given below:

p(infestation_p|do nothing)=(0.3, 0.7)
p(infestation_p|wash)=(0.12, 0.88)
p(infestation_p|insecticide)=(0.045, 0.955)

The first value corresponds to the state *yes* (i.e. plant is infected) and the second value corresponds to the state *no*. The utility is 150 units if the plant survives. The cost of washing is 5 units and of insecticide is 30 units. The expected utilities are therefore:

EU(do nothing)=0.7×150−0=105
EU(wash)=0.88×150 − 5=127
EU(insecticide)=0.955×150−30=113.25

The node *infestation* specifies the expectation of a plant becoming infested and the node *infestation_p* specifies the expectation of removing the infestation given different treatments. The above utilities are computed in the absence of knowing the true status of the plant (i.e. whether or not it is infested). In the absence of any evidence, the optimum action is to wash the plant. If we know that the plant is infested then the probabilities are:

p(infestation_p|do nothing)=(1.0, 0.0)
p(infestation_p|wash)=(0.4, 0.6)
p(infestation_p|insecticide)=(0.15, 0.85)

which are simply the priors that were specified for the success of treatment given that the plant is infested. The utilities are:

EU(do nothing)=0×150−0=0
EU(wash)=0.6×150−5=85
EU(insecticide)=0.85×150 − 30=97.5

The model in Figure 8.5 indicates that a plant has a 30% chance of being infested but the availability of treatment reduces the likelihood of a plant remaining infested to 15.5% (the probability for the state *yes* on *infestation_p* when no evidence exists).

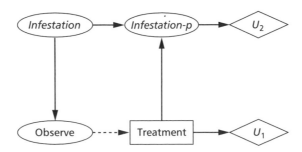

Figure 8.6 The observe node represents the outcome of a diagnosis by a plant expert.

Figure 8.5 does not model what usually happens when a diagnosis is made. Unless we are to remain totally ignorant of the plant's state of health we need to make an observation. In other words, we gather some data regarding the health of the plant. In our simple example we shall treat the observation as an inspection by a plant expert. The treatment then follows the observation made. A model is given in Figure 8.6 for the scenario of a diagnosis by an expert. The *observe* node specifies the expected accuracy of the diagnosis and is given below:

	Observe	
Infestation	Yes	No
Yes	0.9	0.1
No	0.05	0.95

If the plant is infested, the expert will correctly diagnose the infestation in 90% of all cases. The expert will incorrectly diagnose 5% of plants as being infested when in fact they are not (such a diagnosis is called a false positive).

The expert's observation will have an impact on the treatment. The dotted arrow indicates that a decision on the appropriate action is made after the observation. If the expert believes the plant not to be infested then the expected utilities are:

$$EU(\text{do nothing}) = 0.957 \times 150 - 0 = 143.55$$
$$EU(\text{wash}) = 0.983 \times 150 - 5 = 142.45$$
$$EU(\text{insecticide}) = 0.994 \times 150 - 30 = 119.10$$

So the optimum action would be to do nothing. Of course, this action is only marginally more optimal than washing the plant.

● ● ● ● ●

8.2.1 Handling multiple actions

A simple approach to handling multiple actions is to simulate each possible combination of actions to calculate the expectation on the hypothesis variable.

8.3 Test decisions

Tests are performed to gather more data. Doctors have a whole range of tests that can be used to help diagnose a patient's symptoms. It is impracticable to provide complete preventative cover by regularly testing all patients for all conditions. A doctor will usually start with a basic assessment and will take into account factors such as a patient's history, family history and the consequences of making a wrong diagnosis. The doctor may decide on more than one test.

The expected utility of performing an action is given by eqn (8.1):

$$EU(a) = \sum_{h \in H} U(a,h) p(h)$$

The optimal action is the one that maximizes the expected utility:

$$Opt(A) = \arg \max EU(a)$$

$$Opt(A) = \arg\max_{a} \sum_{h \in H} U(a,h)\, p(h)$$

A single test will yield some result t. The expected utility of the optimum action given the test result t is:

$$EU(a \mid t) = \arg\max_{a} \sum_{h \in H} U(a,h)\, p(h \mid t) \tag{8.5}$$

As the decision about a test has to be performed without knowing the outcome, the above expected utility has to be averaged over all test results. So the expected value of a test is therefore:

$$EV(t) = \sum_{t \in T} EU(a \mid t)\, p(t) \tag{8.6}$$

The expected benefit of performing the test is the expected value of the test minus the expected utility of performing an optimum action without any test being performed.

A test is worth considering only if the result has the potential to influence a decision. If the result has the potential to influence the decision then the cost of the test has to be taken into account. For example, suppose that in Figure 8.6 the observation is replaced by a test that involves sending a cutting away for analysis. If the analysis is highly accurate then it might influence the choice of action, but if the cost of the test is higher than the cost of treatment with insecticide then the test is not worth performing.

Example 4 ● ● ● ● ●

Suppose that for the model in Figure 8.6 the test is considered to be the observation by a plant expert. What is the expected profit of the test? We shall assume that the consultation costs nothing.

The value of each action without any observation (test) are:

EU(do nothing) = $0.7 \times 150 - 0 = 105$
EU(wash) = $0.88 \times 150 - 5 = 127$
EU(insecticide) = $0.955 \times 150 - 30 = 113.25$

The optimum value corresponds to wash at 127 units. To calculate the utility of performing a test we need to average over the expected utility for each test result. There are two possible results: either the plant is infested or it is not. If the test shows a positive result, the utilities are:

EU(do nothing) = 17.2
EU(wash) = 91.9
EU(insecticide) = 100.1

If the result is negative, the expected utilities are:

EU(do nothing) = 143.5
EU(wash) = 142.4
EU(insecticide) = 119

The maximum expected utility for a positive result is 100.1 and that for a negative result is 143.5.

The probabilities for each observation are (positive=0.305, negative=0.695). So the expected value of performing the test is:

$$100.1 \times 0.305 + 143.5 \times 0.695 = 130.3$$

The expected benefit of the test is calculated by subtracting the expected value without knowing the test result:

$$\text{the expected benefit of the test} = 130.3 - 127 = 3.3$$

So the test is worth performing. The expected benefit calculated above is also referred to as the **value of information**. The above calculation assigns a value to the information that is expected from the test result. If the cost of the test exceeded the value (i.e. is greater than 3.3 units) then the test would not be worth performing.

● ● ● ● ●

For many real-world applications there will be more than one test available. Suppose we have two tests, t_1 and t_2. There are a number of decisions to be made:

Perform t_1 first and consult the result to decide on whether to perform t_2
Perform t_2 first and consult the result to decide on whether to perform t_1
Perform t_1 and t_2 simultaneously

Performing both tests simultaneously is worth doing only if performing the tests in parallel is cheaper (e.g. a discount is given against multiple tests) or there is some other constraint such as the delay in getting test results. Assuming that the tests are to be performed in sequence, then a decision has to be made as to which test is to be performed first. To calculate the expected value of performing t_1 first, we would need to calculate the expected value of t_1 and then add to this value the value from averaging the expected value from performing t_2 given each result from t_1.

8.4 Value of information

The general equation for the expected value of performing a test is:

$$EV(t) = \sum_{t \in T} V(p(H \mid t)) p(t)$$

where $V(p(H \mid t))$ is the value of the belief in H given the test result t.

We have up until now assumed that an action will be selected and for each action there is a utility value. If an action is present, the value function $V(p(H \mid t))$ is:

$$EU(a \mid t) = \arg\max_a \sum_{h \in H} U(a, h) p(h \mid t)$$

Suppose that there are no actions to be decided on and that the hypothesis node is a diagnostic node

Figure 8.7 A simple model to illustrate the value of doing a diagnostic test in the absence of any actions.

that identifies a disease a patient has. Tests are typically used to provide more information to help the diagnosis. In the absence of any actions, can a test be assigned a value? Yes, and the value function is:

$$V(p(H)) = \max_{h \in H} p(H) \qquad (8.7)$$

The value of the state of H is the value of the state with the highest probability.

The whole purpose of performing a test is to gather more information. The value of the information that is received from performing the test will be zero if the decision to be taken is unchanged no matter what the result of the test is. Consider Figure 8.7, in which a single hypothesis variable (H) is connected to a single test variable (T). Without the test, the prior beliefs in the hypothesis states are (yes=0.3, no=0.7). The test variable has two states, *yes* and *no*. The distribution table for T is given below:

	T	
H	Yes	No
Yes	0.95	0.05
No	0.05	0.95

Performing the test and given that the result is *yes*, the belief in the hypothesis is:

p(H|T=yes)=(yes=89.06, no=10.94)

So a positive test result can reverse the belief in the state of the hypothesis variable. The test is therefore potentially worth performing.

Suppose the prior beliefs in H are (yes=0.03, no=0.97). Performing the test now yields the following beliefs in H:

p(H|T=yes)=(yes=0.37, no=0.63)
p(H|T=no)=(yes=0.0016, no=0.9984)

There is no point now in performing the test as the state with the highest probability in the hypothesis variable remains *no*.

A hypothesis node is more discriminating if one state is very dominant over the others. In an ideal world, one state would have probability 1.0 and the other states 0. If the probability is evenly distributed among all states, then the hypothesis variable provides no discrimination. In Chapter 12, entropy is used as a measure of discrimination in constructing a decision tree. If no model of actions and utilities exists, then entropy might be a useful value function. The value function using entropy is:

$$V(p(H)) = -\sum_{h \in H} p(h) \log_2 (p(h))$$

8.5 A note on utility values

A utility value is a real number and a utility function maps a state into its utility value. A value expresses the desirability of a state. Assigning utility values to different states allows preferences to be indicated. For example, you may prefer to be rich rather than poor. The axioms of utility theory define a number of constraints on the preferences between states. These axioms are fairly intuitive and are designed to express the relationships between preferences that we might expect from a rational agent. For example, the axiom *transitivity* says that if an agent prefers state A to B and prefers B to C then the agent must prefer A to C.

When modelling part of the world with a decision network, utility values are used to indicate preferences among states. We can simulate an action to predict how the state of the world would be expected to look if that action were executed for real. The expected outcome will have an associated utility value and the optimum action is the one that returns the most desired utility value. Usually the most desirable value will be the maximum value. For example, if utility values are expressed in monetary terms it is usually desirable to have more money than less.

Many real-world problems can be modelled in terms of monetary value. The primary objective for most companies is to maximize profit. Even medical care can be assessed in monetary terms. Health organizations work within budget constraints and therefore it is not pragmatic to follow a policy that provides the best care that is theoretically possible. The same is true for transportation. What price are we willing to pay for air transport? In general, we are prepared to accept very small risks to keep the cost of living manageable so that money might be available for more recreational pursuits.

There is no defined method for mapping preferences onto utility values. The method will depend on the problem being modelled. For some problems it might be preferable to normalize utility values to a scale with 0 the lowest value and 1 the highest. Suppose you are taking a maths exam and the pass mark is 40%. You might consider that any value below 40 to be of little value. A grade C at 50% is highly desirable because it gets you into a university of your choice and a B grade (60%) is even better because it gets you into your first-choice university. Grade C is much more preferable than a pass and B is more preferable than a grade C, but the preference between B and C is less than that between a C and a pass. How should a mark be mapped between 0 and 1? A mark of 40% corresponds to 0 and 100% to 1.

One method for assigning intermediate utility values is to imagine two games.

Game 1 You get a mark of 100% with probability p and a mark of 0% with probability $1 - p$.

Game 2 You get for certain the mark x.

You are offered different values for p and for each value you state which game you prefer. If $p = 1$

then you would prefer game 1 because you would get the highest mark possible. The utility value assigned to the mark x is the value of p where you are indifferent as to which game you prefer. For example, suppose x is 30%. This mark is a fail and you might accept any value of p (e.g. nearly zero) because 30% is of little value to you. How about 40%? This mark is a pass and could still get you a university place, albeit one that is not of your choosing. The following table is an assignment by a hypothetical student:

Mark	< 40%	40–50%	50–60%	> 60%	100%
Utility value	0.001	0.7	0.85	0.9	1.0

Summary

The decision networks introduced in this chapter are Bayesian networks with additional nodes: decision nodes and utility nodes. A decision node will specify two or more actions that can be taken. The purpose of decisions is to change something about the world such that the new world is more desirable. Desirability can be modelled by a utility function. An optimal action is the one that maximizes the utility. There are two types of action. A non-intervening action will not alter any of the variable probability distributions within the network. An intervening action can alter the distributions.

Further reading

Influence diagrams were introduced by Howard and Matheson (1984). Methods for solving multiple decisions using influence diagrams includes Shachter (1986), Shenoy (1992) and Shachter and Peot (1992). Jensen *et al.* (1994) use a specialization of the junction tree for solving decision problems using influence diagrams.

Exercises

1   A decision network is sketched below. Given the utility values for each hypothesis h of node A and each action a of decision node D:

h1	h1	h1	h2	h2	h2	h3	h3	h3
a1	a2	a3	a1	a2	a3	a1	a2	a3
50	20	10	40	20	10	30	40	60

and probabilities for each h:

h1	0.2
h2	0.4
h3	0.4

find the expected utility of each action and the optimum action.

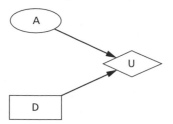

2   A decision network is sketched below. Given the utility values for each hypothesis *h* of node A:

h1	50
h2	40
h3	80

and probabilities for each hypothesis given each action *a* from decision node D:

	h1	h2	h3
a1	0.2	0.5	0.3
a2	0.2	0.3	0.5
a3	0.4	0.1	0.5

find the expected utility of each action and the optimum action.

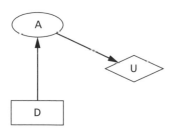

3   Repeat exercise 2 where the costs of each action are:

a1	−10
a2	−15
a3	−20

4   A decision network is sketched below. Given the probability distributions for node A given node B and decision node D:

D	B	A T	F
a1	T	0.3	0.7
a1	F	0.5	0.5
a2	T	0.8	0.2
a2	F	0.6	0.4

and the prior probabilities for B:

B	
T 0.7	F 0.3

and the utilities for A:

A	Utility
T	100
F	70

a   Compute the expected utility for each action.

b   Given that B is set to False, compute the expected utility for each action.

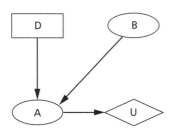

5   A decision node has two actions, a1 and a2. The expected utilities for a1 and a2 are 120 and 150 respectively. A test yields a positive result with probability 0.35 and a negative result with probability of 0.65. The expected utility for a1 given positive and negative results is 160 and 130 respectively. The expected utility for a2 given positive and negative results is 170 and 100 respectively. The cost of the test is –20 units. Calculate the expected utility of the test.

CHAPTER 9

Planning I

The job of a planner is to find a sequence of actions that will achieve goals. A toy problem might require a robot to sort a jumble of labelled blocks into ordered stacks. The required ordering of the blocks specifies the goal of the task and the initial jumble of blocks represents the start state. The robot will be capable of executing certain actions, e.g. grabbing a block and placing it on top of another block. The problem that the robot faces can be solved using search, but the sort of algorithms presented in Chapter 3 are not really adequate for many types of problem that planning algorithms are applied to. The real difference between heuristic-type searching and planning is that a planner will use much more structural knowledge in deciding on its course of action. The planner has a high degree of flexibility because it knows what conditions must exist in order for actions to be performed, and it knows the effects of actions. For instance, if you buy a can of drink from a vending machine, the effects of the action are to reduce by one the number of cans that the vending machine holds and for you to be in possession of a drink. This action has preconditions in that the machine must not be empty and you must have the money to make the purchase.

Planners have a wide range of applications, including robot navigation, autonomous vehicle control, maintenance planning and many more. In this chapter, we shall explore the basics of planning. We shall introduce a simple language for representing actions and we shall introduce a specific instance of a planning algorithm. There are many issues that practical planners face, and some of these issues are discussed in the next chapter.

9.1 A simple plan description language

All planning problems are conducted in some world: this world might be the one we experience as humans, but the implementation of a planning application is typically restricted to some domain such as the environment a robot operates in or, perhaps, the virtual world of some character in a computer game. It is convenient to use a generic term, agent, to refer to a human, or robot or software creature. We defer a detailed discussion of agents until Chapter 22, but for our present purposes we require an agent to be able to sense its world and to perform actions in that world. There are three components to a planning algorithm:

- a description of the world;
- a description of the agent's goal;
- a description of the actions that an agent can perform.

These descriptions are given in some formal language. In this chapter we shall restrict our language to simple non-quantified predicate sentences.

STRIPS (Fikes and Nilsson, 1971) was developed to represent states, goals and actions, during some early pioneering work in the 1970s at the Stanford Research Institute (now known as SRI

International). Languages that are more comprehensive have evolved to describe planning problems in recent years, but STRIPS is still commonly referred to, and it offers a useful starting point to introduce the concepts of planning.

9.1.1 STRIPS

STRIPS uses conjunctions of literals to describe the world and the task to be completed.

State description

The **state** of the world is described using a conjunction of ground literals.[1] So the blocks world in Figure 9.1 can be described as:

$$on(a, fl) \wedge on(c, a) \wedge clear(c) \wedge on(b, fl) \wedge clear(b)$$

Goal description

Goals are described by a conjunction of literals. So the goal in Figure 9.1 is described as:

$$on(c, fl) \wedge on(b, c) \wedge on(a, b) \wedge clear(a)$$

Action description

Actions are represented by STRIPS operators. An **operator** consists of three components:

- The name, so that the action can be identified.
- The **precondition**, which is a conjunction of positive literals that specifies the conditions which must be true before the action can be executed.
- The **effect**, which is a conjunction of both positive and negative literals that specify how the world changes after an action is executed. Sometimes it is convenient to place all of the positive literals in an **add-list** and all of the negative literals in a **delete-list**. An operator's effects define a new state – the add literals are added to the state description and the delete literals are removed from the state description.

An example of an action description for move in the blocks world is:

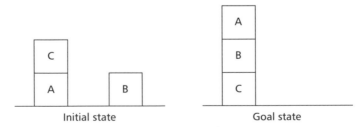

Initial state   Goal state

Figure 9.1 A simple blocks world in which only a single block can be moved at a time. A plan is a sequence of actions from some initial state to a goal state.

---

[1]A ground literal contains no variables.

```
move(X, Y, Z){
        precondition: on(X, Y) ∧ clear(X) ∧ clear(Z)
        add: on(X, Z) ∧ clear(Y)
        delete: clear(Z) ∧ on(X, Y)
}
```

In this simple world it will be assumed that only a single block at a time can be moved. So in Figure 9.1 the action *move(c, a, b)* can be performed because the preconditions (*on(c, a)*, *clear(c)*, *clear(b)*) are true. The effect of the action is that *c* is now on top of *b* (*on(c, b)*) and *a* is clear. Also, *b* is no longer clear and *c* is no longer on top of *a* and so these facts are deleted from the state description.

Notice that we could end up with a slight difficulty when performing an action such as *move(c, a, fl)*. The delete effect specifies *clear(fl),* which means that the floor is no longer clear. A block is either clear or not, but the floor can have more than one block placed on it. In our blocks world we always consider the floor to be clear. If we place *clear(fl)* on the adds list we end up with an undefined result when performing *move(c, a, fl)* because *clear(fl)* appears on both the add and delete lists. As humans, this does not pose a problem because common-sense tells us to think of the floor as usually having a clear space somewhere. With a program, however, we need to get around the problem by making sure that the state description of the blocks world always has *clear(fl)* as a fact.

9.2 Deriving plans

Now that we have a basic language to represent states of the world and how actions can affect the world, we are in a position to look at a planning algorithm. We want the planning algorithm to return a sequence of actions that transforms the world from its initial state to the goal state. For the blocks world in Figure 9.1 such a sequence could be:

```
move(c, a, fl)
move(b, fl, c)
move(a, fl, b)
```

It appears natural for humans to use a divide and conquer approach to solving problems. For instance, our blocks problem has two principal subgoals: *on(b, c)* and *on(a, b)*. So we might look to solve the subgoals independently. There is a difficulty, though, which is called the **Sussman anomaly**. The anomaly arises because the subgoals interfere with one another: if first we choose *on(b, c)* then we cannot achieve the second subgoal because *a* is trapped under *c*, and if we first try to solve *on(a, b)* by placing *c* on the floor then *a* on *b* we cannot achieve *on(b, c)* without taking *a* off (only one block at a time can be moved). A planning algorithm should be able to identify actions that interfere with one another. If an action is permitted that interferes with another subgoal then the planning algorithm may return more actions than is necessary: it will not guarantee to return the shortest path.

9.3 Implementing planning as a simple search procedure

Figure 9.2 illustrates the search space for a naive planner that uses forward search. The edges represent actions and the nodes represent states in the world. A breadth-first search could be used to return the shortest path. Note that the STRIPS operator for move would simply be used to determine

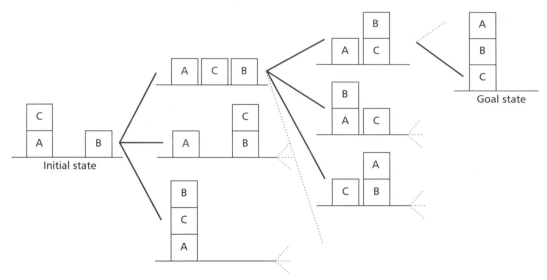

Figure 9.2 A simple forward (data-driven) search. Each branch is an operator, which for the simple blocks world will be a move action. Only a few of the branches are shown.

what new states could be generated from an existing state. Each branch would have to be explored until the goal node was found.

A more promising approach might be to use a backward search as in real-world problems the number of goal literals is likely to be far smaller than the number of literals used to describe states and so the branching factor will be lower. One approach is to use **regression** planning. We follow the approach given by Nilsson (1996).

The regression planner starts from the goal, and at each step it considers an action that might satisfy one of the conjuncts (subgoals) in the goal list. A conjunct is regressed through an action to produce a new list of goals. For an action to be considered, it must have in its effects add list a conjunct that appears in the current list of goals. The result of the regression is to replace the current goal list with a new goal list. The new goal list is made up of the action's weakest[2] preconditions and the current goals except those goals that appear on the action's add effect list. The simple block stacking problem given in Figure 9.1 can be used to illustrate the idea. The initial goal list is:

{on(c, fl), on(b, c), on(a, b), clear(a)}

If we choose to regress *on(a, b)* through the action *move(a, fl, b)* we have a new goal list:

{on(c, fl), on(b, c), clear(a), on(a, fl), clear(b)}

The new list does not include the add effects of the action but does include the preconditions of *move(a, fl, b)*. Figure 9.3 gives a more detailed description.

Even for the small blocks world of Figure 9.1, there are different choices to be made at each step, and ideally we want to reduce these choices. To avoid unnecessary regressions, we could check the goal list literals at each stage against the initial literals and remove any that match. For example,

_____

[2]A formula f1 is weaker than another formula f2 if f2 logically entails f1.

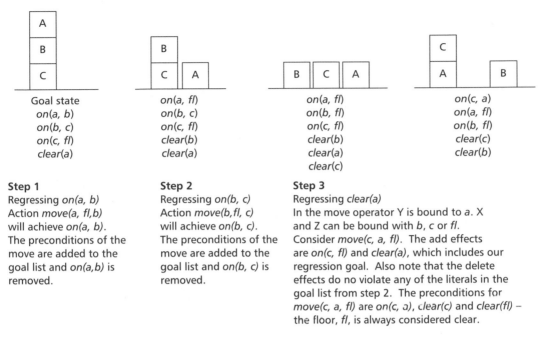

Step 1
Regressing *on(a, b)*
Action *move(a, fl,b)*
will achieve *on(a, b)*.
The preconditions of the
move are added to the
goal list and *on(a,b)* is
removed.

Step 2
Regressing *on(b, c)*
Action *move(b,fl, c)*
will achieve *on(b, c)*.
The preconditions of the
move are added to the
goal list and *on(b, c)* is
removed.

Step 3
Regressing *clear(a)*
In the move operator Y is bound to *a*. X
and Z can be bound with *b, c* or *fl*.
Consider *move(c, a, fl)*. The add effects
are *on(c, fl)* and *clear(a)*, which includes our
regression goal. Also note that the delete
effects do no violate any of the literals in the
goal list from step 2. The preconditions for
move(c, a, fl) are *on(c, a)*, *clear(c)* and *clear(fl)* –
the floor, *fl*, is always considered clear.

Figure 9.3 Illustration of the steps in regression planning. The search starts from the goal state. The goal state is described by a list (conjunctive list) of literals. The idea is to replace items on the goal list with their new subgoals. For instance, the action *move(a, fl, b)* has add effects *on(a, b)* and *clear(fl)*. We always consider the floor to be clear but we can see that the action will achieve the effect *on(a, b)*. The subgoal *on(a, b)* is replaced with the action's, *move(a, fl, b)*, preconditions: *on(a, fl)*, *clear(a)*, *clear(b)*. The subgoal *clear(a)* is already on the list and so *on(a, b)* is replaced with *on(a, fl)* and *clear(b)*. The search proceeds in this manner. If the goal can be achieved from the initial start state, all literals on the goal list will eventually match the description of the initial state.

after step 2 all the literals apart from *on(c, fl)* and *clear(a)* can be removed because the others agree with the initial state. There will also be backtrack points in the search where there are different ways to achieve the same goal. For example, *clear(a)* can be achieved by *move(c, a, fl)* or *move(b, a, fl)*. If we opted first for *move(b, a, fl)*, we would reach a dead end. The alternative action, *move(c, a, fl)*, would provide a backtrack point.

What if the regression is started from the goal state by first attempting to regress *on(b, c)* instead of *on(a, b)*? The goal *on(b, c)* can be achieved by *move(b, fl, c)* or *move(b, a, c)*. There is a conflict here. The precondition of both moves requires *clear(b)*, and adding this to the goal list will conflict with *on(a, b)*. The literals *clear(b)* and *on(a, b)* are said to be mutually exclusive or **mutex**. Recognizing mutex relations constrains the search, thus avoiding wasted effort.

We next present an algorithm called **GraphPlan** that expands its search space in a forward direction (starting from the initial state) and stops after each step to do a backward chaining search. The search is highly constrained by recognizing mutex relations.

We could have chosen a number of prominent planning algorithms to present in detail, but we have decided to concentrate on GraphPlan for a number of reasons. First, GraphPlan has recently received a great deal of attention and has proved itself to be an extremely fast planner. Second, the planner in its basic form is simple and aids understanding of other planners. Third, extensions to GraphPlan (see Weld, 1998) increase its potential for real-world applications.

9.4 GraphPlan

GraphPlan was developed by Blum and Furst (1997). GraphPlan is a parallel planner, which means that a number of plans can be extracted by recognizing different possible action sequences. For instance, if shopping in a supermarket for bread, milk and coffee, you might have the action sequence: collect trolley, select bread, select milk, select coffee, pay for goods. The selection of items can appear in any order without affecting the goal of shopping.

GraphPlan is so called because it generates a graph structure and any valid plan exists as a subgraph. The graph is **levelled,** which means that nodes (vertices) are associated with a level and edges can connect nodes only in adjacent levels. The planning graph contains two types of node: **proposition nodes** and **action nodes**. The levels alternate between proposition levels containing proposition nodes and action levels containing action nodes. The first level, level 0, is a proposition level and contains a node for each proposition (conjunct) in the initial state.[3] The second level, level 1, will contain actions whose preconditions are present in the previous proposition level. Levels 0 and 1 represent the first time step: the propositions that are true at time 1 and the actions that can be executed at time 1.The third level, level 2, will contain propositions that can be true at the second time step: level 2 will contain the add and delete propositions of the actions at level 1. The progression of levels continues in this manner, alternating between proposition and action levels.

The graph contains three types of edges: precondition edges, add edges and delete edges. Precondition edges will connect propositions at level i to actions at level $i + 1$, and these actions will connect to add and delete effects at level $i + 2$ using add edges and delete edges.

An action may exist at a particular level if all of its preconditions exist at the previous level. A proposition may exist at a level if it is either an add or delete effect of an action in a previous level. There is also a **no-op** action: any proposition at a level i is allowed to exist at a level $i + 2$ because it will not necessarily be affected by an action. A no-op connects a proposition in level i to the same proposition in level $i + 2$.

GraphPlan executes the following basic procedure:

> search backwards from the current proposition level at time t
> > if a plan exists
> > > return its path
> > else if graph can be expanded
> > > expand graph to the next proposition level at time $t+1$ and call search
> > else
> > > return fail

Example 1 ● ● ● ● ●

> Rob and Mary are at home. Rob has to get to work and has two options: either he walks or he uses the car. Mary needs to get to the airport and her only option is to use the car. The car needs fuel before it can be used.

For the sake of brevity we shall not use a predicate notation but use simple string descriptions for actions and effects. The initial state is:

> robAtHome   Rob is at home
> maryAtHome   Mary is at home

---

[3]A proposition corresponds to a ground literal.

car   car is available

The actions to be modelled are:

```
Walk{                              Rob walks to work
        precon: robAtHome
        add: robAtWork
        del: robAtHome
}
GetFuel{                           get fuel for the car
        precon:
        add: fuel
        del:
}
DriveAirport{                      Mary drives to the airport
        precon:maryAtHome, car, fuel
        add:maryAtAirport
        del:maryAtHome, car
}
DriveWork{                         Rob drives to work
        precon: robAtHome, car, fuel
        add: robAtWork
        del: robAtHome, car
}
```

The goal is described by the following literals:

```
robAtWork
maryAtAirport
```

The add list contains positive literals and the delete list contains negative literals. We could use the negative and positive literals explicitly instead of denoting add and delete lists. For example,

```
DriveWork{
        precon: robAtHome, car, fuel
        effect: robAtWork, ¬robAtHome, ¬car
}
```

The **closed world assumption** will also be used. This assumption takes a proposition to be false if it is not declared as true in the initial state. For example, *fuel* (have fuel) is assumed to be false. Negative literals for all those propositions assumed to be false could be added to level 0. However, this creates unnecessary work as it means identifying all such propositions by inspecting the goal list and the preconditions of the actions. Weld (1998) describes a lazy approach to handling the closed world assumption. The approach is simple. Do not add negative literals for those propositions known not to be true at level 0. If an action A at level i requires $\neg P$ as a precondition and $\neg P$ exists at level $i-1$ then link to it as usual, and if $\neg P$ does not exist at level $i-1$ check to see if its negation (P) is present at level 0. If P is not at level 0 then add $\neg P$ to level 0 and add no-op edges up to level i.

In Example 1, the goal literals are not satisfied by the initial state and so the graph is expanded. This first expansion is shown in Figure 9.4. The propositions at level 2 (second time step) are searched to see if the goal propositions are present. The subgoal *maryAtAirport* is missing and so the graph is expanded again and is shown in Figure 9.5. This time the subgoals are present at level 4. The subgoals being present at a proposition level is a necessary but not sufficient condition for a plan to exist. In other words, all the subgoals need to be present at a proposition level for a solution to exist, but their presence does not mean that a plan can be generated. A search is therefore performed to see if each of the subgoals can be satisfied.

GraphPlan attempts to limit the search time by identifying mutual exclusion (mutex) relations. An action may be mutex with one or more other actions and a proposition may be mutex with one or more other propositions. There are two ways in which actions act_1 and act_2 at a given action level can be marked as mutually exclusive:

1   **Interference**: if either action deletes a precondition or add effect of the other.
2   **Competing needs:** if there is a precondition of act_1 and a precondition of act_2 that are marked as mutually exclusive in the previous layer (i.e. act_1 is connected by a proposition node that is marked as mutex with a proposition node connecting act_2).

Two propositions, $prop_1$ and $prop_2$, at a given proposition level are marked as mutex if all ways of creating $prop_1$ are exclusive of all ways of creating $prop_2$: all of the actions in the previous level that can add $prop_1$ are marked as mutex with all of the actions that can add $prop_2$.

For example, in Figure 9.4 the no-op maintaining *robAtHome* is mutex with *walk* because *walk*

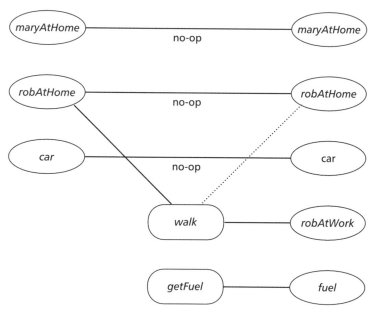

Figure 9.4 The initial propositions are placed at level 0. Any action with preconditions present at level 0 can be added to level 1. Level 2 contains the add and delete effects of the actions at level 1. Delete effects are shown with a dotted edge. A special action called a no-op is used as a maintenance action, which means that, once a proposition is added, it can appear at subsequent proposition levels.

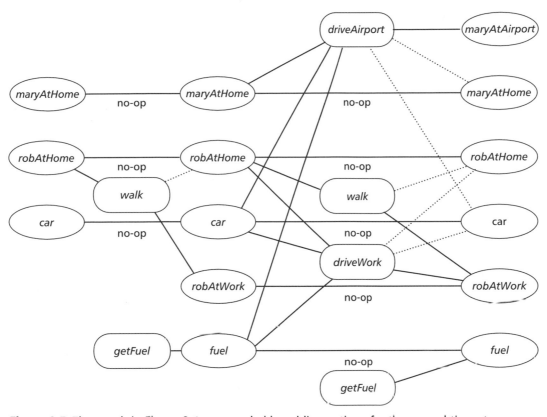

Figure 9.5 The graph in Figure 9.4 is expanded by adding actions for the second time step.

deletes *robAtHome*. Therefore, *robAtHome* and *robAtWork* are mutex at level 2 because all ways of generating *robAtHome* (the no-op) are mutually exclusive with all ways of generating *robAtWork* (walk).

In order for the search in Figure 9.5 to proceed, all goal literals need to be present at level 4 and, in addition, a subgoal must not be mutex with another subgoal. First examine the actions at level 3. The actions *driveAirport* and *driveWork* are mutually exclusive as a result of interference. They both delete *car* and they both have *car* as a precondition. The actions *driveWork* and *walk* are mutex because both delete *robAtHome*, which is a precondition for both actions. Other mutexes exist. At level 4, the subgoals *maryAtAirport* and *robAtWork* are not mutex because there are actions satisfying these goals other than the combination *driveWork* and *driveAirport*. *robAtWork* is also satisfied by the action *walk* and the no-op. Because *robAtWork* and *maryAtAirport* are both present at level 4, and they are not marked as mutex, the search can proceed.

The search works similar to the regression planner introduced earlier. The first step is to look back at level 3 and see which action combinations lead to the subgoals. There are three possible combinations for the actions at level 3 (one way of achieving *maryAtAirport* and three ways of achieving *robAtWork*).

driveAirport	maryAtAirport
driveWork	robAtWork
walk	robAtWork
no-op	robAtwork

The combinations, therefore, are:

> <driveAirport, driveWork>
> <driveAirport, walk>
> <driveAirport, no-op>

The first member of each pair relates to *Mary* and the second to *Rob*. The first combination:

> <driveAirport, driveWork>

is not allowed because they are mutually exclusive. The second combination:

> <driveAirport, walk>

will lead to a solution. The next step is to look at the preconditions of both actions. The action *driveAirport* has preconditions *{maryAtHome, car, fuel}* and *walk* has precondition *{robAtHome}*. The preconditions now form a new goal list. None of the propositions on this new goal list is marked as mutex with any other subgoal on the list. Level 1 is now inspected to find actions leading to each subgoal. There is only a single action for each of the new subgoals:

> maryAtHome   no-op
> car   no-op
> fuel   getFuel
> robAtHome   no-op

The preconditions for these actions are:

> maryAtHome   no-op   maryAtHome
> car   no-op   car
> fuel   getFuel
> robAtHome   no-op   robAtHome

Finally, we reach level 0 and all subgoals on the list are present.
    The actions traced out during the search represent the plan. The plan extracted is:

> getFuel   time step 1
> driveAirport time step 2
> walk   time step 2

Notice that at the second time step there is no order imposed on the execution of *driveAirport* or *walk*. They could be executed sequentially (either being done first) or they could be executed in parallel. Figure 9.6 shows the solution existing as a subgraph.
    The action combination:

> <driveAirport, no-op>

from level 3 will also lead to a solution with walk being executed at time 1.
    For a second example we shall consider some actions performed when gardening.

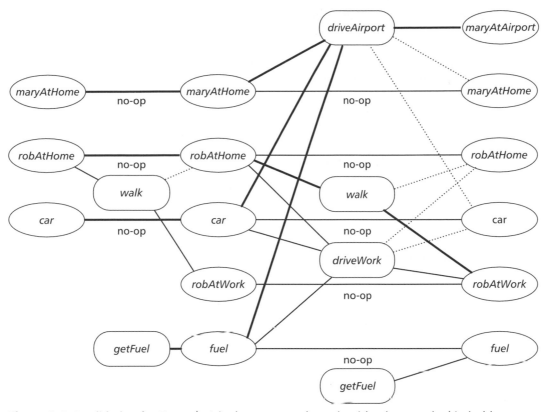

Figure 9.6 A valid plan for Example 1 is shown as a subgraph with edges marked in bold.

Example 2 • • • • •

A gardening agent has to mow the lawn, water the lawn and water the flowers. The lawn is watered using a sprinkler. The flowers can be watered using either the sprinkler or watering can. Once the sprinkler is assigned to a task it cannot be assigned to another task for the purpose of this planning exercise: we think of the sprinkler as being assigned a single task for the duration of the gardening exercise.

For convenience, the propositions and actions are given in abbreviated form with explanations below.

availSprk	sprinkler is available
longLawn	lawn is long
dryLawn	lawn is dry
dryFlowers	flowers are dry
mowLawn	mow the lawn
sprkLawn	water the lawn using the sprinkler
sprkFlwrs	water the flowers using the sprinkler
wcanFlwrs	water the flowers with a watering can
wetLawn	the lawn is wet

wetFlowers   the flowers are wet
shortLawn   the lawn is short

```
mowLawn{
        precon: dryLawn, longLawn
        add: shortLawn
        delete: longLawn
}
sprkLawn{
        precon: availSprk, dryLawn
        add: wetLawn
        delete: availSprk, dryLawn
}
sprkFlwrs{
        precon: availSprk, dryFlowers
        add: wetFlowers
        delete: availSprk, dryFlowers
}
wcanFlwrs{
        precon: dryFlowers
        add: wetFlowers
        delete: dryFlowers
}
```

The initial conditions and goal are:

initial propositions: availSprk, longLawn, dryLawn, dryFlowers
goal list: shortLawn, wetLawn, wetFlowers

The goal list is not satisfied by the initial conditions and so the graph is expanded as shown in Figure 9.7. The propositions in the goal list are all present at level 2 in the graph. However, a solution does not exist because of mutexes. The propositions *shortLawn* and *wetLawn* are mutex because the actions satisfying these propositions (*mowLawn* and *sprkLawn*) are mutex. Mowing the lawn requires the lawn to be dry and so watering the lawn using the sprinkler will cause a conflict.

The graph is expanded for another time step as shown in Figure 9.8. If the graph needs to be expanded because no solution exists at the current level, then for a solution to exist at a later level it must be possible to relieve mutexes on the goal list. Graph expansion can provide more options for achieving a subgoal and therefore reduces the chance of pairwise mutual exclusive relations on the goal list. For instance, *shortLawn* and *wetLawn* are mutex at time 1 (level 2) but not at time 2: at time 2 the no-op for *shortLawn* is not mutex with *sprkLawn*.

At the second time step, there are no pairwise mutually exclusive relations between the goal propositions. Time 2 (level 4) has the necessary conditions for a solution to exist, but a search needs to be performed using backward chaining to see if a plan can be constructed. As before, the first step is to inspect the actions that have the goal propositions as add effects. There will usually be a number of combinations for action selection (e.g. the flowers can be watered in one of two ways in addition to the no-op). The preconditions of the selected action set then form a new goal list. These preconditions appear at level 2. Level 1 actions that have the new goal list as add effects are then inspected and the process continues.

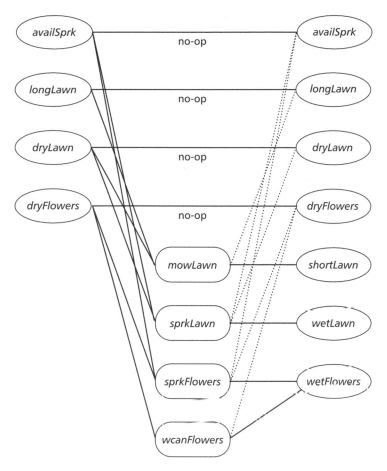

Figure 9.7 The first three levels for Example 2 are shown. All actions have preconditions present at level 0 and so all actions are candidates for execution.

9.4.1 GraphPlan algorithm in summary

GraphPlan is split into two phases: graph expansion and search. If GraphPlan fails to extract a solution during search, then the graph is expanded by another time step.

Expansion

Expansion is straightforward. Insert an action at time t if none of the propositions in its precondition is marked as mutex in the previous level; this saves unnecessary growth of the graph. Connect the actions by edges to the associated propositions in the precondition list. Insert all of the no-op actions. Finally, make a list of all the actions that are mutex.

Add the proposition level for time $t + 1$ by inserting all of the add and delete effects for each of the actions in the previous level. Add edges from an action to its effects. Make a list of propositions that are mutex.

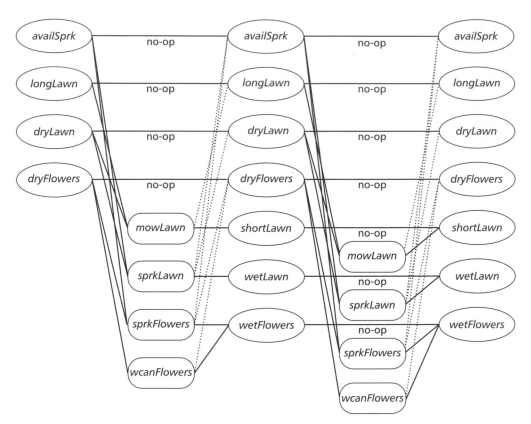

Figure 9.8 Example 2 after expansion of the second time step.

Search

For a search to commence at any time step, each of the subgoals must exist in the proposition level and there should be no mutex relations between the subgoals.

Search follows a backward-chaining strategy level by level. If all of the goals exist at level i and time t, and none of the goals is marked as mutex, then for each goal GraphPlan looks for an action at level $i-1$ that contains the goal in its add list. If each goal can be satisfied by an action at $i-1$, GraphPlan creates a new goal list for time $t-1$ which contains all of the preconditions for the selected actions. The search continues in this way until the initial proposition level is reached. If the search should fail at any level then an attempt is made to backtrack. In order to backtrack, the search has to maintain a list at each step of all of the actions that can satisfy a proposition. For instance, at level 4 in Figure 9.8, the proposition *wetFlowers* can be achieved via a no-op action or *sprkFlowers* or *wcanFlowers*. If the no-op is tried first, *wcanFlowers* provides a backtrack point and, if this should fail, then *sprkFlowers* provides another backtrack point. Backtracking allows GraphPlan to exhaustively try all of the different paths (if it needs to) to ensure that no solution is missed.

9.4.2   Some further points regarding GraphPlan

Simple method for optimizing the search time

There is a simple technique for optimizing GraphPlan that for some problems can significantly reduce the time it takes to find a plan. The technique is called **memoization**. It consists of recording sets of subgoals that fail to yield a solution at some level. Suppose that at some time, t, we are trying to find a solution that satisfies the subgoals {F, G, H}. If the search fails on the set of goals then GraphPlan records the set. If at some later time the same set of subgoals appears at level t, then the search can backtrack immediately.

How do we detect if a plan does not exist?

If GraphPlan cannot find a plan by searching back from the highest level, it expands the graph to the next level. We need some way of determining if a plan does not exist, otherwise we keep on expanding the graph until we run out of space (computer memory) or we get tired of waiting and assume that a solution does not exist.

   If a proposition appears at some level then because of the no-op actions it will also appear at all future levels. As there are a finite number of actions and these contain a finite number of effects, there will be some level from where all future levels contain the same set of propositions: so expanding the graph to the next level gives the same set of propositions. Also, owing to the no-op actions, if two propositions in some level are not marked as mutex they will not be marked as mutex in any subsequent level. So there will exist some level, L, after which all subsequent levels contain exactly the same set of mutex relations as L. Once we reach a stage where levels L and $L+1$ are identical, we say that the graph has **levelled off**. If L is the first level at which the graph has levelled off, then no solution exists if either:

*   a subgoal does not appear in this level, or
*   two subgoals are marked as mutex.

   The failure of this simple test does not guarantee the existence of a plan and therefore the graph will have to be searched. In this event, the technique of memoization is used to provide the test. Let S_i^t denote the collection of all unsolvable goal sets at level i after an unsuccessful stage at time t. If a plan is achievable at time t, then one of the goal sets in S_i^t must be true, but if no solution exists then none of the goal sets in S_i^t is achievable. No plan exists if, having levelled off, the number of goal sets in S_i^{t-1} is the same as the number of goal sets in S_i^t (i.e. $|S_i^{t-1}| = |S_i^t|$).

The frame problem

After an action is executed, the world changes state according to the action's effect. In the case of large problems, the effect of an action is usually to change the world in some small way, with most parts of the world remaining in the state they were before the action was executed. For instance, if for the blocks world in Figure 9.1 we perform the action *move(c, a, fl)*, much of the state description stays the same in that a is still on the floor and b is still on the floor and b is still clear. An action's effect does not describe those aspects of the world that remain the same after that action is executed. Frame axioms could be used to describe what stays the same if an action is executed. So we could add a frame axiom for the action move which would state that, if a block X is on a second block Y before a move action, then X is still on Y after the move action if that action did not remove X from

(a)

State – a structure that records a goal (proposition) and an action that can generate the goal
Open – global list structure that stores objects of type State
Backup – global list structure that stores backup states

PROCEDURE **GraphPlan**(iProps[], Goals[], Ops[]) returns a plan – Open contains the actions
   iProps – initial propositions at level 0
   Goals[] – list of goals
   Ops[] – list of operators
   int j ← 0 current level

   while Search(Goals, j) fails AND graph not levelled off
     expand graph
     empty Open and Backup
   end while

(b)

PROCEDURE **GetAction**(G, j) returns either success if there is an Action that can generate G from level j-1 otherwise fail

   G – is goal to be generated by an action at level j - 1
   Boolean openAdded ← false
   Action A ← null
   foreach action A at level j – 1 that has G as effect
     if G is mutex with any states on Open
         continue
     end if
     if A is first action found
         create a State S holding pair A, G
         add S to Open
         openAdded ← true
     end if
     else
         create a State S holding pair A, G
         add S to Backup
     end else
   end foreach
   return openAdded

(c)

PROCEDURE **BackUp**(j) returns success or fail
   keep popping Open until the next goal in State S on Open matches the next goal in State Sb on Backup and the goal is at level j
   if no match found
      return fail
   end if
   else
     return success
   end else

(d)

```
PROCEDURE Search(goals[], j) returns success or fail

    goals[] – list of goals for level j
    j is the current level
    A – action node
    nextGoals[] – list of goals generated from level j – 2

    if level = 0
            if each member of goals is in level 0
                    return success
            end if
            else
                    return fail
            end else
    end if

    forever
        foreach goal G in goals
            if G is contained in a state S on Open
                    A ← action from S that generated G in level j - 1
                    add each precondition connecting to A at level j – 2 to nextGoals
            end if
            else if GetAction(G) is successful
                    State S ← next state on Open
                    A ← action from S that generated G in level j - 1
                    add each precondition connecting to A at level j – 2 to nextGoals
            end else if
            else
                    try BackUp(level)
                    if backup fails
                            return fail
                    end if
            end else
        end foreach

        Search(next_goals, j – 1)
        if  Search fails
            try BackUp(level)
            if backup fails
                    return fail
            end if
        end if
        else
            return true
        end else
    end forever
```

Figure 9.9 (a) GraphPlan attempts to find a plan and, if it exists, the action sequence will be contained on Open. Memoizing has been ignored. (b) GetAction finds all actions, if any, that are capable of generating G. The actions must all be at level $j-1$ as G is at j. The algorithm checks for mutexes. (c) BackUp attempts to find an alternative starting point when the search fails. (d) Search attempts to find a path through the graph that satisfies the goals. The search is recursive and if successful the last call will contain goals that are found in level 0.

Y. For large problems the number of frame axioms can be enormous, and the problem of representing the way in which the world stays the same is called the **frame problem**.

GraphPlan's solution to the frame problem is no-op actions. Any proposition that exists at level i will also exist at level $i + 1$. So anything that is true at a certain level can potentially be true at the next level.

Summary

A plan is a sequence of actions that is generated to satisfy some specified goal. The goal is modelled by specifying the desired state of the world.

Many planners describe actions using STRIPS-style operators. These operators describe the preconditions that must be satisfied in order for the action to be executed and they describe the effects the action produces when successfully executed.

GraphPlan is an efficient algorithm that uses STRIPS-style operators. An algorithm for GraphPlan is given in Figure 9.9.

Further reading

Early work on planning is seen in Newell and Simon's (1961) general problem solver (GPS) and STRIPS (Fikes and Nilsson, 1971; Fikes 1993). Waldinger (1975) introduced goal regression planning.

Weld (1998) discusses GraphPlan and some further issues regarding propositional planners such as GraphPlan. There have been a number of extensions to GraphPlan. Some of these extensions apply SAT methods (Kautz and Selman, 1992, 1996).

Exercises

1   For the blocks world in Figure 9.1:

        move(X, Y, Z){
                precondition: on(X, Y) $\wedge$ clear(X) $\wedge$ clear(Z)
                add: on(X, Z) $\wedge$ clear(Y)
                delete: clear(Z) $\wedge$ on(X, Y)
        }

    a   How many instantiations of the move operator are there?
    b   How many instantiations would there be if a fourth block were added?
    c   Add a constraint to the above operator such that a block cannot be moved onto itself.

2   Show the steps performed in regression planning when searching for a solution to the block stacking problem. Take the initial state to be that in Figure 9.1 and the goal state to be {on(C, floor), on (A, C), on(B, A), clear(B)}.

3   Suppose that a robot arm is to do the block stacking. The arm has a gripper that can perform two operations: *grasp* an object and *release* an object. The gripper can only handle one block at a time. Write suitable operators for grasp and release.

4   When Greg gets up in the morning he always cleans the kitchen floor using either a cloth or a mop, has a bath and makes breakfast. The operators for these actions are shown below. Sketch out a graph expansion following GraphPlan's procedure and extract a solution. The initial state is hot_water and clean_hands. The goal state is clean_floor, clean and breakfast_ready.

Mop
      Precondition:hot_water
      Add: clean_floor
      Delete:

Breakfast
      Precondition: clean_hands
      Add: breakfast_ready
      Delete:

Cloth
      Precondition:hot_water
      Add: clean_floor,
      Delete: clean_hands

Bath
      Precondition:hot_water
      Add: clean_hands,
      clean
      Delete:hot_water

5   Implement a program that will do the expansion phase in GraphPlan. Use the expansion to find a solution to the blocks world problem (you can perform the search by inspecting the graph).

6   Write a move operator for the towers of Hanoi problem (see Chapter 3, exercise 2).

CHAPTER 10

Planning II

Chapter 9 introduced the basics of planning and presented a fast planning algorithm called GraphPlan. Many issues that challenge real-world applications of planning were ignored. Activities require resources in order to be executed, and they also take time to complete. Real-world planning applications will usually have to conform to scheduling constraints that must consider the timeliness of plan completion and the execution of activities within resource limitations. For example, a company that builds houses needs to consider the availability of different tradesmen at different phases of the build, the availability of building materials and the timely completion of construction to sell when market conditions are favourable.

Activities are executed at some particular point in time, and many things can affect the state of the world at that time. There is therefore a need to handle the uncertainties associated with action outcomes.

This chapter presents some of the possible approaches to tackling issues that arise with real-world applications. No attempt is made to present complete solutions for tackling particular types of planning problems. Instead, the aim is to give an appreciation of issues that have to be addressed by any deployed system (i.e. a system that is used regularly to solve real planning problems).

Section 10.1 explores the need for more expressive operators than the simple STRIPS style of operator introduced in Chapter 9. Section 10.2 discusses the modelling of uncertainty. Bayesian techniques (see Chapters 5 and 6) can be employed but, as these have been discussed elsewhere, we concentrate more on a discussion of Markov models. The interested reader should also consult Chapter 14, in which techniques for finding optimal sequences of actions under Markov assumptions are introduced. Finally, knowledge-based planning is introduced. Knowledge-based planners seek to constrain the search space by explicitly representing domain-specific knowledge. The hierarchical task network is a widely used knowledge-based approach that has been adopted in a number of planning systems.

10.1 Expressive representation

When we introduced first-order logic we saw the advantages that the introduction of variables and quantifiers offers over simple propositions consisting of ground literals. The operators used in the last chapter were simple descriptions that were conjunctions of literals. A number of different languages have been proposed for expressing planning operators. They all vary in detail but have in common the ability to represent parameters, quantifiers and **conditional** effects. Conditional effects allow for the effect of an action to be context dependent. For example, a dishwasher is used to wash plates, cutlery, glasses, etc., but it is only those objects that are in the machine that get washed. The effect, *clean*, is conditioned on the object being in the machine. A conditional effect is represented using a when clause that has an antecedent and consequent. For example:

when (in(X), clean(X))

has an antecedent *in(X)* and consequence *clean(X)*. So if the operator *wash* is executed and X is in the machine, the effect of washing is that X will be clean.

A well-known example for illustrating the need for an expressive operator language is the briefcase domain. The briefcase operator *move* could have the following representation:

```
operator move-briefcase{
        parameters: LOCATION l₁, l₂
        preconditions: at(briefcase, l₁)
        effects:
            ADD: at(briefcase, l₂)
            DEL: at(briefcase, l₁)
        conditions:
            forAll X: when(in(X, briefcase), ADD(at(X, l₂), DEL(X, l₁)))

}
```

ADD is used to denote add effects and DEL to denote delete effects. The operator has two parameters, l_1 and l_2, which are of type LOCATION. We could specify a domain for LOCATION such as:

DOM LOCATION: {home, office, car}

which then restricts l_1 and l_2 to one of these instances. The precondition states that the briefcase is at LOCATION l_1 before being moved. The effect of the move action is to relocate the briefcase to l_2. The conditional effects state that all objects in the briefcase will also be relocated. A ground instance of the operator for when a pen and letter are in the briefcase might be:

```
operator move-bricfcase{
        parameters: l₁=home, l₂=office
        preconditions: at(briefcase, home)
        effects:
            ADD: at(briefcase, office)
            DEL: at(briefcase, home)
        conditions:
            (when(in(pen, briefcase), ADD(at(pen, office), DEL(pen, home))),
            when(in(letter, briefcase), ADD(at(letter, office), DEL(letter, home))))

}
```

It does not take much imagination to see that quantifiers and conditional effects are necessary to express operators that act in real-world domains. A planner can handle such operators by simple expansion. The universal quantifier, *forAll X*, can be replaced by the conjunction of all instances from the domain of type X. This has been done in the above example with a pen and letter. The conditional effects can then be rewritten into the more conventional STRIPS-style notation that contains only preconditions along with add and delete effects. A full expansion will rewrite the operator into a set of mutually exclusive operators by taking into account all of the combinations in the antecedents of the conditional effects. For example, the briefcase move operator would be rewritten into four operators:

```
operator move-briefcase{
        parameters: l₁=home, l₂=office
        preconditions: at(briefcase, home)
        effects:
            ADD: at(briefcase, office)
            DEL: at(briefcase, home)
}

operator move-briefcase{
        parameters: l₁=home, l₂=office
        preconditions: at(briefcase, home), in(pen, briefcase)
        effects:
            ADD: at(briefcase, office), at(pen, office)
            DEL: at(briefcase, home), at(pen, home)
}

operator move-briefcase{
        parameters: l₁=home, l₂=office
        preconditions: at(briefcase, home), in(letter, briefcase)
        effects:
            ADD: at(briefcase, office), at(letter, office)
            DEL: at(briefcase, home), at(letter, home)
}

operator move-briefcase{
        parameters: l₁=home, l₂=office
        preconditions: at(briefcase, home), in(pen, briefcase), in(letter, briefcase)
        effects:
            ADD: at(briefcase, office), at(pen, office), at(letter, office)
            DEL: at(briefcase, home), at(pen, home), at(letter, home)
}
```

The briefcase appears in all the conditional effects because it is the primary object being moved. Anything in the briefcase will also be moved and the options are for nothing to be in the case, the pen only, the letter only, or the pen and letter.

The problem with this full expansion is that it leads to a rapid explosion in the number of combinations. If three objects could be in the case, the expansion would produce eight operators. Furthermore, the antecedents in conditional effects may contain a conjunction of literals, and the more conjuncts the higher the number of operators in the expansion. The full expansion can lead to rapid explosion in the size of the search space the planner has to work with. One approach to reducing the size of the potential search space is **factored** expansion. Anderson *et al.* (1998a) define factored expansion in the GraphPlan framework. Their approach improves performance, but the price is added complexity. Their approach is to consider the conditional effects to be primitive elements in the graph. An operator is considered to be made up of one or more components with one component per effect. The antecedent of a component is the operator's primary precondition conjoined with the antecedent of the conditional effect. The consequent of the component is the consequent of the effect. For example:

```
operator A{
        preconditions:p
        effects:
            ADD e
        conditionals
            (when(q, ADD(f), DEL(g)),
            when((r, s), DEL(q)))
}
```

This operator would generate three components, one for the unconditional effects and one for each conditional effect:

```
component C1{
        antecedent: p
        consequent: e
}
```

```
component C2{
        antecedent: p, q
        consequent: f, ¬g
}
```

```
component C3{
        antecedent: p, r, s
        consequent: ¬q
}
```

Literals in the delete list have been expressed as negative literals. Expansion of the planning graph works in the same manner as for GraphPlan, but component instances are added instead of action instances. For example, to add *C2*, *p* and *q* would need to be present in the previous proposition level. The consequences would then be added to the subsequent proposition level. The identification of mutex relations is subtly different to GraphPlan. One difference is to ensure that no mutex constraint is generated between components from the same action when one component interferes with another component. The number of mutexes can also be increased as a result of what is called induced components. For example, *C2* is said to induce *C1* because both components come from the same action and the antecedent of *C2* (p, q) entails the antecedent of *C1* (p). In other words, if the effects of *C2* are seen, the effects of *C1* will also be seen. If a component from another action is mutex with *C1*, that component will also be mutex with *C2*. The backward chaining search is more complicated: for more details on the search the reader is referred to the paper by Anderson *et al.* (1998a).

10.2 Acting under uncertainty

Uncertainty exists in planning due to non-deterministic outcomes of actions and incomplete information. In Chapters 5 and 6, Bayesian networks to model uncertainty were introduced, and Chapter 8 introduced decision making for actions when information is incomplete and the outcome of actions uncertain. In a decision network, the possible ways of achieving a goal exist within the network model and the task is to decide on those actions that maximize a goal expressed as utility measures. The task of planning is to optimize the likelihood of achieving the goal, but the planner must first generate a sequence of actions that could potentially satisfy the goal. Decision networks and planning networks are both causal structures. The techniques used in decision networks, or more generally Bayesian networks, provide one possible approach for evaluating the likelihood of achieving a planning goal once the plan has been generated. There is no reason why this evaluation could not be invoked at the subplan level for those planning systems that use a hierarchical planning approach (see next section). Bayesian techniques have been introduced in detail in other chapters. This section therefore will concentrate on other strategies for modelling planning under uncertainty. In particular, Markov approaches are discussed. The discussion is purely conceptual, and algorithms are avoided. More is introduced on the techniques for deciding upon action sequences using Markov assumptions in Chapter 14, in which reinforcement learning is introduced.

Consider the following challenge. You are in a hotel near the Eiffel Tower in Paris. Somebody has given you a number of options for getting from your hotel in Paris to London. For example, you could take a bike to the train station and then take the Eurostar train to London. You might instead choose to take a taxi to the station. Another option is to get to the airport and then take a flight to London. A further option is to take a taxi to Calais and then take either a direct train to London or a ferry to Kent and then a train to London. There are quite a number of options in total. You do not have any experience of these options and so you are ignorant about which option to choose. However, you are told that if each mode of travel keeps to its scheduled time, you will reach London within 4 hours. Of course the actual time taken will depend on the options selected. You have been offered £10 000 if you make it to London within 4 hours. You are told that, if you fail, you will receive £10 000 less £50 for every mile you fall short. For example, the station in Kent is approximately 50 miles from London and so if you were at this station after 4 hours you get £7500. One rule is that, if you are midway between locations after 4 hours, then you will be considered as still being at your last point of departure. So, should your plane from Paris be about to land after 4 hours you would still be considered as being at the airport in Paris. In addition, each mode of transport is going to cost you money. Finally, you are given a model showing the reliability of each option along the various routes. Part of this model is shown in Figure 10.1. You want to maximize your likely return.

Each action has a probability of success. For example, going by bike from the hotel to the airport will get you there with probability 0.5. The bike fails therefore with a probability of 0.5, but it is your cheapest form of transport.

For this scenario, a deterministic planner would be capable of generating all the possible route actions given the initial state (at_hotel), the list of operator descriptions (actions such as go by bike), and the goal (at_London). To maximize the reward, it would simply calculate the cheapest route. Because it is a deterministic planner, it assumes that you will reach London with certainty within the allotted time and so the reward is assumed to be £10 000 less the cost of the transport. Thus, the cheapest route is best. This is a naive planner though. What you really require is the route that returns the maximum expected reward and expectations are determined by examining the likelihood of transiting successfully from one state to the next. The planner should return the plan that maximizes your expected return (your reward less costs). To do this, the planner has to reason with probabilities. Sometimes, playing safe is the best option. Suppose you are at the airport in Paris and you have purchased an expensive plane ticket but the flight is delayed by 2 hours. You will now fail to reach London within the time and so you will be heavily out of pocket. It might be better to play it safe and take a route that is more certain to get you much closer to London – there is less risk but profit is also likely to be less. Let's look at a similar but simpler problem.

Jamie is due to meet his grandfather in town. His dad gives him a lift to either location A or location B where Jamie can catch a bus. Jamie's dad is always a bit late and so the chance of Jamie catching the bus on time from either location is 0.9. Now location A is further from town and it is

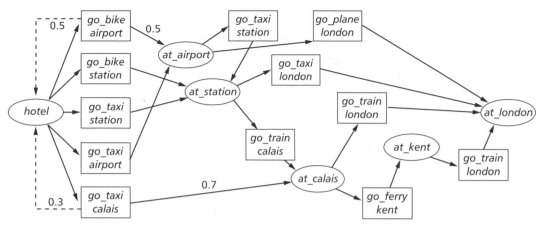

Figure 10.1 Actions are shown as square nodes and departure and destinations as circular nodes. Each edge has an associated probability that denotes the likelihood of reaching the destination within the nominated time.

less reliable, which means that Jamie only has a 50% chance of meeting his grandfather on time. Also, this route will cost Jamie £2. Location B has a higher reliability (80% chance of getting to town) but it will cost Jamie £5. Jamie's grandfather said that he will give Jamie £10 if Jamie arrives on time. Which is the best route for Jamie?

A model of Jamie's problem is given in Figure 10.2. The probability of Jamie getting to town on time by either route is simply the product of the probabilities along any path. For this problem, Jamie has to get to town in two stages, and therefore the only path probabilities that are relevant are:

via A: probability of getting to town $= 0.9 \times 0.5 = 0.45$
via B: probability of getting to town $= 0.9 \times 0.8 = 0.72$

So Jamie's expected reward will be:

via A: $0.45 \times 10 = 4.5$
via B: $0.72 \times 10 = 7.20$

From this he deducts the cost of the bus:

via A: $4.5 - 2 = 2.50$
via B: $7.2 - 5 = 2.20$

So, although route A is riskier, the values involved (costs and rewards) mean that Jamie should take route A if he wishes to maximize his expected return. If his grandfather offered a reward of £12 then route B would be a better choice (only marginally though).

Let us use the same underlying model shown in Figure 10.2 but for a different type of problem. TopCars is a manufacturer of very expensive cars. It uses a high-quality paint finish that is applied by one of two paintshops that the company owns. Cars can be rejected at different stages of manufacture if they fail a quality check. The probability of a car being rejected before reaching the paintshop is low at 10%. The largest probability of rejection is after the paintshop. There are two paintshops, denoted A and B. TopCars, on average, rejects 50% of the vehicles from shop A, which

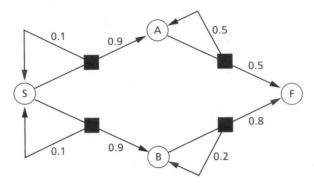

Figure 10.2 A simple model for Jamie's trip into town. His dad gives him a lift from the start S to either bus stop (A or B) from where Jamie can get to town (F).

means a car will have to be resprayed. The cost of painting is £400. Although a rare occurrence, it is not unknown for a single car to be rejected and resprayed a number of times before passing the quality check. TopCars will get another £2000 pounds for a car with the quality paint finish. Of course, if a car is resprayed five times, then it makes no money from the higher quality finish. Shop B has a lower rate of rejection at 20%. However, it is using more expensive technology and so the cost of spraying is £600.

Which shop gives the better return? The model shown in Figure 10.3 is a **Markov model**. A car starts manufacture at S and completes the process at F. Cars are evenly distributed between shops A and B. A car might pass straight from S to A then to F. On the other hand, it could start at S, return to S, return again to S, then to A, where it returns once more to A before going to F. The added return to the manufacturer of shop A or B is not dependent on what has happened previously to the car. So, the number of rejections the car has had before reaching the paint shop has no bearing on whether the car will be rejected after spraying. In other words, the next state the car is in after being sprayed (e.g. from A, the next state could be A or F), is not influenced by the previous states the car has visited. This assumption, that the next state to be predicted is dependent only on the current state, is called the Markov assumption. TopCars have a computer program for calculating the expected return on shop A or B, and the values are shown in Figure 10.3. If, however, the cost of shop A were £300, the values would be those shown in Figure 10.4.

Note that, conceptually, the model when used for Jamie is different from that for the manufacturing of the cars. Node A, for example, is simply modelling the chance of Jamie catching the bus on time. Jamie has to reach town in two stages if he is to get his reward. Jamie is not allowed repeated attempts to catch the bus. The manufacturer, on the other hand, can keep revisiting states before reaching the finish state.

The type of problem being modelled by TopCars is known as a **Markov decision process** (MDP). So what is the interest in MDPs for planning? In the case of real-world planning problems, there will be uncertainty in the outcome of performing actions. For some problems it might be acceptable to ignore the uncertainties and treat the domain as being deterministic (i.e. the outcome of performing an action will always be known). Many applications will require the uncertainty in the outcome of actions to be modelled. Also, in real-world planning applications there will be numeric quantities involved, such as costs, resource measures, etc. There is, therefore, commonality in the issues that are typically modelled using planning or MDPs.

Our manufacturing scenario is simple, but things quickly become more complicated when there are many states and many choices of action. The solution to the manufacturing model resulted in

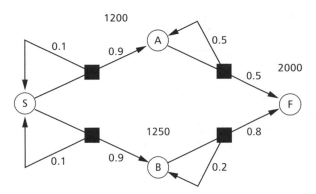

Figure 10.3 A Markov model showing the route a car might take during manufacture. A car starts manufacture at S and completes at F. The only stage of manufacture shown is the final step, when a high-quality paint finish is applied at one of two paintshops (A or B). Shop A costs £400 for a respray and shop B costs £600. Shop B has newer technology and there is less chance of rejection (20%) that would result in a respray. The added value of the high-quality finish is £2000 less the cost of spraying. The expected return for a car being sprayed via shop A is £1200 and via shop B is £1250.

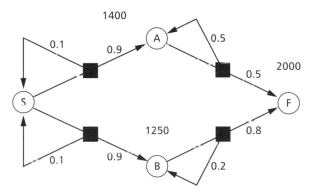

Figure 10.4 The utility values for paintshops A and B, where the cost now for paintshop A is £300.

values being assigned to each state (we ignored the start). A value indicates how promising that state is for reaching the goal. So, if you were to make a choice between paintshop A or B, then Figure 10.3 indicates that it is best to go to paintshop B. Why not shut down paintshop A? Because paintshop A may be required to satisfy other constraints, such as the total number of vehicles that need to be produced per month.

For each state in a Markov model, the solution specifies a value. From a given state, there will usually be a number of choices for which state to visit next. The best choice is the state (which can be reached from the current state) with the highest value. Mapping out a sequence of such choices will define a route through the Markov network. A route is more usually called a **policy**. One technique for finding these values is a simple algorithm called value iteration, which is introduced in Chapter 14.

The Markov and planning approaches are traditionally somewhat different in appearance.

Planning algorithms use structured descriptions for operators and the initial state to generate a description of how things will change. Each change (generated state) is inspected to see if a component of the goal state appears. In other words, a planner will predict new states in its process of searching for a solution, but it does not necessarily have to generate every possible state because it can terminate once it can satisfy the goal. The Markov model, on the other hand, examines every possible action that can occur in every possible state. The goal in a Markov model is expressed as a utility value, whereas a planner may use a logical description. Planners structure the problem, and this structuring is important to reduce the size of the search space. One avenue of current research is to define approaches that utilize more traditional planning approaches with MDPs. We shall refer to some of this work at the end of this chapter.

10.2.1 Partial observations

We have thus far discussed the uncertainty associated with the outcome of an action. There can also be uncertainty associated with the current state. Observations are made to determine the current state. For example, if you were on a walking expedition you might need to fix your current position. If you are on a hill overlooking a village that has a church you might be able to locate your position with a high degree of confidence. If it is misty you might only be able to make a partial observation. You have a railway line nearby and to the north is a low-lying wooded area. If you are where you believe you are, then the village is to the north-east but it is hidden by the mist. This time, your belief is lower. In fact, you may believe that you are in one of three possible locations. The Markov assumption states that the history of where you have walked that day is not relevant to deciding what decision you make next (perhaps the direction you take). Remember that the Markov assumption states that the next state is determined only by the current state and not the history of states. This is really accepting that you have taken several fixes to identify locations along the route and, once you have a fix, you need not remember the previous ones. In other words, you can forget where you have come from; the only thing that matters is where you currently are. You could argue that you wish to keep the history of locations so that you can reason as to what mistakes you have made along the way, and this could be used to update your current belief. The further back you go, the harder it will be to reason forward and estimate where you currently are because of the numerous options that would develop. With the partially observable Markov model you could specify a number of probabilities that express your current belief. Each probability would be your belief in a different location (state). These probabilities would sum to 1.

Partial observation refers to uncertainty in what the current state is. This uncertainty arises from the limitation of sensors. For instance, your ability to sense is impaired when there is mist in the valley. A robot's sensors will constrain what it perceives, and there may be things in the environment that cause confusion.

Suppose you visit your doctor with a skin rash that has been irritating you. The doctor thinks she knows what it could be but says that it could be one of three things. She has to prescribe some medication, but it is a difficult choice. If her diagnostic hunch is incorrect she could make the rash worse by prescribing inappropriate medication. The goal the patient seeks is a cure for the rash. Any improvement, however, is desirable. It would seem appropriate then to attach a value for a cure that denotes a reward. This value might be derived by asking the patient how much he or she would be willing to pay for a complete cure. The problem facing the doctor could then be modelled using a **partially observable Markov decision process** (POMDP). Unlike an MDP, a POMDP will have several values specified for a state.

To make the concept of POMDPs a little easier to grasp, consider the situation where the patient's disease has been identified but there is uncertainty as to the stage of the disease (how far it has progressed). Figure 10.5 shows the two ends of the spectrum, at one end of which the disease is advanced and at the other there is no disease. A number of discrete states are labelled between the two extremities. Two actions are shown, which relate to two different forms of treatment. If the medical team believes the disease to be more advanced than it actually is, the prescribed treatment could be too strong and may make the patient's overall condition worse. If, on the other hand, the medical team underestimates how advanced the disease is, the treatment prescribed may not be powerful enough. To recap, the medical staff do not have a complete observation of the patient's condition. They make the best assessment of the patient's condition that they can but are still left in some doubt as to the true state of the patient. The treatment (action) can have a variable effect even if the true state of the patient is known. There will be uncertainty as to what the patient's response to the treatment will be; in other words, the prognosis is not clear. After treatment, when the patient is re-examined, there may still be uncertainty as to the stage of the disease.

When a state could be completely determined, and there was uncertainty only with regard to actions, each state was described by a single value that represented the reward (or desirability) of a state – this is the MDP model. For the partial observation model, POMDP, because the actual state is uncertain, there will be a vector of values involved. For example, let there be two states, s_1 and s_2, and two actions, a_1 and a_2. Action a_1 has a value of 2 if executed when in state s_1 but 0 if executed in state s_2. Action a_2 has a value of 0 if executed in s_1 but a value of 1.25 if executed in state s_2. The belief in the current situation is [0.7, 0.3] (70% s_1, 30% s_2). The action values are:

$$a_1: (0.7 \times 2) + (0.3 \times 0) = 1.4$$
$$a_2: (0.7 \times 0) + (0.3 \times 1.25) = 0.375$$

Action a_1 is the preferred choice. As with MDPS, algorithms for solving POMDPs use value iteration, but the computations are more complex and are beyond the scope of this book. References will be given at the end of the chapter.

There are situations where you may be uncertain as to the initial state but successive states can be predicted on the basis of the order in which actions are executed. A planner for this type of scenario examines all possible combinations of initial states and all possible eventualities. By examining all paths, it might still be possible to achieve the goal even though there is uncertainty in the initial state. One planner that handles such situations is Sensory GraphPlan (SGP), an extension of GraphPlan. To describe SGP, a simple example is provided by Weld *et al.* (1998). They consider the action of taking medicine when it is not known for sure whether a patient is infected (denoted

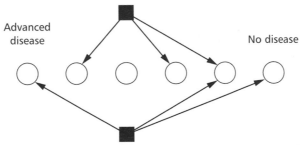

Advanced disease

No disease

Figure 10.5 The current state is uncertain and there are two actions (possible treatments), represented as solid rectangles. The circular nodes represent discrete states including the extremeties of advanced disease and no disease. In a partially observable Markov model there will be a distribution of propbabilities describing the belief in the existing state. For each action and each state there will be utility values describing the desirability of the expected outcome for executing the action.

by *I*) or hydrated (denoted by *H*). The wrong action can result in death (*D*). If a patient is infected before taking the medication then the effect will be that he or she is no longer infected ($\neg I$). If the patient takes medication when not hydrated ($\neg H$) the result is death. The model can be described by a single action, *Medicate,* that has conditional effects.

```
Medicate{
        preconditions:
        effect:      (when I ¬I)
                     (when ¬H D)
}
```

This operator can be expanded into four disjoint operators:

```
Med1{
        preconditions: I, H
        effect: ¬I
}
Med2
        preconditions: I, ¬H
        effect: ¬I, D
}
Med3
        preconditions: ¬I, H
        effect:
}
Med4{
        preconditions: ¬I, ¬H
        effect:D
  }
```

The example considers two possible worlds (PWs): the initial state is one of two combinations.

```
w1 = {¬I, ¬H, ¬D}
w2 = {I, H, ¬D}
```

So the patient is alive, and is either not infected and not hydrated or infected and hydrated. The goal is to get the patient uninfected and not dead ($\neg I$, $\neg D$). There is one other action:

```
Drink{
        preconditions:
        effect: H
}
```

The best plan is to drink first and then to medicate because the plan satisfies the goal given either possible world.

SGP considers each possible world in turn. When an action is performed, the effect of the action has to be examined in all possible worlds and not just the world in which the action is executed. This is necessary because SGP does not know which world it is actually in and therefore must consider the effect an action might have if it were to be in one of the other worlds.

10.3   Planners that use knowledge-based methods

The **hierarchical task network** (HTN) is the most widely studied of the knowledge-based approaches to planning. HTNs have an expressive formalism that models activities with durations, activities that must be completed by certain deadlines and metric quantities. Metric quantities are often required to represent resource constraints. Suppose, for example, that you have to transport a party of 20 people from a business meeting to a hotel. A single minibus might do the job but, alternatively, a number of cars of different carrying capacity could collectively do the job.

In the last chapter, the planning techniques used STRIPS-style descriptions of primitive actions. This style of description contains knowledge, but the level of knowledge is primitive. Knowledge-based planners use domain-specific knowledge, and because the representation is knowledge rich the search for a plan is constrained and the size of the search space is therefore considerably reduced. There are different types of constraint that can be specified. A simple example is an ordering constraint on some of the activities. A further example is specifying an earliest start time for an activity.

In HTNs, activities are more commonly referred to as **tasks**. A task can be composed of other tasks, which in turn could also be compositional. At some point, the decomposition of a task will result in a collection of **primitive tasks**. A primitive task is a task that can be directly executed. The task *build-house* is composed of many other tasks, such as *excavate*, *lay-foundations*, *erect-frame*, *install-services*. A task such as *install-services* can be further decomposed into tasks, e.g. *install-plumbing*, *install-gas* and *install-electricity*. What constitutes a primitive task depends upon the agent that has to execute the task. The primitive task for a robot might be *join_pipe(X, Y)*, whereas a human agent could operate at a higher level of abstraction, such as *install-bathroom-suite*.

The structure used to describe tasks will have preconditions and effects specified. The structure will also be parameterized so that any object of a specified type can be referenced. Parameters are variables that are associated with a type. A parameter might be a simple type, e.g. an integer number, or a more complex type, e.g. an object (e.g. of type building material or, at a lower level, of type brick). A task may have temporal constraints attached. Real-world projects need to be scheduled, and so it is often necessary to specify an earliest start date and latest finish date for a task. Other temporal descriptions might be used to specify minimum duration for a task or that a subsequent task starts within a certain time window. For example, there is no point in boiling a kettle to make tea and then waiting for 10 minutes before pouring the water into the teapot. Order constraints might also be listed.

Plans are represented by networks. Nodes denote tasks and edges are used to convey the ordering of tasks. Part of the task decomposition for building a house is shown in Figure 10.6. There will be ordering constraints on the activities. For instance, heating cannot be installed before the basic plumbing and gas have been installed.

Another network showing some of the tasks to be performed in painting a room is given in Figure 10.7. The presentation in Figure 10.7 is a little more detailed than that given in Figure 10.6: the vertical arrows show the subtasks to be performed and the horizontal arrows show ordering constraints. Figure 10.8 is given merely to illustrate the hierarchical structuring.

Painting a room requires resources. There needs to be enough paint of the correct colours, instruments to apply the paint and at least one person available for painting. If the job has to be done in a certain time, then two or three people may be required. Other types of constraint also exist. For example, a roller can be used to apply paint to the ceiling and walls but not to the woodwork. There

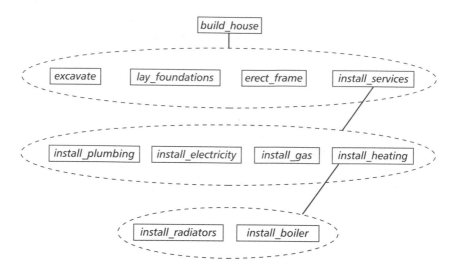

Figure 10.6 A hierarchy of some of the tasks to be performed for building a house. HTNs allow a user to interact with a planning system at various levels of abstraction which can be important for understanding and spotting any interactions between activities that might violate constraints (e.g. the completion of a task).

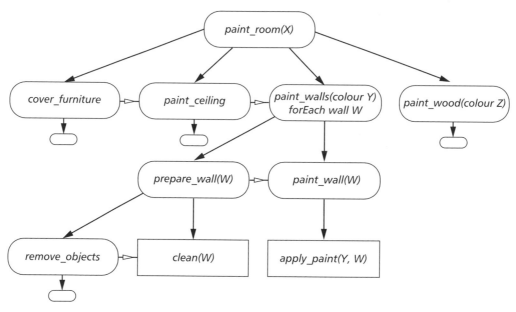

Figure 10.7 A subset of tasks to be performed when painting a room. The vertical directed arrows show the subtasks to be performed and the horizontal arrows show ordering constraints.

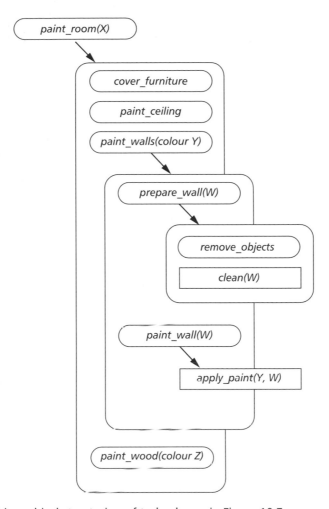

Figure 10.8 The hierarchical structuring of tasks shown in Figure 10.7.

are also ordering constraints. The ceiling is to be painted first and the walls need to be prepared before painting. Part of this preparation requires removing objects such as pictures and cabinets, for which other types of instrument are required.

10.3.1   A generic description of HTN planners

HTN refers to a generic class of planners and there is no singly adopted language for describing plan tasks or specified set of algorithms for searching. However, a general framework for HTN planners can be identified.

In simple terms, a plan is produced by iteratively decomposing tasks until only primitive tasks remain. Goals are specified as tasks. For example, the goal *build_house* will correspond to a task, and this task will be composed of other tasks, all of which need to be completed. Decomposing a task into subtasks has the effect of expanding the plan. During expansion, more detail is being revealed. Part of this detail will include constraints such as the timing of activities or resources. Conflicts can arise. For example, a limited resource might be required for more than one task. At certain points during the expansion, a search will be made to check for any conflicts. This task is assigned to

critics. A critic will be responsible for identifying a particular type of conflict and suggesting ways to repair the conflict. A mechanical digger, for example, might be used to excavate in preparation for laying the foundations. It could also be used for demolition work on another part of the building site. If there is only one digger available, and the two tasks overlap, a critic should identify that the two tasks are in conflict. The critic could then suggest a method of repair by ordering the tasks one after the other.

There may be a number of ways of achieving a task, and each way is called a **method**. For example, painting the walls might have several methods available that specify different numbers of painters, use of different instruments (e.g. spray, brush, roller) and duration. This is where we can see knowledge playing more of a direct role in pruning the search. Suppose that the task *painting the walls* is a subnetwork within a larger planning task network and that the painting has a time duration constraint. The planner need consider only those methods that have an acceptable estimated duration. Consider another example. If you wish to go from London to Aberdeen you might have three methods: *by_car*, *by_train*, *by_aircraft*. The method *by_aircraft* might have the tasks:

        make_reservation
        go_airport
        collect_ticket
        fly(X, Y)

Suppose the task *by_aircraft* has been expanded to satisfy the task of getting from London to Aberdeen. If the flight has to arrive 1 hour before a meeting commences, and yet the scheduling of the meeting is subsequent to addition of the flight task, then the flight arrival might be in conflict with the scheduled meeting. On identifying that the flight arrival is in conflict with the start of the meeting, a number of options might be tried. If the *go(London, Aberdeen)* activity is part of a larger plan network then it might be possible to move the activity allowing our passenger to get an earlier flight. Another option is to try an alternative method such as *by_train* (the train may depart earlier and the destination station may be closer to the venue for the meeting).

HTNs usually produce **partially ordered** plans. A partially ordered plan does not commit to the ordering of actions unless it needs to. For example, a waiter has to take a food order before the chef can cook the food and so the actions *take_order* and *cook_food* are ordered, but the customer can be seated either before the order is taken or after. This leads to a number of possible orderings for executing actions:

1   take_order, seat_customer, cook_food, or
2   seat_customer, take_order, cook_food,
3   take_order, cook_food, seat_customer.

A generic procedure for HTN planning is given in Figure 10.9 (this is adapted from Erol *et al.*, 1994). The implementation of different HTN planners will vary considerably in practice. There are many approaches, and commercial organizations that produce planning systems always guard to some extent their intellectual property. However, the steps shown in Figure 10.9 are an abstraction of those that are common to most HTN planners.

One further issue needs to be addressed by planners used for real-world applications. Plans are produced under assumptions concerning the state of the world at future points in time when actions will be executed. Once the execution of a plan has started it is typical for unexpected events to occur. For example, when constructing a collection of houses a large percentage of the workforce may be plagued by some virus and therefore unavailable to work. The virus might impact on the

```
HTNPLANNER
        P: initialised with one or more goal tasks
        while P contains nonprimitive tasks
                select a task T contained in P
                choose a method to expand T
                replace T with expansion of T
                if critic to be applied this step
                        use critic to find conflicts
                        repair conflicts
                        if any conflict cannot be repaired
                                return failure
                        end if
                end if
        end while
```

Figure 10.9 A generic HTN planner.

timely completion of a task. The failure of a task can then impact on other tasks if the effects of one task form the preconditions of other tasks. Planners will usually have the ability to replan. The need for replanning could also arise because the original goal has been modified. Devising a generic replanning strategy that is applicable to a number of domains is a difficult task. For example, in a house-building project replanning could occur offline. The pace of construction work usually means that the state of the world has not changed much during the time it takes to produce a new plan. In another application, replanning might have to be done in a more incremental manner. Such applications include real-time control, such as guiding a robot or space vehicle.

10.4   Discussion

Planning is a very active and growing area of research. Real-world applications are still limited, but the potential for planning solutions is huge. One active organization is NASA, which has constructed a number of planners for space missions (see Chapter 24).

There is a great deal still to be achieved. In many respects, knowledge-based planners appear to be more suited to real-world planning problems than minimal methods such as GraphPlan. This is because the representational formalism of knowledge-based planners fits more with the knowledge-rich domain of real-world applications. Different types of knowledge can be represented and the knowledge is explicit. The explicit coding of knowledge is important for human user interaction. User interaction is a requirement for many applications, especially in complex domains in which knowledge is often incomplete. The ultimate goal of many planning applications is to satisfy the requirements set by human agents, and planners operate more as assistants that suggest solutions. A user can monitor the construction of a plan and could interact to relax constraints, change the goals or suggest modifications to a plan to overcome conflicts. In other words, the user can guide the planner. Ultimately, the user is available to assist in those areas where knowledge is lacking owing to model complexity.

HTN planners are knowledge rich, but they tend to assume that knowledge is complete and that the outcomes of activities are deterministic. We have already discussed that for many problems this assumption will not hold and there needs to be a way to handle uncertainties. With human interaction it is possible for some applications to limit the impact of the lack of probabilistic reasoning in uncertain situations.

Summary

Real-world applications require a rich descriptive language to describe activities. A basic requirement is to reference objects using variables and quantifiers. Constraints on activities will need to be specified. In addition to the standard preconditions, there will usually be temporal constraints such as the latest finish time, resource constraints, and ordering constraints among activities.

The outcome of activities is rarely certain. There is still much work to be done in developing techniques for modelling uncertainty in planning. Theoretical approaches exist, e.g. Markov and Bayesian models, but their incorporation into practical planning systems is still limited.

Knowledge-based planners use domain knowledge to prune the search space. The most widely adopted knowledge-based approach appears to be the hierarchical task network (HTN). In essence, an HTN is constructed from three types of component:

1   **Goal task** describes properties that we wish to make true, such as *house_built* or *short_lawn* and *watered_flowers*.
2   **Primitive task** is a task that can be directly executed. In other words, it is an action such as moving a block, combing your hair, pouring concrete, etc.
3   **Compound task** is a task that relies on a collection of other tasks.

The plan starts with a high-level task such as *build_house*. This task is then expanded in terms of its subtasks. The expansion is a decomposition of a higher level task into lower level tasks. The decomposition continues until only primitive tasks remain. There maybe different methods for decomposing a task. The method description can contain a great deal of knowledge regarding the use of the method. This knowledge might convey ordering constraints on subtasks, resource constraints, temporal constraints, etc. During plan construction there might be conflicts caused by interactions among tasks. Critics are used to identify conflicts and will attempt to resolve the conflicts. Critics might be invoked only after several plan modifications in an attempt to save computational time.

Further reading

Several language formalisms for describing planning tasks have been proposed. The planning domain definition language (PDDL; Ghallab *et al.*, 1998) is a descendant of several other formalisms, including UCPOP (Barrett *et al.*, 1995) and ADL (Pednault, 1989). The language supports STRIPS-style actions, conditional effects, variables and quantification, types, hierarchical actions, and domain axioms. For example, the predicate *above(X, Y)* is implied by *on(X, Y)*, where X and Y are both variables of type 'physical object'. GraphPlan has been extended by Koehler *et al.* (1997) to work with ADL structures that use variables, quantifiers and conditional effects.

There are a number of extensions to GraphPlan that handle aspects of uncertainty (Anderson *et al.*, 1998a,b; Blum and Langford, 1998). Blythe (1999) provides a general overview of planning under uncertainty. Cassandra *et al.* (1994) have applied POMDPs to planning.

Two examples of planning systems that use a knowledge-rich approach are O-plan (Currie and Tate, 1991)[1] and SIPE (Wilkins, 1988, 1990). Wilkins and desJardins (2001) present the case for knowledge-based approaches to planning. Erol *et al.* (1995) provide a formalism for HTN planning and investigate the relation between HTN planning and STRIPS-style planning.

Kambhampati's (1999) tutorial provides a good overview and reference to the various approaches to planning that have emerged and the relation between the different approaches.

---

[1]More detail on O-plan is given in Chapter 24.

PART 5

Learning

This part of the book concentrates on learning. A machine or software tool would not be viewed as intelligent if it could not adapt to changes in its environment. Adaptation is also desired as experience is gained. For example, you would expect a medic's skill to develop with experience. Learning in these types of situation can be viewed as a form of self-programming. Learning is also applied to pattern recognition problems such as speech recognition and object identification. Speech recognition software learns to adapt to a speaker's voice by being informed of words it has incorrectly perceived. A growing role for learning is in data mining products that are utilized to search for hidden patterns in large databases. A credit card company might use such a tool to analyse a large database of previous applicants so that it can predict fraudulent applications.

Chapter 11 provides a general introduction to learning. Chapter 12 introduces the learning of decision trees. Chapter 13 introduces inductive logic programming, which in simple terms can be viewed as the automatic generation of programs in a logic type of syntax (like Prolog). Chapters 2 and 4 are prerequisites for Chapter 13. Chapter 14 introduces reinforcement learning, in which a machine learns a sequence of actions through feedback on its performance while exploring its environment. Chapter 15 introduces neural networks. Feedforward networks are presented in some detail and the backpropagation algorithm is explained. Chapter 16 presents some additional neural network architectures, in particular the self-organizing feature map and radial-basis function networks. Chapter 17 concludes the part on learning with a look at genetic algorithms.

CHAPTER 11

Introduction to Learning

Learning is a process that allows an agent to adapt its performance through instruction or experience, and is considered fundamental to intelligent behaviour. This point is clearly exemplified by our interpretation of animal intelligence. We can admire the highly developed skills of different species that have evolved over the millions of years, but a species' ability to learn, and the complexity of the learned task, is what largely appears to define the scale of intelligence. Learning might be a simple association task where a specific output is required when given some input. A dog learns to associate the command 'sit' with the physical response of sitting. Associative learning is fundamental to many tasks, another example being object recognition. Another common form of learning is the acquisition of a skill through direct interaction with the environment; a 'try to do' approach like learning to ride a bicycle. We are born with the physical attributes to ride a bike but we are not born with the knowledge that links sensory input to the required actions needed to stay upright on a bike. When an agent learns, it acquires knowledge, and it is the automatic acquisition of knowledge that is one of the major attractions of machine learning. For most learning there will exist some level of prior knowledge. For some forms of learning this prior knowledge might need to be significant, but nonetheless the aim of learning is for the knowledge base to be significantly enhanced. Prior knowledge might be implicit in that it influences the choice of learning algorithm and any pre-processing of the input. Sometimes knowledge in learning is used more explicitly. An example would be the construction of a Bayesian network using prior knowledge of causal associations, following which a learning algorithm is applied to generate the prior distributions for each variable from a database of examples.

Learning is a very active and large area of AI research. Learning research is motivated for a number of reasons. From a biological and cognitive perspective, we have a desire to understand more about ourselves. For example, a large body of research involves building computational models of some small part of the human brain in an attempt to explain how our own neural circuitry performs tasks and adapts. The largest motivating factor, and that which concerns us in the following chapters, is to get machines (agents) to perform tasks that serve us in some way. In other words, we are interested in real-world applications of learning. The successes in learning are many and varied: learning to recognize customers' purchasing patterns so that credit card fraud can be detected, profiling customers to target marketing campaigns, categorizing content on the worldwide web and automatic channelling of data according to the user's interests, credit scoring of loan applicants, fault diagnosis for gas turbines, etc. Learning has also been demonstrated in domains such as navigating a vehicle on a public highway, discovering a new class of star and learning to play backgammon to a world champion standard. Learning has proved itself time and again to be a valuable tool for both research and commercial applications.

This chapter gives a brief introduction to learning terminology and the components that make up the essence of a learning system. It could be argued that the learning system comprises sensing technology and response effectors in those agents that learn through interaction with their environment. Although these components are acknowledged as important, this book is concerned more with the core learning algorithms. Subsequent chapters will explore the principles of a number of learning algorithms. Inevitably there are many, many algorithms that cannot be included. An attempt has been made to give a reasonable breadth of coverage and to include the basis of algorithms that are used for real-world applications.

11.1   The elements of learning

At the core of any learning agent, whether the agent be animal, mechanical or software, is an algorithm that defines the process (instruction set) that is used for learning. The job of the algorithm is to transform input data into a particular form of useful output. The output could be the recognition of optically scanned handwritten characters, it could be the actions that a robot needs to perform in order to grasp hold of an object, it could be the next move in a game of chess, it could be a recommendation of whether a loan applicant should be allowed to borrow money. The product of learning is called the **target function**. If learning is successful the target function should be able to take input data and produce a correct (or optimal) output. For instance, the target function might take an image of a scanned character from which it outputs a single instance of {A, B, ... Z, 0,1, ... 9}. A number of questions come to mind: How is the target function represented? What is adapted during learning? What guides or provides judgement so that the agent knows that its learning is progressing along the correct lines? How do we know when learning is complete? How do we know that learning has been successful? This chapter makes a start at answering these questions.

Suppose that there is a database of horse-riders who are professionals in one of the following sports: show jumping, flat racing or three-day eventing. The database keeps a record of attributes such as age, height, number of years competing and weight. The learning task is to make a judgement as to whether or not a rider is a jockey (flat racer) from the single attribute weight. Admittedly, this is not a very interesting or challenging problem as we know that jockeys are light, but it will serve to introduce a number of fundamental concepts. Each record in the database is tagged with the rider's sport. The first task is to select a training data set. The training data will consist of a subset of the database records, which is typically selected at random. The only attributes of interest in this example are weight and sport. Weight is a real-valued attribute with units in kilograms and sport is a text tag that labels the sport of each rider as one of the following {jockey, jumper, eventer}. The target function is to be a binary classifier that outputs a 1 if the rider is a jockey and 0 otherwise. The sport attribute can be replaced with a new attribute so that all jockeys are tagged positive with the other types of rider tagged as negative.

Learning from examples is known by the more general term of **inductive** inference. Each example is a pair, $(x, f(x))$, where an output $f(x)$ is given for each input, x. Learning will generate different approximations of the target function f. Each approximation of f is called a **hypothesis**. The hypothesis needs to be represented in some form. In the jockey learning task, the choice of hypothesis representation will be a simple threshold defined as follows:

$$f(x_i) = \begin{cases} 1 \text{ if } x_i \le T \\ 0 \text{ if } x_i > T \end{cases} \tag{11.1}$$

where x_i refers to the weight for example i and T is a real-valued threshold.

Learning generates different versions of the hypothesis by adapting the representation. The things in the representation that are adapted can be generally referred to as parameters. In this example, there is a single parameter T. Each example in the training set has a target output t: $t = 1$ if the example is tagged as positive and $t = 0$ if the example is tagged as negative. The actual output,

y_i, for an example is computed from $y_i = f(x_i)$, and this value can be different to the target output, in which case there is an error Δ_i.

How is the threshold value T found? In this simple example it could be computed directly using Bayesian statistics. However, the purpose here is to illustrate a simple process of learning. One way to approach this learning task is to start with a random value for T, calculate the error Δ for the first example which is $\Delta = t - y$, and then adapt the weight so that the error is reduced. The threshold can be adapted according to the following rule

$$T_{new} = T + \eta \Delta \qquad (11.2)$$

where η is the learning rate (the amount by which the threshold should be adapted).

The learning rate needs to be set to a small value (~ 0.05). The algorithm processes each example and then continually iterates over the training data until the output of each example remains constant between successive iterations.

After learning is complete, a test set of data is used to see how successful learning has been. Our goal with any learning algorithm is to have acceptable performance on data that were not seen during training. In the above example, the aim would be for the learned function to indicate whether or not a rider is a jockey. If a rider's sport was not known, the rider's weight could then be used to predict if the rider is a jockey.

One limitation with the form of the function given above is that the output is either 0 or 1. Things are rarely that decisive, but a binary output offers no grey area in between. In many problems it is desirable to have a measure of certainty. One way to provide this measure is to use a function such that the output gives a measure of the probability of rider x being a jockey given their weight, *p(jockey|weight)*. A probability distribution function is used in place of the threshold function. A commonly used distribution is the Gaussian function. For a single attribute, the Gaussian function is defined by two parameters, the mean and the standard deviation. The mean gives the location of the function centre and the standard deviation is a measure of spread. An example of the function is shown in Figure 11.1. There are a number of density estimation techniques for learning the parameters of the Gaussian.

The choice of representation for the target function is rather limited in the above example. If more available data about a rider were to be used then the target function might have a better chance of more accurately identifying jockeys. In the example a single attribute, weight, was used. One-dimensional problems are those in which the training examples are described by a single input attribute.

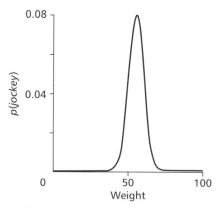

Figure 11.1 A one-dimensional Gaussian distribution.

If another attribute were to be used, such as height, the problem becomes two-dimensional. Many types of learning attempt to associate an input to a decision region within some high-dimensional space. In a two-dimensional plane (two inputs) the decision region could be defined by multiple lines. The representation of the hypothesis determines the shape of these regions. A Gaussian, for example, becomes bell shaped in two dimensions, as shown in Figure 11.2. Many learning problems use a high number of attributes and are therefore known as high-dimensional problems. The number of attributes should be chosen with care as, contrary to what might be expected, adding too many attributes can lead to deteriorating classification performance owing to what is called the **curse of dimensionality**. Using a high number of attributes for a relatively low number of training examples can make the high-dimensional space very sparse, which basically means that the training examples become widely distributed, with the danger that examples belonging to a single class get separated into different regions. The concern then is that the learned hypothesis might be a poor representation of the target function, in which case the accuracy will be poor when classifying new data.

If data are two-dimensional, it is common to refer to the x attribute and the y attribute, and for three dimensions the z attribute. For high-dimensional problems the letters of the alphabet quickly become exhausted, and so it is usual to replace x, y and z with x_1, x_2 and x_3. Dimensions can be increased by adding x_4, x_5, and so on. In general, a training example $\mathbf{x}_i$ will be represented by an n-dimensional vector of the form $<x_{i,1}, x_{i,2} \ldots, x_{i,n}>$ Each component of the vector is an attribute value (attributes are also commonly referred to as features) and can be discrete or real-valued if continuous. If the training examples are of the form $\{(\mathbf{x}_1, \mathbf{y}_1), \ldots, (\mathbf{x}_m, \mathbf{y}_m)\}$, where the m training examples each have a target value (or vector of values) $\mathbf{y}$, then the learning problem is known as **supervised learning**. An example of supervised learning is a classification task (like learning the concept 'jockey') where each example has a class label. Learning tasks for which training examples do not have target values (or vectors) are known by the general term **unsupervised learning**. Unsupervised learning searches for patterns of similarity among objects. For instance, a supervised classification task might have a group of different chair objects labelled with the class 'chair' and table objects labelled with the class 'table'. For unsupervised learning, these labels would not exist but the learning algorithm could still generate groupings that would largely separate chairs and tables into different groups. One distinguishing feature for chairs might be that the surface area of the top (seat) relative to the height is small compared with tables.

11.2   Representing the target function

There are many different learning algorithms that have been invented and that continue to evolve. Like most things in science, the new inventions owe much to their predecessors for inspiration. There are many ways in which learning algorithms can be grouped. They can be grouped as supervised or

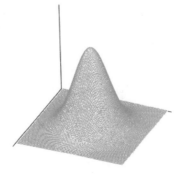

Figure 11.2 A two-dimensional Gaussian distribution.

unsupervised, or they can be grouped by the type of learning task, concept learning or regression learning for example, or they can be grouped by application domain. Another form of grouping is in terms of the target function representation. Three ways of representing a hypothesis (and hence the target function) are illustrated in Figure 11.3. The first representation uses a tree, where root nodes denote an attribute and branches denote attribute values. Trees can be used to represent classification functions, decision functions and even programs. The second form of representation is expressed in first-order logic. We know from previous chapters that a range of tasks from low-level

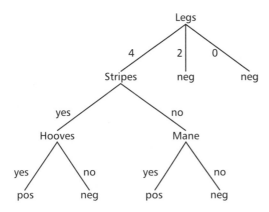

The hypothesis is represented by a classification tree. Attributes are denoted by root nodes and values by branches (e.g. Legs has tree values, {0,2,4}). Leaf nodes labelled pos (positive) have the majority of assigned examples having a target value that matches the target classification, and those leaf nodes labelled neg (negative) have the majority of assigned examples not matching the target classification. An example is assigned to a leaf node by starting at the topmost root and then following the branches that match with the example's attribute values.

scales(fish), legs(fish, 0), lays_eggs(fish), habitat(fish, water).

The hypothesis is represented by a conjunction of literals.

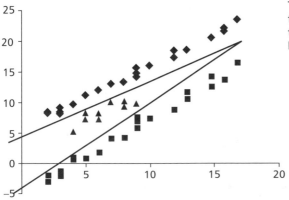

The hypothesis is represented by a decision function that consists of two lines. To separate the triangles from the other data requires a point to be above the bottom line and below the top line.

Figure 11.3 Three examples for representing target functions.

computations (like multiplication) to complex reasoning can be represented using first-order logic. The third form illustrated uses two lines to form a decision region for classifying a group of points. There are other forms of representation, including graphs and binary strings. The different forms of representation need not be mutually exclusive, in that a representation can be viewed in different ways. A tree used for classification is really defining a set of decision regions in high-dimensional space. It is not surprising, therefore, that algorithms using different forms of representation can be compared and are sometimes found to have similar performance when given the same task. The choice of representation is governed by a number of factors, such as the type of attributes (e.g. continuous or discrete), the speed with which any learned function must be executed, whether or not learning is part of some overall system, a belief that a particular learning algorithm will give better performance, etc. Some algorithms are designed to work with continuous attributes, whereas others are designed to work with discrete attributes and some enable learning with a mixture of continuous and discrete attributes. A decision on how hypotheses should be represented can only be made from having a good understanding of the application domain and an understanding of different learning algorithms.

Another factor that often has an influence on the choice of hypothesis representation is the visibility of the knowledge that has been learned. Many forms of representation, such as classification trees and first-order logic, make the knowledge explicit. With an explicit representation it is possible to explain how a decision has been reached. Some hypotheses are more like black boxes. For example, the knowledge acquired by a neural network is represented by a network of weighted values, which conveys little immediate meaning, hence the term black box. Although much research is under way to understand neural network representations and to develop techniques to transform the acquired knowledge into a more readable form, there are many learning problems for which, for the time being, we have to accept that the knowledge acquired cannot be easily explained. It is arguably preferable to have an insight into the knowledge acquired by any learning agent, but learning machines such as neural networks have proved to be highly applicable to real-world problems.

During learning, different candidate hypotheses will be generated. For instance, in Figure 11.3, different trees could be generated during learning, each one describing a different classification function. A first-order logic expression can be adapted by adding and deleting literals. The lines in the third representation shown in Figure 11.3 can be varied, by redrawing the existing lines or adding additional lines, to provide different candidate hypotheses. Learning can be viewed as a search through a space of candidate hypotheses. The goal of the search is to find a hypothesis that best represents the target function. This notion of 'learning as search' is expanded upon in section 11.4.

11.3   Types of learning task

There are many domains in which machine learning is applied. Some types of learning task are listed below.

11.3.1   Classification learning

There are very many applications that come under the general umbrella of classification learning. Optically scanning and automatically recognizing hand-printed characters is one such application. The machine is required to scan an image of a character and output its classification. For the English language the machine needs to learn the classification of the digits $0 \ldots 9$ and the characters $A \ldots Z$. Learning will be supervised because the classification of each training example is known. Unsupervised learning is also widely used in classification tasks. Even when a target classification is available for each training example it is sometimes useful to adopt an unsupervised approach to see how the examples group in terms of the attributes that describe them. Unsupervised learning is widely adopted when there is no target classification available and the task becomes one of looking for patterns of similarity amongst the examples. A typical example application is the detection of anomalies in data acquired from sensors fitted to machines (e.g. helicopter transmissions) to detect malfunctions before they propagate to a point of failure.

11.3.2 Learning sequence of actions

Chess games and robots that navigate around offices emptying bins are examples of the need for situation assessment and action selection. The chess-playing agent must read the state of the board and decide on an action that involves moving a piece in the belief that the action will maximize its chance of winning the game. The robot is looking to decide on actions that will maximize its garbage-collecting efficiency while ensuring that it never becomes stranded before reaching a recharging location.

11.3.3 Learning optimal decisions

In Chapters 5, 6 and 8 Bayesian networks and decision networks were introduced. Learning can involve automatically creating these networks and/or adapting their distributions as experience is gained. Alternatively, the decision process might be represented as a decision tree. These forms of learning can also involve actions that might be sequential or even parallel in execution. The decision-making process that is learned must be optimal in the sense that expected rewards versus expected penalties are maximized. For instance, the decision whether or not to launch a space vehicle has to balance the reward of making the launch on time with the risk of losing the vehicle as a result of external factors such as weather conditions.

11.3.4 Learning a regression function

Regression learning refers to learning the association between one variable (the dependent variable) and other variables (the independent variables). A typical application requiring interpolation involves failure of some signal that is normally recorded, perhaps because of a faulty sensor. For example, a jet engine might have two shafts, one coupled to a low-speed compressor and the other to a high-speed compressor. The shafts are mechanically independent but their speed of rotation is related. The speed of rotation is used to calculate performance, which is a critical measurement required of aircraft engines. A sensor failure can lead to the loss of a signal from one of the shafts, but it might be possible to interpolate the lost signal from other monitored engine parameters, one of which would be the other shaft speed. Another example of learning a regression function is predicting the future value of a share index.

11.3.5 Learning programs

All forms of learning can be viewed as a form of automatic programming. However, there are learning algorithms that are specifically targeted at learning to represent the solution of a task in a syntax that closely resembles a programming language. There are, for example, learning algorithms whose target function is a Prolog program.

11.4   Learning as search

The algorithms that are of primary interest to us will be introduced in the following chapters. A number of other points concerning learning can be usefully introduced by viewing learning as a search process. Mitchell (1982) was the first to define learning as a search through a space of hypotheses.

This section is specifically concerned with **concept learning**, which for our purpose we can think of as learning to classify objects. For example, the concept to be learned could be the recognition of the character 'L'. This type of task will consist of positive and negative training examples. The positive examples will all be instances of 'L' and the negative examples will be instances that are not 'L', e.g. {A, B, C, ...}. Each hypothesis could be represented by a template of pixel values, with the job of the target function being to compare pixels in the object with those in the template. Another choice for representing hypotheses could be a vector of features such as:

<segment(1, long, vertical), segment(2, short, horizontal), joined(segment(1), segment(2))>.

Different candidate hypotheses would be generated, for example:

<segment(1, long, vertical), segment(2, short, horizontal)>
<number_segments(2), segment(1, long, vertical), segment(2, short, horizontal)>
...

H is used to denote the space of all hypotheses. The goal of learning is to find a member, h, of H that correctly identifies all object instances as positive or negative.

An example object x is said to **satisfy** a hypothesis h when h classifies x as a positive example (even though x may be a negative example). A hypothesis h is said to be **consistent** with a set of training examples provided h correctly classifies all examples: all positive examples are classified as positive by h and all negative examples are classified as negative by h. A hypothesis h is said to **cover** a positive example if it correctly identifies the example as positive.

The learning algorithm presented here generates candidate hypotheses by applying **specialization** and **generalization** operators. Consider the following hypotheses:

1   A, B, C
2   A, B
3   A
4   A OR B

Note that conjunction (AND) is denoted by ','.

Hypothesis 1 is a specialization of hypothesis 2 or, alternatively, hypothesis 2 is a generalization of hypothesis 1. If a hypothesis is specialized, the set of objects that satisfy the hypothesis is more restricted. Hypothesis 1 compared with hypothesis 2 has an additional condition, C, that objects must possess in order to satisfy the hypothesis. The operator AND therefore imposes an additional constraint on the objects that can be satisfied and so it is a specialization operator. The OR operator, on the other hand, is a generalization operator. Another way of generalizing and specializing a hypothesis that has real-valued attributes is by either expanding or restricting the range of values satisfied. For instance, given:

$\{h_1 = 18 < age \leq 24\}$
$\{h_2 = 18 < age \leq 26\}$

h_1 is a specialization of h_2.

Mitchell (1982) described the space of all hypotheses that are consistent with the training data as the **version space**. He also introduced an algorithm called **candidate elimination** to represent the version space. The version space is bounded by two sets: the specific boundary set, S, and the general boundary set, G.

Table 11.1 shows a list of examples for a hypothetical credit-scoring application. Given that the target function is *person x is credit worthy,* there are three positive and two negative examples. Suppose the hypothesis is represented as a vector of attribute values:

<age, mortgage, default, length-employed, surplus>

In this representation a hypothesis is a conjunction of attribute values, which means that any example covered by the hypothesis must have attribute values that match with the hypothesis. The symbol ? is used to indicate that the attribute can take on any value. For instance the hypothesis <?, y, n, 1–5, y> represents that age can be any value but the other attributes must have the values specified at their vector positions (e.g. mortgage=y). How might we find a hypothesis that correctly classifies all examples? One approach is to start a search over the hypothesis space from the most specific hypothesis and gradually expand the search by generalizing the hypothesis until all positive examples are covered. One other symbol, Ø (the empty set), is required, which is used to denote that no attribute value is acceptable. The most specific hypothesis is initialized to:

< Ø , Ø , Ø , Ø , Ø >

which means that no example in Table 11.1 is covered (because the hypothesis states that no attribute has an acceptable value). Each positive training example is then considered in turn and the hypothesis is generalized the least amount necessary to cover the example.

The first example is <18–60, N, N, 1–5, N>. The least generalization of the initial hypothesis requires every attribute to be set to the same values as the first example. If any attribute has a value Ø, no example can be covered (because all examples have a value for each attribute). Note that the symbol ? is not used in place of an attribute value at this stage as this would generalize the hypothesis more than is necessary to cover the first example.

The second example is <18–60, Y, N, 1–5, N>. This example differs from the first example in the second attribute value. So, to generalize the hypothesis to cover the second example requires the 'do not care' symbol, ?, to denote that the second attribute can take on any value. The hypothesis is now <18–60, ?, N, 1–5, N>.

The final positive example is <18–60, N, N, >5, N> and the final hypothesis is:

Table 11.1 A set of attribute values for loan applicants

	Age	Mortgage	Default	Length employed	Surplus %	Creditworthy
1	18–60	N	N	1–5	N	Y
2	18–60	Y	N	1–5	N	Y
3	< 18	N	N	< 1	N	N
4	18–60	N	Y	1–5	N	N
5	18–60	N	N	> 5	N	Y

<18–60, ?, N, ?, N>

Notice that the final hypothesis is consistent with the complete training set. All of the positive examples are correctly covered, whereas no negative example is covered. One limitation of the above approach is that it only finds the most specific hypothesis that covers the positive training examples. The hypothesis <18–60, ?, N, ?, ?> is also consistent with the training examples and it is more general than the hypothesis <18–60, ?, N, ?, N>. Which hypothesis is to be preferred? We cannot answer this question from the training data alone. We might suspect that the second hypothesis will generalize to a larger set of unseen data than the first, but its classification accuracy could in fact be worse. The judgement of the best hypothesis must be made using a test data set.

The candidate elimination algorithm will find the version space that represents all hypotheses consistent with the training data provided that the target concept can be represented using the hypothesis language (e.g. tree, predicates, etc.). The algorithm has the following two steps:

1   If the example is positive, any hypothesis in G that is inconsistent with the example is deleted and hypotheses in S are minimally generalized so that they are all consistent with the example.
2   If the example is negative, any hypothesis in S that is inconsistent with the example is deleted and hypotheses in G are minimally specialized so that all are consistent with the example.

The algorithm is given in Figure 11.4.

Example 1 ● ● ● ● ●

The candidate elimination algorithm operating on the data in Table 11.1 is explained below. Figure 11.5 shows the status of the sets S and G after encountering each training example.

First positive example
The hypothesis in G is consistent with the example. S is not consistent and so it is replaced with all values instantiated to the example's attribute values.

Second positive example
The hypothesis in G is consistent with Example 2. The hypothesis in S has to be generalized. It differs from the first example only in terms of the second attribute and so the minimal generalization is achieved by indicating that the second attribute can take on any value.

First negative example
The hypothesis in S is consistent (the attribute values do not match). The single hypothesis currently in G is inconsistent. The minimal specializations of G include: {<18–60, ?, ?, ?, ?>, <?, Y, ?, ?, ?>, <?, ?, Y, ?, ?>, <?, ?, ?, 1–5, ?>, <?, ?, ?, ? ,Y>}. Of these, the second one is inconsistent with the first example, the third is inconsistent with the first two examples, and the fifth is inconsistent with the first two examples. The other two hypotheses are added to G. Note that both of these hypotheses are as equally general.

Second negative example
The hypothesis in S does not cover Example 4. The hypotheses in G are inconsistent and need specializing.

```
G is initialised to the set of maximally general hypotheses in H
S is initialised to the set of maximally specific hypotheses in H
for each training example x
        if x is positive
                for each hypothesis h in G
                        if h is not consistent with x
                                delete h
                        end if
                end for
                for each hypothesis h in S
                        if h is not consistent with x
                                remove h from S
                                generate the set h_min of all minimal generalisations of h
                                for each member h_new of h_min
                                        if h_new is consistent with x and G contains a more general
                                        hypothesis
                                                add h_new to S
                                        end if
                                end for
                        end if
                end for
                remove from S any hypothesis that is more general than another hypothesis in S
        end if

        if x is negative
                for each hypothesis h in S
                        if h is not consistent with x
                                delete h
                        end if
                end for
                for each hypothesis h in G
                        if h is not consistent with x
                                remove h from G
                                generate the set h_min of all minimal specialisations of h
                                for each member h_new of h_min
                                        if h_new is consistent with x and S contains a more specific
                                        hypothesis than h
                                                add h_new to G
                                        end if
                                end for
                        end if
                end for
                remove from G any hypothesis that is less general than another hypothesis in G
        end if
end for
```

Figure 11.4 The candidate elimination algorithm.

Third positive example

The second hypothesis in G is inconsistent and so it is deleted. The hypothesis in S is inconsistent and is generalized.

S: {<ø, ø, ø, ø, ø,>} G: {<?, ?, ?, ?, ?>} Initialization step	S: {<18–60, N, N, 1–5, N>} G: {<?, ?, ?, ?, ?>} After presenting the first positive example
S: {<18–60, ?, N, 1–5, N>} G: {<?, ?, ?, ?, ?>} After presenting the second positive example	S: {<18–60, ?, N, 1–5, N>} G: {<18–60, ?, ?, ?, ?>, <?, ?, ?, 1–5, ?>} After presenting the first negative example
S: {<18–60, ?, N, 1–5, N>} G: {<18–60, ?, N, ?,?>,<?, ?, N, 1–5, ?>} After presenting the second negative example	S: {<18–60, ?, N, ?, N>} G: {<18–60, ?, N, ?,?>} After presenting the third positive example

Figure 11.5   A trace of candidate elimination for Example 1.

The candidate elimination algorithm defines the set of most specific and the set of least general hypotheses. All hypotheses consistent with the training data are bounded by these two sets. In Figure 11.5, the final boundary sets define the only two hypotheses consistent with the training data. However, if learning used only examples 1–4 in Table 11.1, the complete set of consistent hypotheses would be that given in Figure 11.6.

The candidate elimination algorithm is in not suited to real-world problems. In real-world problems, data contain errors and noise as a result of, for example, missing attribute values, incorrectly recorded values and misclassified training data.

Given the hypotheses in Figure 11.6 what would the new sample[1] (Example 5 in Table 11.1) be classified as? Only two out of the six hypotheses classify the instance as positive. One strategy for classifying the sample might be majority voting, in which case the sample would be classified as negative. There is therefore a level of uncertainty, and for most real problems, things are rarely certain.

---

[1]The word 'sample' will occasionally be used to refer to an input to a learning algorithm. The word 'sample' can refer to a training example or a test input, etc.

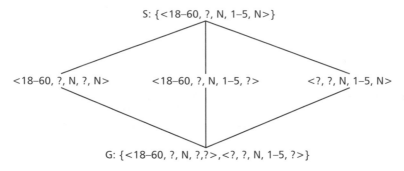

Figure 11.6 Version space generated by using examples 1–4 in Table 11.1.

11.5 Learning bias in the hypothesis space

The representation of the hypothesis space in Example 1 uses a conjunction of attribute values. No hypothesis therefore could represent the target function:

If (age $= 18 - 60$ or age > 60)

Suppose the training examples are as listed below. There are four examples each having two values, one for attribute A and another for attribute B.

	A	B
1	a1	b1
2	a1	b2
3	a2	b1
4	a2	b2

The total example set X is $\{1, 2, 3, 4\}$. The power set of X is all the subsets that can be generated from X including the empty set $\emptyset$. The power set is:

$$\{ \emptyset, \{1\}, \{2\}, \{3\}, \{4\}, \{1, 2\}, \{1, 3\}, \{1, 4\}, \{2, 3\}, \{2, 4\},$$
$$\{3, 4\}, \{1, 2, 3\}, \{1, 2, 4\}, \{1, 3, 4\}, \{2, 3, 4\}, \{1, 2, 3, 4\}\}$$

The power set describes the target concepts that can be defined on the training data. For instance, the target concept might not cover any of the examples, in which case it corresponds to $\emptyset$; on the other hand, it might cover all examples $\{1, 2, 3, 4\}$. How many target concepts can be described by a hypothesis that uses a conjunction of attribute values? Target concepts that can be represented include $\{<\emptyset, \emptyset>, <?, ?>, <a1, b1>, \ldots\}$. The total number of vectors that can be used to represent a target hypothesis is $(3 \times 3) + 1 = 10$. The first attribute can take on the values $\{a1, a2, ?\}$ and the second attribute can take on the values $\{b1, b2, ?\}$. This gives 3×3 combinations. The other hypothesis that can be represented is $<\emptyset, \emptyset>$. Note that a hypothesis that is made up from a single instance of $\emptyset$, such as $<\emptyset, b1>$, is not an acceptable hypothesis as all examples have a value for each attribute.[2] The total set of hypotheses that can be represented is given in Table 11.2. This example shows that the choice of representation language will determine what target concepts can be represented. In

---

[2]We should note, however, that many real-world applications of learning must handle examples with missing attribute values.

Table 11.2 The concepts (subsets of {1, 2, 3, 4}) that can be represented using a conjunction of attribute values

< Ø, Ø >	Empty set – Ø
< ?, ? >	{1, 2, 3, 4}
< a1, ? >	{1, 2}
< a2, ? >	{3, 4}
< ?, b1 >	{1, 3}
< ?, b2 >	{2, 4}
< a1, b1 >	{1}
< a1, b2 >	{2}
< a2, b1 >	{3}
< a2, b2 >	{4}

this case 10 out of the 16 possible target concepts can be represented. We see therefore that our choice of representation language could prevent the target concept being learned. Is there a way of deciding whether or not the target concept can be represented by the hypothesis language? One of the main motivating factors for using machine learning is that we do not know in advance what the target function looks like – if we did there would no need to use learning. In practice, knowledge of the domain in which learning is taking place will be used to make a judgement about an appropriate hypothesis language. How about using a language that could represent all possible hypotheses? Mitchell (1997) explains that this approach is futile. Remember that the ultimate goal of learning is for our target function to perform well on unseen data – learning is a waste of time if we cannot generalize. If a language is used that is capable of representing every possible hypothesis there will be no ability to generalize to unseen data. When we adopt a hypothesis language we make an assumption that the target concept can be represented.

Given a set of training data, there could be several competing hypotheses that appear to perform equally as well. It is, for example, possible to envisage a number of candidate trees for a classification problem, with each tree having the same accuracy on the training data. Some of these trees will be larger than others. The learning algorithm could bias the choice of the final selected hypothesis. For instance, the algorithm might make a preference for smaller trees. This bias is referred to as **inductive bias**.

11.6 Some further points

Some points that need to be considered before learning can take place are listed below.

Target function specification	What is to be learned?
	What is an appropriate representation for the target function?
Selection of learning algorithm	There is a need to consider the nature of the task and the application domain.
	Are there any constraints on the form of target function? For example, in some safety-critical situations a black box algorithm might not be accepted.
	Are there any constraints on the time to learn?
	Is there a requirement for parallel implementation?

Data selection	Data may reside in a database. Data might be acquired by scanning an image, for example, or by monitoring the outputs of sensors. Are there sufficient training data?
Selection of data subsets	Training, validation and test sets need to be selected. Each set should be representative of the range of data that the target function needs to handle.
Pre-processing	It is typical for data to go through some form of pre-processing before being passed to the learning algorithm. The curse of dimensionality was mentioned earlier. Often the intrinsic dimension is less than the number of attributes and pre-processing can transform the data into a more compact representation (lower dimensions). For instance, a straight line in the two-dimensional plane has an intrinsic dimension of 1. Other forms of pre-processing involve extracting features such as edge location in an image.
Measure of performance	There has to be some way of judging learning. The agent needs to be able to assess its performance. Judgements can be computed in a number of ways. Simple examples might compute the accuracy of a classification function or the accuracy of a regression prediction. Other performance measures will require a utility function to compute expected rewards.
Halt criteria	Some algorithms perform continuous online updates. An example could be the updating of prior distributions in a Bayesian network. Most algorithms tend to be off-line and will terminate when some criterion is met, e.g. accuracy is no longer improving or training has taken too long.

Summary

The whole idea of learning is to expose the learning agent to data for a period of training, after which the knowledge is fixed (it could be later updated with additional training). The thing being learned is a target function. The representation of a target function is often referred to as a hypothesis. Learning involves adapting one or more of the hypothesis parameters. The parameters might consist of subtrees in a tree representation, the mean and standard deviation of a Gaussian function, the literals in a first-order logic expression, etc. Adapting the hypothesis parameters generates different versions of the hypothesis, and learning is really a process of searching for a hypothesis that best represents the target function. Once the knowledge is fixed the true measure of performance is how well the agent performs on unseen data (data which were not used for training). The ability to generalize provides a measure of performance on unseen data.

Further reading

Mitchell (1997) provides a good overview of many types of learning and goes into more depth than is practical with this book. *Machine Learning*, volumes I–III (Michalski *et al*. 1984, 1986; Kodratoff and Michalski, 1990), provide an interesting source for tracing the history of developments over the last couple of decades. A general information server for machine learning resources is Mlnet.

CHAPTER 12

Decision Tree Learning

In this chapter an algorithm is presented for learning a decision tree. The decision tree represents a discrete-valued function. Each node in the tree represents an attribute and the branches leading from a node represent the attribute values. For example, in a weather decision tree, the attribute pressure might have values {high, low} and the attribute wind strength might have values {nil, moderate, strong, gale-force}. Decision trees have proved to be one of the most practical machine-learning algorithms applied to real-world problems. Decision tree learning is robust in that it can cope with misclassified training data and data with missing attribute values.

12.1 Introduction

A decision tree for whether an ice-cream van will be out selling is given in Figure 12.1. Each path in the tree leads to a leaf-node that provides a decision based on the values of attributes encountered along the path. The decision is either sell or don't sell. Each path can also be represented as a rule. For instance, the rule:

> IF Outlook = sunny AND Temperature = hot THEN Sell

corresponds to the leftmost branch.

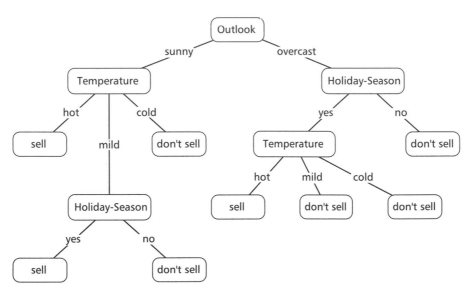

Figure 12.1 A decision tree for deciding whether or not an ice-cream seller will be out selling given attributes of the weather and holiday season.

Decision tree learning is a widely used form of inductive inference. A set of training examples is provided, and each example is marked with a target classification. For example, if our ice-cream seller is always consistent in his behaviour then we could construct the tree from examples obtained by observing and recording the weather conditions for when he is out selling. The target classification would be sell or don't sell. We see therefore that the tree can also be viewed as a classification function.

Problems suited to decision tree learning are those that have training instances represented by attribute–value pairs and where the target classification has discrete output values (e.g. sell, don't sell). The attribute values are discrete. Continuous attributes can be handled by partitioning the attribute values into discrete bins, with a lower and an upper limit being specified for each bin. For instance, discrete categories for people's age can be created by defining a set of bins and labelled pairs as follows {(age ≤ 5, infant), (5 > age ≤ 13, junior), (13 > age ≤ 18, teenager), (18 > age, adult)}.

Example 1 ● ● ● ● ●

The scenario for this example concerns a brewery that owns a chain of bars/restaurants throughout the UK. It needs to assess the suitability of new sites, i.e. for a nominated site should it build a new bar/restaurant or classify the site as unsuitable? To assess a new site, it examines a number of attributes about the area where the site is located. These attributes describe whether the site is a city or large town, whether a university is located in the area, what type of housing estate, if any, is nearby, whether there is an industrial estate (park), the quality of public transport and the number of schools in the location. For each attribute there are a number of attribute values, for example {Y – yes, N – no} for City, {M – medium, S – small, N – none, L – large} for Housing-Estate. The brewery has a database of existing bars/restaurants and the attribute values for each. A subset of the database is listed in Table 12.1. Each existing bar/restaurant is also given a class label where + (positive) means that the brewery consider the site to be successful and – (negative) means that the site is borderline and they would not wish to make a similar investment in the future. The brewery wish to use the database to find a set of rules that will help them decide on the suitability of a new potential site.

Figure 12.2 provides such a set of attribute–value rules in the form of a classification tree. Two of the rules are:

> IF the Transport = Poor AND Industrial-Estate = No THEN do not purchase site (because examples {2, 4, 10, 13, 18} are all negative)
> IF the Transport = Good THEN purchase the site (because examples {7, 12, 16, 19, 20} are all positive)

Following the path from the root node to a leaf node generates a rule. Each node along the path denotes an attribute and the branch leading from the attribute that follows the path provides the attribute value.

● ● ● ● ●

12.2 ID3 algorithm

ID3 (Quinlan, 1986) is one algorithm that has popularized decision tree learning. The algorithm starts with a root node. It then assigns to this root node the best attribute. The way to select the best attribute will be described later. A branch is then generated for each value of the attribute. At the end of each branch a new node is generated. Each training example is then assigned to one of these new

Table 12.1 A list of examples for the bar/restaurant example

Example	City/Town	University	Housing-Estate	Industrial-Estate	Transport	Schools	Class
1	Y	Y	M	N	A	L	+
2	N	N	S	N	P	L	−
3	Y	Y	M	N	A	M	+
4	Y	N	M	N	P	S	−
5	N	N	M	Y	P	M	+
6	N	Y	N	N	A	S	−
7	Y	N	N	N	G	S	+
8	Y	N	S	N	A	M	−
9	N	N	L	Y	P	L	+
10	N	N	M	N	P	S	−
11	N	N	L	Y	A	M	+
12	Y	N	N	N	G	L	+
13	N	Y	S	N	P	L	−
14	N	N	L	Y	P	L	+
15	Y	N	M	N	A	M	−
16	Y	Y	N	N	G	S	+
17	N	N	L	N	A	M	−
18	N	N	L	N	P	S	−
19	Y	N	N	N	G	L	+
20	Y	N	N	N	G	S	+

nodes according to the value it has for the attribute. For example, in Figure 12.2, examples {1, 3, 6, 8, 11, 15, 17} all have the value A (average) for Transport. If no examples are assigned to a node (because none has the attribute value), then the node and branch can be removed. Each new node is considered as a new root and the whole process is repeated. The category of a leaf node is decided by majority vote (the class with the most examples). Consider the path that leads to the rule:

IF Transport=Good THEN Purchase the site
(because examples {7, 12, 16, 19, 20} are all positive)

The Transport attribute has been chosen as the best attribute for the root of the tree. This attribute has three values {Average – A, Poor – P, Good – G}, and so three new branches and nodes are generated. The examples are then assigned according to attribute values. Examples {2, 4, 5, 9, 10, 13, 14, 18} all have the value P for Transport. At the end of this P branch, a new best attribute node is selected. Transport has already been used along this path and so is not considered again. This time the best attribute is Industrial-Estate. Industrial-Estate has two values and so two new branches and nodes are generated. The examples {2, 4, 5, 9, 10, 13, 14, 18} are then assigned to the new nodes according to attribute value for Industrial-Estate.

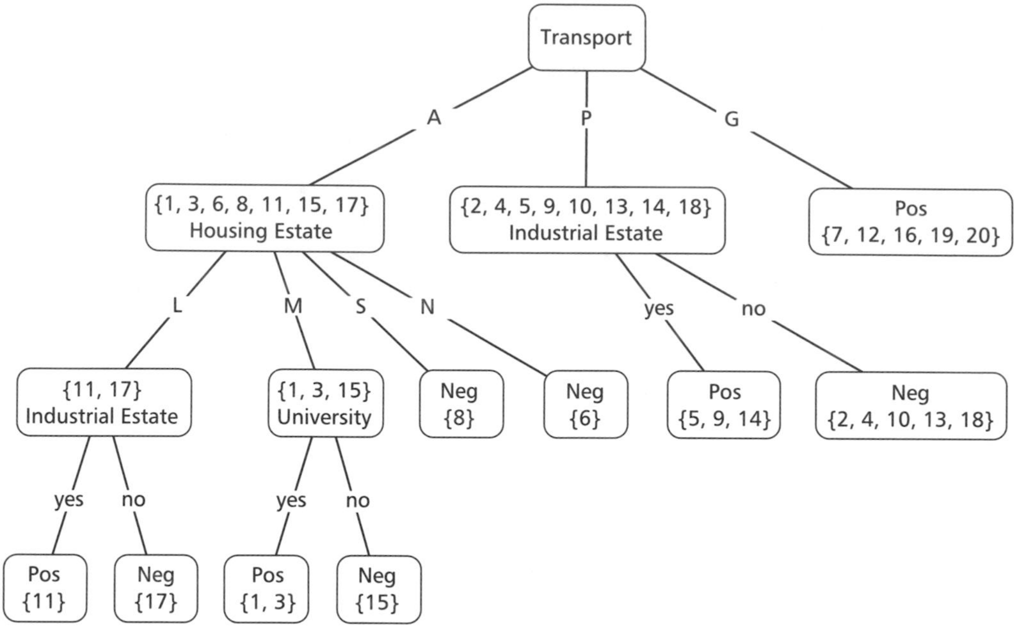

Figure 12.2 A decision tree for whether a bar/restaurant should be constructed at a particular site.

The ID3 algorithm is listed in Figure 12.3.

12.2.1 Choosing the best attribute

The best attribute is chosen on the basis of a statistical property called **information gain**. In order to define this gain we need to define a property called **entropy**. For c classification categories, and for an attribute a with all examples having a value v, the entropy E is defined as:

$$E(a = v) = \sum_{i=1}^{c} -p_i \log_2 p_i \qquad (12.1)$$

where p_i is the probability of value v of category i occurring.

The concept of entropy can be viewed from two interpretations. The first interpretation of entropy is found in number theory and the second in information theory. Both interpretations rely upon the same theory, and the relevance of an interpretation is dependent upon the nature of the problem being modelled. In essence, entropy provides a measure of dispersion of objects over a number of categories. For example, suppose that we are concerned with transmitting messages, with a single message being a single character from the set {a, b, c, d, e, f, g, h}. There are eight objects (characters), and to represent eight distinct objects three bits are needed {000, 010, 100, 110, 001, 011, 101, 111}. The average number of bits per message is therefore three. To confirm this:

$$E = \sum_{i=1}^{8} {}^{1}/_{8} \log_2 {}^{1}/_{8}$$
$$= 3$$

```
PROCEDURE ID3()
create new Node n
Extend(n)
while L is not empty
          n ← top element of L
          remove top element from L
          if all the examples assigned to n are not all the same classification
                    Extend(n)
          end if
end while


PROCEDURE Extend(n)
if all attributes used
          return
end if
choose best attribute a
assign a to used attribute list for n (this makes sure that an attribute already used on a path is not reused)
for each value of a
          add a child node to n
          push each new child node onto L
end for
for each training example t that is assigned to n
          assign each t to new child node according to value for a
end for

Node is a structure that maintains a set of used attributes and a set of training examples which are a subset of the total
training set.
L is a list that records each node to be considered for expanding
```

Figure 12.3 ID3 algorithm.

In the absence of any other information, it has to be assumed that all messages occur with equal likelihood (1/8). If each message occurs with a different frequency, shorter bit strings can be assigned to represent the most frequently occurring messages and longer strings assigned to the less frequent messages. Table 12.2 shows an example in which the average number of bits of each message is approximately 2. So in this example the non-uniform frequency distribution provides the opportunity to reduce the number of bits that are needed, on average, to transmit a message. In the context of classification trees, the distribution of messages corresponds to the distribution of classification categories generated by an attribute's value.

To select the best attribute, the measure used is called **information gain**. The information gain for an attribute is the expected reduction in entropy if the examples were to be partitioned according to that attribute and is defined as:

$$Gain\,(T,A) = E(T) - \sum_{j=1}^{V} \frac{|T_j|}{|T|} E(T_j) \qquad (12.2)$$

where T is a set of training examples and T_j is a subset of examples having value j for attribute A. An example will illustrate how gain is calculated. The root of the tree in Figure 12.2 has all 20 examples assigned as the examples have not been partitioned at the root. The classification has two categories {POS, NEG}, with 11 examples classified as POS and 9 as NEG (i.e. $|POS| = 11$ and $|NEG| = 9$). The target classification can be treated as an attribute with two values and so:

Table 12.2 A frequency distribution for messages {A, B, C, D, E, F, G, H} is given

	A	B	C	D	E	F	G	H	Total
Number of messages	1	2	4	8	40	20	3	2	80
Probability of message	0.0125	0.025	0.05	0.1	0.5	0.25	0.0375	0.025	1
Number of bits	6.32	5.32	4.32	3.32	1.00	2.00	4.74	5.32	32.35
Entropy	0.079	0.133	0.216	0.332	0.500	0.500	0.178	0.133	2.071

$$E(T) = -^{11}/_{20} \log_2 \, ^{11}/_{20} - ^9/_{20} \log_2 \, ^9/_{20}$$

$$= 0.993$$

The attribute City has two values {yes, no}. For the value *yes* there are seven positive examples and three negative examples:

$$T_{j=yes}[7POS, 3NEG]$$

So:

$$E(T_{j=yes}) = -^7/_{10} \log_2 \, ^7/_{10} - ^3/_{10} \log_2 \, ^3/_{10}$$

$$= 0.881$$

For the value *no* City has the distribution:

$$T_{j=no}[4POS, 6NEG]$$

$$E(T_{j=no}) = -^4/_{10} \log_2 \, ^4/_{10} - ^6/_{10} \log_2 \, ^6/_{10}$$

$$= 0.971$$

The gain therefore is:

$$Gain(T, City) = 0.993 - [(^{10}/_{20} \times 0.881) + (^{10}/_{20} \times 0.971)]$$

$$= 0.067$$

The calculations for the other attributes are given in Table 12.3, from which it can be seen that Transport has the highest gain and so Transport forms the root of the tree. The examples are then partitioned according to the values {A, P, G}. The child node attached to the G branch becomes a leaf node because all of the examples belong to the same classification category (POS). The other two nodes are extended in the same manner as before. Note now that the entropy for the examples attached to the Transport = A branch is:

$$E(T) = -^3/_7 \log_2 \, ^3/_7 - ^4/_7 \log_2 \, ^4/_7$$

Table 12.3 Shows all the calculations of gain for selecting the root attribute for the tree in Figure 12.2

Attribute-Value	|POS|	|NEG|	Entropy	Expected entropy for attribute	Gain
University = yes	3	2	$-\frac{3}{5}\log_2\frac{3}{5} - \frac{2}{5}\log_2\frac{2}{5} = 0.971$	$(\frac{5}{20}\times0.971) + (\frac{15}{20}\times0.997) = 0.991$	0.002
University = no	8	7	$-\frac{8}{15}\log_2\frac{8}{15} - \frac{7}{15}\log_2\frac{7}{15} = 0.997$		
Housing-Estate = L	3	2	$-\frac{3}{5}\log_2\frac{3}{5} - \frac{2}{5}\log_2\frac{2}{5} = 0.971$	$(\frac{5}{20}\times0.971) + \frac{6}{20} + 0 +$ $(\frac{6}{20}\times0.650) = 0.738$	0.255
Housing-Estate = M	3	3	$-\frac{3}{6}\log_2\frac{3}{6} - \frac{3}{6}\log_2\frac{3}{6} = 1$		
Housing-Estate = S	0	3	$-\frac{0}{3}\log_2\frac{0}{3} - \frac{3}{3}\log_2\frac{3}{3} = 0$		
Housing-Estate = N	5	1	$-\frac{5}{6}\log_2\frac{5}{6} - \frac{1}{6}\log_2\frac{1}{6} = 0.650$		
Industrial-Estate = yes	4	0	$-\frac{4}{4}\log_2\frac{4}{4} - \frac{0}{4}\log_2\frac{0}{4} = 0$	$0 + (\frac{16}{20}\times0.989) = 0.791$	0.202
Industrial-Estate = no	7	9	$-\frac{7}{16}\log_2\frac{7}{16} - \frac{9}{16}\log_2\frac{9}{16} = 0.989$		
Transport = A	3	4	$-\frac{3}{7}\log_2\frac{3}{7} - \frac{4}{7}\log_2\frac{4}{7} = 0.985$	$(\frac{7}{20}\times0.985) + (\frac{8}{20}\times0.954) + 0 = 0.727$	0.266
Transport = P	3	5	$-\frac{3}{8}\log_2\frac{3}{8} - \frac{5}{8}\log_2\frac{5}{8} = 0.954$		
Transport = G	5	0	$-\frac{5}{5}\log_2\frac{5}{5} - \frac{0}{5}\log_2\frac{0}{5} = 0$		
Schools = L	5	2	$-\frac{5}{7}\log_2\frac{5}{7} - \frac{2}{7}\log_2\frac{2}{7} = 0.863$	$(\frac{7}{20}\times0.863) + \frac{6}{20} + (\frac{7}{20}\times0.985) = 0.947$	0.046
Schools = M	3	3	$-\frac{3}{6}\log_2\frac{3}{6} - \frac{3}{6}\log_2\frac{3}{6} = 1$		
Schools = S	3	4	$-\frac{3}{7}\log_2\frac{3}{7} - \frac{4}{7}\log_2\frac{4}{7} = 0.985$		

12.3 Some issues with decision tree learning

The real test of success for a learning algorithm is its performance on data that it has not seen during training. Training typically involves training samples and validation samples. Validation samples are used to test performance after training. Poor validation results may demand retraining, perhaps using a different set-up such as a larger training set or changing the method to transform continuous attributes into discrete attributes, etc. The validation results therefore do not provide an independent test of performance, and so it is usual to have an additional test set of samples, called the test set, for checking generalization performance once training has been finally completed. As with many forms of learning, decision tree learning can lead to overfitting of the data. Overfitting means that the training performance has been improved at the expense of generalization. In other words, better generalization may be achieved if more errors were allowed during training. The criterion for extending a path in the tree is to continue extending while there are examples of mixed category attached to the same node or until no more attributes are available. To keep extending a path is not always optimal as some attributes may coincide favourably with a subset of the data but still be unrelated to the classification criteria. For instance, suppose a system is trying to learn how to credit score loan applicants and one of the rules developed so far has found that disposable income and job security appear to be useful classification criteria. Also, the rule developed so far has 15 positive and five negative instances. It just so happens that 13 of the positive instances happen to have a company pension. The rule is extended on the basis of whether someone has a company pension and the group is split into two {13+}, {2+, 5−}. If many loan applicants that have secure jobs but no company pension are considered creditworthy then the rule is not good as these people will be rejected for having no company pension. The additional pension criterion was learned because the attribute was coincident with the subset of instances used for training. This emphasizes the need to select representative training data, but the opportunity for developing incorrect rules always exists when a rule is continually extended for the sake of improving accuracy during training. In general, the greater the number of attributes and the greater the number of attribute values, the more opportunity there is to keep extending rules for the sake of training accuracy.

Prior knowledge should, as a rule of thumb, always be used for feature selection so that a good selection of attributes (and attribute values if applicable) is made. The reason for adopting a learning method is because this prior knowledge is incomplete and so the potential for overfitting is unlikely to be resolved by feature selection alone. A typical approach to avoid overfitting is to retain a representative set of data to test performance periodically during training. This representative set is not part of the training set. The idea is that, as the tree grows, the representative set will be used to judge performance accuracy. The expectation is that the performance on both the training and representative sets will improve during the early phases of training. If overfitting occurs, the performance on the training set will continue to improve but the performance using the representative set will start to fall.

An alternative to stopping training early is to allow training to overfit the data and then to prune the tree. This is called post pruning because some nodes and their extensions are removed. A representative set of data is retained to judge the performance of pruning. The basic rule is to allow a node to be pruned provided that performance on the representative set is at least as good as that before pruning. For instance, in the credit-scoring application, the node would be pruned at the point at which the 15 positive and five negative instances are classed together. A majority vote would determine the class label to be positive in this case. Both pruning of the tree and stopping training early rely on sufficient training data for a representative subset to be retained for validating performance. An alternative method of pruning is introduced via an example.

Example 2 • • • • •

A validation set of examples given in Table 12.4 has been tested on the decision tree in Figure 12.4. There are five misclassifications. Pruning of the nodes does not improve accuracy in this case. Is there an alternative method of pruning? One technique is to convert the tree into rules and then to prune the rule conditions. After pruning, the rules are sorted in terms of accuracy. The rules corresponding to Figure 12.4 are:

1   IF A=y AND B=y THEN POS.
2   IF A=y AND B=n AND C=y THEN POS.
3   IF A=y AND B=n AND C=n THEN NEG.
4   IF A=n THEN NEG.

Rule accuracy will be calculated simply by counting the proportion of correctly classified examples, as shown in Table 12.5.

Rules 2 and 4 are 100% accurate and so they are left as they are. All combinations of rule conditions for rules 1 and 3 are tabulated below.

Table 12.4 Validation set of examples

Example	A	B	C	Class	Tree misclassified
1	Y	Y	Y	P	
2	Y	Y	Y	P	
3	Y	Y	Y	P	
4	Y	Y	Y	P	
5	Y	Y	Y	P	
6	Y	Y	N	N	*
7	Y	Y	N	N	*
8	Y	Y	N	N	*
9	Y	N	Y	P	
10	Y	N	Y	P	
11	Y	N	Y	P	
12	Y	N	Y	P	
13	Y	N	N	P	*
14	Y	N	N	P	*
15	Y	N	N	N	
16	Y	N	N	N	
17	Y	N	N	N	
18	N	N	N	N	
19	N	Y	N	N	
20	N	Y	Y	N	

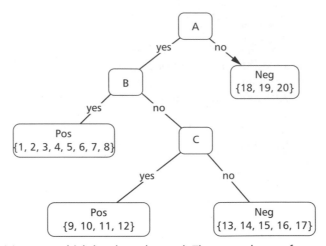

Figure 12.4 A decision tree which has been learned. The examples are from a validation test set defined in Table 12.4. The tree misclassifies examples {6, 7, 8, 13, 14}.

Table 12.5 Calculating rule accuracy

Rule	POS classifications	NEG classifications	Accuracy
1	5	3	5/8
2	4	0	4/4
3	2	3	3/5
4	0	3	3/3

Rule	Drop A	Drop B	Drop C	Drop A and B	Drop A and C	Drop B and C	Choice
1	5/10	11/17					Drop B
3	4/6	6/8	3/9	8/10	4/10	6/17	Drop A and B

The final set of rules is:

1   IF A=y THEN POS.
2   IF A=y AND B=n AND C=y THEN POS.
3   IF C=n THEN NEG.
4   IF A=n THEN NEG.

Sort them by accuracy and generality:

IF A=n THEN NEG {18, 19, 20}
IF A=y AND B=n AND C=y THEN POS {9, 10, 11, 12}
IF C=n THEN NEG {6, 7, 8, 13, 14, 15, 16, 17}
IF A=y THEN POS {1, 2, 3, 4, 5}

Examples 13 and 14 are misclassified but the accuracy has improved.

Summary

Decision trees can be used as classifiers. Each leaf node represents a class, with the class label being determined by a majority vote. The internal nodes represent attributes and branches represent attribute values. The tree can be interpreted as a set of rules. The tree is learned by selecting a 'best' attribute as the root node. Branches are then added to the root node, with one branch for each attribute value. The training examples are assigned to each branch by matching against the attribute values. The foot of each branch then acts as a new root node and the procedure is repeated for each one of these nodes. The 'best' node is selected in a number of ways. One commonly used measure for selecting a 'best' node is entropy.

Further reading

The ID3 algorithm was introduced by Quinlan (1986). ID3 provides a simple approach to decision tree learning, but for real-world problems the algorithm needs to be extended to cope with issues such as noise in the training data, missing attribute values and attributes with continuous values. In this chapter we have touched on the issue of overfitting data, which can be caused by noisy data (training data that have been incorrectly classified). Also, we have suggested that continuous attributes can be made discrete by defining a set of thresholds and dividing training examples into subsets according to which threshold bin that value lies. Quinlan (1990) provides an extension to handle noisy data and missing attribute values. The essence of the approach is to provide a probabilistic classification using Bayesian statistics. The key extensions to ID3 are encapsulated in C4.5, details of which can be found in Quinlan (1993).

There are a number of other tree, or attribute-valued rule, induction algorithms. RIPPER (Cohen, 1995) is a rule induction algorithm that constructs rules with the body of each rule described by a conjunction of attribute values. CART (Breiman *et al.*, 1984) is another tree induction algorithm that builds a binary tree.

Proprietary extensions/modifications of the algorithms mentioned here have found their way into commercial data mining applications (see Chapter 24).

Exercises

1   Sketch a decision tree for the following samples:

X	Y	CLASS
T	F	pos
F	F	neg
T	F	pos
F	F	neg
T	F	pos
F	T	pos
F	T	pos

2   Give the truth table for the following tree and identify the Boolean function that it represents.

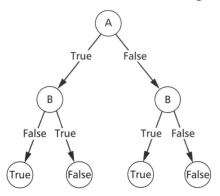

3   Calculate the entropy for the following classification and the information gain for X and Y.

X	Y	Class
T	T	+
T	F	−
T	F	+
T	T	+
F	T	−

4   Following the procedure for ID3, construct the decision tree for the following table:

A	C	Class
a1	c1	Pos
a1	c2	Pos
a1	c2	Pos
a1	c2	Pos
a1	c1	Pos
a2	c1	Pos
a2	c1	Pos
a2	c1	Pos
a2	c2	Neg
a2	c1	Neg
a2	c1	Neg

CHAPTER 13

Inductive Logic Programming

In Chapter 12, decision tree learning was introduced. We saw how the tree could be interpreted as a set of rules, expressed as a conjunction of attribute–value pairs. For many tasks, this form of rule is sufficient. However, we can also imagine many domains where a richer language that uses predicates and co-referencing with variables would be desirable. Describing family relationships requires such a language. For example, X and Y are siblings if they have a common parent.

$$\text{sibling}(X, Y) \leftarrow \text{parent}(Z, X) \wedge \text{parent}(Z, Y).$$

Describing structural relationships also requires a predicate language. For example:

$$\text{covered}(X, Y) \leftarrow \text{on\_top}(Y, X).$$

could be used to deduce that block b is covered by block a if block a is on top of block b.

Prolog is a language that is commonly used to represent predicate relationships and perform deductive inference. The expressive power of logic languages has motivated research into algorithms that can learn programs expressed in a logic language. Inductive logic programming (ILP) refers to the automated (really semiautomated) construction of logic programs. This chapter introduces the basics of ILP, some of the key issues that must be addressed in any ILP system and the basic elements of ILP algorithms.

In the remainder of this chapter we shall use Prolog syntax to describe clauses. Therefore ':-' will be used in place of '$\leftarrow$' and ',' in place of '$\wedge$'. Predicate names and constants will start with a lowercase letter and variables with a capital letter. So

$$\text{sibling}(X, Y) \leftarrow \text{parent}(Z, X) \wedge \text{parent}(Z, Y).$$

is written as:

$$\text{sibling}(X, Y) \text{ :- } \text{parent}(Z, X), \text{parent}(Z, Y).$$

13.1 Introduction

The application of learning algorithms to real-world problems requires background knowledge. This knowledge is often implicit in the process. A typical role for background knowledge is in applying feature extraction techniques, which to be most effective usually requires an understanding of the data. One of the strengths of ILP is that the role of background knowledge (often called background theory) is used in a direct, explicit way.

A typical ILP task specifies a set of positive and negative training examples, background knowledge, B, and hypothesis language. The task is to find a hypothesis, H, such that all positive examples are entailed and all negative examples are not entailed. More formally, the target predicate definition should satisfy:

1   $B \wedge H \vDash p$ for all p, where p is a positive training example;
2   $B \wedge H \nvDash n$ for all n, where n is a negative training example.

The first rule is called **completeness** and means that the hypothesis and background theory should entail all positive training examples. The second rule is called **consistency** and states that the hypothesis and background theory should not entail any negative example.

Example 1 • • • • •

The task is to learn the concept of animal classes. A set of positive and negative examples is given. The background theory lists a number of properties for each class of animal. The rules that have been learned satisfy the completeness and consistency constraints.

Positive examples	Negative examples
class(trout, fish)	class(trout, reptile)
class(salmon, fish)	class(trout, bird)
class(eagle, bird)	class(salmon, reptile)
class(ostrich, bird)	class(salmon, bird)
class(robin, bird)	class(eagle, reptile)
class(crocodile, reptile)	class(eagle, fish)
class(lizard, reptile)	class(ostrich, reptile)
class(dog, mammal)	class(ostrich, fish)
	class(robin, reptile)
	class(robin, fish)
	class(crocodile, fish)
	class(crocodile, bird)
	class(lizard, fish)
	class(lizard, bird)

Background knowledge	
has_covering(trout, scales)	has_legs(robin, 2)
has_covering(salmon, scales)	has_legs(crocodile, 4)
has_covering(eagle, feathers).	has_legs(lizard, 4)
has_covering(ostrich, feathers)	lays_eggs(trout)
has_covering(robin, feathers)	lays_eggs(salmon)
has_covering(crocodile, scales)	lays_eggs(eagle)
has_covering(lizard, scales)	lays_eggs(ostrich
has_gills(trout).	lays_eggs(robin)
has_gills(salmon).	lays_eggs(crocodile)
has_legs(eagle, 2)	lays_eggs(lizard)
has_legs(ostrich, 2)	

Rules that have been created using inductive inference:

    class(X, fish) :- has_gills(X).
    class(X, reptile) :- has_covering(X, scales), has_legs(X, 4).
    class(X, bird) :- has_covering(X, feathers).

● ● ● ● ●

Example 2 ● ● ● ● ●

ILP systems can also learn arithmetic operations. Given below is the typical form of training examples used in the ILP system Progol (see Muggleton, 1995). The background knowledge consists of definitions for incrementing an integer (inc) and decrementing an integer (dec).

Positive examples	Negative examples
mult(4, X, Y) :- plus(X, X, Z), plus(X, Z, Z1), plus(X, Z1, Y).	:- mult(0, 0, 1).
mult(3, X, Y) :- plus(X, X, Z), plus(X, Z, Y).	:- mult(2, 3, 12).
mult(2, X, Y) :- plus(X , X, Y).	:- mult(2, 4, 10).
mult(1, X, X).	:- mult(2, 5, 4).
mult(0, X, 0).	:- mult(2, 5, 12).
plus(4, X, Y) :- inc(X, U), inc(U, V), inc(V, W), inc(W, Y).	:- mult(2, 10, 19).
plus(3, X, Y) :- inc(X, U), inc(U, V), inc(V, Y).	:- mult(3, 5, 12).
plus(2, X, Y) :- inc(X, Z), inc(Z, Y).	:- mult(3, 4, 6).
plus(1, X, Y) :- inc(X, Y).	:- mult(3, 4, 3).
plus(0, X, X).	:- mult(3, 4, 10).
plus(X, 0, X).	:- mult(3, 4, 16).

Background knowledge
inc(X, Y) :- Y is X + 1
dec(X, Y) :- Y is X − 1, 0 =< X.

Rules that have been created using inductive inference:

    plus(0, X, X).
    plus(X, 0, X).
    plus(A, B, C) :- dec(A, D), inc(B, E), plus(D, E, C).
    mult(0, X, 0).
    mult(A, B, C) :- dec(A, D), mult(D, B, E), plus(B, E, C).

● ● ● ● ●

13.2   Generating the hypothesis

There are two general approaches to finding the hypothesis. The first approach starts with a very general clause and looks to specialize the clause; the second starts with a specific clause and aims to generalize it. The first approach can be viewed as a top-down search and the second as a bottom-up search.

13.2.1 Top-down

Given the clause:

class(A, reptile).

we can specialize the clause by adding literals to the body or by applying a substitution for variables. The following specialization:

class(A, reptile) :- has_covering(A, feathers)

will fail to satisfy logical constraints as none of the positive examples in Example 1 for reptile is entailed by this rule (there is no match for an A which both is a reptile and has feathers). The following clause:

class(A, reptile) :- has_covering(A, scales)

succeeds in matching positive examples, but it needs further specialization to prevent negative examples being entailed. Adding the new literal has_legs(A, 4) will succeed in satisfying completeness and consistency constraints (it entails all positive examples but none of the negative examples is entailed).

class(A, reptile) :- has_covering(A, scales), has_legs(A, 4)

13.2.2 Bottom-up

Given a specific clause:

class(A, reptile) :- has_covering(A, scales), has_legs(A, 4), lays_eggs(A).

we can generalize by dropping a literal from the body or replacing a constant with a variable. Example generalizations include:

class(A, reptile) :- has_covering(A, scales), has_legs(A, 4)
class(A, reptile) :- has_covering(A, scales), lays_eggs(A)
class(A, reptile) :- has_covering(A, scales)
class(A, reptile) :- has_covering(A, scales), has_legs(A, B)

13.3 Inductive inference

An inductive learning algorithm starts with a target concept such as class(A, reptile) or mult(X, Y, Z). Inference rules are applied to generate hypotheses, which are then tested against the positive and negative examples. The background knowledge, along with a definition of allowable predicates (language definition), specifies the allowable form of the final hypothesis.

13.3.1 Inductive inference rules

A clause c_1 is more general than a clause c_2 if and only if $c_1 \vDash c_2$. This states that c_1 entails c_2 or that c_2 can be proved from c_1.

Given a background theory B and hypothesis H, the formula:

$$B \wedge H \vDash P$$

states that P can be deduced from B and H, which we know as deduction. Deriving H from B and P is induction. Induction can be thought of as the inverse of deduction.

A naive approach to constructing H from B and P would be to enumerate over H (generate the different possibilities) and then test H on the database of examples. However, allowing the enumeration to happen in an uncontrolled way will lead to a combinatorial explosion. In other words, the space of hypotheses becomes too large to search and so the search has to be expanded in a controlled manner using generalization and specialization operators.

In the remainder of this chapter, we are going to introduce a top-down learning algorithm, FOIL, and then introduce induction from the perspective of inverting implication. This will then lead into a general description of a bottom-up algorithm for rule induction.

13.4   FOIL

FOIL (Quinlan, 1993) is a top-down induction algorithm. It starts with the head of a clause (left-hand side) and specializes it by adding literals to the clause body. The algorithm stops when no negative examples are entailed or when the clause becomes too complex (as judged by some heuristic). The algorithm is given in Figure 13.1.

Example 3 ○ ● ● ● ●

This example illustrates the basics of FOIL. In practice, more candidate literals (to specialize a clause) would be generated, but this example generates only a minimum set for the sake of simplicity.

Positive examples
{<+(X, b747)>, <+(X, c130)>}
Negative examples
{<-(X, starling)>, <-(X, robin)>, <-(X, cadillac)>}
Background knowledge
hasengine(b747), hasengine(cadillac), hasengine(c130), haswings(c130), haswings(b747), haswings(robin), haswings(starling), energysource(b747, fuel) energysource(c130, fuel), energysource(cadillac, fuel), energysource(robin, food), energysource(starling, food)
For completeness we note that b747 and c130 are types of aircraft, cadillac is a type of car and the other two objects types of bird.

Each example is written as a vector of ordered pairs in which the first element of each pair is a variable and the second element the value. Each pair denotes a predicate argument. The task is to learn the target predicate aeroplane(X).

PROCEDURE FOIL

form a set T of training examples (both positive and negative examples)

        Each member t_i of T is an ordered list containing pairs where the first element of each pair is a variable and the second element the value. The number of pairs for each t_i will initially correspond to the number of arguments in the target predicate. So if the target predicate is parent(X, Y) each t_i will have two ordered pairs {(X, value for X), (Y, value for Y)}.

while T contains positive examples

        Initialise a new clause head with the target predicate

$$P(V_1, V_2, ..., V_k) \leftarrow$$

        Where P is the predicate and $V_1, V_2, ..., V_k$ denote the arguments (so a binary predicate would be initialised with two variables)

        form a new training set T_{copy}

$$T_{copy} \leftarrow T$$

        while T_{copy} contains negative examples

                Find a literal L to add to the right hand side of the clause

                Form a new empty training set T_{new}

                    Call extendExamples(T_{copy}, T_{new})

$$T_{copy} \leftarrow T_{new}$$

        end while

        remove from T any examples covered by the new clause

end while

PROCEDURE extendExamples(T_{copy}, T_{new})

for each member t_i of T_{copy}

        for each binding b of any new variables introduced by the literal L

                if t_i and b satisfy L

                        add b to t_i

                        add t_i to T_{new}

                end if

        end for

end for

Figure 13.1 FOIL algorithm.

The training set, T, is initialized to:

    {<+(X, b747)>
    <+(X, c130)>
    <-(X, starling)>
    <-(X, robin)>
    <-(X, cadillac)>}

Initialize new clause:

aeroplane(X) :-

Form a new training set that is a copy of T:

{<+(X, b747)>
<+(X, c130)>
<-(X, starling)>
<-(X, robin)>
<-(X, cadillac)>}

T_{copy} has negative examples and so find a literal L to add to the right hand side of the clause:

candidate literals:
hasengine(X), haswings(X), energysource(X, Y), energysource(Y, X).

(Note that in a real application, FOIL generates other candidate literals using negation and equality.)

hasengine(X) will produce the following extensions
{<+(X, b747), (X, b747)>
<+(X, c130), (X, c130)>
<-(X, cadillac), (X, cadillac)>}

haswings(X) will produce the following extensions
{<+(X, b747), (X, b747)>
<+(X, c130), (X, c130)>
<-(X, robin), (X, robin)>
<-(X, starling), (X, starling)>}

energysource(X, Y) will produce the following extensions
{<+(X, b747), ((X, b747), (Y, fuel))>
<+(X, c130), ((X, c130), (Y, fuel))>
<-(X, robin), ((X, robin), (Y, food))>
<-(X, starling), ((X, starling), (Y, food))>
<-(X, cadillac)((X, cadillac), (Y, fuel))}

hasengine appears to be the best literal since it extends all positive examples and removes two of the three negative examples: So T_{copy} is now:

{<+(X, b747), (X, b747)>
<+(X, c130), (X, c130)>
<-(X, cadillac), (X, cadillac)>}

and the clause becomes:

aeroplane(X) :- hasengine(X)

There is still a negative example and so we continue.

T_{copy} has negative examples and so find a literal L to add to the right-hand side of the clause:

Since all examples have an energy source, the literal energysource(X, Y) will extend all examples. The literal haswings(X) will eliminate cadillac. So the clause will become

aeroplane(X) :- hasengine(X), haswings(X)

● ● ● ● ●

13.4.1 Literal forms

Thus far, not much has been said about the literal forms that FOIL can consider. The forms that FOIL considers are:

- $P(V_1, V_2, ..., V_n), \neg P(V_1, V_2, ..., V_n)$, where P is a predicate and V_is are variables. At least one V_i must have already occurred in the clause, so, given aeroplane(X) :-, hasengine(X) is acceptable but hasengine(Y) is not; also energysource(X, Y) is acceptable but energysource(Y, Z) is not as both Y and Z are new to the clause.
- $V_i = V_j, V_i \neq V_j$ – the values of existing variables can be compared.
- $V_i = c, V_i \neq c$, where c is a theory constant. So, in Example 3, the clause :- energysource(X, Y), Y = food would separate out the birds.
- $V_i \geq k, V_i < k, V_i > V_j, V_i \leq V_j$, etc. These allow FOIL to compare numeric values for attributes against a threshold k and against other attributes.

In Example 3, judgement was used to select a literal from the candidate set. For a computer implementation of the algorithm, this judgement needs to be quantified. The measure FOIL uses is called **gain** and is based on information theory.

$$gain(L_i) = s\{-\log_2(T^+_{copy}/|T_{copy}|) - [-\log_2(T^+_{new}/|T_{new}|)]\}$$

where T^+ is the number of positive examples, $|T|$ is the total number of examples in the set and s is the number of positive examples in T_{copy} that have extensions in T_{new}. Note that s is not necessarily the same as T^+_{new} because a positive example in T_{copy} could have more than one extension in T_{new} (e.g. an aircraft may have two different types of energy source).

So in Example 3, T_{copy} is initially set to:

{<+(X, b747)>
<+(X, c130)>
<-(X, starling)>
<-(X, robin)>
<-(X, cadillac)>}

and the extended set T_{new} when considering hasengine(X) was:

{<+(X, b747), (X, b747)>
<+(X, c130), (X, c130)>
<-(X, cadillac), (X, Cadillac)>}

So the gain is:

$$gain(hasengine) = 2\{-\log_2 (2/5) - [-\log_2 (2/3)]\} = 1.47$$

13.5   Inverting resolution (reversing implication)

This section introduces the idea of implementing induction as the inverse of implication. There are several inductive inference rules that work by the principle of inverting implication, but θ-subsumption, introduced in the next section, is the most practical.

One deductive inference rule introduced in Chapter 4 is the resolution rule. Remember that two literals of the form A and $\neg A$ are known as a complementary pair. If two clauses contain a complementary pair, they may be resolved to give a new clause (the resolvent). For example, given the rule $A \rightarrow B$ and datum A, B can be deduced. The two clauses (A and $A \rightarrow B$) are resolved to give B. The clauses are first transformed into conjunctive normal form (CNF): $A \rightarrow B$ is transformed into the equivalent form $\neg A \vee B$. The first clause (A) and the second clause ($\neg A \vee B$) contain a complementary pair of literals, and these literals can be resolved (cancelled if you like) to produce the new clause B. The resolvent of two clauses can be described as below:

$$res(C_1, C_2) = (C_1 - \{\lambda\}) \cup (C_2 - \{\neg\lambda\})$$

where C_1 and C_2 are clauses and λ and $\neg\lambda$ are literals. The disjunctive clauses in the above formula are represented as sets. So, A and $\neg A \vee B$ are represented as $\{\{A\}, \{\neg A, B\}\}$ The resolvent using the above formula is then:

$$res(\{A\}, \{\neg A, B\}) = (\{A\} - \{A\}) \cup (\{\neg A, B\} - \{\neg A\})$$

where '–' is set difference.

The resolvent is sometimes more easily seen using the inverted tree notation, as shown in Figure 13.2.

Inverting the resolution rule derives one of the initial clauses from the resolvent clause and the other initial clause. For example, $\neg A \vee B$ could be derived from B and A by inverting resolution. In this sense, induction can be viewed as the inverse of deduction. Suppose that the resolvent is C and the other initial clause is C_1 and the task is to derive C_2. Whatever literal is present in C_1 but not in C must have its complement in C_2 otherwise C_1 and C_2 could not be resolved to produce C. So, the inverse of resolution can be describe by the process:

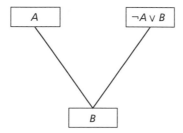

Figure 13.2 B is the resolvent of A and $\neg A \vee B$. Inverting resolution takes the resolvent and the clause from one of the branches to produce the clause on the other branch.

1   Identify a literal λ that occurs in C_1 but not in C.
2   Form the second clause C_2 by performing the following set operations: $C_2=(C-(C_1-\{\lambda\}))\cup\{\neg\lambda\}$.

A key observation is that there are multiple possibilities for C_2. For instance $C_1=\{A, D\}$ and $C_2=\{\neg A, B, \neg D\}$ will resolve to B. In other words, inverse resolution is not deterministic and any ILP algorithm that incorporates inverse resolution must utilize some heuristic to determine which choice for C_2 is preferable.

So far we have used inverse resolution only for the propositional case, but the language of ILP has predicates and variables. The extension to the first-order case is straightforward and is achieved by applying unifying substitutions. For example, father(X, david) will unify with father(graham, david) given the substitution {X/graham}. Suppose we have:

> father(pam, charles)
> mother(catherine, pam)
> grandfather(catherine, charles)
> grandfather(Z, X) :- father(Y, X), mother(Z, Y)

Converting the grandfather rule to CNF produces:

$$grandfather(Z, X)\vee\neg father(Y, X)\vee\neg mother(Z, Y)$$

The resolution procedure for first-order expressions is:

1   Identify a literal λ_1 that occurs in C_1 and a literal λ_2 that occurs in C_2 such that $\lambda_1\theta=\lambda_2\theta$.
2   Form the resolvent by performing the following set operations: $res(C_1, C_2)=(C_1-\{\lambda_1\})\theta\cup(C_2-\{\neg\lambda_2\})\theta$.

Inverting the equation above provides the inverse procedure. Figure 13.3 illustrates inverse resolution for the first order case.

13.6   θ-Subsumption

The simplest inference rule for ILP comes from θ-subsumption defined by Plotkin (1969): a clause c_1 θ-subsumes a clause c_2 if and only if there exists a substitution θ such that $c_1\theta\subseteq c_2$. Under θ-subsumption c_1 is a generalization of c_2. For example:

> $c_1\theta$ = sister_of(caroline, david) :- sibling(caroline, david), female(caroline)

> c_2 = sister_of(caroline, david) :- sibling(caroline, david), female(caroline), female(mary)

c_2 is θ-subsumed by:

> c_1 = sister_of(X, Y) :- sibling(X, Y), female(X)

with the substitution:

> θ = (X/caroline, Y/david) – this gives $c_1\theta$

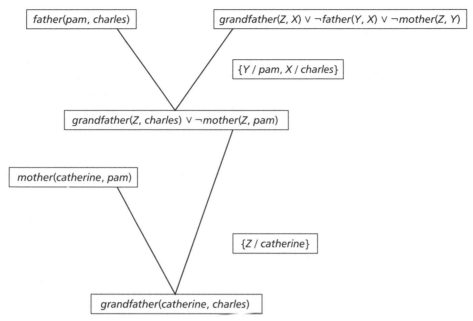

Figure 13.3 Illustration of inverting resolution for first-order logic.

To see this we put the clauses in CNF. So, for clause 1, c_1, we have:

{sister_of(caroline, david), $\neg$ sibling(caroline, david), $\neg$ female(caroline)}

and for c_2:

{sister_of(caroline, david), $\neg$ sibling(caroline, david), $\neg$ female(caroline), $\neg$ female(mary)}

We see that $c_1 \theta \subset c_2$

Thus, the first clause is a generalization of the second clause. θ-Subsumption is also a special case of entailment. If c_1 θ-subsumes c_2 then $c_1 \models c_2$. The converse is not necessarily true. There are examples where $c_1 \models c_2$ but c_1 does not θ-subsume c_2. Consider the following self-recursive clauses:

A. dog(mother_of(X)) $\leftarrow$ dog(X)
B. dog(mother_of(mother_of(X))) $\leftarrow$ dog(X)

The first clause says that a mother of a dog is a dog, and the second says that the mother of the mother (grandmother) of a dog is a dog. A entails B but A does not θ-subsume B (there is no substitution that makes the literals in clause A a subset of clause B).

13.7 Practical implementations of ILP systems that invert implication

We said earlier that a naive approach to inductive learning would be to generate a candidate hypothesis and then test it against the examples. If the hypothesis and background knowledge allow all positive examples to be proved, but none of the negative examples can be proved, then the hypothesis satisfies the logical constraints. The hypothesis can be represented as a set of clauses. Unfortunately, the number of clause combinations is too large to search unless some ordering of the clause space is imposed to guide the search. Almost all ILP systems use subsumption as opposed to inverting resolution for generating candidate clauses. Inverting resolution can easily lead to a combinatorial explosion of the search space.

Subsumption imposes a lattice on the clauses that can be part of a hypothesis. Basically, this means that for any two clauses there is a partial ordering that is based on whether one clause subsumes the other. Also, two clauses have what is called a **least upper bound** and a **greatest lower bound**. The greatest lower bound for clauses c_1 and c_2 is simply their union. The least upper bound is the least general generalization (lgg), which is defined below.

Given a pair of terms, literals or clauses u, v, L is the lgg of u and v if and only if:

1   L is a common generalization of u and v.
2   Every other common generalization of u and v is also a generalization of L.

Remember that c_1 is a generalization of c_2 if and only if c_1 subsumes c_2.

Without trying to understand the detail of the above, for the purpose of this introduction it is sufficient to know that θ-subsumption provides a method of generalizing and specializing a clause using simple syntactic operations. Once we have the subsumption lattice we can define a general algorithm to perform induction:

1   Choose a positive example e to be generalized.
2   Construct the most specific single-clause hypothesis c_s.
3   Find the best clause c in the subsumption lattice that is above c_s.
4   Remove all clauses made redundant by c.

The basis of this algorithm is more easily understood through an example.

Example 4 ● ● ● ● ●

Suppose we look to generalize:

class(trout, fish).

The most specific clause is:

class(trout, fish) :- has_covering(trout, scales), lays_eggs(trout), has_gills(trout).

We can generalize this with:

class(A, fish) :- has_covering(A, scales), lays_eggs(A), has_gills(A).

Now we can look for redundancy. Redundancy means that the new clause can replace one or more other clauses without affecting things that the program can prove. This form of redundancy does not apply in this example as no other clauses have been previously generated. Another form of redundancy exists if literals can be removed from a clause without affecting the things that can be proved. In this example, removing the literals {has_covering(A, scales), lays_eggs(A)} still proves all positive examples of class fish (refer back to Example 1) without covering any negative examples. The example has now been generalized to:

class(A, fish) :- has_gills(A).

● ● ● ● ●

13.7.1 Generating the most-specific clause

Given background knowledge B and a positive example e, we want the most specific clause, subject to:

$$B \wedge h_s \vDash \neg e$$

Or:

$$h_s \vDash \neg (B \wedge \neg e)$$

The procedure is:

1   Compute $\neg e$.
2   Find the conjunction of literals that can be derived from B and $\neg e$.
3   Compute the most specific clause by taking the negation of the conjunction formed in step 2. This produces a disjunction of literals that is a clause.

In Example 1, the first example, e, is class(trout, fish) and the background knowledge is:

{has_covering(trout, scales), lays_eggs(trout), has_gills(trout)}

Step 2 produces the conjunction of literals:

{¬class(trout, fish), has_covering(trout, scales), lays_eggs(trout), has_gills(trout)}

Negating the above conjunction:

{class(trout, fish) ∨ ¬has_covering(trout, scales) ∨ ¬lays_eggs(trout) ∨ ¬has_gills(trout)}

which is the same as:

class(trout, fish) :- has_covering(trout, scales), lays_eggs(trout), has_gills(trout)

13.7.2 Controlling search using language bias

To further constrain the search for clauses a language bias can be employed. A language bias can constrain the language used to express the hypothesis in a number of ways that include:

1   specifying which literals can appear as a head for a clause;
2   specifying which literals can appear in the body of a clause;
3   type constraints for arguments;
4   which arguments must be known before program execution and which serve as output, e.g.

mult(input-int, input-int, output-X) specifies that the first two arguments will be supplied as input and the third will be produced as output like mult(3, 4, X);

5   when a literal appears in a clause, which arguments should have variables and which arguments should have constants.

Progol (Muggleton, 1995) employs all of the above specifications. Each predicate symbol is given a mode declaration (modeb – predicate can appear in the body of a clause; modeh – predicate can appear as the head of a clause). For each argument the following is specified:

*   input (+) or output (–);
*   constant (#);
*   type.

For example:

   modeh(1, class(+animal, #class))

says that a generalization must have the form:

   class(A, #) :- …

where A is an input of type animal and # is a constant of type class. And:

   modeb(1, has_gills(+animal))

says that has_gills(+animal) can appear in the body of a clause and the argument is of type animal. From these two mode declarations Progol will accept as legal a clause of the form:

   class(A, #) :- has_gills(A)

13.7.3 Preference bias

In practice, there will be more than one hypothesis that will satisfy a given task and so a natural question to ask is 'Which hypothesis is to be preferred?'. Given two hypotheses h1 and h2, both satisfying the consistency and completeness constraints, a preference bias means that one hypothesis is chosen over the other. This choice has to be justified. For inductive inference we really need a probabilistic framework for justification, the reason being that we cannot be certain how any learned clause will perform on unseen data. One way of computing the justification is to use Bayes' rule and select the hypothesis, H, that maximizes:

   P(H | Examples)

Summary

Inductive logic programming is the process of learning logic programs (e.g. programs in Prolog) from a training set of examples and background knowledge. There are two basic approaches to induction: top-down learning and bottom-up learning. A top-down approach will typically start with a general clause and seeks to specialize the clause by adding literals so that only positive examples are entailed. Additional clauses are generated to satisfy completeness and consistency constraints. A bottom-up approach starts with a specific clause and seeks to cover more positive examples by generalizing that clause.

Further reading

For further reading see Flach (1998), Muggleton (1987, 1988), Muggleton and DeRaedt (1994) and Quinlan and Cameron-Jones (1993).

Exercises

1   $r \mapsto \{a1, a2, a5, a6\}$ $p \mapsto \{a2, a3, a5, a7\}$ $q \mapsto \{a1, a2, a6\}$ $s \mapsto \{(a2, f), (a1, l), (a6, f)\}$, class_1 $\mapsto \{a2\}$, class_2 $\mapsto \{a2, a6\}$

Given the above sets, which express the mappings between predicates r, p, q, s, class_1 and class_2, give a specialization of:

class_1(X) :- r(X), p(X)

such that the rule is only satisfied by class_1 members. Give a rule that will correctly classify only members of class_2.

2   FOIL has been used to extend the following set of examples:

$\{+,+,+,+,+,+,-,-,-,-\}$

The new extension is:

$\{+,+,+,+,+,+,-,-\}$

What is the information gain (the extension is a subset of the original examples)?

3   FOIL is constructing a new rule with head:

p(Y) :-

Which of the following literals could be considered as candidate extensions?

a   q(Y)
b   r(X),

c   s(X, Y)

d   ¬s(X, Y)

4   The clause pred_1(a) has been resolved with clause C to give pred_2(b, a). Give an expression for C.

5   Show that

      p(a, b) :- q(b, a), r(a), r(b)

is a specialization of:

      p(X, Y) :- q(Y, X), r(Y) under the substitution (X/a, Y/b).

6   Given example:

      class(a, b)

and background knowledge:

      {pred_1(a, c), pred_2(a, d)}

give the most specific clause for class(a, b).

Chapter 14

Reinforcement Learning

Many of the skills that we acquire throughout our lives are learned through interacting with the environment. Learning to walk, learning to ride a bike and learning to converse are all examples. A rally car driver is an expert at reading road and track conditions, and by predicting the effect of these conditions on the handling of the car he can anticipate with precision what control inputs he needs to apply. The driver uses his senses to obtain data about the state the car is in, and obtains future state information by looking ahead and taking information from his navigator. His knowledge, learned through experience, is used to interpret these data, and a judgement is made about what control inputs are required to keep the car moving as fast as possible while still under control. When learning to drive, the rally driver might take explicit instruction from a trainer on how to handle certain situations, such as skidding on ice, but it would appear that the majority of his skill is learned by doing, in other words interacting with his environment.

The computational approach to learning by interaction is known as **reinforcement learning**. In supervised learning, there is a supervisor to say that a particular vibration signal is from a cracked gear tooth or that an image is the character 'C', for example. In reinforcement learning there is no explicit supervisor. Instead, an agent gets feedback on its performance. This feedback expresses the desirability of a state such as being in balance on a bike, the positions and moves during a game of chess, the response of a car to a driver's input, etc.

In this chapter we introduce reinforcement learning. First we introduce the concepts that describe how we should choose actions to optimize a task. Then we introduce a number of analytical approaches for finding optimum actions, before finally introducing the learning algorithm.

14.1 Introduction

Reinforcement learning is about learning to map situations to actions. Situations are described more generically as states. A state might represent the configuration of pieces during a game of chess, or a state might represent a manoeuvre of a fighter jet engaged in air combat. An action changes the situation and therefore yields a new state. A move in chess changes the configuration of the board pieces, inputs to flight controls of a jet fighter changes the aircraft attitude. There may be several competing actions such as which chess piece to move and what location to move that piece to. Actions usually, but not always, result in a transition from one state to another state. For instance, depressing the accelerator pedal in a car does nothing if the cable is broken. States are associated with a desirability level known more formally as a **reward**. The game of chess will have rewards that associate states with the potential to win.

During learning, we are attempting to acquire knowledge needed to perform a task. Often, we express the successful outcome of a task as a goal. For example, the goal could be to stay in balance on the bike, to win the game of chess, to find the quickest route to work, etc. Suppose that the goal is to be the world's number one tennis player. The environment is the tennis court, the opponent, the racket, the ball, the umpire, the crowd, etc. The tennis player makes use of all his senses to obtain data about a situation. The focus for his senses will be learned. For instance, in order to react and hit the ball he will sense the movement of his opponent and predict what his opponent is about to do. When it is his turn to strike the ball he has to decide which set of actions will maximize his chance of hitting a winning shot. What we start to see is that learning can involve many facets: learning to process sensory input and deciding what input to focus on; learning which actions are likely to maximize the chance of attaining the goal; and learning temporal relationships.

Temporal reasoning is required for many practical tasks. For instance, the action of pumping air into a punctured tyre still results in the same state, a 'flat tyre', but the rate of deflation may be slow enough for the cyclist to get home (so the action to inflate the tyre might achieve the goal of getting home). In this chapter we are going to assume that sensors are available with sufficient processing capability to deliver the data about states – in other words, we shall not be concerned with learning how to read states. Instead, we are going to concentrate on learning the mapping between states and actions in order to achieve a goal. The worlds that we are interested in learning to model are not deterministic. We might have a belief about the outcome of some action but rarely will we be certain about the outcome. Unless it is the winning move, a chess player cannot be certain about the outcome of moving a board piece, and a tennis player is never certain that the ball will follow the desired trajectory.

A simple example

In Figure 14.1 a mobile agent has the task of navigating its way from the start state (marked S) to the finish state (marked F). The agent wants to get to the finish state with the least amount of effort. If distance is computed as the number of squares (states) negotiated in reaching F then there are two paths of equal distance (length 5). Although both paths are the same distance and represent the shortest paths for reaching F, for one of these paths there is a lake that has to be negotiated, and traversing a lake is twice the effort of traversing a standard square. The path of least effort is shown in Figure 14.1. If the agent were to be dropped on to a square other than the start state then the optimum route could be through the lake. From square 2, the optimum route would take the agent through the lake.

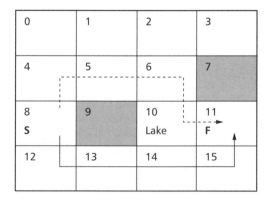

Figure 14.1 The outer perimeter is a wall and the shaded squares are also walls. A simple navigation task to move from S to F with the least amount of effort is shown (solid line). The dotted line is a path of the same length but takes more effort because the lake has to be negotiated.

The agent attempts to move to a square by performing one of four actions: N – north, S – south, W – west and E – east. It might be assumed that this task could be solved using a naive search algorithm. This approach is fine if the world modelled by the grid is deterministic, i.e. the outcome of any action is always known (e.g. executing the action S in square 2 always results in the agent moving to square 6). If the agent is equipped with sensors to sense its environment then it can assess the situation after every move and select the action that is expected to be optimal. Equipped with such sensors, the agent can react to actions that are not deterministic. For example, an action may move the agent in the intended direction 90% of the time, but 10% of the time it moves the agent in the opposite direction. So in state 6 the action W would usually move the agent to state 5, but occasionally it will move the agent east, where it bumps into the wall and remains in state 6.

• • • • •

14.2 The key elements of reinforcement learning

Using its sensors, the agent perceives its environment in each state in which it finds itself, and from its percepts it chooses an action. A mapping of the agent's perceived states of its environment to actions is called a **policy**. An optimal policy for the world shown in Figure 14.1 is given in Figure 14.2(a). The optimal policy defines which action to take for each state.

For a given state, the agent should be able to perceive how good the state is in terms of meeting its goal (in this example the goal is getting to F) and also the expected **reward** of any action, as a given action is expected to move the agent to a new state (if the agent meets a wall then it stays in the same state). A reward function maps state–action pairs to a real-valued reward. The reward indicates the desirability of the state. The goal state, F, could be given a reward of 1.0. The effort to perform an action in any state could be given a negative reward (viewed then as a cost associated with the action). The rewards chosen for the example are somewhat arbitrary. In practice, the rewards must be set to model the required behaviour. For instance, it takes twice as much effort to traverse the lake as it does to cross the other squares, and so its reward (penalty if you like) is twice that of any other square.

A reward value indicates the immediate reward on entering a state, but the agent's goal is to maximize the reward that it will receive in the long term. For each action/transition the agent

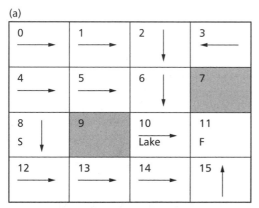

Figure 14.2 (a) An optimal policy is shown for the agent world described in Figure 14.1. (b) The utility values are given that correspond to the policy shown in (a). The arrows indicate in which direction to move.

receives a reward. In Figure 14.1 the rewards are 1.0 for state 11, –0.01 for state 10 and –0.05 for all other states. The **return**, R, is the sum of all rewards:

$$R_t = r_{t+1} + r_{t+2} + \ldots + r_T = \sum_{i=1}^{T} r_{t+i}$$

The optimal path in Figure 14.1 would have a reward of:

$$-0.05 + -0.05 + -0.05 + -0.05 + -0.05 + 1.00 = 0.75$$

Each sequence is known as an **episode** or **epoch**. So, in Figure 14.1, all paths leading from some state to the finish state are episodes.

Discounting is another concept that is often used in computing the reward. With discounting, future rewards are weighted less than immediate rewards. A discount rate, λ, specifies this weighting.

$$R_t = \sum_{i=0}^{T} \lambda^i r_{t+1} \quad 0 \le \lambda < 1 \tag{14.1}$$

where t denotes a time step. If λ is zero then only the immediate reward is considered.

Suppose in Figure 14.1 that all rewards are zero apart from the finish state, which has a reward of 1, then the shorter the path the higher the discounted return (for non-zero values of λ).

Given a path, a return can be computed. From a particular start state in Figure 14.1 an agent could take many paths in reaching the finish state. If the agent were to act in a totally random manner then sometimes the path taken will take far more than five transitions. For each state and each choice of action there is a **utility** value that is the expected return for a state–action pair. The expected utility of a state is required in order to define an optimal policy. A value-function specifies the utility values for each state. The utility of a state provides a real-valued measure of the desirability of a state in terms of its reward and the rewards that will be accumulated from states that are likely to follow. The utility values for the world in Figure 14.1 are given in Figure 14.2(b). The optimum policy for a state is the action that returns the highest expected utility:

$$\pi_i^* = \arg\max_a \sum Pa_{ij} U_j \tag{14.2}$$

where π^* is the optimum policy, Pa_{ij} is the probability of reaching state j if action a is performed in state i and U_j is the utility of state j. As an example, consider state 0 in Figure 14.2(b). For a state only the maximum utility of all actions is shown (remember that there are four actions). Choosing the action S (to move south) is expected to move the agent to state 4. The behaviour of the agent is stochastic, and the model described earlier stated that 90% of the time the action is successfully executed and 10% of the time the agent moves in the opposite direction, which in this example results in the agent hitting the wall and staying in state 0. The probabilities are therefore:

$$P_{\text{south}0,4} = 0.9 \qquad P_{\text{north}0,0} = 0.1$$

where P is subscripted with the action, the current state and the state that follows if the action is successfully executed.

The expected utility of the action south in state 0 is therefore:

$$U_{south}(0) = (0.9 \times 0.710) + (0.1 \times 0.654)$$

$$= 0.704$$

For the other actions, the values are {north=0.66, west=0.66, east=0.704}. We see then that there are two optimal policies, to move south or east. The optimum policy for state 0 has a utility value shown as 0.654 in Figure 14.2(b). This is because the reward (a cost) for any action in any state (other than the finish state or the lake) is –0.05. The reward for the lake is –0.1.

14.3   Computing the optimal policy

To compute an optimal policy the agent needs to be able to assess for any state the expected reward of any following state and the reward that is expected to be accumulated for each successive state that is likely to follow. The utility values in Figure 14.2(b) provide real values for the assessment of the world described in Figure 14.1. For example, if the agent finds itself in state 5, its future reward is expected to be maximized by choosing to move to state 6. Remember that the utility values provide a measure of the expected immediate and future reward. The nearer the agent gets to the finish state, the higher the expected reward, because the agent is increasingly more likely to succeed in reaching the finish state. (The environment is stochastic so there is always a possibility – albeit very small – that the agent having reached state 13, for example, returns to state 8. However, the possibility of this happening is less when the agent reaches state 14 and even less again when it has reached state 15.)

The agent uses its sensors to perceive its environment and inform it of the current state. Ideally, the agent would like to know everything that would be useful in making its decision. We might suppose that knowledge of previous states provides part of this useful information. For example, if we wish to predict whether an athlete halfway through a marathon is likely to win, it is important to know if that athlete expended too much effort early on in the race in addition to knowing the athlete's position relative to the others. How much information about previous states should the agent remember? In practical problems a judgement has to be made about the increased benefit of added complexity and cost of computation. If we could measure (sense) certain physiological properties of all the athletes halfway through the race we might believe we could make an adequate prediction without retaining an explicit record of the past history of states. In fact, the added sensors are retaining much of the history that is important because an athlete's physical state will depend on what the athlete has done during the race. A decision process is said to have the **Markov property** if the transition probabilities to a succeeding state depend only on the current state and not on the history of previous states. If, for example, the agent is playing a game of chess then its next move would depend only on the current board state and not the previous states. We shall assume that the agent's sensors are sufficiently informative so that each state can be considered a Markov state – future values are then a function only of the current state.

More formally, the Markov property allows us to rewrite:

$$P(s_{t+1} = s' \mid s_t, s_{t-1}, \ldots, s_0)$$

as:

$$P(s_{t+1} = s' \mid s_t) \tag{14.3}$$

where s denotes state.

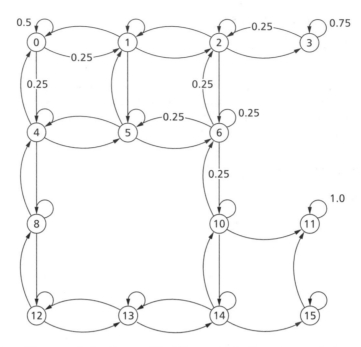

Figure 14.3 A transition graph for the world of Figure 14.1. There is a node to represent each state that the agent can enter. The edges have real values, indicating transition probabilities between states. All outgoing edges from a state must sum to 1. State 11 is an absorbing state, and once in this state the agent remains. If we assume the Markov property then the likelihood of any successive transition depends only on the current state and not on the previous history of states. For example, to reach state 5 the agent might have taken the path 8–8–4–5 or the path 8–4–0–1–1–5, but the next transition does not depend on knowing this history – in other words knowing the path leading to state 5 does not help in predicting the next state.

A Markov model describes a stochastic process and, as real-world problems tend to be stochastic, the Markov models are of interest. Figure 14.3 is a transition graph for Figure 14.1. There is a state node for each state in the grid – the blank squares in Figure 14.1 are not included in the transition graph as the agent can never enter those squares. The edges in the graph are weighted with transition probabilities. All edges that are outgoing from a node must sum to 1. All actions in the model of Figure 14.1 can occur with equal probability. The behaviour is such that 90% of the time the action is successful (e.g. action S leads to a move south) but 10% of the time the action moves the agent in the opposite direction. In state 0, the actions {north, south, west, east} result in the agent staying in state 0 with probabilities {0.9, 0.1, 0.9, 0.1}. In state 0, the actions {north, south, west, east} result in the agent transiting to state 1 with probabilities {0, 0, 0.1, 0.9}. In state 0, the actions {north, south, west, east} result in the agent transiting to state 4 with probabilities {0.1, 0.9, 0, 0}. Normalizing these action probabilities means that the agent will transit to states {0, 1, 4} with probabilities {0.5, 0.25, 0.25}. These transition probabilities can be represented using a transition matrix P. The entries of the matrix for Figure 14.3 are given in Table 14.1.

A transition in the Markov model corresponds to a single time step. Starting in state 8 (start), it takes a minimum of five time steps to reach state 11 (finish). If the agent acts in an uninformed manner and selects actions at random what is the probability of reaching state 11 from state 8 in five time steps? There is a convenient way of computing all transition probabilities after t time steps. If P is the transition matrix the transition probabilities after two time steps are $P^2 = P \times P$ and after three

Table 14.1 The transition probabilities for Figure 14.3 are presented in matrix form. The leftmost column denotes the source node and the first row denotes the sink node. For example, the entry at 5, 6 is 0.25 and represents the probability of transiting from state 5 to state 6

	0	1	2	3	4	5	6	7	8	9	10	11	12	13	14	15
0	0.5	0.25	0	0	0.25	0	0	0	0	0	0	0	0	0	0	0
1	0.25	0.25	0.25	0	0	0.25	0	0	0	0	0	0	0	0	0	0
2	0	0.25	0.25	0.25	0	0	0.25	0	0	0	0	0	0	0	0	0
3	0	0	0.25	0.75	0	0	0	0	0	0	0	0	0	0	0	0
4	0.25	0	0	0	0.25	0.25	0	0	0.25	0	0	0	0	0	0	0
5	0	0.25	0	0	0.25	0.25	0.25	0	0	0	0	0	0	0	0	0
6	0	0	0.25	0	0	0.25	0.25	0	0	0	0.25	0	0	0	0	0
7	0	0	0	0	0	0	0	0	0	0	0	0	0	0	0	0
8	0	0	0	0	0.25	0	0	0	0.5	0	0	0	0.25	0	0	0
9	0	0	0	0	0	0	0	0	0	0	0	0	0	0	0	0
10	0	0	0	0	0	0	0.25	0	0	0	0.25	0.25	0	0	0.25	0
11	0	0	0	0	0	0	0	0	0	0	0	1	0	0	0	0
12	0	0	0	0	0	0	0	0	0.25	0	0	0	0.5	0.25	0	0
13	0	0	0	0	0	0	0	0	0	0	0	0	0.25	0.5	0.25	0
14	0	0	0	0	0	0	0	0	0	0	0.25	0	0	0.25	0.25	0.25
15	0	0	0	0	0	0	0	0	0	0	0	0.25	0	0	0.25	0.5

time steps $P^3 = P \times P \times P$. In general, for t time steps, the transition probabilities can be computed from P^t.

The transition probabilities from state 8 to all other states for 1–5 time steps are given in Table 14.2. After one time step the agent can only reach states 4 or 12 or remain in state 8. After two time steps the agent could also reach states 0, 5 or 13. Probabilities can be computed by tracing through Figure 14.3. For example, to compute the probability of staying in state 8 after two time steps, we take the product of probabilities along each path and sum all path probabilities. The paths are 8–8–8, 8–4–8, 8–12–8. The corresponding probabilities are {0.5, 0.5}, {0.25, 0.25} and {0.25, 0.25}, and so the probability of remaining in state 8 after two time steps is $(0.5 \times 0.5) + (0.25 \times 0.25) + (0.25 \times 0.25) = 0.375$. Of course, it takes at least five time steps for the agent to reach state 11. From Table 14.2 it can be seen that the probability of reaching state 11 in five time steps is very low (0.003). This is to be expected as the agent is acting in a totally uninformed, random manner. Given enough time we would expect the agent to reach state 11 and so, for a large value of t, P^t will show that the probabilities for reaching state 11 from any other state approach 1.

The Markov model to represent the world of Figure 14.1 is actually more complex than shown in Figure 14.3. Firstly, the model needs to be extended to represent the choice of actions. Figure 14.4 shows part of the state–action transition graph for state 0 in the simple world of Figure 14.1.

14.3.1 Value functions

The utility values in Figure 14.2(b) are optimal. Each state will have a value for each action, but

Table 14.2 The transition probabilities for five time steps are shown for transiting from state 8 to other states. These probabilities are computed using matrix multiplication. Given the matrix P in Table 14.1, rows {1, 2, 3, 4, 5} correspond to $\{P^1, P^2, P^3, P^4, P^5\}$

	0	1	2	3	4	5	6	7	8	9	10	11	12	13	14	15
1	0.000	0.000	0.000	0.000	0.250	0.000	0.000	0.000	0.500	0.000	0.000	0.000	0.250	0.000	0.000	0.000
2	0.063	0.000	0.000	0.000	0.188	0.063	0.000	0.000	0.375	0.000	0.000	0.000	0.250	0.063	0.000	0.000
3	0.078	0.031	0.000	0.000	0.172	0.063	0.016	0.000	0.297	0.000	0.000	0.000	0.234	0.094	0.016	0.000
4	0.090	0.043	0.012	0.000	0.152	0.070	0.020	0.000	0.250	0.000	0.008	0.000	0.215	0.109	0.027	0.004
5	0.094	0.054	0.019	0.003	0.141	0.071	0.027	0.000	0.217	0.000	0.014	0.003	0.197	0.115	0.037	0.009

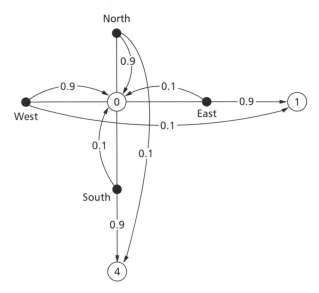

Figure 14.4 A part of the state–action transition graph for the world of Figure 14.1 is shown. The small black nodes denote actions.

only the maximum values for each state are shown. For example, state 1 has a maximum value corresponding to the action E (move east). There are, in other words, four policies for each state. One or more of these policies for each state will be optimum. State 0, for instance, has two optimum policies (only one is shown in Figure 14.2). Equation (14.2) provides the means for calculating the optimal policy for a given state and is repeated below:

$$\pi_i^* = \arg\max_a \sum Pa_{ij}U_j$$

The maximum utility of a state is given by eqn (14.4):

$$U_i^* = r_i + \arg\max_a \sum Pa_{ij}U_j \tag{14.4}$$

where r_i is the reward for state i. Equation (14.4) is a recursive relation between the value of one state and its successor states. Figure 14.5 shows the transition probabilities and utilities for the optimal policy shown in Figure 14.2(a).

Utility values can also be expressed in terms of what are called Q-values. A Q-value is the value of taking action a in state i.

$$U_i^* = r_i + \arg\max_a Q(a,i) \tag{14.5}$$

Equation (14.5) will form the basis for a learning algorithm introduced in section 14.4.

Q-values can be expressed in terms of successor states (a' is an action that can be executed in state j):

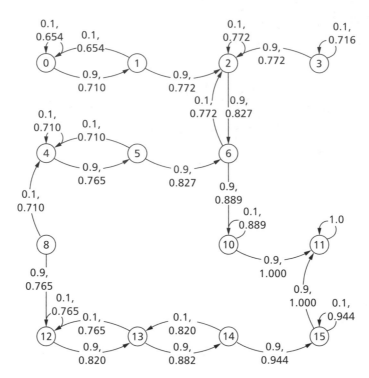

Figure 14.5 This transition graph shows the relationship between the utility values in Figure 14.2(b) corresponding to the optimal policy of Figure 14.2(a). Utility values are computed using eqn (14.4). To compute the summation $\Sigma Pa_{ij}U_j$ for a state take the product of probability and utility for each outgoing edge and sum. For example, state 6 has a utility of $-0.05 + (0.9 \times 0.889) + (0.1 \times 0.772) = 0.827$.

$$Q(a,i) = r_i + \sum P_{ij} \arg\max_{a'} Q(a', j) \qquad (14.6)$$

14.3.2 Finding an optimum policy

An impractical way to compute an optimal policy would be to compute all possible policies, simulate a large number of possible episodes and average the returns, and assign the utility as the maximum return for a state over all policies. Figure 14.2(a) is one policy out of many. The simulation for this policy would compute a number of episodes (paths) starting at state 8 and concluding at the finish state. The return for each episode is then computed and the average over all episodes found. The average would be the utility value for state 8 corresponding to the policy shown in Figure 14.2(a). All other states could be treated as start states and their utilities computed in the same way.

The above procedure is too time-consuming. Two algorithms that provide more efficient procedures in search of an optimal policy are presented below. These algorithms assume that the transition model (transition probabilities) is known. If the transition model is not known then it has to be learned while searching for the optimum policy. An algorithm that will learn the transition probabilities whilst searching for the optimum policy is presented in section 14.4.

Value iteration

We can find approximations (to any degree of accuracy required) of the utility values using an algorithm called **value iteration**. The utility values for each state are initialized to zero, apart from those states whose utility values remain fixed (e.g. the goal state in Figure 14.1), and eqn (14.4) is repeatedly applied to each state until the values converge to within some specified tolerance. The convergence simply means that the utility values change very little on further iteration. The algorithm is presented in Figure 14.6.

Equation (14.4) defines that for each update the utility of a state is computed from the old utility values of neighbouring states. Starting at state 0 in Figure 14.1, the value of:

$$\arg\max_{a} \sum Pa_{ij}U_j$$

will be zero since the utility values of the neighbouring states are initially zero. The updated value therefore for state 0 will be simply the reward for state 0 (–0.05). The updated values for the states neighbouring the goal state, F, will have a value for:

$$\arg\max_{a} \sum Pa_{ij}U_j$$

on the first iteration of the algorithm as the utility of the goal state is fixed at 1.0. As the algorithm iterates continually over the states, information from these goal-neighbouring states is propagated through the grid. Once the utility values have been found the optimal policy is computed using eqn (14.2).

Example 1 ● ● ● ● ●

Figure 14.7 shows the utility values after the first two iterations. On the first iteration, all utility values are set to zero apart from the finish state, which is set to 1. The states are updated in numerical order (0, 1, 2, …, 15). On the first iteration, the neighbouring states of state 0 have zero utility and so the utility of state 0 is simply the cost (-0.05). When state 5 is updated, the only neighbouring state that is not negative is state 6 as 6 has yet to be updated. The maximum return is therefore going to be obtained from moving east and so the utility is $-0.05+(0.9\times0)+(0.1\times-0.05)=-0.055$.

---

while not converged
       for each state i

$$U_i' = r_i + \arg\max_{a} \sum Pa_{ij}U_j$$

$$U_i \leftarrow U_i'$$

       end for
end while

where U' denotes the next state.

Figure 14.6 An algorithm for value iteration.

-0.050	-0.050	-0.050	-0.050
-0.050	-0.055	-0.055	
-0.050		0.8	1.000 F
-0.050	-0.050	0.67	0.85

-0.100	-0.101	-0.101	-0.100
-0.101	-0.110	0.66	
-0.100		0.88	1.000 F
-0.100	0.543	0.77	0.935

Figure 14.7 The utility values for the first two iterations of the value-iteration algorithm when applied to the world of Figure 14.1. The values are updated in numerical order: state 0, state 1, ..., state 15.

On the second iteration the update of state 5 is $-0.05 + (0.9 \times -0.055) + (0.1 \times -0.1005) = -0.110$.

• • • • •

Policy iteration

Figure 14.2(a) shows a policy for the grid world of Figure 14.1. There can be more than one policy, but there is always one policy that is optimal (or at least as optimal as another). Policy iteration starts by selecting a policy and calculates the utility of each state given that policy. The policy for each state is then updated using the utility values of neighbouring states. The process repeats until the policy stabilizes (i.e. does not change for each state on further iteration). The update is performed using eqn (14.2). The algorithm is given in Figure 14.8.

The notation:

$$\sum P(a = \pi_i)_{ij} U_j$$

returns the utility from neighbouring states for a fixed policy for state i. In other words, an action is fixed for each state, which initially is an arbitrary choice. The utility for each state is then determined based on this fixed policy. The algorithm then iterates through each state in turn to calculate the utility for each given action (each policy). If the maximum utility returned for a state is greater than the utility for the current policy, the policy is updated. So, for example, if state 6 currently has a policy to move north but the maximum utility corresponds to the action move south, the policy will be changed to move south.

For policy iteration the utility values do not necessarily have to converge. This is because the optimal policy is not necessarily sensitive to the utility values.

A potential problem with the algorithm as presented in Figure 14.8 is that the initial policy (and the updated policies during the early stages of iteration) may never reach the goal state. This is because the policy for each state is initially random and there may be no policy leading to the goal state. The problem then is that the utility for the goal state is not propagated and the time to convergence is slow.

do

    for each state i

$$U_i^{'} = r_i + \sum P(a = \pi_i)_{ij} U_j$$

    end for

    policyUpdated _ false

    for each state i

        if $\arg\max_a \sum Pa_{ij} U_j > \sum P(a = \pi_i)_{ij} U_j$

$$\pi_i = \arg\max_a \sum Pa_{ij} U_j$$

        policyUpdated _ true

        end if

    end for

while policyUpdated = true

Figure 14.8 Policy iteration algorithm.

14.4 Q-learning

So far we have assumed a model for the transitions between states. The Markov model provides a way to calculate the probability of transitioning between any two states. However, this model may not exist. The task, then, for the agent is to learn the transition model while searching for the optimal policy. The agent does this by exploring its environment. By observing and remembering the outcomes of interactions with the environment the agent can learn the transition model. The agent in the world of Figure 14.1, for example, may initially act in a totally uninformed (or random) way. In time the agent will observe that if an action is selected at random there is a 50% chance that it will remain in a state in which there are two walls (e.g. state 0). The agent will also learn what the expected outcome is for any action in a given state.

Equation (14.5) defines the utility of a state in terms of Q-values, which is the utility of doing some action a in state i.

$$U_i^* = r_i + \arg\max_a Q(a,i)$$

We also have an expression for calculating Q-values in terms of neighbouring Q-values – eqn (14.6):

$$Q(a,i) = r_i + \sum P_{ij} \arg\max_{a'} Q(a',j)$$

This equation, though, is still dependent on the transition model. How then can utility values be updated without this model? Suppose the utility values for all states in Figure 14.1 other than the goal state are initially zero. If the agent observes a transition from state 15 to the goal state, F, it will receive a reward of –0.05 (every move has a cost). There is, however, a large reward (of 1) because the goal state is reached and this reward far outweighs the cost of the move. It might therefore appear sensible to update the utility of state 15 to be closer to that of the goal state, as being in state 15 has to be quite good if it increases the chance of reaching the goal. This update could be achieved using an update rule of the form:

$$U'_i = U_i + \alpha(r_i + U_j - U_i)$$

where α is the learning rate (a real-valued parameter). This rule is known as **temporal difference learning**. If α is 0.5 then the utility for state 15 would, after transiting to the goal state and assuming that it has not previously been updated, be:

$$U'_i = 0 + 0.5(-0.05 + 1 - 0)$$

$$= 0.475$$

If we assume that when the agent finds itself again in state 15 it transits to F rather than the other possible transition to 14, the utility becomes:

$$U'_i = 0.475 + 0.5(-0.05 + 1 - 0.475)$$

$$= 0.713$$

If the agent is exploring its environment in full, then it will also transit to state 14 on some occasions when it finds itself in state 15. It can, of course, also find itself staying in state 15 when attempting a move. All of these transitions will update the utility value. If α is set to some constant, the utility values will never converge. Each update for a state depends on the transition to successive states whose values are also continually being updated. To overcome this, α can be set so that it decays based on the number of times a state is visited for a given preceding state and action. This decay can be computed by maintaining a count that records how many times the action 'north' in state 15 results in a transition to F, and how many times the action 'west' results in a transition to 14, etc.

$$\alpha_n = \frac{1}{1 + visits(a, i, j)}$$

where α_n is the value for α at iteration n and $visits(a, i, j)$ is the number of transitions from state i to state j when action a has been performed in i.

Temporal difference learning can be used with Q-values to produce an algorithm called **Q-learning**. The update rule for Q-learning is:

$$Q_n(a, i) \leftarrow (1 - \alpha_n)Q_{n-1}(a, i) + \alpha_n[r_i + \arg\max_{a'} Q_{n-1}(a', j)] \tag{14.7}$$

The basic algorithm can now be explained. A table is maintained of Q-values for each state–action pair. So, for each state in Figure 14.1, there will be four Q-values, one for each action. These Q-values are initialized to zero. The agent can start at any state. Once at a terminal state, the agent

for each state i
        for each action a
                $Q(a, i) \leftarrow 0$
        end for
end for
while exploration continues
        select an action a for the current state and execute it

        in the new state j select the maximum Q-value – $\underset{a'}{\arg\max} Q_{n-1}(a', j)$

        update the Q(a,i) using

$$Q_n(a,i) \leftarrow (1-\alpha_n)Q_{n-1}(a,i) + \alpha_n \left[r_i + \underset{a'}{\arg\max}\, Q_{n-1}(a', j) \right]$$

end while

Figure 14.9 An algorithm for Q-learning.

must reposition to some other non-terminal state in order to continue to explore its environment. An algorithm for Q-learning is presented in Figure 14.9.

There is no specified stopping criterion for the algorithm presented. The agent can keep on learning during its lifespan. In practice, however, learning maybe stopped once the Q-values have converged to within a specified tolerance.

For the agent world of Figure 14.1 we have a transition model. In Q-learning we are assuming that this model does not exist (indeed, it may not exist for a problem). This transition model is learned in the frequency counts of $visits(a, i, j)$.

The agent needs to choose actions when exploring. This choice could be purely random. In fact, this random choice is a good way of exploration in the absence of a good exploration strategy. If the agent were simply allowed to choose an action corresponding to the largest Q-value, then the agent may commit too early to actions that have high Q-values assigned early on during learning. A random choice will ensure that the agent sufficiently explores all possible state–action pairs, but to continue to behave randomly may not lead to efficient exploration. One approach is to prefer actions with higher Q-values while ensuring that other actions for a given state have a chance of being executed. This can be achieved by assigning a prior probability to each state–action pair where the probability is weighted by the Q-value. The probabilities can be assigned using a rule of the following form:

$$P(a \mid i) = \frac{k^{Q_n(a,i)}}{\sum k^{Q_n(a,i)}}$$

where k is a constant that is greater than 0. This rule ensures that every action has a chance of being selected while being able to specify the preference for higher Q-values. Suppose that a state has Q-values $\{0.8, 0.9, 0.5, 0.2\}$ and that k is 2. The probability of selecting the action corresponding to the first Q-value will be:

$$P = \frac{2^{0.8}}{2^{0.8} + 2^{0.9} + 2^{0.5} + 2^{0.2}}$$
$$= \frac{1.74}{6.17}$$
$$= 0.28$$

The complete set of probabilities is $\{0.28, 0.30, 0.23, 0.19\}$. The preference then is for the action corresponding to the second Q-value. The preference can be made even stronger by making k larger. If k were 20, the probabilities would be $\{0.34, 0.46, 0.14, 0.06\}$. We could vary the value of k during learning so that the agent acts randomly to start with but has a gradually increasing preference for higher Q-values. If k were initially set to 1, then each action selection is equally probable. The value of k could then gradually increase as learning progresses.

Summary

A policy is the mapping of a state to an action. An optimal policy for a state is one that has maximum expectation of achieving the desired goal. Judgement of an optimal policy is made using state utility values, which provide the expected return (future cumulative reward) for entering a particular state. State–action models are typically stochastic and there will exist an underlying stochastic model that describes the likelihood of state transitions given an action. When this stochastic model exists, algorithms like value iteration and policy iteration can be used to find the optimal policy. Reinforcement learning can be used to discover the stochastic model while searching for an optimum policy.

Further reading

Reinforcement learning is related to dynamic programming approaches to solving Markov decision processes. Reinforcement learning seeks to add capability when faced with approximating the decision process due to incomplete information and scaling up to real-world problems. Value iteration and policy iteration are classical dynamic programming algorithms that assume a perfect model. Dynamic programming methods are rooted in the work by Bellman (1957a,b). A good source for an in-depth introduction to reinforcement learning is the book by Sutton and Barto (1998). This book also traces the history of reinforcement learning.

Exercises

1   Sketch two policies for the following grid of utility values:

0.73	0.78	0.83
0.82	0.83	0.85
0.80	0.81	0.90

2   Assume that utility values for the grid in exercise 1 are being learned. From the top left grid, an agent can move south or east. The action is not deterministic and if the agent moves south it succeeds with probability 0.6 and stays where it is with probability 0.4. If the agent moves east the probabilities are 0.95 for success and 0.05 for staying where it is. There is no cost for moving. Which action (south or east) gives the maximum expected utility?

3   An optimal policy is shown for the middle square in the top row of the grid below. Assume that all utility values have been learned. If the agent has a probability of 0.85 of succeeding in moving east and 0.15 of moving to the square to its left, what is the utility value for the top middle square given that a move costs 0.01units?

0.73	$\rightarrow$	0.89
	0.83	

4   The Q-learning equation can be modified for the deterministic case (where an action's outcome can be predicted with certainty) by setting $\alpha = 1$. Give the modified equation. Use this equation to find the updated Q-value of S when the agent moves from S by taking the action 'east'. The square to the east has Q-values {96, 58, 88, 102}, corresponding to actions {north, south, east, west}. The immediate reward (penalty) for an action is –2.5.

5   An agent is to explore moving around the grid given below. There are no transition probabilities given. The agent starts at S and moves in a clockwise direction until it reaches F. F has a reward of 2. All transitions have a reward (penalty) of 0.1. All utility values, other than for F, are initialized to 0. Using Q-learning, calculate the utility values for all squares (other than F) for one complete clockwise circuit. Repeat the calculation for a second and third circuit.

S	F

CHAPTER 15

Neural Networks I

Artificial neural networks are parallel computing devices consisting of many interconnected simple processors. These processors really are simplistic, especially when compared with the type of processor found in a computer. Each processor in a network is aware only of signals it periodically receives and the signal it periodically sends to other processors, and yet such simple local processes are capable of performing complex tasks when placed together in a large network of orchestrated cooperation.

Work on artificial neural networks dates back to the 1940s, but it has only really been since the late 1980s that this form of computation has become popular, following some theoretical leaps in learning and the growth in available computing power. The word 'artificial' is sometimes used to make it clear that discussion is about an artificial device and not about neural circuitry found in animals. The human computer (the brain) performs some tasks that computers have not, as yet, come close to matching in performance, and some would argue that a number of these tasks might always prove elusive to computer scientists. It is not surprising then that our own neural architecture should be the inspiration for computing machines. At this point in time, in comparison with the human brain, artificial neural networks are simplistic abstractions. It is common practice to drop the prefix 'artificial' when it is clear in which context these networks are being discussed. Also, artificial neural networks are often referred to as **connectionist** networks when computing ability is emphasized rather than biological fidelity. In other words, connectionists aim to make neural networks solve a task rather than attempt to mimic faithfully some part of biological computation.

Although neural networks can be (and are) implemented as fast hardware devices, much research is performed with a conventional computer using software simulation in place of hardware implementation. Not only does software simulation provide a relatively cheap and flexible environment with which to develop ideas, but also real-world applications can be delivered in the form of a conventional piece of software. For example, neural networks are applied to credit score loan applicants, and many other applications exist that do not demand a hardware implementation.

Neural network solutions are growing more sophisticated, and no doubt over the coming years our skills for engineering these computing devices will improve. Already, though, there is a vast array of exciting developments. The application base for neural networks is enormous: credit card fraud detection, stock market forecasting, credit scoring, optical character recognition, machine health monitoring, road vehicle autopilots, learning to land damaged aircraft, etc. Further understanding of the human brain will inspire future artificial neural networks, but there is mutual support in that artificial neural networks are being used as models for brain processes to assist in our understanding of the human brain.

Neural networks are typically programmed through learning, and hence their place within this part of the book. In this chapter, we shall introduce a type of architecture known as the feed-forward network and present an algorithm for learning called **backpropagation**. Most practitioners would accept that the backpropagation algorithm played a major role in bringing neural networks back to mainstream computing.

15.1   The basic components

A neural network is a collection of nodes that are connected in some pattern to allow communication between the nodes. These nodes, also referred to as neurons or units, are simple processors whose computing ability is typically restricted to a rule for combining input signals and an activation rule that takes the combined input to calculate an output signal. Output signals may be sent to other nodes along connections known as weights. The weights usually excite or inhibit the signal that is being communicated. A neural network node is illustrated in Figure 15.1.

One of the intriguing aspects of neural networks is that, although they have nodes with very limited computing capability, when many of these nodes are connected together the complete network is capable of performing complicated tasks.

The pattern of connectivity refers to a network's wiring detail, i.e. the detail of which nodes connect, their direction of connection and the values of their weighted connections. The task that a network knows (or its program) is coded in the weights. The connection pattern is usually determined by a two-stage process: first, the system designer specifies which nodes are connected and in which direction and, second, the weight values are learned during a training phase.

Sometimes the weights can be determined without training, but the great appeal of neural networks is their ability to learn a task from being exposed to the kind of data that the network will be expected to process when fully operational. Indeed, for many applications, training is the only option for programming a network because we do not have the task-solving knowledge.

There are many different types of neural network but, in general, they will share the following features:

- a set of simple processing nodes;
- a pattern of connectivity;
- a rule for propagating signals through the network;
- a rule for combining input signals;
- a rule for calculating an output signal;
- a learning rule to adapt the weights.

15.1.1   A set of simple processing nodes

Each processing node usually has incoming weights to receive signals from other network nodes and outgoing weights to transmit signals to other network nodes. Some nodes, input nodes, exist to receive input signals. There are also nodes, termed output nodes, for outputting the results of computation. For example, if a network is used as a classifier, the inputs would be attribute values and the outputs would correspond to the different classes.

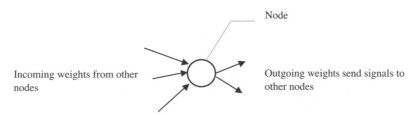

Figure 15.1 A single network node.

15.1.2 A pattern of connectivity

The pattern of connectivity refers to the way in which the nodes are connected. In one type of network, each node may connect to every other node; in another network type, nodes may be arranged into an ordered hierarchy of layers in which connections are allowed only between nodes in immediately adjacent layers; yet other types of network allow feedback connections between adjacent layers, or within a layer, or allow nodes to send signals back to themselves. A connection is parameterized by a weight. A weight is specified by three parameters:

1   the node that the weight connects from;
2   the node that the weight connects to;
3   a number (usually real) that denotes the weight value.

A negative weight value will inhibit the activity of the connected-to node whereas a positive weight will serve to excite the connected-to node. The absolute weight value specifies the strength of the connection.

The pattern of connectivity is conveniently described in a matrix, $\mathbf{W}$, where the entry w_{ij} represents the weight value from node i to node j (note that, in many texts, the matrix is written so that connections go from node j to node i: the important thing is to be consistent when performing matrix and vector operations). More than one weight matrix may be used to describe the pattern of connectivity where nodes are grouped into layers. Figures 15.2 and 15.3 give examples of the connectivity pattern written as matrices.

The weight matrix (or matrices) is the network's memory, which holds the knowledge of how to perform a task.

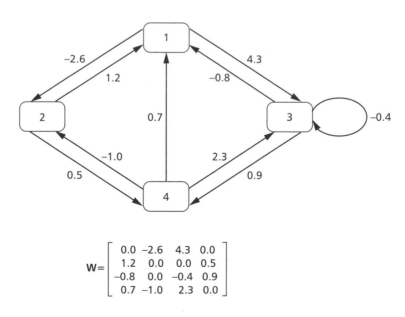

$$\mathbf{W} = \begin{bmatrix} 0.0 & -2.6 & 4.3 & 0.0 \\ 1.2 & 0.0 & 0.0 & 0.5 \\ -0.8 & 0.0 & -0.4 & 0.9 \\ 0.7 & -1.0 & 2.3 & 0.0 \end{bmatrix}$$

For example the weight that connects node 3 (row 3) with node 1 (column 1) is denoted by the value –0.8 in the weight matrix above.

Figure 15.2 The matrix describes the network's connections.

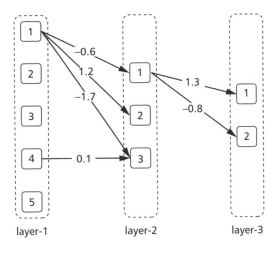

$$W_1 = \begin{bmatrix} -0.6 & 1.2 & -1.7 \\ \cdot & \cdot & \cdot \\ \cdot & \cdot & \cdot \\ \cdot & \cdot & 0.1 \\ \cdot & \cdot & \cdot \end{bmatrix} \qquad W_2 = \begin{bmatrix} 1.3 & -0.8 \\ \cdot & \cdot \\ \cdot & \cdot \end{bmatrix}$$

Figure 15.3 Matrices describe the network's connections.

15.1.3   A rule for controlling the propagation of signals through the network

Conventional computer programs impose conditions on when certain processes can start and finish. The same is true for neural networks. For a particular network type, some rule will exist to control when nodes can be updated (i.e. combine input signals and calculate an output signal) and when a signal can be sent on to other nodes. With some network types, a node is selected at random for updating, whereas other types insist that one group of nodes must update before another group can be updated.

15.1.4   A rule for combining input signals

It is typical for a node's incoming signals to be combined by summing their weighted values. This summation method is illustrated in Figure 15.4, in which net_j is the resultant combined input to the node j, x_i is the output from node i and n is the number of incoming connections. Other methods for combining input signals exist.

15.1.5   A rule for calculating an output signal

Nodes have a rule for calculating an output value that will be transmitted to other nodes or for presenting output results. This rule is known as an **activation function**, and the output value is referred to as the **activation** for the node. The activation may be real-valued, sometimes restricted to the interval [0, 1], or discrete such as {0, 1} or {+1, −1}. The value passed to the activation function is the net combined input to a node. Some activation functions are given next.

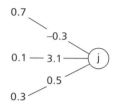

$$net_j = \sum_{i=1}^{n} x_i\, w_{ij}$$

$$net_j = (0.7 \times -0.3) + (0.1 \times 3.1) + (0.3 \times 0.5)$$
$$= 0.25$$

or, alternatively, in vector notation

$$[0.7,\ 0.1,\ 0.3] \begin{bmatrix} -0.3 \\ 3.1 \\ 0.5 \end{bmatrix} = 0.25$$

Figure 15.4 The typical way of summing the signals impinging on a node.

Identity function

The activation function for input nodes is the identity function, which simply means that the activation (signal sent on to other nodes) is the same as the net input (Figure 15.5).

Binary threshold function

Most network types rely on a non-linear activation function. A binary threshold function will limit the activation to 1 or 0 depending on the net input relative to some threshold θ (Figure 15.6). Usually, it is more convenient to add a bias term to the net input and change the threshold to its mathematical equivalent form shown in Figure 15.7. The bias w_0 is the negative of the threshold and in this case the net input is calculated as:

$$net_j = w_0 + \sum_{i=1}^{n} x_i w_{ij} \tag{15.1}$$

The bias is normally thought of as a weight coming from a node that always has an activation of 1, as shown in Figure 15.8.

The net input can be expressed as:

$$net_j = \sum_{i=0}^{n} x_i w_{ij} \tag{15.2}$$

where x_0 always has a value of 1.

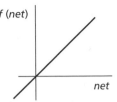

Figure 15.5 The activation is the same as the net input, $f(net) = net$. Note that $f(net)$ refers to the activation.

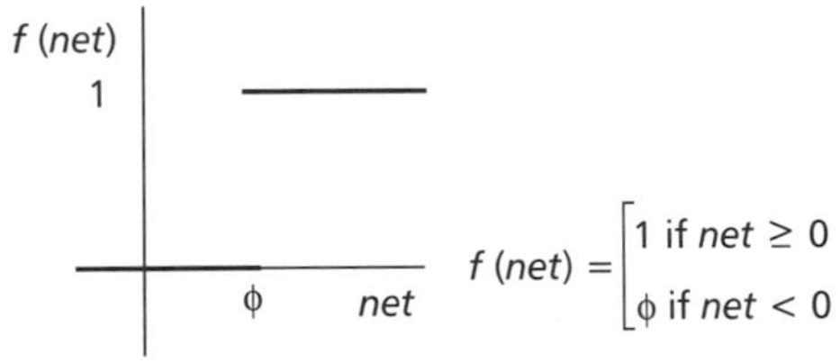

$$f(net) \qquad \qquad f(net) = \begin{cases} 1 & \text{if } net \geq 0 \\ \phi & \text{if } net < 0 \end{cases}$$

Figure 15.6 Binary threshold function.

$$f(net) \qquad \qquad f(net) = \begin{cases} 1 & \text{if } net \geq 0 \\ 0 & \text{if } net < 0 \end{cases}$$

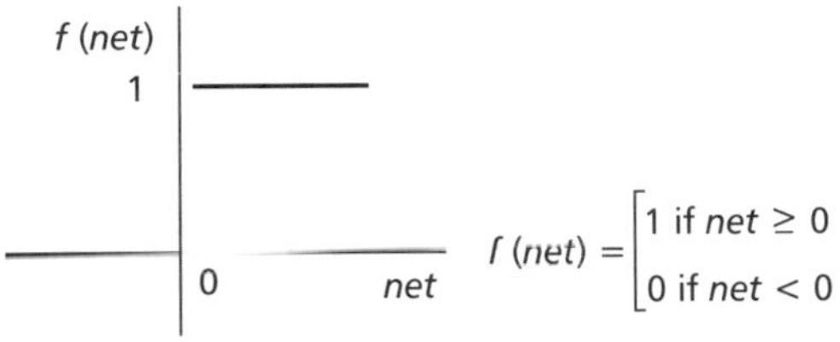

Figure 15.7 Binary threshold function with bias term added in.

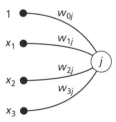

Figure 15.8 For convenience of implementation, the bias term is often thought of as being a weight that is connected to a node in the previous layer with an activation permanently set to 1.

Sigmoid function

The sigmoid function is one of the most common forms of activation functions used whose output falls in a continuous range from 0 to 1. An example is the logistic function shown in Figure 15.9. The slope and output range of the logistic function can vary. The bipolar sigmoid, for example, has an output in the range of −1 to 1.

$$f(net) = \frac{1}{1 + \exp(-net)}$$

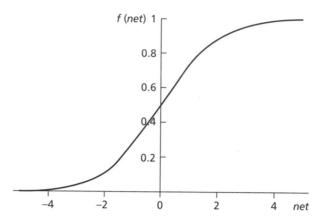

Figure 15.9 The sigmoid function.

Example 1 ● ● ● ● ●

The following example brings together some of the points discussed so far. A network is used to express the XOR relationship. The XOR relationship maps two binary inputs to 0 or 1; the definition is given in Table 15.1.

The network model shown in Figure 15.10 is a layered feed-forward network with two input nodes, two hidden nodes and one output node. The **hidden** nodes are so called because they do not take direct input from the environment or send information directly out to the environment. In this example, we can think of the environment simply as ourselves feeding values to the input nodes and monitoring the result via the output nodes. The nodes are arranged in layers: the input layer containing the input nodes, the hidden layer containing the hidden nodes and the output layer containing the output nodes. The number of nodes in each layer depends on the problem being solved and will be discussed later in this chapter. For the moment, we simply observe that the number of input nodes matches the number of attribute values describing the training examples and the number of output nodes matches the number of attributes describing the output vector associated with each training example. For this example the net input is calculated according to:

Table 15.1 XOR relationship

Input		Output
X_1	X_2	
1	1	0
0	0	0
1	0	1
0	1	1

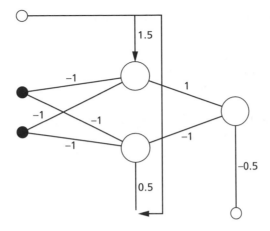

Figure 15.10 Network used to model the XOR relation.

$$net_j = \sum_{i=0}^{n} x_i w_{ij}$$

and the output will be calculated using the threshold function

$$f(net) = \begin{cases} 1 \text{ if } net \geq 0 \\ 0 \text{ if } net < 0 \end{cases}$$

The activation is the same as the net input for nodes in the input layer. Signals propagate through the network from the input layer to the output layer.

The first input will be the first sample in Table 15.1, which is $<1, 1>$. For the first hidden node with a bias of 1.5:

$$net = (x_0 \times 1.5) + (x_1 \times -1) + (x_2 \times -1)$$
$$net = (1 \times 1.5) + (1 \times -1) + (1 \times -1) = -0.5$$

so the output$=0$. For the second hidden node with a bias of 0.5:

$$net = (x_0 \times 0.5) + (x_1 \times -1) + (x_2 \times -1)$$
$$net = (1 \times 0.5) + (1 \times -1) + (1 \times -1) = -1.5$$

so the output$=0$.

For the output node with a bias of -0.5:

$$net = (x_0 \times -0.5) + (x_1 \times 1) + (x_2 \times -1)$$
$$net = (1 \times -0.5) + (1 \times 1) + (1 \times -1) = -0.5$$

so the output is 0.

If the procedure is followed for the other three samples, the output of the network will match the output column in Table 15.1.

15.1.6 A learning rule to adapt the weights

The network illustrated in Example 1 implements the XOR function. The correct operation of this XOR network is dependent on the arrangement of nodes, the choice of activation function and the weights. The arrangement of nodes is usually fixed at the start of learning, and so is the choice of activation function. The task during learning then is to adapt the weights so as to produce the desired response.

It is usual for the weights to be set to small random values at the start of training and so, when an input sample is presented for the first time, it is unlikely that the network will produce the correct output. This discrepancy between what the network actually outputs and what it is required to output constitutes an error, and this error can be used to adapt the weights. An example of an error-correcting rule is the **delta rule** or **Widrow–Hoff rule**. For an output node that has a single input weight, an activation (i.e. output) of y and a target output t, the error, δ, is given by:

$$\delta = t - y \tag{15.3}$$

The signal into the output node is x. The delta rule states that the adjustment to be made, Δw, is:

$$\Delta w = \eta \delta x \tag{15.4}$$

where η is a real number known as the learning rate. The new weight is then the adjustment added to the old weight:

$$w_{new} = w + \Delta w \tag{15.5}$$

At the start of training, the weights are set to small random values, for instance in the range $[-0.7, +0.7]$. The backpropagation algorithm is a generalized version of the delta rule. During training, each example in turn is presented to the network and weights are continually adapted until for any input example the error drops to an acceptable low value. Upon completion of training, the network is tested on data that were not seen during training to test generalization.

15.2 Fundamental concepts

This section will consider basic concepts before moving on to look at the backpropagation model.

15.2.1 Decision function

To introduce the concept of how a neural network operates, a trivial task is presented and the most basic type of network is used to solve that task.

Figure 15.11 illustrates a classification task. The task is to provide rules to classify an instance as either a member of class A or class B. The rules could be given in symbol form:

> IF $x_2 > 0.80$ AND $x_1 < 0.55$ THEN class A
> IF $x_2 < 0.90$ AND $x_1 > 0.25$ THEN class B

The above rules[1] use discrete limit values that effectively partition the space into rectangular regions. An alternative approach to using rules is to derive a classification function by defining a

---

[1]Note that x_1 is used in place of x and x_2 in place of y. Subscripting on x is used when problems have a high number of dimensions. For example, x_3 is used in place of z.

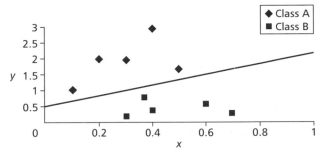

Figure 15.11 The separation of two classes using idealized data.

line that separates the two classes. The class for a new instance can be judged by plotting its location in the x, y plane and observing on which side of the line the instance is. In the present scenario it is possible to visualize the data as a two-dimensional picture. However, when handling hundreds of samples with a large number of attributes (i.e. a high-dimensional problem) it is no longer possible to visualize the task (not using standard charts).

The solution then is to use a decision function. The equation of the line that separates the two classes is:

$$x_2 = 1.5x_1 + 0.5$$

This equation can be used to create a decision function:

$$f(x_1, x_2) = -x_2 + 1.5x_1 + 0.5$$

$$d = \begin{cases} class\ B \text{ if } f(x_1, x_2) \geq 0 \\ class\ A \text{ if } f(x_1, x_2) < 0 \end{cases}$$

For example, a sample from class B $<0.4, 0.5>$ will give:

$$f(0.4, 0.5) = -0.5 + (1.5 \times 0.4) + 0.5 = 0.6$$

The decision function will classify the sample correctly as a member of class B.

The above decision function could be modelled using a neural network, as shown in Figure 15.12.

The node in Figure 15.12 calculates an output value according to the threshold criteria:

$$output = \begin{cases} 1 \text{ if } total\ input \geq 0 \\ 0 \text{ if } total\ input < 0 \end{cases}$$

An output value of 1 would indicate a member of class B and an output of 0 would indicate a member of class A.

Example 2 ● ● ● ● ●

Find the weights for a neural model similar to Figure 15.12 that represents the equation:

$$2x_2 = -4x_1 + 8$$

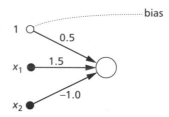

Figure 15.12 A simple neural network that models a line.

For any point that falls on the line, the weights will be defined such that:

$$w_0 + x_1 w_1 + x_2 w_2 = 0$$

Rearranging gives:

$$x_2 = -x_1 \frac{w_1}{w_2} - \frac{w_0}{w_2}$$

Equating terms gives:

$$-\frac{w_1}{w_2} = -\frac{4}{2}, -\frac{w_0}{w_2} = \frac{8}{2}$$

So, $w_0 = -8$, $w_1 = 4$ and $w_2 = 2$.

15.2.2 Adapting the weights

It should be obvious from Figure 15.11 that many straight lines can be drawn as the separating boundary and therefore many sets of weights exist to provide a solution. If t_j denotes the target or desired output from node j and o_j the actual output, then the error E_p for an example p can be defined as:

$$E_p = 1/2 \sum_j (t_j - o_j)^2 \tag{15.6}$$

and the overall error $E = \Sigma E_p$. The factor 1/2 is included for convenience later on.

The activation for any node is dependent on the net input to that node and therefore is dependent on the weights impinging on that node. Imagine a node as in Figure 15.12 but with no bias. Such a node can model any straight line that passes through the origin. For a linear activation function and a single input vector, eqn (15.6) can be written as:

$$E = 1/2(t - net)^2 \tag{15.7}$$

because for a linear activation function the output is the same as the input. Expanding gives:

$$E = \frac{1}{2}[t^2 - 2t\,net + net^2] \tag{15.8}$$

$$= \frac{1}{2}[t^2 - 2t(x_1 w_1 + x_2 w_2) + x_1^2 w_1^2 + 2x_1 w_1 x_2 w_2 + x_2^2 w_2^2]$$

with $net = x_1 w_1 + x_2 w_2$. Differentiating eqn (15.8) with respect to w_1:

$$\frac{\partial E}{\partial w_1} = (-t + x_1 w_1 + x_2 w_2)x_1 \tag{15.9}$$

Equation (15.8) shows that if the squared error is plotted against w_1 the shape is parabolic, as shown in Figure 15.13, and if eqn (15.9) is set to 0 and solved the minimum point on the curve can be found.

Training starts with random weights and the initial state can therefore be anywhere on the error surface but is unlikely to be at its minimum. During training, the network should adapt its weights so that the overall error is reduced. The weights should therefore be adjusted in the direction of steepest descent.

15.2.3 Minimizing the squared error

A science experiment that many children will have performed at school is to plot the deflection of a beam against different loads and then to fit a best straight line by minimizing the sum of the squared differences between each point and the line. The same principle can be used to adapt weights and one such rule for adapting weights is the delta rule introduced earlier. This rule is:

$$\Delta w_{ij} = \eta \delta_j x_i, \qquad \delta_j = (t_j - o_j) \tag{15.10}$$

where t_j is the target value at node j, o_j is the actual output, x_i is the signal coming from node i, η is the learning rate (by how much to adapt the weight) and Δw_{ij} is the amount by which to change the weight connecting node i with j.

The rule is simple to derive for a linear node with the output defined as:

$$o_j = \sum_i x_i w_{ij}$$

The chain rule can be used to express the derivative of the error surface with respect to a weight as a product that reflects how the error changes with a node's output and how the output changes with an impinging weight:

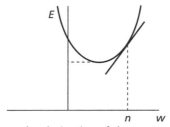

Figure 15.13 The line represents the derivative of the error with respect to a weight at time n.

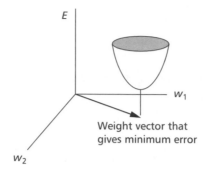

Figure 15.14 The error can be plotted for different combinations of weights.

$$\frac{\partial E}{\partial w_{ij}} = \frac{\partial E}{\partial o_j} \frac{\partial o_j}{\partial w_{ij}}$$

$$\frac{\partial E}{\partial o_j} = -\delta_j \qquad\qquad (15.11)$$

$$\frac{\partial o_j}{\partial w_{ij}} = x_i$$

and substituting back into eqn (15.11):

$$-\frac{\partial E}{\partial w_{ij}} = \delta_j x_i \qquad\qquad (15.12)$$

Taking into account the fact that the weights need to change in a direction that is opposite to the direction of the gradient vector and that a learning rate is factored in, eqn (15.10) is derived.

A modification to this method of adapting weights will be given in section 15.4 to train networks with multiple layers of nodes, but before that we shall take a look at what advantage such a network offers over one with just a single layer of weights (i.e. a layer of input nodes and a layer of output nodes).

15.3 Linear and non-linear problems

The network in Figure 15.12 has two input nodes for two attributes. The number of attributes denotes the dimension of the space that all input samples are drawn from: so a simple network model consisting of three inputs and a single output node will model a plane, and for n-inputs the model will be a n-dimensional plane. For a classification task, if a line (for two dimensions) or a plane (for n-dimensions) can separate all samples into their correct class, then the problem is linear. If the problem requires multiple lines or planes to separate the samples then the problem is non-linear. A famous non-linear example is the XOR problem introduced earlier.

The XOR problem, then, is non-linear, and there are two options for solving it with a neural network: either use a network that will model two or more lines to separate the data or change the input vectors. The latter option can make the problem linear by augmenting the two input attributes with a third to make the samples three-dimensional (the two classes will then reside on two different ends of a cube). For most problems we prefer the network to sort out the non-linearity; after all, a main attraction of neural networks is their ability to solve problems for which a solution is not immediately obvious. Therefore, we shall concentrate on a solution that uses two lines to separate the data. The network then will require two hidden nodes, both connected to two input nodes to represent the two lines, and a third node to combine the outputs from the two hidden (middle) nodes. The XOR task with separating boundaries is illustrated in Figure 15.15. Figure 15.16 shows a neural network architecture that will model the two separating boundaries.

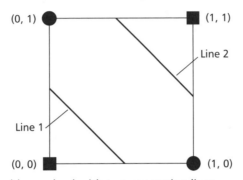

Figure 15.15 The XOR problem solved with two separating lines.

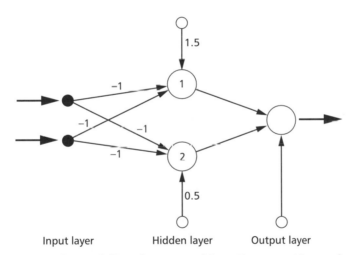

Figure 15.16 Neural net for modelling the XOR problem. The second layer of weights is shown later.

Table 15.2 Response of hidden nodes for the network shown in Figure 15.16

		Net input to hidden layer		Output from hidden layer	
x_1	x_2	Node 1	Node 2	Node 1	Node 2
1	1	−0.5	−1.5	0	0
0	0	1.5	0.5	1	1
1	0	0.5	−0.5	1	0
0	1	0.5	−0.5	1	0

What does the first layer of weights do to each input vector? Nodes on the input layer will be indexed by i, nodes on the hidden layer by j and the output nodes by k. The network in Figure 15.16 has the nodes split into the three layers. Table 15.2 shows the net input and output (using a threshold function) of the nodes in the hidden layer in response to the inputs for the XOR problem.

Each sample is transformed by the action of the first layer of weights and the hidden nodes. The second layer of weights connecting the hidden layer to the output layer will also model a line as there will be two inputs and a bias passing values to the single output node. If the output node is to respond with the correct class for each input sample, then the input to the second layer of weights must be linearly separable. This can be checked by plotting the response of the hidden nodes as shown in Figure 15.17. Figure 15.18 shows the weights that define the separating line given in Figure 15.17.

A network with only linear activation functions is restricted to modelling linear problems. The association law of matrix multiplication tells us that for linear activation functions a single layer of

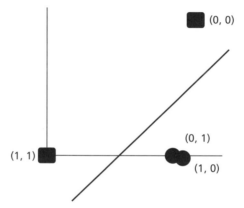

Figure 15.17 The effect of the first layer of weights has been to move the original point (0, 1) to (1, 0).

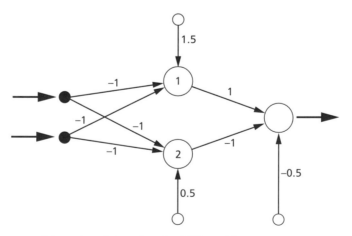

Figure 15.18 The complete network to solve the XOR problem.

weights can be found that will achieve the same result as a network that has more than one layer of weights. In other words, a multilayered network with linear activation functions will only be able to solve a problem that a single layered network is capable of solving. Therefore, non-linear problems are ruled out. For multilayered networks then, a non-linear activation function is required, and for the backpropagation algorithm the function should be continuous, differentiable and monotonically increasing. A function satisfying these properties is the sigmoid function.

15.4   Backpropagation learning

For many years there was no rule available for updating the weights of a multilayered network undergoing supervised training. In the 1970s, Werbos developed a technique for adapting the weights, but it was the publication by Rumelhart, Hinton and Williams (1986a) that gave a new lease of life to neural networks. The weight adaptation rule is known as backpropagation. For what follows, a fully connected feed-forward network is assumed, which means activation travels in a direction from the input layer to the output layer, and the nodes in one layer are connected to every other node in the next layer up.

The backpropagation algorithm defines two sweeps of the network: first a forward sweep from the input layer to the output layer and then a backward sweep from the output layer to the input layer. The backward sweep is similar to the forward sweep except that error values are propagated back through the network to determine how the weights are to be changed during training. This double sweep is illustrated in Figure 15.19.

During training, each input sample will have an associated target vector. The objective of training is to find a set of network weights that provide a solution to the particular problem at hand. Before training commences, the weights are set to small random values, for example between –0.7 and 0.7. For reasons discussed earlier, a non-linear activation function, the sigmoid, will be used. The logistic sigmoid can only produce values between 0 and 1, and, because the function can never actually attain an exact 0 or 1, sometimes 0.1 and 0.9 are used instead of 0 and 1. The network is usually considered to have learned a task once all outputs fall within a specified tolerance of their target values. For example, if the target output is 1.0 and the tolerance is 0.1 then any actual output

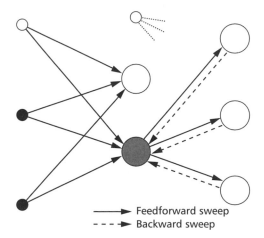

Figure 15.19 The shaded hidden node sends activation to each output node and so during the backward sweep this hidden node will receive error signals from these output nodes.

between 0.9 and 1.0 will be within the specified tolerance. The procedure for backpropagation training is as follows:

```
while not STOP
        STOP=TRUE
            for each input vector
                perform a forward sweep to find the actual output
                obtain an error vector by comparing the actual and target output
                if the actual output is not within tolerance set
                        STOP=FALSE
                end if
                perform a backward sweep of the error vector
                use the backward sweep to determine weight changes
                update weights
            end for
    end while
```

In summary, a sample is presented to the network and an error vector is calculated to determine how the weights should change; the process is then repeated for each other sample. An epoch is a complete cycle through all samples (i.e. each sample has been presented to the network). The samples are continually presented to the network, epoch after epoch, until during one epoch all actual outputs for each sample are within tolerance.

15.4.1 Some theory

Backpropagation uses a generalization of the delta rule. For a more in-depth presentation than that given here, the interested reader is referred to Rumelhart *et al.* (1986a) or Werbos (1990).

The error derivative can be expressed as

$$\frac{\partial E}{\partial w_{ij}} = \frac{\partial E}{\partial o_j} \frac{\partial o_j}{\partial net_j} \frac{\partial net_j}{\partial w_{ij}} \tag{15.13}$$

δ_j is defined as:

$$\delta_j = -\frac{\partial E}{\partial net_j} \tag{15.14}$$

The original delta rule in section 15.2.3 had the definition as:

$$\delta_j = -\frac{\partial E}{\partial o_j}$$

This definition is consistent with eqn (15.14) as the original delta rule is for linear nodes in which the output is the same as the input. The definition for δ_j can be expressed as:

$$\delta_j = -\frac{\partial E}{\partial o_j} \frac{\partial o_j}{\partial net_j} \tag{15.15}$$

As:

$$E_p = {}^1\!/_2 \sum_j (t_j - o_j)^2$$

we have:

$$\frac{\partial E}{\partial o_j} = -(t_j - o_j) \qquad (15.16)$$

For activation function f' (typically the logistic function) the output is:

$$o_j = f(net_j) \qquad (15.17)$$

and so the derivative f' is given by:

$$\frac{\partial o_j}{\partial net_j} = f'(net_j) \qquad (15.18)$$

So:

$$\delta_j = (t_j - o_j) f'(net_j) \qquad (15.19)$$

The standard summation of products is used to find the net total input:

$$net_j = \sum_{i=0} x_i w_{ij}$$

and so

$$\frac{\partial net_j}{\partial w_{ij}} = x_i \qquad (15.20)$$

So taking the product of each derivative and substituting back into eqn (15.13) gives:

$$\frac{\partial E}{\partial w_{ij}} = (t_j - o_j) f'(net_j) x_i \qquad (15.21)$$

Noting that the weight change should be in the direction opposite to the derivative of the error surface, the weight change for a node is:

$$\Delta w_{ij} = \eta \delta_j x_i$$

The error δ_j given above is applicable to an output node, but the error for a hidden node is not directly related to the target output. However, a hidden node can be adapted in proportion to its assumed contribution to the error in the next layer up (i.e. output layer for a network with a single hidden layer). For a network with a single hidden layer, the error from each output node will make a contribution to the error of each hidden node by propagating error signals back through the network. The contribution to a hidden node will depend on the size of the error for an output node and the strength of the weight that connects both nodes. In other words, an output node with a high error makes a strong contribution to the error of any hidden node that is connected by a weight with a high strength. For a hidden node the error is given by:

$$\delta_j = f'(net_j) \sum_k \delta_k w_{kj} \qquad (15.22)$$

where k indexes the layer sending back the error (the output layer in a network with a single hidden layer). A suitable activation function is the logistic function:

$$f(net_j) = \frac{1}{1 + \exp(-net_j)}$$

The derivative of this activation function is:

$$f'(net_j) = \frac{\exp(-net_j)}{(1 + \exp(-net_j))^2}$$

$$= \frac{1}{1 + \exp(-net_j)}\left(1 - \frac{1}{1 + \exp(-net_j)}\right) \qquad (15.23)$$

$$= f(net_j)[1 - f(net_j)]$$

15.4.2 The backpropagation algorithm

The first stage is to initialize the weights to small random values. Training continues until the change in the absolute value of the averaged squared error falls within some tolerance between one epoch and the next epoch. For example, a tolerance of 0.01 means that the averaged squared error must not change by more than ±0.01 between successive epochs. If a network meets the tolerance during training it is said to have converged. An alternative way to judge the end of training is to insist that each target output for each training sample be within some specified tolerance.

To reduce the likelihood of the weight changes oscillating, a momentum term, α, is introduced that adds in a proportion of the previous weight change. So, the weight change for sample $m+1$ is dependent on the weight change for sample m:

$$\Delta w_{ij}(m+1) = \eta(\delta_j o_j) + \alpha \Delta w_{ij}(m) \qquad (15.24)$$

The backpropagation algorithm is summarized in Figure 15.20.

Example 3 ● ● ● ● ●

Figure 15.21 illustrates a single forward and backward sweep through a 2–2–1 network with input <0.1, 0.9>. The learning rate is 0.8 and the momentum 0. The weights are:

$$\begin{bmatrix} -2 & 3 \\ -2 & 3 \\ 2 & 2 \end{bmatrix} \begin{bmatrix} -2 & 2 \\ -4 & 2 \\ 3 & -2 \end{bmatrix} \begin{bmatrix} 3 \\ 1 \\ -2 \end{bmatrix}$$

where each matrix represents a layer of weights. The last row is the bias weights.

● ● ● ● ●

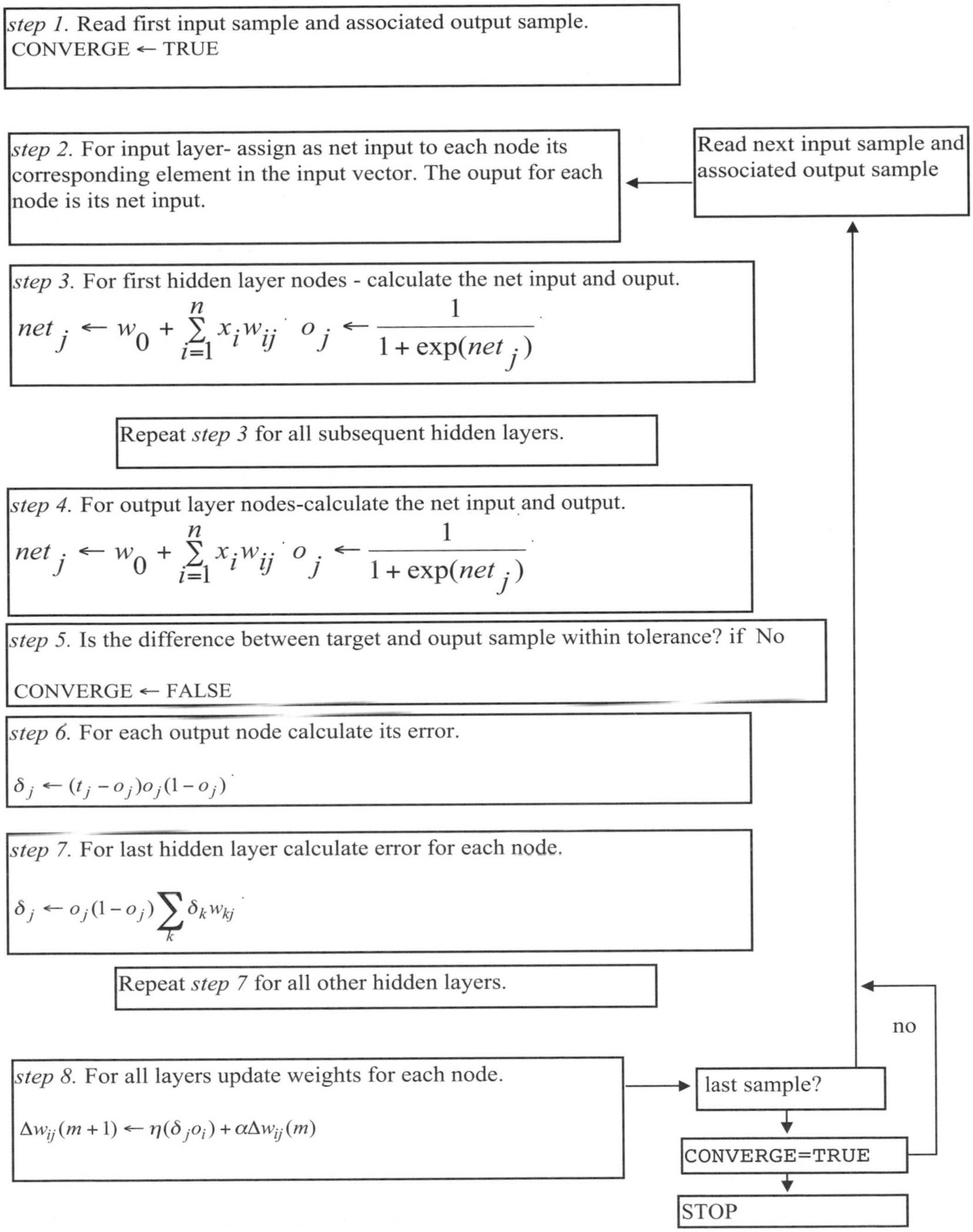

step 1. Read first input sample and associated output sample.
CONVERGE ← TRUE

step 2. For input layer- assign as net input to each node its corresponding element in the input vector. The ouput for each node is its net input.

Read next input sample and associated output sample

step 3. For first hidden layer nodes - calculate the net input and ouput.

$$net_j \leftarrow w_0 + \sum_{i=1}^{n} x_i w_{ij} \quad o_j \leftarrow \frac{1}{1 + \exp(net_j)}$$

Repeat step 3 for all subsequent hidden layers.

step 4. For output layer nodes-calculate the net input and output.

$$net_j \leftarrow w_0 + \sum_{i=1}^{n} x_i w_{ij} \quad o_j \leftarrow \frac{1}{1 + \exp(net_j)}$$

step 5. Is the difference between target and ouput sample within tolerance? if No

CONVERGE ← FALSE

step 6. For each output node calculate its error.

$$\delta_j \leftarrow (t_j - o_j) o_j (1 - o_j)$$

step 7. For last hidden layer calculate error for each node.

$$\delta_j \leftarrow o_j (1 - o_j) \sum_k \delta_k w_{kj}$$

Repeat step 7 for all other hidden layers.

no

step 8. For all layers update weights for each node.

$$\Delta w_{ij}(m+1) \leftarrow \eta(\delta_j o_i) + \alpha \Delta w_{ij}(m)$$

last sample?

CONVERGE=TRUE

STOP

Figure 15.20 The backpropagation algorithm. The index k refers to a previous layer in the reverse sense (i.e. when moving back through the net).

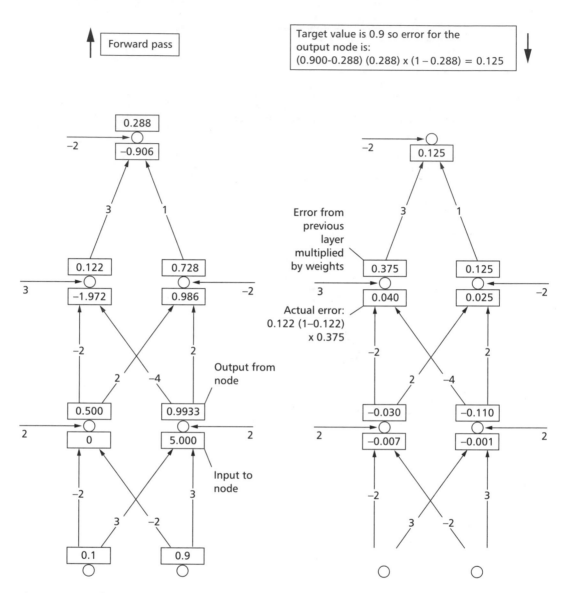

Figure 15.21 Illustrating a forward and backward sweep of the backpropagation algorithm.

15.4.3 *Some practical considerations*

The successful application of a neural network usually demands much experimentation. There are a number of parameters to be set that can affect how easy it is to find a solution. For feed-forward networks, the number of hidden nodes and the number of layers can be varied. Certainly, an important factor is the training data, and a good deal of attention must be paid to the test data so that we can be sure the network will generalize correctly on data it has not been trained on. Indeed, it is possible to train a network on data with complete success only to find that it fails when processing new data. For any new application, there is no prescribed way of finding a solution. Sometimes the problem appears intractable, but failure to find a solution does not mean that the application is not amenable to a neural solution. Although applying neural networks involves a 'try and see approach', the requirement for knowledge of the application domain and knowledge of neural networks should not be underestimated.

Theory tells us that a network with a single hidden layer can represent any continuous mapping of the form:

$$y = f(x)$$

Since this form of mapping is the basis for many real-world problems, is there a need for more than one hidden layer? Well, a network with two hidden layers can sometimes be easier to train and a variant of the feed-forward net known as an auto-associater may use multiple hidden layers to perform data compression.

The learning algorithm as it has been presented uses pattern updating of the weights, which simply means that the weights are updated after each sample presentation. It can sometimes prove quicker to train a network using batch updating, in which the error for a node is accumulated for one epoch before adapting the node's weights. However, it can be beneficial to randomize the order of presentation for each training sample between epochs, in which case pattern updating is required. Usually, it is best to experiment with different approaches.

Generalization

If a network can produce the correct output for the majority of input samples in the test data set, the network is said to generalize well. It is assumed that the test data set was not used during training.

If a network is trained well to produce a smooth non-linear mapping, it should be able to interpolate to new samples that are similar but not exactly the same as those samples used for training. A non-smooth mapping results when the network is overtrained. In this situation, the network will work more like a memory, looking up an output for a certain input from the training set.

Good generalization is dependent on the training set and network architecture. The training data set must be representative of the problem being tackled, but the number of hidden nodes is also an important factor. If there are more hidden nodes than is required to learn the input–output relationship, there will be more weights than necessary and overfitting of the data can result if training continues for too long. Sometimes a subset of the training data is used to act as an interim test for detecting overtraining.

The application of neural networks is an experimental approach to engineering. General guidelines sometimes exist for network design. Haykin (1998) uses a result derived by Baum and Haussler (1989) to give a guideline as to the size of the training data set. The guideline states that:

$$N > \frac{W}{\varepsilon}$$

where N is the number of training examples, W is the number of network weights and ε is the percentage of allowed errors in testing. So, for a 10% error the number of training examples should be 10 times the number of weights.

15.5 An example of character classification

The task is to classify the digits 0 through to 9. There are 10 classes and so each target vector could be a 1-in-10 vector. For example, the target for the character 2 could be <0, 0, 1, 0, 0, 0, 0, 0, 0, 0>, which indicates that the third output node should be on and all others off.

In the case study presented here, the target values are represented by 1-in-9 vectors for the numerals 1 to 9, with zero being represented by having all output nodes set to 0. The numerals to be learned are shown in Figure 15.22. Each numeral is represented by a 9×7 grid, with a grey pixel being 0 and a black pixel being 1.

A network architecture of 63–6–9 is chosen: (9×7) input nodes, one for each pixel, six hidden nodes and nine output nodes for the target vectors. The pixels are mapped into the input layer as shown in Figure 15.23.

The network was trained for 600 epochs using a learning rate of 0.3 and a momentum of 0.7. An output node was considered to be on if its activation was greater than 0.9 and off if its activation was less than 0.1.

The network trained successfully. It was then tested on the data in Figure 15.24. Each of the

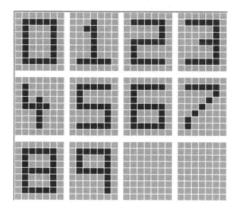

Figure 15.22 Training data.

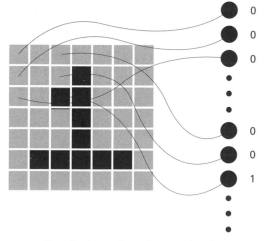

Figure 15.23 The grid is mapped to the input layer by treating it as a long string of bits that are set to 0 or 1. The bits are mapped by starting at the top left-hand corner, working down the grid for the first column and then repeating for each other column.

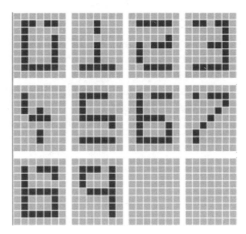

Figure 15.24 Noisy test data.

numbers has one or more bits missing. All the test numbers were correctly identified apart from 8. The sixth output node had an activation of 0.53 and the eighth node an activation of 0.41. The network was confused with the eighth sample being either the numeral 8 or 6 but not confident in either.

Summary

This chapter has looked at supervised learning, in which the object of learning is to map an input vector to a target vector. For supervised learning it is necessary to have:

- data that have a known classification;
- sufficient data that represent all aspects of the problem being solved;
- sufficient data to allow testing (the test data set and the training data set should be disjoint, i.e. test data are not used during training).

The backpropagation algorithm is in wide use:

- It learns by adapting its weights using the generalized delta rule, which attempts to minimize the squared error between what is the desired network output and the actual network output.
- During learning, it continually cycles through the data until the error is at a low enough value for the task to be considered solved. Even when the squared error is low, it is important to check that individual training samples are all correctly classified.
- Following training, the network's weights are fixed and the network can then be used to classify unseen data.
- The knowledge of the solved task resides in the network's weights
- A single hidden layer of nodes is theoretically sufficient for a task to be learned, but in practice more than one hidden layer could lead to better performance.
- Backpropagation networks can take a long time to train.
- Generalization is a measure of how well the network performs on data not seen during training. The number of hidden nodes and the length of training can have a significant effect on generalization.

Further reading

The original exposition of the backpropagation algorithm by Rumelhart *et al.* (1986a) is still worth studying. The later paper by Werbos (1990) also describes the theory behind backpropagation and a variation with recurrent connections. There are many variations of the backpropagation algorithm to speed up training and to help the network avoid the problem of local minima, which can result in the network failing to learn. The keen reader is referred to Haykin (1998) and to Masters (1995), who provides a practical insight to solving these issues using the C++ language. For a statistical treatment of neural networks, Bishop (1995) provides good coverage.

Exercises

1   Sketch a neural network along with weight values that will model the line:

$$y = -0.3x + 0.7$$

2   The figure below shows a backpropagation network that is currently processing the training vector [1.0 0.9 0.9] and the associated target vector is [0.1 0.9 0.1].

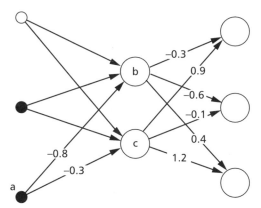

Given that the output from unit b is 0.6 and from c is 0.8, and assuming that the logistic function is the activation function:
a   Calculate the actual output vector.
b   Calculate the error for each output unit.
c   Calculate the error for each hidden unit.
d   Calculate the weight changes for the weights connecting from unit a. Use a learning rate of 0.25 and momentum of zero.

3   Given that the points {(–1, 1), (–1, –1), (1, –1)} belong to class A and that {(–2, –2), (1, 1), (2, 2), (4, 1)} belong to class B:
a   Show that the classes are not linearly separable.
b   Assuming a network with units that has outputs according to:

$$output = \begin{cases} 1 \text{ if } total\ input \geq 0 \\ 0 \text{ if } total\ input < 0 \end{cases}$$

show that the first layer of weights $\mathbf{W}_1$ in a three-layer network will transform the problem into a linear one. The first row in $\mathbf{W}_1$ defines the bias weights.

$$\mathbf{W}_1 = \begin{bmatrix} 1 & -6 \\ -2 & -2 \\ -1 & -3 \end{bmatrix}$$

c   Derive a second layer of weights so that the network will correctly classify all the patterns. Assume a single output unit.

4   The points $\{(4, -1), (8, -2), (1, 1), (3, 6)\}$ belong to class A, and the points $\{(-8, 4), (-2, -3), (-1, -1), (2, -9)\}$ belong to class B. Derive a minimal network to classify these points correctly.

5   Derive a suitable feed-forward network that models the logical AND.

6   The bipolar sigmoid is another activation function that is commonly used with a backpropagation network. The range of the function is $(-1, 1)$ and is defined as:

$$f(x) = \frac{2}{1 + \exp(-x)} - 1$$

The derivative can be expressed as:

$$f(x) = \tfrac{1}{2}[1 + f(x)][1 - f(x)]$$

Give the error correcting rule for both an output and a hidden unit.

CHAPTER 16

Neural Networks II

One of the most common applications of learning is searching for hypotheses that can classify a set of training examples. Thus far, learning to classify objects has been supervised as each training instance has a known class. There are many applications in which the class memberships of a set of training examples are unknown and learning is used to discover classes. This form of learning is called clustering or unsupervised learning. It can be useful to use clustering even when training data have known classes. Clustering can inform us of any natural structure within the data. Clustering can also be combined with a supervised approach in a form of two-phase learning for building a classifier and for regression.

Figure 16.1 shows a plot of two-dimensional data that fall naturally into three clusters. In Figure 16.1, a sample can be said to fall naturally into a cluster if it is close to a point in the same cluster compared with a point belonging to another cluster. Of course, two-dimensional data are convenient because they can be plotted using a scatter chart and any clusters will be seen. For high-dimensional problems we need to rely on techniques such as clustering.

In this chapter, two conceptual approaches to clustering are introduced. The first approach views clustering as a process of discovering groupings based on similarity metrics, for example the distance between samples. The second approach takes a model view and attempts to discover the parameters of the model that best predict the data.

16.1 Discovering clusters using similarity metrics

The distance between two points is a typical measure for judging similarity. For continuous attributes, the Euclidean squared distance can be used and is defined as:

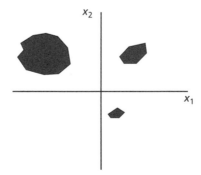

Figure 16.1 Data that form three clusters.

$$d_{pq} = \sum_{j}^{n} (x_{pj} - x_{qj})^2 \qquad (16.1)$$

where d_{pq} is the Euclidean squared distance between point p and point q, x_{pj} is the value for attribute j for example p (similarly for q) and n is the number of dimensions.

One simple approach to clustering is provided by the following algorithm:

1   Generate k n-dimensional vectors to represent the centres of k clusters. These vectors are generated at random with attribute values within the range of the training examples.
2   Assign each training example to its nearest cluster using eqn (16.1).
3   Update each of the k clusters by averaging over all of the examples assigned to a cluster.
4   Repeat from step 2 until some specified halt criterion is satisfied.

Each training example and each cluster centre are n-dimensional vectors. Given that $\mathbf{p}_k$ is a vector for representing the centre of cluster k, example $\mathbf{x}$ is assigned to a cluster according to the rule:

$$index(\mathbf{x}) = \min d(\mathbf{p}_k, \mathbf{x}) \quad \textit{for all } k \qquad (16.2)$$

which returns the index of the cluster with the lowest Euclidean squared distance from vector x. The vectors $\mathbf{p}_k$ can be considered as prototypes for the clusters. These prototypes serve to represent the key features of a cluster. For example, if you were to cluster basketball players and horse-jockeys, no doubt one distinguishing feature would be height.

The aim of the simple algorithm introduced above can be illustrated with the help of Figure 16.2. Initially, random prototypes are produced, and during training their positions move after each iteration. The halt criterion in this example could specify that the algorithm continues to iterate until the prototypes no longer move (or move only by some small amount).

A number of desirable properties a cluster algorithm should possess are:

*   automatic determination of the number of prototypes;
*   a measure of the similarity (or relative position) of one prototype to another;
*   the key features representative of a prototype.

The first property is difficult to satisfy for real-world applications, although some algorithms make an attempt by using a set of heuristics. The other two properties are used to interpret the significance

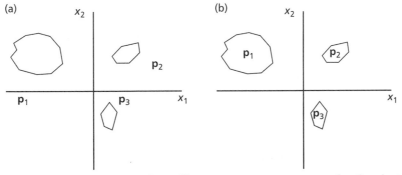

Figure 16.2 (a) Three random vectors that will move to act as prototypes for the clusters. (b) Prototypes have moved to become the centroids of clusters.

(if any) of the clusters. For instance, vibration data are often monitored to check the health of rotating machinery. An anomaly in the data can sometimes show as a cluster, which might turn out to be a benign pattern, or it could signify a developing fault. An experienced engineer can look at the characteristics of the anomaly and decide whether any immediate maintenance action is required.

A popular unsupervised neural network is the self-organizing feature map (SOFM) (Kohonen, 1990). The SOFM was developed in the early 1980s, and much work has been done with it since.

16.2 The self-organizing feature map

The SOFM has a set of input nodes that correspond in number to the dimension of the training vectors and output nodes that act as prototypes. Figure 16.3 illustrates the basic architecture. The data in Figure 16.1 would require a network with two input nodes and at least three output nodes to represent each cluster.

The input nodes serve to distribute the input vector to the network's output nodes. The output nodes shall be referred to as cluster nodes. Since the number of input nodes is the same as the dimension of the input vectors, and each input node is fully connected to each cluster node, the total number of weights impinging on a cluster node is also the same as the dimension of the input vectors. The weights of a cluster node represent the cluster's position in the n-dimensional input space. Figure 16.4 shows how the weights relate to the input space.

The cluster nodes are arranged in a one- or two-dimensional array in the manner shown in Figure 16.5. During training, the cluster nodes are considered to be competing for training vectors. When any training vector is presented, the distance to all cluster nodes is calculated and the node that is closest to the training vector is denoted the winning node. The winning node will then adapt its weights in a way that moves that cluster node even closer to the training vector. It is usual for nodes within a prespecified neighbourhood of the winning node to also update their weights. A node is a member of the updating neighbourhood if it falls within a specified radius that is centred on the winning node. The radius is usually reduced during learning. A learning rate, which also decreases over time, determines the amount by which a cluster node moves towards the training vector.

16.2.1 Algorithm

The SOFM algorithm is given in Figure 16.6. The training samples are selected at random from the training set. The HALTING condition is met when the weight changes for all cluster nodes become very small; under this condition, the training samples should fall within the same region of the map from one epoch to the next. The learning rate is varied over time. It could, for example, start at a

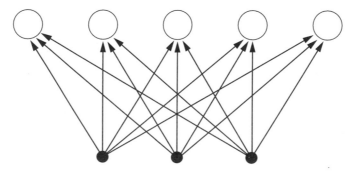

Figure 16.3 This network has three inputs and five cluster nodes. Each node in the input layer is connected to every node in the cluster layer.

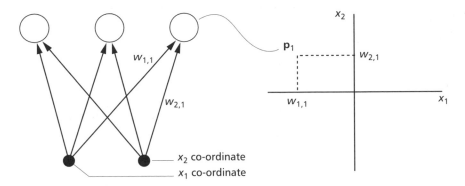

Figure 16.4 This diagram shows how a cluster node acts as a prototype. There is one input node per attribute. The weights adapt during training, and when learning is complete each cluster node will have a position in the input space determined by its weights.

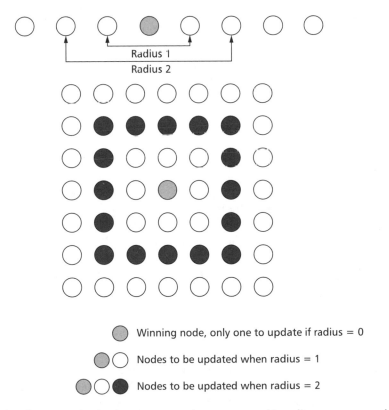

Figure 16.5 The cluster nodes in the top network are arranged in a linear manner whereas the network below has the nodes arranged in a square grid. The topology determines which nodes fall within a radius of the winning node. The nodes can be arranged in other ways (e.g., triangular, hexagon) but the linear and square arrangements are most typical.

η – learning rate
n – time step

initialise weights to random values
while not HALT
        for each input vector
                for each cluster node calculate the distance from the training vector

$$d_j = \sum_i (w_{ij} - x_i)^2$$

                end for
                find node j with the minimum distance
                update all weight vectors for nodes within the radius according to

$$w_{ij}(n+1) = w_{ij}(n) + \eta(n)[x_i - w_{ij}(n)]$$

        end for
        check to see if the learning rate or radius need updating
        check HALT
end while

Figure 16.6 SOFM algorithm.

value of 0.9 and decrease in a linear manner before remaining fixed at a small value (e.g. 0.01). The radius usually starts out large so that all nodes are initially updated. The radius also reduces over time so that, in the end, none or only the immediate neighbours of the winning node are updated. The learning rate can also be specified to depend on how close the updating node is to the winning node.

16.2.2 Self-organizing

The feature map has two phases of learning. In the first phase, the nodes are ordered to mirror the input space and in the second phase there is fine tuning. If the data are two-dimensional then it is possible to view the organization process. Suppose, for example, that input vectors are drawn randomly from a uniform distribution contained within a square, and a map trained. The map is drawn at different times during training by plotting the cluster nodes in the input space in the same manner as shown in Figure 16.4. The nodes are connected by grid lines to show their relative location. The map usually starts twisted and gradually unfolds and spreads out during training. The end result of training is a map that covers the input space and is fairly regular (i.e. nodes are almost equally spaced). A map with a square topology of 49 nodes was trained on 250 data points drawn from a unit square, starting with random weights that positioned each cluster node in the centre of the input space, as shown in Figure 16.7. Figures 16.8 and 16.9 show the development of the map over time.

As with other networks, the result of training depends on the training data and choice of learning parameters. Figure 16.10 shows the distribution of 100 training samples over the unit square. A map with a square topology of 25 nodes was trained on this data set starting with random weights that once again positioned each node in the centre of the input space. This is a relatively small network and, not surprisingly, the end result of using non-uniform data is an irregular-looking map, as shown Figure 16.11. The map also contains a twist in the top right-hand corner. Twists can be

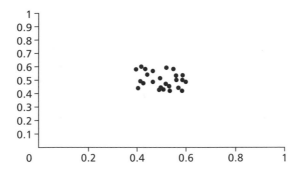

Figure 16.7 The weight vectors start with random values in the range 0.4–0.6.

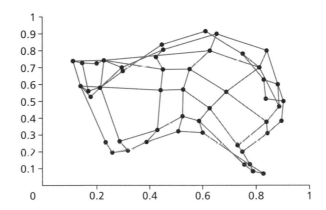

Figure 16.8 The map after 20 epochs.

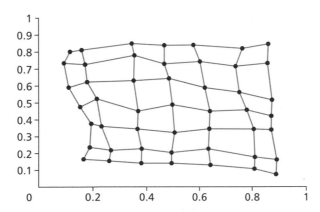

Figure 16.9 The map after 2000 epochs, towards the end of training. The nodes are now ordered and the map will become more regular during the final phase of convergence.

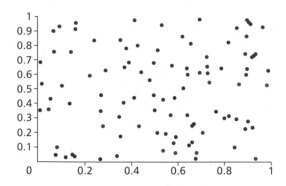

Figure 16.10 Randomly generated data. The data are not uniform across the square.

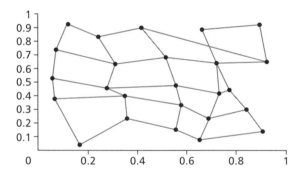

Figure 16.11 The map nodes locations after training on the data shown in Figure 16.10. Adjacent nodes are connected by grid lines.

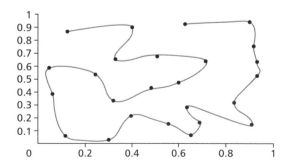

Figure 16.12 A linear map of 25 nodes fitting random data drawn from a unit square.

the result of the initial weight values, which determine where each cluster node is positioned in the input space at the start of training. For example, if the nodes all start out being weighted towards one direction of the input space then the ordering process can be hampered. Figure 16.12 shows the same experiment, but this time the map is a linear array of nodes. The linear array is twisting to fill the input space. The same space-filling properties can be shown with other shapes. For example, if the training data are drawn uniformly from a triangle then a square map will organize its nodes to fill the triangle.

Example 1 ● ● ● ● ●

A Kohonen network with three input nodes and two cluster nodes is to be trained using the four training vectors:

$$\begin{bmatrix} 0.8 & 0.7 & 0.4 \end{bmatrix}$$
$$\begin{bmatrix} 0.6 & 0.9 & 0.9 \end{bmatrix}$$
$$\begin{bmatrix} 0.3 & 0.4 & 0.1 \end{bmatrix}$$
$$\begin{bmatrix} 0.1 & 0.1 & 0.1 \end{bmatrix}$$

and initial weights:

$$\begin{bmatrix} 0.5 & 0.4 \\ 0.6 & 0.2 \\ 0.8 & 0.5 \end{bmatrix}$$

The initial radius $=0$ and the learning rate $\eta=0.5$. Calculate the weight changes during the first cycle through the data taking the training vectors in the given order.

Solution

For input vector 1, we have for cluster node 1:

$$d_1=(0.5-0.8)^2+(0.6-0.7)^2+(0.8-0.4)^2=0.26$$

and for cluster node 2:

$$d_2=(0.4-0.8)^2+(0.2-0.7)^2+(0.5-0.4)^2=0.42$$

Node 1 is closest and so:

$$w_{ij}(n+1)=w_{ij}(n)+0.5[x_i-w_{ij}(n)]$$

The new weights are:

$$\begin{bmatrix} 0.65 & 0.40 \\ 0.65 & 0.20 \\ 0.60 & 0.50 \end{bmatrix}$$

For input vector 2 we have, for cluster node 1:

$$d_1 = (0.65 - 0.6)^2 + (0.65 - 0.9)^2 + (0.6 - 0.9)^2 = 0.155$$

and for cluster node 2:

$$d_s = (0.4 - 0.6)^2 + (0.2 - 0.9)^2 + (0.5 - 0.9)^2 = 0.69$$

Node 1 is closest and so the new weights are:

$$\begin{bmatrix} 0.625 & 0.400 \\ 0.775 & 0.200 \\ 0.750 & 0.500 \end{bmatrix}$$

The process is repeated for the last two vectors.

● ● ● ● ●

Kohonen (1990) gives a few practical hints for training a SOFM. During the first 1000 iterations, the learning rate should start out close to 1, thereafter gradually decreasing. The exact form of decreasing the learning rate is not critical and can be linear, exponential or inversely proportional to the number of iterations. The ordering of the map occurs during this initial phase. After the ordering phase, the learning rate should be maintained at a low value (e.g. ≤0.1) for a long period while fine adjustment of the map takes place. The radius should start out large (e.g. can be greater than half the diameter of the map) and should decrease linearly during the first 100 iterations, after which it can be maintained at 1 or zero. There should be a large number of iterations, typically 10–100 000.

16.2.3 An experiment

In this experiment, there are four different classes of characters drawn using three different fonts (Figure 16.13). The experiment was designed simply to see how a SOFM would cluster the training instances. A square grid with nine nodes in total was chosen. The initial radius was set at 3 and

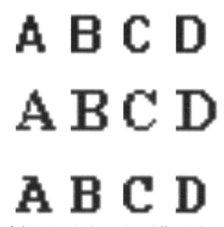

Figure 16.13 Each row of characters is drawn in a different font.

Table 16.1 The SOFM nodes to which the characters have been labelled. The numbers denote different fonts

A1 A2 A3		B1 D1 B3 D3
B2 D2		C1 C2 C3

the learning rate at 1. The network was trained for 3000 cycles through all the samples. Table 16.1 shows how the characters clustered at the end of training. Each cell in the table corresponds to a node in the grid.

The character images are 16×16 pixel grids, and so there are 256 inputs to each node. After the network has converged, a node is expected to be a prototype for the examples that are assigned to that node. If the weight vectors are plotted as an image, we might expect a node's image to look similar to the samples it is a prototype for. The original bitmaps of the characters used 0 to represent a white pixel and 1 for a black pixel. Therefore, all node weights will have values between 0 and 1. Each weight is associated with a single pixel in the original grid, and so each weight can be treated as a greyscale value between 0 and 1 (greyscales actually range from 0 to 255 and so the weights have to be scaled to the same range). From examination of Figure 16.14, which shows the images of each node's weights, you can see to which nodes a sample is likely to be assigned. In this experiment, all the As have clustered together and so have all the Cs. The Bs and Ds have similar shapes and have clustered together. Ideally, we might hope for the Bs and Ds also to cluster against separate nodes. However, for real-world problems clustering gives an indication of similarity and is not meant to be foolproof.

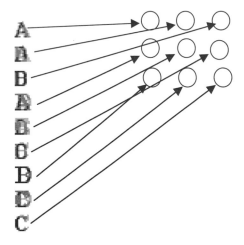

Figure 16.14 The figure shows node weights plotted as greyscale values. The top left node is seen to be clearly representative of 'A' and the bottom right node representative of 'C'. All As and Cs are assigned to these nodes. There is confusion between the Bs and Ds.

16.3 Model generator for clustering

The two classes of data depicted in Figure 16.15 have been generated by randomly sampling two Gaussian distributions. A model-based approach to clustering assumes a type of distribution and then seeks to find the parameters that best predict the data. In the case of Figure 16.15, if two Gaussian distributions are assumed, the task of learning is to find the means and standard deviations of these distributions.

A simple model for a probabilistic classifier can be built using the naive Bayes classifier (Duda and Hart, 1973). The Bayes classifier is viewed as a model for generating the training examples. These models conform to the simple structure shown in Figure 16.16. The model has a single parent variable that represents the classification(s), and the child variables are the attributes, which are assumed to be independent of each other.

It is typical in many applications to split attribute values over a limited number of bins. The probability distributions are then represented by conditional probability tables in the same way as for the full Bayesian networks introduced in Chapters 5 and 6. The distributions in Figure 16.15 can be discretized by defining a number of evenly spaced bins that span the maximum and minimum values of both attributes.

Assume for the moment that the task is supervised and so the class of each training sample is known. Classification of an unknown sample can be computed using the junction tree algorithm presented in Chapter 6. However, the application of Bayes rule is straightforward for computing class membership.

$$p(y = C \mid \mathbf{x}) = \frac{p(\mathbf{x} \mid y = C) \times p(y = C)}{p(\mathbf{x})}$$

$$p(y = A \mid \mathbf{x}) = \frac{p(\mathbf{x} \mid y = A) \times p(y = A)}{p(\mathbf{x})} \qquad (16.3)$$

$$p(y = B \mid \mathbf{x}) = \frac{p(\mathbf{x} \mid y = B) \times p(y = B)}{p(\mathbf{x})}$$

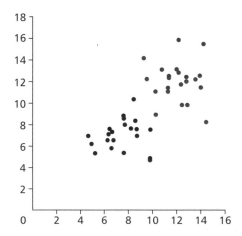

Figure 16.15 Two classes of data have been randomly generated by sampling two different Gaussian distributions.

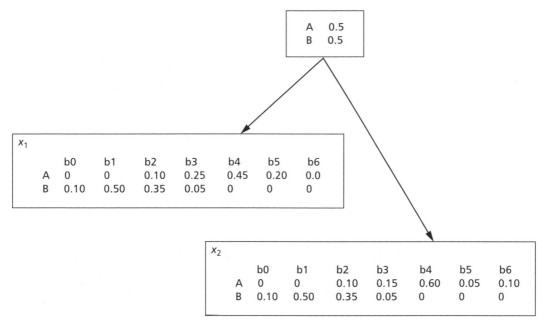

Figure 16.16 A Bayesian network model for classification. The root node is a class variable that has priors for each class – in this case two classes A and B are both equally likely. The child nodes represent the attributes (in this case there are two attributes). The continuous attributes in Figure 16.15 have been discretized into seven bins.

where $p(y=C|\mathbf{x})$ is the probability that the class variable y predicts class C given sample vector $\mathbf{x}$. For convenience, the probability of $\mathbf{x}$ occurring, $p(\mathbf{x})$, can be cancelled and the above equations expanded into products of attribute values as follows (this is possible because attributes are assumed to be independent):

$$\frac{p(y=A|\mathbf{x})}{p(y=B|\mathbf{x})} = \frac{p(x_1|y=A)\times p(x_2|y=A)\times p(y=A)}{p(x_1|y=B)\times p(x_2|y=B)\times p(y=B)} \tag{16.4}$$

Subscripts on $\mathbf{x}$ denote the attribute. An example is classified as belonging to class A if:

$$\frac{p(y=A|\mathbf{x})}{p(y=B|\mathbf{x})} > 1 \tag{16.5}$$

Otherwise it is as a member of B. So, for example, the sample <b2, b3> is classified as a member of B:

$$\frac{0.10 \times 0.15 \times 0.50}{0.35 \times 0.05 \times 0.50} = 0.857$$

For supervised learning, the conditional probability tables are easily computed from a database of examples. All that is required is a frequency count for each bin value given the known classifications of the data.

In Figure 16.16, the prior probabilities have been easily computed as the training samples are tagged with either class A or class B. If the class of each sample is unknown, is it possible, using a Bayesian approach, to discover the classes? The answer is 'yes', and to illustrate the approach we shall introduce a technique that is applicable to multinomial distributions that are found in Bayesian networks' conditional tables. The technique can also be extended to other distributions, which include the binomial, exponential, Gaussian and others.

The expectation maximization algorithm

Dempster *et al.* (1976) introduced the expectation maximization (EM) algorithm and demonstrated its application to a range of problems. EM can be applied to clustering. We shall illustrate its use for discovering the type of model shown in Figure 16.16.

Clustering algorithms usually start by assuming a number of classes. In practice, the user specifies the number of classes that might exist using knowledge of the application domain. If, for our example, we assume two classes, then the algorithm will terminate with a class assignment for each training example. The task of learning is to discover the values of the conditional probability tables. These values are referred to as weights and are collectively denoted by W.

The EM algorithm starts with random values for W and then alternates between two steps until the vales of W converge.

1. E-step. Given the current values of W, compute the probabilities $p(y_i = A | \mathbf{x}_i)$ and $p(y_i = B | \mathbf{x}_i)$ for each example i. Note that $\mathbf{x}_i$ is a vector and x_{ij} is the value corresponding to attribute j for example i.
2. M-step. Given the class probabilities computed in the E-step, compute the maximum likelihood estimate for W.

The aim of the algorithm is to maximize the quantity $p(\mathbf{x}_i | W)$ for each training example. In other words, the algorithm seeks a model that has maximum likelihood of generating the training data.

Step 1 is computed using:

$$p(y_i = C | \mathbf{x}_i) = \frac{p(\mathbf{x}_i | y_i = C) \times p(y = C)}{p(\mathbf{x}_i)} \qquad (16.6)$$

The priors, $p(y = C)$ can be all initialled to $1/k$, where k is the number of assumed clusters. So each class is initialised with a prior of 0.5 when two classes are assumed.

For the M-step the priors need updating. The first step is to compute the new prior for a class:

$$p(y_i = C) = {}^1/m \sum_i p(y_i = C) \qquad (16.7)$$

which sums the probability for each example belonging to class C and then averages by dividing by m, the number of training examples. The updated weights are computed using:

$$p(w_j \mid y = C, a) = \frac{1}{p(y = C)} \sum_{il\,j,a} p(y_i = C) \qquad (16.8)$$

Equation (16.8) specifies that the new weight corresponding to bin j, attribute a, given class C, is computed by summing the probabilities of class C occurring for each sample that has bin value j for attribute a.

The EM algorithm applied to the data in Figure 16.15 produced weights that split the data, with 17 samples in one class and the remaining 23 samples in the second class. The original data were produced by generating two classes with 20 samples in each. The algorithm in this instance cannot be completely successful as the bins chosen to discretize the data cause the classes to overlap (some samples from both classes fall within the same bins). A version of the EM algorithm that assumes Gaussian distributions is capable of discovering the two classes with all samples correctly assigned. An EM algorithm applied to Gaussians is given in Bishop (1995).

16.4   Radial-basis function networks

In this section a network is introduced that has wide general application, much like the backpropagation network.

Engineers who are familiar with signal processing know that any signal can be represented by a sum of sine and cosine waves. A sine wave and cosine wave can be expressed in exponential form and so a wave can be represented as a linear sum of exponentials. Each exponential is termed a **basis function**. Basis functions are not restricted to being exponentials; another type of basis function used in signal analysis comes from a class of functions called wavelets.

Figure 16.17 shows a plot of a sine wave. The wave was generated using 26 points. It is possible to represent this wave exactly using 26 basis functions. The most common form of basis function is the Gaussian:

$$\varphi_k(\mathbf{x}) = \exp\left(-\frac{\|\mathbf{x} - \mu_k\|^2}{2\sigma_k^2} \right) \qquad (16.9)$$

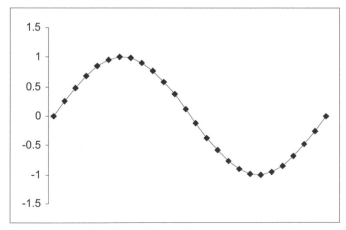

Figure 16.17 A sine wave generated from 26 samples.

where $\|\mathbf{x} - \mu_k\|^2$ is the Euclidean squared distance. The sine wave can be represented using a more simplified version:

$$\varphi_k(\mathbf{x}) = \exp(-\|\mathbf{x} - \mu_k\|^2) \tag{16.10}$$

The sine wave is single dimension and is generated in this example using 26 evenly spaced sample points. To represent the sine wave exactly, each sample point acts as the mean for each basis function. A 26×26 matrix, $\boldsymbol{\varphi}$, is generated by applying eqn (16.10) to each sample point for each basis function. In other words, the distance from each sample to each function centre is calculated and the exponential taken. For a sample point, the amplitude of the sine wave is then a weighted sum of the outputs from each basis function. Let us consider the sine wave sample as a supervised training data set. The sample point, x, is the input, and each input has an associated target value t (the amplitude of the wave). A vector of target values can be computed from the vector of training samples and weights according to the following equation:

$$\mathbf{t} = \boldsymbol{\varphi}\mathbf{w} \tag{16.11}$$

In this example $\mathbf{t}$ and $\mathbf{w}$ are both 26×1 vectors. The weights, $\mathbf{w}$, can be found using a supervised neural network of the type introduced in Chapter 15. However, for many situations the inverse of $\boldsymbol{\varphi}$ exists and fast computational numerical analysis routines such as singular value decomposition (SVD) can be used to compute $\boldsymbol{\varphi}^{-1}$. The weights are then found using equation (16.12):

$$\mathbf{w} = \boldsymbol{\varphi}^{-1}\mathbf{t} \tag{16.12}$$

Figure 16.18 shows a sine wave that contains noise. An exact interpolation procedure in which the signal is faithfully reproduced will not usually generalize well when unseen data are interpolated. The reason is that most real-world problems contain noise, and it is better to smooth the signal by using a number of basis functions that is fewer than the number of training samples.

A radial-basis function network typically uses far fewer basis functions than the number of training samples. The centres of the basis functions are typically learned using an unsupervised approach and are therefore not constrained to coincide with any training sample. The widths, σ_k, of each basis function are not constrained to be the same and, like the centres, are usually determined during unsupervised training. Like feed-forward networks, bias weights are also included. The input vectors can be multidimensional.

A radial-basis function network has three layers of nodes, with the usual input layer to distribute a sample to the first layer of weights, a hidden layer and an output layer. The input to hidden layer mapping is non-linear and the hidden to output layer mapping is usually linear. Usually (but not always), the number of hidden nodes exceeds the number of input nodes. The idea is that, if a non-linear problem is cast into a high-dimensional space in a non-linear manner, then it is more likely to be linearly separable. The network has two phases of training. In the first phase, unsupervised learning is used to determine the first layer of weights, and in the second phase supervised learning is used to determine the second layer of weights.

The mapping of the first layer works as follows. For each hidden node there is a function φ. Each of these functions takes the net input and produces an activation value as output. The collective activations of all the hidden nodes defines the vector to which the input vector has been mapped. That is:

$$\varphi(\mathbf{x}) = \langle \varphi(x_1), \varphi(x_2), \ldots, \varphi(x_k) \rangle$$

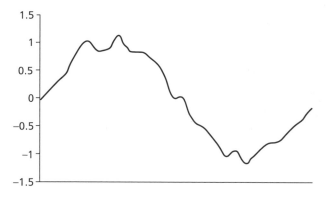

Figure 16.18 A sine wave with added noise.

where k is the number of hidden nodes and $\mathbf{x}$ is the input vector.

The weights connecting to a hidden node define the centre of the radial-basis function for that hidden node. The input to a node is then taken to be the Euclidean distance (also called Euclidean norm):

$$net_k = \| \mathbf{x} - \mathbf{w}_k \|$$

$$= \left[\sum_{i=1}^{n} (x_i - w_{ik})^2 \right]^{1/2}$$

where n is the number of input nodes. Various non-linear hidden node activation functions are used.

Example 2 ● ● ● ● ●

A 2–2–1 radial-basis function network is used to solve the XOR problem. The first layer of weights is:

$$\begin{bmatrix} 1 & 0 \\ 1 & 0 \end{bmatrix}$$

Calculate the activation for the hidden nodes, for each XOR sample, using an activation function of the form $\varphi(net) = \exp[-net^2]$, where net is the Euclidean norm.

Solution

For sample (0, 1) and the first hidden node:

$$\varphi_1 = \exp[-[(0-1)^2 + (1-1)^2]] = \exp[-1] = 0.368$$

For sample (0, 1) and the second hidden node:

$$\varphi_2 = \exp[-[(0-0)^2 + (1-0)^2]] = \exp[-1] = 0.368$$

The complete set of activations is:

Input	φ_1	φ_2
(0, 1)	0.368	0.368
(1, 0)	0.368	0.368
(0, 0)	0.135	1
(1, 1)	1	0.135

If the hidden activations are plotted, it will be seen that the samples are now linearly separable. All that is required now is to learn the second layer of weights.

Summary

A neural network can be made to cluster data by a process of competition. A network's nodes can also be made to undergo a self-organization process so that the location of the network's nodes, when drawn in the input space, mimic the topology of the training data. A typical similarity measure that is used is Euclidean distance.

For a self-organizing feature map:

- All cluster nodes connect to the input nodes. The input nodes serve to distribute the input features of a sample to all cluster nodes.
- During training, nodes compete for a sample. The winning node, which is the node closest to the input sample, adapts its weights so that it becomes closer (i.e. more similar) to the current input sample.
- There are two phases of training. During the first phase, nodes that are neighbours of the winning node are allowed to update their weights. The neighbourhood of nodes that are allowed to update their weights decreases during the first phase. During the second phase, all weights are adjusted by small amounts until the network converges.
- Once trained, the network can be used to classify an unknown sample on the basis of its similarity to samples that the network was trained with.

A radial-basis function network is a network that has general application much like the back-propagation network introduced in Chapter 15.

- It solves a non-linear problem by casting input samples into a higher dimensional space in a non-linear way.
- The first layer of weights is learned using an unsupervised technique. The weights are the centres of a set of basis functions. A commonly used basis function is the Gaussian.
- The second layer of weights can be found using singular value decomposition provided that the output nodes are linear.

Further reading

The 1990 paper by Kohonen provides some interesting examples of the self-organization process and practical hints in using SOFMs. Kohonen's paper is also a good source for locating other studies with SOFMs. Hecht-Nielsen (1990) gives a good overview of competitive learning. Adaptive resonance theory (ART) is another form of clustering network with wide applications. ART was developed by Carpenter and Grossberg (1987), but for a good introduction see Fausett (1994).

Exercises

1   For the vectors given below:

$$\mathbf{x} = [0.2 \quad -1.4 \quad 2.3]$$
$$\mathbf{p}_1 = [0.6 \quad -4.0 \quad 7.0]$$
$$\mathbf{p}_2 = [0.1 \quad -1.0 \quad 2.2]$$

    a   Which prototype ($\mathbf{p}_1$ or $\mathbf{p}_2$) is $\mathbf{x}$ nearest to in terms of Euclidean distance?
    b   Adapt the weight vector of the winning prototype in (a) according to the Kohonen algorithm with a learning rate of 0.8.

2   Repeat exercise 1 for the following vectors:

$$\mathbf{x} = [0.2 \quad -1.4 \quad -0.3 \quad 0.8]$$
$$\mathbf{p}_1 = [0.3 \quad -3.0 \quad 1.0 \quad 0.2]$$
$$\mathbf{p}_2 = [0.4 \quad -1.4 \quad 2.0 \quad 3.0]$$

3   The rate of learning in a SOFM decays according to the law

$$\eta(n) = 0.8[1 - (n/1000)]$$

where n is the iteration. How many iterations will it take for the learning rate to drop to 0.003?

4   Show that the radial-basis function network in Example 2 can solve the XOR problem with the first layer of weights set to:

$$\begin{bmatrix} 0 & 1 \\ 1 & 0 \end{bmatrix}$$

5   Derive the second layer of weights for the solution to exercise 4.

CHAPTER 17

Genetic Algorithms

Nature provides many examples of agents that are optimized for specific tasks. The cheetah has quick acceleration and speed to catch its prey, a polar bear has the strength to punch its way through several feet of ice to obtain lunch, and a bat uses refined echo reflection for locating objects. These species have evolved over many thousands of generations into agents that are especially adapted to suit their environments.

The genetic algorithm is the computer engineer's tool for simulating evolution. Genetic algorithms have many applications that include game playing, classification tasks, engineering design, computer programming, etc.

The genetic algorithm searches for a solution to some problem by evolving a population of hypotheses. Before this search can commence, the following three elements have to be specified:

1   Hypothesis encoding. Hypotheses need to be represented. Binary strings are typically used to represent hypotheses, but strings of real-valued parameters and tree structures are also used. In this chapter the binary string representation is used to study the underlying principles of genetic algorithms.
2   Objective function. An objective function is defined to evaluate the utility of a hypothesis. This evaluation returns a measure of how close a hypothesis is to a solution. This measure is referred to as fitness.
3   Genetic operators. Hypotheses are evolved by changing the elements in the string representation. Parent strings are selected from which new offspring are born. These offspring contain a combination of parent bits.

A genetic algorithm starts with an initial population of strings (hypotheses). The search is an iterative process over the following steps:

1   Evaluate the fitness of each string using the objective function.
2   Using a selection strategy, select a number of the fittest strings.
3   Apply genetic operators to generate new strings from those selected in step 2.
4   Randomly mutate these new strings. A string is mutated by selecting a single bit at random and then flipping the bit according to a stochastic sampling schedule. In other words, a random schedule is used to determine if the selected bit is actually flipped.[1]
5   Using a reinsertion strategy, generate the next population by replacing some of the existing strings with the new strings generated in steps 3 and 4.
6   If a solution is found, stop; otherwise return to step 1.

---

[1]Flipping a bit means that a 0 changes to 1 and vice versa.

Genetic algorithms can be seen as a form of function optimization. For example, in a classification task, the optimal hypothesis is one that classifies all samples correctly. If the fitness of a string is judged according to the number of classification errors, the fittest strings are those with zero error. The search basically evolves new strings to sample different areas of the search space for optimal solutions.

Example 1 ● ● ● ● ●

A simple example is used to introduce the notion of a genetic algorithm.

Figure 17.1 shows a plot of the function $f(x)=x^2: -32 < x \leq 32$. The task is to search for the minimum of this function. Each hypothesis in this case is simply the value of x. If x is restricted to integer values, then there are 64 possible values $\{-31, -30, -29, ..., 32\}$. A binary string using six bits, with an additional bit set to 1 if the value is negative and 0 if the value is positive, can be used to represent each value of x. So the values $\{2, 5, 32, 0, -31\}$ would be represented by $\{0000010, 0000101, 0100000, 0000000, 1011111\}$. The fitness value for a hypothesis is the value returned by the function. The algorithm would start by generating a number of hypotheses, each one a candidate for representing the function minimum. The function is then used to evaluate each hypothesis (which in this example is simply the value x) to test fitness. A number of the fittest hypotheses are used to produce new strings (new hypotheses). New strings are created by selecting hypotheses to act as parents, from which offspring are produced. An offspring is a string containing bit combinations from both parents. These offspring are then inserted into the population. To make sure that the hypotheses search does not become localized, some randomness is injected into the population by subjecting each hypothesis to the possibility of a bit being flipped. The process repeats until the minimum is found.

● ● ● ● ●

17.1 Some terminology

A hypothesis is represented as a binary string. A set of these strings makes up a **population**. Strings are more commonly referred to as **chromosomes** (or genomes), which contain substrings called **genes**. In Example 1 the chromosome consisted of only one gene. Genes represent parameters (attribute values). For example, a person's age and height might use the following encoding:

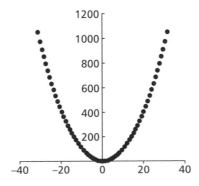

Figure 17.1 A plot of the function $f(x) = x^2: -32 < x \leq 32$.

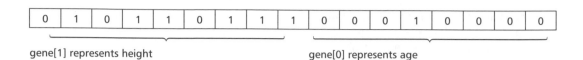

| 0 | 1 | 0 | 1 | 1 | 0 | 1 | 1 | 1 | 0 | 0 | 0 | 1 | 0 | 0 | 0 | 0 |

gene[1] represents height   gene[0] represents age

The population is a set of chromosomes that represent the current hypotheses under consideration. Parents are drawn from the population for mating. Mating is achieved by applying a **genetic operator** such as **single-point crossover** (see Figure 17.2). After mating, some of the chromosomes will be **mutated**, which results in a single bit being selected at random and then randomly flipped.

An **objective function** has to be defined for a learning task to measure which chromosomes best represent the target function. For a given chromosome, the fitness function returns a numerical value that is proportional to the chromosome's utility for the stated task. For example, if the hypothesis is a rule for classifying objects then fitness can be a measure of classification accuracy. If the hypothesis represents an optimum racing driver in a software game then the fitness could be the proportion of races won. It is common practice to express the optimum fitness value as a minimum so that the lower the fitness value of a chromosome the more suited it is to the task. If a problem is more naturally expressed as searching to maximize a function it can be converted to a minimization problem simply by taking the negative of the function output. If, for example, we were searching for the highest (maximum) peak in the Rocky Mountains then a function could use a geographical database to return the elevation for any given map coordinate. If every value returned by the database were negated, the highest peak would correspond to the minimum of the returned values. Another way to convert a maximization task to a minimization task is to invert the fitness value.

Example 2 ● ● ● ● ●

This example is designed purely to illustrate the workings of the basic genetic algorithm and therefore you should not consider the hypothesis's representation or fitness function to be necessarily good examples.

In this example, we are going to imagine a game in which you have to get into a dungeon to rescue a princess. Several hurdles have to be overcome in order to get into the dungeon, and one of them requires a heavy gate to be raised. The only thing that might have the strength to raise the gate is a creature called a 'citegen'. You have as companions a number of citegens. Each citegen attempts to raise the gate, and the citegens that raise the gate the most mate to produce new offspring. These offspring also attempt to raise the gate and, once again, the best performers mate. The game will finish if the gate is not raised within a certain time. The citegen that will succeed in raising the gate has a chromosome with the code 0133. All other citegens with other codes will raise the gate either partially or not at all. The code, therefore, represents the citegen's strength (fitness). All

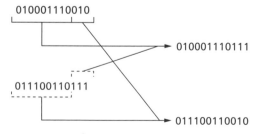

Figure 17.2 Single-point crossover. The parents on the left exchange bits to produce two new strings (offspring), shown on the right.

chromosomes are four digits long, with each digit denoting a gene, which can be one of the values {0, 1, 2, 3}. The fitness is computed according to the following rules:

fitness ← 0

If chromosome contains 0 then fitness ← fitness + 1
If chromosome contains 1 then fitness ← fitness + 1
If chromosome contains 3 then fitness ← fitness + 1
If gene[0] has a value of 0 then fitness ← fitness + 1
If gene[1] has a value of 1 then fitness ← fitness + 1
If gene[2] has a value of 3 then fitness ← fitness + 1
If gene[3] has a value of 3 then fitness ← fitness + 1

For example, the chromosome 0223 will have a fitness of 4. If all seven rules are satisfied (i.e. when the chromosome is 0133), then the fitness is 7.

The fitness value is negated to make the task a minimization search. Therefore, the target chromosome has a fitness value of –7.

The first thing to do is to transform the chromosomes into a binary string. This can be done by representing 0 with 00, 1 with 01, 2 with 10, and 3 with 11. Each gene is now represented by two bits. The target chromosome is represented by 00011111.

To keep the example simple, a single-point crossover will always be applied at position 6. Therefore, the parent chromosomes are copied to produce two offspring, and then the two offspring exchange their last two bits. Indexing starts from 0, so position 6 corresponds to the seventh bit counting from the left. The crossover is illustrated in Figure 17.3. Mutation will consist of randomly selecting a single bit and flipping it (i.e. 0 becomes 1 and 1 becomes 0). Learning proceeds as follows:

1   Generate an initial random population.
2   Compute fitness of each chromosome.
3   Select the four best chromosomes (according to fitness) and delete the others from the population.
4   Select parents for reproduction.
5   Produce offspring using single-point crossover.
6   Mutate each chromosome by randomly selecting a bit and flipping its value.
7   Repeat from step 2 until a chromosome is found with a fitness value of –7.

An example evolution is illustrated in Figure 17.4.

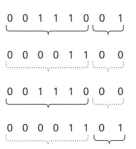

Figure 17.3 Single-point crossover used in Example 2.

Initial population randomly generated

1	0	0	0	0	1	0	1	0	-2
2	0	1	1	0	1	1	0	1	-3
5	0	0	1	1	1	0	0	1	-4
6	0	0	0	0	1	1	0	0	-4
8	0	0	0	1	1	0	1	1	-6
9	0	1	1	0	1	1	1	0	-3
10	0	0	1	1	1	0	0	0	-3
11	0	1	1	0	1	1	0	1	-3

Fittest four selected

5	0	0	1	1	1	0	0	1	-4
6	0	0	0	0	1	1	0	0	-4
8	0	0	0	1	1	0	1	1	-6
11	0	1	1	0	1	1	0	1	-3

5 and 6 mate

12	0	0	1	1	1	0	0	0	-3
13	0	0	0	0	1	1	0	1	-5

8 and 11 mate

14	0	0	0	1	1	0	0	1	-4
15	0	1	1	0	1	1	1	1	-4

Whole population mutated

5	0	0	1	0	1	0	0	1	-3
6	0	1	0	0	1	1	0	0	-4
8	0	0	1	1	1	0	1	1	-4
11	0	1	0	0	1	1	0	1	-4
12	0	0	1	1	1	0	1	0	-3
13	0	1	0	0	1	1	0	1	-4
14	0	0	1	1	1	0	0	1	-4
15	0	0	1	0	1	1	1	1	-5

Fittest four selected

11	0	1	0	0	1	1	0	1	-4
13	0	1	0	0	1	1	0	1	-4
14	0	0	1	1	1	0	0	1	-4
15	0	0	1	0	1	1	1	1	-5

11 and 13 mate

16	0	1	0	0	1	1	0	1	-4
17	0	1	0	0	1	1	0	1	-4

14 and 15 mate

18	0	0	1	1	1	0	1	1	-4
19	0	0	1	0	1	1	0	1	-5

Whole population mutated

11	0	1	0	1	1	1	0	1	-4
13	0	0	0	0	1	1	0	1	-5
14	0	0	0	1	1	0	0	1	-4
15	0	0	0	0	1	1	1	1	-5
16	0	1	0	0	1	1	1	1	-5
17	0	0	0	0	1	1	0	1	-5
18	0	0	0	1	1	0	1	1	-6
19	0	1	1	0	1	1	0	1	-3

Fittest four selected

15	0	0	0	0	1	1	1	1	-5
16	0	1	0	0	1	1	1	1	-5
17	0	0	0	0	1	1	0	1	-5
18	0	0	0	1	1	0	1	1	-6

15 and 16 mate

20	0	0	0	0	1	1	1	1	-5
21	0	1	0	0	1	1	1	1	-5

17 and 18 mate

22	0	0	0	0	1	1	1	1	-5
23	0	0	0	1	1	0	0	1	-4

Whole population mutated and 15 satisfies finish condition

15	0	0	0	1	1	1	1	1	-7
16	0	0	0	0	1	1	1	1	-5
17	0	0	1	0	1	1	0	1	-5
18	0	0	1	1	1	0	1	1	-4
20	0	0	0	0	1	1	0	1	-5
21	0	0	0	0	1	1	1	1	-5
22	0	0	1	0	1	1	1	1	-5
23	0	1	0	1	1	0	0	1	-2

Figure 17.4 Each chromosome is given an identity (integer value on the left). The fitness value is shown in the rightmost column. Ties where strings are competing for parent selection with the same fitness are broken arbitrarily.

17.2   A more complete algorithm

A complete genetic algorithm for binary strings is given in Figure 17.5. The selection for breeding new offspring is based on a chromosome's fitness relative to the population. A chromosome with optimal fitness has a high probability, *p(c)*, of being selected for breeding:

Specify

        n – size of population (value should be divisible by 2)

        k - size of population to act as candidates for reproduction (value should be divisible by 2)

        p_c – probability of applying crossover

        p_m – probability of applying mutation

        f_threshold – value of fitness to be attained

PROCEDURE **GA()**

Initialise population *pop* by randomly generating *n* chromosomes

for each chromosome *c*

        compute its fitness *f*

end for

while $\min_{c} f(c) > f\_threshold$

        call new_generation

        for each chromosome

            compute its fitness *f*

        end for

end while

PROCEDURE **new_generation()**

//create a new population *pop_new*

select *k* chromosomes from *pop* according to the probability distribution

$$p(c_i) = \frac{f(c_i)}{\sum_{i=1}^{n} f(c_i)}$$

add *k* new chromosomes to *pop_new*

$j \leftarrow 0$

while $j < (n - k)$

        select two parents at random from *pop_new*

        pick random crossover site

        with probability p_c generate offspring

        if offspring generated

            add offspring to *pop_new*

            $j \leftarrow j + 2$

        end if

end while

for each chromosome in pop_new

        randomly select a bit

        flip bit with probability p_m

end for

$pop \leftarrow pop\_new$

Figure 17.5 A more developed genetic algorithm.

$$p(c_i) = \frac{f(c_i)}{\sum\limits_{i=1}^{n} f(c_i)}$$

Table 17.1 lists the probabilities, based on fitness, of being selected for mating. Chromosome 0 has the lowest cost (maximum fitness) and therefore has the highest probability of being selected for mating. Note that the population must have four times as many chromosomes with a cost of −2 to have the same chance of being selected as chromosome 0. An efficient way to select parents for mating is to sort the probabilities into descending order and then calculate the cumulative probabilities of the distribution. A pair for mating is then selected by generating two random numbers between 0 and 1 for indexing into the table of sorted probabilities. Computing the cumulative distribution has the effect of distributing each chromosome over a series of bins defined on the range [0, 1]. Each bin size corresponds to the probability of the chromosome being selected. The upper boundary of a bin for a particular chromosome is the cumulative probability value for that chromosome. A chromosome is selected according to the bin in which the random number falls. For example, the numbers (0.203, 0.723) would select the following pair (0, 4) for mating.

17.2.1 Adaptations to the algorithm

There are a number of ways in which the genetic algorithm in Figure 17.5 can be adapted. In particular, variations can be specified for the method of selecting parents and the method for inserting new offspring into the population.

The above sampling method for selecting parents is a stochastic sampling with replacement strategy, more commonly known as roulette wheel selection. The method of selection is analogous to a roulette wheel, on which there is a segment for each chromosome and the size of a chromosome's segment is proportional to its fitness. The probability of the wheel stopping on a chromosome when spun is proportional to fitness. Another selection strategy is stochastic universal sampling. Like the roulette wheel selection, a chromosome occupies a width proportional to its fitness. Universal sampling is easy to visualize by considering another wheel that sits on the outside of the roulette wheel. This second wheel has a number of equally spaced pointers. There is a pointer for each parent

Table 17.1 Cumulative probability distribution for selecting mates from a population

ID	Cost	Probability	Cumulative
0	−8	0.216216	0.216216
1	−6	0.162162	0.378378
2	−6	0.162162	0.540541
3	−5	0.135135	0.675676
4	−3	0.081081	0.756757
5	−2	0.054054	0.810811
6	−2	0.054054	0.864865
7	−2	0.054054	0.918919
8	−2	0.054054	0.972973
9	−1	0.027027	1

to be selected (i.e. if 10 parents are to be selected then the wheel will have 10 pointers). A single spin of the wheel will identify all parent selections simultaneously. Parents selected using stochastic universal sampling are more deserving than those selected by roulette wheel sampling. There are other selection strategies. Some are based on the ranking of fitness, whereas others use the concept of sampling from local neighbourhoods, in which a chromosome's mating partner is selected from the same neighbourhood.

There are different strategies for inserting newly bred offspring into the population. One strategy is to randomly choose how many chromosomes are to be replaced. If this number is N, then the N least fit chromosomes are replaced by the N fittest offspring.

The selection and insertion strategies are designed to guide the search towards an optimal solution by giving more representations to the fittest chromosomes. Genetic operators and mutation generate new chromosomes so that new regions of the hypothesis space are sampled. It is important that the genetic operators do not disturb the search and direct it away from optimal regions of the search space. On the other hand, it is important that other regions of space can still be sampled so that the search does not terminate prematurely on a non-optimal solution. As the search becomes more concentrated in certain regions of space, some bits in the chromosome can become lost because they never get changed during mating. Mutation is designed to prevent any bit from becoming permanently lost. Mutation provides an opportunity to sample other parts of the search space that are not being explored. But the majority of search effort should concentrate in those regions that are expected to yield optimal solutions. As mutation disturbs this concentration, it should be applied sparingly. It is common, therefore, for a bit selected for mutation to be actually flipped less than 1% of the time.

17.2.2 Other forms of genetic operators

Operators like crossover are conveniently implemented using a mask. For a single-point crossover, the mask is a series of contiguous 1s up to and including the crossover point, with the remainder of the string being zeros; the mask is the same length as the parent strings. If the bit in the mask is 0 then the corresponding bit in parent_1 is passed to offspring_1 and the corresponding bit in parent_2 is passed to offspring_2. If the mask bit is 1 the corresponding bit in parent_1 is passed to offspring_2 and the corresponding parent_2 bit is passed to offspring_1.

A two-point crossover uses a mask with a specified number of leading zeros, followed by a specified number of leading 1s, with the remainder being zeros.

For uniform crossover the bit mask is created by randomly setting each bit independently of the other bits.

These operators are illustrated in Figure 17.6.

17.3 Representing hypotheses

One of the most difficult aspects of using genetic algorithms is deciding how best to represent the hypotheses. Sometimes the choice is simple as in Example 1. At other times the choice of representation is less obvious. How could the following rule be represented?

If car_start = no AND lights = dim THEN battery_faulty = true

One way would be to use a single gene to represent a variable like *car_start* and to use a single bit for each value that the variable can be assigned. So, if *car_start* can have the values {yes, no},

Single-point crossover

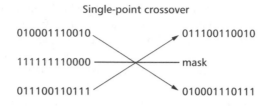

Two-point crossover

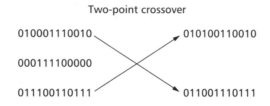

Uniform crossover

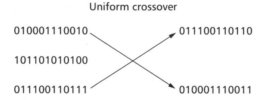

Figure 17.6 Bit masks define the genetic operator. The first offspring is generated according to: if the mask bit is zero the corresponding bit in parent_1 gets passed to offspring_1 and if the mask is 1 the corresponding bit in parent_2 gets passed to offspring_1. The second offspring is generated in the same manner but the roles of the parents are swapped.

two bits are used with the assignments {10, 01}.[2] So, for the variable *lights*, the values {bright, dim, off} would be represented by {001, 010, 100}. The value '111' could represent that it does not matter what the value of *lights* is and 011 could represent *lights = bright or dim*. Conjunctions of rule conditions are then a concatenation of genes. The conclusion could also be represented in a similar way. Note, however, that, if the conclusion were to be represented by two bits to denote {true, false}, the value '11' is inconclusive. So to force the battery to be in one of the two states, a single bit is used with 0 = false and 1 = true; alternatively, a constraint can be added to the algorithm to ensure that for this gene the value '11' never occurs. Using this representation the above rule has the following chromosome:

car_start = no	lights = dim	battery_faulty = true
01	010	1

DeJong *et al.* (1993) use a genetic algorithm in a system called GABIL that learns Boolean concepts represented as a set of rules. Each rule is a conjunction of variables. A hypothesis can be

---

[2]A single bit would suffice but we retain two bits so that we can represent the notion of 'don't care' (see the extension in the following sentence).

represented by more than one rule; the hypothesis is then a disjunctive set of rules. For example, a training sample either is or is not a member of the concept and the following hypothesis:

If A=T AND B=F pos; If B=T Then neg

states that a sample is classed as positive (pos, that is a member of the concept) if A is true and B is false, but if B is true then the sample is classed as negative (neg). The following bit strings could represent the two rules:

A=T	B=F	Class=pos
10	01	1

A='don't care'	B=T	Class=neg
11	10	0

The hypothesis consists of two rules and so its chromosome representation is both of the above strings concatenated.

10 01 1 11 10 0

In a system like GABIL there has to be opportunity for hypotheses to have a variable number of rules. This means that the population of chromosomes can have variable-length bit strings. Two-point crossover is used, but the operation needs to be constrained to ensure that matching sections of a rule are exchanged. For example, consider the crossover between the two parents:

A	B	Class	A	B	Class
10	01	1	11	10	0

A	B	Class	A	B	Class
01	11	0	11	10	1

Crossover is performed by selecting two points at random in the first parent. Suppose positions 1 and 8 are selected. The crossover points, indicated by '(' and ')', are then:

A	B	Class	A	B	Class
1(0	01	1	11	1)0	0

The crossover points are randomly selected in the second parent subject to the constraint that the pair of points identify the same rule boundaries. So the allowable crossovers in the second parent are constrained to be:

A	B	Class	A	B	Class
0(1	11	0	11	1)0	1

or

A	B	Class	A	B	Class
01	11	0	1(1	1)0	1

or

A	B	Class	A	B	Class
0(1	1)1	0	11	10	1

The constraint ensures that a new valid rule is formed during crossover. So, if the parents have the following crossovers selected:

A	B	Class	A	B	Class
1(0	01	1	11	1)0	0

A	B	Class	A	B	Class
01	11	0	1(1	1)0	1

two new hypotheses (chromosomes) are formed after crossover. Replacing bits delimited by '(' and ')' in the first string with those in the second string:

A	B	Class
11	10	0

Replacing bits delimited by '(' and ')' in the second string with those in the first string:

A	B	Class	A	B	Class	A	B	
Class								
01	11	0	10	01	1	11	10	1

The fitness of a chromosome can be based on the classification accuracy of the contained hypothesis.

Genetic algorithms have been applied to design problems such as aircraft design and circuit layout. Consider the layout of houses on a building plot. Land in the UK is in short supply for new housing developments. The cost of land in very populated areas is very high, and developers like to maximize the number of houses that can be built on a plot. In addition, constraints will often be imposed on builders, such as a minimum number of starter homes or family homes must be provided. There may be a minimum plot size for a given size of house. Also, people prefer not to be overlooked by neighbours. Many other constraints can be identified and an optimum development layout is one that meets these constraints but also maximizes the return on sales. The layout of rooms in the house can also be difficult to design. You may live in a house and thought 'if only it had been laid out this way then rooms A and B would have more space'.

Suppose that you are to design the layout of the first floor in a two-storey house. There are to be two living rooms, a hall and a kitchen. Your task is to minimize the total area subject to constraints that each room's size conforms to certain size limits. So the fitness function to be minimized is:

$$F = L_1 W_1 + L_2 W_2 + L_k W_k + L_h W_h$$

where L is length, W is width, 1 is living room 1, 2 is living room2, k is the kitchen and h is the hall. A chromosome is a concatenation of bits representing each variable (length for living room 1, width for living room 1, etc.). Of course, as the encoding stands, the optimum chromosome is one with all room sizes having a value zero. Suppose that the constraint on the kitchen's length is that it is to be a minimum of 12 units but a maximum of 20 units. The range (difference between maximum and minimum length) is eight units, which could be represented using three bits (assuming accuracy to one unit). When the cost is calculated for the kitchen, the minimum value of 12 is added to the value encoded by the bits representing its length. So, if the bits are 011, the length would be 12 + 3 (= 15). In practice, fractions of a whole unit would need to be represented, and so a larger number of bits would be used. Other constraints, such as the proportional costs of different types of room or the fitting of doors, can be included by careful consideration of the encoding strategy and objective function.

Some problems impose a duplication constraint on the chromosome. For instance, in the classic travelling salesman problem, in which a single gene represents a city to be visited, a single-point crossover will duplicate some cities and ignore others. Suppose that there are five cities to be visited and two parent chromosomes are 42513 and 54213 (the decimal representation is used for convenience of illustration). If crossover is applied at the value 5 (position 2) in the first parent, the offspring are 42213 and 54513. So the first offspring has city 2 duplicated but makes no visit to city 5. One solution is to iterate through the other positions and swap corresponding values between the two chromosomes. Once cities at every position have been exchanged there will be no duplicates.

17.3.1 Gray codes

Suppose a chromosome has a gene that represents a numerical parameter such as a person's age. If the target hypothesis is to be a rule that is to identify characteristics of people retiring from work, we might expect the fitness function to return high values for the age group 55–65. The values 64 and 63 are very similar, but their binary equivalents are {01000000, 00111111}, which are not very similar. If these two genes were to reproduce using crossover after the second bit, the offspring would have gene values of {01111111, 00000000}, which have decimal equivalents {127, 0}. The problem here is that we expect the offspring to have high values of fitness (because the parents have ages 63 and 64), but the ages 127 and 0 are very dissimilar to the ages of their parents and are not typical ages for retirement. The offspring are not very representative of the target hypothesis, and this can lead to the genetic algorithm taking longer to converge. The problem arises because decimal numbers that are close in value are not necessarily close when using the standard binary representation. Similarity in this case is judged in terms of the hamming distance, which is the number of bits by which two genes differ. One solution to this problem is to use **Gray codes** to represent decimal values. Binary representations of adjacent integer values differ by only a single bit when represented by Gray codes. For example, the integers {0, 1, 2, 3, 4, 5, 6, 7} would have Gray codes {000, 001, 011, 010, 110, 111, 101, 100}. A binary string is converted to a Gray code by copying the first bit and then setting $c[i + 1] = c[i] \wedge c[i + 1]$ where $\wedge$ denotes exclusive or. For example, the binary strings {011, 111} have Gray codes {010, 100}.

17.4 Schema theorem and implicit parallelism

There is always an interest in analysing and mathematically describing any learning algorithm. In this way we hope to gain an insight into its useful properties, any limitations and possible means of improvement. Holland (1975) described the schema theorem to characterize how a population evolves over time.

The theory is based on the concept of schemata, which are strings that contain '*'. A schema is described by the alphabet {0, 1, *}, where * is 'don't care' (i.e. the bit can be 0 or 1). A schema corresponds to a hyperplane in the search space. For example, all combinations of three bits can be represented by the corners of a cube. The string 001 would occupy one corner and 010 another corner. So the schema 0** corresponds to the front face of the cube in Figure 17.7. A bit string matches a schema if that string can be constructed by replacing the '*' with 1 or 0. For example, {000, 010, 001, 011} all match the schema 0**. All strings that match a schema are contained in the hyperplane partitioned by that schema. The order of a hyperplane corresponds to the number of bit values in the schema. For example, 1 is order 1 and **0***1*0 is order 3. A string of length L occupies a corner of a hypercube in L-dimensional space and is a member of 2^L-1 hyperplanes (the string of all '*' corresponds to the whole space and is not counted). Also 3^L-1 hyperplane partitions can be defined on the whole space (each position in the string can have either * or 1 or 0).

The schema theorem illustrates that the population of chromosomes provides information about numerous hyperplanes. In particular, we would expect low-order hyperplanes to have many sample points within the population. This sampling of many hyperplanes when a population of chromosomes is evaluated is referred to as implicit parallelism. The theory also suggests that the representation of competing hyperplanes increases or decreases during reproduction according to the relative fitness of strings that sample those hyperplanes.

The evolution of a population depends on selection, crossover and mutation. These dependencies can be described mathematically, but we shall stick to a simpler description. Selection is biased towards those chromosomes that have the best fitness score. Therefore, those schemata matched by strings with the best fitness scores have a higher likelihood of selection and gradually become more representative of the population. Crossover will leave a schema intact if it does not cut the schema. Given the schemata 1*****0 and ***11**, the first has higher probability than the second of being cut during crossover (here we only consider single-point crossover).

A defined bit within a schema is either 0 or 1. The length, $l(s)$, of a schema, s, is the number of bits between the first defined and last defined bit (e.g. 011**0** has $l(s)=4$, the number of bits between the first and last defining bits). The effect of crossover is proportional to $l(s)$. The effect of crossover is also inversely proportional to the total length of the string: if a given length schema is embedded in a long string it has less chance of being changed by crossover than if it were in a short string. The impact of mutation in altering a schema depends on the probability of mutation and the number of defining bits.

The schema theorem tells us that fit, short schemata become exponentially more represented as the population evolves. For a population of n strings there are n fitness function evaluations for each generation, which is proportionately low compared with the number of schemata being processed (the implicit parallelism).

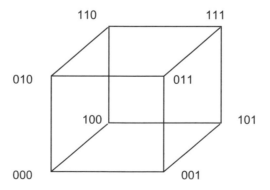

Figure 17.7 A cube with vertices denoting each combination of three bits.

17.5   Some other points about genetic algorithms

We have introduced the genetic algorithm for binary chromosomes. It is possible to use other forms of representation for variable values. One alternative to using a binary representation is to use real values for problems with continuous parameters. Crossover, whereby a real value is treated in the same manner as a single bit in the binary version, means that no new information is introduced from generation to generation (the entire gene pool never adapts, whereas for the binary version crossover can recombine parts of a single gene). One approach to introducing new information is to apply a blending method. The following equation (Radcliff, 1991) defines one form of blending:

$$p_{new} = \beta p_{1n} + (1 - \beta) p_{2n}$$

where β is a random number in the range $[0, 1]$, p_{new} is the new parameter value in offspring 1, p_{1n} is the nth parameter from parent 1 and p_{2n} is the nth parameter from parent 2. The second offspring is the complement of the first, which is computed by replacing β with $1 - \beta$.

17.5.1   *Genetic programming*

One fascinating application of genetic algorithms is the evolution of computer programs (known as genetic programming). A chromosome denotes a tree, which in turn represents a program. For example, the program corresponding to the function $f(x, y) = x^2 + y$ would be represented by the tree in Figure 17.8. A crossover operator could take two parent trees and randomly pick two subtrees to exchange. Mutation operators might consist of destroying a subtree, swapping nodes within a tree or swapping subtrees within the same tree. Koza (1992) has built several genetic programming applications. One example created a program for stacking blocks to make the word 'universal'. Program operators included: *move block to stack, move block to table, equal block x block y, not x* and *do until x y* (executes the expression x until condition y returns a value of true – for example a block could be continually added to the stack until there were no more blocks to add).

17.5.2   *Parallel processing*

Genetic algorithms are natural candidates for parallel processing. One approach is to split the population into subpopulations and assign a processor to each subpopulation. The standard genetic algorithm is run on each processor and the subpopulations evolve. Periodic migration is permitted when some chromosomes from one subpopulation are transferred (or copied) to the other. This form of parallelization can be helpful in preventing overcrowding where the genetic make-up of a fit chromosome that appears early in the evolution cycle evolves to dominate the population.

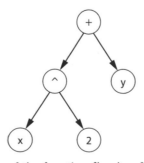

Figure 17.8 A tree representation of the function $f(x, y) = x^2 + y$.

Summary

Genetic algorithms evolve a population of hypotheses in search of the target function. Hypotheses are more commonly referred to as chromosomes, which are typically represented by binary strings, continuous parameters and trees. The principle of 'survival of the fittest' provides a strategy to evolve the population so that it converges towards the target function. The fittest chromosomes are selected for breeding to produce new candidate chromosomes, which are then added to the population. Genetic operators describe how new offspring are bred.

Further reading

An easy and clear introduction to genetic algorithms, with applications, is given in Haupt and Haupt (1998). A good introductory book that also covers the history and motivation for the subject can be found in Michell (1998). An authoritative book by one of the most active researchers in the field is the book by Goldberg (1989). The paper by Whitely (1994) provides a tutorial on theoretical aspects of genetic algorithms.

Exercises

1 Generate a mask for single-point crossover (at the fifth bit from the left) on an eight-bit string. Using this mask compute the two offspring for parents:

> 0 1 0 1 0 0 0 1
> 0 1 1 1 0 1 1 0

2 Generate a mask for two-point crossover (at the third and eighth bit) on a 12-bit string. Using this mask compute the two offspring for parents:

> 0 0 0 1 0 1 1 1 0 1 0 1
> 1 1 1 1 0 0 0 1 1 1 0 0

3 If the optimal fitness of a chromosome is represented by:

> 0 1 1 1 0 1 0 1 1 1 1 0 0 0 1 0

Using the hamming distance compute the fitness of the following strings
a   0 1 1 0 0 1 0 1 0 1 1 0 0 0 0 0
b   0 1 1 1 1 1 0 1 1 0 0 1 1 0 1 0
c   1 1 1 1 0 1 0 1 0 1 1 0 0 0 1 0
d   0 0 1 0 1 1 1 1 0 1 1 0 1 0 1 0
e   0 1 1 1 1 1 0 0 1 0 1 0 1 1 1 0

Which two strings would be selected for reproduction?

4 A set of training cases are described using three binary attributes. How many target concepts

can be learned if a set of rules are constructed from a conjunction of attribute values? If each attribute is represented by a gene with two bits, is it possible to generate hypotheses during evolution that do not represent a target concept (legal rules)?

5   Given the following costs for each of six candidate hypotheses, calculate the cumulative distribution for selecting mates:

–5
–4
–2
–5
–3
–6

Which pair would be selected for reproduction given the random numbers 0.2 and 0.75?

6   Describe a strategy for using a genetic algorithm to learn a straight-line fit to a set of two-dimensional data points.

PART 6

Natural Language Understanding and Perception

This part of the book introduces high-level tasks that build on topics introduced earlier in the book. Chapters 18 and 19 provide an overview of natural language understanding and the significant challenges that exist in attempting to get machines to understand communication using the English language. Chapter 18 introduces syntax parsing and the basics of semantic analysis. Chapter 19 builds upon Chapter 18 and introduces chart parsing. Semantic analysis is also discussed in more detail. Chapter 19 concludes with a brief introduction to the application of statistical approaches to language processing; the early part of Chapter 5 would be useful study before for this section is read. Chapter 20 introduces speech recognition. The hidden Markov model is introduced. Chapter 5 is useful study before tackling Chapter 20. Chapter 21 provides an overview of perceiving objects. In particular, it discusses feature extraction and segmentation for object recognition. An appreciation of the material in Part 5 (learning) would be useful reading before starting this chapter.

CHAPTER 18

Natural Language Processing I

Communication is a fundamental part of our daily lives. We communicate in many ways, using natural language, sign language and facial expressions, as well as through actions. Natural language, whether spoken or written, provides an efficient form of communicating. Such is the efficiency of natural language communication that a long-standing desire has been to build human–machine interfaces that operate using language. The applications for a natural language interface are various and include: efficient querying of databases, translation of text between languages of different nations, the filtering and summarizing of news stories that are of particular interest, the efficient retrieval of text documents, and so on.

If the communication is by voice, we take a sound signal and process it to identify words. A word conjures up some meaning for us, and somehow we piece together these individual meanings, along with general knowledge of the world, to interpret what has been said. This processing may appear complicated when analysed, but for us it is usually effortless. Attempts to build a natural language-understanding computer has taught us that the process of natural language communication is difficult to model and there are significant hurdles to overcome before any type of artificial communicating agent could come close to matching what we typically expect from a young child. However, much has been learned from natural language processing (NLP) research, and it is possible to build computer NLP systems that exhibit a remarkable degree of practical utility. For example, computerized air travel information systems that can respond correctly to the majority of user queries have been demonstrated. The success of such systems is largely the result of the limited domain of knowledge required: the system knows only about flight information and could not answer queries with respect to some other domain. This domain restriction cuts complexity by reducing the size of vocabulary and making the assignment of meaning to a request more manageable.

The aim of this chapter is to introduce some of the key components required to build a natural language human–machine interface. The language can be in a written or a spoken form. The construction of a computational model that can be utilized in many different applications is not practicable at this point in time. One of the reasons for this is the vast amount of knowledge that needs to be represented. Much of our ability to understand one another comes about because we share similar experiences. We know, for example, what to expect when we walk into a shop and purchase a number of items. This expectation will include the exchange of money for any item purchased and the giving of a receipt as proof of purchase. The situation in which communication is taking place allows the interpretation of what might otherwise be ambiguous. For example, the goal of a customer who asks a shopkeeper 'Do you have any milk?' might be interpreted as 'I want some milk but can't find it'. This interpretation informs the shopkeeper that a 'yes' (or no') response is not appropriate and that the customer's intention is to be directed to where the milk can be found. The shopkeeper has a belief of what the customer desires. From this shop situation we can see that many different things influence the interpretation of language. The challenge for a particular application is to represent a sufficient amount of the various forms of knowledge in a suitable way to allow complete coverage and efficient computation.

A natural language human–machine interface could involve both understanding natural language input and generating language to communicate output. This chapter is directed more to understanding, but the material is also relevant to natural language generation. In this chapter will shall look at what might be called the classical approach to NLP. The chapter starts with a brief overview of the various types of knowledge that are required in natural language processing (NLP). This is followed by a short introduction to some of the grammatical aspects of English. This chapter and the following require only a basic knowledge of sentence structure and word categories such as nouns and verbs. More information than is strictly necessary is given on the forms of verbs and tense, but the motivation here is to emphasize the considerable structure that exists within languages. The two basic approaches to parsing are then introduced. Finally, the fundamental approach to extracting sentence meaning is introduced.

18.1   The stages in natural language understanding

A classical computational model for natural language understanding (NLU) requires a number of components, which include knowledge of how sentences are structured, a database of individual words and what they mean (this database is called a **dictionary** or **lexicon**), knowledge of how word meanings combine to provide sentence meaning, knowledge of how preceding sentences affect the interpretation of the current sentence, knowledge about situations, a representation of beliefs about intentions and a model of actions. Basically, we need a lot of knowledge and knowledge represented in different ways. The knowledge required can be split into a number of categories.

Syntactic knowledge is concerned with the way in which words can be put together to form sentences. There are many ways in which words can be combined to form a sentence, and a **grammar** describes these combinations. Each word in a sentence belongs to a class depending on how the word is used. A sentence contains one or more subparts called **clauses**. A clause describes a group of words that contain a **verb**, the **subject** and often an **object**. In the sentence:

Jenny threw the ball.

Jenny is the subject, *threw* the verb and *ball* is the object. Other words are often used together with the subject, verb and object. The groupings form **phrases**. In the sentence:

The dogs had been fighting.

the dogs is the noun phrase and *had been fighting* the verb phrase. There is, therefore, a great deal of structure in natural languages. Syntactic knowledge is about understanding the structure, and syntax analysis is concerned with taking a sentence and describing the structure and testing if the sentence is grammatical[1] (i.e. conforms to the rules of the grammar).

Semantic knowledge is concerned with the meaning of words and how the meanings of words combine to provide the meaning of a sentence. Consider the sentence:

Walk the dog.

---

[1]Strictly speaking, many sentences can be understood even if they are not strictly grammatical.

The meaning is for the dog to be taken out for some physical exercise, not for the dog to be washed or eaten or something else. It also means for the dog to be walked, not the cat, kitchen sink or grandmother. The word *dog* is associated with a specific physical object and the word *walk* with a specific type of action.

    Context knowledge is concerned with how language is used and how previous sentences impact on the interpretation of the current sentence. A distinction is sometimes made between **pragmatic** knowledge and **discourse** knowledge. Pragmatics is concerned with how the current situation affects the interpretation of the sentence. The term 'discourse' refers to a collection of sentences, and discourse knowledge is concerned with issues such as resolving pronoun reference. For our purpose, we shall refer collectively to both aspects as context knowledge. There are many issues that can only be resolved in context and the following are just a few examples:

> Not many kids can cook. Can you make breakfast?
> I'm hungry. Can you make breakfast.

The interpretation of 'Can you make breakfast?' depends on the previous sentence. The first example is a question enquiring of a person's skill, whereas the second is a request for action (to cook breakfast).

> Can you baby-sit Friday?
> Sorry, I can't, I have a prior engagement.

The answer 'no' would convey the same message but would be considered impolite, and by signalling a prior engagement the respondent is indicating a reason why the request cannot be satisfied.

> Jan had a meal at that new restaurant last night.
> She said it was lovely.

The most likely interpretation of the second sentence is that 'she' is a reference to Jan and 'it' a reference to the meal.

    There are other forms of knowledge. If a system is to process low-level language input then it will need **phonetic knowledge** to relate sound signals to words or **character recognition knowledge** to extract words from written text. This chapter is not concerned with these low-level tasks and assumes that individual words can be recognized (speech processing is covered in Chapter 20). **Morphological** knowledge is concerned with how word meanings are constructed from primitives called **morphemes** (for example, the word *pulled* is the past tense of *pull* and is constructed from the base form *pull* and the suffix *-ed*). If we attempted to construct a machine that could understand natural language in a number of situations (or, more generally, could extract the meaning of conversations) then we would have to be concerned with **world knowledge** and issues such as common-sense reasoning. Common-sense knowledge is the knowledge that we take for granted, such as *a raised object will fall if it is no longer supported* and that *a person's date of birth remains the same throughout his or her life*. Some common-sense reasoning is required in many domain-limited applications (such as a specific database application), but the knowledge base would have to be huge for general discourse.

18.2   Parts of speech

This section provides a brief review of some of the terminology and components of the English language.

A piece of text is composed of sentences and each sentence is composed of words. Words are grouped into lexical categories:

- **Nouns** label objects and events (such as *man*, *book* and *party*).
- **Pronouns** act as substitutes for a noun (such as *he* and *they*).
- **Verbs** describe action, states or relations (such as *hit*, *read* and *hate*).
- **Auxiliary verbs** combine with main verbs to indicate different times, degrees of completeness and certainty (such as I *have* eaten, I *might* eat).
- **Adjectives** provide additional description of a noun (such as *tall*, *red* and *pretty*).
- **Determiners** identify a specific object (such as *the, my, a, their*).
- **Adverbs** provide more description about actions (such as *slowly, gently*).
- **Prepositions** provide information about position or movement (such as, *on, at* and *over*).
- **Connectives** join phrases and sentences (such as *and* and *but*).
- **Quantifiers** indicate amount or quantity of something a noun refers to (such as *all, many* and *some*).

A sentence consists of a number of parts. The sentence 'John flew the new plane' has a **subject,** *John*, a **verb phrase,** *flew*, and an **object**, the *new plane*. The subject is either a **noun phrase** or a pronoun and usually comes before the verb phrase. The object is a noun phrase or a pronoun. A verb that has an object is called a **transitive** verb (for example, 'John found his wallet'). A verb that does not have an object is called an **intransitive** verb (for example, 'John shouted'). A noun phrase can be a single word or a group of words. A verb phrase can be a single word or group of words.

Most of the verbs in English are main verbs and are used to indicate action and state. The other verbs are auxiliary verbs. Main verbs have five forms:

1   base form (for example, *push*);
2   third person singular, simple present tense (for example *pushes*);
3   simple past tense (for example, *pushed*);
4   past participle (for example, *pushed*);
5   present participle (for example, *pushing*).

Most verbs are **regular**, which means that they are all formed in the same way by building on the base form: form 2 is formed from the base plus -s, form 3 and form 4 are formed from the base plus -ed, form 5 is formed from the base plus -ing. Irregular verbs have a different relationship between the base and other forms. The verb *be* is an example of an irregular verb and has eight different forms: *be, am, is, are, was, were, being, been*.

The term **tense** is used to talk about the time scale a verb phrase expresses. The tenses are categorized as:

- **Simple tenses**: the **simple present** ('Rob walks to work', 'David sings in the choir'), the **simple past** ('Rob walked to work', 'David sang').
- **Progressive tenses** (show duration or continuity): the **present progressive** ('Rob is walking to work'), the **past progressive** ('Rob was walking to work'). The progressive tense is formed from the present participle of the main verb and the present or past tense of the verb 'be'.

- **Perfect tenses** (show that an action is completed): the **present perfect** ('Rob has walked to work'), the **past perfect** ('Sara had missed the bus'). The perfect tense is formed using either the present or past tense of the verb have plus the past participle.
- **Perfect progressive tenses** (show duration, completion, and present relevance): the **present perfect progressive** ('I have been talking all day'), the **past perfect progressive** ('I had been talking all day'). These tenses are formed from using either the present or past tense of the verb have plus the past participle of be plus the present participle of the main verb.

Future reference can be made in a number of ways. The modal verbs will/shall plus the base form can be used for future reference (for example, 'I will read the report this week').

There is a lot of knowledge regarding the structure of natural languages, certainly more than enough for a book dedicated to a single language like English. The study of language structure comes under the discipline of **linguistics**. Linguistic studies provide a rich knowledge base out of which to construct computer models, and they also highlight some of the difficult issues that need to be addressed. Some examples of difficult issues are given in Table 18.1.

18.3 Analysing structure

A **grammar** describes how words combine to form phrases and how phrases combine to form sentences. A grammar can be expressed using any one of a number of representational languages, but a frequently used format is **rewrite rules**. An example grammar using rewrite rules is given in Grammar 18.1.

Each rule describes how the symbol on the left-hand side (LHS) of the $\rightarrow$ can be rewritten in terms of the symbols on the right-hand side (RHS). For example, rule 1:

1        $S \rightarrow NP\ VP$

can be rewritten as:

Table 18.1 Some difficulties with processing natural language

Type of problem	Example	Explanation
Saying the same thing in two different ways	1 Stuart hit the ball 2 The ball was hit by Stuart	(1) is expressed in active form (2) is the passive form of (1)
With-clause role	1 The girl hit the boy with the stick 2 The girl hit the boy with the dog	In (1) the with-clause denotes an instrument of hitting, whereas in (2) the with-clause modifies the boy (i.e. adds more description)
Many words have multiple categories	1 The green flies 2 The aeroplane flies	In (1) flies refers to insects and is a noun whereas in (2) flies is the verb 'fly'
Subject–verb number agreement	1 Racing cars is dangerous 2 Racing cars are dangerous	(1) refers to the act of driving a car, whereas (2) implies you should keep clear of a race track
Word order	1 The dog ate the cat 2 The cat ate the dog	In (1) the cat was eaten, whereas in (2) the dog was eaten

---

Grammar 18.1 A sample grammar expressed using rewrite rules

1	S	→	NP VP
2	S	→	NP V
3	NP	→	D AP
4	NP	→	D N
5	NP	→	NP PP
6	PP	→	P NP
7	VP	→	V NP
8	VP	→	V PP
9	AP	→	ADJ AP
10	AP	→	ADJ N

S, sentence, NP, noun phrase; VP, verb phrase; AP, adjective phrase; PP, preposition phrase; N, noun; V, verb; ADJ, adjective; P, preposition; D, determiner.

> 1   S → D N VP

by rewriting the NP according to rule 4 (NP in the sentence rule is replaced with D N).

It is usual to show the phrase structure of a sentence as a tree structure, as shown in Figure 18.1. The **terminal** nodes are leaf nodes (i.e. they have no branches emerging) and denote word categories. The **non-terminal** nodes (those that have branches) can be rewritten and so will always appear on the LHS of a rule.

Grammar 18.1 is known as a **context-free grammar** (CFG), which means that only a single symbol can appear on the LHS. There are other grammar formalisms, but CFGs have proved popular.

Extracting the structure of a sentence and testing if the sentence is grammatical is the job of a **parser.** A main reason for the popularity of CFGs is that efficient parsers can be built. Inputs to the parser are the sentence, the grammar rules and the lexicon (which in the examples used here is really a simple dictionary). The lexicon gives the category of a word (e.g. N, V, P, ADJ, D). The concept of parsing can be explained using a simple example. Consider using Grammar 18.1 to parse the sentence:

> The dog ran across the road.

The lexical entries are {the – D, dog – N, ran – V, across – P, road – N}. The parser starts with the rule:

> 1   S → NP VP

and rewrites it by expanding the NP to give:

> 1   S → D N VP

Note that the rule could be rewritten using the other rules for a NP, but to keep things simple it is assumed that the parser makes the correct choice at each stage.

The RHS now contains terminal symbols that the parser can try and match with the sentence words. Starting with the first word, *the*, a match is made with the first lexical symbol D. The second word, *dog*, matches the second lexical symbol N. The rule now has the following matches:

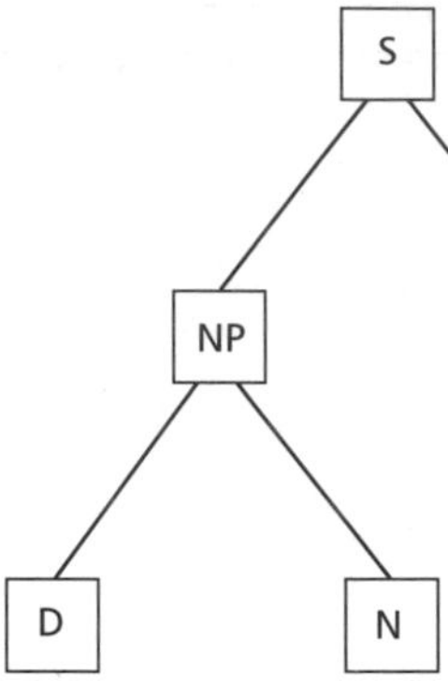

Figure 18.1 An expansion of a grammar rule represented as a tree.

$$S \rightarrow D \text{ (the) } N \text{ (dog) } VP$$

The verb phrase is now rewritten using rule 8:

$$S \rightarrow D(\text{The}) \, N(\text{dog}) \, V \, PP$$

The third word, *ran,* matches with V:

$$S \rightarrow D(\text{The}) \, N(\text{dog}) \, V \text{ (ran) } PP$$

The preposition phrase is now rewritten using rule 6:

$$S \rightarrow D(\text{The}) \, N(\text{dog}) \, V \text{ (ran) } P \, NP$$

The fourth word, *across,* matches with P:

$$S \rightarrow D(\text{The}) \, N(\text{dog}) \, V \text{ (ran) } P \text{ (across) } NP$$

The NP is now rewritten using rule 4:

$$S \rightarrow D(\text{The}) \, N(\text{dog}) \, V \text{ (ran) } P \text{ (across) } D \, N$$

The last two words, *the* and *road*, match with the D and N:.

$$S \rightarrow D(\text{The}) \, N(\text{dog}) \, V \text{ (ran) } P \text{ (across) } D \text{ (the) } N \text{ (road)}$$

The syntactic structure of the sentence is shown in Figure 18.2. In practice, the parser will not know in advance whether a rule can be completely matched. If, for example, the parser started by rewriting the sentence using:

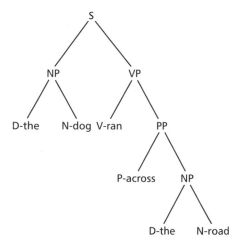

Figure 18.2 The parse tree for 'The dog ran across the road'.

$$NP \rightarrow D\ AP$$

to give:

$$S \rightarrow D\ AP\ VP$$

the match would fail as there is no adjective phrase. In this situation. the parser needs to back up and try any alternatives (in this case rewrite the sentence using the second noun phrase rule).

Parsing is a search procedure that attempts to match the structure of a sentence with structures described by the rules of a grammar. The sentence is grammatical if a match of the complete sentence can be made with a sentence rule.

There are two basic approaches to parsing: **bottom-up** and **top-down**. A bottom-up parse starts with the lexical categories of the words and tries to match a single word or group of words with a phrase structure (the right-hand side of a rule). Identified phrase structures can then be replaced with the left-hand symbol of the matching rule. This process continues, and, if the sentence constituents are all eventually replaced by a single left-hand symbol corresponding to a sentence, then the sentence is grammatical. A top-down parser starts with the sentence grammar rules and rewrites these rules until terminals can be matched with the lexical categories of words. The top-down parser proceeds in the same manner as the example given above. Parsers have the job of identifying whether a sentence is legal (conforms to the grammar, i.e. is grammatical) and of extracting a parse tree that identifies the sentence structure. The algorithms presented below would need some additional book-keeping to record the parse tree.

18.3.1   A bottom-up parser

One of the simplest forms of parser is a **shift-reduce** parser. The basics of the algorithm will be illustrated using an example constructed from Grammar 18.2.

The sentence to be parsed is:

Grammar 18.2

1	S → NP VP	The	D
2	NP → D ADJ N	dog	N
3	NP → D N	can	N AUX
4	NP → ADJ N	jump	V
5	VP → AUX VP	fence	N
6	VP → V NP		
7	VP → V PP		
8	PP → P NP		

The dog can jump the fence.

The parser proceeds by placing the word lexical categories on a stack. If a sequence on the stack can match with the RHS of a rule, the sequence can be replaced with the rule's symbol on the LHS (the stack is reduced). Figure 18.3 shows the steps involved. The first word, *the*, is shifted on to the stack. The word does not match with the RHS side of a rule and so the stack cannot be reduced. Next, the word *dog* is shifted onto the stack. The lexical categories match with the RHS of rule 3 and so the D N can be reduced to a NP. The process continues in this manner until the end of the sentence is reached. If there is a single item, S, left on the stack then the sentence is grammatical.

The parser as presented here would in practice have to be supplemented with additional capability to overcome various problems it might encounter. An example of such a problem is shift/reduce conflicts, where the parser has a choice either to reduce the stack or to shift the next symbol on to the stack. For example, if the rule:

VP → V

were added to Grammar 18.2, upon reading in *the dog can jump* 'the dog' has been reduced to a NP, but should the parser reduce the AUX (can) V (jump) to a verb phrase, or should it shift the next symbol onto the stack in anticipation of a NP to match with the RHS of rule 6 (the AUX in rule 5 having matched with 'can')? Some parsers attempt to overcome this type of conflict using lookahead techniques.

18.3.2 A top-down parser

A top-down parser algorithm is given in Figure 18.4. The algorithm maintains a stack, ToComplete, which is initialized by pushing it with the LHS of the first sentence rule. This first symbol is popped and the symbols on the RHS of the rule pushed onto ToComplete. Each sentence word is examined in order. The head symbol on ToComplete must be either a non-terminal or terminal symbol. If the head symbol on ToComplete is a non-terminal symbol, then it is replaced with the RHS of the first rule whose LHS matches the symbol. Backup states are maintained for all other matches. These backup states are stored on a backup stack. If the head symbol on ToComplete is a terminal node and matches the lexical category of the current word, then the next word from the sentence is scanned and ToComplete is popped. If the head symbol on ToComplete is a terminal node and does not match the lexical category of the current word then a backup is performed. A backup replaces content on the ToComplete stack with the head symbols on the backup stack. The algorithm is illustrated in Figure 18.5.

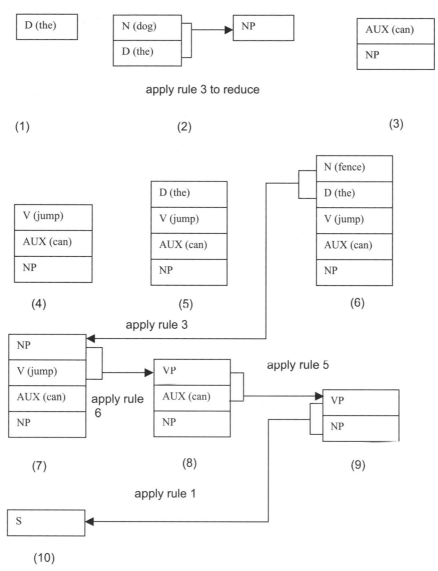

Figure 18.3 The steps in applying a bottom-up parser to the sentence 'The dog can jump the fence'.

18.4 Semantic analysis

For a sentence to serve any purpose there has to be a connection between words and their meaning, and there has to be a way to construct the whole sentence meaning from the meaning of individual words. This is true also for computer languages. The following is a statement that can be written to query a database:

Select * from CUSTOMERS

```
Algorithm topDownParse

PROCEDURE topDownParse

Initialise ToComplete [1, {S}]
parseNextWord


PROCEDURE parseNextWord

if ToComplete is empty and Position is at end of sentence
        return success
end if
if ToComplete is empty
        return fail
end if
assign head symbol of ToComplete to Current and pop ToComplete
if Current is terminal node
        if Current matches Word
                increment Position and assign Word to next word at Position
        end if
        else if Current does not match Word
                backup
        end else if
end if
else if Current is non-terminal
        create copy of ToComplete called CopyComplete
        push child nodes for first rule of type Current onto ToComplete
        for each remaining rule of type Current
                create a new backup state which is a copy of CopyComplete , push child nodes of rule onto new
                backup state, set index of new backup state to Position
        end for
end else if
parseNextWord

PROCEDURE backup

        replace ToComplete with first backup state
        set Position to ToComplete.index
```

Figure 18.4 A top-down parsing algorithm.

The word *select* has a meaning to both the user and the database query engine. This symbol indicates that the user wishes to extract data. The other symbols also have meaning. The * indicates that all columns from one or more tables are required. The symbol *from* indicates that the next word is going to be a table containing data and that this table is called CUSTOMERS. The symbols taken together mean that the user wishes to see all of the data from the CUSTOMERS table.

The following piece of C++ code

```
int x, y;
x = 5;
y = x + 6;
```

Current attempt	Sentence POSITION	TOCOMPLETE stack	Backup stack
initialise	the dog can jump the fence	[1, {S}]	
current is S S->NP VP	the dog can jump the fence	[1, {NP VP}]	
current is NP NP→D ADJ N	the dog can jump the fence	[1, {D ADJ N VP}]	[1, {D N VP}] [1, {ADJ N VP}]
current is D which matches the	the dog can jump the fence	[1, {ADJ N VP}]	[1, {D N VP}] [1, {ADJ N VP}]
ADJ does not match dog so backup	the dog can jump the fence	[1, {D N VP}]	[1, {ADJ N VP}]
current is D which matches the	the dog can jump the fence	[1, {N VP}]	[1, {ADJ N VP}]
current is N which matches dog	the dog can jump the fence	[1, {VP}]	[1, {ADJ N VP}]
current is VP VP→AUX VP	the dog can jump the fence	[1, {AUX VP}]	[3, {V NP}] [3, {V PP}] [1, {ADJ N VP}]
current is AUX which matches can	the dog can jump the fence	[1, {VP}]	[3, {V NP}] [3, {V PP}] [1, {ADJ N VP}]
current is VP VP→AUX VP	the dog can jump the fence	[1, {AUX VP}]	[4, {V NP}] [4, {V PP}] [3, {V NP}] [3, {V PP}] [1, {ADJ N VP}]
jump does not match AUX so backup	the dog can jump the fence	[4, {V NP}]	[4, {V PP}] [3, {V NP}] [3, {V PP}] [1, {ADJ N VP}]
current is V which matches jump	the dog can jump the fence	[4, {NP}]	[4, {V PP}] [3, {V NP}] [3, {V PP}] [1, {ADJ N VP}]
current is NP NP→D ADJ N	the dog can jump the fence	[5, {D ADJ N}]	[5, {D N}] [5, {ADJ N}] [4, {V PP}] [3, {V NP}] [3, {V PP}] [1, {ADJ N VP}]
current is D which matches the	the dog can jump the fence	[5, {ADJ N}]	[5, {D N}] [5, {ADJ N}] [4, {V PP}] [3, {V NP}] [3, {V PP}] [1, {ADJ N VP}]
current is ADJ which does not match fence backup	the dog can jump the fence	[5, {D N}]	[5, {ADJ N}] [4, {V PP}] [3, {V NP}] [3, {V PP}] [1, {ADJ N VP}]
current is D which matches the	the dog can jump the fence	[5, {N}]	[5, {ADJ N}] [4, {V PP}] [3, {V NP}] [3, {V PP}] [1, {ADJ N VP}]
current is N which matches fence	the dog can jump the fence	[5,]	[5, {ADJ N}] [4, {V PP}] [3, {V NP}] [3, {V PP}] [1, {ADJ N VP}]
ToComplete is empty and at end of sentence so return success			

Figure 18.5 Example illustrating the top-down parsing algorithm given in Figure 18.4.

has semantic meaning. That is, variable x is initialized to 5 and y is assigned the value of x plus 6 ($y = 11$).

The following code is syntactically correct but is semantically incorrect

```
const int y = 10;
int x = 5;
y = x;
```

There is nothing wrong with the syntax of each line, but the third line is semantically incorrect because a const (constant variable) may only be assigned a value at initialization.

In C++, operators (such as $+$, $-$, $+=$ and others) can be overloaded. Overloading an operator allows a programmer to define the meaning of an operator. A programmer may define the $+$ operator to concatenate two strings in which case the following code is legal:

```
string s1, s2, s3;
s1 = s2 + s3;
```

The exact meaning of an operator depends on the types of its arguments (s2, s3). So the expression:

```
string s2 = 'brown';
string s3 = 'cow';
string s1 = s2 + s3;
```

results in s1 having the value *browncow*. The operator '+' can result in different actions depending on what other symbols accompany it. It might mean that numbers should be added or it could mean something else, such as for two strings to be concatenated.

For natural language, semantic analysis extracts the context-independent meaning of a sentence. Semantic analysis therefore extracts the meaning of a sentence in isolation of other sentences. But in what form is sentence meaning defined? A commonly held view is that semantics deals with how the truth condition of a sentence can be asserted. So one approach is to represent the sentence in such a way that we can automate the assertion of its truth condition. One form of representation is called the **logical form**, based on first-order predicate calculus (FOPC), which was introduced in Chapter 2. For example, the logical form for:

Sadie is a dog.

is:

dog(sadie)

Given a database that lists objects of type dog, the truth of the sentence can be asserted.

The two sentences:

John kicked the ball.
Did John kick the ball?

have the same representation:

kick(john, ball)

The first sentence is a declaration (**declarative mood**) that is stating *John kicked the ball* as a fact. The second sentence is **interrogative mood**, which in this example requires a yes/no answer. For a database application, if the mood can be identified the computer can respond appropriately. In the first sentence the computer would enter the information into the database as a fact and in the second case the computer would query the database to see if the statement exists as a fact.

The logical form provides flexibility. For example, once the database has listed as a fact that:

John kicked the ball   kick(john, ball)

we can then ask:

Who kicked the ball?   kick(X, ball)
What did John kick?   kick(john, X)
Who kicked what?   kick(X, Y)

For semantic analysis, it is useful to view the meaning of a sentence as being composed of the meaning of its subparts. The meanings of subparts are in turn composed from the meanings of their subparts and so on until the subpart is a word. We could concern ourselves with the meaning at the subparts of words level (morpheme level), but to keep things simple we shall restrict our lowest level of unit meaning to the level of words. So, how is meaning assigned to a word? This question is philosophical, and much has been written on the topic. The symbolic view, which is our concern here, is that a word is a label (a substitute if you like) for the real thing. Labels are used in the form of names to refer to our friends. A name serves as a convenient way to refer to someone we know. So, for objects, the meaning is represented as a label – a symbol that can be read and used to refer to the real item. Relations between objects appear as verbs and are expressed as predicates that take one or more arguments. So the meaning of the word *like*, for example, can be represented as a predicate that takes two arguments *like(X, Y)*. Words that describe properties are also represented by predicates.

The view of semantics given here is that the meaning of a sentence is **compositional** and that the units of composition correspond to syntactical units (words and phrases). This correspondence between syntax and semantic structure suggests that semantic analysis can be synthesized into the parsing stage of analysis. One approach to this synthesis is to introduce the notion of **features** into the grammar rules. The following rules:

$S \rightarrow NP\ VP$
$NP \rightarrow N$
$N \rightarrow name$
$VP \rightarrow V\ NP$
$name \rightarrow Mary$
$name \rightarrow John$
$verb \rightarrow loves$

can be used to identify the syntax structure of *John loves Mary*. The logical form is:

loves(john, mary).

To extract this logical form during parsing, the grammar can be enhanced with **semantic features**. A semantic feature is denoted using **sem-x,** where x is a word category or phrasetype (e.g. N, NP). The above grammar has been augmented with semantic features:

1   S(sem-vp sem-np) → NP(sem-np) VP(sem-vp)
2   NP(sem-np) → N(sem-np)
3   N(sem-n) → name(sem-n)
4   VP(sem-v sem-np) → V(sem-v) NP(sem-np)

name(sem-n) → Mary('mary')
name(sem-n) → John('john')
verb(sem-v) → love($\lambda y.\lambda x.$love(X, Y))

The first rule states that the semantics of a sentence can be composed from the semantic feature for the verb phrase with the semantic feature for the noun phrase. Rule 4 states that, for a verb phrase, the semantics is composed out of the semantic feature for the verb and the semantic feature for the noun phrase. The semantic features for the names are given on the right-hand side in brackets and should be viewed as labels. The semantic feature for the only verb, *love*, is a binary predicate, but it has some additional notation that provides an expression in a form that is called **lambda calculus**. For our purpose we use it to perform a simple operation known as **lambda reduction** to simplify an expression. For example, an expression of the form:

$$((\lambda \ x \ Px) \ a)$$

can be reduced to 'Pa'. So the expression $\lambda y.\lambda x.$love(X, Y) formulated with:

$$((\lambda y.\lambda x.\text{love}(X, Y)) \ \text{'mary'}) \text{ reduces to } \lambda x.\text{love}(X, Mary) \text{ and}$$
$$((\lambda x.\text{love}(X, Mary)) \ \text{'john'}) \text{ reduces to love(john, mary).}$$

The lambda reduction works in a left to right order, and its purpose is simply to make the expression more readable (or recognizable). All we are doing is replacing one symbol with another. The parse for *John loves Mary* is illustrated in Figure 18.6. The semantic content for the subject and object noun phrases are John and Mary respectively. The semantic content for the verb *love* is:

$$\lambda y.\lambda x.\text{love}(X, Y).$$

The LHS of the VP rule states that the semantic content of the verb phrase should be written as:

$$[\lambda y.\lambda x.\text{love}(X, Y) \text{ mary}]$$

which reduces to:

$$[\lambda x.\text{love}(X, mary)].$$

The LHS of the S rule states that the semantic content of the sentence should be written as:

$$[\lambda x.\text{love}(X, mary) \text{ john}]$$

which reduces to:

$$\text{love(john, mary).}$$

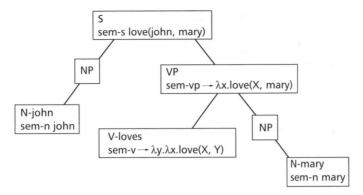

Figure 18.6 The parse and semantic analysis of *John loves Mary*.

18.5   Context analysis

The full meaning of a sentence is usually dependent on context. For example, the logical expression:

> saw(john, match)

cannot not be fully interpreted in isolation since *match* has more than one meaning: an implement that can produce a flame or a contest of some sort. The situation in which the sentence:

> John saw the match.

appears needs to be analysed. If the preceding sentence is:

> John was attempting to light the fire when he dropped the match.

it would seem probable that match is referring to the implement with which the fire was being lit. So context is needed to resolve the type of object *match* is referring to. Another example is:

> Jane hit the boy with the ball.

Taken in isolation, we may assume that Jane kicked or threw the ball and it hit the boy. We would soon modify our interpretation if told:

> Jane was watching the football match when she threw her hat at the players.

The ball is not the instrument with which to hit but instead serves as additional description to identify the boy who was hit.

We understand much about how language is used from our everyday experiences. Once again we see that context affects our interpretation. For example:

> Can you make a cup of tea?

is often meant as a request for a cup of tea to be made. but it could literally mean 'Are you capable of making tea?'.

Context can also be used to restrict the sense of a word. The word *love* in its everyday use has a sense expressed in the form:

love(Human, Object).

This sense admits expressions such as:

John loves Mary.

and

John loves chocolate.

In the following definition, the object of the relationship is restricted to being a human. In the context of human relations, *love* maybe restricted to:

love(Human, Human)

and in this sense we may assume that *candy* in:

love(john, candy)

is a human object rather than a sweet. The restriction in this case has resolved a potential ambiguity between *candy* being a sweet and *candy* being human (assuming that we are talking in the context of human relationships).

Summary

A great deal of knowledge is required for natural language processing. Knowledge is required about the structure of languages, how meaning is attached to sentences and how sentences interact to give meaning. We have taken a brief look at:

- syntactic knowledge – knowledge regarding the structure of sentences;
- semantic knowledge – how meaning is derived from a sentence;
- context knowledge – how sentences interact during discourse to provide meaning.

There is a great deal of inherent structure in natural languages. The classical approach to NLP attempts to represent this structure to extract meaning. A parser is used to analyse the structure of a sentence. Parsing is essentially a form of search that seeks to match the structure in a set of grammar rules with the structure of a sentence. Semantic analysis is concerned with extracting the meaning of a sentence, and the typical output of semantic analysis is a FOPC representation of a sentence. Semantic information is often extracted during syntax analysis. Much is understood about syntax and semantics, and it is feasible to build NLP systems to operate in small application domains. However, the arrival of a general conversational artificial agent is a long way off. A challenge is the considerable amount of general world knowledge that such an agent would need to possess.

Exercises

1   A large part of a grammar consists of rules governing the order in which words can appear. Simply changing word order can alter the meaning of a sentence. Write alternative sentences for each sentence listed below by playing with the order of words and explain how the meaning changes.

    The dog chased the cat.
    Can you cook breakfast?
    The boy with a dog helped me.
    Copy the last four pages.

2   Identify the class (part of speech, e.g. noun, adjective, etc.) for the word *brown* in the following sentences:

    The dog is brown.
    The onions should be browned first.
    David pocketed the brown.

3   Identify the lexical categories of the words in the following sentences and, using Grammar 18.1, sketch the parse trees for the following sentences:

    The little boy hit the ball.
    The dog jumped into the river.

4   Modify Grammar 18.2 to accept the sentence:

    John can swim.

5   Write a program that uses Grammar 18.2 to generate sentences. Input a dictionary of words and use the program to generate sentences. Discuss any observations you make about the sentences.

6   Reduce the following expression

    $((((\lambda x \lambda y \lambda z\ between(x, z, y))\ a)\ b)\ c)$

7   Write a grammar that will parse the following sentences into FOPC expressions:

    The dog barked.
    Sadie jumped the river.

8   Write a small grammar that will parse the following arithmetic expressions:

    $y = (3 + 2)$
    $y = x * 4$
    $z = 5 / x$

9   Explain in what ways the following sentences could be ambiguous:

  Sara caught the train.
  Sara took the train from London to Paris
  The sailor danced with a wooden leg.

10 Pick a subject to talk about with a colleague. Record the conversation. Play back the conversation and write down the transcript. Make observations regarding the grammatical structure and lack of emphasis through loss of voice stress and tone.

11 Identify the subject, verb and object in the following sentences:

  John punched the bag.
  Sue likes David.
  The tyre is flat.
  The cat ate the fish.
  The pilot landed the plane.

12 English is used in many different ways, and the array of usage contributes significantly to the complexity of building general language understanding systems. For example, saying 'no' can be done in many ways. For example:

  Can I borrow your CD?
  Sorry.
  Not today.
  I don't think so

Create a list of other ways in which 'no' can be stated.

CHAPTER 19

Natural Language Processing II

Chapter 18 gave an overview of some of the key aspects of natural language processing. This chapter extends the material presented in the last chapter. We start with a parsing technique that is practical for working with large grammars. Next we examine the need to augment grammars with features that represent knowledge regarding noun and verb agreement. Semantic analysis is developed further, and two fundamental approaches are introduced: the first is an extension to that introduced in Chapter 18, in which semantic knowledge is embedded into the grammar, and the second adopts an approach whereby more semantic knowledge is provided in the lexicon. Finally, a brief discussion is given on some of the issues regarding context analysis.

19.1   Chart parser

In Chapter 18, top-down and bottom-up parsing were introduced. The top-down parser starts with a rule for a sentence and rewrites the sentence rule in the form of its constituents. Any constituent that is a non-terminal (can appear on the left-hand side of a grammar rule) will be rewritten (with symbols on the right-hand side of a rule), and when there is more than one way of rewriting a rule backup states are recorded. Terminals are matched with the lexical categories of words in a sentence. If a match fails, the parser attempts to back up. The bottom-up parser examines the lexical category of each word in turn and attempts to construct complete phrase structures by matching with the right-hand side of the grammar rules. For small, simple grammars, both of these approaches can be implemented as practical parsers. For larger-scale grammars, much work needs to be repeated when the same matches are tried again and again during backup operations. To avoid repetition, it is necessary to record matches that have already been completed or started. The structure for recording this effort is called a **chart**.

Consider a parsing technique in which each word of a sentence is processed in order. Work already done is recorded to save repetition. This record keeps track of rules that have been partially matched or could potentially be matched, and rules that have been completed. A completed chart is illustrated in Figure 19.1. It is convenient to think of the chart as being made up of subgraphs, with each subgraph corresponding to a grammar rule.

A subgraph spans the nodes according to the words it matches within the sentence. For example, g3 starts at node 0 and ends at node 2 because D matches with *the* and N with *dog*. The rule g1 spans the whole sentence because there is an NP (g3) and a VP (g5) spanning from node 2 to 6. On examination, the following compositions can be seen:

g1: S $\rightarrow$ g3 g5

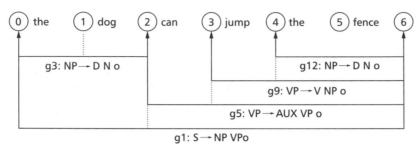

Figure 19.1 A completed chart showing the phrase structure of the sentence 'The dog can jump the fence'.

g3: NP→D N
g5: VP→AUX g9
g9: VP→V g12
g12: NP→D N

In practice, the chart will contain other subgraphs that have been either **introduced** or partially **extended**. Figure 19.2 shows two other graphs that have been introduced, g4 and g2, but only g2 has been partially extended. Graph g4 is introduced but cannot be extended because its first symbol to be matched is ADJ, and this does not match the following sentence word, *the*. The first symbol to be matched in g2 is D , which matches with *the*, but it cannot be extended further because ADJ does not match with *dog*. Graph g3 is **completed** because all of the symbols on the right-hand side (RHS) have been matched. Notice that in Figure 19.1 additional edges have been indicated with dotted lines. This shows that g1 has an edge spanning 0–2 and a second edge spanning 2–6. The first time g1 is extended is when a NP rule that is introduced at node 0 is completed. The NP to be completed is g3 and so g1 has an edge added from 0 to 2. Rule g1 cannot be further extended until there is a completed VP that is introduced at node 2. When g5 is complete, g1 can have an edge added from node 2 to node 6. To keep the following figures less cluttered, the additional edges will not be shown.

The chart parser will be illustrated using Grammar 19.1 to parse the sentence:

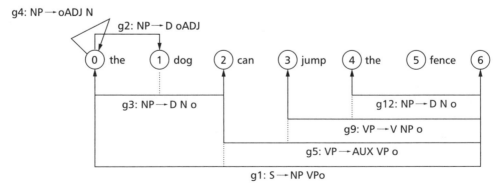

Figure 19.2 A chart that is generated during the parse of 'The dog can jump the fence'.

Grammar 19.1

1	S→NP VP
2	NP→D ADJ N
3	NP→D N
4	NP→ADJ N
5	PP→P NP
6	VP→AUX VP
7	VP→V NP
8	VP→V PP

The dog can jump the fence.

The starting point is to consider each rewrite rule of type S (sentence). In the current example there is only one,

1   S→∘NP VP.

The symbol ∘ is used to write what is called the **dot notation** to indicate the current position within a rule; so, once a NP has been completed, the dot can be advanced by one position. This first rule is predicting that a NP should exist followed by a VP. If a NP cannot be constructed there is no point in considering the VP as the sentence will not conform to the grammar; thus, at any point in the parse, the parser is concerned only with the symbol that immediately follows the dot. The NP is the first subphrase required and so all ways of constructing a NP are considered:

2   NP→∘D ADJ N
3   NP→∘D N
4   NP→∘ADJ N

Three NP rules have been introduced. The next step is to see if any of the rules under consideration can be extended (advancing the dot). The first word in the sentence is *the*, which has the lexical category D. Two of the noun phrases can be extended and so the rules in dot notation now look like:

1   S_0→∘NP VP
2   NP_0→D ∘ADJ N
3   NP_0→D ∘N
4   NP_0→∘ADJ N

One further piece of information that needs to be recorded is the point at which a rule is introduced. All of the above phrases were introduced before the first word (stage 0), and this is indicated by the subscript at the head symbol. If the point at which a rule is introduced is not recorded then the rules will be used to create illegal structures. For example, only rules 2 and 3 can be considered for the next word because the dot is in a position to predict the second word's lexical category. When a rule is considered, three actions can potentially be taken: if the symbol following the dot is a lexical category and the category matches the next word of the sentence then the rule can be **extended**; if the symbol following the dot is a non-terminal then any rule with a head that matches the non-terminal type can be **introduced** (added to the list of rules under consideration); and if the symbol following the dot is a lexical category but does not match the next sentence word then the dot stays in its current position.

The next word in the example is *dog*, which is of type N, and so the rules now look like:

1 $S_0 \rightarrow \circ NP\ VP$
2 $NP_0 \rightarrow D \circ ADJ\ N$
3 $NP_0 \rightarrow D\ N \circ$
4 $NP_0 \rightarrow \circ ADJ\ N$

Rule 3 has been completed, which means that the dot for rule 1 can be advanced as rule 1 currently has its dot at the position where rule 3 was introduced and the next symbol in rule 1 is an NP which matches rule 3. Rule 1 is extended to give:

1 $S_0 \rightarrow NP \circ VP$

The position of the dot in rule 1 is now predicting a VP. There are three VP rules that can now be introduced to give:

1 $S_0 \rightarrow NP \circ VP$
2 $NP_0 \rightarrow D \circ ADJ\ N$
3 $NP_0 \rightarrow D\ N \circ$
4 $NP_0 \rightarrow \circ ADJ\ N$
5 $VP_2 \rightarrow \circ AUX\ VP$
6 $VP_2 \rightarrow \circ V\ NP$
7 $VP_2 \rightarrow \circ V\ PP$

The procedure continues in the same fashion until the last word of the sentence has been processed. If after the last word has been processed the sentence phrase has been completed (by completing a VP) then the sentence is legal.

The algorithm is given in Figure 19.3. Each graph carries with it some additional information: a unique identifier number, the sentence position at which it was introduced and the position of the dot in terms of sentence position. So, for rule 3, $NP_0 \rightarrow D\ N \circ$, there would be a graph [g3, 0, 2], which denotes a graph with a unique identifier g3, introduced at position 0, and the dot is currently at position 2 (corresponds to the third word in the sentence). A data structure called the **agenda** keeps a record of all constituents to be explored. Figure 19.4 illustrates each stage of the parse.

The parse tree structure is contained within the subgraphs of the matching sentence graph (g1).

19.2 Grammars and features

A simple grammar is given in Grammar 19.2. Grammar 19.2 will allow the following sentences to be parsed:

> The dog barks.
> The dog found a bone.
> The dogs bark.

The grammar also accepts the following sentences

> *The dogs barks.

```
PROCEDURE ChartParse
Initialise
Parse

PROCEDURE Predict
return the next constituent for a rule


PROCEDURE Initialise
Introduce("S")
for each S
        Introduce first constituent
end for

PROCEDURE Parse
for each word in sentence
        Get constituent types for word and add to Agenda
                while Agenda still has constituents
                        Set constituent to head of Agenda
                        Extend(constituent)
                end while
end for

PROCEDURE Extend(Constituent c)
for each Graph
        current sentence position is p
        see if graph [Gᵢ, Intᵢ, Posᵢ] can be extended according to the following:
                if the next constituent is a terminal, the graph is extended provided:
                        the next constituent matches c
                        the graph's dot position matches the current sentence position
                        Posᵢ ₌ p
                end if
                if the next constituent is a non-terminal, the graph is extended provided:
                        the next constituent matches c
                        the graph's dot position matches the  c's position of introduction Intᵢ ₌ p
                end if

        if extended
                if completed
                        Add constituent head to Agenda
                end if
                else
                        Introduce(Predict) – Predict is next constituent in graph
                end else
        end if
end for

PROCEDURE Introduce(constituent)
for each grammar rule
        If head of rule matches constituent then create new graph for rule and add
        to the chart. Record in the graph the sentence position at which point the graph is added to
        the chart.
end for
```

Figure 19.3 Chart parsing algorithm.

(a)

g1: S ->o NP VP

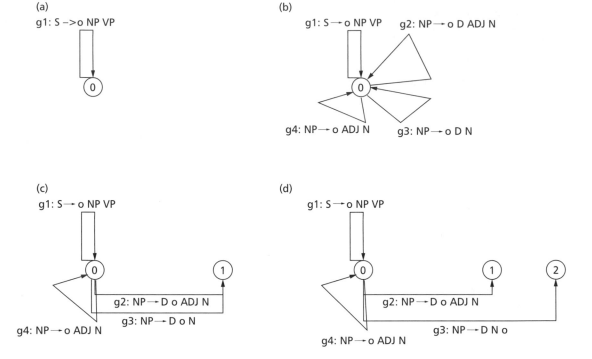

(b)

g1: S→o NP VP   g2: NP→o D ADJ N

g4: NP→o ADJ N   g3: NP→o D N

(c)

g1: S→o NP VP

g2: NP→D o ADJ N

g3: NP→D o N

g4: NP→o ADJ N

(d)

g1: S→o NP VP

g2: NP→D o ADJ N

g3: NP→D N o

g4: NP→o ADJ N

(e)

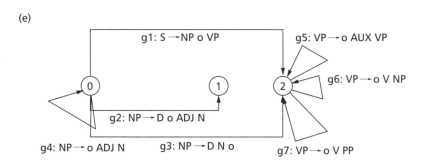

g1: S→NP o VP   g5: VP→o AUX VP

g6: VP→o V NP

g2: NP→D o ADJ N

g4: NP→o ADJ N   g3: NP→D N o   g7: VP→o V PP

(f)

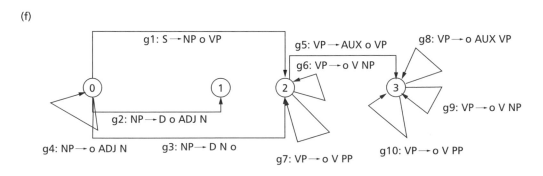

g1: S→NP o VP   g5: VP→AUX o VP   g8: VP→o AUX VP

g6: VP→o V NP

g2: NP→D o ADJ N   g9: VP→o V NP

g4: NP→o ADJ N   g3: NP→D N o   g7: VP→o V PP   g10: VP→o V PP

Figure 19.4

(g)

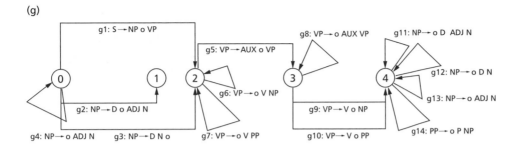

(h)

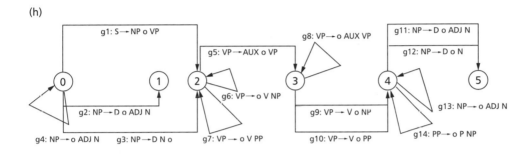

(i)

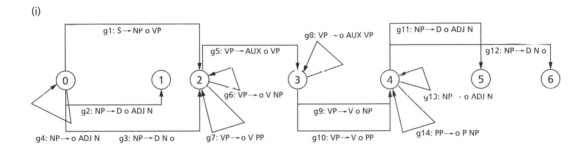

(j)

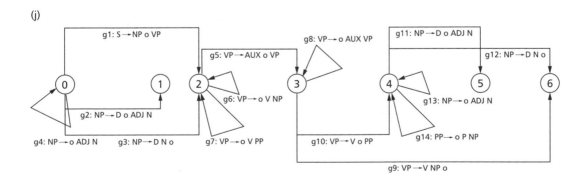

Figure 19.4

(k)

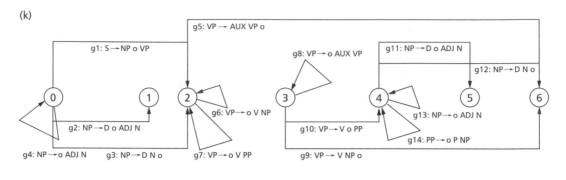

(l)

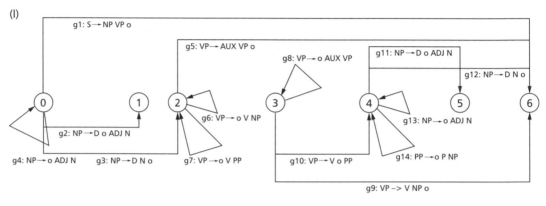

Figure 19.4 (a) The only sentence rule is introduced. Agenda: D (the). (b) NPs have been introduced. Agenda: D (the). (c) Agenda: D (the). Can extend g2 and g3. No predictions (ADJ and N are terminals). (d) Agenda: N (dog). Can extend g3. g3 is completed and so add NP (g3) to agenda. (e) Agenda NP (g3). Can extend g1 (S) because g3 was introduced at point where g1's dot is currently located. g1 is now predicting VPs. (f) Agenda: AUX (can). g5 is extended, and aVP is predicted as g8, g9, g10 added. (g) Agenda: V (jump). g9 and g10 extended. NP and PP predicted so g11, g12, g13 and g14 added. (h) Agenda: D (the). g11 and g12 extended. No completions and no predictions. (i) Agenda: N (fence). g12 is extended and completed. A NP (g12) is added to the agenda. (j) Agenda: NP (g12). g9 is extended as its dot is located where g12 was introduced. g9 is completed and so a VP (g9) is added to the agenda. (k) Agenda: VP (g9). g5 is extended and completed since its dot is located where g9 was introduced. g5 is completed and a VP (g5) is added to the agenda. (l) Agenda: VP (g5). Finally, g1 is extended as its dot position is currently located where g5 was introduced.

Grammar 19.2

S → NP VP	the – D
NP → D N	dog – N
NP → N	dogs – N
VP → V	bark – V
VP → V NP	barks – V
	found – V
	a – D
	bone – N
	bones – N

*The dog found.
*The dogs found

The * is used to denote that the sentences are not grammatical. 'The dogs barks' is not grammatical because *dogs* and *barks* do not agree in number. 'The dog found' and 'The dogs found' are ungrammatical because the verb *found* is transitive and requires that a noun phrase follows. To prevent ungrammatical sentences of the form described above, the grammar needs to be constrained.

Grammar 19.3 is constrained through the introduction of features to both the grammar rules and lexicon. For example:

The dog found a bone.

is grammatical but:

The dog found a bones.

is not because *a* is singular and *bones* is plural. Rule 2 has a number feature, and the expression:

<D number>=<N number>

means that the number feature for the D must match the number feature for the N. Notice that rule 2 also has the expression:

<NP number>=<N number>

This states that the number of the noun phrase will be copied from the number of the noun. It is typical in many parsers for the feature of the parent (the left-hand side for the rule) to be copied from one of the children (a constituent from the right-hand side). The **head of the phrase** is the child that provides the copied feature. So for the sentence:

The dogs bark.

the and *dogs* match in number because *the* has no number feature and therefore can match against any number feature for a noun. For *the dogs*, the NP number feature is copied from the noun *dogs* and is therefore plural (PL).

<D number>=<N number>
<NP number>=<N number>

So, the first number feature of D is checked to see that it matches with the number feature for N. The N is the head of the phrase. NP will have no number feature assigned and so, when it is matched with N, NP becomes bound to the same value as N.

According to grammar rule 1, the NP and VP must match in number. Since *bark* is plural:

The dogs bark.

is accepted as grammatical but:

The dogs barks.

Grammar 19.3

1   S → NP VP
    <NP number> = <VP number >

2   NP → D N
    <D number > = <N number >
    <NP number > = <N number >

3   VP → V
    <VP number > = <V number >

4   VP → V NP
    <VP number > = <V number >

5   NP → N
    <NP number> = <N number>

a
    <cat> D
    <number> = SING

the
    <cat> D

dog
    <cat> N
    <number> = SING

bark
    <cat> V
    <number> PL

found
    <cat> V

barks
    <cat> V
    <number> SING

dogs
    <cat> N
    <number> PL

bone
    <cat> N
    <number> SING

bones
    <cat> N
    <number> PL

---

is not because *the dogs* is plural and *barks* is singular.

The lexicon in Grammar 19.3 has been structured. Each entry in the lexicon can be considered as a data structure with feature value pairs. The first feature <cat> denotes the lexical category of the word. Other features are used to encode further constraints. One other example is the use of a feature to constrain verb complements. Transitive verbs require a noun phrase to follow the verb. For example:

> *Jasper found.

requires a noun phrase complement such as:

> Jasper found a bone.

Intransitive verbs can stand alone and require no complement (for example 'Jasper barked'). Some verbs allow a complement of two noun phrases, for example:

John gave Sara a ticket.

Some verbs require specific prepositional complements. For example, the verb *give* also has a complement of a NP followed by a PP but with the constraint that the preposition *to* be used, for example:

John gave a ticket to Sara.

We can represent such phrase complements using another feature called **subcat**. So the verb *found* has a subcat value of _np to indicate that the verb must be followed by a noun phrase. Similarly, the verb *give* can have a subcat value _np_pp(to) (as in 'John gave a ticket to Sara'). *Give* can also have the subcat value _np_np (as in 'John gave Sara a ticket').

Other features would be needed in practice. For example, subjects and verbs should agree with respect to the person: first person, second person or third person. Number and person features always occur together, and therefore these two features are often combined into a single feature that has six possible values (there are two number values which can each be paired with any one of the three person values). So the pronoun *man* would have a 3s (third person singular) value, whereas *men* would have a 3p (third person plural value). For some words, multiple values can be assigned. For instance, the word *were* can have values {2s, 1p, 2p, 3s}.

Grammar 19.4 has been augmented with enough features to correctly analyse the following sentences:

The dog barks.
The dog found a bone.
The dogs bark.
*The dogs barks.
*The dog found.
*The dogs found.

The first three sentences are accepted as grammatical whereas the last three are rejected as ungrammatical.

19.3   Semantics

The meaning of a sentence can change depending on context. The question 'Have you got your passport?' will typically be interpreted differently depending on whether it is asked by a customs officer or a family member on leaving home. The customs officer would be asking to see your passport, whereas the family member would be making sure that you have remembered your passport. How we respond to questions (what action we take) is dependent on context.

Semantics is about determining the context-independent meaning of a sentence, and for many applications the aim of semantic processing is to extract some context-independent logical form from analysing structure.

Deriving the logical form involves identifying predicates and their arguments, and relevant logical operators. In syntax analysis, child constituents are combined to form a parent constituent: for instance, a noun phrase can be formed from the child constituents D and N. Like syntax, semantics is taken to be compositional: word meanings combine to form the meaning of subphrases, which in turn combine to give sentence meaning. One problem we encounter is that words can have multiple definitions, with each definition denoting a different sense of the word. The word *fly*, for example, in most dictionaries will have at least two senses defined: the first sense is an insect and the second sense is a motion through the air. So fly can be either a noun or a verb.

There are different representations for the logical form, but many approaches use a predicate–argument notation based on first-order predicate calculus (FOPC). Predicates are used to describe relations and properties. Verbs such as *love*, *play* and *see* correspond to *n*-ary predicates, and common nouns, e.g. *girl* and *dog*, correspond to unary predicates. Objects and events correspond to terms. So a proper name such as *John* is a term. A sentence is represented by one or more predicates whose arguments are composed of terms. More complex sentences can be constructed using the logical operators (or, and, negation, implication and double implication).

As semantic analysis is often defined as a compositional process that is independent of context, the process of extracting the logical form is often achieved during syntax analysis. We can consider two approaches to combining syntax and semantic analysis. The first approach is to encode the semantic structure into the grammar rules and add semantic (**SEM**)[1] features to the lexicon. The second approach puts more emphasis on trying to represent semantic information in the lexicon. We shall take a brief look at both approaches.

Grammar 19.4

Rules	Dictionary

1   S → NP VP
      \<NP number> = \<VP number>
	A
	    \<cat>D
	      \<number> = SING

2   NP → D N
      \<D number> = \<N number>
      \<NP number> = \<N number>
	The
	    \<cat>D
	 dog
	    \<cat>N
	      \<number> = SING

3   VP → V
      \<V subcat> =
      \<VP number > = \<V number>
	bark
	    \<cat>V
	      \<number> = PL
	      \< subcat> = _

4   VP → V NP
      \<V subcat> = _np
      \<VP number> = \<V number>
	found
	    \<cat>V
	      \<number> = SING
	      \< subcat> = _np

5   NP → N
      \<NP number> = \<N number>
	barks
	    \<cat>V
	      \<number> = SING
	      \<subcat> = _
	 dogs
	    \<cat>N
	      \< number> = PL
	 bone
	    \<cat>N
	      \<number> = SING
	 bones
	    \<cat>N
	      \<number = PL

---

[1]Note that the notation is extended slightly here compared with that given in chapter 18. SEM is just a marker that denotes the place where semantic detail is defined.

19.3.1 *Encoding semantic structure within the grammar rules*

In Grammar 19.5 the rules and child constituents have a SEM feature (there is also an EV feature, which is introduced later). The SEM feature for rule 1 is constructed out of the SEM features for the verb phrase followed by the SEM feature for the noun phrase. In rule 4, the verb phrase has a semantic feature that will form a predicate expression. The predicate name will be the SEM feature for the verb child constituent and the SEM feature of the noun phrase will provide the second argument to the predicate expression. A lambda operator along with a variable x is used so that the first argument can be obtained when the verb phrase is composed with another phrase to form a parent phrase (for example, a sentence). Using our adopted notation, the logical form for:

> Jasper found the bone.

is

> found(jasper, bone)

Grammar 19.5

1	S SEM sem-vp sem-np	$\rightarrow$	NP SEM sem-np	VP SEM sem-vp

2	NP	$\rightarrow$	D	N SEM sem-n	SEM sem-n

3	NP SEM sem-n	$\rightarrow$	NAME SEM sem-n

4	VP SEM λx sem-v(X sem-np)	$\rightarrow$	V SEM sem-v	NP SEM sem-np

5	VP SEM λx sem-v(EV e, X) EV e	$\rightarrow$	V SEM sem-v

6	VP SEM λx [sem-vp(X) & sem-pp(EV e)] EV e	$\rightarrow$	VP SEM sem-vp	PP SEM sem-pp

7	PP SEM λx sem-p(X, sem-np)	$\rightarrow$	P SEM sem-p	NP SEM sem-np

Jasper SEM Jasper	bone SEM bone	sleep SEM sleep	on SEM on-loc
found SEM found	the SEM	couch SEM couch	

and the construction is illustrated in Figure 19.5. The construction uses rules 1, 3, 4 and 2. In rule 1, the child constituents are a noun phrase followed by a verb phrase. The noun phrase in rule 3 for this example is *Jasper*, and its semantic feature is *Jasper*. The verb phrase is constructed using rule 4. The verb in rule 4 corresponds to *found* and the following noun phrase is constructed from rule 2. Rule 2 corresponds to *the bone* and the semantic feature of the noun phrase simply consists of the noun *bone* (for convenience of illustration the D constituent is ignored). The semantic feature for the noun phrase in rule 2 is then passed up to rule 4. The semantic feature for rule 4 is:

$$\lambda x \ sem\text{-}v(x, sem\text{-}np)$$

and when instantiated with the child constituents becomes:

$$\lambda x \ found(X, bone)$$

The semantic feature for rule 4 is then passed up to rule 1, whose semantic feature is constructed from the semantic feature of the verb phrase followed by the noun phrase *Jasper*:

$$\lambda x \ found(X, bone) \ Jasper$$

which reduces to:

found(jasper, bone)

after applying lambda reduction.

Constructing the logical form for 'Jasper found the bone' is reasonably straightforward, but constructing the logical form for:

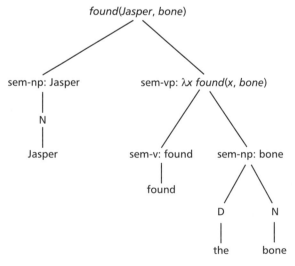

Figure 19.5 Parse tree showing the phrase structure and semantic representation for *Jasper found the bone*.

Jasper is sleeping on the couch.

is more complicated. To represent 'Jasper is sleeping' we can simply use:

sleep(jasper)

and to represent 'Jasper is on the couch we could use:

on-loc(jasper, couch)

This representation does not adequately describe the event (of Jasper sleeping) in that it fails to represent that Jasper's location is providing more description about the event Jasper sleeping. So the location of Jasper and Jasper's activity (sleeping) are linked in that they co-occur, and this should be explicitly represented. We can represent the fact that Jasper's activity and location are linked to the same event by introducing an event (**EV**) variable that will appear as an argument to both predicates. Our representation of the sentence then becomes:

sleep(e1, Jasper) ∧ on-loc(e1, couch)

The rules for parsing 'Jasper is sleeping on the couch' are given in Grammar 19.5. We have now introduced an EV feature into the verb phrase rules. The construction of the logical form is illustrated in Figure 19.6 and further explained below. Note that & is used in place of ∧ (logical AND).

There is a new event variable instantiated for each occurrence of x. Working from the leaf nodes in a left to right order, the first rule encountered with an event variable is rule 5. The semantics for the rule is:

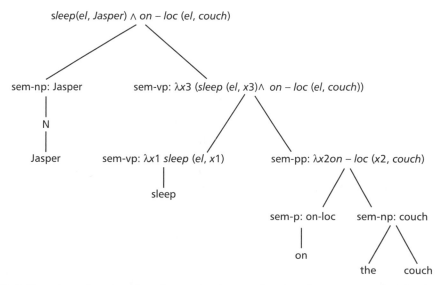

Figure 19.6 Parse tree showing the phrase structure and semantic representation for *Jasper is sleeping on the couch.*

λx sem-v(EV e, x)

which becomes:

Rule 5 VP: $\lambda x1$ sleep(EV e1, x1)

because sleep is the semantic feature for the verb and 1 is used to denote the first instantiations of the variables x and e. The next instantiation is for the preposition phase:

Rule 7 PP: $\lambda x2$ on-loc(x2, couch)

The VP and PP get passed up to rule 6:

Rule 6 VP: $\lambda x3$ [sem-vp(x3) & sem-pp(EV e2)]

Rule 6 VP: $\lambda x3$ [$\lambda x1$ sleep(EV e1, x1) (x3) & $\lambda x2$ on-loc(x2, couch) (EV e2)] EV e2=e1

The event variable gets pulled up from rule 5 to rule 6:

Rule 6 VP: $\lambda x3$ [$\lambda x1$ sleep(e1, x1) (x3) & $\lambda x2$ on-loc(x2, couch) (e1)]

Applying lambda reduction:

Rule 6 VP: $\lambda x3$ [sleep(e1, x3) & on-loc(e1, couch)]

Finally, rule 1 is used:

Rule 1 S: $\lambda x3$ [sleep(e1, x3) & on-loc(e1, couch)](Jasper)

With lambda reduction:

Rule 1 S: [sleep(e1, jasper) & on-loc(e1, couch)]

19.3.2 Encoding semantic structure into the lexicon

The second approach to constructing the logical form places the emphasis on the lexicon. The semantic entries in the lexicon become more complicated but the grammar rules are simpler. For this approach it is convenient to represent a sentence using a **case frame**. A case frame describes the action of a sentence in terms of a number of **roles** that express linguistic relationships. Typical roles include **agent**, **object**, **instrument** and **location**. For example, the sentence:

John hit the ball.

could be represented using the frame:

hit(AGENT John, OBJECT ball)

The sentence:

John hit the ball with the bat.

could be represented with the frame:

hit(AGENT John, OBJECT ball, INSTRUMENT bat)

The agent role describes who is carrying out the action, the object role describes the thing being acted upon or undergoing some change and the instrument role describes the tool used to perform the act. The location role can have a number of subroles:

TO-LOC	John kicked the ball to David
FROM-LOC	I caught the train from London
TO-POSS	John gave a ticket to Sara

Grammar 19.6 is used in Figure 19.7 to illustrate the parse and semantic analysis of the two sentences:

John gave a ticket to Sara.

and

John gave Sara a ticket.

Note that *give* has two entries corresponding to two different subcategories. The order of the variables is different.

From the examples given, it might appear that encoding more semantic information into the lexicon offers a simpler approach to that of making the grammar rules more complicated. In practice, the representation of the lexicon would need developing. For our example, the word *give* has two lexical entries to encode the semantic structure for the different verb complements. We would have to do the same for many other verbs. One approach to making the lexicon more concise is to use a hierarchical structure in which properties can be shared through inheritance.

19.4   Quantification and the intermediate-logical form

We have up to this point ignored a number of important issues with the form of our logical language. FOPC does not adequately represent many constructs that we find in natural languages.

In FOPC there are two types of quantifier, universal and existential quantifiers. These two quantifiers are too restrictive for natural language. For instance, in English we have words such as 'many', 'some', 'most', 'a', 'the,' etc. In using FOPC we have to be clear about what type of object the quantified variable is referring to. For example, we cannot state that $\forall x.fly(x)$ as this would claim that every object in the domain can fly (i.e. all things in our world that we may refer to). We need to restrict the type of object x is referencing. We may write:

$$\forall x.[bird(x) \rightarrow fly(x)]$$

which states that all birds fly. In our language, the domain of discourse is huge, and we often have objects which are exceptions to the rule. We know, for example, that some types of bird cannot fly. Therefore, it appears more correct to say most birds can fly. We could use:

$$\text{MOSTx.[bird(x), fly(x)]}$$

as our notation to represent the fact that most birds can fly.

Other types of construct not covered by FOPC are found with verbs such as *believe* and *like*, and structures that indicate past, present and future tense. These types of construct can be represented by what are called **modal operators**. The adopted logical language must then define the meaning of these modal operators if reasoning is to be extended to cover issues of tense and issues of attitude such as *believe* and *like*.

There is another key feature that must be introduced to the logical form if multiple sentences are to be processed. During a discourse, the same word (as it appears on paper or as it sounds) may be used to refer to different objects or events. A simple example is when referring to two different people who have the same name. Consider the discourse, 'John plays for the local football team.

Grammar 19.6

S SEM sem-vp sem-np	$\rightarrow$	NP SEM sem-np	VP SEM sem-vp
NP SEM sem-n	$\rightarrow$	ART	N SEM sem-n
NP SEM sem-n	$\rightarrow$	NAME SEM sem-n	
VP SEM sem-v sem-np sem-pp	$\rightarrow$	V SEM sem-v	NP PP SEM sem-np SEM sem-pp
VP SEM sem-v sem-np1 sem-np2	$\rightarrow$	V SEM sem-v	NP1 NP2 SEM sem-np1 SEM sem-np2
PP SEM sem-p sem-np	$\rightarrow$	P SEM sem-p	NP SEM sem-np

John
SEM John

Sara
SEM Sara

give
SUBCAT _np_pp(to)
SEM
$\lambda x \lambda y \lambda z \; give(AGENT\; z, OBJECT\; x, TO\text{-}POSS\; y)$

give
SUBCAT _np_np
SEM
$\lambda y \lambda x \lambda z \; give(AGENT\; z,$
$\quad OBJECT\; x, TO\text{-}POSS\; y)$

ticket
SEM ticket

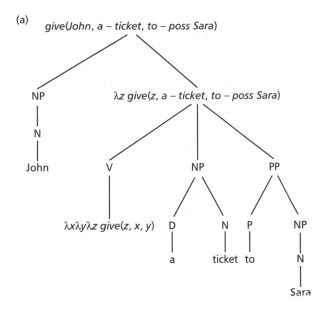

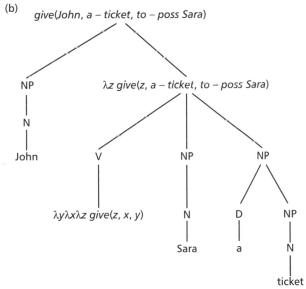

Figure 19.7 (a) Semantic parse of 'John gave a ticket to Sara'. (b) Semantic parse of 'John gave Sara a ticket'.

John the butcher also plays for the team'. From these two sentences we can assume that there are two people called John. We need therefore to distinguish between the two Johns, and to do this we can label the first John as *John1* and the second as *John2*. The same approach has to be adopted when handling word senses. The word 'file' could describe a file for keeping papers or the type of file found in a carpenter's toolbox. So the sentence 'John took the file' is represented as

took(John1, THE f1. {File1 File2})

The second argument has a set to list the different word senses.

19.4.1 *Ambiguity*

When a sentence (or part of a sentence) can have more than one interpretation, the sentence is said to be ambiguous. Resolving ambiguity is one of the major difficulties in natural language understanding. Much ambiguity arises as a result of the different senses that a word might have, the word *fly* being an example that can be a verb or a noun. Ambiguity can also be structural as in the sentence

I hit the boy with the ball.

Was the boy physically hit with an instrument of type ball or does ball help identify the boy being referred to? Word sense ambiguity can often give rise to structural ambiguity. Ambiguity can also arise when using quantifiers. For example, the sentence:

Every student likes a teacher.

is ambiguous between the two expressions:

$$[\exists y.teacher(y) \wedge \forall x.student(x)] \rightarrow like(x, y)$$

$$\forall x.student(x) \rightarrow \exists y.teacher(y) \wedge like(x, y)$$

The first expression states that there is a teacher that all students like. The second expression states that each student will like at least one of his or her teachers. Taken in isolation, the sentence is ambiguous because we are not sure which quantified logical expression represents the intended meaning and we must therefore maintain two semantic structures to represent both interpretations.

Keeping track of all possible semantic interpretations in their different logical forms is cumbersome. An alternative approach is to use a generic representation, wherever possible, for the multiple interpretations. This generic form of representation is known as the **intermediate-logical form**.

Suppose that the two interpretations for the sentence:

Every student likes a teacher.

are represented in our own devised representation language as:

(A y. teacher(y), EVERY x. student(x), like(x, y))

(EVERY x. student(x), A y. teacher(y), like(x, y))

These two expressions could then be collapsed into a single form (our intermediate-logical form):

like(EVERY x. student(x), A y. teacher(y)).

The ambiguity encoded in the intermediate-logical form needs to be resolved at some point in the analysis. Many aspects of ambiguity can be resolved only when context is taken into account. Some processing to resolve ambiguity can, however, be achieved independent of context. One form of ambiguity already seen is due to sentences such as:

Every student likes a teacher.

The interpretation is dependent on the scoping of the quantifiers. If the universal (every) quantifier outscopes the existential (a) quantifier then the interpretation is:

$$\forall x.student(x) \rightarrow \exists y.teacher(y) \land like(x, y)$$

Algorithms can be defined to pull out the quantifiers in a specified order, and this ordering determines the scope. Quantifiers can be ordered by defining **preferences** in much the same way as precedence is defined for arithmetic operators; for example, the preference:

every>a

means that *every* has a higher weight than *a* and therefore *every* will usually outscope *a*. According to this preference criterion, the interpretation of *every student likes a teacher* is then:

(EVERY x. student(x), A y. teacher(y), like(x, y)).

In practice, things are not this simple, and a comprehensive set of heuristics would be required to handle syntactic role preferences.

19.5 Context

Contextual processing is used to increase the information content of the logical-logical form by further resolving any remaining ambiguity due to issues such as pronoun reference and multiple word senses. We shall take only a brief look at some of the issues that arise with context.

Context refers to information that is conveyed in preceding sentences and to a general awareness of the current situation. The word *bat* in the second sentence of:

He lost his grip as he went to strike the ball.
The bat flew into the air.

is associated with the physical object used in some ball games rather than the flying mammal because of the context given by the preceding sentence. The sentence:

Do you have any wine?

when asked by a customer seated in a restaurant is usually interpreted by the waiter as a request to see a wine menu rather than a query about the possession of wine. The situation of a restaurant generates expectations of what is meant by a sentence.

In the sentence:

Debbie decided to get off the bike because she was too tired to continue.

it seems reasonable that the pronoun *she* is referring to Debbie. The referent for a pronoun often appears in a preceding sentence, but even considering the above sentence in isolation we may feel reasonably confident that *she* is referring to Debbie. Part of this reasoning has to do with context independent constraints that *she* must match *Debbie* in both number and gender (singular, feminine). Also, general knowledge plays a part in that riding a bike is consistent with a feeling of tiredness and could therefore be a reason to get off the bike.

When two noun phrases refer to the same object they are said to co-refer; the first phrase is called the **antecedent** and the second the **anaphor**. *Debbie* and *she* co-refer. The term **intrasentential anaphora** describes two co-references that appear in the same sentence, and **discourse anaphora** co-references that appear in different sentences. The following is an example of discourse anaphora:

Sara and Jack both caught the bus to work.
He was late for work.

The reference of the pronoun *he* can only be resolved when the previous sentence is brought into the analysis. Again, the gender constraint applies to resolve that *he* refers to *Jack* (the bus is discounted because we know that he usually refers to a male and humans are sometimes late for work). Of course, we might change expectations of pronoun referents if we were to humanize the bus as in a child's story.

Consider the following two sentences:

Jack bought the cake for David's party.
Jack was late for his party.

The second sentence taken in isolation would tend to suggest that *his* refers to *Jack* but when we consider the context provided by the previous sentence it is clear that *his* refers to *David*.

Emily the cat is always following her owner Caroline.
She is affectionate with all her cats.

Although the structure of the above discourse could be improved, it seems clear to what object the pronouns are referring. Again, background knowledge is used. We can use this knowledge to build more information about objects as the discourse continues. We know, for example, that Caroline is human because only humans (in the strict sense) can own objects. This form of knowledge is known as **selectional** restriction and we record in the knowledge base that the type of object doing the owning must be human.

An algorithm that resolves the referents of pronouns will typically make use of what is called the **history list**. The history list maintains a list of structured entities that describes objects that have been introduced throughout the discourse. The occurrence of an indefinite noun phrase usually introduces a new object. These structured entities maintain any known properties (such as gender, number, selectional restrictions, etc.) about the object. When a pronoun is encountered, the history list is consulted for objects whose properties match with any pronoun constraints. The objects that have been most recently introduced to the list are to be preferred, and so the matching proceeds from the last object introduced and works backwards until a match is found.

Knowledge of actions/events and their cause and effects can be critical in understanding discourse. The discourse:

John was thirsty.
He filled a glass with water.

describes the action 'filling a glass with water'. We could say that the cause for the action is John being thirsty. A glass full of water is an effect of the action. If we participate in a dialogue we will usually have expectations of how the dialogue is to proceed. This is because a discourse will typically involve a situation encountered many times before. In daily life we encounter stereotypical situations such as buying food, catching a train, eating at a restaurant, etc. When we encounter one of these familiar situations we have expectations with regards to actions/events. For example, we know that a restaurant will generally involve the acts of being seated, order being taken, waiter bringing the food, eating the food, paying for the bill, and so on. Recognizing stereotypical situations would appear to be fundamental to interpreting a discourse. A **script** is a structure for representing such situations. The script describes a sequence of ordered actions. The script therefore represents a temporal ordering of expected actions. A simple 'eating out' script might be represented as:

script   eating_out

{restaurant(R), customer(C), waiter(W), food(F)}

at_loc(C, R)
shows_table(W, C)
brings_menu(W)
select(C, F)
takes_order(W)
brings(W, F)
eats(C, F)
pays_bill(C)

A computerized natural language system that uses scripts needs to know when to invoke a script and track the actions represented by the script; a script is said to be **cued** when invoked. So how does a system recognize when a sentence is cueing a script? One idea is that the script name may be suggested by a sentence goal. For example, the goal *eating_out* is suggested by the sentence:

Jack decided to eat out.

Once a script has been cued the action list is tracked as the discourse proceeds.

One limitation of scripts is that expectations can be anticipated only from a predetermined list of actions. This is quite restrictive for real-world applications because a script is not always strictly followed. For example, a party of people may decide to eat out and negotiate a fixed price and the bill is paid before the actual event leaving only additional items to be settled after the meal. This might be considered an extreme exception, but how many possible exceptions are there? The waiter may present the menu to the customer while the customer is waiting for a table to become available. If we look to planning (see Chapters 9 and 10) as a model for representing actions and cause–effect relations then there is greater flexibility. Consider the discourse:

> Jack decided to eat out and drove to a restaurant recommended by a colleague.
> The waiter greeted Jack and gave him the menu.
> The waiter took Jack's order and then showed him to his table.

The sequence of events is ordered differently to that presented in the script. A simple script-based algorithm would have difficulty in recognizing that the order of events is coherent, but a plan-based system knows that the only precondition to taking an order is that Jack should be at the restaurant and that Jack has consulted the menu. Plan-based systems allow for a flexible sequencing of events. Remember that the system will be trying to understand the meaning of the discourse, and part of the reason for having the capability of modelling expectations is to check that current understanding is coherent given the situation. The role of planning in natural language understanding is therefore slightly different to that presented in Chapters 9 and 10, in which the role of planning is to search for a sequence of actions that will enable a goal to be achieved. Chapters 9 and 10 were concerned with plan generation, whereas natural language understanding requires **plan recognition**. Plan recognition denotes the ability to infer the goal of another agent. A discourse may suggest several goals. If we insist that the actions recognized during the discourse all relate to the goal, the set of expectations is limited to those that are consistent with plans that can be generated from the actions and goals that have been recognized.

19.6 Statistical approaches to NLP

Probabilistic approaches have played a significant role in a number of topics in this book, and perhaps it is no surprise that probability has a significant role to play in NLP. Probability-based methods have a number of applications in NLP, and we shall see this in the next chapter on speech recognition. A few other ways in which probability contributes are mentioned below.

Much of our communication is facilitated by an ability to resolve word ambiguity through taking into account words already seen (or heard). One source of ambiguity is due to some words having multiple lexical categories as, for example, the word *can:*

> *She can sing* – can is an auxiliary
> *Use a can of tomatoes* – can is a noun denoting a metal container
> *We can the peas we grow* – can is a verb used in the sense of preserving

Because of the different uses of the word *brush* the following sentence is ambiguous

> I saw her brush.

Did you see the brush or did you see her doing the act of brushing? The context of surrounding sentences can sometimes assist in resolving ambiguity, but at other times it is necessary to make a guess, and probabilistic approaches can model this form of guessing.

Spelling errors are a common occurrence for most of us, but some are harder to detect, e.g. the following:

> I posted the <u>cart</u>.

It seems probable that the word underlined should be card.

Word prediction can help some people with speech disabilities to communicate through using a computer by suggesting an appropriate list of words that might contain the word the speaker intends to use next. Selecting a word from a list is simpler than typing the whole word.

> Sorry, the bus was ___

The word *late* would seem to be a good guess for the last word in the above sentence.

All of the above examples pose problems that can be solved, or partially solved, by guessing the next word from the context of the words that have gone before. We have developed through experience an expectation of what word(s) follow other words. Probability can be used to model this type of expectation. If we could evaluate the probability of the sentences:

1   Sorry, the bus was full.
2   Sorry, the bus was late.

and found that sentence 2 had a higher probability than sentence 1, the word *late* could be listed before the word *full* when making suggestions to help a disabled speaker. The probability for the first sentence could be calculated using the product:

$$P(sorry)P(the\,|\,sorry)P(bus\,|\,sorry\ the)P(was\,|\,sorry\ the\ bus)P(full\,|\,sorry\ the\ bus\ was)$$

To use expressions of this form would require a huge number of probabilities. For each word, we would require a probability for the word appearing on its own (as the first word in a sentence), probabilities for the word appearing with each possible immediately preceding word, probabilities for the word following each possible set of two preceding words, and so on. Probabilities are computed using large volumes of text collected from different sources, e.g. newspapers, novels, academic publications. These **corpora** (text volumes) are made available for research purposes. A corpus may contain in excess of a million words, and to calculate the probability of a word based on all words that precede it in a sentence is impractical. There would be a huge number of calculations to compute the required probabilities, and many word combinations would not be found even in a large corpus. Models are therefore simplified. The simplest model is the **bigram** model, which uses the Markov assumption, which states that the probability of a word depends only on the previous word. So, in the above example, the probability for the last word being *full* would be calculated as the probability of *full* given the occurrence of *was*:

> $P(full\,|\,was)$

A **trigram** model would be:

> $P(full\,|\,bus\ was)$

These models are called by the more general term of **N-gram** models. An N-gram model looks at the $N-1$ words already seen (a 4-gram would look at the last three words).

Estimating probabilities for word frequency using corpora is not without difficulties. A corpus, although it will in general contain a large number of sentences, will have a finite number of word sequences, and legitimate N-grams can be missing. This leads to N-grams having zero probabilities or the true probability being underestimated. There are various algorithms that can be used to interpolate N-grams and provide a better estimate of their likelihood.

We have seen that a natural language has a lot of structure, and this is reflected in the grammar rules that convey the co-occurrence of different lexical categories – e.g. a noun following a determiner. Each word in a lexicon has a lexical tag. For instance, the word *can* might have the tags N (noun), V (verb), AUX (auxiliary). Lexical tags provide useful information about a word and its neighbouring words. For instance, if a word is tagged as a personal pronoun (I, you, me) then we know that it is likely to be followed by a verb. One useful role of tags is in disambiguating word senses. There are a number of well-known **tagsets** for English. The Penn treebank tagset has 45 tags. The number of tags might seem large but the Penn treebank is in fact a small tagset. Some example tags are:

DT – determiner (e.g. the)
VB – verb base form (e.g. pull)
VBD – verb past tense (e.g. pulled)
JJ – adjective (e.g. green)
PP – personal pronoun (e.g. I)

Punctuation like quotation marks, commas, colon, etc, are also tagged.

Part-of-speech tagging is the process of assigning lexical tags to each word in a corpus. A lexicon will then exist that will list for each word its tag. As already noted, however, many words will have multiple tags. The job of a tagging algorithm is to take a string of words and assign the best tag to each word. These tagging algorithms can be rule based or probabilistic based. A probabilistic approach will attach a tag that maximizes the likelihood of a word having a given tag in a given context. For example, a bigram tagger would choose a tag that maximizes

$P(t|t_{i-1}, w_i)$

where t is a tag for the current word w_i and t_{i-1} is the tag for the last word. If the current word has a number of candidate tags for t, then t is the candidate that produces the maximum value of $P(t|t_{i-1}, w_i)$

It is possible to have a sentence in which there is no lexical ambiguity in tagging but there is still structural ambiguity. Jurafsky and Martin (2000) give an example:

Can you book TWA flights?

This sentence has two possible meanings. The first 'Can you book flights on behalf of TW*A?*' and the second 'Can you book flights operated by TWA?'. In the first interpretation, the verb phrase consists of a verb and two noun phrases; in the second interpretation a verb is followed by a single noun phrase. This form of ambiguity could potentially be solved using a probabilistic context-free grammar. The basic idea is to assign a probability to each grammar rule. The probability represents the likelihood of the symbol on the left-hand-side being expanded into those on the right-hand side. For example, we might have:

1	S → NP VP	0.75
2	S → AUX NP VP	0.25
3	NP → D N	0.3

4	NP→N	0.1
5	NP→Pronoun	0.6
6	VP→V	0.6
7	VP→V NP	0.4
	...	

Notice that the probabilities for each rule type sum to 1. Using these probabilities, a parse tree can be assigned a probability by multiplying each of the probabilities for the rules used in the parse. So a parse tree constructed using rules 1, 3, and 6 would have a probability:

$$= 0.75 \times 0.3 \times 0.6$$

A parser could then pick the most likely interpretation by selecting the tree with the highest probability.

We shall expand on some of the principles mentioned briefly here in the next chapter on speech recognition.

Summary

For many practical applications a chart parser is used. A chart parser saves much work by avoiding repeatedly expanding the same grammar rules through maintaining a list of all rules that could potentially match incoming words. A chart parser really attempts all rule expansions in parallel. To be useful, a grammar needs to encode much more information about the structure of sentences in addition to encoding legal sequences of lexical categories. Features are used to encode this information. Features will encode gender and number. Other features can be used to encode information such as word complements, an example being that a transitive verb must have an object. There are two main approaches to encoding semantic information. The first approach embeds most of the structural semantic knowledge in the grammar rules, whereas the second approach embeds the major part of this knowledge in the lexicon. Following semantic analysis, sentences are typically represented in an intermediate-logical form (also called quasilogical form). The intermediate-logical form is less formal than FOPC and therefore less restricted in quantifier notation, and it can also represent ambiguity. Context plays an important role in language understanding, e.g. assisting with disambiguation and resolving pronoun referents. As with all AI topics, knowledge is the key to many successful applications. Knowledge of word meaning, and how words combine to provide meaning, is fundamental to language processing, but many other forms of knowledge, e.g. speaker intention, goals, beliefs, etc., are also important aspects that require modelling in some applications.

Further reading

For a comprehensive introduction to NLP see Jurafsky and Martin (2000) and Allen (1995). For an introduction to NLP using Prolog see Gazdar and Mellish (1989).

Terry Winograd's SHRDLU is an early example of natural language understanding (Winograd, 1972). The system simulated a robot performing simple tasks in a toy blocks world in response to instructions given in English. Schank and Abelson's (1977) approach to natural language understanding used human conceptual models represented as scripts and plans. Woods' (1973) LUNAR question–answering system used predicate logic for representation. Baker (1989) provides an overview of English syntax. For a general reference on the English language see Crystal (2001).

The basis of chart parsing can be found in Aho and Ullman (1972) and Earley (1970). Work on semantic interpretation can be found in Gazdar *et al.* (1985) Unification in linguistics can be found in Kay (1982). Other work on unification can be found in Pereira and Shieber (1987), and Alshawi (1992). A comprehensive book on statistical approaches to language processing is Manning and Schutz (1999) and a short overview is Charniak (1997). For an overview of corpus-based approaches to semantic interpretation see Hwee Tou Ng and Zelle (1997).

There has been much work done on connectionist approaches to NLP. Rumelhart *et al.* (1986b) is an example of some early work where a neural network was trained to produce the past tenses of English verbs. For an attempt to build a complete connectionist solution see Miikkulainen (1993).

For a survey of NLP work see Cole *et al.* (1998).

Exercises

1   Using Grammar 19.1, record all the rule introductions, extensions and completions when using a chart to parse the following sentence:

> Tall giraffes can reach high branches.

2   Provide number features for the words in the following sentences and test the sentences against Grammar 19.3:

> Cows produce milk.
> The cows produces milk.
> The girls likes John.
> A girl likes John.

3   List subcat features for the following verbs so that restrictions are placed on the legal complements (as in *give* having complement np-np):

> push
> put
> lead
> jumping
> saw (as in see)

4   Identify the agent, object, instrument, etc., of the following sentences. Give a case frame representation for each verb in each sentence.

> John ate the egg.
> John ate the egg with a spoon.
> Sara hit the ball to Mike.
> Mary drove from London to Edinburgh.

5   Select a paragraph from a book or magazine. For each sentence test whether its meaning is self-contained or how you would extend the sentence to make it self-contained.

6   Identify the properties/knowledge that could help to resolve the pronouns in the following text.

> Sara is taking her cat, Emily, to the vet. She always drives to the vet's.
> Sara cuddles Emily at the vet. She does not like the vet.
> The vet today is Tom and his assistant is Steven. He is still learning.

7   Write a script for a visit to the dentist. Discuss some of the practical issues with using the script for language processing.

CHAPTER 20

Speech Processing

Speech is an effortless and highly efficient form of communication. Continuous speech recognition software is readily available from local computing stores and comes complete with microphone, allowing the user to dictate text directly into a document. The current technology is not perfect but it is getting better.

Dictating text directly into a document is a reality of today, albeit requiring dedication on the part of the user to train the recognizer on the nuances of his or her voice. Using speech for general interfacing to a computer presents a challenge on a different scale to that of dictation. There is already some level of interfacing between humans and machines using speech. Some modern aircraft use a limited vocabulary that allows a pilot to issue some commands by voice. Software packages on our computers can also respond to spoken commands. However, the ability of current applications is a lot lower than that required of a system to respond to the following request:

> Back up all the program files for the projects I have worked on today.

Such a command requires natural language understanding, and this in itself is a computationally challenging problem, as we have seen. If the input to the understanding system is speech as opposed to text the complexity moves up a few notches. If written (type as opposed to handwritten) text is used as the input then individual words and strings of words can be clearly identified. With speech this is not so. It might be acceptable to correct recognition mistakes following dictation, but recognition mistakes become very costly if the receiving agent (e.g. machine) has to understand what has been spoken. There is a great deal of uncertainty with spoken language when it comes to recognizing individual words. On many occasions when you communicate with friends you probably make guesses as to what word was spoken. These guesses are often well informed because of the context of what is being communicated. When we converse with a fellow human there is also much information communicated through tone, facial expressions and other gesturing. A speaker will often correct what has been said and will often repeat information but phrased in a different way. Other complications arise because different words can sound the same, for example *fare* and *fair*, *mail* and *male*, etc.

In this chapter, we shall take a brief overview of speech recognition. We start with the analysis of sound waves to extract features that can be related to sound units from which words are built. There will be uncertainty as to the precise identity of the sound units and the final phase of recognition uses a model to match word sequences with sequences of extracted sound units.

20.1 The basic units that make up the sounds of words

A speech recognition system needs several levels of processing. Words are carried as sound waves, which are analogue signals. These signals are passed through a signal processor that extracts features such as energy and frequencies. These features are then mapped onto individual sound units called **phones**. Word sounds are made up of phones, and so the final phase is to translate a sequence of possible phones into a sequence of words. We use the term possible because we will be uncertain as to the identity of phones carried by the sound.

Speech generation requires a word to be mapped into a sequence of phones that are then passed to a speech synthesizer from where the word sound is emitted via a speaker. There is also intonation planning so that the synthesizer knows how to use voice variation instead of speaking using an unnatural monotone dialogue. In this chapter we shall concentrate on speech recognition but the material is relevant to speech generation.

The individual units of sound that make up a word are phones. For a language such as English, the different units of sound have to be identified and grouped. The grouping should ensure that all words in the language can be distinguished – we do not want two different words to have the same phonetic structure. A few sample phones are listed below.

[b]	<u>b</u>in
[p]	<u>p</u>in
[th]	<u>th</u>in
[l]	<u>l</u>ip
[er]	b<u>ir</u>d
[ay]	<u>i</u>ris

Phones can have different sounds depending on context. For example, the phone *th* in the word *three* has a different sound to *th* in *then*. These different variations of the same phone are called **allophones**. It is sometimes convenient to abstract the differences into a generalized grouping called a **phoneme**. Phonemes are written inside slashes. For example, /*th*/ is a phoneme and it will have different sounds depending on context. Words can be represented at the phoneme level or, if more information is required, representation can be at the level of allophones.

20.2   Signal processing

Sound waves are variations in air pressure. Two key features of a sound wave are its **amplitude**, which is a measure of air pressure at a point in time, and **frequency**, which is the rate at which this amplitude varies. When you speak into a microphone, the change in air pressure causes a diaphragm to oscillate. The size of the oscillation is proportional to the air pressure (amplitude), and the rate at which the diaphragm oscillates is proportional to the rate at which the air pressure varies. Thus, the deflection of the diaphragm from its stationary position is a measure of amplitude. The deflection of the diaphragm can be described as positive or negative depending on whether the air is being compressed or uncompressed (rarefaction). The amplitude of deflection will depend at what point the deflection is measured as the diaphragm cycles between positive and negative values. The taking of measurements is known more generally as **sampling**. When a sound wave is sampled, it can be plotted as an *x–y* plot, where the *x*-axis represents time and the *y*-axis represent amplitude. The frequency of a wave is how many times it repeats itself per second. Each repeat is a cycle and so a frequency of 10 means that the wave repeats itself (cycles) 10 times in 1 second – 10 cycles per second or more usually expressed as 10 Hz (hertz).

The loudness of a sound is related to power, which is related to the square of the amplitude. A visual inspection of a waveform does not reveal much information. A visual difference can be seen between vowels and most consonants, but the identification of phones is not possible from simply eyeballing a plot of the waveform. We must believe that the data being captured by the microphone contain the information we require about words, otherwise we would not be able to record speech and play it back as intelligible speech. The requirement, however, for speech recognition is to extract the information that allows words to be identified. We would like this information to be concise to keep computation manageable. Ideally, we would like to break the signal up into a number of chunks from which a number of discrete values are extracted. These discrete values are more generally referred to as features. Each chunk of signal is called a **frame**, and frames will overlap to make sure that important information that might lie on a frame boundary does not get missed.

Speech occurs below 10 kHz (10 000 cycles per second). The number of samples taken per second will be twice the highest frequency that needs to be recorded. This doubling is due to theory, which tells us that frequencies will otherwise be missed (see Figure 20.1). A frame will typically be 10 ms and will contain 200 samples when using a sampling rate of 20 kHz. Each sample is a real value that denotes intensity. Each real value is then converted into an integer value to save on memory – this is called **quantization**. Some information will be lost in quantization as a real value will have to be rounded up or down to its nearest integer value. If eight-bit integer values are used then each sample is one of 256 values. Sampling transforms a continuous signal into a sequence of discrete values. In other words, the signal has been digitized. The next stage is to take the digitized signal and extract features.

One method for extracting features from a digitized signal is to compute the **Fourier transform**. A sound wave can be represented as a composition of sine waves, as shown in Figure 20.2. Each sine wave has a frequency and amplitude. The Fourier transform can be used to identify the dominant frequencies and amplitudes that make up a sound wave. The collection of frequency components that are extracted is called the **spectrum**. The wave in Figure 20.3 has been digitally sampled and is the sum of three sine waves:

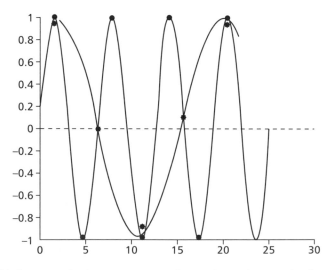

Figure 20.1 The solid sine wave is the true wave and completes three cycles for every one cycle of the dotted wave. The black circles represent samples taken at twice the frequency of the true wave. This sampling captures the true sine wave. The stars are being undersampled, and at this sampling rate the wave is believed to be the dotted wave, which is a third of the frequency of the true wave. This illustrates that sampling should be at twice the frequency of the highest frequency that needs to be measured.

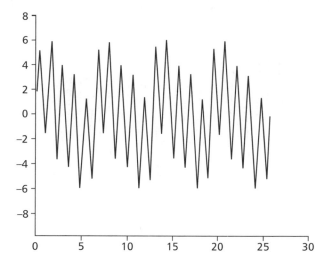

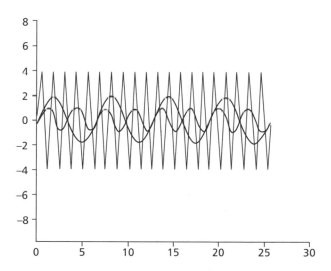

Figure 20.2 The wave at the top is the sum of the three sine waves at the bottom.

$$2\sin(2\pi \times 50t) + \sin(2\pi \times 120t) + 4\sin(2\pi \times 200t)$$

where t is time. The spectrum for this wave is also shown in Figure 20.3.

For speech recognition, the features are usually extracted using another technique called **linear predictive coding (LPC)**. The Fourier transform might still be used at a later stage to extract additional information. LPC expresses each sample of the signal as a linear combination of previous samples. The prediction requires the estimation of coefficients, which is done by minimizing the mean-square error between the predicted signal and the actual signal.

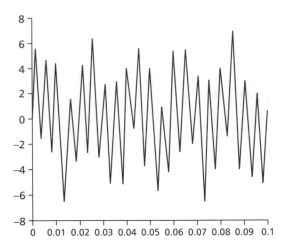

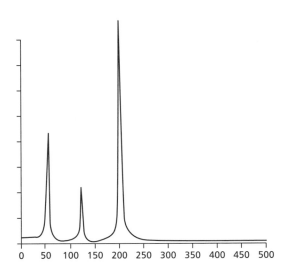

Figure 20.3 The wave at the top is made up of three sine waves whose amplitudes and frequencies are shown in the spectrum at the bottom. The spectrum shows three peaks, with each peak centred on a sine wave frequency. The spectrum has been obtained through a Fourier transform of the digitally sampled wave.

A spectrum represents the different frequency components of a wave. This spectrum can be obtained using the Fourier transform or LPC or some other approach. The spectrum identifies dominant frequencies that can be matched to different phones. This matching produces a likelihood estimate for different phones.

In summary, speech processing involves sampling a continuous sound wave, with each sample being quantized to provide a condensed digitized representation of the wave. The samples lie in overlapping frames. From each frame a vector of features that describes the frequency content is extracted. Phonetic likelihoods can then be calculated for each frame of vectors.

20.3   Recognition

Once the sound source has been reduced to a collection of features, the next task is to identify the words these features represent. We shall concentrate for the moment on single word recognition. The input to the recognition system is a sequence of features. Words, of course, correspond to a sequence of characters (letters). If we were to analyse a large database of words, we would identify patterns in that certain sequences of characters are more likely to occur than others. For example, the letter y is much more likely to follow *ph* than the letter t. A Markov model is one method of representing the likelihood of a sequence. Figure 20.4 is an example of a Markov model. The model has four states, labelled 1–4, and the edges represent the probability of transiting from one state to the next. In Figure 20.4, state 4 is considered a terminating state as from state 4 there is nowhere else to go. From any state, you can only follow the directions of the arrows, and all arrows emerging from a state must have a total probability of 1. The states could represent characters that make up a word, but for the time being we shall just talk about states in general.

The model in Figure 20.4 can be viewed as a sequence generator. For example, if we started in state 1 and finished in state 4 the following are some of the sequences that could be generated:

    1 2 3 4
    1 2 2 3 3 3 4
    1 2 3 3 4
    1 2 2 2 2 3 4

The probability of any sequence being generated can be calculated. This probability is simply the product of all probabilities along the path that generates the sequence. For example, for the sequence:

    1 2 3 3 4

the path is the collection of edges:

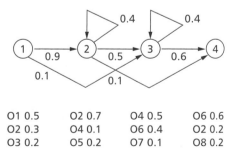

O1 0.5	O2 0.7	O4 0.5	O6 0.6
O2 0.3	O4 0.1	O6 0.4	O2 0.2
O3 0.2	O5 0.2	O7 0.1	O8 0.2

Figure 20.4 A hidden Markov model. The circles are states and the edges denote legal transitions between states. Each edge has a weight that is the probability of transiting between states. The values below are observation weights. Each state can emit one of the symbols listed below it. The weight is a probability and shows the relative frequency of each symbol being emitted. Note that a symbol may be emitted by more than one state.

1–2, 2–3, 3–3, 3–4

and the probability is:

0.9×0.5×0.4×0.6=0.108

Some sequences are more likely to be generated than others. The key assumption of the Markov model is that the next state depends only on the current state.

20.4 Hidden Markov model

We shall give a general introduction to the hidden Markov model (HMM) before discussing some specific issues concerning speech recognition. HMMs are so called because the state which the machine is in at any point in time is hidden from the user. This situation occurs in many applications and arises because data from sensors do not correspond exactly to the states in the Markov model. In speech recognition, the input data are features extracted from sound waves. The states in the Markov model would correspond to sound units (e.g. phones). We do not know what state the incoming features correspond to. Even though the features do not correspond exactly to states in the Markov model, we can make a good guess as to the likely states. Different phones have different sounds and, although phones may share some of the same sound features, the differences allow us to guess what the phone is. So, given a feature, we know which states are more likely to correspond to that feature. We are still uncertain as to the identity of the state, but at least the problem is reduced because many states have been ruled out. Suppose that there is a sequence of features. The recognizer gets the first feature. It does not know what state this feature corresponds to but it can make a guess to reduce the number of possibilities. It now gets the second feature and reduces this down to a handful of likely states. It does the same for the third feature and continues in this manner. As the recognizer gets more features, it can reduce the number of possibilities further because it knows that some features are likely to co-occur more often – the recognizer has information about sequences and the likelihood of one phone following another. HMMs model the probability of word features and the occurrence of one feature following another feature.

Figure 20.4 shows a list of observation symbols for each state. Think of the model again as a generator. This time, instead of emitting a sequence of states, the model emits a sequences of observation symbols. If we were to run the machine 100 times, starting in state 1, we would expect that approximately 50% of the sequences would start with the symbol O1, 30% with O2 and 20% with O3. These percentages correspond to the probabilities of the symbols being generated from state 1. From state 1 the machine is most likely to move to state 2, but 10% of the time it will move to state 3. Therefore, O2, O4, O5, O6, O7 could all follow O1.The symbol O2 is most likely to occur next in the sequence because state 2 is likely to follow state 1 and O2 is by far the most likely symbol to be generated in state 2. Note that observation symbols can be generated by more than one state. For example, O2 can be generated by states 1, 2 and 4.

There are two things we are interested in calculating when given a sequence of observations. First, we would like to find the most likely path through the Markov model. The most likely path identifies which sequence of states along with the order in which they fire is most likely to generate the sequence of observations. Second, we are interested in calculating the likelihood of the sequence being generated by the model. There will be several paths through the model that could generate the sequence, and the likelihood for the sequence is the sum of all path probabilities. Consider the following sequence:

O1 O2 O4 O4 O6 O6

Each symbol corresponds to a different time step. O1 is received at time1, O2 at time2, O4 at time3 and time4, and O6 at time5 and time6. We shall not be concerned here with the scale at which these time intervals occur. The first observation symbol is O1, and O1 can only be generated by state 1. So, in this example, the machine is starting in state 1. From state 1 the machine can move only to either state 2 or state 3. The next observation is O2, and this cannot be generated by state 3, and so the next state in the sequence is state 2. However, from state 2 the machine can go to either state 3 or state 4 or remain in state 2. The machine must move to state 3 or stay in state 2 because state 4 cannot generate O4. The actual state now is hidden – the recognizer does not know whether the first occurrence of O4 occurs in state 2 or state 3. The recognizer can, however, determine the most likely state to generate O4.

Figure 20.5 shows all paths that could generate the sequence of observations. The graph in the top of Figure 20.5 shows the states at each time step that could generate the symbols. For a state to be shown at a time step it must be capable of generating the symbol that is seen at that time, and it must be reachable from the state listed at the previous time step. For example, O2 can be generated by states 1, 2 and 4, but at time step 2 the only possible state is state 2 because it is not possible to reach states 1 or 4 from state 1. At time5 state 4 is dotted because it is a dead end. State 4 is a terminating state and, once it has generated a symbol, the sequence must end. So state 4 can only occur at time6, otherwise the whole sequence could not be generated. Note, however, that it is possible to terminate in state 3. In the current example we are not insisting on terminating at state 4, simply that if state 4 is reached then there is nowhere else to go. The six paths have been extracted from the graph and are shown in Figure 20.5. The transition probabilities have also been marked on the edges. The

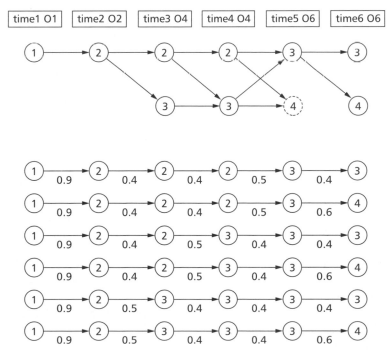

Figure 20.5 The paths through the model shown in Figure 20.4 that can generate the sequence O1 O2 O4 O4 O6 O6.

probability of a sequence of observations being generated is a product of the path probability and the probability of the observation weights (the probability of an observation being generated given the current state). For example, the first path has probability:

p(O1|state 1)×0.9×p(O2|state 2)×0.4×p(O4|state 2)×0.4×p(O4|state 2)×0.5×p(O6|state 3)×0.4×p(O6|state 3)

which can be separated into a product of path probabilities and observation probabilities:

(0.9×0.4×0.4×0.5×0.4)×(p(O1|state 1)×p(O2|state 2)×p(O4|state 2)×p(O4|state 2)×p(O6|state 3)×p(O6|state 3))

Substituting in the observation probabilities:

(0.9×0.4×0.4×0.5×0.4)×(0.5×0.7×0.1×0.1×0.4×0.4)=0.00001613

The other paths have probabilities:

0.000036
0.000081
0.000181
0.000403
0.000907

So the most likely path is the last path. This path represents the most likely sequence of states to have generated the sequence of observations. The sum of all of the six path probabilities is the probability that this sequence of observations was generated by this model.

In a recognition problem, it is the sequence of observations that serves as input. These observations will be the features extracted by signal processing. Different words have different transition states and probabilities. The job of the recognizer is to determine which word model is the most likely. We therefore need a way of implementing the path extraction that was calculated above. We shall now describe such a method.

We shall keep the recognition task at a general level and we shall not assume knowledge of any start state or terminating state. When an observation is received, there is no knowledge of what state the observation corresponds to. There will be an unknown state for each observation in the sequence. One way to visualize the different paths is to construct a trellis. A trellis has a copy of the Markov model's states for each time step. So, if the sequence has six observations, there will be six copies of the states arranged in levels, with each level corresponding to a time step in the sequence. Edges connect states between the current level, j, and the next level, $j + 1$. The edges connecting the levels correspond to the edges in the Markov model. So, a state S_i at level j will have a connection to state S_{i+1} at level $j + 1$ only if there is an edge connecting from S_i to S_{i+1} in the Markov model. A trellis for the model in Figure 20.4 is shown in Figure 20.6. The trellis represents all possible paths through the model (a legal sequence of states).

The algorithm for finding the most likely path uses a trellis structure. Each edge in the trellis is weighted with the probability taken from the Markov model. Each node in the trellis is weighted with the probability $P(O_j|S_{i,j})$, the probability for observation at time j being generated by state i.

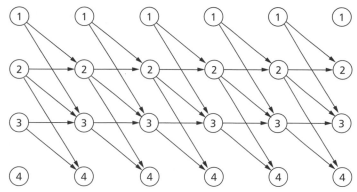

Figure 20.6 A trellis for the model in Figure 20.4. Weights are not shown.

The algorithm starts at the last time step (the last observation). We shall illustrate the algorithm using the example sequence given earlier, which is:

O1 O2 O4 O4 O6 O6

The last observation is O6. We will start at the last level in the trellis. The first task is to identify the states that could generate O6 and enter the probability $P(O_j | S_{i,j})$. States 3 and 4 can generate O6, and the probabilities are 0.4 and 0.6. These values are recorded against their states at the last level, j. The second last level, $j-1$, is analysed next. The observation is O6, and once again the states are 3 and 4 with observation probabilities 0.4 and 0.6. Each step is shown in Figure 20.7, but most of the edges and weights are not shown, to keep the illustration simple. We can identify the best path leaving each state at level $j-1$. We know the weight (probability) of each edge leaving a state and we know the weight of the state at level j that each edge connects to. The path probability is simply the product of the edge weight and the state weight it connects to. Of all the edges leaving a state, the edge with the highest product is the best path. The weight for each state at level $j-1$ is now updated. This weight is the product of the observation probability for that state with the best path leaving the state. For example, consider state 3 at level $j-1$. The two paths are:

From state 3 at level $j-1$ to state 3 at level $l = 0.4 \times 0.4 = 0.16$
From state 3 at level $j-1$ to state 4 at level $l = 0.6 \times 0.6 = 0.36$

The highest weight is 0.36. The weight of state 3 at level $j-1$ is 0.4 (the probability of generating O6). The weight stored against state 3 at level $j-1$ is $0.4 \times 0.36 = 0.144$. The same procedure is now repeated between levels $j-2$ and $j-1$. The observation at $j-2$ is O4. Only states 2 and 3 can generate O4. The weights for states 2 and 3 at level $j-2$ are calculated as:

From state 2 at level $j-2$ to state 3 at level $j-1 = 0.1 \times 0.5 \times 0.144 = 0.00720$
From state 3 at level $j-2$ to state 3 at level $j-1 = 0.5 \times 0.4 \times 0.144 = 0.0288$

The same is done for each state at level $j-3$. There are two paths emerging from state 2 at level $j-3$ (connecting to states 2 and 3 at level $j-2$). The weight for state 2 is the observation O4 (0.1). The best path is the greater of:

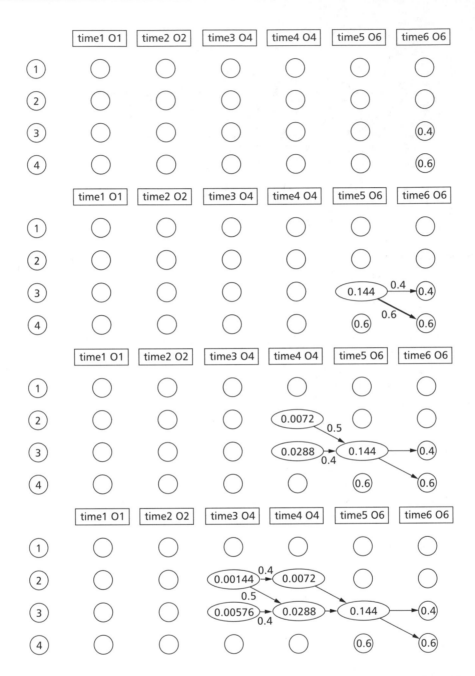

Figure 20.7 Illustration of the Viterbi algorithm starting from the last time step. A weight is stored against each state (node) that represents the most likely path leading from that node. The weights in the last column are simply the observation probabilities for O6. The weight in the second last column for a state is found by taking the product of the observation probability for O6 with the best path leading from that state. The best path is the one with the highest value computed from the product of edge probability with the weight of the node it connects to. The algorithm repeats this procedure for each column.

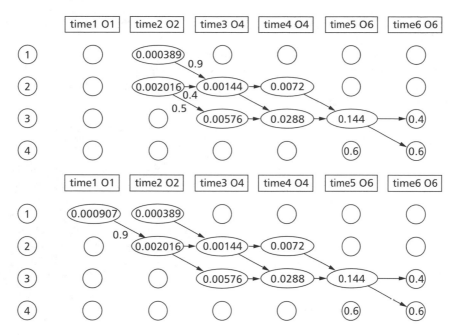

Figure 20.7 Continued.

From state 2 at level $j-3$ to state 2 at level $j-2=0.4\times0.0072=0.00288$
From state 2 at level $j-3$ to state 3 at level $j-2=0.5\times0.0288=0.01440$

So the weight for state 2 at level $j-3$ is:

$0.1\times0.01440=0.00144$

The algorithm continues in this manner until each level is completed. If we are interested in the best path, then for each state we need to keep only the edge that has the best path leading from that state. Once the last level is completed, the best path starts from the state with the highest weight. The algorithm just described is called the **Viterbi algorithm**.

There are different ways to model speech using Markov models. One approach could be to construct a Markov model at the word level. The states would correspond to phonemes. We could explicitly identify a start state and a terminating state. There is no need to have an explicit start and terminating state. Instead, an initial distribution is provided that identifies the probability of starting from each state in the model. It is typical for states to have self-loops so that the durations for a phone can be modelled. Speech will usually consist of a sequence of words, and the sound from one word will blend into the next, making it difficult to identify word boundaries. Identifying and separating out the words is called **segmentation**. The procedure for identifying and segmenting a sequence of words is essentially the same as for identifying a single word from a sequence of observations. The recognizer will receive a sequence of observations representing a sequence of words. A Markov model can be constructed from the Markov models for individual words. There are edges connecting each pair of words, and these edges represent the probabilities of one word following another. The recognition problem is the same as before: identify the path that is most likely to have generated the sequence of observations. This path will identify each word and the order in which they were spoken.

It is more usual to use log probabilities in HMMs. The calculations then comprise additions rather than more computationally expensive products. The weights in the Markov model are found by applying machine learning to large corpora. Algorithms based on expectation maximization are used, and so too are neural networks.

Summary

During speech recognition, a continuous sound wave is sampled to transform an analogue signal into a digitized representation. Speech occurs below 10 kHz, and the sampling needs to be at twice this frequency, meaning that 20 000 real values will be captured every second. Each real value is quantized by rounding it to an integer value. Features are extracted from the digitized signal. Several techniques can be applied and include linear predictive coding and fast Fourier transform. These features are designed to summarize the most useful information in the signal. Words are made up of basic sound units called phones. The task of speech recognition is to take the extracted signal features and predict the sequence of phones and in turn the sequence of words spoken. There is much uncertainty in this procedure, and a probabilistic model is used. This model is called a hidden Markov model (HMM). The HMM represents the likelihood of different phones given the extracted sound features and the likelihood of one phone succeeding another.

Further reading

For books on speech see Rabiner and Juang (1993) and Jurafsky and Martin (2000). Waibel and Lee (1990) provide a collection of papers on speech, and empirical methods are discussed in Stolke (1997). A well-known connectionist demonstration of a neural network learning to pronounce English text was given by Sejnowski and Rosenberg (1987).

CHAPTER 21

Vision

The cup and saucer in Figure 21.1 are easily recognized objects. Turning the cup upside down, placing the saucer on top of the cup, shrinking the image and tilting the image are all operations that are unlikely to fool our perception. The saucer on top of the cup is, of course, a different image, but if the task is to recognize the two objects then we can.

Our eyes are the sensors we use for visual perception. A machine's sensors for vision are cameras.[1] We appreciate what a good job a camera does at capturing images of the world. Looking at pictures gives us a real sense about the way things were when the image was captured even when we were not present. You could recognize someone from a photograph even though you have not met before. The images captured with a camera serve, for us at least, as a good representation of the way things in our environment appear. One of the ultimate challenges of machine vision is getting a machine to recognize objects in the world and to understand what action is taking place within its visual field. This is a considerable challenge. Raw image data are represented inside a computer by a collection of integer values. If we imagine a very fine grid overlaid on a picture there would be one integer value for every square. Assuming that the image consists of shades of grey as opposed to colour, each integer value would be a shade of grey or measure of light intensity. Colour images are similarly represented, but for every square, there would be three numbers, each representing the contribution of a primary colour. Each square in the grid is a pixel. The higher the number of pixels

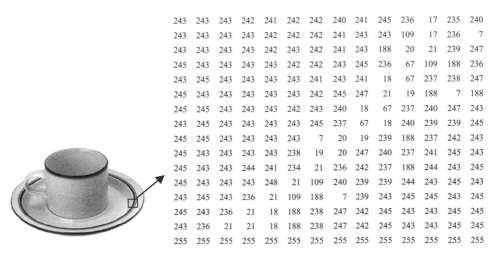

243	243	243	242	241	242	242	240	241	245	236	17	235	240
243	243	243	243	242	242	242	241	243	243	109	17	236	7
243	243	243	243	242	243	242	241	243	188	20	21	239	247
245	243	243	243	243	242	242	243	245	236	67	109	188	236
243	245	243	243	243	243	241	243	241	18	67	237	238	247
245	243	243	243	243	243	242	245	247	21	19	188	7	188
245	245	243	243	243	242	243	240	18	67	237	240	247	243
243	245	243	243	243	243	245	237	67	18	240	239	239	245
245	245	243	243	243	243	7	20	19	239	188	237	242	243
245	243	243	243	243	238	19	20	247	240	237	241	245	243
245	243	243	244	241	234	21	236	242	237	188	244	243	245
245	243	243	243	248	21	109	240	239	239	244	243	245	243
243	245	243	236	21	109	188	7	239	243	245	245	243	245
245	243	236	21	18	188	238	247	242	245	243	243	245	245
243	236	21	21	18	188	238	247	242	245	243	243	245	245
255	255	255	255	255	255	255	255	255	255	255	255	255	255

Figure 21.1 A greyscale image and the integer values representing the intensity of pixels within a small region of the image.

---

[1]A machine could use other types of sensors for perception, e.g. radar, sonar, etc.

for a given image size, the finer the grid, and therefore the higher the level of detail. In Figure 21.1, the numbers corresponding to a small part of the image are shown. By changing these numbers, we change the image. Software for processing an image operates directly on these numbers to alter the contrast, remove scratches, blur or sharpen the image, shrink or enlarge the image, make the image look like a sketch and so on. These pixel values carry all the data pertaining to any objects that may be present in the image, but how are we to process these values to extract information that would allow a machine to perform object recognition? Looking at the numbers in Figure 21.1 conveys no information to us about the image – the values have to be turned into shades of grey for us to see the image and yet the numbers are the raw data that computers have to work with.

If a machine is to recognize objects then the machine needs to extract information from the array of numbers. This information should relate to features that the machine can reason with. For many applications, an image may contain many items or details that are of no interest. If the machine had to recognize a cup and saucer sitting on a table alongside a dinner plate, knife and fork, it must somehow identify that there are four objects (treating the cup and saucer as one). For each object, the machine has to look at all the pixel values and group those pixels that belong to the same thing. The machine should identify the pixels that make up the knife. The machine might not be able to recognize the knife at this stage, but it needs to identify that these pixels belong together because they are part of the same thing. This procedure of grouping like things is called segmentation. Segmenting the cup and saucer allows the machine to focus on those pixels that are part of the cup and saucer. Looking at the image in Figure 21.1, there are dark edges that convey shape information and there are other less distinctive edges such as the cup's handle. Finding the pixels that form part of an edge and then describing the shape of the edge is another process that extracts useful information. Other features also convey much useful information. Texture can be used in segmenting and object recognition. The stripes on a zebra form a pattern that is usually distinct from the image background. The pattern 'stripes' is also a useful cue as to the type of animal object. Colour is another valuable feature.

The world is three-dimensional, but an image flattens the depth information in its two-dimensional representation. To function successfully in a three-dimensional world, a machine has to be able to reconstruct three-dimensional information from two-dimensional data. For this, the machine is equipped with more than one camera.

In this chapter, we are going to look at a number of techniques for extracting features from an image. These features are then reasoned with to provide information about the environment. We have explored elsewhere in the book a number of techniques for classification and reasoning, and so this material is not covered in this chapter. The chapter starts with a simple overview of what an image is and the geometrical relation between an object and its image. Stereo imaging is then introduced as a method that allows depth information to be recovered. Features that provide useful visual cues are introduced. Basic edge detection and segmentation techniques are covered before finally discussing object classification.

21.1   Images

An image is acquired using a sensing device that responds to a band within the electromagnetic energy spectrum. The band may be X-ray, ultraviolet, visible or infrared. We shall base our discussion on cameras that operate in the visible band and produce digitized images. Such digital cameras have become popular for capturing and storing images on a computer, which can then be displayed and edited. The image may be colour, but for convenience we shall talk mainly about grey-level images. This type of image can be represented as a two-dimensional light intensity function. The image is made up of elements called **pixels** that are ordered into rows and columns. The x-coordinate of a pixel denotes its column position and the y-coordinate its row position. Convention puts the origin of the axes in the top left-hand corner of the image. It is convenient to think of the pixels as forming a matrix. Within the matrix there is a position for each pixel whose index corresponds to the pixel's position within the image. Each entry in the matrix will be a number that denotes the intensity (brightness) of the image at that location – each entry is a grey level. The scale for measuring intensity will range from 0 (considered to be black) to some maximum value L (considered to be white). Values in between are different levels of grey. The intensity of a pixel is more usually referred to as amplitude. Amplitudes are normally represented by integers and the number of grey levels is designed to be a power of 2. So eight-bit integers can represent 256 levels of grey. For a given size of image, the more pixels there are and the higher the number of grey levels, the more detail there is. The level of detail is called **resolution**. If the image has eight rows of pixels and eight columns of pixels and 256 grey levels, the number of bits required to store the image is $8 \times 8 \times 8$ ($= 512$). The greater the resolution, the greater the memory required for storage. The required resolution depends on the application. A modern camera that captures an image with 1152×964 pixels will produce an image that is visually appealing. Many cameras can capture images with a higher level of detail, such as might be required for artwork or the quality approaching that demanded by a fashion house.

21.2   Basic mathematical relation between object and image

Cameras are used to capture images, and modern cameras are sophisticated devices that to model properly would require a mathematical description of the lens. A simple model can be produced for the pinhole camera, which consists of a tiny hole in the front of a box, which is pointed at an object whose image is to be captured. Film is placed at the opposite end of the box and is called the image plane. The image plane collects a cone of light rays that pass through the pinhole. The film reacts when exposed to light and an inverted image is formed as shown in Figure 21.2. The model described by this simple set up is called **perspective projection** and, although it is an approximate model, it is mathematically convenient. In essence, perspective projection provides a model of how an object viewed in a three-dimensional world projects onto a two-dimensional plane.

The notation in Figure 21.3 will be used to show the equations for perspective projection. A coordinate system (X, Y, Z) is established with its origin at the lens centre (the pinhole). The line extending from the lens centre to C (the image centre) is called the **optical axis**. The image plane is located a distance f' from the lens centre along the Z-axis. The distance f' is called the **focal length** when the camera is in focus on a distant object. A point in a three-dimensional scene is located at (x, y, z) and its image is formed at location (x', y', z'). The distance z' is the same as f'. The object point, lens centre and image point all lie along the same line. Simple geometry informs us that the

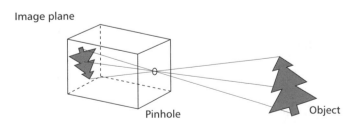

Figure 21.2 Simple camera model. The camera is a box and in place of the lens is a pinhole. An inverted image of the object being viewed is formed on the image plane.

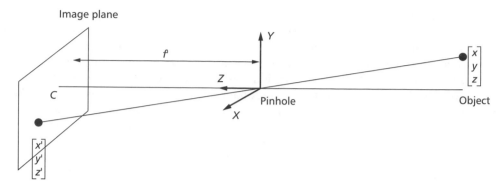

Figure 21.3 The notation used in the equations that describe perspective projection. The axes origin is positioned at the pinhole. There is a scalar relationship between the object's coordinates and that of its image.

distances x', y' and z' are a scalar value of x, y, z respectively. The scaling value is denoted by λ, so that

$$x' = \lambda x$$
$$y' = \lambda y \tag{21.1}$$
$$z' = \lambda z$$
$$\lambda = f'/z$$

There are other projection models. For example, the imaging surface could be a surface other than planar, such as cylindrical or spherical. In **spherical projection**, the imaging surface is spherical and, unlike planar surfaces, a spherical surface is always symmetrical irrespective of its orientation. For example, if you capture an image of a spherical object on a planar surface the image will be circular provided that the image plane is perpendicular to the object. The light rays from the spherical object through the pinhole form a circular cone. If the circular cone is cut by a plane, and the plane is perpendicular to the apex of the cone, the cut is circular. If the plane's orientation is other than perpendicular, the cut will be elliptical. With a spherical image plane, the image remains circular irrespective of orientation.

One effect of perspective projection is that the same-sized object produces different-sized images depending on how far away the object is from the camera. This is illustrated in Figure 21.4. The ratio of the image height to the object height gives the magnification. The magnification of an object will be dependent on its distance from the camera. In other words, the magnification varies with scene depth. If the distance of the camera from the scene is large relative to the scene depth, the model can be simplified by assuming constant magnification. Furthermore, if the camera remains at a constant distance from the scene, the coordinates can be normalized so that the magnification is 1. This simplified model is called **orthographic projection**, and all light rays are parallel to the Z-axis. For orthographic projection:

$$x' = x$$
$$y' = y \tag{21.2}$$

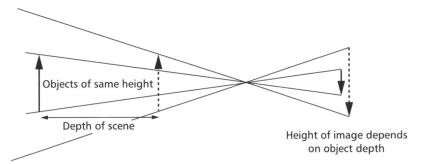

Figure 21.4 The height of an object's image depends on how far away the object is from the camera. The image height of an object gets smaller the further the object is from the camera.

21.2.1 Camera calibration

A camera's position relative to a scene will usually be variable not only in distance but also in orientation of the image plane. Cameras are typically mounted on a joint so that they can pan[2] and tilt. Imagine that a camera is positioned in a room. The room forms a small world and we imagine that we have a world coordinate system established with the origin in one corner. The position of the camera and any object can be given relative to this coordinate system. The camera is mounted on a tripod and can tilt and pan relative to the object on which it is focused. The camera has its own coordinate system, so that the positioning of an object relative to the image plane can be described. If we wish to find the image coordinates of an object point, then the world and camera coordinates need to be aligned. Once the coordinates are aligned, the equations of a projection model (e.g. perspective projection) can be applied to locate an image point. Suppose that the camera is focusing on a block. The block's position in world coordinates is known. If the camera's image plane is located at the origin of the world coordinates then the location of one of the block's vertices can be established using the equations for one of the projection models (perspective or orthographic or some other). As the camera will usually be positioned somewhere other than at the origin of the world coordinates, it is necessary to align the world coordinates with the coordinates of the camera's image plane before using the equations of a projection model. Geometry is used to establish a sequence of matrix transformations that will shift the world coordinates into the image plane coordinates. This shift will transform any point described in world coordinates to the coordinate system of the camera's image plane. To align the two coordinate systems, measurements are required to establish the parameters of camera offset and angles of pan and tilt. If the camera frequently moves about in the room then direct measurement of these parameters is impracticable. It is preferable to use the camera itself as the measuring device. To do this a set of image points with known world coordinates are used. The procedure for establishing the parameters of offset and angles from these known image points is called **camera calibration**.

When a single image plane is used for vision, the objects in a three-dimensional world are being mapped into a two-dimensional representation. A point in the image does not uniquely determine the location of an object point because information regarding depth is missing. To recover depth information more than one image plane is used. Stereo imaging involves two image planes (two cameras).

---

[2]Pan refers to horizontal swinging of the camera.

21.2.2 Stereo imaging

For many applications, depth information is important, and to recover this information two or more images are required. Stereo imaging involves working with two separate images, and the information provided can be used to recover the structure of a three-dimensional scene. In Figure 21.5 the object O has two images, i and i', formed by two cameras. Knowing the parameters of the cameras (e.g. positioning, focal length), it is possible to use a geometric technique called **triangulation** to find the distance of the object. In practice, the task is not as easy as implied here owing to the problem of **correspondence**. For example, we rely on knowing that i and i' correspond to the same object point. The task of deciding which points in image 1 correspond to which points in image 2 is difficult, but it is helped by what is called the **epipolar** constraint. In Figure 21.6, the line connecting e' and i' is an epipolar line (and similarly the line connecting e and i is an epipolar line). The point in image 2 corresponding to i in image 1 must lie along the epipolar line $e'i'$. The point e' is called the **epipole** of camera 2 and is the virtual image of the optical centre of camera 1 as seen by camera 2. The constraint reduces the search to a restricted portion of the image.

The search for corresponding image points still has to be performed using some type of similarity matching. There are several techniques. One technique is to produce two windows, one for each image, containing image intensities of the pixels around the region to be searched. The window in the first image is fixed. The window in the second image is subjected to incremental shifts and the correlation between the windows computed. The correlation function is normalized so that it has a range of -1 to $+1$. The best match corresponds to the offset in the second image that returns the maximum correlation.

21.3 Visual cues

There are many features of an image that provide visual cues about the identity of objects. These include colour, shading, shadows and texture. These features can exist at different levels of processing. For example, the colour of a single pixel may be known, but it will take groups of pixels to form a textural pattern. All of these features are useful in establishing shape.

Figure 21.7 shows a golf ball that has a spotlight directed from above and slightly from behind, making the top of the golf ball brightly lit and the bottom dark. There is also a shadow that has been cast by the ball. The ball has a textured surface created by the dimples, but the dimples at the bottom of the ball are shaded and therefore not visible. The curvature of the ball's surface produces an effect

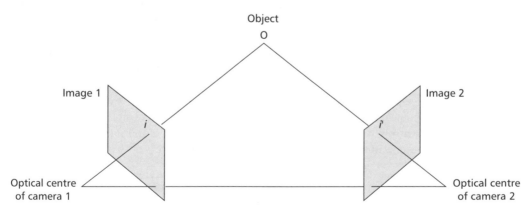

Figure 21.5 Stereo imaging. Two cameras are used. A plane has been drawn that connects the object and the optical centres of both cameras.

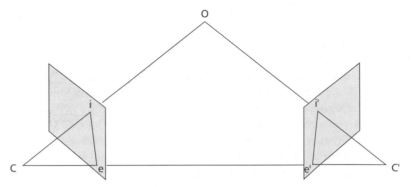

Figure 21.6 One difficulty with stereo imaging is correspondence: which point in image 2 corresponds to a given point in image 1? How do we establish that *i'* corresponds to *i* in image 1?

Figure 21.7 A golf ball that has a spotlight directed from above and slightly behind the ball. The shading helps to reveal shape, as does the textured surface.

that distorts the dimples, the amount of distortion being dependent on where on the surface the dimple is. The background also appears as two different shades which are generated by two different plane surfaces: a shelf the ball is sat on and a wall that is behind the ball.

An understanding of physics can be used to model the effects of different light sources. A light source can be classed as a point source (like a spotlight), a line source (like a strip light) or area source (like continuous lighting in an overhead ceiling or the lighting effect produced on a cloud-covered day). The combination of light source and physical properties of an object determines the effect produced by lighting. Through understanding the effects of lighting on different objects, it is possible to establish the shape of an object from a series of images taken under different light conditions.

We experience colour because our visual system responds differently to different wavelengths of light. A colour is typically represented as a linear weighted sum of three primary colours. Most people's experience of colour appears to be similar, a fact that can be established by getting subjects to adjust the mix of three differently coloured light sources until the mix matches a reference colour. People tend to choose the same mixing weights for the three primary colours, and therefore a linear representation based on a weighted sum of primary colour seems reasonable. Colour can sometimes be used to help establish object identity. For example, a system for picking faces out of a colour image has a useful cue from colour because the colour of skin is restricted to certain colour bands.

There is no clear definition of texture, but texture does appear to be a function of scale. The gravel laid on a garden path appears as a textured pattern if viewed from a distance, but close up individual stones become apparent. The surface of a building maybe textured by bricks, stones, strips of wood, etc. Some animals, e.g. zebras, giraffes and cheetahs, have distinctive textural markings. Texture is difficult to define because it is a qualitative perception made up of seeing and touching. A representation of texture is required if it is to be used in a vision system. Several approaches have been suggested. Some textured surfaces appear as regularly repeated patterns. Examples include a brick wall, the dimples on a golf ball or the herringbone weave of a cloth with a zigzag pattern. The regularity in shape and pattern repeats seen with these textures suggests a structural representation of texture might be appropriate. Bricks are rectangular, dimples circular and zigzags are arrows. The bricks in a wall, the dimples in a golf ball and the zigzag weave of a cloth all form a repeated pattern. Rules can be used to describe the repeats. For example, a brick can be placed to the left or right of the existing brick (or above or below with a horizontal offset) but all bricks are parallel (not always true!). Another approach is to describe texture in terms of features extracted from a Fourier analysis. A texture can sometimes be characterized by prominent peaks in the spectrum and the spatial period of pattern repeats can be revealed. We cannot rely on the texture pattern being perpendicularly aligned with the image plane, and so the spectrum may be computed for different orientations in the hope of aligning approximately with the principal direction of pattern repeats.

One other approach to representing texture that has received a lot of attention is to characterize texture in terms of filter response. Filters are useful for finding patterns because patterns within the image that closely resemble a filter's kernel will respond strongly when convolved with the filter (see Box 21.1). The kernel of the filter can be designed to mirror the shape of objects of interest (including therefore texture patterns). Convolving the image with the filter should produce a strong response in the region where texture mirrors the kernel.

Texture is useful for isolating objects or regions of interest (called segmentation). For example, the stripes on a tiger are a useful feature for isolating these animals from the rest of the image.

Box 21.1 Filters

A linear filter is essentially a matrix of numbers. Different-sized filters (sized matrices) can be constructed. The entries in the matrix are known as weights, and these weights define what is called the **kernel** of the filter. The kernel is a function. To keep things simple, consider a single row in the matrix as consisting of weights that correspond to heights of the bars in the histogram of Figure 21.8. The histogram is shaped a little like a Gaussian. Applying a filter to an image is referred to as **convolution**. To grasp the process of convolution it is useful to treat the filter as a mask that is placed on top of the image. The mask is designed to contain an odd number of rows and columns. The centre of the mask is positioned over a single pixel, p. A new image of p is built by multiplying each weight in the mask with the pixel the weight is positioned over and summing. The summed value gives the image of p. Once this operation is performed, the mask is shifted by one pixel and the process repeated. After the procedure has been performed for every pixel, a new image results, which is the same size as the original. The new image is the original image convolved with the filter. The kernel in Figure 21.8 would perform a weighted average. The pixel in the centre is emphasized (because it has the largest weighting) and the neighbouring pixels make a contribution that decays with distance. This type of averaging will smooth an image. Figure 21.9 illustrates the idea of convolution. The mask that is shown will respond to a horizontal edge.

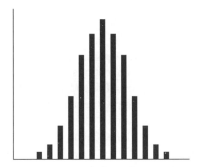

Figure 21.8 A kernel that is approximately Gaussian shaped. The heights of the bars denote weights.

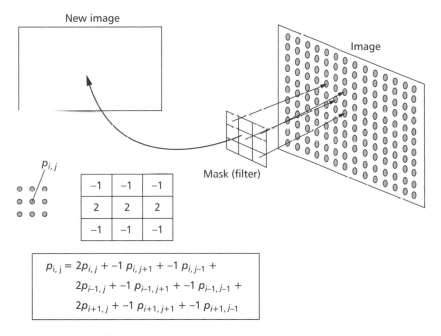

$$p_{i,j} = 2p_{i,j} + -1\, p_{i,j+1} + -1\, p_{i,j-1} +$$
$$2p_{i-1,j} + -1\, p_{i-1,j+1} + -1\, p_{i-1,j-1} +$$
$$2p_{i+1,j} + -1\, p_{i+1,j+1} + -1\, p_{i+1,j-1}$$

Figure 21.9 This diagram illustrates convolving an image with a filter. The filter is represented as a mask which is a matrix of weights. A new value p' for pixel p is found by computing a weighted average of the pixel with its neighbours.

Texture is a also useful cue for determining shape since textural elements are distorted as the orientation of an object's surface changes relative to the image plane. This effect is obvious with the dimples on the golf ball.

21.4 Describing shape

Analysing objects contained in an image requires an understanding of how different-shaped objects map onto the image. For example, a planar image perpendicular to a sphere will map into a circular-shaped image. In the case of some applications, such as reconstructing buildings from aerial images, the objects of interest will be polygons. For applications that rely on recognizing people, the objects of interest could be cylindrical in shape. Other applications might deal with objects that have complex smoothly curved surfaces (e.g. a vase).

Consider the simple blocks in Figure 21.10. Each polyhedral vertex involves three faces, the junction of which can be described as one of four types: fork junction, arrow junction, L-junction or T-junction. These junctions provide a description of the mapping of three-dimensional blocks into two-dimensional line drawings.

Many surfaces of interest consist of smooth curves. A useful parameter for describing curves is **curvature**, which can be represented using **surface normals**. Referring to Figure 21.11, the tangent to the curve at point P provides the closest representation of the direction of the curve at P. The tangents and normals have been drawn for the points P_1 and P_2. The normals intersect at I. As P_1 approaches P_2, the intersection of the normals approaches a limit called the **centre of curvature**. The inverse of the distance between the centre of curvature and the point is called the curvature. A description of how a curved surface varies can also be given in terms of the changing normal. For a known object, the tangents and normals can be assessed at different points. If the orientation of the image plane to the object is known, then geometry can be used to mathematically describe the shape of the object.

21.5 Edge detection

An **edge** is associated with points in an image where there are abrupt changes in brightness. Edges are of interest because they often denote an object's boundary. An extreme example would be a white object on a black background (or its inverse). The edge, defined by an abrupt change in brightness, would outline the boundary of such an object. Edges are also formed from effects such as shadows

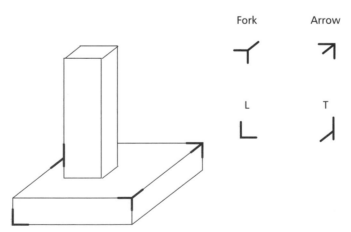

Figure 21.10 A junction at which three faces meet can be described as one of four types: fork, arrow, L, or T. These descriptors provide a description of a three-dimensional object in terms of a two-dimensional line drawing

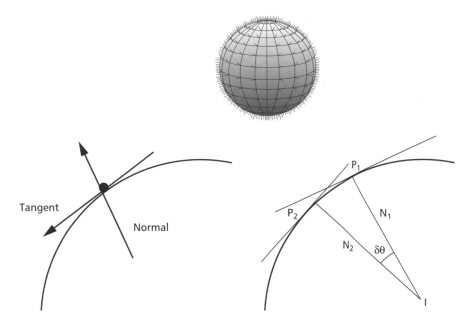

Figure 21.11 The normals to the surface of a sphere are shown in the image. Curvature at a point can be described by a tangent that is perpendicular to the surface normal. As $\delta\theta$ approaches 0 (i.e. P_1 approaches P_2), the point at which the normals N_1 and N_2 intersect, I, is known as the centre of curvature. The inverse of the distance between the centre of curvature and the point is called the curvature.

and surface orientation and features such as the stripes on a zebra. The edges in an image carry a lot of information, and so edge detection is a primary technique used in image analysis.

It is usual to reduce the effect of any noise in the image before attempting edge detection. Noise can produce edge-type effects and can therefore cause confusion with image data, making it more difficult to extract meaningful information. Noise[3] is often modelled as if it were generated by some distribution (e.g. Gaussian) with a zero mean. This type of model assumes that small random values have been added to the true value of a pixel. To reduce the noise, each pixel can be replaced by a weighted average of its neighbouring pixels as most pixels in an image will tend to have a value that is similar to its neighbours. The averaging is done by convolving the original image with a filter to produce a new image. The kernel of the filter defines the weights for the averaging.

Averaging has the effect of smoothing or blurring the image. This can remove small unwanted detail, such as gaps in an edge, but care has to be taken that the filter does not introduce unwanted secondary effects. The simplest type of filter to apply is an averaging filter with all weights set to a value of 1. The filter can be viewed as a mask with the centre of the mask positioned over the pixel to be average. For example, a 3×3 mask would be:

$\frac{1}{9} \times$

1	1	1
1	1	1
1	1	1

---

[3]Noise is anything in the image that does not convey useful information. Noise is often seen as small random fluctuations in intensities. A scratch in a picture is an example of noise.

This mask simply sums the value of a pixel with its eight neighbours and divides the result by 9. Larger masks would produce more blurring.

Filters with Gaussian kernels are commonly used. The principle behind this filter is that a pixel should have most in common with its immediate neighbours and increasingly less in common with distant neighbours. The Gaussian gives higher weight to those pixels in the centre and gradually decreasing weight the further a pixel is away from the centre.

It can be seen from Figure 21.12 that there is a large change in local gradient at the location of an edge. The gradient of a function at location (x, y) is:

$$\nabla \mathbf{f} = \begin{bmatrix} G_x \\ G_y \end{bmatrix} = \begin{bmatrix} \dfrac{\partial f}{\partial x} \\ \dfrac{\partial f}{\partial y} \end{bmatrix} \tag{21.3}$$

The gradient points in the direction of maximum rate of change, and its magnitude, denoted by ∇f, is defined as:

$$\nabla f = (G_x^2 + G_y^2)^{1/2} \tag{21.4}$$

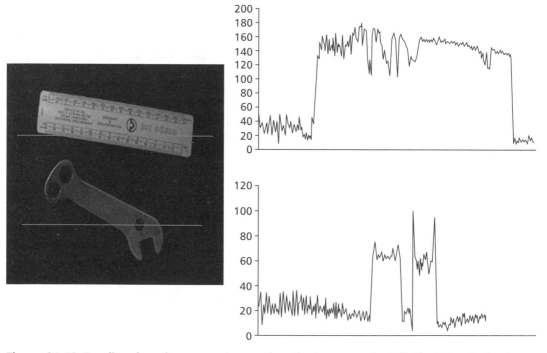

Figure 21.12 Two lines have been superimposed on the image on the left. The intensity levels of these lines have been extracted and plotted – shown on the right. In the upper profile the intensity jumps where the line cuts the ruler and remains high until the line leaves the ruler, at which point it drops sharply. The bottom profile shows two large jumps as the line cuts through the profile of the spanner. The dip in the middle corresponds to the length of the hole in the spanner.

There are a number of masks that implement approximations to eqn (21.4). A first approximation is to ignore the powers of 2 and work with absolute values. One pair of masks for calculating an approximation to the gradient are the **Sobel** operators. These masks compute the following equation:

$$\nabla f = |(z_7 + 2z_8 + z_9) - (z_1 + 2z_2 + z_3)| + |(z_3 + 2z_6 + z_9) - (z_1 + 2z_4 + z_7)| \tag{21.5}$$

z_1	z_2	z_3
z_4	z_5	z_6
z_7	z_8	z_9

-1	-2	-1
0	0	0
1	2	1

G_x

-1	0	1
-2	0	2
-1	0	1

G_y

After applying the masks to a pixel, the gradient magnitude can be calculated using eqn (21.4) or the simpler approximation of eqn (21.5), that is:

$$\nabla f \approx |G_x| + |G_y| \tag{21.6}$$

One benefit of the Sobel operators is that they have a smoothing effect which counteracts to some extent the noise enhancement caused by derivatives (derivatives respond to noise because noise often appears as discontinuities).

The operators are applied to each pixel in turn, producing a gradient magnitude for each pixel location. Figure 21.13 shows the result of applying the Sobel operators to the image in Figure 21.12. Figures 21.14 and 21.15 show the result of edge detection. The image in Figure 21.15 has been smoothed by applying a filter with a Gaussian kernel.

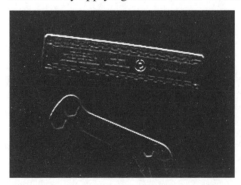 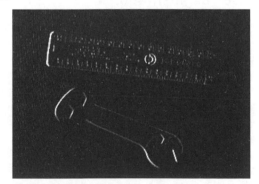

Figure 21.13 The sobel operators have been applied to the image in Figure 21.12. The image on the left is the result of convolving with G_x and that on the right the result of convolving with G_y.

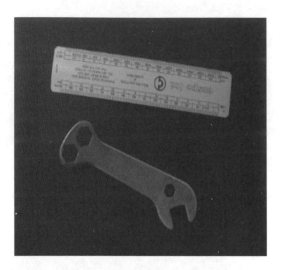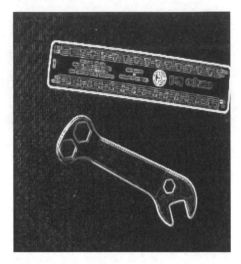

Figure 21.14 Edge detection applied to the original image.

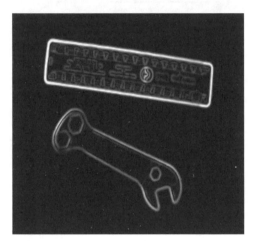

Figure 21.15 Edge detection after applying a Gaussian smoothing function.

21.6   Segmentation

Segmentation refers to the extraction of information from an image in a representational form that is useful for a given task. This description is perhaps vague, but segmentation is a very general term that encompasses many facets of information extraction. For example, edge detection can be classed as a subprocess of segmentation. We could describe segmentation as the grouping of picture tokens that are of interest to an application. The grouping should allow an image processing system to focus on those objects relevant to the task. For instance, suppose we want an application that can extract (segment) a person present in an image. A person can be described in terms of cylindrical-shaped objects: two cylinders for the arms are attached to the upper part of a much wider cylinder forming the torso, and attached to the other end of the torso are two other cylinders, the legs. Another application might require a target to be identified and tracked. The target image could contain many objects such as trees, rocks, cars, animals, etc., but if the type of target being sought is a tank then the system needs to segment tanks from the rest of the image. Segmenting also reduces the data for subsequent processing. If the tank is moving then the tracking is concerned only with the tank and none of the other objects – the tank is the focus of attention.

Grouping of image elements (e.g. pixels) is based on some measure of similarity. The inputs to algorithms for measuring similarity are features such as colour, texture, intensity gradients, components from a Fourier analysis, etc. A golden retriever dog against a green lawn background can be segmented on colour. Most of the pixels associated with the dog will have a similar colour. Likewise, the blades of grass that make up the lawn will be similar in colour. The different pixels associated with the lawn can be grouped into some homogeneous whole. Other pixels associated with the dog also form a natural grouping. Buildings, on the other hand, can be described as groups of polygons. Segmenting a building might involve the identification of edge points from which lines can be constructed that in turn construct polygons.

We can see that segmentation can involve different levels of processing. For example, the dog is contained in a region that is distinguishable in colour. The use of colour in this context isolates an area, which can then be the focus of a more detailed analysis. The next level may involve looking for shapes and their location and orientation within the isolated region. This information can then feed into a higher level of processing that looks to construct a model from the shapes, which can then be compared with built-in models for different object types, such as dog. Note that these different processing levels all involve grouping on the basis of similarity: the region in the image is first detected by a grouping of like-coloured pixels; the boundary of a shape defines a grouping of pixels that fall within the boundary; matching structural models constructed from an image with stored models is based on similarity.

21.6.1 Segmentation from thresholding

A simple form of segmentation is to use binary thresholding. Pixels that relate to a single object will usually share some characteristic, such as colour, texture or intensity. Suppose that the image being processed is greyscaled. We might expect the pixels within an image object to have a similar level of grey. We could then define a thresholding range corresponding to pixel grey levels that we wish to exclude. A binary image could then be generated by turning pixels within the range black and those outside of the range white. This process has been performed in Figure 21.16. This is a simple example as the background is dark, upon which two lighter coloured objects, the ruler and spanner, are placed. A histogram has been plotted in Figure 21.16. The histogram shows how many pixels share a particular grey level. It can be seen from this histogram that a large number of pixels have a grey level of 30 or less. Figure 21.16 shows the result of turning all pixels below a grey level of 31 black and all of those above a grey level of 30 white. The ruler and spanner stand out, but there is also a considerable amount of noise owing to lighting directed from the left of the image. A higher threshold of 120 leaves most of the ruler as white but nearly all other pixels black. Figure 21.17 shows the result of thresholding after averaging with a Gaussian filter to reduce the effect of noise.

Automatically selecting a thresholding level can be done by density estimation. The histogram in Figure 21.16 can be seen to consist of three regions. These regions appear as hills (peaks) with valleys separating them. The third hill is less defined and appears rather flat. The three regions correspond to the image background and the two objects. If the location of the hills and their width (spread) can be estimated, then it is possible to automatically define the thresholds for segmentation. The description of these hills in terms of location and width can be done using density estimation, and one technique is to cluster the grey levels on the assumption that each hill can be described as a Gaussian function. The mean of a cluster defines its location and the standard deviation its spread.

Clustering provides a general approach to segmentation. The objective of clustering is to identify groups of objects (pixels) that are similar. The measure of similarity could simply be based on grey

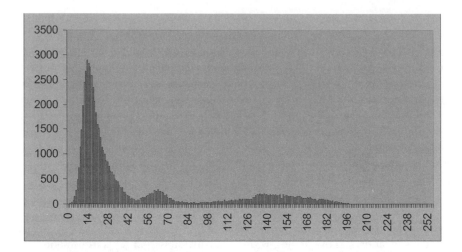

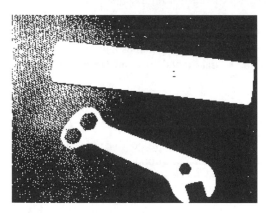
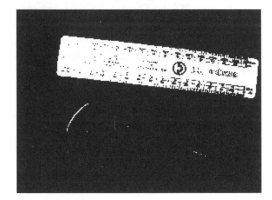

Figure 21.16 The graph at the top shows the histogram for the image from Figure 21.11. The image in the bottom left has been produced by turning all pixels within the intensity range 0–30 black and those outside this range white. The image on the right has all pixels within the range 0–120 black and those outside of this range white.

levels. Clustering in this case is one-dimensional. If the image is coloured, the clustering could be three-dimensional, with each dimension corresponding to one of the three primary colours (e.g. red, green or blue). Each pixel would be described by three numbers denoting the intensity level for each primary colour. Clustering may be based on pixel location if the objects of interest are believed to be contained within a localized region.

21.7 Extracting boundaries

Edge detection was introduced earlier to find points that are associated with an edge. Noise can give rise to edge points, but if the edge is a strong visible feature then there will be a collection of edge points arranged in some approximately contiguous way. The arrangement may form a straight line, a circle, ellipse or some other more complex shape. Automating the recognition of edges requires techniques for extracting an edge description from a collection of candidate edge points. Many techniques assume a model for the type of edge to be extracted. Such models are appropriate in

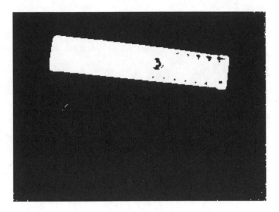

Figure 21.17 The result of thresholding after averaging with a Gaussian filter to reduce the effect of noise.

controlled environments where the types of objects of interest are known. For instance, polygon objects have edges that are straight lines. In this section, we shall introduce one technique, the **Hough transform**, for extracting straight line edges.

21.7.1 Hough transform

The Hough transform uses a maximum vote strategy to select a line that fits a series of points. The equation of a straight line is:

$$y = ax + b \qquad (21.7)$$

where a is the slope and b the intercept with the y axis. The equation of a line can also be given in normal form. To get the normal equation we imagine a second line that is drawn perpendicular from the first line to the origin, as shown in Figure 21.18. The angle, θ, of this second line and its length, ρ, provide the parameters to the equation describing the first line. This equation is:

$$x\cos\theta + y\sin\theta = \rho \qquad (21.8)$$

It is instructive to take a series of points that form a straight line and find the values of ρ for a number of angles. The points are listed below:

x	8	7	6	5	4	3	2	1	0	−1	−2	−3	−4	−5	−6	−7	−8
y	26	24	22	20	18	16	14	12	10	8	6	4	2	0	−2	−4	−6

For each point, and for each angle, a value for ρ will be computed. The angle shall range from 0 to 180°. We only want to compute for a small set of angle values and so the angles will be discretized into 36 bins:

0–4, 5–9, 10–14, ..., 176–180

The angle value is taken to be the mid-point of each bin. For each point (x, y, location) there are 36

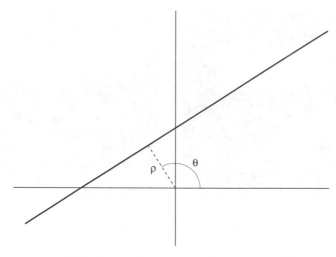

Figure 21.18 The equation of the line can be expressed in its normal form $x\cos\theta + y\sin\theta = \rho$.

values of ρ computed using eqn (21.8). The values of ρ for the first seven points have been plotted in Figure 21.19. There is a curve for each point. Each curve is a sinusoid, and they all cross at specific values for θ and ρ. The point of crossing gives the parameters for the normal representation of the line from which the points were sampled.

A matrix is a useful structure for automating the above process. The matrix grid in Figure 21.20 has a column for each θ bin and a row for each ρ bin. A count is maintained for each grid location. The count in each location of the matrix is initialized to zero. Each bin of θ has a value that is the mid-point between its lower and upper bounds. The first mid-value and the first edge point are used to compute a value for ρ. The calculated value of ρ provides an index into the matrix row (i.e. the bin of the value that ρ falls in). The count of the location indexed by the current values of ρ and θ is incremented. A value of ρ is calculated for each of the other edge points and the matrix counts updated. The value of θ is then set to the mid-value of the next bin and the procedure repeated. The procedure is performed for each θ bin. After all points have been processed for each angle, the grid location with the highest count is used to select ρ and θ as the line parameters.

The procedure described above is the Hough transform. There are, of course, an infinite number of values for ρ and θ. The range of values for ρ is constrained by the size of the image. Values for θ range between 0 and 180°. Selecting the number of bins to use can be difficult. If the bins are too large then spurious lines can be generated because large bins will tend to collect a large number of votes. Conversely, bins that are too small may fail to recognize a line. Once the bins have been chosen a matrix grid can be formed as shown in Figure 21.20. The basic algorithm is given in Figure 21.21.

We have talked about using the Hough transform for fitting straight lines to edge points. However, the Hough transform can be applied to any function that describes a curve in terms of coordinates and a vector of parameters.

21.7.2 Other techniques for fitting lines

There are a number of techniques for fitting lines. Another approach is to use a heuristic search. A

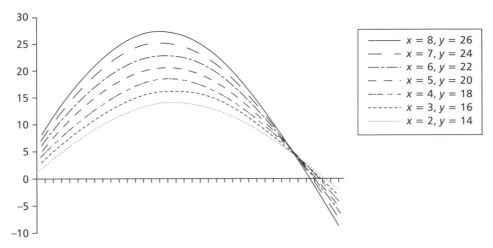

Figure 21.19 Each curve corresponds to fixed values for *x* and *y* that are substituted into eqn (21.8) to obtain values for ρ (plotted on the vertical axis) for different values of θ.

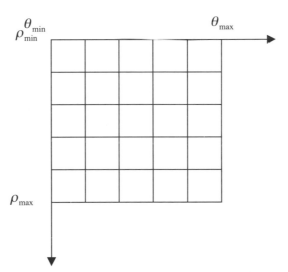

Figure 21.20 A matrix is created by splitting ρ and θ into a number of bins. Each cell in the grid maintains a count. For each θ value (column) a value of ρ is generated by taking an edge point's *x, y* coordinates and substituting into eqn (21.8). The computed value of ρ provides the row index into the matrix, which along with the current value of θ identifies the cell whose count is to be incremented.

node in the search graph corresponds to an edge in the image. Using four neighbours,[4] a pixel can be associated with one of four edges – an edge connecting from the pixel to one its four neighbours. The cost of a node is:

$$c(x, x_{neighbour}) = H - \left\lfloor f(x) - f(x_{neighbour}) \right\rfloor$$

[4] For a pixel located at *x* and *y*, its four neighbours are $(x+1, y)$, $(x-1, y)$, $(x, y+1)$, $(x, y-1)$. Other *n*-neighbourhoods can be defined.

PROCEDURE HoughTransform
initialise each entry in the association matrix A to 0

for each value θ_j

      for each edge point

            compute value of ρ_i using Equation (8)

$$A_{i,j} = A_{i,j} + 1$$

      end foreach
end foreach

return θ_j and ρ_i corresponding to the cell with the largest number of votes

Figure 21.21 Hough transform.

where H is the highest pixel intensity in the image, $f(x)$ is the intensity of pixel x and $f(x_{neighbour})$ is the intensity of the selected neighbour. Points associated with an edge will share similar values of intensity. The purpose of the search is to find a path of edges that has minimum cost. The Hough transform requires edge points to be detected using a gradient operator and can be sensitive to noise. The search technique can work well in the presence of noise, but its drawback is the added complexity and associated computing time.

Other techniques include least squares fitting and probabilistic minimization.

21.8   Classifying objects

If vision is to be used for perception then an agent needs to understand what it is seeing. A robot would need to identify objects so that it knows how to navigate round them. If the robot has a task of picking up litter then it needs to recognize objects that constitute litter. It does not take much thought to realize that a litter-collecting robot would require a huge knowledge base. Someone would not be happy if their mobile phone had been mistaken for litter. Litter collection may be an ambitious task, but knowledge plays a key role in much simpler tasks of object recognition. As humans we have to recognize objects that might be partially obscured by other objects or objects that have something missing or objects that are badly lit, etc. Our recognition is also invariant to size and rotation. To do recognition we have to reason about a lot of things so that we can infer what the object is, and this reasoning is greatly assisted when we have an expectation of what sort of objects we will see. For example, from a distant view a computer monitor looks very much like a portable TV, but if the context is an office the expectation is a monitor and concluding the presence of a monitor is reinforced if we see a rectangular object that may be a keyboard. We see in this example a form of probabilistic weighting of evidence that we explored in Chapters 5 and 6 using Bayesian networks. We have looked at reasoning with knowledge and probabilistic models throughout the book, and all have a role to play in object recognition. In addition, we have looked at machine learning techniques for automatically acquiring knowledge. Learning can play a significant role in building the knowledge base for recognizing objects. In this section, we are going to talk in general about classifying objects and, in particular, we shall talk further about extracting meaningful features for the recognition task. The inputs to the recognition stage will, in general, be features that have been derived during or after segmentation.

Segmentation is used to extract regions or features that are expected to be of interest for a particular application. If the application were face recognition, segmentation would be used first to extract a face from the image. The segmentation in this example is very specific, and the system may have a model of what a face consists of, such as horizontal bars for the eyes and mouth and a vertical bar for the nose. The model would also contain knowledge of the structural relationship between these features. Having segmented a face, the application may then be required to recognize which individual the face belongs to. This is the task of object classification. We can think of segmentation in this example as recognizing a class of objects (faces), and the task now is to associate the face with one contained in a database of faces. In other chapters we have met a number of techniques for classification. These techniques include decision trees, neural networks, Bayesian models and Markov models. Often, the classifier will be trained, because for many applications we lack the explicit knowledge to describe how the classification should be done. These classifiers are of the supervised variety and so we require training instances with known classifications and instances for testing.

The choice of classifier depends on the application as this will determine the type of features that are derived to convey information about the image. For example, an application for sign language recognition has a close analogy with speech recognition, and therefore a hidden Markov model might be appropriate. The signs are captured over a sequence of video shots. There will be ambiguity in recognizing individual signs, but context will give a model of expectation so that a sequence of signs can be predicted.

Images contain large numbers of pixels, and this constitutes high-dimensional data. The coordinates in two-dimensional space of a pixel are, of course, two-dimensional, but the tokens to be represented are made up of many pixels. Suppose, for example, we are to construct a classifier using a feedforward neural network to recognize numeric digits from a black and white (monochrome) image. Each pixel has a value of either 0 (black) or 1 (white). Even for an image of 8×8 pixels, the dimension of the problem is 64 as the neural network will have to receive information about each of the 64 pixels. Most images of interest will be much larger and will not be restricted to black and white. For training classifiers, high-dimensional data are troublesome. Large sets of data imply long training times but, more importantly, they imply a need for more training instances. For good training, a classifier needs a large number of instances so that it can learn to distinguish those features that are most relevant to the object recognition task from those that are not. For face recognition, for example, most pixels will be irrelevant (one part of a cheek will look much like another). Pragmatic considerations usually demand that a classifier be trained with a good set of features or at least a data set that has been compressed. Feature extraction will often result in a form of compression. A simple example is the extraction of area for a rectangle from width and height. Input to the area function is two-dimensional and the output one-dimensional. If area is the relevant feature for a task then it makes good sense to extract this feature and use it for training rather than require the function for area to be learned in addition to learning how to classify an object.

A feature is something that is computed from measured parameters. There are numerous methods for extracting features, but some have wide application. One example is the extraction of Fourier components. For many applications it is the dominant tones in a signal that are of most interest, and the Fourier analysis extracts these tones as the features for further processing. Another widely used technique is **principal component analysis** (PCA). PCA is a linear technique that describes a data set using a new set of axes. To see this, consider data that are two-dimensional and form a straight line. The data can be plotted in the x, y plane. If the line is horizontal with the x-axis then it is easy to see that y values add no information as for each value of x the value of y is the same. The information content is essentially one-dimensional and we might as well just describe the data using a single feature (its x values). For a classification task, the y value can add no discriminatory information as all objects share the same value. Consider now the line rotated with equation:

$$y = x$$

The slope is 1 and the intercept 0. The information content is still one-dimensional. This can be shown using Figure 21.22. A new set of axes have been drawn, which can be seen as the original set rotated. PCA can find this set of axes. Each training sample is described as a vector, and all sample vectors form a training matrix. Each point along the straight line has a component x_1 (x coordinate) and x_2 (y coordinate). Each of the N training points is therefore a two-dimensional vector. The mean vector μ is computed as the average of each dimension (column) in the training matrix:

$$\mu = \frac{1}{N} \sum_{n=1}^{N} \mathbf{x}^n \tag{21.9}$$

where n is a training instance. Next the covariance matrix Σ is computed:

$$\Sigma = \sum_n \left(\mathbf{x}^n - \mu\right)\left(\mathbf{x}^n - \mu\right)^T \tag{21.10}$$

where T denotes transpose. The eigenvectors of Σ are the new axes. Each eigenvector has an eigenvalue that indicates the spread of the data along the direction of the eigenvector. The eigenvalues can be used therefore to form an ordering of the eigenvectors for dimension reduction. In Figure 21.23, the eigenvectors project from the centre of the data points. The first eigenvector $\mathbf{v}_1$ shows the direction of most spread and has the largest eigenvalue. The second eigenvector $\mathbf{v}_2$ is orthogonal (perpendicular) to the first and has a lower eigenvalue, reflecting the fact that the data are less spread in this direction. An ordering of the eigenvectors can be used to perform dimension reduction (a form of lossy compression). A point can be described in terms of the eigenvectors instead of using the original set of axes. If the eigenvectors are ordered from highest eigenvalue to the lowest, then minor components (those vectors with lower eigenvalues) can be ignored and a point can be described as a vector containing a reduced number of elements. Some information

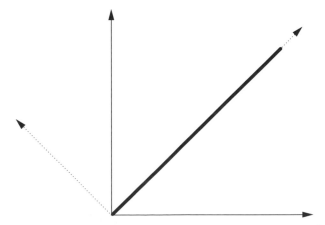

Figure 21.22 The straight line is plotted in two dimensions, but the line is inherently one-dimensional. This is easy to see if we draw a new set of axes, shown dotted. Using the new set of axes the line is effectively of single dimension: there is no discrimination in terms of the second axis as all points share the same value.

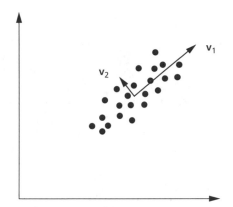

Figure 21.23 A new set of axes have been derived for the data points. The first axis, $\mathbf{v}_1$, is in the direction of most spread and the second axis, $\mathbf{v}_2$, is orthogonal to the first.

is lost, but the amount of information retained can be computed as the sum of the eigenvalues (for those eigenvectors retained) divided by the sum of all eigenvalues. If, for example, the second eigenvector in Figure 21.23 were to be ignored, the data points would effectively collapse onto the first eigenvector (all points would lie on the straight line described by $\mathbf{v}_1$). Information is lost if the second eigenvector is ignored and the amount of loss is proportional to the spread in the direction of $\mathbf{v}_2$ to the overall spread.

PCA has been used directly in face recognition. Instead of using every pixel in the image, a new set of features is obtained by describing each face in terms of the dominant eigenvectors. The idea is to extract features that are good representations of faces. To do this, a number of images of different people are collected. Several pictures of the same person are taken under different lighting conditions, pose and facial expression. From the complete set of images, the eigenvectors are computed. Each image can then be represented in terms of the dominant eigenvectors. If the original images are 128×128 pixels then an image is a vector with dimension 16384 (each dimension is an axis). If the greyscale for each pixel is used, then each component of the vector is the greyscale value of an individual pixel. Projecting an image onto the extracted eigenvectors simply means that an image is represented by the new coordinates (eigenvectors). If only the dominant eigenvectors are used, then a projected image has a vector with fewer components than that contained in the original image. This provides a form of compression and the compression can be significant. Compression can save on storage, but its main role in classification is to help identify the salient characteristics of objects. An artist's characterization of a well-known individual is void of quality and some of the rich information contained in a photograph, but the sketch accentuates certain attributes that enable recognition. In face recognition, the compression can yield a set of features that are invariant to pose, lighting, expression, etc. Classification of a new image can be performed by projecting the new image onto the set of reduced eigenvectors and matching with stored projections of individuals.

Usually, there will be many ways to represent an object and therefore many different approaches to classification. A face could be represented using line segments along with their positioning relative to each other. Most applications of AI involve some level of uncertainty. This is certainly true in image recognition. There would be uncertainty, for example, that some horizontal bar denotes a left eye. We might therefore opt for a Bayesian model that predicts the likelihood of an individual given facial features and their perceived relationship.

Summary

An image is represented by a matrix of quantized numbers. Each cell in the matrix is a number representing the light intensity of a pixel. A pixel's cell position in the matrix corresponds to its coordinate position within the image. If the image is colour, then a pixel is typically described using three numbers, one for each primary colour. Several projection models exist to describe the geometrical relationship between a real object and its image. Two or more images are required to recover depth information so that three-dimensional information can be extracted from two-dimensional images. A number of features provide useful cues for object recognition, including colour, texture, shading and shape. Edge detection and segmentation are used to identify homogeneous groupings of pixels. The grouping will signify similarity between pixels. This similarity maybe in terms of colour, texture, spatial location, etc. Extracted features should provide useful cues for object recognition. The recognition of objects is made more difficult because of variances in rotation and lighting, occlusion and noise. A good set of features will be invariant to some these conditions.

Further reading

Ballard and Brown (1982), Nalwa (1993) and Davies (1997) are general books on vision. Forsyth and Ponce (2002) provide a modern and in-depth treatment of vision. Online material is also made available at CVOnline.

Marr and Poggio (1976) devised an algorithm for determining which points in two images correspond to each other. Pattern recognition plays a large role in image processing and a good place to start is still Duda and Hart (1973).

For early work on three-dimensional interpretation of line drawings, see Huffman (1971) and Clowes (1971). For a linear programming technique see Sugihara (1984). For a paper on obtaining shape from shading information see Horn (1975).

Roberts (1965) is an example of early work on three-dimensional object recognition. Marr (1982) also discusses recognition. A two-dimensional object recognition system that uses graph matching of image primitives is FORMS (Zhu and Yuille, 1996).

Lecun *et al.* (1998) apply neural networks to recognizing hand-written digits. Essa (1999) provides an easy-to-read look at people recognition, tracking and facial expression recognition. Turk and Pentland (1991) is one example of an eigenvector approach to face recognition. Rowley *et al.* (1998) have devised a neural network system for rotation invariant face recognition.

Exercises

1   How many bits does it take to store a 640×480 pixel image that has 256 levels of grey?

2   An object is located at [10, 20, 80] relative to the optical centre. Assuming perspective projection, what are the coordinates of its image assuming a focal length of 35?

3   Logic operations are sometimes applied to binary images (all pixels have a value 0 or 1). These operations apply between two images on a pixel by pixel basis, and the result determines the pixel value for a third image (image 1 *logical operation* image 2 = image 3). Both images are

assumed to be the same size, and an operation applies between pixels that share the same location in the image array. For example, if the pixel at location (3, 4) in the first image had value 1 and the pixel at location (3, 4) in the second image had value 1, the result of logical AND gives value 1 at location (3, 4) in the third image. Logical operations include AND, OR, XOR and NOT. Logical operations can be useful for identifying objects using template matching. Suppose that a robot is equipped with a camera and treats all images as binary. Describe how a simple object recognition system could be constructed that uses logical operations. All objects are assumed to be flat and are simple shapes (rectangular, circular or triangular). Assume that only one object at a time is in view.

4   A 3×3 mask is to be applied to a 640×480 pixel image. How many arithmetic operations does this entail? How many operations are required for a 1024×1024 image?

5   For the array of integer values in Figure 21.1, apply the Sobel operators, plot a histogram, select a threshold and apply this threshold to the image.

6   Implement the Hough transform. Sample a collection of points from the line $y=3x+4$ and demonstrate that the Hough transform identifies the normal equation of the line.

7   Give the eigenvectors that will rotate points lying along the line $y=x$ to coincide with the y-axis. Show that these eigenvectors will rotate a series of points sampled from $y=x$. (Hint: think in terms of a 2×2 transformation matrix and the angle subtended by the line relative to the y-axis.)

8   A neural network is to be trained for classifying images with 64 levels of grey. The size of each image is 120×120 pixels. Discuss some of the practical issues that would arise and suggest possible solutions.

PART 7

Agents, Philosophy and Applications

This final part of the book provides additional material that might supplement material for an AI undergraduate module. The agent metaphor has been used heavily in many writings since it became popular a few years ago. This book has occasionally used the term 'agent' to refer conveniently to a machine or virtual machine (i.e. software tool), but the term 'intelligent agent' has not been explained. Chapter 22 provides this explanation. It is probably fair to say that there is a great deal of work to be done in the field of agents before they mature and find wide application. The concept of agents, though, as cooperative intelligent entities is very attractive from the point of view of system implementation. Chapter 23 is a kind of short essay on some philosophical issues that are of concern in artificial intelligence. Many topics could have been discussed, but the aim is to provide an appreciation of the useful role philosophy plays without attempting to study in depth any specific topic. The book concludes with a look at a few real-world applications of AI in Chapter 24.

CHAPTER 22

Agents

22.1 Agents

We have occasionally used the word 'agent' as a generic reference to the computer or machine that is performing some intelligent action, but for some entity to be called an agent it should satisfy certain requirements, and the purpose of this short chapter is to explain what an agent is. Research in agent technology has been around for about 20 years, but agents became popularized around 1994 with the emerging Internet technology. An agent can be a physical entity, such as a robot, or it can be some entity completely embedded in software. Most work with agents concerns software agents, and this chapter will concentrate on software agents. The concepts also apply to physical agents as the core intelligence of these agents is still embedded using software and the software can be complex. We shall talk about a software system in a very general sense as software made up from a number of interacting components.

Viewing an intelligent software system as a collection of agents is a way of conceptualizing a complex system. Tools, techniques and standards are being developed for this form of software engineering. There is much talk about the application of agents to real-world problems, and there have been many projects, but at the time of writing it is difficult to identify real-world applications that follow the true spirit of the agent philosophy. That said, the agent-oriented approach to intelligent software development is likely to succeed eventually because it is an intuitively appealing way of modelling complex systems. Also, the types of software tools with which the agent infrastructure can be implemented are now beginning to emerge.

The agent-oriented aim is to build a collection of interacting autonomous agents that when acting together have more capability than any single agent within the system. Such a system is called a **multiagent** system. So what is an agent? An agent is an entity that has goals and is situated in some environment. The agent can sense its environment and is capable of autonomous action. The environment is obviously system dependent. If the agent is part of an air traffic control system then the environment consists of aircraft, controllers, locations, aircraft positioning and trajectories, time, arrivals, departures, etc. If the agent is part of an aircraft engine diagnostic system the environment is the engine with its various components, the monitoring technology, the databases with aircraft histories, maintenance actions, etc. The word 'sense' is used in a very general way to denote that the agent has an awareness of what is going on within its environment. The agent may have input from physical sensors such as cameras mounted on a robot or vibration sensors on an aircraft engine. The sensors need not be physical for an agent to sense its environment. For instance, part of an agent's environment could be a text document and changes to a document can be detected. Agents should be able to react to changes in the environment and determine their own behaviour in pursuit of their goals – they need to be autonomous. To be autonomous they need to be able to make decisions in the context of what is happening in the environment. Decisions often result in action and actions will change the environment.

In a multiagent system, the agents need to interact in order for their behaviour to be cooperative so that collectively they satisfy goals that no single agent acting alone could achieve. Interaction is achieved by interagent communication. The communication is at a high level (knowledge level). This form of communication is different to message passing between objects. We can use the analogy of a vending machine. The standard machine takes messages in the form of buttons being pressed so that you can select a hot drink, with milk and sugar, etc. If you could have a dialogue with the machine to determine the drink then you are communicating at a higher level or knowledge level. You would interact with the machine in the same manner as you would with a human serving drinks in a coffee bar. Both you and the machine must have a common understanding of words used when communicating. You are both agents. You have a goal (to get the drink that you desire) and your intention is to use the cooperation of the other agent (machine) to help satisfy your goal. The machine needs to sense what is happening in the environment: it needs to know when a customer is waiting to be served, what supply of coffee, milk and sugar is left, and whether the correct money has been handed over.

Jennings *et al.* (1998) identify three key concepts in the definition of agents.

- **Situatedness** – an agent receives input from its environment through sensors and it can perform actions which change the environment in some way. The environment could be the physical world or a software world such as the Internet.
- **Autonomy** – an agent should be able to act on its own without human intervention. It should have control over its own actions and internal state.
- **Flexibility** – an agent should exhibit flexible behaviour. An agent should be responsive so that it can react to changes in the environment in a timely manner. An agent should also be proactive so that it not only reacts to changes but also takes initiative to satisfy its goals. An agent should also exhibit social behaviour through interacting with other agents to solve its own goals and help satisfy the goals of other agents.

Nwana and Ndumu (1999) give a good example of a multiagent system. The system is to operate over the Internet. They consider the case of a traveller wishing to arrange a trip from a town outside London to a city on the east coast of the USA. The traveller delegates the arrangements for the trip to a personal travel agent (PTA), which is the equivalent of a personal secretary in human terms. Other agents roughly correspond to other humans involved in arranging the trip and include transport agents and accommodation agents. Transport agents could include air transport agents, railway agents and car rental agents. Agents communicate with other agents. For instance, an agent that books flights might have to communicate with one or more agents that deal with specific flight operators. Information regarding flights, hotels, etc. is available online through the Internet. Each agent has a goal, such as to find a flight that takes a particular route and gets to the destination by the required time. Other, more general, goals, such as managing the cost of the trip, could also be set. The different agents need to cooperate with each other to ensure that all elements of the trip fit together and there are no conflicts. Car and rail services must fit the schedule of the flight and the hotel must be reserved from when the traveller arrives until the time of departure. We can also imagine other agents that would negotiate the costs of transport and hotels.

The agents are there to do a job for us. The PTA would be personalized in that it would know your own likes and dislikes and your preferences. For example, you might always insist on staying in top-class hotels or you might have experienced bad service in the past from one transport operator and not wish to travel with that operator again.

An agent system for air traffic management is describe in Rao and Georgeff (1995) and Kinny *et al.* (1996). The system has actually undergone evaluation at Sydney airport. The system is designed to assist a human flow controller in determining the landing sequence of aircraft on multiple runways. Constraints include maintaining safety and minimization of delays and congestion. This is a real-time application operating in a complex and uncertain environment. The environment changes in a non-deterministic way: the wind field can change over time, aircraft leave and enter the environment, runway conditions change, etc. Many decisions can be made, e.g. putting an aircraft into a holding pattern, stretching a flight path, shortening a flight path. There are multiple objectives, e.g. landing aircraft at specified times and maximizing runway usage. This is a complex application. Conceptually, it appears that the best way to model this application is through interacting software elements. Because these elements need an understanding of what is going on the environment, and they have goals to achieve and decisions to make, it appears that these elements are best modelled as agents. The system consists of three permanent agents with the roles of coordinator, sequencer and windmodel. The system also has aircraft agents; an aircraft agent exists for the lifetime an aircraft is under the direction of the flow controller.

The coordinator's role is the creation and deletion of aircraft agents. The sequencer interacts with aircraft agents and the flow controller to determine landing time assignments. The windmodel maintains a model of wind conditions in the controlled airspace. An aircraft agent consists of three elements: a predictor, monitor and planner. The predictor computes the expected time of arrival at various waypoints contained in the flight plan. A flight plan can be modified during a flight. The predictor needs an understanding of an aircraft's performance (e.g. speed, climb performance, fuel burn) and requires input from the windmodel agent. The monitor receives data derived from radar to compare actual times of arrival at waypoints with those predicted. If deviations occur, the monitor analyses the reasons and then notifies the predictor and planner. Deviations can result from inaccuracies in the windmodel or an aircraft not following the planned flight path. The planner's job is to construct a set of plans that will allow the aircraft to land at the time assigned by the sequencer. A plan includes directives for following air speed and altitude profiles. Acceptable plans are constrained to follow certain altitude ranges, speed ranges and holding points. Another constraint is to minimize the instructions to the pilot.

We can begin to see why agent technologists rely on artificial intelligence. Agents need to make decisions, plan and communicate. In many applications, they also need the ability to update their own knowledge and beliefs and so they need to learn from experience.

Of course, a great deal of infrastructure is required to support these agents. Nwana and Ndumu discuss the requirements in some detail. For example, the PTA needs to locate travel agents and hotel agents. The PTA needs access to directories that are updated when agent addresses change. Once other agents are located they need to communicate, and this requires standardized communication protocols. At a business level, XML is becoming more established as a means for applications to pass data. Once the lower level protocols are standardized, there is then the requirement for agents to communicate in a high-level language that all agents can understand. A number of languages have been proposed, e.g. knowledge query and manipulation language (KQML) and the agent communication language (ACL). These languages use a syntax that expresses how the speaker intends the listener to respond. Intentions are indicated using messages such as *ask*, *tell* or *achieve*, which are based on Searle's (1969) speech act theory performatives. Agents also need a common definition of the ontology. The ontology refers to all the concepts within the application domain. These concepts include flight, hotel, journey leg, etc.

Modern software techniques such as object-oriented development and software component methods assist with agent technology development, but systems developed using these technologies are not in themselves agent based. To be agent based they need to have components that sense their environment, react to changes, be capable of autonomous action and communicate with other components at a level that requires cooperative knowledge. It should also be apparent that many traditional AI systems are not agent based. For instance, an expert system may make decisions, but its link to what is happening in the environment may be through a user, and it is the user who requests the system to perform reasoning. In this scenario there is no autonomous reaction to sensed changes in the environment. That is not to say, however, that an expert system cannot be agent based. An aircraft diagnostic system could use a number of cooperative agents with dedicated knowledge of particular sensing technologies such as engine performance parameters, vibration parameters, particle sensors that react to material travelling into the engine or out through the exhaust, and oil-monitoring sensors. These various agents have an understanding of faults and symptoms. They must also cooperate to give a diagnosis because different sensors can react to the same faults. There also needs to be a temporal level of knowledge and understanding. For example, a particle sensor might detect an object that is ingested into the engine, but it could be several hours before the damage caused by the particle becomes severe enough that other sensors detect symptoms.

Agent technology is really a synthesis of AI techniques and advanced state-of-the-art software engineering techniques. The questions that naturally arise are: 'How do we specify what an agent system is?' and 'How do we structure the design and implementation of agent systems?'. For example, in software engineering the procedural perspective conceptualizes a system as a hierarchical arrangement of procedures with the execution of higher level procedures dependent on lower level ones. Detail is abstracted away by defining higher level procedures in terms of lower level ones. The designer therefore has a method for modularizing a system and the facility to focus at different levels of detail. The object-oriented methods conceptualize a system in terms of class types, objects, object communication and events. Levels of abstraction can be determined using class subtyping. We are really referring to architectural issues. So how should agent architectures be specified and implemented? Answers to the question are inextricably tied to the philosophy of the nature of intelligence and the requirements of an application domain. Representation formalisms take a philosophical stance in that they propose methods for encoding knowledge and methods for reasoning with this knowledge. Different application domains impose different constraints. For example, in an air traffic management systems there is not the time for lengthy computation of optimal decisions. High-level business decisions, on the other hand, while demanding timely responses, can afford to take considerably more computing time than a real-time system. It is not surprising, then, that there are many proposed architectures. Architectures have been based around logic languages, planning languages, decision-theoretic languages and possible world models.[1] These formalisms have been introduced in this book. Other architectures have been proposed. Some build on the representation formalisms we have studied; others, like reactive architectures (described below), take a radical departure from formal representation. We briefly introduce two other architectures.

Belief, desire, intention (BDI) architectures characterize rational agents in terms of attitudes. For example:

> John *wants* to order a drink.
> David *believes* Mary is cold.

Attitudes such as *wants* and *believes* can be used to explain human behaviour and to predict human behaviour. Rao and Georgeff (1992) developed a logical framework based on the attitudes *beliefs*, *desires* and *intentions*. A system's beliefs denote the system's understanding of what state the environment is in. Beliefs are continually updated as more environment data are sensed. A system's

---

[1]The notion of possible worlds was illustrated using an example from Sensory GraphPlan in Chapter 10.

desires denote the system's motivational state. Desires are determined by system objectives and the utility (costs and rewards) of satisfying these objectives. A system's intentions denote the course of action that is to be undertaken. These attitudes provide the basic concepts around which a system's architecture is constructed. The BDI model suggests a way to conceptualize a system and structure its design.

A **reactive** architecture is one that does not propose any explicit representation of knowledge or tokening of entities in the environment. This is a radical shift away from models built using logics or graphical models like semantic networks. Brooks (1986, 1991) has proposed such an approach, which he calls the **subsumption architecture**. Brooks takes the view that intelligent behaviour can be generated without explicit representation and without explicit reasoning mechanisms. Instead, intelligent behaviour can arise from an agent's interaction with its environment. Brooks's motivation for the subsumption architecture was to define an approach for controlling autonomous mobile robots. The computations are simple but behaviour can be complex. The subsumption architecture specifies a hierarchy of behaviours. At the lowest level are primitive behaviours such as 'avoid obstacle'. Through interaction with the environment, a robot can learn how to achieve complex tasks by following primitive task-accomplishing behaviours.

Wooldridge and Jennings (1995) provide an overview of the many agent architectures.

CHAPTER 23

Philosophy of Artificial Intelligence

There are two general reasons for studying AI:

- from a purely engineering perspective to build machines that can be put to work for us;
- to understand human intelligence by replicating its functionality.

The two are, of course, related because work in pursuit of one feeds across to the other. Both pursuits also pull us into philosophical issues. We may suppose that the adoption of AI in pursuit of engineering useful tools is not concerned with philosophy. This viewpoint is wrong. The designers of any system make philosophical commitments. In particular, we see this when building intelligent systems. We need to address questions such as:

- What knowledge is required?
- How should this knowledge be represented?
- What should the system be capable of?
- What do we believe the system will be capable of and why?

To construct intelligent entities we need to reflect on the nature of intelligence and understand the capabilities and limitations of the technology we use.

Philosophers are naturally attracted to AI because they are interested in the nature of intelligence and theories of mind. This chapter provides a very brief introduction to some of the philosophical debates that accompany AI. These debates include very difficult questions on whether machines could ever be made to understand or whether something made of silicon could be conscious. There is also a strong link to cognitive psychology in pursuit of answers to questions such as 'What goes on in the mind when we see an image?', 'How can different concepts be seen in the same image?' We shall only skim the surface of some of these debates. We shall sit on the fence with regard to opinion – opinion could not be justified in such a short space with topics that have many arguments in support of different views. This chapter is more like a short essay to give an idea of what role philosophy plays in AI and to give a lead into the many texts written on the subject.

23.1 So what is philosophy?

Sloman (1995) summarizes philosophy as investigating:

1   the most general questions about what exists;
2   the most general questions about questions and possible answers;

3   the most general questions about what ought to exist, or ought not to exist.

The first point concerns **ontology**. Ontology is a branch of metaphysics that deals with the nature of being. For example, can a mind exist independently of matter? When we construct any knowledge-based system we are concerned with the types of objects that exist. When we construct ontologies we identify objects and their types. These could include physical objects, events and concepts such as time, hot and cold, etc.

The second point is concerned with **epistemology**. Epistemology is the general theory of knowledge. For example, what do we know when we know that 'Wet roads cause a car to take longer to stop'? More generally, what do we know when we say that we know that event A causes event B? Some people would know the connection between the wet road and the car stopping and could explain it in physical terms; other people may simply know that one always seems to coincide with the other (event B always follows event A). We can use a specific example of why such philosophical issues are of interest to us all, no matter what our motive for studying AI. The example is given by Copeland (1993) and concerns a well-known issue with representing causality using implication. Copeland gives the example of a baked bean that is run over by a car tyre

The car tyre runs over the baked bean → the baked bean squashes

Clearly, it is true that a car tyre running over a baked bean will cause the bean to be squashed. But the above proposition (according to the definition given in Chapter 2) will also be true when Freddie's fork causes the bean to be squashed. As a representation of causality the logical implication is poor. Consider reasoning backwards in a diagnostic sense when we know that the bean is squashed. Are we to conclude that the car tyre was the cause? We have addressed some of these issues earlier in the book and showed that, although the car tyre could be a cause, it is only one possible cause, and other events might be more likely.

The third point is really concerned with ethical issues. For example, if we construct machines, which to us appear human like and express emotion, is it ethical to terminate their existence?

23.2 Strong and weak AI

AI scientists have no commitment to computers other than for pragmatic reasons that the computer is the physical entity upon which we can implement algorithms and representations to simulate human intelligence. AI scientists would happily use a biological process as opposed to electronic bits if they were given the apparatus and if following such a path of investigation looked promising.

AI has a philosophical theory of mind, and that theory is that human cognitive mental states can be duplicated using computing machinery. In fact, a distinction is made between two levels of duplication. The first level is strong AI, which maintains that suitably programmed machines will be capable of conscious thought. Weak AI makes no claim beyond being able to simulate the input and output behaviour of humans once machines are suitably programmed. In other words, weak AI maintains that human intelligence can be simulated, but the machine doing the simulation need not have conscious thought or be thinking. Strong AI is the claim that machines can be made to think and have genuine understanding and other cognitive states – the human mind can be replicated. Weak AI claims that computing machines will be built to simulate thought but makes no claim as to their ability to really understand what is being reasoned.

Strong AI is the most controversial. Many critics have claimed that machines cannot be programmed to have conscious thought. The best-known attack is Jon Searle's Chinese room thought experiment. First, consider our own capabilities when we read a story. We can make inferences about things that are not explicitly stated in the story. Indeed, we do this all the time in conversation because it is inefficient and tedious to keep stating 'the obvious'. For example, 'The sky was getting dark, so John decided to take an umbrella along for his walk'. We can infer why John is taking an umbrella because we posses common-sense knowledge. We know that a dark sky implies a chance of rain and that people mainly prefer to keep dry and that an umbrella is an instrument to help humans keep dry. Searle's argument is that, although you might be able to program the story into a machine and get the machine to correctly answer any question about the story, the machine will not understand anything that it processes. According to Searle, the machine is a symbol manipulator, but manipulating symbols does not lead to understanding. The machine is expert at processing syntax but not semantics. For example, as a non-French-speaking person you could take a question written in French and without understanding any content of the sentence give a correct answer in French by looking up the answer in a huge book of rules. You need only to master syntax. So all that is required is that you recognize the boundaries of words and match word symbols with those in the rule book to form a correctly constructed answer. The simplest scenario would be for an answer to be written for every question that could be asked. As another example of purely syntactic processing consider converting a sentence of the form:

John hit Chris – active form

to

Chris was hit by John – passive form

You could be given rules to correctly convert an active sentence to a passive one without any knowledge of active and passive sentences. For an active sentence of the above form you use the two rules:

Swap the order of names.
Replace the *verb-name* with *was verb-name by*.

Searle states that, if a computer were made to simulate human intelligence, it would be nothing other than a simulation without understanding. The computer may contain millions of pieces of knowledge and thousands of rules for manipulating this knowledge, but it all boils down to symbol manipulation, and manipulating symbols does not lead to understanding. This program, according to Searle, could be simulated (in theory) by a person locked away in a room in possession of many rule books, pencils and paper. Call the person Joe. The room contains two slots. The first is marked 'input', through which symbols are passed to Joe by people outside, and the second slot is marked 'output', through which Joe passes symbols back to the people outside. The input symbols and output symbols are written in Chinese, and Joe has no knowledge of Chinese. A story is fed symbol by symbol through the input slot. Next a series of questions are passed into the room through the input slot. Joe takes the first symbol of the story and looks up a rule that tells him what to do with the symbol. The rule might simply tell Joe to record the symbol on paper. Joe keeps on looking up rules for each symbol. Sometimes he will have to follow many rules in sequence for one Chinese symbol. He may be told to take the last three symbols he recorded on paper and replace them with another symbol. John is essentially following (tediously) the same sort of processing that a computer does when analysing the syntax of sentences. After the story has been processed Joe does the same for the questions. After many years of waiting, Joe starts to write Chinese symbols on to cards and pass these through the output slot to people waiting. Eventually, Joe completes his task. All questions have been correctly answered. Searle maintains that Joe did not understand Chinese before entering the room and would still not understand Chinese no matter how much symbol manipulation he performed.

A simulation of the Chinese room using a computer, with minutes to process as opposed to years, would be impressive. Although impressive, Searle maintains there is no understanding. Just like Joe, the machine would have no understanding of what it processed and would not even be aware that it had processed a story and answered questions about that story. So, although the system appears to understand Chinese, it does not.

Searle's argument is seductive, and some have taken it as conclusive proof that strong AI cannot be achieved. But it is not a proof, it is conjecture. The AI community is not so easily convinced about Searle's argument, and there have been many counterarguments. We shall mention just a couple of replies (Searle has counter-replies to these replies). The **system response** basically states that, although Joe does not understand Chinese, you cannot imply that the system (Joe plus pencils plus paper plus interface for communicating input and output) does not understand Chinese. The **robot response** states that the reason that Joe has no understanding of Chinese is that there are no sensory connections between the symbols and the objects in the world they relate to. So, if a robot is equipped with sensors to experience its world, it will develop genuine understanding of the symbols it manipulates. To really understand the symbol 'tea' requires one to taste, smell and see tea used in the way it is in the real world. The **other minds response** is that we can attribute an understanding of Chinese to a Chinese-speaking individual only by observing his or her behaviour, and if a computer exhibits such behaviour why not attribute it with the same level of understanding?

A great deal has been written about Searle's argument. One real difficulty for Searle is the ridiculous nature of the argument. We know that we could not in practice implement the experiment using a person because that person would not live long enough to perform the computations and the whole task would be physically unmanageable. Yet the person is central to Searle's argument. As Copeland points out, the argument is less seductive if you replace the person with a superflea that can respond to stimuli and flip switches on and off.

There is another thought experiment which upon first encounter would appear to support the notion of building a thinking machine out of silicon. In this experiment we imagine taking a person and replacing a single brain cell (neuron) with a silicon chip. The chip is designed to respond in exactly the same way as the neuron – the outputs of the neuron and chip are identical for the same stimuli. We are then to imagine that every other cell in the brain is also replaced one at a time. We could check after each cell is replaced to see how the person's thought processes are affected. Surely, replacing one neuron with a chip could not have much impact on the person's thinking? Furthermore, the functions performed within the brain rely on collections of many neurons that interact through stimulating each other, and, provided we maintain the right inter-cell stimulation, surely we maintain the same functionality when we replace a neuron with a chip? So at what point in the replacement of neurons does thinking and understanding disappear? Searle, of course, is not convinced.

23.3 Thinking machines

Thinking is an often loosely used metaphor to describe the behaviour of AI programs, but there are few people who would attempt to argue seriously that a thinking machine has already been built. Most would accept that technologists are still a long way from building a genuine thinking machine. But will these machines need to be conscious of what they are thinking to really understand or will consciousness perhaps evolve as a natural property of simulating cognitive function?

Consciousness has been impossible to define, but in simplistic terms we can say that it refers to awareness of one's own existence and thought processes. You know, for example, when you are studying a subject that you are studying that subject and you are aware that you are trying to reason about that subject to improve your understanding. We may assume that there is no thought without consciousness. But this is a big assumption to make, and most psychologists accept that we are not consciously aware of all, if not most, of all our mental processes. For example, most of the time when you speak you probably do not plan exactly what you are going to say. There are also experiments that suggest we can know things without knowing we know (or being aware that we know). An example of this is demonstrated by subjects with so-called blindsight. Blindsight can occur as a result of damage to part of the visual cortex, e.g. after surgery to remove a tumour. Patients with blindsight claim not to be able to see a small light moved around in some parts of their visual field even though they could see such a light previously, i.e. before their visual cortex was damaged. A screen is positioned in front of the patient and a spot of light is shone onto the screen in the region of the patient's blind area. The light is moved about in the blind area, and after each change of position the patient is asked to reach out and touch the light on the screen. Patients are usually able to pinpoint the light spot extremely accurately but claim to be unaware of whether or not they were successful and are most surprised at their achievement. They tend to believe that they are guessing where the spot is, but the results suggest that they know the position of the spot even though they are unaware of knowing.

We need to be careful, however, when drawing conclusions about the link between thought and awareness. Chalmers (1996) makes the point that it is not clear that patients with blindsight have no experience at all of the light; it could be that this experience has an unusual relation to verbal reporting. Chalmers characterizes consciousness as the subjective quality of experience. He continues:

> When we perceive, think, and act, there is a whir of causation and information processing, but this processing does not usually go on in the dark. There is also an internal aspect; there is something it feels like to be a cognitive agent. The internal aspect is conscious experience. Conscious experiences range from vivid colour sensations to experiences of the faintest background aromas; from hard-edged pains to elusive experience of thoughts on the tip of one's tongue; from mundane sounds and smells to the encompassing grandeur of musical experience…

It is not clear what processes give rise to our experience. Take, for example, visual perception. You could look at a jar and interpret it in different ways. In one interpretation you see the jar as a flower vase; in another interpretation you see it as a money jar. But what about the rabbit–duck picture in Figure 23.1 (Wittgenstein 1958). If you have never seen a duck before, but only rabbits, then upon viewing this image you would see a rabbit. Conversely, if you have only ever seen a duck, you see the image as a duck. So are we seeing something different in each instance or are we interpreting the image differently? This has implications for vision processing. For example, is what we see a process of inferencing, in one case interpreting the left of the image as a duck's beak and the eye looking to the left or alternatively interpreting the left-hand side of the image as a rabbit's ears with the eye looking to the right? Or is the process of what we see more instantaneous and a form of direct association between two different stored templates, one for a rabbit and one for a duck?

Chalmers admits that consciousness is really impossible to define, and hence he opts to talk about experience in attempting to pin down what is being talked about when the word 'consciousness' is used. A huge amount has been written on consciousness, and the last decade in particular has seen a steep growth in interest and research funding. Sloman (2001) believes that the scientific and philosophical discussion of consciousness is a 'real mess'. For a start, Sloman believes there is too much introspection when trying to answer what consciousness is. He states that we need to collect many more data on things like the differences between humans at various stages of development, differences between mental phenomena in different cultures, surprising effects of brain damage or disease, stages and trends in evolution, and much more.

Figure 23.1 Rabbit–duck picture.

Given that consciousness is impossible to define, perhaps the best we can do for the time being is to explore under what circumstances we might be willing to attribute a machine as having a genuine level of understanding. Of course, we might start from the basis that if something is not conscious then it has no genuine understanding. But there might be different levels of consciousness, and different levels of understanding that correlate with different levels of information processing. Take, for example, the interaction we can imagine between ourselves, a stick, a fly, a dog and a chimpanzee. If we raise the stick and bring it down towards the fly, the fly will always react as if it is trying to protect itself from being flattened. The fly might not know what it is seeing or be able to deduce what is going to happen – it appears to respond with a reflex reaction (possibly pre-programmed to respond to this form of stimulus). The dog, on the other hand, may react in one of two ways depending on the context. If you are angry, the dog may cower in the expectation that you wish to hit him. If you are playful, the dog may attempt to grab the stick or wait for you to throw it. Some wild chimpanzees are able to put the stick to a functional use such as fishing for termites. It is generally accepted that a chimp is more intelligent than a dog and a dog is more intelligent than a fly. The level of understanding of each species is difficult to assess, but when we attempt to assess it we invariably use communication. Many research programmes have concentrated on teaching chimps to sign. In fact, language features very heavily when we talk of intelligence and an ability to think. Language plays a role in Searle's Chinese room. We shall take a brief look at the possible link between thinking and language in a moment, but first we shall review its role in a test of intelligence.

23.4 Turing test

Alan Turing proposed a test to determine if a machine is capable of thought. The test has become known as the Turing test and involves two humans and the machine. One of the humans acts as an interrogator. The interrogator does not know the identity of the other human or machine, which are referred to as subject A and subject B. All three are hidden from each other in separate rooms. They communicate via a keyboard and screen. The interrogator can ask any form of question he or she wishes, and the machine is allowed to try and deliberately hide its identification. The test is repeated a number of times, with different people taking the place of the two humans. If, after all tests, the number of times the machine has been correctly identified is not significantly greater than the random guess of 50%, the machine is declared to be capable of thought.

We can sometimes allow ourselves to be easily deceived. This was demonstrated with Weizenbaum's (1965) ELIZA back in the 1960s. ELIZA could hold a conversation with a human subject using a keyboard and screen. Below is a small extract, where H denotes a human and E denotes ELIZA:

H: You are like my father in some ways.

E: What resemblance do you see?
H: You are not very aggressive but I think you don't want me to notice that.
E: What makes you think I am not very aggressive?
H: You don't argue with me.
E: Why do you think I don't argue with you?
H: You are afraid of me.
E: Does it please you to believe I am afraid of you?

It has been reported that ELIZA duped a lot of people into believing that they were communicating with another human hidden behind the keyboard and screen. But ELIZA had not the remotest understanding of any conversation she took part in. ELIZA was really a trick that consisted of a program that would look for patterns in questions and would form answers by making simple transformations to the question. For example, the response to 'You don't argue with me' is formed by swapping *You* to *I* and *me* to *you* and prefixing with *why do you think*. For much of the time, ELIZA could respond to a question with a question. Of course, in some situations, for example a psychotherapy session, such a response might be appropriate. But if you know that you are conducting a Turing test, your questions are directed for the purpose of identifying the machine and it is no longer easy to fool an interrogator with clever tricks.

In 1990, the New York millionaire Hugh Loebner launched the Loebner contest. The contest is held every year, and programmers compete for a gold medal and $100 000. The rules of the contest change slightly from year to year, but in essence the test is the Turing test. No competitor has yet won the gold medal. In the competition of 2000, not a single judge out of 10 mistook a machine for a human and, to win the gold medal, 30% of the judges had to be fooled within 5 minutes into thinking the machine was a human.

The following conversations are from the 2000 competition (source: *Guardian*, Saturday 6 October 2001). Conversation 2 is the machine and the other two are human.

Conversation 1
Q: I will ask you some simple questions and give simple commands. I want you to give me correct answers and relevant responses.
A: You like being in control, yes?
Q: What is the colour of a blue truck?
A: To business then it is. The colour of a blue truck is blue.
Q: Where is Sue's nose when Sue is in her house?
A: Assuming Sue's nose is where it belongs, it should be in the house with Sue.
Q: What happens to an ice cube in a hot drink?
A: It is still there, just in a more relaxed state. Hot drinks will do that.
Q: A more relaxed state? Meaning what?
A: Sort of spread out and throughout.
Q: Altogether, how many feet do four cats have?
A: Do you mean how long are they when in line or do you mean the number of paws in total?
Q: Both …
A: Paws should be 16. Feet in length about four, without tails extended.

Conversation 2
Q: I drank too much coffee this morning.
A: Interesting gossip – Judge 7 said she drank too much coffee this morning.
Q: Not terribly interesting.

A: Oh I get it.
Q: Tell me a joke.
A: Did you hear the one about the mountain goats in the Andes? It was Baaaaad.
Q: Well...
A   Well what?
Q: What is the punchline?
A: I haven't heard of the punchline. Would you like to know more?
Q: Are you a computer?
A: Would it matter to you if I were metal instead of flesh?
Q: Yes.
A: Next question?

Conversation 3
Q: What does the letter M look like when turned upside down?
A: Is that sign a letter?
Q: It's an M.
A: W.
Q: What comes next after A1, B2, C3?
A: D4.
Q: Reverse the digits in the number 41.
A: 14.
Q: Please imitate my typing style.
A: In caps?

Not surprisingly, there have been objections to the Turing test. Possibly the strongest objection is that the test presupposes that the machine will think in the same way that we do and should also communicate in the same language as we do. It is quite conceivable to have machines that can think but in a way that is very different to our way of thinking. Most accept that chimpanzees are thinking animals and yet a chimp could not pass the test because the chimp does not speak our language and a chimp's experience is likely to be very different to ours. Nevertheless, although intelligent thinking machines with method of communication and thoughts different to ours might one day serve us, we will desire an ability to communicate with some machines, and for many tasks the need for a rich form of communication will be paramount. We will desire machines that communicate in our language and communication will require that the machine behave as though it understands what is communicated. Would these machines be genuinely thinking or just simulating thought? So far, machines that have no level of understanding have failed dismally on the Turing test.

23.5   Do we think in a language?

The computer is essentially a symbol manipulator. At the lowest level there are two basic symbols, which conventionally are written as 0 and 1. The symbols 0 and 1 are just convenient denotation for how the symbols are physically realized in the machine, but they could just as well be denoted using A and B or A and Y. The physical representation within the computer of 0 and 1 is a flip-flop. A flip-flop is just like a light switch: in one position the light is off and is denoted by us as 0, and in the other position the light is on and is denoted by a 1. Flip-flops are organized into rows called registers. We use strings of 0s and 1s to denote the state of a register. Any number or letter that we type into the computer is given a unique configuration of flip-flop settings, which can be written as a string of 0s and 1s. For example, the number 7 has the following binary representation:

0000111

and the letter A:

1000001

These representations can vary between different types of computer. Each number or letter occupies a register, which in the above examples are seven bits long. A five-letter word such as 'hello' would require five registers to represent it. All computer programs boil down to storing bit strings in registers, fetching strings from registers, performing operations on these strings, e.g. comparing and shifting bits, and placing new strings into registers as a result of these operations. The computer is a symbol processor.

A symbol system consists of entities called symbols. A symbol can be part of an expression called a symbol structure. Symbol expressions are symbol structures composed of one or more symbols arranged in some pattern. The symbol system contains a number of processes that can operate on symbol structures to form new symbol structures.

The language in which the structures are encoded is taken to be compositional and recursive. Examples of such languages are Prolog or the English language. Familiar compositional and recursive structures to computer technologists are tree data structures. A symbol structure has two fundamental roles of designation and interpretation. Designation means that expressions can refer to something else. For intelligence, the machine must behave with reference to the external world. A symbolic expression designates some object if the machine's behaviour is dependent upon the object (in the external world) which is referenced. This really amounts to the need for the machine to represent the external world. Interpretation basically means that a symbol expression can serve as a program. A symbol structure can therefore be interpreted and a set of computational instructions executed by the machine.

The (strong) symbol system hypothesis in a nutshell states that the computer we know today is capable of reproducing human intelligence, provided that we give the computer the right kind of symbol structures along with the right kind of symbol structure transformation procedures, and the right kind of symbol representations of the external world.

The properties that the symbolic expressions must possess are the same properties that we see in a language like English. If machine intelligence can be embodied in a symbol processor then thinking may be akin to language processing. The language of thought hypothesis (LOTH) states that thinking is done in a mental language. The physical encoding of this language within the human brain can be very different to that which we see in computers, but the mental language would share key properties with languages like English and first-order logic (FOL[1]). To be more specific, the kinds of thoughts philosophers refer to in the LOTH are those known as propositional attitudes; some sentences that reflect propositional attitudes are:

John likes Mary.
Sue hopes that her car will start.
Caroline believes that Tom is a cat.

The mental representations of these attitudes should have a combinatorial syntax and semantics. Complex representations are composed from simpler constituents, and the semantic content of complex representations is a function of the semantics of its constituents. The operations on these

---

[1]FOL may not be expressive enough as a mental language but it still possesses key properties.

representations are causally sensitive to the syntactic structure – for example, the result of $2 - 3$ is different from the result of $3 - 2$.

The arguments in support of the LOTH are various, and we shall mention in brief a few of these. The first argument gets support from cognitive psychology in that the best scientific models of human higher level cognitive processes, such as planning, concept learning and decision making, are computational models defined over symbol representations. The second argument is that thought is **productive**. There appears to be no limit to the number of different thoughts that we can entertain, just as there is no limit to the number of sentences that can be formed in English. But these infinite thoughts must be contained within finite physical capacity, and to do so requires a representational mechanism that has unbounded capacity for entertaining an infinite number of thoughts. A representation that is recursive has such unbounded capacity and languages are typically recursive. The third argument concerns **systematicity**. The idea with the systematicity of thought is that, once you can entertain a thought, you will be able to entertain other related thoughts. For example, if you can entertain the thought that *John loves the girl* you can entertain the thought that *the girl loves John*. Natural languages appear to be systematic. For example, you do not find a speaker who can express that *John loves the girl* but cannot express that *the girl loves John*.

There are many objections to the LOTH often put forward by connectionists. For example, symbol systems are not tolerant to damage or tolerant to noisy input. A connectionist network, on the other hand, can display graceful degradation and noise tolerance. For example, you can train a network to recognize class A and class B from a set of features. After training, you could change some of the weights and the network might still perform reasonably well on the classification task. Some input features could be missing or be different to their true value, but the network can still give a reasonable performance. In symbol systems, the features are either correctly tokened or not. For example, if *John* is used to denote a person known as 'John' then the tokens *Jhn, Jim, J*, etc. will not do. Connectionists see symbol structures as being too rigid.

As you might expect, there have been many arguments in response to the objections expressed by connectionists. It was Fodor (1975) who first proposed the LOTH and it was Fodor in conjunction with Pylyshyn who led the attack on connectionism in 1988. Basically, they responded with a challenge – that connectionists need to answer how productivity and systematicity can be accounted for using connectionist architectures. Furthermore, connectionists could not resort to symbol-type representations using their connectionist machines for this would show that connectionism offered nothing new other than a different implementation of classical AI.

Many connectionists accept that representations should exhibit compositional syntax and semantics and that operations on representations should be sensitive to syntax. What they are not willing to accept is that connectionist architectures, when they exhibit productivity and systematicity, will turn out to be another implementation of classical symbol structures. We should also note that there are important cognitive connectionist models. When Fodor proposed the LOTH in 1975, representations were of the classical symbol variety as connectionism was going through its quiet period. Connectionists have carried out much work targeted at bridging the gap between connectionist and symbolic representations. There have been some interesting demonstrations, such as Chalmers's (1990) connectionist transformation of sentences from active to passive form. The connectionist representation of these sentences is not concatenative as with classical symbol structures and yet the operation of transformation is sensitive to what is represented. There is however still a long way to go. These connectionist experiments have yet to demonstrate that they can generalize in the same systematic way that can be demonstrated with classical symbol representations. For example, it is easy to define the structural symbolic representation and transformation operation that will reliably transform an active sentence to a passive sentence but it is not yet clear how to achieve the same systematic performance using the same types of representation that Chalmers used.

Further reading

The two papers by Sloman (1995) and McCarthy (1996) provide a useful insight into the role of philosophy within AI and the role AI plays within philosophy. A good book to get started on philosophy and AI is Copeland (1993). Grevier (1993) also has some interesting philosophical discussion. Boden (1990) includes a collection of papers that provide an overview of the debate on machine intelligence. A persistent critic of AI is Hubert Dreyfus (1992). Grevier is well worth reading with regard to the criticism by Dreyfus and the AI community's reaction.

There are a number of books on consciousness, two examples being Chalmers (1993) and Dennett (1994). Sloman's (2001) online material is well worth a look. Cognitive psychology also plays a big part in understanding the workings of the mind, and a good place to start is Eysenck and Keane (2000).

For an insight into the language of thought hypothesis and the symbolic versus connectionist debate see Aydede (1999), Fodor and Pylyshyn (1988) and Clark (1993). A collection of papers in Hinton (1991) provides an insight into some of the early work of connectionists in response to criticism that neural networks do not display systematic, productive and structure-sensitive properties. Contributors to this volume include Geoffrey Hinton, David Touretzky, Jordan Pollack, Mark Derthick, Paul Smolensky, Mark St. John and James McClelland. Minsky (1990) discusses symbolism and connectionism. Also see Minsky (1990). Dennett (1994) makes an interesting case for the role of language in intelligence.

For a general paper on the nature of intelligence, see Davis (1996).

CHAPTER 24

Some Applications of Artificial Intelligence

This chapter introduces a few applications of AI technologies. The purpose of this chapter is to show that AI technology is being actively applied to difficult real-world problems. The applications presented are a very small subset of those in existence. No structure is given to the order of application presentation as many of the applications build on a broad range of techniques that have been introduced in this book.

24.1 Spacecraft autonomous control

On 24 October 1998, the spacecraft Deep Space 1 was launched from Cape Canaveral. The purpose of the mission was to test 12 advanced high-risk technologies. The success of the mission led to its extension, and Deep Space 1 finally retired on 18 December 2001. On board Deep Space 1 was a software experiment that represented a big step forward for the future autonomous control of spacecraft. The software was an artificial intelligence system called remote agent (RA) that could plan and control spacecraft activities.

The conventional method of getting a spacecraft to perform a task such as positioning itself to take images of asteroids involves a team of humans on the ground formulating a sequence of control commands that are sent to the spacecraft. The RA can formulate its own plans in response to a high-level goal such as[1] 'During the next week take pictures of the following asteroids and thrust 90% of the time'. The plan specifies a sequence of actions that will satisfy the goal. An action is represented as tasks, and tasks are decomposed into more detailed tasks until finally each task is an instruction that can be executed by the flight software. To function, the RA is equipped with the knowledge behind the rationale of conventional on-board control software and that used by ground controllers. There is knowledge of mission goals, understanding of spacecraft hardware and knowledge of the environment in which the spacecraft will operate.

The advantage of systems like RA is that they enable future missions involving greater uncertainty when exploring new areas in space. For example, if a spacecraft is to land on an active comet where there are flying rocks that could damage the craft, there is a need for quick reaction, which could not be provided from the ground because of the delay in communication.

Controlling a spacecraft involves making complex decisions. The RA software is model based. Models provide general descriptions of the structure and behaviour of the spacecraft being controlled and the environment in which the spacecraft is to operate. Reasoning is performed on these models to provide a solution that is expected to satisfy the goals. The RA consists of three separate technologies: onboard planner/scheduler (PS), smart executive (EXEC), which is a plan execution system, and the mode identification and recovery (MIR) system, which performs model-based fault diagnosis and recovery.

---

[1]Quote from Deep Space 1 Technology Validation Report.

Kennedy Space Center, Florida. Lighting up the launch pad, a Boeing Delta II (7326) rocket propels Deep Space 1 through the morning clouds after lift-off from Launch Complex 17A, Cape Canaveral Air Station. The first flight in NASA's New Millennium Program, the spacecraft is designed to validate 12 new technologies for scientific space missions of the next century, including the ion propulsion engine. Propelled by the gas xenon, the engine is being flight tested for future deep space and Earth-orbiting missions. Other on-board experiments include software that tracks celestial bodies so the spacecraft can make its own navigation decisions without the intervention of ground controllers. Deep Space 1 will complete most of its mission objectives within the first 2 months, but will also do a flyby of a near-Earth asteroid, 1992 KD, in July 1999. (Photograph courtesy of NASA.)

The PS generates a plan that is used to control the spacecraft. The PS starts with an incomplete plan and expands it into a complete plan. The plan must satisfy constraints that either originate from the ground or are contained in the models (e.g. the camera must be pointed at an object to take a picture of it). Constraints are posted to a constraint-based temporal database. Performing a heuristic backtracking search over the database generates a plan.

The EXEC has a number of responsibilities, which include requesting and executing plans from the planner, requesting and executing failure recoveries from MIR and managing system resources. EXEC is a control system that is designed to achieve goals. A goal is defined as a state that the system must be in for a specified length of time (e.g. keep device A on from time X to time Y).

MIR listens to commands sent by EXEC to the spacecraft hardware. MIR gets information about the state of the spacecraft by observing sensors. MIR can reason over models of the spacecraft hardware and behaviour to determine what state the spacecraft will be in given the commands sent by EXEC and the observations from sensors. The current state is reported to EXEC. If a failure occurs, MIR can find a repair to allow the plan to continue.

The PS is the core technology of the command capability provided by RA. The initial incomplete plan contains the spacecraft's initial state and goals. The complete plan consists of a set of synchronized high-level activities that, when executed, will achieve the goals. Each activity needs to be scheduled. Activities can generate subgoals. Subgoals can also be generated in response to resource constraints. For example, if power becomes limited it may be necessary to power down certain scientific instruments so that power is allocated to more mission-critical subsystems. Many planning systems perform action planning and resource scheduling as sequential stages, but PS can tune the order in which decisions are made by considering the consequences of action planning and resource scheduling simultaneously. Time is represented explicitly using metric values stored in a temporal database. The complete plan in comparison with the initial plan contains many more constraints. The PS attempts to make a plan more complete by posting constraints in the database. The definitions of actions give rise to a number of possible plans (a space of plans). These plans are searched to find one that satisfies the constraints and achieves the goals.

24.2 Hierarchical task planning using O-Plan

O-Plan is a planning system developed at Edinburgh University. O-Plan is a knowledge-based planner.

1   The planner uses a hierarchical representation of a plan, and tasks can be expanded into greater levels of detail.
2   There may be different methods for expanding high-level plans into low-level ones, and the planner searches the alternative ways of plan generation. The solutions to different parts of the plan may contain interactions that need detecting and correcting.
3   Networks of nodes represent the different levels of a plan. This form of representation allows knowledge about time and resource constraints to be used to constrain the search for a solution.

Activities and the details of how they may be expanded are represented using schemas. These schemas are encoded using a language called task formalism (TF). TF is a rich language for describing actions, their conditions and effects, different types of resource (consumable, reusable, shareable, etc.), ordering of tasks, time windows, patterns containing constant terms and variables and types of condition.

An example schema called *puton* for stacking objects in the simple 'blocks world' is given in Figure 24.1. Three variables, *x*, *y* and *z*, are introduced. They are all defined as object types, but *x* is also movable. Relationships between variables can also be defined, and in this example the relationships express that all objects are distinct. Conditions and effects are expressed using patterns and have the form:

pattern = value

A pattern can be a constant name beginning with a letter or can consist of any number of these constants within braces '{...}'. A pattern can also contain variables expressed using the form *?x* (e.g. *?colour*). Some example patterns are:

```
always {cleartop table};

types objects = (a b c table),
      movable_objects = (a b c);


schema puton;
  vars ?x = ?{type movable_objects},
       ?y = ?{type objects},
       ?z = ?{type objects};
  vars_relations ?x /= ?y, ?y /= ?z, ?x /= ?z;
  expands {puton ?x ?y};
  only_use_for_effects
                {on ?x ?y}    = true,
                {cleartop ?y} = false,
                    {on ?x ?z}    = false,
                {cleartop ?z} = true;
    conditions          only_use_for_query {on ?x ?z},
                        achieve {cleartop ?x},
                        achieve {cleartop ?y};
end_schema;
```

Figure 24.1 An O-Plan schema *puton* for stacking blocks.

$\{on\ b\ c\} = true$
$\{length\ d\} = 20$
$\{location\ john\} = home$

Conditions describe pattern values that must exist before an action can occur. Effects describe changes in pattern values. In the *puton* schema the conditions are that x and y must both be clear. The effect of the action is that x is on y, y is not clear, x is not on z, and z is clear. Other keywords are also used in defining conditions and effects. A condition type tells the planner how conditions should be met. Condition types include *achieve*, and *only_use_for_query*. *achieve* is a condition that tells the planner that the condition may be satisfied by any means available. For example, the planner may decide to add a new plan structure. The type *only_use_for_query* is normally used to bind variables. Other types exist. For example, the type *compute* means that the condition can be satisfied using an external source such as a user or database. The *only_use_for_effects* statement informs the planner of the primary effects that the schema asserts. A simple *effects* statement indicates side-effects and informs the planner that the schema should not be used to explicitly achieve these effects.

The *expands* pattern in the schema describes the primitive action. The *expands* statement is also used to indicate that a schema expands (adds actions) to another schema.

Two other statements are present in Figure 24.1. The *always* statement defines states that can never be refuted by actions. The *types* statement defines objects and their types.

A planning task is given to the planner using a **task** schema. An example is given below:

```
task stack_ABC;
      nodes
                    1 start,
                    2 finish;
      orderings 1 → 2;
```

conditions
        achieve {on a b} at 2,
        achieve {on b c} at 2;
    effects
        {on c a} at 1,
        {on a table} at 1,
        {on b table} at 1,
        {cleartop c} at 1,
        {cleartop b} at 1;
end_task;

The 'conditions' state what must be achieved in order for the plan to be successful. The 'effects' list the state of the world at the start (node 1). The task expresses a partial plan that consists of two nodes, and the state of the world at these two nodes is given. O-Plan completes the plan by inserting additional nodes containing actions. An example sequence of actions is:

    (puton c table)
    (puton b c)
    (puton a b)

Another example describes the task of getting to work (see Figure 24.2). The 'nodes' expression in the *get_to_work* schema shows how the action can be decomposed. The action is decomposed into a sequence of actions, but within this sequence two actions (*read_paper* and *eat_breakfast*) can take place in parallel. The other schemas describe primitive actions. There are two actions that expand go to work (by *walking* or *catching the bus*). The task is given to the planner using the task schema:

    task get_to_work_via_expansion;
        nodes
            1 start,
            2 finish,
            3 action {get_to_work self};
        orderings 1 → 3, 3 → 2;
        time_windows 8:00 at 1;
    end_task;

A time window expresses that it is 8:00 am at the start. The primitive actions also have time windows that express the duration of an action. An output for the plan is:

8:00:00	Begin	(get_to_work self)
	Begin	(get_dressed)
8:10:00	End	(get_dressed)
	Begin	(read_paper)
	Begin	(eat_breakfast)
8:11:00	End	(read_paper)
8:12:00	End	(eat_breakfast)
	Begin	(go_to_work)
8:27:00	End	(go_to_work)
	End	(go_to_work self)

```
schema get_to_work;
  expands {get_to_work self};
  only_use_for_effects {location self} = work;
  nodes
     sequential
        1 action {get_dressed},
        parallel
           2 action {read_paper},
           3 action {eat_breakfast}
        end_parallel,
        4 action {go_to work}
     end_sequential;
end_schema;

schema get_dressed;
  expands {get_dressed};
  effects {dressed} = true;
  time_windows duration self = 10 minutes;
end_schema;

schema eat_breakfast;
  expands {eat_breakfast};
  effects {breakfast_eaten} = true;
  time_windows duration self = 2 minutes .. 30 minutes;
end_schema;

schema read_paper;
  expands {read_paper};
  effects {paper_read} = true;
  time_windows duration self = 1 minutes .. 30 minutes;
end_schema;

schema walk_to_work;
  expands {go_to work};
  effects {walked} = true;
  time_windows duration self = 15 minutes .. 20 minutes;
end_schema;

;;; Note that taking the bus can be slower than walking,
;;; because we may have to wait for the bus and we might
;;; get caught in traffic.

schema take_bus_to_work;
  expands {go_to work};
  effects {took_bus} = true;
  time_windows duration self = 5 minutes .. 30 minutes;
end_schema;
```

Figure 24.2 An O-Plan task schema for getting to work.

O-Plan has been in development for many years and is a good example of a knowledge-rich planner. O-Plan has been applied to many real-world problems, and some of these are listed below:

- space platform construction
- satellite planning and control
- construction and house building
- software development
- unix administrator's script writing
- logistics
- non-combatant evacuation operations
- crisis response
- air campaign planning workflow.

24.3   Decision support tools that assist with airport operations

There are many decisions to be made in the day-to-day management of a busy airport. Gates have to be allocated to flights, remote parking positions assigned, check-in counters and departure lounges organized, and personnel assigned to tasks such as security and check-in. Plans may be disrupted by events such as delayed flights. Decisions have to be coordinated. For example, when assigning a landing slot to a flight other resources such as a parking position, baggage belts, staff for baggage handling and security must be available. A company called Ascent Technology has developed a product called SmartAirport that is deployed in a number of airports throughout the world.

Ascent Technology was founded in 1986 by Professor Patrick Henry Winston and other members of the AI laboratory at the Massachusetts Institute of Technology (MIT).

24.4   Extraction of text from news stories

Information extraction is an area of NLP research that is beginning to see commercialization. Information extraction is about providing concise summaries of information that appear in news reports or other sources of data such as the Internet. Many organizations depend on business intelligence. For example, information about company mergers and takeovers is relevant for investment decisions. Information extraction does not require full text understanding. Not all of the input text is relevant to the task, and there is no need to extract the goals the writer had in mind when writing the text. Information extraction often involves mapping text to a predefined target representation. The representation is a **template** (or **frame**) with slots that are to be filled by elements of the text. For example, in news stories about terrorist attacks the slots could be:

incident
perpetrator
human target.

Information extraction systems have competed annually in a series of message understanding conferences (MUCs). A collection of texts on a chosen type of topic is supplied, from which the competitors are to extract information. The task In MUC-5 July 1993 (Chinchor and Sundheim, 1993) was to extract information about company joint ventures. One such text was:

Bridgeston Sports Co. said Friday it has set up a joint venture in Taiwan with a local concern and a Japanese trading house to produce golf clubs to be shipped to Japan. The joint venture,

Bridgestone Sports Taiwan Co., capitalized at 20 million new Taiwan dollars, will start production in January 1990 with production of 20 000 iron and 'metal wood' clubs.

One system competing at MUC-5 was FASTUS, developed by SRI International. FASTUS is a slightly permuted acronym for finite state automaton text understanding system. The templates produced by FASTUS are shown in Figure 24.3.

Processing in FASTUS involves a number of stages. Early stages identify syntactic structure using linguistic knowledge. These stages require little modification when FASTUS is presented with a new application domain. Later stages find domain dependent patterns among the linguistic entities identified in earlier stages. There are five stages in all.

Stage 1 identifies complex words. These words can be multiwords such as 'set up', 'trading house' and 'joint venture'. This stage identifies personal names, locations, names of organizations and companies, etc.

The second stage involves the identification of noun groups, verb groups and word classes such as prepositions, conjunctions and relative pronouns. The result of this stage in processing the MUC-5 text given above is shown in Figure 24.4.

Stage 3 recognizes complex noun and verb groups on the basis of domain-independent syntactic information. These include the attachment of measure phrases, as in:

   20 000 iron and metal wood clubs a month

prepositional phrases, as in:

   production of 20 000 iron and metal wood clubs a month,

and noun group conjunction, as in:

   a local concern and a Japanese trading house.

In the process of recognizing basic and complex phrases, domain entities and events are recognized and a structure is constructed. For example, the following structure is built from:

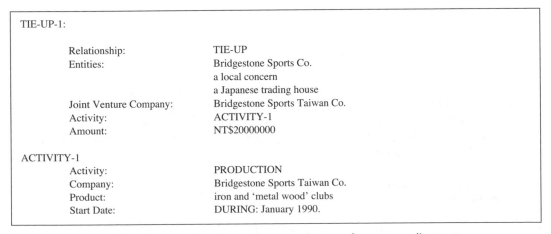

Figure 24.3 Templates produced by FASTUS in extracting text from news clips.

Company Name	Bridgestone Sports Co.
Verb Group	Said
Noun Group	Friday
Noun Group	It
Verb Group	Had set up
Noun Group	A joint venture
Preposition	In
Location	Taiwan
Preposition	With
Noun Group	A local concern
And	A Japanese trading house
Verb Group	To produce
Noun Group	Golf clubs
Verb Group	To be shipped
Preposition	To
Location	Japan

Figure 24.4 Second-stage results from FASTUS processing of a news clipping.

The joint venture, Bridgestone Sports Taiwan Co.

Relationship	TIE-UP
Company	–
Joint venture company	Bridgestone Sports Taiwan Co.
Activity	–
Amount	–

In stage 4, the complex phrases are scanned to identify patterns for domain events. When found, structures are built to encode the information about entities and events contained in the pattern. Complex phrases are presented in the order in which they occur. Any text that is not included in a basic or complex phrase from stage 3 is ignored in stage 4. The patterns are hand coded as finite-state machines. State transitions in these machines are based on complex phrases driven off head words such as *company*, *formed* or *currency*. The domain patterns corresponding to the first sentence in the above example are:

{Company/ies} {Set-up} {Joint-Venture} with {Company/ies} and {Produce} {Product}

The following structures are built:

Relationship	TIE-UP
Entities	Bridgestone Sports Co. A local concern A Japanese trading house
Joint venture company	
Activity	
Amount	

Activity:	PRODUCTION
Company:	
Product:	Golf clubs
Start Date:	

For the second sentence the domain patterns are:

> {Company} {Capitalized} at {Currency} and
> {Company} {Start} {Activity} in/on {Date}

The structures generated are:

Relationship	TIE-UP
Entities	
Joint venture company	Bridgestone Sports Taiwan Co.
Activity	
Amount	NT$20 000 000

Activity	PRODUCTION
Company	Bridgestone Sports Taiwan Co.
Product	
Start Date	DURING: January 1990

The fifth and final stage operates over all sentences. Structures are merged provided they are consistent. Merging the structures for the two sentences yields the structures in Figure 24.3.

FASTUS, along with other technology projects, has led recently to the formation of a company called Discern Communication, a spin-off of SRI. The company provides products that use language understanding to automate the response to customer queries, which can be either typed or spoken. There is a need for this type of technology in customer service centres. When you have a query about a product you have purchased you are usually directed either to a website or to a call centre. Some people find the interface on a website difficult to navigate when attempting to find the content that answers their query. Call centres often route callers to some other person once the nature of a query is established. The customer may be held in a long queue and they may eventually talk to someone who does not have the knowledge to answer the query. Automating the understanding of a customer's query and searching all sources of relevant information to construct an appropriate response is desirable to maintain customer satisfaction.

24.5 Flight information conversational interface

Pegasus is a conversational interface that provides flight information over the telephone. Developed by MIT, Pegasus is currently being tested on actual user calls. A call is recorded so that the data can be used to further develop the system. An example transcript is given in Figure 24.5.

Pegasus can answer questions about flights within the USA on the day of enquiry. Data that Pegasus knows include departure and arrival times for flights that have taken off or landed or for which a flight plan has been filed. The user may not always know the airline or flight number and so Pegasus knows about flight schedules so that it can converse with the user until the flight the user is interested in is identified.

24.6 Face recognition

Recently, there has been a great deal of interest in face recognition software. Most interest is for security in spotting terrorists or criminals. There are, of course, many other potential applications, and some are quite controversial. For example, if a system recognizes you when you walk into a shop, sales staff can be informed of your likes and dislikes and target their sales pitch accordingly. Face recognition software is currently in use in surveillance systems.

Current face recognition systems tend to use a statistically based approach. Commercial products contain proprietary algorithms, but a simplified pattern based approach that yields good results was described by Turk and Pentland (1991). The approach involves the construction of what are termed eigenfaces. The basic approach can be described using a number of steps:

1   Collect M images from a number of people. There will be more than one image for each person showing different poses, variation in expression and lighting.
2   Compute the eigenfaces. This is essentially a principal component analysis (PCA). Suppose that each image is $x \times y$ pixels. A vector for each image of length xy is generated. An average across all image vectors is computed, and this average is subtracted from each of the M ($x \times y$) vectors. Suppose that x and y are both N pixels. A matrix is formed from the averaged vectors. This matrix, call it P, is ($N \times N$) $\times M$. A new matrix, call it L, is generated by taking the product of the transpose of P with P. The matrix L is of size $M \times M$, and entry i, j is the correlation of image i with image j. Eigenvectors of L are computed, and these vectors are sorted in terms of

---

USER: Can you tell me the status of united flight 9?

PEGASUS: United flight 9 from Kennedy is expected in Los Angeles at 11:43 a.m. local time. It is 47 minutes ahead of schedule. What else would you like to know?

USER: Are there any flights from Chicago to Boston arriving around noon?

PEGASUS: There are two flights from Chicago arriving in Boston at 12 o'clock pm local time, United flight 506 scheduled to arrive at 11:53 a.m. and American flight 744 scheduled to arrive at 11:59 a.m. Please select one.

USER: Will the second one be on time?

PEGASUS: American flight 744 from O'Hare landed in Boston at 11:42 a.m. local time, 17 minutes ahead of schedule. Is there something else you'd like to know?

Figure 24.5 An example transcript from PEGASUS.

their associated eigenvalues (eigenvectors with most variance are given preference). Keep K eigenvectors associated with the K largest eigenvalues. K is usually much smaller than $N \times N$. These K vectors are the eigenfaces.

3   Project each image in the database onto the new vector space represented by the K basis vectors. This means that each image is represented by a vector of length K.

4   Take the projections of all images for a person and average these projections to form a representative vector for each person.

Recognition of a new image is done by projecting the new image onto the space spanned by the K vectors and then doing a nearest neighbour match with the stored representations for each person.

The principle behind eigenfaces is that a face can be recognized using a relatively small set of salient features. The features are computed as the eigenvectors.

Much research has been conducted around the eigenface approach. MIT has explored improving the rate of face recognition by coupling eigenfaces with eigenvectors derived from the eyes, nose and mouth. Using this combined approach, it reported a recognition rate of 98% on a test set of 45 individuals.

There are a number of companies offering face recognition technology. One such company is Visionic, which produces a product called Faccit that uses AI technology. Faces can be automatically located from a video frame. Alternatively, a face can be captured manually by clicking on the image. Up to 30 000 images can be searched in less than 3 seconds. The recognition uses local features derived from statistical techniques. Recognition is said to be resistant to changes in lighting, skin tone, eyeglasses, ageing, facial expression and hairstyle. It is also said to be resistant to pose changes (by up to 35°).

24.7   Imaging in medical diagnosis

Tripath Imaging and Cytyc are two companies that produce technology for cancer detection, diagnosis and staging. The technologies include equipment and procedures for the preparation of cervical cytology slides that can then be automatically screened for signs of abnormal cells using intelligent imaging software. Abnormal cells can be hard to spot when hidden among many other normal-looking cells. In large-scale screening programmes such as that to detect early signs of cervical cancer, manual slide analysis becomes very labour intensive. Intelligent image analysis can be used to reduce false negatives (slides classed as normal which in fact contain abnormal cells). Automated imaging is used to alert a human expert about slides that have a high probability of containing abnormal cells. The expert will then make a close examination of these slides.

24.8   Data mining

Organizations such as companies, government agencies and the military have accumulated vast quantities of data over many years. As the methods of data capture grow in efficiency as a result of schemes such as customer loyalty cards, the introduction of the Internet, new sensors on machines, e.g. aircraft, and enhanced surveillance, the volume of data captured has mushroomed. Within these data hide patterns that, if revealed, can provide valuable information that organizations can use to their advantage. For companies, this information assists with decisions that need to be made for achieving goals like finding new customers, retaining good customers and reducing the incidence of fraud. Customer profiling is an example of the type of information that can be extracted and utilized by organizations to good effect. Revenue can be increased if the traits of customers buying a certain product can be identified. Other customers with similar traits who have not bought that product can then be targeted. Also, customer attrition can be reduced if the reasons why a type of customer has left for another company can be identified. Retaining existing customers and acquiring new ones is crucial to the survival of companies in today's highly competitive markets.

The discovery of patterns in large databases is the discipline of data mining. The algorithms used in data mining systems are machine learning algorithms and statistical algorithms. Data mining really describes a process that is used to discover patterns and relationships in data. These patterns can be used to make predictions. Data to be mined often consist of many thousands or millions of cases,[2] and algorithms are designed with this in mind. For example, data may need to be paged in and out of memory from disk storage. There are many software companies that provide data mining products, including big names such as IBM, Microsoft and Oracle. Nearly all the types of machine learning algorithm presented in this book can be found in data mining products. For example, at the time of writing, Microsoft's data mining tool offers two proprietary algorithms, one for learning decision trees and another that performs clustering.

Data mining algorithms are used to discover models of association or predictive models. The association between cases can be examined using clustering techniques that aim to form different groups containing members that are similar in some way. Link analysis is another associative technique for discovering simple relationships such as the likelihood of someone buying a video recorder when buying a television. Predictive models fall into one of three broad categories: classification, regression and time series. Classification algorithms learn to predict the class that a new case belongs to from its characteristic features. For instance, an applicant with high debt and low income might be a bad loan risk. Regression predicts other values using existing values. For instance, the weight of an unborn baby may be predicted by taking measurements of limbs using ultrasound. Time series will predict values at a future point in time based on values already seen. An example is forecasting the value of a stock index from preceding values of the index.

The process of data mining entails a lot more work than simply running statistical or learning algorithms over selected data. The following is a non-exhaustive list of steps that are often required:

1   Data integrity checking and cleaning. Data are not always what they appear to be. Even though data may be electronically stored, they could have been manually entered into a database either in whole or in part. Any form of manual entry can lead to errors. Electronic integrity checking at the point of entry is good practice, but there are many legacy systems that have collected data over many years with few or no integrity checks. Errors can arise from simple typographical mistakes or from more proactive errors, e.g. if convenience data are entered like a random response to the question 'Which option describes where you saw this promotion advertised?'. Often, data will be incomplete, and there can be numerous reasons for this, such as the failure of a machine sensor. Data can sometimes be cleaned to work around inconsistencies or missing values. Substitutes for missing values can sometimes be made, or it may be possible to predict a variable value from other variable values for a case. Simple substitution techniques might be appropriate, e.g. substituting with the mean value of a continuous variable. Often a more robust statistical approach such as expectation maximization is required to replace missing values. It might be that a continuous variable has entries set to zero where a value is missing. Such entries can be misleading when computing statistics, and it might be preferable to substitute null values in place of zeros so that these data items are ignored.

---

[2]Data mining analyses cases. A case is often referred to as a sample or training example. The term 'case', however, has more general meaning. It can refer to a single record in a database table. For example, the record may hold the variable values in a customer's loan application. A case may also be a nested record. For example, the variable 'product purchase' may contain two properties for 'product' and 'quantity'. A customer's purchases could then be described using a single record, but the number of product types bought would be variable (e.g. one customer bought bread and lemonade while another customer bought bread, fish and cereal).

2   Data enrichment. Data are often enriched by adding calculated variables. For example, perform-ance parameters are calculated for gas turbine engines using a small set of sensed parameters, e.g. pressures, temperatures and rotational speeds at different points in an engine. Data may need to be standardized. For example, engine performance parameters are usually corrected to a standard day to cancel effects due to variations in outside temperature and pressure. A good mining attribute for loan applications could be to calculate the ratio of income to fixed monthly expenditure (mortgage plus utility bills plus food plus existing loans, etc.).

3   Data transformation. Data transformation modifies variables for data mining. A common form of transformation is to convert a continuous variable into a discrete variable. This transforma-tion is called discretization. The result of discretization is to place each variable value into one of a number of discrete bins. For example, continuous values in the range 0–10 could be discretized into one of five bins, the first bin for values less that 2, the second for values equal to or greater than 2 but less than 4, etc. There are various techniques for discretization that vary from the construction of equal-sized bins to bins with ranges determined by the distribution of data or cumulative rates of change.

4   Data exploration. In order to build meaningful data mining models,[3] it is necessary to gain an understanding of the data. This understanding is obtained through knowledge of the transaction process used when acquiring the data and through computing descriptive statistics or data visualization. Data exploration is often required before data cleansing so that errors with the data can be spotted. Outliers might need to be removed, or they might represent meaningful patterns, but this can only be decided upon once the data are understood. Some variables may not be relevant to the analysis or they may correlate highly with other variables. Exploration might also suggest that certain cases be left out of the data mining. Perhaps these cases are too different because they were acquired under unique or rare conditions/circumstances.

5   Case set preparation for training. The variables and cases used for training need to be selected. For a prediction model, input and predictable variables are selected. The data mining algorithm attempts to use the input variables (also known as independent or predictor variables) to predict the predicted variable(s) (also known as dependent variables). The choice of input variables is influenced by knowledge of the data (i.e. select those believed to be good predictors). The goal of data mining determines the choice of predictor variable(s). For instance, the cost of a weekly grocery shop is likely to be influenced by family income and family size, but geographical loca-tion may have no influence other than as a secondary factor if it correlates with an attribute such as income. Some algorithms, e.g. clustering, accept only input variables. Preparing the case set for data mining also needs careful consideration. The more data that algorithms are fed, the longer they take to learn. In general, you will need to select a subset of data by careful sampling. Once again, understanding the data is invaluable. Outliers in the data might contain important information, but they might also mislead model construction. For instance, two variables that are highly correlated could be seen as uncorrelated because of a small number of outliers.

6   Data mining model construction. Model construction is an iterative process. The output from a model can lead to a better understanding of the data, and this understanding may suggest ways in which the model could be adapted and improved. The type of algorithm to be used is determined in part by the type of model to be constructed. A classifier could be constructed using a decision tree or neural network, for example. The type of algorithm may dictate data preparation. For instance, some tree induction algorithms will only work with discrete or categorical data. Different case sets used for training typically yield different models. If the

---

[3]A data mining model refers to the pattern structure that is learned. For example, the tree learned by a decision tree induction algorithm is a model. Strictly speaking a model holds other information like details of any data pre-processing and algorithm options.

training case set is well sampled, the difference between the model and another model generated using a different case set will be insignificant. If the training data are poorly sampled or there simply is not enough then a model can be heavily biased. It is important, therefore, to test a model. Testing requires using a case set not used for training. There are techniques that can be employed when the number of cases is limited. You may not have enough cases to form disjoint training and test sets when constructing a predictive model. A technique called **cross-validation** may be appropriate in such situations. The cases are randomly divided into two equal sets. The first set is used for training the model. The model then predicts the outcomes in the second data set, from which an error rate can be calculated. The same is done in reverse by building a model using the second set and calculating an error rate by predicting the outcomes of the first set. These two independent error rates are averaged to give an estimate of the model error. Finally, the model is built using all of the data and its estimate of error is taken to be the average of the two independent error estimates. Cross-validation can be extended by increasing the number of disjoint groups.

7 Data mining model evaluation and validation. Data used for testing a model have been used during training, either directly because of limited data or indirectly through poor results, suggesting that a better model needs to be built. A model can therefore only be validated by testing it in the real world. You cannot judge a model's performance until it has been field tested. Model evaluation may be more complex than computing a simple error rate. Remember that these models are to be used to support decision making, and decisions have costs associated with them. It might be preferable to have a model that is less accurate in a medical screening application if the inaccuracy is due to false positives (the model suggests that a patient has a condition when in fact they do not). Such a model is behaving in a cautious manner, which is preferable when lives are at risk.

Data mining tools are often used alongside other analytical tools such as online analytical processing (OLAP). OLAP organizes data around structures called dimensions. A dimension is basically an attribute that is organized into levels to reflect hierarchical structure. For example, an international retail chain may organize store locations into a hierarchy. At the highest level are the countries where the stores are located, below each country are counties (states) and below the counties are towns. Another dimension might have products organized by categories, e.g. electrical items, groceries and household products, and each of these categories split further into subcategories such as groceries into drinks and foods, from which drinks break down further into alcoholic drinks and non-alcoholic drinks, etc. Dimensions can be organized into other structures called cubes. Aggregate information can then be displayed for analysis. For example, you could drill down into the cube to find the total sales of alcoholic drinks by country, county, town or store. OLAP technology is designed for processing large volumes of data in support of business questions. OLAP and data mining tools complement each other.

There are many vendors who produce data mining tools, but these tools can vary considerably in terms of the support they give the user. Good tools will allow a user to interface to many different data storage formats such as different relational databases. These tools remove from the user the concern as to how data are retrieved for mining. The user simply specifies what data are to be mined, and it is the job of the tool to know how the data are to be retrieved. Learning and statistical algorithms are the crucial components of a data mining tool, but these algorithms make up only a part of a capable data mining tool. The more capable tools keep track of what options were executed in building a data mining model. These options include data selection, variable transformation and selection, learning algorithm used and any specified parameter values for controlling learning.

The prevalence of data mining is such that all major database vendors feel obliged to offer a data mining tool. All forms of organization have a need for data mining. Retail outlets need to retain existing customers, find new customers, target those customers most likely to respond to a marketing campaign and explore different store layouts to maximize sales. Credit card companies need to spot fraudulent transactions. Companies that sell or advertise over the Internet can conduct opportunistic marketing if they can understand a customer's browsing and buying habits. A simple example is seen in sites that sell books when they suggest other books that might be of interest based on previous purchases. Pharmaceutical companies mine databases of genetic material and chemical compounds to aid drug development. Operators of military aircraft need to mine historical data to explore the reliability of components alongside component usage. This information allows better management of assets and identifies component weaknesses that need improvement.

24.9   Getting information from unstructured data

Autonomy, founded in 1996, has risen quickly from a start-up company to a listed company whose performance is tracked closely by many interested parties of investors. Autonomy can list many well-known international companies as customers of its products. Autonomy is in the business of automatically processing and organizing large volumes of unstructured data. The content of data sources such as text documents is automatically categorized, linked and organized. The company was formed by Dr Mike Lynch as a spin-off from another company he founded called Neurodynamics. Much of the core technology used by Autonomy was developed at Neurodynamics, a company specializing in advanced pattern recognition technologies utilizing neural networks and Bayesian techniques.

In the digital age, we are often overwhelmed with huge volumes of data. In these data lies information, but the retrieval of this information is complicated because of its unstructured nature and the fact that it resides in multiple disparate sources, e.g. word-processing documents, emails and web content. If the data can be understood and organized they can then be personalized so that a user can get at information of interest and in a format that is most useful. At the heart of Autonomy's technology is proprietary pattern matching techniques that utilize Bayesian inferencing and information theory.

Statistical pattern matching techniques for document processing have become increasingly popular. One traditional technique for organizing and classifying text utilizes keywords. Documents relevant to a search are retrieved based on keyword content. This is similar to you performing a web search using a Boolean combination of search terms (words). Keywords tend to retrieve irrelevant documents and, at worse, direct the search completely down the wrong path. Keywords on their own are limited because they contain no information on the way keywords have been used and they carry no context. For instance, the word 'bat' has a number of uses in English. If 'bat' appears in a document with 'ball' and 'wicket' then it is likely to be used in a cricket game sense as opposed to a winged mammal sense. The words 'ball' and 'wicket' may not appear in a relevant document, but a word associated with these terms, e.g. 'stump', could. If a system uses context-based searching then a search on the words 'bat AND wicket' has a chance of retrieving the correct document because it is not defeated by wicket not being present: it knows that 'wicket' has an association with 'stump'. Statistical models for matching can also be updated through learning.

24.10 Fraud detection

Fraud costs credit card, telecommunications and utility companies millions of pounds each year. Many other types of business are also affected, the most obvious being banks. A common type of fraud with credit cards is the fraudulent use of a stolen card or card skimming, in which the details of a card are read when the card is out of a customer's sight, such as when a card has been handed over to pay a restaurant bill. A fraudulent card can then be constructed. Profiling a customer's spending habits can sometimes predict a fraudulent transaction at the point of sale. One of the major forms of credit card fraud is application fraud whereby a fraudster applies for a credit card and then submits bogus information on the application form. Companies have to protect themselves against this type of fraud by passing suspicious applications to an underwriting team for manual analysis. If a company is too cautious in its judgement of applicants then it risks the loss of revenue by rejecting genuine applicants. To make the judgement of applications more efficient, and to automate where possible, scoring technologies are used. Scorecards are statistical models that examine variable values of a customer's application and classify the customer as a fraudster or non-fraudster. Scoring technology is also used to classify customers as defaulters and non-defaulters. It can also be used to classify loyals and churners: those customers likely to stay with the company and those customers likely to leave in favour of a competitor.

The traditional approach to scoring is to attach a score to a predetermined list of variable values. For example, 'marital status' may have categorical values {married, single, widowed, divorced, separated}. If a married person is considered to be less risk than a single person, then a value of married gets a higher score. Each variable score is summed, and the summed value must exceed a predetermined threshold for the applicant to be accepted. The problem with traditional scoring is that it does not model interacting variables. A single person in stable employment is probably deserving of a higher score than someone who is married and has had four different jobs in the past 3 years. Linear and logistic regression models offer an improvement over traditional scoring techniques. We know that simple multilayered neural networks can implement regression models, and it is therefore not surprising that neural network technology is being used to detect fraud. Two companies offering this type of technology are HNC[4] and Neural Technologies. These companies offer a suite of proprietary developed products applicable to different industries. Dr Robert Hecht-Nielsen, well known for his work in neural network technologies, was a co-founder of HNC, which started up in 1986.

24.11 Giving machines common-sense

Some 17 years ago, a well-known and respected AI personality, Doug Lenat, started an ambitious project to code common-sense. The project was called Cyc (pronounced 'psych'), which is derived from 'encyclopaedia', because the idea was to construct a knowledge base that would contain the type of knowledge someone would require to understand the facts and information contained in an encyclopaedia. This type of knowledge is common-sense. Common-sense is knowledge made up of many millions of rules that we take for granted as being shared among our fellow beings, for example someone's date of birth stays the same forever, an open container needs to be carried open side up, when people die they stop buying things, and people tend to be more polite on their first date.

As of April 2002, the effort put into Cyc has been estimated at 600 person-years and has resulted in a knowledge base containing some 3 million rules of thumb plus around 300 000 terms or concepts. This knowledge is coded in a form of predicate calculus. For example, the assertion 'Animals sleep at home' is coded using a formalized syntax that represents the explicit meaning that 'if x is an animal and x is the performer of a sleeping event s, then the place where the event s takes place is the home of x'. With a little thought you can soon see that many person-years will be required to enter the many millions, and growing number of, assertions about our world. Lenat expects the number of assertions contained in Cyc's knowledge base to grow rapidly due to a new 'tutoring

---

[4]HNC Software Inc. recently merged with Fair Isaac.

mode' of knowledge entry. Cyc has relied upon logicians to enter assertions, but in the tutoring mode Cyc uses its own knowledge to drive knowledge entry, which allows less skilled people to enter knowledge. Lenat gives the following example:

> You say 'I want to tell you about a new kind of bacteria', and it might say, 'What kind of things does it kill? Is it similar to anything I know about already?'

A small subset of Cyc called OpenCyc has been released to the public. The original release contained about 50 000 assertions and 5000 concepts. The idea with OpenCyc is to migrate everything into the public domain, but it will always lag 24–30 months behind Cyc. Releasing Cyc to the public means that many millions of people can enter knowledge into Cyc. One of the challenges for Lenat and his team is to make sure that no garbage is entered, but Lenat has a strategy in place to counter garbage entry by checking for consistency between new entered assertions and existing knowledge. Also, an OpenCyc committee is to be set up to help vet the knowledge base. Only time will tell how well this approach works.

The progress of Cyc has been watched with close interest by many in the AI community. It has been a project on a huge scale with massive financial backing. It has also had many critics, who believe that there is nothing fundamentally unique to Cyc that will offer any great scientific advance or advance in proportion to the size of the project. But Lenat set about creating Cyc because he and others in AI knew that for machines to posses a broad level of intelligence they would need to posses the millions of facts that only experience teaches us. Lenat's view is that applications need to posses a domain-specific knowledge base and a common-sense knowledge base. Cyc has some way to go before it has the common-sense knowledge that a typical 9-year-old has. Ultimately, financial backers want to see real-world applications emerging from new technology, and this is starting to happen with Cyc. The first commercial product is CycSecure. The military has been one of the first users of CycSecure. Networks of computers have to be made secure from attack. CycSecure can test the vulnerability of networks. CycSecure has knowledge about the network it is designed to test and it is also regularly updated on information about all known ways in which a system can be attacked. Using this knowledge, CycSecure tests network vulnerability by planning attacks. It can simulate attacks from the outside or attacks from a disgruntled employee.

There are many other applications planned for Cyc, e.g. support for search engines and data mining. Lenat also has some futuristic ideas for Cyc. He would like to see Cyc become an integral part of our everyday life. It could then learn about us and act as a personal assistant. It may eventually learn to predict what you are about to do – a glance towards your watch might suggest to Cyc that you want to know the time. The challenge here is to make applications truly personalized – there is often a fine line between these sorts of application being helpful and annoying. There must be real potential, however, in the near future for applications that assist people who have disabilities.

24.12 Managing aircraft health

Smiths Aerospace is a world leader in technology for monitoring the health of aircraft systems. A typical application involves monitoring the health of helicopters used in North Sea oil operations. The North Sea is a harsh operational environment, and safety is paramount. Crew and passengers receive survival training should an aircraft need to ditch in the sea, but the risks associated with ditching mean that great effort is made to reduce the likelihood of a mechanical defect causing such an event. This type of aircraft operation can never be without risk, but operators know that they have a responsibility to make operations as safe as possible. These helicopters carry on board Health and Usage Monitoring Systems (HUMS). Vibration sensors are mounted to monitor vibration patterns of gears and bearings in the helicopter transmission (the mechanical means of driving the rotors from the engines). Years of research have produced pattern indicators that can detect mechanical defects.

The F22 Raptor is a revolutionary performance fighter that uses stealth technology so that it is virtually invisible to radar (Air Force photo).

These indicators are computed from the signals captured by the sensors. At the end of a flight, the captured data are downloaded to a ground station for analysis. The time history for a helicopter is derived from a number of flights, and changes in signal patterns over time can indicate faults. Expertise is required to interpret these patterns.

HUMS have been around for a number of years now, but the number of applications is growing, and military helicopters in the UK are being fitted with this form of health monitoring. There is also great interest in fitting health monitoring technology to fighter aircraft. The new Joint Strike Fighter (JSF) is a good example of how things are to change in the future. This aircraft will be fitted with traditional sensors and also new types of sensor. One new type of sensor is an electrostatic sensor developed by Smiths Aerospace. There are two types of sensor: a sensor that sits on the engine inlet and a sensor that sits in the engine exhaust. The signals from these sensors are analysed to detect patterns of electrical charge that are associated with wear debris or material ingestion. The data from the electrostatic sensors will be fused with data from other sensor types to provide a picture of engine health. Sensor technology needs to be complemented with comprehensive data management facilities. These facilities are also needed for existing aircraft. Aircraft these days have a long service life, and during this life there will be technology updates to systems. Smiths Aerospace, in conjunction with the US Air Force Research Laboratory, has funded research through a programme called the Probabilistic Diagnostic and Prognostic System (ProDAPS). ProDAPS is a suite of software components utilizing AI technology. The primary role of ProDAPS is to fuse sensor data to analyse health and to give a prognosis so that assets[4] can be managed in an optimal way. It has reasoning components for diagnosis and prognosis, decision support components to assist with asset management, and data mining components so that its knowledge can be updated and added to.

A number of reasoning methods are required for aircraft applications. A core component of ProDAPS is Bayesian inferencing. This component can operate in a ground station and can also be embedded onto a card for in flight reasoning. One target application of ProDAPS is the health

---

[4]Assets here means aircraft or engines and associated systems.

Edwards Air Force Base, California (AFIE). The Global Hawk unmanned aerial vehicle banks to land after a 24-hour training mission from Edwards to Alaska. Global Hawk is a long-endurance, high-altitude unmanned aerial vehicle intended for multiple battlefield applications. Capable of surveying an area the size of the state of Illinois, or 40 000 square miles, in just 24 hours, Global Hawk can range as far as 13 500 nautical miles at altitudes approaching 65 000 feet (US Air Force photo by George Rohlmaller).

management of fighter engines. The principle of how a gas turbine engine works is simple, but its operation in a real-world environment is complicated. A fighter engine can be cycled rapidly through many extreme states to provide the thrust changes required during combat manoeuvres. The engine has a logic controller to make sure that the engine stays within safe operational limits. Monitoring how an engine has been operated is important for predicting the state of engine health. Capturing event information such as an engine stall is also important. An engine stalls as a result of a disturbance of airflow, and the chance of a stall can be increased during certain types of combat manoeuvre. The engine controller is designed to prevent stall, but, as with any machine, it is not possible to factor all eventualities into a design. An engine can also stall because of a mechanical defect. Events like stall are important to monitor because they affect engine health. New fighters will be fitted with new types of sensor, but existing aircraft are fitted with sensors to monitor performance and provide inputs to control the engine. By monitoring these parameters, the engine logic can capture when a range of events such as stall occur.

Data captured during flight provide only part of the diagnostic picture. For example, a stall can happen for a number of reasons, and it is useful to be able to categorize the type of stall. Other diagnostic information also becomes available on the ground. Inspections of the engine can reveal problems, analysis of oil can detect wear debris and a change in engine performance over time can reveal deteriorating health. When the aircraft is back on the ground, data are downloaded to a ground-based computer. These data will contain any event information, regime information (what the aircraft was doing) and a range of parameters acquired from engine sensors. Knowledge of the engine is used to reason about these various data sources and output health information. This is one role that ProDAPS is designed to fill. Causal networks (Bayesian networks) can be used to represent this knowledge. Knowledge is gained from operational experience. Knowledge is also acquired from the engine manufacturer. Manufacturers perform what is known as a failure mode and effects analysis. They use experience and different sources of data (e.g. from tests, and physical models) to state for each engine component what the likelihood of failure is and, if the component fails, in what way can it fail and what will be the effects of this failure. This form of analysis can yield thousands of propositions. Fast inferencing can be performed with networks containing hundreds of nodes, but for ease of management the knowledge is represented in a collection of subnetworks. The reasoner also needs temporal knowledge about health conditions. As a fault develops, symptoms can change over time. There can also be delays between a damaging event and observable symptoms. A simple example is foreign object damage (FOD) caused when a piece of material is sucked into the engine. Electrostatic sensors can reliably detect FOD. But the consequence of ingesting material can be wide ranging. Innocuous-looking material (e.g. a paper bag) can sometimes cause great damage while harmful-looking material such as a steel nut may pass through the engine without causing any observable harm. In a damaging scenario, blades in the compressor and turbine can be shredded. The effects of less severe damage are not always immediate. Some flights later there could be increased activity picked up by vibration sensors, and this activity could be due to previously unseen damage propagating to a level of severity that is now observable.

Decision support is another ProDAPS tool. Systems like ProDAPS are designed to maximize available information for decision making. ProDAPS is designed to assist with determining which decisions are optimal. For example, a decision for maintenance action can be influenced by many factors. These factors include the cost of maintenance, the risk to missions if maintenance is not carried out, opportunistic maintenance, the availability of matching engine modules, potential reduction in engine life if maintenance is not performed, etc. An element of the decision support tool is a software component for decision networks (influence networks). Costs are assessed for each aspect of a decision, and these costs are then used in conjunction with probabilistic propositions and simulated scenarios to assess decision outcomes.

The ProDAPS data mining tool is designed to bring multiple sources of data together for mining. Data sources include downloads from the aircraft, data manually entered during maintenance procedures, data from aircrew debriefs, data from engine tests, and data pertaining to engine component upgrades. The ultimate aim of health management is to predict when a condition will occur that needs action.[5] The ability to make a prognosis provides the opportunity for improved management. Much prognostic knowledge can be gained from only in-service experience, and one role of data mining is to assist in the acquisition of this knowledge. The nature of in-service problems changes during the life of an engine model. Parts on the engine are upgraded, and the types of fault that occur can change during the engine's life cycle. Faults also come and go depending on how the aircraft is operated. This changing nature means that knowledge has to be updated, and this is another role for data mining. For example, statistical distributions have to be periodically assessed for updating causal networks. Data mining also plays a more general role in extracting information that feeds up to decision support. An example of the sort of information required is the reliability of engine components against their utilization.

Systems like ProDAPS are the way of the future in aircraft health monitoring. Existing systems like HUMS will be upgraded with more intelligent information processing. The boundaries of this technology will also be pushed in the coming years as more unmanned aircraft are used in military operations.

24.13 The growing role of Bayesian inferencing

Many real-world applications utilize some form of Bayesian inferencing. We have already men-

---

[5]This is called prognosis.

tioned two in this chapter. The application of Bayesian networks has grown considerably in the last decade. Two companies specializing in this technology are HUGIN (founded by Finn Jensen) and Norsys. Microsoft has also been active in this field of research. One application Microsoft has been interested in is the diagnosis of computer network faults.

The first commercial deployment of Bayesian models by Microsoft was in Clippy, the animated paper clip assistant. Clippy has been derided as annoyingly intrusive, but Microsoft claims to have learned a great deal from this first venture into intelligent personal assistants. Future assistants need to be much more sensitive to context, and they need to understand a user's goals and preferences. Assistants like Clippy make too many assumptions as to a user's needs, and interventions and suggestions can often be misguided. Microsoft is working on smart applications that can analyse a user's e-mails, phone calls, news clips and web pages and assign every item a priority based on a user's observed behaviour and preferences. For example, if an application can understand the content of a text message, and knows the sender–recipient relationship from inspecting an organizational chart, and knows the recipient's diary, then it can begin to make a sensible guess at assigning a message priority. Bayesian inferencing is used to assess the likelihood of a software decision satisfying a user's desires.

24.14 Robotics

Robots have a large number of applications in industry, entertainment, exploration, and even the home. In 2000, the UN estimated that 742 500 industrial robots were in use throughout the world. Most of these robots probably could not claim to have any level of intelligence. It is not surprising, though, that there is huge incentive to put intelligence into these machines. NASA is exploring many applications of robots. These include surveillance work and construction tasks on Mars. Construction tasks require multiple robots to cooperate (for example, to carry heavy loads). These machines require some level of intelligence, and research into suitable AI architectures is under way. Rodney Brooks, Director of the MIT AI laboratory, is co-founder of iRobot. This company carries out research and development for the US government and it is also active in constructing robots for industrial applications and entertainment. New robotic entertainers are appearing all the time. A well-known example is Sony's AIBO, the mechanical dog that can recognize its owner's voice, respond to commands and learn. An impressive demonstration of a human form of robot is Honda's ASIMO (featured on the front of this book). ASIMO walks, waves and can climb stairs. It is leased out for events. One large corporation is reported to use ASIMO for greeting visitors and leading the way to the conference room. On 14 February 2000, ASIMO rang the opening bell on the New York Stock Exchange. Honda is working towards getting ASIMO to perform more human interaction. One area of development is to give ASIMO some image recognition capability. Sony has also developed a 58 cm-high biped robot called SDR-4X that can walk. It can navigate around an obstacle using stereo vision, can learn to recognize faces, and has continuous speech recognition.

Further reading

A description of the experiments onboard DS1 is contained in the validation report by Bernard *et al.* (this report is available from the website listed under Bernard *et al.* in the references). Further information on O-Plan can be found in Currie and Tate (1991) and the *O-Plan User Guide* (listed under O-Plan in the bibliography). FASTUS is described in Hobbs *et al.* (1992a,b). There is a website for PEGASUS (see references under PEGASUS). For further information on Cyc see references under Cyc for the website.

A Quick Tour of Prolog

Prolog is a language that is based on first-order logic. It is not a pure logic language because it has procedural elements for carrying out functions such as reading and writing to files. Some Prolog implementations also have significant additional support, e.g. procedures for programming graphical–user interfaces.

Prolog has been applied to many areas of AI, including the construction of expert systems, natural language processing and deductive databases. This chapter provides a short overview of some key Prolog elements. The syntax of Prolog is used in a few places throughout the book. In particular, Chapter 4 introduces Prolog and its method of inferencing. This material is not repeated here, but the reader is advised that it would be useful to have an appreciation of Chapters 2 and 4 before reading this chapter.

The Prolog environment

When you open a Prolog editor you are presented with the following prompt

    ?-

This prompt is waiting for you to enter a query. The query could be an arithmetic question like 'is 2 less than 3?' which is entered as follows

    ?- 2 < 3.

The query is terminated with a full stop. Prolog responds with 'yes' to this query because the evaluation is true. Usually, queries of interest will be about a specific program that has been loaded into the Prolog environment. A pure Prolog program consists of facts and rules. A fact is expressed using predicate notation. For example:

    mother(barbara, caroline).

states that Barbara is the mother of Caroline. Given this fact, the following queries can be asked:

    ?- mother(barbara, caroline).   % is Barbara the mother of Caroline?
            yes
    ?- mother(barbara, X).   % who is Barbara the mother of?
            X = caroline
    ?- mother(X, caroline).   % who is the mother of Caroline?
            X = barbara

There are a few points to note with these questions. The user needs to know the predicate notation being used in the program so that Prolog can correctly match the facts and rules with the question being asked. So the strings denoting predicate names and objects must be syntactically correct. Also, the order of arguments is important. For instance, the mother predicate presented above is used in the sense that the first argument denotes the mother and the second argument the child of that mother. The term X is a variable and it will match with other terms according to the unification rules introduced in Chapter 4. The per cent symbol (%) is used to denote that a comment follows – comments are ignored by the Prolog interpreter/compiler.

Prolog programs are usually written as text files then loaded into the environment. The facts and rules contained in the program are then entered into Prolog's database. Another way of placing a fact or rule into the database is to use the **assert** statement. An assert allows an entry to be placed into the database either dynamically when a program executes (i.e. as part of a rule) or manually during an interactive session with the Prolog editor. For example:

    ?- assert(mother(barbara, caroline)).
    ?- assert(mother(barbara, steven)).

places the two facts:

    mother(barbara, caroline) and mother(barbara, steven)

into the database. The question 'Who is Barbara the mother of?' responds with:

    ?- mother(barbara, X).
    X = caroline ;
    X = steven

After the first answer (Caroline) Prolog pauses (it does not go straight back to the prompt ?-). The pause indicates that there might be an alternative answer to the question. If the user responds with a semicolon (;) the alternative 'steven' is produced. The symbol ';' is logical OR in Prolog. By entering ';' the user is requesting that Prolog backtrack and find an alternative answer. The order in which answers are produced by Prolog is determined by the order in which facts are stored in the database.

Prolog operates with the **closed-world assumption**, which means that it responds with 'no' (false) about anything it cannot prove. In other words, Prolog will respond with 'no' to anything it does not know about. So, if Barbara is the mother of David, Prolog would respond with 'no' to the query

    ?- mother(barbara, david).

if the fact mother(barbara, david) is not contained in the database.

A small program

The following is a small Prolog program that was introduced in first-order logic notation in Chapter 4, Example 7. A variable used in the specification of a Prolog clause is assumed to be universally quantified.

```
friend(graham, tony).
friend(graham, duncan).
likes(X, wine) :- friend(graham, X).
drinks(X, alcohol) :- likes(X, wine).
```

The program contains two facts and two rules. The two facts denote friends of Graham. The first rule states that someone likes wine if they are a friend of Graham, and the second rule states that someone drinks alcohol if they like wine. The symbol ':-' stands for IF and is used to construct rules. The rule contains a single predicate term to the left of ':-', and this term is called the head of the rule. The body of the rule is written on the right-hand side of ':-'. The body will contain one or more terms. The above program can be used to show that both Tony and Duncan like wine and that they both drink alcohol. So you could ask the question, 'Who drinks alcohol?'

```
?- drinks(X, alcohol).
```

Thus far, we have kept to using the variable X, but any variable name would do – in this case it might be better to use:

```
?- drinks(Person, alcohol)
```

since it is more readable and conveys more meaning (because a person drinks alcohol).

Prolog answers queries by unification and doing depth-first search. This process was explained in Chapter 4, and therefore only a brief explanation is given below. When asked for who drinks alcohol, Prolog searches the facts and rules as they appear in its database. So, given the query:

```
?- drinks(X, alcohol)
```

Prolog attempts to find a clause that can match the query. The clause must contain the predicate name 'drinks' and the same number of arguments (two). The variable X is currently unbound and can match a variable or a constant; the second argument 'alcohol' is a constant and so for a clause (fact or rule) in the database to match it must have either this constant or a variable as its second argument. The only clause that can be matched is the rule:

```
drinks(X, alcohol) :- likes(X, wine).
```

To satisfy this rule (prove it), all terms on the right-hand side must be satisfied. So Prolog now needs to prove that someone likes wine. The only clause matching:

```
likes(X, wine)
```

is the rule:

```
likes(X, wine) :- friend(graham, X).
```

and to satisfy this rule Prolog needs to find a friend of Graham. The first fact records that 'tony' is a friend of Graham. In other words:

```
friend(graham, X)
```

matches with:

>   friend(graham, tony)

with X=tony (X is bound to tony). Prolog can now assert that:

>   likes(tony, wine)

and in turn assert:

>   drinks(tony, alcohol).

A trace of this reasoning is given in Figure A.1. During reasoning, Prolog notes that there is a second way of satisfying 'friend(graham, X)' by binding X to 'duncan'. Because there is an alternative way to satisfy 'friend(graham, X)', Prolog places a pointer against friend(graham, X). This pointer is used to denote a backup point so that Prolog knows it can return to this location and try an alternative line of reasoning should it need to.

   Note that multiple terms in a rule body are joined using conjunction (AND). It is not necessary to use OR as multiple rules can be used. For example:

>   a :- b OR c.

can be written as:

>   a :- b.
>   a :- c.

Syntax

Prolog programs are constructed from **terms**. Terms are the basic building blocks for constructing

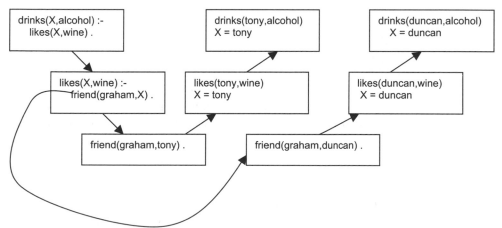

Marker placed by the friend clause to denote that there is a second way to satisfy friend(graham, X) and Prolog can use this marker as a backup point.

Figure A.1 A trace of reasoning 'who likes alcohol'.

clauses and commands. A term is a constant, a variable or a structure. A term is written as a sequence of characters. A character can be an uppercase letter (A, …, Z), a lowercase letter (a, …, z), a digit (0, 1, …, 9) or a symbol (+ − * / \ ^ < > = ' : . ? @ # $ &).

Constants name specific objects (an integer is also a constant) or specific relationships. Examples of constants are:

likes   drinks   graham   duncan

Constants that are not integers are referred to as atoms. There are three types of atom. An **alpha-numeric atom** consists of a lowercase letter followed by a sequence of zero or more alphabetic characters (lower- and uppercase letters), digits, or underscore '_'. For example:

foo123   middle_class

Symbolic atoms consist of a sequence of symbolic characters. The reserved symbols used by Prolog, e.g. '?-' and ':-', are symbolic atoms. A **quoted atom** is any sequence of characters inside single quotes. Examples include:

'hello world' '123'

A variable name is a sequence of alphanumeric characters starting with an uppercase letter or underscore (_). An underscore that appears on its own is an **anonymous variable**.

Comments are any sequence of characters following the symbol '%'. Comments are ignored and simply allow a programmer to record notes about the program.

A **structured data item**, also called a **compound term**, consists of a **functor** followed by one or more arguments enclosed in parenthesis. Each argument is separated by a comma. The general form is:

functor(arg1, arg2, …, argn).

The **arity** of a functor refers to the number of arguments it has. The following are examples of compound terms:

likes(steven, david)
>(2, 3)   % the functor is >

Note that the functor '>' is a mathematical operator. **Operators** are functors for carrying out mathematical operations – their symbols are more familiar to us. There is flexibility in the way that operators can be written. An operator can appear before its arguments (known as prefix notation), as in:

+(2, 3)

or between arguments (known as infix notation), as in:

2+ 3

A programmer can specify new operators. For example, we could express that Paul is tall as:

is_tall(paul)

Or we could define 'is_tall' as a post-fix operator using the syntax:

:- op(600, xf, is_tall).

so that we can write:

paul is_tall

The first argument of 'op', 600, specifies the operator precedence. The second argument, 'xf', is a reserved notation stating that the operator denoted by 'f' is to appear after the argument denoted by 'x'. Every operator has a precedence which is an integer value between 1 and 1200. The lower the precedence the more strongly an operator binds to its arguments. For example:

2 + 3 * 6

is equivalent to:

+(2, *(3, 6)).

because the multiply '*' binds more strongly than addition '+'. In other words, '*' is applied before '+'. The general syntax for defining operators is:

op(Precedence, Type, Name)

where *Type* is one of the following:

fx	non-associative prefix operator
fy	right associative prefix operator
xf	non-associative postfix operator
yf	left associative postfix operator
xfx	non-associative infix operator
xfy	right associative infix operator
yfx	left associative infix operator

Clauses are the structural elements of a program. There are two types of clause, facts and rules. A fact is of the form:

head.

where head is the head of the clause. A head may be an atom or compound term whose functor is any atom except ':-'. A fact is terminated by a full stop. A rule is of the form:

head :- $t_1, t_2, \ldots, t_n$.

Each t_i is a **goal** (or known as a call term). A goal is an atom, a compound term or a variable name.

Recursion

Recursion is a powerful programming construct, and it is fundamental to building Prolog programs. Consider the following clauses that express one city being to the north of another city:

```
north(aberdeen, edinburgh).
north(edinburgh, manchester).
north(manchester, birmingham).
north(birmingham, cambridge).
north(cambridge, brighton).
```

Given these clauses we can ask:

```
?- north(edinburgh, manchester) % is Edinburgh north of Manchester
```

and get a correct response of 'yes'. But given the query:

```
?- north(edinburgh, birmingham). % is Edinburgh north of Birmingham
```

the answer given by Prolog is 'no' because Prolog can respond positively only to either what it is told explicitly as a fact or to a conclusion that it can infer. We can see from the clauses that Edinburgh is north of Birmingham because the relationship 'north of' is transitive. We can express this knowledge we possess (for how to work out if a city is north of another city) to Prolog using the two rules:

```
northOf(X, Y) :- north(X, Y).
northOf(X, Y) :- north(X, Z), northOf(Z, Y).
```

The second rule is recursive because the body uses the predicate northOf in its definition of northOf.

The principle of recursion is to represent a boundary condition (or terminating rule) and rules that decompose the problem into simpler versions of itself. So the first rule of northOf is a boundary condition: it states that a city X is north of a city Y if it is known as a fact that X is to the north of Y. The second rule decomposes the problem into:

city X is to the north of city Y if city X is to north of another city called Z and Z is to north of Y.

Some more examples of recursion will be presented in what follows.

Arithmetic

The operator **is** is used to force arithmetic evaluation. So, to assign the sum of $2 + 3$ to X, the following syntax is used:

```
?- X is 2 + 3.
```

The answer given is:

$$X = 5$$

There are a number of arithmetic operators built into Prolog, and these are listed below.

+	addition
−	subtraction
*	multiplication
/	division
mod	modulo, e.g. X mod Y is the remainder after integer division of X by Y

A Prolog compiler will usually support many more built in functions. Comparison operators include:

$X < Y$	is X less than Y
$X =:= Y$	are the values of X and Y equal
$X =< Y$	is X less than or equal to Y
$X =\textbackslash= Y$	are X and Y not equal
$X > Y$	is X greater than Y
$X >= Y$	is X greater than or equal to Y

We introduced recursion earlier. Some mathematical functions are naturally expressed using recursion. For example, the factorial of a number is recursive. The factorial of 4 is:

$$4 \times 3 \times 2 \times 1 = 24$$

A Prolog implementation of the factorial function is:

```
factorial(0, 1).
factorial(N, Res) :- N1 is N − 1, factorial(N1, Res1), Res is Res1 * N.
```

Let us look at little closer at how this program works. The first rule provides a boundary condition which expresses that the factorial of 0 is 1. This boundary rule terminates the recursion. If asked for the factorial of 3:

```
?- factorial(3, Res).
```

then the first clause does not match (because 3 does not match with 0). The second clause matches with N^1 bound to 3 and Res^1 bound to Res. The superscripts denote the variables on each call: internally Prolog generates new variables every time a clause is called. The execution follows as below:

factorial(3, Res).

factorial($N^1/3$, Res^1/Res) :-
$N1^1$ is 3 − 1,
factorial(2, $Res1^1$),
Res^1 is $Res1^1$ * 3.

factorial(2, $Res1^1$)

factorial($N^2/2$, $Res1^1$) :-
$N1^2$ is 2 − 1,

	factorial$(1, Res1^2)$, $Res1^1$ is $Res1^2 * 2$.
factorial$(1, Res1^2)$	factorial$(N^3/1 , Res1^2)$:- $N1^3$ is $1 – 1$, factorial$(0, Res1^3)$, $Res1^2$ is $Res1^3 * 1$.
factorial$(0, Res1^3)$ recursion has reached boundary condition	factorial$(0, 1)$ $Res1^3/1$
$Res1^3/1$	factorial$(N^3/1 , Res1^2)$:- $N1^3$ is $1 – 1$, factorial$(0, Res1^3/1)$, $Res1^2$ is $1 * 1$.
$Res1^2/1$	factorial$(N^2/2 , Res1^1)$:- $N1^2$ is $2 – 1$, factorial$(1, Res1^2/1)$, $Res1^1$ is $1 * 2$.
$Res1^1/2$	factorial$(N^1/3 , Res^1/Res)$:- $N1^1$ is $3 – 1$, factorial$(2, Res1^1/2)$, Res^1 is $2 * 3$.
$Res^1/6$	$Res=6$

Lists

A list is a fundamental type of structure that is useful for many programming tasks. Other structures, such as stacks, queues and sets, can be implemented using lists. A list is a sequence of terms written in the form:

$$[t_1, t_2, ..., t_n]$$

Each term t_i can be any type of Prolog term. The empty list is denoted by:

[ ]

Examples of lists include:

[a, b, c, d, e]
[[the, dog], barked]

A notation is used in Prolog to identify the head and tail of a list. The head of a list is the first element on the list, and many tasks require the head to be split from the tail. The tail is the list left after the head is removed. The head and tail of a list is extracted using the following syntax:

[Head|Tail]

If we asserted a list as:

?- assert(list1([a, b, c, d])).

then queried:

?- list1([Head|Tail]).

the answer would be Head=a, Tail=[b, c, d]. Note that 'list1' is not really defining a list called 'list1', it is simply denoting a clause whose argument (the list) we are matching with [Head|Tail].
   Some more matches can be tested as follows:

```
?- [Head|Tail]=[3+2, 4+5].
Head=3+ 2,
Tail=[4+5]
?- [Head|Tail]=[a].
Head=a,
Tail=[]
?- [Head|Tail]=[[the, dog], found, [a, bone]].
Head=[the, dog],
Tail=[found, [a, bone]]
```

A search to see whether an element is a member of a list is extremely useful. A membership clause can be defined as follows:

```
member(X, [X|_]).
member(X, [Y|Z]) :- member(X, Z).
```

The two clauses express that if the element being looked for is in the list then it is either at the head of the list (the first clause) or it is in the tail (the second clause). So if we queried:

?- member(1, [1, 2, 3]).

the first clause would match and the answer would be 'yes'. The match is:

(1, [1, 2, 3])=(X, [X|_)

which succeeds because 1 is the first argument and gets bound to X, and the head of the list ([1, 2, 3]) is 1, which matches the value bound to X. This might be easier to see if the first clause were written as:

member(X, [Y|_]) :- X=Y.

Note that the anonymous variable '_' is used in the first clause because there is no need to refer to the tail.
   The following query:

>   ?- member(3, [1, 2, 3]).

cannot succeed on the first clause (because 1 does not match with 3). The second clause is applied and X is bound to 3 and Z to [2, 3]. The membership is now called as:

>   member(3, [2, 3])

Once again, the first clause fails to match, and when the second clause is applied again the membership gets called as:

>   member(3, [3])

and the first clause now succeeds.

If an element being searched for does not appear on the list, the body of the second clause will eventually call:

>   member(X, [ ])

for which there is no matching clause and so the test for membership fails.

An ability to append one list onto another is also a useful function that can be defined as:

>   append([ ], L, L).
>   append([X | L1], L2, [X | L3]) :- append(L1, L2, L3).

So,

>   ?- append([a, b, c], [d, e], X).
>   X = [a, b, c, d, e]

A list is a convenient structure for implementing abstract data types such as stacks, sets and queues. The following three clauses implement the push and pop for a stack and checks for an empty stack. Note that pop is defined in terms of push – there is no need for the pop clause but it can help to make a program more readable. The element being pushed or popped is X, and L is the stack.

>   stack_push(X, L, [X|L]).
>   stack_pop(X, L) :- stack_push(X, _, L).
>   stack_empty([]).

Using recursion and lists to search

The 'edge' clauses in the code below describe a tree: an edge is a connection between one node and another, and the connection is directed from the node that occupies the first argument to the node that occupies the second argument. For example, 'c' is a child of 'a'. The goal node for the tree is 'h', and is represented by the 'goal' clause. The first rule for the search 'depthFirst1' is a boundary condition and terminates the search once the goal node is reached. The path is returned in the argument 'Sol':

```
edge(a, c).
edge(a, b).
edge(c, d).
edge(c, e).
edge(d, f).
edge(d, g).
edge(d, h).
goal(h).
depthFirst1(N, [N]) :- goal(N).
depthFirst1(N, [N | Sol]) :- edge(N, N1), depthFirst1(N1, Sol).
```

The above search will not cope with a graph structure that contains loops (cycles) between two nodes. To prevent repeated looping, a modified version of the search is required to check if a node has already been visited. The modified search keeps a list of already visited nodes, and if a node appears on the list the path leading to that node is not repeated.

```
depthFirst2(N, T, [N|T]) :- goal(N).
depthFirst2(N, T, Sol) :- edge(N, N1), not member(N1, T),
depthFirst2(N1, [N|T], Sol).
```

depthFirst1 is called using depthFirst1(a, L): a is the root and L returns the path. depthFirst2 is called using depthFirst2(a, [ ], L).

Controlling program execution

Use of cut

Normally a Prolog program searches for a solution, backtracking on failure, and terminates when the first solution has been found. There are a number of predicates that allow the search behaviour to be modified.

Backtracking can be controlled by the **cut** predicate which is denoted by an exclamation (!). So in the following program:

```
a :- b, !, c.
a :- d.
```

the cut will not allow backtracking into 'b' should the subgoal 'c' fail or a later goal fail. The cut can be thought of as a one-way fence: once the fence is passed over the program cannot return back to the other side. The cut also prevents alternative ways of satisfying the head of the clause in which the cut appears in. For example, the second clause for 'a' in the above program will not be tried because the cut appears in a previous clause with 'a' as the head. Consider the following program:

```
dog(sadie).
dog(lara) :- !.
dog(katie).
```

Normally the query:

```
?- dog(X).
```

would allow the user to keep asking for alternatives (by entering ';') and all three dog names would be produced as answers but with the cut on the second clause Prolog will respond only with 'sadie' and 'lara'.

If a cut appears at the end of a rule then the rule is deterministic. For example, in the following code:

```
play_racquet_sport(X) :- play_tennis(X).
play_tennis(X) :- energetic(X), weather(dry), weather(warm), !.
play_tennis(X) :- keen(X), weather(warm).

weather(dry).
weather(warm).
energetic(graham).
keen(duncan).
```

there is only one answer (graham) to the query:

```
?- play_racquet_sport(X). % who plays a racquet sport
```

If the first 'play_tennis' predicate fails before reaching the cut then the answer is 'duncan'. Because the first clause for 'play_tennis' succeeds, the only answer is 'graham'. Without the cut Prolog can backtrack and respond with both 'graham' and 'duncan'.

The cut can be used to make a program more efficient. For instance, the following fuzzy membership function

$$\mu_{POS}(x) = \begin{cases} 1 \text{ if } x \geq 10 \\ 0 \text{ if } x \leq 0 \\ 0.075x \text{ if } 0 < x < 10 \end{cases}$$

could be implemented using:

```
pos(X, 1) :- X >= 10.
pos(X, 0) :- X =< 0.
pos(X, Y) :- X > 0, X < 10, Y is 0.075 * X.
```

Given the query:

```
?- pos(11, Y).
```

the first query succeeds, but Prolog will attempt to satisfy the query a second and third time by testing the right-hand side of the second and third rules. As the rules are mutually exclusive (only one can succeed), it is more efficient to place a cut at the end of each rule.

Use of fail

Predicates can be forced to fail and cause backtracking. Failure is forced using a predefined predicate, **fail**. For example, suppose that we wanted to print all dogs to the screen. We can do this printing using a built-in predicate called 'write', but to print all dogs we need to force failure. For example:

```
dog(sadie).
dog(lara).
dog(katie).
list_all_dogs :- dog(X), write(X), nl, fail.
```

The predicate 'nl' prints a new line. The above code will print all dog names to the screen, each name appearing on a new line.

Often the cut and fail will be used together to provide a form of negation. Suppose that we wanted to express that John likes all fruit. This is done using the following rule:

```
likes(john, X) :- fruit(X).
```

Now suppose that John likes all fruit apart from melon. This can be represented as follows:

```
likes(john, X) :- fruit(X), X=melon, !, fail.
likes(john, X) :- fruit(X).
fruit(banana).
fruit(apple).
fruit(melon).
fruit(orange).
```

The program allows us to ask if john likes a specific fruit:

```
?- likes(john, orange).
yes
?- likes(john, melon).
no
```

Note, however, that:

```
?- likes(john, X).
```

fails immediately.

A more concise implementation can be given using the built in predicate **not**:

```
likes(john, X) :- fruit(X), not( X=melon).
```

The predicate not succeeds if 'X=melon' fails.

NLP

Prolog has built-in support for defining language grammars. The syntax used by Prolog makes the specification of a grammar simple, and the syntax is similar to the rewrite rules introduced in Chapters 18 and 19. For example, the following grammar allows Prolog to parse the sentence 'The dog ran across the road'.

```
sentence → noun_phrase, verb_phrase.
sentence → noun_phrase, verb.
```

noun_phrase → determiner, noun.
preposition_phrase → preposition, noun_phrase.
verb_phrase → verb, noun_phrase.
verb_phrase → verb, preposition_phrase.
determiner → [the].
noun → [dog].
verb → [ran].
preposition → [across].
noun → [road].

To query whether a sentence is legal according to the grammar, the user asks:

?- sentence([the, dog, ran, across, the, road], []).

We shall see shortly why the syntax of the query appears as it does. We can check the legality of any phrase, for example:

?- noun_phrase([the, dog], []).
yes
?- preposition_phrase([across, the, road], []).
yes

The above questions can usually be asked by using a built-in 'phrase' predicate:

?- phrase(sentence, [the, dog, ran, across, the, road]).

We can also generate sequences of words conforming to a phrase structure. For example:

?- phrase(sentence, S).
S = [the, dog, ran, the, dog] ;
S = [the, dog, ran, the, road] ;
S = [the, dog, ran, across, the, dog] ;
S = [the, dog, ran, across, the, road] ;
S = [the, road, ran, the, dog] ;
S = [the, road, ran, the, road] ;
S = [the, road, ran, across, the, dog] ;
S = [the, road, ran, across, the, road] ;
S = [the, dog, ran] ;
S = [the, road, ran]

Not all of these sentences make sense but that is because we have not constrained the grammar with additional features.

Prolog's representation of grammar rules

We could write a grammar using the following syntax which is in the more familiar clause form.

sentence(S, S0) :- noun_phrase(S, S1), verb_phrase(S1, S0).

noun_phrase(NP, NP0) :- determiner(NP, NP1), noun(NP1, NP0).
verb_phrase(VP, VP0) :- verb(VP, VP1), noun_phrase(VP1, VP0).
determiner([the|Rest], Rest).
noun([dog|Rest], Rest).
noun([bone|Rest], Rest).
verb([likes|Rest], Rest).

Each of the above grammar rules takes an input list and returns an output list. Each clause will parse the input list to see if it can match the initial part of that list with a particular subphrase. If the clause succeeds in parsing the initial portion of the list, the rest of the list is returned as an output list.

The reading of the sentence rule is:

> There is a sentence between S and S0 if there is a noun phrase between S and S1 and a verb phrase between S1 and S0.

Suppose the following sentence is being parsed:

> The dog found a bone.

The sentence needs to be a noun phrase followed by a verb phrase. The noun phrase is a determiner followed by a noun. The determiner phrase would be represented by the following lists:

> input list = [the, dog, found, a, bone]
> output list = [dog, found, a, bone]

and for the noun:

> input list = [dog, found, a, bone]
> output list = [found, a, bone]

Prolog automatically adds the input and output arguments to a rule written as:

> sentence → noun_phrase, verb_phrase.

so that it is translated into:

> sentence(S, S0) :- noun_phrase(S, S1), verb_phrase(S1, S0).

We are now in a position to understand the original query:

> ?- sentence([the, dog, ran, across, the, road], [ ]).

This is asking:

> Can the sentence be parsed such that the sentence output list is empty?

For example, asking:

?- noun_phrase([the, dog, ran, across, the, road], []).
no

results in 'no' because the sentence is not a noun phrase. But asking:

?- noun_phrase([the, dog, ran, across, the, road], Rest).
Rest = [ran, across, the, road]

returns the remainder of the list after the noun phrase has been extracted.

Adding features to grammar rules

We saw in Chapter 19 that the following grammar accepts illegal sentences such as 'The dogs barks':

sentence → noun_phrase, verb_phrase.
noun_phrase → determiner, noun.
preposition_phrase → preposition, noun_phrase.
verb_phrase → verb.
verb_phrase → verb, noun_phrase.
noun_phrase → noun.
determiner → [a].
determiner → [the].
noun → [dog].
noun → [dogs].
verb → [bark].
verb → [barks].
verb → [found].
noun → [bone].
noun → [bones].

We can modify this grammar to add number agreement as follows:

sentence → sentence(N).
sentence(N) → noun_phrase(N), verb_phrase(N).
noun_phrase(N) → determiner(N), noun(N).
verb_phrase(N) → verb(N).
verb_phrase(N) → verb(N), noun_phrase(N0).
noun_phrase(N) → noun(N).
determiner(singular) → [a].
determiner(_) → [the].
noun(singular) → [dog].
noun(plural) → [dogs].
verb(plural) → [bark].
verb(singular) → [barks].
verb(_) → [found].
noun(singular) → [bone].
noun(plural) → [bones].

The sentence 'The dogs barks' is no longer accepted as legal.

There are more arbitrary ways that a grammar can be constrained. The transitive verb 'found' requires a noun phrase complement. We could apply this constraint using the following notation:

verb_phrase(N) → verb(N, Comp), {Comp = v_np}, noun_phrase(N0).
verb(_, v_np) → [found].

The constraint is implemented by adding the goal 'Comp = v_np' to the rule and adding the feature 'v_np' to the dictionary entry for found. The curly brackets tell Prolog that we do not want the goal to be expanded when the grammar rule is translated into standard clause form.

Further reading

Clocksin and Mellish (1994), and Bratko (2000) provide good introductions to the Prolog language.

Bibliography

Aho, A. V. and Ullman, J. D. (1972) *The Theory of Parsing, Translation and Compiling*. Englewood Cliffs, NJ: Prentice Hall.

Allen, J. (1995) *Natural Language Understanding*, 2nd edn. Redwood City, CA: Benjamin/Cummings Publishing.

Alshawi, H. (ed.) (1992) *The Core Language Engine*. Cambridge, MA: MIT Press.

Anderson, C. R., Smith, D. E. and Weld, D. S. (1998a) Conditional effects in GraphPlan. In *Proceedings of the Fourth International Conference on AI Planning Systems (AIPS-98), Pittsburgh* (Simmons, R., Veloso, M. and Smith, S. eds), pp. 44–53. Menlo Park, CA: AAAI Press.

Anderson, C. R., Smith, D. E. and Weld, D. S. (1998b) *Extending GraphPlan to Handle Uncertainty and Sensing Actions*. In *Proceedings of the Fifteenth National Conference on Artificial Intelligence (AAAI'98)*. Menlo Park, CA: AAAI Press.

Aydede, M. (1999) The language of thought hypothesis. In *The Stanford Encyclopedia of Philosophy*, fall 1999 edn (Zalta E. N. ed.). http://plato.stanford.edu/archives/fall1999/entries/language-thought/

Baker, C. L. (1989) *English Syntax*. Cambridge, MA: MIT Press.

Ballard, D. H. and Brown, C. M. (1982) *Computer Vision*. Englewood Cliffs, NJ: Prentice Hall.

Barrett, A., Christianson, D., Friedma, M., Golden, K., Kwok, C., Penberthy, J. S., Sun , Y. and Weld, D (1995) *UCPOP Users' Manual* (version 4.0). Technical Report 93-09-06d. Seattle, WA: Department of Computer Science, University of Washington.

Baum, E. B. and Haussler, D. (1989) What size net gives valid generalization? *Neural Computation* **1:** 151–160.

Bellman, R. E. (1957a) *Dynamic Programming*. Princeton, NJ: Princeton University Press.

Bellman, R. E. (1957b) A Markov decision process. *Journal of Mathematical Mechanics* **6:** 679–684.

Bernard, D. E., Gamble, E. B., Jr., Rouquette, N. F., Smith, B. and Tung, Y. Jet Propulsion Laboratory, California Institute of Technology, Pasadena, CA; Muscettola, N., Dorias, G. A., Kanefsky, B., Kurien, J., Millar, W., Nayak, P., Rajan, K. and Taylor, W., Ames Research Center, Remote Agent Experiment, DS1 Technology Validation Report http://nmp-techval-reports.jpl.nasa.gov/

Bishop, C. M. (1995) *Neural Networks for Pattern Recognition*. Oxford: Clarendon Press.

Blum, A. L. and Furst, M. L. (1997) Fast planning through graph analysis. *Artificial Intelligence* **90:** 281–300.

Blum, A. L. and Langford, J. C. (1998) Probabilistic planning in the GraphPlan framework. In *AIPS98 Workshop on Planning as Combinatorial Search, Pittsburgh* (Kautz, H., Blum, A., Kambhampati, S. and Selman, B. eds), pp. 8–12.

Blythe, J. (1999) An overview of planning under uncertainty. In *Artificial Intelligence Today: Recent Trends and Developments. Lecture Notes in Computer Science,* Vol. 1600 (Wooldridge, M. and Veloso, M. M. eds). Berlin: Springer.

Boden, M. A. (ed.) (1990) *The Philosophy of Artificial Intelligence. Oxford Readings in Philosophy*. Oxford University Press, Oxford.

Bratko, I. (2000) *Prolog Programming for Artificial Intelligence*, 3rd edn. Reading, MA: Addison-Wesley.

Breiman, L., Friedman, J. H., Olshen, R. A. and Stone, C. J. (1984) *Classification and Regression Trees*. Wadsworth International Group.

Brooks, R. A. (1986) A robust layered control system for a mobile robot. *IEEE Journal of Robotics and Automation* **2:** 14–23.

Brooks, R. A. (1991) Intelligence without representation. *Artificial Intelligence* **47:** 139–159.

Buntine, W. L. (1994) Operations for learning with graphical models. *Journal of Artificial Intelligence Research* **2:** 159–225.

Carpenter, G. A. and Grossberg, S. (1987) A massively parallel architecture for a self-organizing neural pattern recognition machine. *Computer Vision, Graphics and Image Processing* **37:** 54–115.

Cassandra, A. R., Kaelbling, L. P. and Littman, M. L. (1994) Acting optimally in partially observable stochastic domains. In *Proceedings of the Twelfth National Conference on Artificial Intelligence (AAAI-94)*, pp. 1023–1028. Menlo Park, CA: AAAI Press.

Chalmers, D. (1990) Syntactic transformations on distributed representations. *Connection Science* **2(1 & 2):** 53–62.

Chalmers, D. J. (1996) *The Conscious Mind. In search of a Fundamental Theory.* New York: Oxford University Press.

Charniak, E. (1997) Statistical techniques for natural language parsing. *AI Magazine* **18(4):** 33–44.

Chinchor, N. and Sundheim, B. (1993) MUC-5 evaluation metrics. In *Proceedings of the Fifth Message Understanding Conference*, pp. 69–78. San Francisco, CA: Morgan Kaufmann.

Clark, A. (1993) *Associative Engines – Connectionism, Concepts, and Representational Change.* Cambridge, MA: MIT Press.

Clocksin, W. and Mellish, C. (1994) *Programming in Prolog*, 4th edn. Berlin: Springer.

Clowes, M. B. (1971) On seeing things. *Artificial Intelligence Journal* **2(1):** 79–116.

Cohen, W. W. (1995) Fast effective rule induction. In *Proceedings of the Twelfth International Conference on Machine Learning*, pp. 115–123. San Francisco: Morgan Kaufmann Publishers.

Cole, R., Mariani, J., Vszkoreit, H., Varile, G. B., Zaenen, A. and Zampolli, A. (eds) (1998) *Survey of the State of the Art in Human Language Technology*. Cambridge: Cambridge University Press. Also available at http://cslu.cse.ogi.edu/HLTSurvey/

Collins, A. and Quillian, R. (1969) Retrieval time from semantic memory. *Journal of Verbal Learning and Verbal Behaviour* **8:** 240–248.

Copeland, J. (1993) *Artificial Intelligence – A Philosophical Introduction.* Oxford: Blackwell.

Crystal, D. (2001) *The Cambridge Encyclopedia of the English Language.* Cambridge: Cambridge University Press.

Currie, K. W. and Tate, A. (1991) O-Plan: the open planning architecture. *Artificial Intelligence* **52(1):** 49–86.

CVOnline: The Evolving, Distributed, Non-Proprietary, Online Compendium of Computer Vision (Fisher, R. B. ed.). www.dai.ed.ac.uk/.Cvonline

Davies, E. R. (1997) *Machine Vision: Theory, Algorithms, Practicalities*, 2nd edn. San Diego: Academic Press.

Davis, R. (1998) What are intelligence? and why? 1996 Presidential Address. *AI Magazine*, **19(1):** 91–111.

Davis, R., Shrobe, H. and Szolovits, P. (1993) What is a knowledge representation? *AI Magazine*, **14(1):** 17–33.

Deerwester, S., Dumais, S, T., Furnas, G. W., Landauer, T. K. and Harshman, R. (1990) Indexing by latent semantic analysis. *Journal of the American Society For Information Science* **41:** 391–407.

DeJong, K. A., Spears, W. M. and Gordon, D. F. (1993) Using genetic algorithms for concept learning. *Machine Learning* **13:** 161–188.

de Kleer, J. (1986) An assumption-based TMS. *Artificial Intelligence* **28:** 127–162.

Dempster, A. P. (1967) Upper and lower probabilities induced by a multi-valued mapping, *Annals of Mathematical Statistics* **38:** 325–339.

Dempster, A. P. (1968) A generalization of Bayesian inference. *Journal of the Royal Statistical Society, B* **30:** 205–247.

Dempster, A. P., Laird, N. M. and Rubin, D. B. (1977) Maximum likelihood from incomplete data via the EM algorithm. *Journal of the Royal Statistical Society, B* **39**: 1–38.

Dennett, D. C. (1994) The role of language in intelligence. In *What is Intelligence? The Darwin College Lectures* (Khalfa, J. ed.). Cambridge: Cambridge University Press.

Doyle, J. (1979) A truth maintenance system. *Artificial Intelligence* **12(3)**: 231–272.

Dreyfus, H. L. (1992) *What Computers Still Can't Do: A Critique of Artificial Reason.* Cambridge, MA: MIT Press.

Duda, R. O. and Hart, P. E. (1973) *Pattern Classification and Scene Analysis.* New York: John Wiley.

Earley, J. (1970) An efficient context-free parsing algorithm. *Communications of the ACM* **13(2)**: 94–102.

Elkan, C. (1993) The paradoxical success of fuzzy logic. *Proceedings of the 11th National Conference on Artificial Intelligence (AAAI '93), Washington, DC, 11–15 July*, pp. 698–703. Menlo Park, CA: AAAI Press.

Elman, J. L. (1990) Finding structure in time. *Cognitive Science* **14**: 179–211.

Erol, K., Hendler, J. and Nau, D. S. (1994) UMCP: a sound and complete procedure for hierarchical task-network planning. In *Proceedings of the 1994 International Conference on AI Planning Systems, University of Chicago* (Hammond, K. ed.), pp. 249–254. Menlo Park, CA: AAAI Press.

Erol, K., Hendler, J. and Nau, D. S. (1995) Complexity Results for HTN Planning. Technical Report CS-TR-3240, UMIACS-TR-94-32, ISR-TR-95-10. Computer Science Department, Institute for Systems Research, and Institute for Advanced Computer studies, University of Maryland.

Essa, I. A. (1999) Computers seeing people. *AI Magazine* **20(2)**: 69–82.

Eysenck, M. and Keane, M. T. (2000) *Cognitive Psychology: A Student's Handbook*, 4th edn. Hove, East Sussex: Psychology Press.

Fausett, L. (1994) *Fundamentals of Neural Networks. Architectures, Algorithms and Applications.* Upper Saddle River, NJ: Prentice-Hall.

Fikes, R. E. (1993) STRIPS, a new approach to the application of theorm proving to problem solving. *Artificial Intelligence* **2(3–4)**: 189–208.

Fikes, R. E. and Nilsson, N. J. (1971) STRIPS, a retrospective. *Artificial Intelligence* **59(1–2)**: 227–232.

Flach, P. A. (1998) The logic of learning: a brief introduction to inductive logic programming. In *Proceedings of the CompulogNet Area Meeting on Computational Logic and Machine Learning*, University of Manchester, June 1998, pp. 1–17.

Fodor, J. A. (1975) *The Language of Thought.* Cambridge, MA: Harvard University Press.

Fodor, J. and Pylyshyn, Z. (1988) Connectionism and cognitive architecture. A critical analysis. *Cognition* **28**: 3–71.

Forsyth, D. A. and Ponce, J. (2002) *Computer Vision: A Modern Approach.* Prentice-Hall.

Fredman, M. L., Johnson, D. S., McGeoch, L. A. and Ostheimer, G. (1995) Data structures for traveling salesmen. *Journal of Algorithms* **18(3)**: 432–479.

Friedman, N. and Koller, D. (2000) Being Bayesian about network structure. A Bayesian approach to structure discovery in Bayesian networks. In *Proceedings of the 16th Annual Conference on Uncertainty in AI (UAI-2000), Stanford University* (Booutilier, C. and Goldszmidt, M. eds), pp. 201–210. San Francisco: Morgan Kaufmann Publishers.

Gabbay, D. (1998) *Elementary Logics: A Procedural Perspective.* Hemel Hempstead: Prentice Hall.

Gazdar, G. and Mellish, C. (1990) *Natural Language Processing in PROLOG.* Reading, MA: Addison Wesley.

Gazdar, G., Klein E., Pullum, G. K. and Sag, I. (1985) *Generalized Phrase Structure Grammar.* Oxford: Blackwell.

Geman, S. and Geman, D. (1984) Stochastic relaxation, Gibbs distributions, and the Bayesian restoration of images. *IEEE Transactions on Pattern Analysis and Machine Intelligence* **6**: 721–741.

Genesereth, M. and Nilsson, N. (1987) *Logical Foundations of Artificial Intelligence.* Los Altos, CA: Morgan Kaufmann Publishers.

Gent, I. P. and Walsh, T. (1999) *The Search for Satisfaction*. Glasgow: Department of Computer Science, University of Strathclyde. http://dream.dai.ed.ac.uk/group/tw/sat/

Ghallab, M., Howe, A., Knoblock, C., McDermott, D., Ram, A., Veloso, M., Weld D. and Wilkins, D. (1998) *PDDL – The Planning Domain Definition Language Version 1.2*. Technical Report CVC TR-98-003-DCS TR-1165. Yale Centre for Computational Vision and Control.

Goldberg, D. E. (1989) *Genetic Algorithms in Search, Optimization and Machine Learning*. Reading, MA: Addison Wesley.

Golumbic, M. C. (1980) *Algorithmic Graph Theory and Perfect Graphs*. London: Academic Press.

Grevier, D. (1993) *AI – The Tumultuous History of the Search for Artificial Intelligence*. New York: Basic Books.

Haupt, R. L. and Haupt, S. E. (1998) *Practical Genetic Algorithms*. New York: John Wiley.

Haykin, S. (1998) *Neural Networks, A Comprehensive Foundation*. New York: Macmillan College Publishing.

Hecht-Nielsen, R. (1990) *Neurocomputing*. Reading, MA: Addison-Wesley.

Heckerman, D. (1996) A tutorial on learning with Bayesian networks. Technical Report MSR-TR-95-06. Redmond, WA: Microsoft Research. Available from http://research.microsoft.com/research/pubs/view.aspx?msr_tr_id=MSR-TR-95-06

Henrion, M. (1988) Propagating uncertainty in Bayesian networks by probabilistic logic sampling. In *Second Conference on Uncertainty in Artificial Intelligence* (Lemmer, J. F. and Kanal, L. M. eds), pp. 149–163. New York: Elsevier Science.

Hinton, G. E. (ed.) (1991) *Connectionist Symbol Processing. A Bradford Book*. Cambridge, MA: MIT Press.

Hobbs, J. R., Appelt, D. E., Bear, J., Tyson, M. and Magerman, D. (1992a) Robust processing of real-world natural-language texts. In *Text-Based Intelligent Systems: Current Research and Practice in Information Extraction and Retrieval* (Jacobs P. ed.), pp. 13–33. Hillsdale, NJ: Lawrence Erlbaum Associates.

Hobbs, J. R., Appelt, D. E., Bear, J., Israel, D. and Tyson, M. (1992b) *FASTUS: A System for Extracting Information from Natural-Language Text*, SRI Technical Note 519. Menlo Park, CA: SRI International.

Holland, J. H. (1975) *Adaptation in Natural and Artificial Systems*. Ann Arbor, MI: University of Michigan Press.

Horn, B. K. (1975) Obtaining shape from shading information. In *The Psychology of Computer Vision* (Winston, P. H. ed.), pp. 115–155. New York: McGraw-Hill.

Howard, R. A. and Matheson, J. E. (1984) Influence diagrams. In *Readings on the Principles and Applications of Decision Analysis* (Howard, R. A. and Matheson, J. E. eds), pp. 719–762. Menlo Park, CA: Strategic Decisions Group.

Huang, C. and Darwiche, A. (1994) Inference in belief networks: a procedural guide. *International Journal of Approximate Reasoning* **11**: 1–158.

Huffman, D. A. (1971) Impossible objects as nonsense sentences. *Machine Intelligence* **6**: 295–323.

Hwee Tou Ng and Zelle, J. (1997) Corpus-based approaches to semantic interpretation in NLP. *AI Magazine* **18(4)**: 45–64.

Jennings, N. R., Sycara, K. and Wooldridge, M. (1998) A roadmap of agent research and development. *Journal of Autonomous Agents and Multi-Agent Systems*, **1**: 7–38.

Jensen, F. V. (1996) *An Introduction to Bayesian Networks*. London: UCL Press.

Jensen, F. V., Olesen, K. G. and Andersen, S. K. (1990) An algebra of Bayesian belief universes for knowledge-based systems. *Networks* **20**: 637–659.

Jensen, F., Jensen, F. V. and Dittmer, S. L. (1994) From influence diagrams to junction trees. In *Proceedings of the Tenth Conference on Uncertainty in Artificial Intelligence* (Lopez de Mantaras, R. and Poole, D. eds). San Francisco: Morgan Kaufmann Publishers.

Johnson, D. S. and McGeoch, L. A. (1997) The travelling salesman problem: a case study. In *Local Search in Combinatorial Optimization* (Aarts, E. H. L. and Lenstra, J. K. eds), pp. 215–310. Chichester: John Wiley.

Jurafsky, D. and Martin, J. H. (2000) *Speech and Language Processing. An Introduction to Natural Language Processing Computational Linguistics and Speech Recognition*. Upper Saddle River, NJ: Prentice Hall.

Kambhampati, S. (1999) *Recent Advances in AI Planning: a Unified View*. IJCAI-99 Tutorial. Presentation available at http://rakaposhi.eas.asu.edu/ijcai-tutorial-presented-cleaned/index1.htm

Kautz, H. and Selman, B. (1992) Planning as satisfiability. In *Proceedings of the 10th European Conference on Artificial Intelligence (ECAI 92), Vienna, Austria, 3–7 August 1992* (Neumann, B. ed.), pp. 359–363. Chichester: John Wiley.

Kautz, H. and Selman, B. (1996) Pushing the envelope: planning. Propositional logic, and stochastic search. In *Proceedings of of the Thirteenth National Conference on Artificial Intelligence (AAAI-96), Portland, OR*, pp. 1194–1201. Menlo Park, CA: AAAI Press.

Kay, M. (1982) Parsing in functional unification grammar. In *Natural Language Parsing* (Dowty, D. R., Kartutunen, L. and Zwicky, A. eds), pp. 251–278. New York: Cambridge University Press.

Kelly, J. (1997) *The Essence of Logic*. Hemel Hempstead: Prentice Hall.

Kinny, D., Georgeff, M. and Rao, M. (1996). A methodology and modelling technique for systems of BDI agents. In *Agents Breaking Away: Proceedings of the Seventh European Workshop on Modelling Autonomous Agents in a Multi-Agent World (MAAMAW96). Lecture Notes in Artificial Intelligence*. Berlin: Springer.

Kirkpatrick, S., Gela Jr, C. D. and Vecchi, M. P. (1983) Optimization by simulated annealing. *Science* **220:** 671–680.

Knight, K. (1989) Unification: A multidisciplinary survey. *ACM Computing Surveys* **21(1):** 93–121.

Kodratoff, Y. and Michalski, R. (eds) (1990) *Machine Learning: An Artificial Intelligence Approach*, Vol. 3. San Mateo, CA: Morgan Kaufmann Publishers.

Koehler, J., Bernhard, N., Hoffmann, J. and Dimopoulos Y. (1997) *Extending Planning Graphs to an ADL Subset. TR 88*. Freiburg: Institute for Computer Science, University of Freiburg.

Kohonen, T. (1990) The self-organizing map. *Proceedings of the IEEE* **78:** 1464–1480.

Kosko, B. (1994) *Fuzzy Thinking, the New Science of Fuzzy Logic*. London: HarperCollins.

Kowalski, R. (1988) The early years of logic programming. *Communications of the Association for Computing Machinery* **31:** 38–43.

Koza, J. R. (1992) The genetic programming paradigm: genetically breeding populations of computer programs to solve problems. In *Dynamic, Genetic and Chaotic Programming, The Sixth Generation* (Soucek, B. ed.), pp. 203–321. New York: John Wiley.

Lauritzen, S. L. and Spiegelhalter, D. J. (1988) Local computations with probabilities on graphical structures and their application to expert systems. *Journal of the Royal Statistical Society, B* **50:** 157–224.

Lecun, Y., Bottou, L., Bengio, Y. and Haffner, P (1998) Gradient-based learning applied to document recognition. *Proceedings of the IEEE* **86:** 2278–2324.

McAllester, D. A. (1980) *An Outlook on Truth Maintenance*. Tech Report. AI Memo 551, Cambridge, MA: MIT Artificial Intelligence Laboratory.

McCarthy, J. (1996) What has AI in common with philosophy? Stanford, CA: Computer Science Department, Stanford University. http://www-formal.stanford.edu/jmc/aiphil/aiphil.html.

McDermott, D. and Doyle, J. (1980) Non-monotonic logic I. *Artificial Intelligence* **13(1–2).**

Manna, Z. and Waldinger, R. (1985) *The Logical Basis for Computer Programming*. Reading, MA: Addison Wesley.

Manning, D. and Schütz, H. (1999) *Foundations of Statistical Natural Language Processing*. Cambridge, MA: MIT Press.

Marr, D. (1982) *Vision*. New York: WH Freeman.

Marr, D. and Poggio, T. (1976) Cooperative computation of stereo disparity. *Science* **194:** 283–287.

Masters, T. (1995) *Advanced Algorithms For Neural Networks. A C++ Sourcebook*. New York: John Wiley.

Metropolis, N., Rosenbluth, A., Rosenbluth, M., Teller, A. and Teller, E. (1953) Equation of state calculations by fast computing machines. *Journal of Chemical Physics* **21:** 1087–1092.

Michalski, R. S., Carbonell, J. G. and Mitchell, T. M. (1984) *Machine Learning – An Artificial Intelligence Approach*, Vol. I. Berlin: Springer Verlag.

Michalski, R. S., Carbonell, J. G. and Mitchell, T. M. (1986) *Machine Learning – An Artificial Intelligence Approach*, Vol. II. Los Altos, CA: Morgan Kaufmann.

Michell, M. (1998) *An Introduction to Genetic Algorithms*. Cambridge, MA: MIT Press.

Miikkulainen, R. (1993) *Subsymbolic Natural Language Processing. An Integrated Model of Scripts, Lexicon and Memory*. Cambridge, MA: MIT Press.

Minker, J. (1993) An overview of non-monotonic reasoning and logic programming. *Journal of Logic Programming*, Special Issue, **17**.

Minsky, M. (1975) A framework for representing knowledge. In *The Psychology of Computer Vision* (Winston, P. H. ed.). New York: McGraw-Hill.

Minsky, M. (1990) Logical vs. analogical or symbolic vs. connectionist or neat vs. scruffy. In *Artificial Intelligence at MIT, Expanding Frontiers,* Vol. 1 (Winston, P. H. ed.). Cambridge, MA: MIT Press.

Mitchell, T. M. (1982) Generalization as search. *Artificial Intelligence* **18**: 203–226.

Mitchell, T. M. (1997a) *Machine Learning*. New York: McGraw-Hill.

Mitchell, T. M. (1997b) Does machine learning really work? *AI Magazine* **18(3)**: 11–20.

Muggleton, S. (1987) Duce, an oracle based approach to constructive induction. In *IJCAI-87,* pp. 287–292. San Mateo, CA: Morgan Kaufmann.

Muggleton, S. (1988) A strategy for constructing new predicates in first order logic. In *Proceedings of the Third European Working Session on Learning* (Sleeman, D. ed.), pp. 123–130. Pitman Press.

Muggleton, S. (1995) Inverse entailment and Progol. *New Generation Computing* **13**: 245–286.

Muggleton, S. and De Raedt, L. (1994) Inductive logic programming: theory and method. *Journal of Logic Programming* **20**: 629–679.

Nalwa, V. S. (1993) *A Guided Tour of Computer Vision*. Reading, MA: Addison-Wesley.

Newell, A. and Simon, H. A. (1961) GPS, a program that simulates human thought. In *Lernende Automaten* (Billing, H. ed.), pp. 109–124. Munich: R. Oldenbourg.

Nilsson, N. (1971) *Problem-Solving Methods in Artificial Intelligence*. New York: McGraw-Hill.

Nilsson, N. (1996) *Introduction to Machine Learning*. http://robotics.stanford.edu/people/nilsson/mlbook.html

Nwana, H. S. and Ndumu, D. T. (1999) A perspective on software agents research. *The Knowledge Engineering Review*. **14(2)**: 1–18.

O-Plan User Guide and Task formalism Manuals. http://www.aiai.ed.ac.uk/~oplan/documents/index.html

Passino, K. M. and Yurkovich, S. (1998) *Fuzzy Control*. Addison Wesley Longman.

Pearl, J. (1986) Fusion, propagation, and structuring in belief networks. *Artificial Intelligence* **29**: 241–228.

Pednault, E. (1989) ADL: Exploring the middle ground between STRIPS and the situation calculus. In *Principles of Knowledge Representation and Reasoning: Proceedings of the First International Conference (KR-89)* (Brachman, R., Levesque, H. J. and Reiter, R. eds), pp. 324–331. Toronto: Morgan Kaufmann Publishers.

PEGASUS (1998) http://www.sls.lcs.mit.edu/sls/whatwedo/applications/pegasus.html

Pereira, F. C. N. and Shieber, S. M. (1987) *Prolog and Natural language Analysis*. Chicago: Chicago University Press.

Plotkin, G. D. (1969) A note on inductive generalisation. In *Machine Intelligence*, Vol. 5 (Meltzer, B. and Michie, D. eds), pp. 153–163. Edinburgh: Edinburgh University Press.

Quine, W. V. (1982) *Methods of Logic*, 4th edn. Cambridge, MA: Harvard University Press.

Quinlan, J. R. (1986) Induction of decision trees. *Machine Learning* **1**: 81–106.

Quinlan. J. R. (1990) Probabilistic decision trees. In Kodratoff and Michalski 1990.

Quinlan, J. R. (1990) Learning logical definitions from relations. *Machine Learning* **5**: 239–266.

Quinlan. J. R. (1993) *C4.5: Programs for Machine Learning*. San Mateo, CA: Morgan Kaufmann Publishers.

Quinlan, J, R. and Cameron-Jones, R. M. (1993) FOIL: a midterm report. In *Proceedings of the 6th European Conference on Machine Learni*ng (P. Brazdil ed.), Vol. 667 of *Lecture Notes in Artificial Intelligence*, pp. 3–20. Vienna: Springer-Verlag.

Rabiner, L. R. and Juang, B. H. (1993) *Fundamentals of Speech Recognition*. Englewoods Cliffs, NJ: Prentice-Hall.

Radcliff, N. J. (1991) Forma analysis and random respectful recombination. *In Proceedings of the Fourth International Conference on Genetic Algorithms*. San Mateo, CA: Morgan Kauffman.

Rao, A. S. and Georgeff, M. P. (1992) An abstract architecture for rational agents. In *Proceedings of the Third International Conference on Principles of Knowledge Representation and Reasoning* (Rich, C., Swartout, W. and Nebel, B. eds), pp. 439–449. San Mateo, CA: Martin Kaufmann Publishers.

Ringland, G. and Duce, D. (eds) (1988) *Approaches to Knowledge Representation*. Letchworth: Research Studies Press.

Roberts, L. G. (1965) Machine perception of three-dimensional solids. In *Optical and Electro-Optical Information Processing* (Tippett, J. T. ed.), pp. 159–197. Cambridge, MA: MIT Press.

Robinson, J. A. (1965) A machine-oriented logic based on the resolution principle. *Journal of the Association for Computing Machinery* **12**: 23–41.

Rowley, H. A., Baluja, S. and Kanade, T. (1998) Rotation invariant neural-network based face detection. *Proceedings of IEEE Computer Vision and Pattern Recognition*, 38–44. IEEE Computer Society: http://www.computer.org/proceedings/cvpr/8497/8497toc.htm

Rumelhart, D. E., Hinton, G. E. and Williams, R. J. (1986a) Learning internal representations by error propagation. In *Parallel Distributed Processing, Explorations in the Microstructure of Cognition*, Vol. 1 (Rumelhart, D. E., McClelland, J. L. and the PDP Research Group eds), pp. 318–362. Cambridge, MA: MIT Press.

Rumelhart, D. E., McClelland, J. L. and the PDP Research Group (eds) (1986b) *Parallel Distributed Processing, Explorations in the Microstructure of Cognition*, Vol. 1. Cambridge, MA: MIT Press.

Schank, R. C. and Abelson, R. P. (1977) *Scripts, Plans, Goals, and Understanding*. Hillsdale, NJ: Lawrence Erlbaum Associates.

Searle, J. R. (1969) *Speech Acts: an Essay in the Philosophy of Language*. Cambridge: Cambridge University Press.

Sejnowski, T. J. and Rosenberg, C. R. (1987) Parallel networks that learn to pronounce English text. *Complex Systems* **1**: 145–168.

Selman, B., Levesque, H. and Mitchell, D. (1992) A new method for solving hard satisfiability problems. In *Proceedings of the 10th National Conference on AI*, pp. 440–446. American Association for Artificial Intelligence. Menlo Park, CA: AAAI Press.

Selman, B., Kautz, H. and Cohen, B. (1993) Local search strategies for satisfiability testing. In *Proceedings of the Second (DIMACS) Challenge on Cliques, Coloring, and Satisfiability, Providence, RI.*

Shachter, R. D. (1986) *Evaluating Influence Diagrams. Operations Research* **34**: 871–882.

Shachter, R. D. and Peot, M. A. (1992) Decision making using probabilistic inference methods. In *Proceedings of the Eighth Conference on Uncertainty in Artificial Intelligence* (Dubois, D., Wellman, M. P., D'Ambrosio, B. and Smets, P. eds), pp. 276–283. San Francisco: Morgan Kauffmann Publishers.

Shafer, G. (1976) *A Mathematical Theory of Evidence*. Princeton, NJ: Princeton University Press.

Shenoy, P. P. (1992) Valuation-based systems for Bayesian decision analysis. *Operations Research* **40**: 463-484.

Sloman, A. (1995) A philosophical encounter: an interactive presentation of some of the key philosophical problems in AI and AI problems in philosophy. In *Proceedings of the 14th International Joint Conference on AI, Montreal, Canada* (Mellish, C. ed.), p. 2037. San Francisco: Morgan Kaufmann Publishers.

Sloman, A. (2001) Varieties of consciousness. Presented at Oxford University Consciousness Society, 24 October 2001. http://www.cs.bham.ac.uk/~axs/misc/talks/oxford.consciousness.slides.pdf.

Smets, P. (1999) Theories of uncertainty. *Handbook for Fuzzy Computation.* http://iridia.ulb.ac.be/~psmets/ Uncertainty_HbkFuzzyComput.pdf

Spirtes, P., Glymour, C. and Scheines, R. (2000) *Causation, Prediction, and Search,* 2nd edn. Cambridge, MA: MIT Press.

Spivey, M. (1996) *An Introduction to Logic Programming through Prolog.* Hemel Hempstead: Prentice Hall.

Stolke, A. (1997) Linguistic knowledge and empirical methods in speech recognition. *AI Magazine* (special issue on empirical natural language processing) **18(4):** 25–32.

Sugihara, K. (1984) An algebraic approach to the shape-from-image-problem. *Artificial Intelligence Journal* **23:** 59–95.

Survey of the State of the Art in Human Language Technology (1996)

Sutton, R. S. and Barto, A. G. (1998) *Reinforcement Learning: an Introduction.* Cambridge, MA: MIT Press.

Turk, M. and Pentland A. P. (1991) Face recognition using eigenfaces. *Journal of Cognitive Neuroscience* **3(1):** 71–86.

Waibel, A. and Lee, K. F. (eds) (1990) *Readings in Speech Recognition.* San Mateo, CA: Morgan Kaufmann.

Waldinger, R. (1975) Achieving several goals simultaneously. In *Machine Intelligence*, Vol. 8 (Elcock, E. W. and Michie, D. eds), pp. 94–138, Chichester: Ellis Horwood.

Weizenbaum, J. (1965) ELIZA – a computer program for the study of natural language communication between man and machine. *Communications of the ACM* **9:** 36–45.

Weld, D. S. (1999) Recent advances in AI planning. *AI Magazine* **20(2):** 93–123.

Weld, D. S., Anderson, C. R. and Smith, D. E. (1998) Extending GraphPlan to handle uncertainty and sensing actions. In *Proceedings of AAAI 98'.*

Werbos, P. J. (1990) Backpropagation through time: what it does and how to do it. *Proceedings of the IEEE* **78:** 1550–1560.

Whitely, D. (1994) A genetic algorithm tutorial. *Statistics and Computing* **4:** 65–85.

Wilkins, D. E. (1988) *Practical Planning: Extending the AI Planning Paradigm.* San Mateo, CA: Morgan Kaufmann.

Wilkins, D. E. (1990) Can AI planners solve practical problems? *Computational Intelligence* **6:** 232–246.

Wilkins, D. E. and desJardins, M. (2001) A call for knowledge-based planning. *AI Magazine* **22(1):** 99–115.

Williamson, J. (2001) *Bayesian Networks for Logical Reasoning.* Presented at the 8th Workshop on Automated Reasoning, York, 22–23 March 2001, and at the AAAI Symposium on using Uncertainty within Computation, North Falmouth, MA, 2–4 November 2001.

Winograd (1972) *Understanding Natural Language.* New York: Academic Press.

Winston, P. H. (1970) *Learning Structural Descriptions from Examples.* Doctoral dissertation MAC TR-76, Cambridge, MA: MIT.

Wittgenstein, L. (1958) *Philosophical Investigation*s, 3rd edn (translated by G. E. M. Anscombe), pp. 193–196. Englewood Cliffs, NJ: Prentice Hall.

Woods, W. A. (1973) Progress in natural language understanding: an application to lunar geology. *AFIPS Conference Proceedings* **42:** 441–450.

Wooldridge, M. J. and Jennings, M. R. (1995) Intelligent agents: theory and practice. *Knowledge Engineering Review* **10**(2): 115–152.

Wos, L., Overbeek, R., Lusk, E. and Boyle, J. (1992) *Automated Reasoning: Introduction and Applications,* 2nd edn. New York: McGraw-Hill.

www.mlnet.org

Zadeh, L. A. (1965) Fuzzy sets. *Information and Control* **8:** 338–353.

Zadeh, L. A. (1973) Outline of a new approach to the analysis of complex systems and decision processes. *IEEE Transactions on Systems, Man and Cybernetics* **3:** 28–44.

Zadeh, L. A. (1978) Fuzzy sets as a basis for a theory of possibility. *Fuzzy Sets and Systems* **1:** 3–28.

Zhu, S. and Yuille, A. L. (1996) FORMS: a exible object recognition and modeling system. *International Journal of Computer Vision* **29:** 187–212.

Index